MIGRANT WORKERS IN INTERNATIONAL HUMAN RIGHTS LAW

Migrant Workers in International Human Rights Law

Their Protection in Countries of Employment

RYSZARD CHOLEWINSKI

CLARENDON PRESS · OXFORD

This book has been printed digitally and produced in a standard specification in order to ensure its continuing availability

OXFORD
UNIVERSITY PRESS

Great Clarendon Street, Oxford OX2 6DP

Oxford University Press is a department of the University of Oxford.
It furthers the University's objective of excellence in research, scholarship, and education by publishing worldwide in

Oxford New York

Auckland Bangkok Buenos Aires Cape Town Chennai
Dar es Salaam Delhi Hong Kong Istanbul Karachi Kolkata
Kuala Lumpur Madrid Melbourne Mexico City Mumbai Nairobi
São Paulo Shanghai Taipei Tokyo Toronto

Oxford is a registered trade mark of Oxford University Press in the UK and in certain other countries

Published in the United States
by Oxford University Press Inc., New York

Reprinted 2003

ISBN 0-19- 825992-1

Preface and Acknowledgements

The plight of migrant workers and their families is one of those intractable issues in the field of human rights. In the current anti-immigration climate in many developed industrialized countries, economic migrants are often misunderstood. They are easy targets for politicians and the media in difficult economic times and are considered a threat to the host society, particularly those that enter the country of employment without authorization. Illegal migrants are frequently perceived as 'scroungers' on the welfare state, as criminals, or as potential trouble-makers. The hardships these people face and the many difficulties they have to overcome in countries of employment are rarely reported at any length. Occasionally, we are informed of the very dangerous conditions irregular migrants experience in transit at the mercy of unscrupulous traffickers, stories which often have a tragic conclusion.

In international law, migrant workers and their families share a common feature with refugees, namely they are aliens in the host society. As non-citizens and without formal membership of the community in which they reside, migrant workers and their families are at greater risk from the discretionary whims of the sovereign state. Unlike refugees, however, they have traditionally been provided with far less attention and protection by the international community, even though they outnumber refugees considerably. In recent years, the closing of borders to involuntary migrants has also resulted in great hardships for those who voluntarily seek to make a better life for themselves beyond their countries of origin. Despite this perceived lesser status, international human rights standards have not neglected this vulnerable group and one of the aims of this book is to highlight the norms that exist.

My interest in the plight of migrant workers and their families was first stirred by a series of excellent and informative lectures given by Virginia Leary at the University of Strasbourg in July 1987 at the 18th study session of the International Institute of Human Rights. The enthusiasm and devoted efforts of Virginia Leary in the human rights field have always served as inspiration for my own work.

The origins of this book lie in a doctoral thesis that was written at the University of Ottawa in Canada between 1989 and 1992. My interest in the subject would probably have not been realized but for the financial assistance that enabled me to undertake studies in Canada. Consequently, I remain grateful to those that made this possible. Bill Pentney, the former Acting Director of the Human Rights Research and Education Centre, and Eugene Meehan, the former Head of Graduate Studies at the Faculty of Law in Ottawa, were very instrumental in making the necessary administrative and financial arrangements which enabled me to travel to Ottawa and study there. During my studies, my sponsors consisted of the Ontario Ministry of Colleges and Universities (in the form of Ontario Graduate scholarships), the Faculty of Graduate Studies and Research at the University of Ottawa, the Common and Civil Law sections of the Faculty of Law, and the Human Rights Research and Education Centre. The basis of the research for this book was conducted at the Human Rights Research and Education Centre, a lively and stimulating environment for work in the human rights field. I am particularly grateful to the following persons: Bill Black, my thesis supervisor and the Director of the Centre at that time, who provided untiring guidance and assistance; Magda Seydegart, the former long-serving Executive Director, who made me feel very welcome and who found space for me in which to work; and to Iva Caccia, the Head Documentalist at the Centre, who drew my attention to relevant bibliographical material. Moreover, I wish to acknowledge the many genuine and interesting people who passed through the Centre and with whom I was able to discuss my ideas. I would also like to thank my examiners, Guy Goodwin-Gill, Christopher Granger, Virginia Leory, and Donald McRae, for the very helpful observations in their reports on my doctoral thesis.

I am grateful to a number of colleagues and former colleagues in the Faculty of Law at the University of Leicester for their advice and support in completing this extensive project, in particular Andrew Choo and Matthew Craven. The students who have participated during the last 3 years in my post-graduate course on the International Protection of the Human Rights of Migrants have also helped me, through their enthusiasm, interest and questions, to consider anew and afresh some of the topics in this book.

Most of all, I am thankful for the support of members of my family, both in the United Kingdom and Canada, and for their patience and understanding. This book is dedicated to my mother and to the memory of my father.

I have striven to state the law as it stood on 31 August 1996, although I have also referred to a number of legal developments that have occurred after this date. Any errors and omissions remain my responsibility alone.

RYSZARD CHOLEWINSKI
Leicester, January 1997

Contents

Abbreviations

ACHPR	African Charter on Human and Peoples' Rights
ACHR	American Convention on Human Rights
AEHRYB	All-European Human Rights Yearbook
ACP	African-Caribbean-Pacific
AJIL	American Journal of International Law
Am. Soc. Int'l L. Prcdgs	American Society of International Law Proceedings
C97	ILO Convention No. 97 of 1949 concerning Migration for Employment (Revised)
C143	ILO Convention No. 143 of 1975 concerning Migrations in Abusive Conditions and the Promotion of Equality of Opportunity and Treatment of Migrant Workers
California Western L. Rev.	California Western Law Review
CCME	Churches Commission for Migrants in Europe
CHR	UN Commission on Human Rights
CMLR	Common Market Law Reports
CML Rev.	Common Market Law Review
COE	Council of Europe
Comp. Lab. L.J.	Comparative Labour Law Journal
CSCE	Conference on Security and Cooperation in Europe
D & R	Decisions and Reports (European Commission of Human Rights)
DLR	Dominion Law Reports
Duke J. Int'l & Comp. L.	Duke Journal of International and Comparative Law
EC	European Community
ECE	European Convention on Establishment
ECHR	European Convention on Human Rights
ECR	European Court (of Justice) Reports
ECRI	European Commission against Racism and Intolerance
EEA	European Economic Area
EEC	European Economic Community

EFTA	European Free Trade Association
EHRR	European Human Rights Reports
EIRR	European Industrial Relations Review
EJIL	European Journal of International Law
EMW	European Convention on the Legal Status of Migrant Workers
ESC	European Social Charter
ETS	European Treaty Series
EU	European Union
Eur. Ct. H.R. Ser. A	Publications of the European Court of Human Rights, Series A: Judgments and Decisions
FAS	ILO Committee on Freedom of Association
FDI	Foreign Direct Investment
GA	UN General Assembly
GDP	Gross Domestic Product
German YBIL	German Yearbook of International Law
GISTI	Groupe d'information et de soutein des travailleurs immigrés
HRLJ	Human Rights Law Journal
HRQ	Human Rights Quarterly
Georgetown Immigration L.J.	Georgetown Immigration Law Journal
ICCPR	International Covenant on Civil and Political Rights
ICERD	International Convention on the Elimination of All Forms of Racial Discrimination
ICESCR	International Covenant on Economic, Social and Cultural Rights
ICLQ	International and Comparative Law Quarterly
ICMW	International Convention on the Protection of the Rights of All Migrant Workers and Members of their Families
IGC	Intergovernmental Conference
IHRR	International Human Rights Reports
IJCLLIR	International Journal of Comparative Labour Law and Industrial Relations
IJRL	International Journal of Refugee Law
ILM	International Legal Materials

ILO	International Labour Organization
ILO SLB	ILO Social and Labour Bulletin
ILPA	Immigration Law Practitioners' Association
ILR	International Labour Review
IM	International Migration
IMR	International Migration Review
Industr. & Lab. Rel. Rev.	Industrial and Labor Relations Review
INLP	Immigration and Nationality Law and Practice
JCMS	Journal of Common Market Studies
JO	Journal Officiel des Communautés Européennes
LIEI	Legal Issues of European Integration
LNTS	League of Nations Treaty Series
Mich. J. Int'l L.	Michigan Journal of International Law
Mich. L. Rev.	Michigan Law Review
MLR	Modern Law Review
MN	Migration News
MNS	Migration News Sheet
NAFTA	North American Free Trade Agreement
Netherlands YBIL	Netherlands Yearbook of International Law
NGO	Non-Governmental Organization
Nordic J. Int'l L.	Nordic Journal of International Law
NQHR	Netherlands Quarterly of Human Rights
OAU	Organization of African Unity
ODA	Official Development Assistance
OECD	Organization for Economic Cooperation and Development
OJ	Official Journal of the European Communities
OOPEC	Office for Official Publications of the European Communities
OSCE	Organization for Security and Cooperation in Europe
R86	Recommendation No. 86 of 1949 concerning Migration for Employment (Revised)
R100	Recommendation No. 100 of 1955 concerning the Protection of Migrant Workers in Underdeveloped Countries and Territories

R151	Recommendation No. 151 of 1975 concerning Migrant Workers
RPG	Refugee Policy Group
SEA	Single European Act
SIS	Schengen Information System
SOPEMI	Continuous Reporting System on Migration
TEU	Treaty on European Union
Texas Int'l L.J.	Texas International Law Journal
UBC L. Rev.	University of British Columbia Law Review
UDHR	Universal Declaration of Human Rights
UN GAOR	United Nations General Assembly Official Records
UNCTAD	United Nations Conference on Trade and Development
UNESCO	United Nations Educational, Scientific and Cultural Organization
UNHCR	United Nations High Commissioner for Refugees
UNTS	United Nations Treaty Series
Wisconsin L. Rev.	Wisconsin Law Review
YBECHR	Yearbook of the European Convention on Human Rights
YBEL	Yearbook of European Law
YBILC	Yearbook of the International Law Commission

Table of Cases

1. EUROPEAN CONVENTION ON HUMAN RIGHTS

European Court of Human Rights

European Commission of Human Rights

2. EUROPEAN COMMUNITY

European Court of Justice

3. NATIONAL CASE LAW

4. ARBITRATION DECISIONS

5. COMMUNICATIONS BEFORE THE HUMAN RIGHTS COMMITTEE

6. COMMUNICATIONS BEFORE THE COMMITTEE ON THE ELIMINATION OF RACIAL DISCRIMINATION

Table of National Legislation

Belgium

France

Germany

Greece

Italy

Japan

Netherlands

Norway

Portugal

Spain

Sweden

United Kingdom

United States

Table of Treaties and Other International Instruments

EC Draft Agreements

UN Resolutions

UN General Assembly

UN Economic and Social Council

UN Commission on Human Rights

UN Sub-Commission on Prevention of Discrimination and Protection of Minorities

UN Human Rights Treaty Bodies—General Comments and Recommendations

Human Rights Committee

Committee on Economic, Social and Cultural Rights

Committee on the Elimination of Racial Discrimination

Table of European Community and Council of Europe Instruments

EUROPEAN COMMUNITY

Regulations

Directives

Decisions

Joint Actions

Declarations

Resolutions

Recommendations

Presidency Conclusions

Proposals

Miscellaneous

COUNCIL OF EUROPE

Resolutions

Recommendations

Miscellaneous

Introduction

The focus of this work is on the protection of the rights of migrant workers and their families in countries of employment under international human rights law. The rights under examination are economic, social, cultural, political, and residence rights, which are arguably of most concern to migrants once they are in the host country. For the purpose of this study, economic and social rights are defined as follows: employment rights, which incorporate the right to equal treatment with nationals in respect of work and employment conditions and the right of access to employment; trade union rights; social security rights; the right to health, which covers rights to healthcare and occupational health and safety; the right to housing, including private ownership of property; the right to family reunion; and the right to education, which comprises both the education of migrant children and workers' education, such as vocational training and language instruction. The cultural rights of migrant workers and their families embrace the right to retain and develop their culture and language as well as the right of the children of migrants to be taught their culture and language or to be educated in their language. The political rights of migrants encompass a right to political activity and a general right to participate in the decision-making process concerning their interests, including the right to vote and to stand as a candidate in local elections. The study also considers the residence rights of migrants, broadly defined as: the right to remain in the host country while in work and for some time after the termination of employment; rights to permanent residence and naturalization; and protection against arbitrary or unfair expulsion. Clearly, residence rights are integral to the enjoyment of the other enumerated rights.

The protection of migrants before they leave their country of origin, whilst in transit, and during their reception in the state of employment is not discussed. Rights pertaining mainly to the migration process, such as the right to information,[1] are therefore excluded. So-called basic or fundamental rights and freedoms, such as the right to life, the right not to be subjected to torture or to cruel, inhuman or degrading treatment or punishment, and the right to freedom of thought, conscience or religion are not discussed in any depth. Because of the interdependence of all rights, however, these fundamental rights and freedoms clearly interact with some of the rights under consideration and references are therefore made

[1] For a synopsis of what is understood by the right of migrant workers to information, see generally T. Hujanen, 'The Role of Information in the Realization of the Human Rights of Migrant Workers' (Conference Report of the Final Conference of the Joint Study held at Crêt-Bérard, Lausanne, 23–27 Oct. 1988) (1989) 23 IMR 105. See also T. Hujanen, (ed.), *Role of Information in the Realization of the Human Rights of Migrant Workers*, Report of International Conference, Tampere, 19–22 June 1983 (Tampere: University of Tampere, Department of Journalism and Mass Communication, 1984).

to them where appropriate. For example, an argument might be advanced that the denial of family reunion could, in certain exceptional circumstances, constitute a form of inhuman or degrading treatment.

TERMINOLOGY

Throughout this work, the terms 'migrant worker', 'foreign worker' and 'immigrant worker' are used interchangeably. The term 'guest worker', which comes from the German word *gastarbeiter*, is also used, principally in the context of the traditional approach taken in Europe where, by and large, labour migration has been treated as a temporary phenomenon.[2] The expression 'migrants' is used in two senses depending on the context: to refer globally to all immigrants regardless of whether they migrate to take up employment, and to refer to migrant workers and their families taken together. Likewise, the terms 'illegal migrant worker', 'non-documented' or 'undocumented migrant worker', 'clandestine migrant worker' and 'migrant worker in an irregular situation' or 'irregular migrant worker' are equivalent. States of employment are also referred to as 'receiving' or 'host countries', whereas migrants' states of origin are also called 'sending countries'. Although many sending countries are developing states and most receiving countries are developed and highly industrialized states, these terms are not necessarily synonymous.[3] Indeed, migration for employment, particularly that taking place outside of Europe and North America, does not necessarily conform to this rubric.[4] It is also noteworthy that a number of countries both export and import labour, such as Malaysia and Portugal.[5]

[2] D. G. Papademetriou and P. L. Martin, 'Labor Migration and Development: Research and Policy Issues' in D. G. Papademetriou and P. L. Martin, (eds.), *The Unsettled Relationship: Labor Migration and Economic Development* (New York: Greenwood Press, 1991) 3, 7 (n. 9).

[3] Moreover, the distinction between developed and developing countries is not always clear. According to the World Bank, developing countries generally comprise those countries with low-income (GNP per capita of $695 or less in 1993) or middle-income (GNP per capita of more than $695 but less than $8,626 in 1993) economies, although it recognizes that some high-income economies are classified as developing by the UN or are regarded as developing by the authorities of the countries concerned: World Bank, *World Development Report 1995. Workers in an Integrating World* (New York: Oxford University Press for the World Bank, 1995) ix. What is clear, however, is that there are far more developing countries in the world than developed countries. In a classification of 132 countries in its *World Development Report 1995*, 162–3, the World Bank considered only 24 countries to be high-income economies and the remainder to be low-income or middle-income economies.

[4] For example, Kritz and Zlotnik observe that 'though migration from developing to developed countries is considerable, large flows also take place . . . between countries at comparable levels of development, and still other flows originate in developed countries and end in the developing world': M. M. Kritz and H. Zlotnik, 'Global Interactions: Migration Systems, Processes, and Policies' in M. M. Kritz, L. L. Lim and H. Zlotnik, (eds.), *International Migration Systems: A Global Approach* (Oxford: Clarendon Press, 1992) 1, 15.

[5] See OECD, *Trends in International Migration—Continuous Reporting System on Migration—SOPEMI 1994* (Paris: OECD, 1995) 57 and 114–15 respectively. Indeed, as Kritz and Zlotnik, n. 4 above, point out: 'In an increasingly inter-connected world, few countries can be simply categorized

DEFINITION OF 'MIGRANT WORKER'

References are made throughout the study to international definitions of migrant workers and their families. The concept of 'migrant worker' is defined explicitly in a number of universal and regional instruments concerned with the protection of migrants. With regard to other relevant instruments and regimes, a definition has to be implied, either from the pertinent text, or from the interpretation of these instruments and regimes by the supervisory bodies charged with their implementation.

Broadly speaking, foreign workers may either be long- or short-term immigrants.[6] The first category includes workers and their families who migrate with a view to settling permanently in the receiving country. Examples of such persons are immigrants to Australia, Canada, and the USA, who are usually admitted as permanent residents and who eventually become eligible for naturalization after a certain period of residence in the country. The second category comprises workers lawfully admitted on temporary work permits (of a finite duration), usually for specific employment (bearing in mind, of course, that work permits may be extended or renewed while workers are in the country of employment). This describes the approach that has been taken and, to some extent, is still being taken in Western European states of employment which do not consider themselves to be 'countries of immigration'. It is also the preferred approach in other migrant-receiving countries, such as the Gulf States and South Africa.[7] Short-term migrants also include frontier and seasonal workers[8] and those studying and pursuing their careers abroad. Self-employed workers may fall into both categories. Not all of these groups are covered by the various definitions of 'migrant worker' in international instruments. Moreover, students, trainees and those sent by their employers to another country to perform a specific job are explicitly excluded from all the international definitions of 'migrant worker'.

The two categories of long- and short-term immigrants are by no means mutually exclusive.[9] For example, migrant workers who initially intended to work

as "receivers" or "senders" of migrants, and only the adoption of a wide perspective with regard to migration can advance our understanding about the coexistence of inflows and outflows of migrants from the same country or of the simultaneous admission of highly skilled workers and low-skilled ones by another'.

[6] See UN Division of Human Rights, *Report of the Seminar on the Human Rights of Migrant Workers*, Tunis, Tunisia, 12–24 Nov. 1975, UN Doc. ST/TAO/HR/50, 30, para. 115.

[7] Papademetriou and Martin, n. 2 above, 7 (n. 9), describe these immigrant workers as 'contract workers'. Their employment in the host country is frequently sanctioned by arrangements between that country and the state of origin.

[8] Seasonal workers are usually nationals of countries bordering receiving states employed in agriculture, construction, or hotel and catering; e.g., Mexican farm workers in the USA and migrant workers in Switzerland's tourist industry. Cf. T. Ansay, 'Legal Problems of Migrant Workers' (1977) *Recueil des Cours* 1, 8; Papademetriou and Martin, n. 2 above.

[9] One possible general distinction between these categories is that the latter group retain the intention, however vague or unrealistic, of returning home. Cf. A. Segal, *An Atlas of International Migration* (London: Hans Zell, 1993) 146.

abroad for a limited period of time and then to return home may be permitted to settle on a permanent basis.[10] Indeed, this has occurred with respect to many of the migrant workers in Western Europe, who are now effectively settled in the country of employment. They have obtained permanent residence status and have been joined by their families. On the other hand, migrant workers may intend staying longer in a country or be admitted for permanent residence there without intending to make that country their home. At all times, they may consider their place of origin to be their permanent home.[11]

Migrant workers may also be residing and working in a country illegally or without authorization. Illegal migrants are expressly excluded from the definition of 'migrant worker' in most relevant international instruments with the exception of the recent UN International Convention on the Protection of the Rights of All Migrant Workers and Members of Their Families.

The following categories of illegal migrants are discernible. Migrants may attempt to cross a frontier wholly concealed from the authorities or may enter a country by means of false documentation or other kinds of misrepresentation. The first form of clandestine migration frequently takes place into countries with particularly long borders, such as the migration of undocumented workers into the USA from Mexico across the 3,000 kilometre border between these two countries.[12] Although the former method can be achieved on the migrant's own initiative or with the assistance of relatives, both methods, and especially the latter, increasingly involve the participation of criminal organizations with substantial resources.[13] Clandestine crossings arranged by traffickers often expose immigrants to many forms of exploitation. Immigrants not only pay a large sum of money for these services, but also face blackmail by traffickers for long periods after entry together with confiscation of their travel documents. Moreover, illegal migrants are particularly vulnerable to dangerous, unhygienic, and very uncomfortable conditions of transport to their destination.[14]

[10] See also Kritz and Zlotnik, n. 4 above, 5.

[11] I am grateful to Bill Black for bringing this point to my attention.

[12] UN Commission on Human Rights, Sub-Commission on Prevention of Discrimination and Protection of Minorities, 27th Session, *Exploitation of Labour Through Illicit And Clandestine Trafficking* (Preliminary Study prepared by Ms. H. E. Warzazi, Special Rapporteur), UN Doc. E/CN.4/Sub.2/351 (17 June 1974) 17, para. 46. This report has been consolidated in UN Doc. E/CN.4/Sub.2/1986/6.

[13] *Ibid.* 17–18, paras. 45–50. See also UN GA Res. 48/102 of 20 Dec. 1993 on Prevention of the Smuggling of Aliens. For a discussion of the pertinent issues in this area, see G. Gunatilleke, 'Seminar Report: International Response to Trafficking in Migrants and the Safeguarding of Migrant Rights (Eleventh IOM Seminar on Migration, Geneva, 26–28 Oct. 1994)' (1994) 32 IM 593. This seminar took place in response to the General Assembly's request to the relevant specialized agencies and intergovernmental organizations, including the International Organization for Migration (IOM), 'to consider ways and means, within their respective spheres of competence, to enhance international cooperation to combat the smuggling of aliens' (para. 11). Res. 48/102 also 'reaffirms the need to observe fully international and national law in dealing with the smuggling of aliens, including the provision of humane treatment and strict observance of all the human rights of migrants (para. 10)'.

[14] *Ibid.* 19, paras. 51–3. The hardship that such irregular crossings may cause was publicized in 1973 when a truck carrying 59 Africans from Mali, packed into it like sardines with little food, water, or air, broke down after having passed into France from Italy through the Mount Blanc tunnel. These

In many cases, however, illegal migrant workers actually enter a country by legal means. They may enter as 'tourists' without the necessary papers for employment and then find themselves in an 'irregular situation' when they start working.[15] Irregular labour migration also frequently encompasses those migrants who are entitled to residence and not to work and yet are employed, as well as those who have both residence and work permits but nevertheless work illegally in 'informal' jobs. In this instance, illegal migration for employment is inextricably bound up with legal labour migration.[16] The numbers of illegal migrants may be inflated substantially by the family members of migrant workers. These may accompany a clandestine entrant, join a legally residing migrant worker in contravention of immigration requirements, or become workers in an irregular situation by finding employment without permission, even though their entry into, and their residence in, the host country are sanctioned by law.

The diverse definitions of 'migrant worker' found in the various international instruments indicate that it is necessary to embrace a broad understanding of this concept for the purpose of this study. The adopted definition applies to both long- and short-term immigrants. So long as these persons have not acquired the citizenship of the state of employment and are working or have worked in that country, they are included.[17] Self-employed and seasonal migrant workers and those studying and training abroad but also working are therefore covered. A special interest is also reserved in this work for illegal migrants, who constitute the most vulnerable class of migrants and who are most likely to be subject to exploitation and to suffer from human rights abuses. The persons excluded under this broad definition are Geneva Convention and *de facto* refugees,[18] tourists, and those migrating to a country for the purpose of retirement, unless it is to the country in which they completed their work life.

people had paid a great deal of money to be smuggled into France. See V. Leary, 'Migrant Workers and Human Rights' in *Materials for the 18th Study Session of the International Institute of Human Rights*, Strasbourg, France, July 1987 (Strasbourg: International Institute of Human Rights, 1987) 6.

[15] J. Power, *Western Europe's Migrant Workers*, Minority Rights Group Report No. 28, rev. ed. (London: Minority Rights Group, 1978) 24.

[16] R. Rogers, 'Western Europe in the 1980s: The End of Immigration?' in R. Rogers, (ed.), *Guests Come to Stay: The Effects of European Labour Migration on Sending and Receiving Countries* (Boulder, Colorado: Westview Press, 1985) 285, 294–5. This link is also established whenever undocumented migrant workers in the country of employment are regularized (under an amnesty programme): Kritz and Zlotnik, n. 4 above, 5.

[17] Therefore, persons *seeking* employment for the first time in a country other than their own are not included, even though EC law on the free movement of workers applies to those seeking employment, at least for a certain period of time. See Case C-292/89, *R* v. *Immigration Appeal Tribunal, ex parte Antonissen* [1991] ECR I-745, [1991] 2 CMLR 373. This decision is discussed in Ch. 6.

[18] Namely, refugees who are not encompassed by the definition in the Geneva Convention Relating to the Status of Refugees (189 UNTS 137), but who nonetheless find themselves in 'refugee-like situations', for example by fleeing internal conflict, serious public order disturbances, or generalized violence. Indeed, such persons are considered 'refugees' by pertinent regional instruments, such as the OAU Convention Governing the Specific Aspects of Refugee Problems in Africa of 1969 (UNTS 14691) (Art. I(2)) and the Cartagena Declaration on Refugees of 1984 (OAS/Ser. L/V/II.66, Doc. 10, rev. 1, 190–3) in Latin America. Unsuccessful asylum seekers, who in reality turn out to be 'economic migrants', are included in the definition of migrant worker adopted for the purpose of this study.

ORGANIZATION

Part I of the study, entitled International Migration for Employment, Aliens and Citizens, sets out the broad context within which the concerns surrounding the need to protect effectively the rights of migrant workers and their families are located.

Chapter 1 provides an overview of international migration for employment with a sketch of the history and causes of such migration, its impact on receiving and sending societies, and its relationship with the right to development. Although the overall focus of this work is on the international protection of the rights of migrants in the country of employment, it is recognized that an analysis of the relevant safeguards would be incomplete without an examination of the forces which propel labour migration in the first place. Successful sustainable development in countries of origin is seen as a pre-requisite to reducing this migration in the long term, and would therefore go some way towards alleviating the human rights' problems experienced by migrants in countries of employment.

In addition to the problems faced by all workers and associated with labour everywhere, migrant workers and their families are further burdened by their status as aliens and by the particularly difficult consequences which accompany this status. The obstacles that alienage poses to the realization of their rights are substantial. Chapter 2 focuses on migrant workers *as aliens*. It traces the history of the treatment of aliens and the basic international legal rules which evolved from the concept of the 'minimum standard' in the international law of state responsibility to the development of international human rights norms protecting *all* persons. It then examines the applicability of general international and regional human rights norms to aliens, in particular as they pertain to the protection of their economic, social, cultural, political, and residence rights. Although the universal thrust of these norms holds out much promise for safeguarding the rights of aliens, a closer examination reveals that this protection is not so comprehensive. The chapter concludes with an appraisal of the Declaration on the Human Rights of Individuals who are not Nationals of the Country in Which They Live, adopted by the UN General Assembly on 13 December 1985.

Part II of the study examines the universal standards within the International Labour Organization (ILO) and the UN, which specifically relate to the protection of migrant workers and their families. The oldest multilateral body concerned with the protection of migrant workers is the ILO. Chapter 3 contains a general appraisal of the protection of human rights by the ILO and the unique mechanisms in force for their supervision and enforcement. Within this context, it evaluates ILO standards found in conventions and recommendations expressly concerned with the protection of migrant workers and their families. This analysis is not limited, however, to rights concerned with labour alone and includes an examination of the protection of the other rights under examination in this work, such as rights to education and cultural and political rights. Strictly-speaking, the protection of these rights falls outside of the competence of the ILO. Nonetheless, this chapter shows that the ILO *is* concerned with these rights, largely because the question of labour cannot be considered in isolation from the broader social, cultural, and political context in which migrants find themselves. The UN International Convention on the Protection of the Rights of All Migrant Workers and Members of Their Families, adopted in December 1990 after 10 years of negotiation, is the focus of Chapter 4, which evaluates the Convention's provisions on the rights of migrant workers and their families in countries of employment. In doing so, it refers extensively to the *travaux préparatoires* in order to assess the potential extent of this protection, the position of some key countries of employment towards the Convention, and the prospects for its ratification.

Part III (Chapters 5 to 8) constitutes a comprehensive and detailed evaluation of the regional human rights standards found in Europe, which are relevant to the protection of the economic, social, cultural, political, and residence rights of migrant workers and their families.

Europe has been chosen as the most suitable region of study for a number of reasons. First, international migration for employment has a lengthy history in Europe, particularly since the Second World War when it began to resemble other major population movements in history. Hence the volume of human beings involved is hardly insignificant. Secondly, there is a plethora of developed international standards in Europe applicable to the human rights of aliens and foreign workers, which are not found in other regions of the world. Thirdly, these standards flow from an intergovernmental organization, the Council of Europe (COE), and from a series of overlapping economic regional regimes which also provide for free movement of labour among member countries, in particular the European Community (EC) and, to a lesser extent, the Nordic Common Market and the regime operating between the Benelux countries. The comparative study of these systems is an interesting and challenging task. Fourthly, the continent today is undergoing dramatic and far-reaching political and economic changes, especially in central and eastern Europe, which have led to the expected increase (albeit minor at present) in labour migration from east to west. Finally, political and economic migrants from the Third World have always flocked to Europe, and in particular to the western half of the continent. Given the ever-widening gulf between the countries of the developed North and the developing South, this migratory flow will without doubt continue.

An attempt is also made in the case study to provide an overview of the legal condition of migrant workers and their families in some of the major European labour-receiving countries. Because the principal purpose of the case study, however, is to examine the protection of migrant workers and their families from a regional human rights perspective, this overview by no means purports to constitute a comprehensive treatise on the treatment of migrants in each country. It is recognized, however, that regional protection is not necessarily superior and that in some cases, national law or bilateral agreements between labour-sending and receiving states might afford migrant workers and their families greater protection. Indeed, examples of such superior protection are provided where appropriate. Moreover, the multifarious international standards pursuant to the protection of migrant workers and their families in Europe should not be considered in isolation from universal norms, such as those contained in the International Bill of Rights examined in Chapter 2, and those exclusively focusing on migrants, such as the specific ILO instruments and the recent UN Convention analysed in Chapters 3 and 4 respectively. Chapter 5 introduces the relevant treaties and systems in Europe for the protection of the rights of migrant workers and their families. Chapter 6 proceeds to analyse the various definitions of 'migrant worker', the particular legal situation of non-EC or 'third country' migrants and the level of protection which irregular or undocumented migrants might expect to receive on the continent. Chapter 7 undertakes an examination of the way these treaties and systems implement the principle of equal treatment between migrants and nationals in the country of employment, and Chapter 8 focuses in detail on the protection of the economic, social, cultural, political, and residence rights of migrant workers and their families.

The principal instruments of protection examined in Part III are the human rights treaties adopted under the auspices of the COE and the relevant provisions of EC law on free movement of workers which are more advanced than the analogous COE provisions.[19] The liberal EC standards, however, operate in a uniquely integrated system, and, for the time being at least, are less relevant outside of the EC context.[20] In general, therefore, EC standards only apply to the most 'privileged' class of migrants on the continent. In a similar vein, COE instruments, with the exception of the European Convention on Human Rights,

[19] This study does not discuss the legally non-binding provisions on migration adopted under the auspices of the Conference on Security and Cooperation in Europe (CSCE), renamed as the Organization on Security and Cooperation in Europe (OSCE) with effect from 1 Jan. 1995. For a consideration of the relevance of the CSCE/OSCE for the protection of migrant workers and their families, see the following: U. Gibson and J. Niessen, *The CSCE and the Protection of the Rights of Migrants, Refugees and Minorities in Europe*, CCME Briefing Paper No. 11 (Brussels: Churches Commission for Migrants in Europe, March 1993); K. Groenendijk, 'Migration Policy in Europe and the Role of the CSCE' in A. Bloed and W. de Jonge, (eds.), *Legal Aspects of a New European Infrastructure* (Utrecht: Europa Instituut and the Netherlands Helsinki Committee, 1992) 119; J. Niessen, 'The Conference on Security and Cooperation in Europe and other European Fora on Migration' (1994) 28 IMR 580; and, with particular reference to the right to family reunion, R. Cholewinski, 'The Protection of the Right of Economic Migrants to Family Reunion in Europe' (1994) 43 ICLQ 568, 578–80, 593–4. A recent development was the seminar on migrant workers held in Warsaw in March 1994 by the Office for Democratic Institutions and Human Rights (ODIHR) under the Human Dimension of the CSCE/OSCE. The documents relating to this seminar can be found in Commission on Security and Cooperation in Europe, *CSCE Human Dimension Seminar on Migrant Workers: Report, Briefing, Documentation*, Warsaw, Poland, 21–25 March 1994 (Washington, D.C.: Commission on Security and Cooperation in Europe, April 1994).

[20] T. Stein and S. Thomsen, 'The Status of the Member States' Nationals under the Law of the European Communities' in Max Planck Institute of Comparative Law, (ed.), *The Legal Position of Aliens in National and International Law*, vol. 2 (Berlin: Springer Verlag, 1987) 1775–6. The adoption by the EC of association and cooperation agreements with an increasing number of non-member countries has altered this situation somewhat. See the discussion in Ch. 6.

are only applicable to nationals of those states parties which have ratified the instrument in question. Therefore, the most vulnerable groups of migrant workers and their families in Europe, in most cases, may only claim protection under the European Convention on Human Rights and under the ILO instruments examined in Chapter 3 of the work, assuming of course that these apply. The advanced protection afforded by EC law to EC nationals should not, however, be considered in isolation, without reference to the global context. With the trend in the world today towards economic regionalization in the shape of 'free trade' arrangements, EC standards are bound to gain importance elsewhere as countries in other regions seek to bring down trade barriers and consider implementing free movement of labour.

In the concluding chapter, a hypothetical appraisal is undertaken of the position in international human rights law of a particularly vulnerable group of migrant workers and their families residing in Western Europe. These migrants come from European countries, which are not members of the EC or which have not ratified any of the COE instruments, or from developing countries outside of Europe, such as the Mahgreb region of North Africa. The tendency to exclude these migrant workers and their families from national life must be resisted and should not be translated into similar moves to exclude them from the protection of regional economic regimes, such as the EC, or from other regional trading blocks or systems, established or in the process of being established elsewhere, which might plan to implement free movement of labour on a similar basis to that within the EC. The concluding chapter contends that the realization of the rights of alien migrant workers and their families is a test of our humanity and can only serve to advance the rights of *all* human beings.

PART I

International Migration for Employment, Aliens and Citizens

I

International Migration for Employment: An Overview with Reference to the Right to Development

[A]nthropologically-speaking, migration is an irrepressible human urge. People have always wanted to move to places with more spiritual freedom, greater political liberty or higher standards of living (and the satisfaction of basic needs in their country of origin does not constitute a threshold at which the urge to migrate suddenly vanishes or loses legitimacy). The more tolerant the receiving State, the more attractive its spiritual freedom and political liberty; the richer it is, the stronger its economic pull. When tolerance and wealth go hand in hand, man-made laws can attempt to regulate migration but they cannot suppress it . . . Economically-speaking, migration represents for the individual an escape from poverty (relative or absolute) and it relieves his home country of mouths to feed and bodies to clothe and shelter—even if it does not necessarily boost its productive capacity or afford it other gains as it does the individual and the country of employment.[1]

These are fascinating and extraordinary times, but also precarious and unpredictable. Since 1989, there have been many political changes, particularly in Europe. With the collapse of the Berlin Wall, the great ideological barrier between East and West has been swept aside. In its place, uncertainty reigns. Many states have regained their political freedom after a long period of oppression. Many more have entered the arena of international affairs for the very first time. War has raged in the heart of Europe—in the newly independent states of the former Yugoslavia and especially in Bosnia-Herzegovina. Conflict and unrest have spread to many corners of what was once the Soviet Union, where nations and peoples have sought to assert themselves after a long dark period of totalitarian rule. In Africa, genocidal atrocities, on an unprecedented scale, have been committed in Rwanda. These recent events, as is often the case, have eclipsed those unchanging concerns which have constantly preoccupied the international community, such as the scourge of poverty and the continuing and widening economic divide between the poor developing countries of the South and the prosperous developed nations of the North.

In this transitional and uncertain world order, the migration of people, both involuntary and voluntary, remains a familiar and perennial concern. From the earliest times, people have migrated across frontiers for numerous and various

[1] W. R. Böhning, *Studies in International Labour Migration* (London: ILO (published by Macmillan Press), 1984) Ch. 1, 'International Migration and the International Economic Order' 3, 13.

reasons. War, famine, environmental and man-made disasters, political and religious persecution, and forced expulsions have caused and continue to cause the involuntary migration of individuals and groups all over the globe. One appalling example of forced migration was slavery. This profound affront to human dignity led to the deportation of whole peoples and depopulated Africa. According to the UN Special Rapporteur, the practice of slavery, together with colonialism, contributed greatly to the present economic gulf between developed and developing countries by restraining the socio-economic development of the latter.[2] The inequitable socio-economic disparity between the North and South is also the principal cause of voluntary international migration. Indeed, most of international migration today is still in large part voluntary and constitutes the manifestation of a quest for a better life; hence the term 'economic refugees'. Labour migration is simply one facet of this voluntary international migration.[3]

Although the timeless nature of international migration reflects the dynamism of this phenomenon, it is evident that the instability in the world which many experience today and to which the events described above have undoubtedly contributed, has overshadowed the positive aspects of migration to the detriment of individual migrants:

> Migration has been a positive force in the world over time and history—linking nations and people, opening trade opportunities, creating communication links and contributing to the cross-fertilization of ideas and cultures. However, we are witnessing an unfortunate and troubling shift in perception among many about the idea of migration in general. World recession, coupled with political and economic instability which has followed some of the startlingly sudden changes in the post-Cold War period . . . are making migration a phenomenon inspiring fear and resentment in many parts of the world. And migrants themselves are bearing the brunt of the new fortress mentalities we see emerging.[4]

[2] *Exploitation of Labour Through Illicit And Clandestine Trafficking* (Preliminary Study prepared by Ms. H. E. Warzazi, Special Rapporteur) (hereinafter *Warzazi Preliminary Report*) 8, para. 17.

[3] The distinction between involuntary and voluntary international migration is not hard and fast given the multiple factors involved in migration decisions. It must be emphasized that the use of the term 'voluntary migration' connotes the absence of 'physical coercion', and it is recognized that many other forms of 'coercion' exist. See A. Segal and L. Marston, 'Maps and Keys—World Voluntary Migration 1500–1980' (1989) 27:1 *Migrationworld Magazine* 36. See also A. Segal, *An Atlas of International Migration* (London: Hans Zell, 1993) 14. For example, Martin writes: 'Much of today's migration is unwanted by the migrants as well as by the countries they seek to enter. Refugees are driven from their homes by persecution and many economically motivated migrants would remain at home if they could find jobs there': P. L. Martin, 'Epilogue. Reducing Emigration Pressure: What Role can Foreign Aid Play?' in W. R. Böhning and M. Schloeter-Paredes, (eds.), *Aid in Place of Migration?: Selected Contributions to an ILO–UNHCR Meeting*, A WEP Study (Geneva: International Labour Office, 1994) 241. Indeed, on a more abstract level, similarities can be found between refugees and economic migrants. For example, the migration of refugees fleeing political persecution in their homelands and illegal migrant labourers 'shares at least one common characteristic—it is an act born of desperation and a lack of hope and viable alternatives, not true choice': Employment and Immigration Canada, *An Approach to International Migration* (Immigration Policy Group, Jan. 1993) 2.

[4] *An Approach to International Migration*, n. 3 above, 3.

1.1 HISTORICAL BACKGROUND

Improvements in ocean travel during the latter half of this millennium resulted in mass migrations overseas, primarily from Western Europe to the Americas. Voluntary migrants were usually colonial settlers. Between 1506 and 1650 it is estimated that just under half a million persons migrated from Spain to the Caribbean and to Central and South America and Mexico, and that by 1815, one million migrants had settled in North America from the United Kingdom and Ireland.[5] Their numbers, however, were considerably less than those forced to migrate,[6] such as slaves,[7] indentured labourers,[8] convicts, and refugees.

The nineteenth century witnessed the expansion and acceleration of voluntary migratory movements. Contributing factors included the industrial revolution, the demographic and economic situation of Europe, the attraction of spaces to be settled and developed in the New World, technical advances in transportation, and the relaxation of government controls on movements of people.[9] Between 1815 and 1914, there were considerable intercontinental movements: about 60 million people migrated from Europe and elsewhere to the Americas, Oceania, and South and East Africa; an estimated 10 million persons migrated from Russia to Siberia and central Asia; approximately 12 million Chinese and 6 million Japanese moved to eastern and southern Asia; and 1.5 million persons emigrated from India to South-east Asia and South and East Africa.[10]

The nineteenth century also saw the development of migration for paid employment, which initially consisted of the large-scale importation of indentured agricultural labour to sustain the plantation economies of European colonial empires.[11] The importation of Indian Tamils by the British to work in the coffee and tea plantations in Ceylon (Sri Lanka) is just one example. The consequences of this migration, like the effects of slavery in the USA, have proven to be the source

[5] Segal, n. 3 above, 14. [6] Segal and Marston, n. 3 above, 36.

[7] For example, the slave trade accounted for the departure of an estimated 15 million people from Africa between 1550 and 1850: S. Ricca, *International Migration in Africa. Legal and Administrative Aspects* (Geneva: International Labour Office, 1989) 10.

[8] According to Segal, n. 3 above, 169, indentured labour for a designated period of time is considered, historically, as voluntary migration.

[9] *Warzazi Preliminary Report*, n. 2 above, 8–9, para. 18. Segal, n. 3 above, 161, notes that this mass migration 'probably served to reduce social tensions stemming from land shortages, lack of social mobility, and demographic pressures'. He adds that 'emigration as a historic "escape valve" for discontent, and potential social unrest has characterized much voluntary migration'.

[10] Segal and Marston, n. 3 above, 37. See also Segal, *ibid.* 16.

[11] *Warzazi Preliminary Report*, n. 2 above, 9, para. 18. Between 1834 and 1937, over 30 million indentured workers were brought from the Indian sub-continent to work in (other) colonies in Asia, the Indian Ocean, and the Caribbean. Although these migrants were not strictly-speaking slaves, they toiled in slave-like conditions. See R. Appleyard, *International Migration: Challenge for the Nineties* (Geneva: International Organisation for Migration, 1991) 11, 42 citing from K. Davis, *The Population of India and Pakistan* (Princeton, N.J., 1951) 99.

of human rights problems and international tensions today.[12] In Europe, industrialization created a demand for labour which was initially met by internal resettlement from rural to urban areas within countries and then by intra-European migration.[13] Until the beginning of the twentieth century, one characteristic of labour migration was its permanency. The temporary nature of such migration today is essentially a recent phenomenon.[14]

International voluntary migration continued during the inter-war period, but at a slower rate due to the introduction of restrictive immigration policies and the Great Depression of the 1930s; the latter resulting in a drastic decline in international trade, mass unemployment in many countries, and the phenomenon of large-scale forced and voluntary repatriation (as the USA and Argentina, for example, repatriated many Mexican and Italian migrants respectively).[15]

The end of the Second World War brought about a significant increase in migration generally. In addition to the forced migration of refugees and settlers from former colonies, many foreign workers flocked to Western Europe, mainly from southern Europe and the Mahgreb region of North Africa. These 'guest workers' contributed significantly to the reconstruction of Western Europe after the devastation of the war and to the creation of economic prosperity shortly afterwards. Indeed, the influx of foreign labour in many Western European countries appeared to spiral uncontrollably upwards until the beginning of the 1970s. In the Federal Republic of Germany, for example, there were 165,000 foreign workers in 1959. In 1960, this figure reached 280,000 and by 1971 it had climbed to a staggering 2.2 million.[16] Workers also migrated in significant numbers after 1945 in other parts of the world: to the USA from Mexico, Latin America and the Caribbean; to Argentina and Venezuela from Uruguay and Colombia respectively; to the Gulf States from Egypt, Jordan, and Asia; to the Ivory Coast and Nigeria from other parts of West Africa; to the former apartheid economy of South Africa from neighbouring countries;[17] and more recently within the East

[12] V. Leary, 'Migrant Workers and Human Rights' (1987) 1–2. The problems of adjustment of modern-day migrant workers and their families to their new milieu are also acute and have international repercussions. *Ibid.*

[13] *Warzazi Preliminary Report*, n. 2 above, 9, para. 18. Internal rural-urban migration within European countries is also considered to be a catalyst for this emigration. Cf. R. Appleyard, 'International Migration and Development—An Unresolved Relationship' (1992) 30 IM (Special Issue—Migration and Development) 251, 258.

[14] T. Ansay, 'Legal Problems of Migrant Workers' (1977) 7; cf. P. L. Martin and A. Richards, 'International Migration of Labor: Boon or Bane?' (1980) 103:10 Monthly Labor Review 4; cf. 'Introduction' in D. G. Papademetriou and P. L. Martin, (eds.), *The Unsettled Relationship: Labor Migration and Economic Development* (1991) ix, x.

[15] Segal and Marston, n. 3 above, 39; Segal, n. 3 above, 18.

[16] *Warzazi Preliminary Report*, n. 2 above, 9, para. 19, citing from International Labour Office, 188th Session of the Governing Body, Nov. 1972, ILO Doc. G.B. 188/5/9, para. 106. In 1972, there were 11 million migrant workers and their families in Western Europe. Of these, 7 million were to be found in seven countries, namely Belgium, France, the Federal Republic of Germany, the Netherlands, Sweden, Switzerland and the United Kingdom. *Ibid.*

[17] *Warzazi Preliminary Report*, 9–10, para. 20; Segal and Marston, n. 3 above, 40–1; Segal, n. 3 above, 20.

and South-east Asian region.[18] Many of these included illegal migrant workers who entered countries without authorization to take up paid employment.

Labour migration to Europe declined significantly as a result of the recession which followed the 1973–74 oil crisis. Nonetheless, many migrant workers remained in their countries of employment, and the total number of migrants actually increased because of family reunification. Migration for employment to Europe, however, is likely to increase again, particularly in view of the continuing economic disparity between North and South, the 'opening of borders' in central and eastern Europe, the disintegration of the former Soviet Union, and the implementation of the single economic market between EC member states.

1.2 CURRENT GLOBAL LABOUR MIGRATION MOVEMENTS AND FUTURE PROJECTIONS

This brief historical survey indicates that international labour migration is truly a global phenomenon, taking place in every region of the world. Estimates for 1993 place the global number of economically active migrant workers at approximately 30–35 million; 8 million in Europe (excluding the former Soviet Union and former Yugoslavia); 7 million in North America; 3–5 million in Central and South America; 5–6 million in Africa; 2–4 million in South, South-east and East Asia; and 5 million in West Asia (Gulf region).[19] Together with their dependants, the current migrant population world-wide is probably between 70 and 85 million.[20] This number is expected to increase as a result of entry pressures created by rapid demographic growth in developing countries.[21] More significant for

[18] See R. Skeldon, 'International Migration Within and From the East and Southeast Asian Region: A Review Essay' (1992) 1 *Asian and Pacific Migration Journal* 19, 44–9.

[19] ILO, IOM, UNHCR, *Migrants, Refugees and International Cooperation*, A joint contribution to the International Conference on Population and Development (Geneva; ILO, IOM, UNHCR, 1994) 2. The Director General of the International Organization for Migration (IOM) suggested in 1990 that the number of illegal migrants alone could be as high as 30 million. J. N. Purcell Jr., 'Opening Address by the Director General of the International Organization for Migration: Ninth IOM Seminar on Migration: South–North Migration, Geneva, 4–6 Dec. 1990' (1991) 29 IM 157, 160. See also Appleyard (1991), n. 11 above.

[20] *Migrants, Refugees and International Cooperation*, n. 19 above. One recent estimate places the number of international migrants in the world, including refugees, at more than 125 million, about half of whom are found in developing countries. The number of migrants entering the principal receiving countries of the developed world has increased in recent years at a rate of 1.4 million annually, with two-thirds originating in developing countries: *Report of the International Conference on Population and Development*, Cairo, 5–13 Sept. 1994, UN Doc. A/CONF.171/13 (18 Oct. 1994) Annex, Programme of Action, 70, para. 10.1.

[21] Global population is expected to increase from the present 5.2 billion to 8.4 billion in 2025. The expected increase in the developing world during this period is 3 billion in contrast with a mere 147 million in industrial countries. As a result, developing countries' share in the global population will rise from 68% to 84% in 2025. See B. Ghosh, 'Trends in World Migration: the European Perspective' (Sept.–Oct. 1991) *The Courier* (African–Caribbean–Pacific (ACP)–European Community) 46, 48–9. A good exemplar of this population growth in individual developing countries is Egypt. Egypt's population rose from 9.7 million in 1897, to 19 million in 1947, and to 48.2 million

international labour migration is the projected *increase* in the number of people of working age in less developed countries which stood at 1.8 billion in 1990 and is expected to rise by 733 million by 2010. When compared with a labour force in more developed countries of 586 million in 1990, this is a staggering statistic indeed.[22] Despite these demographic data, the percentage of people in a state who cross national boundaries as migrants is still fairly small.[23] The salient feature of current migration flows 'is that direction is more global and composition more diverse'.[24]

1.3 CAUSES OF AND FACTORS FACILITATING INTERNATIONAL LABOUR MIGRATION

The causes of international labour migration are numerous and complex, and this section only focuses on what are arguably the principal causes. On a basic level, migration for employment is caused by complementary 'push' and 'pull' factors; the former is characterized by poor living conditions in the country of origin and the latter by the availability of well-paid work (in relative terms) in the country of employment. The labour migration process is then facilitated by improving communications, the availability of transportation, and by social or ethnic networks.[25]

in 1986. In 1989, it stood at 54 million. These figures represent an annual population growth of 2.7%. Note, Egypt, 'Population Growth and Jobs' (1989) ILO SLB 292. In Mexico, the population more than tripled from 20 million in 1940 to 67 million in 1980. In the 1980s it rose further to 88 million. Commission for the Study of International Migration and Cooperative Economic Development, 'Immigration and Economic Development' in *The Unsettled Relationship: Labor Migration and Development*, n. 14 above, 221, 241, originally the Executive Summary to: US Commission for the Study of International Migration and Cooperative Development, Report to the US Congress, *Unauthorized Migration: An Economic Development Response* (Washington DC: US Government Printing Office, July 1990) (hereinafter *US Study on Unauthorized Migration and Development*). (The Commission was set up by the US Immigration Reform and Control Act 1986 with the mandate 'to examine the conditions in Mexico and such other sending countries which contribute to unauthorized migration to the United States and [to explore] mutually beneficial, reciprocal trade and investment programs to alleviate such conditions' (s. 601) *ibid.* 221).

[22] Ghosh, n. 21 above, 49: A. Golini, G. Gerano, and F. Heins, 'South–North Migration with Special Reference to Europe' (1991) 29 IM 253, 255. In Mexico, 1 million persons enter the labour market each year, compared with 2 million in the USA which has nearly three times Mexico's population: *US Study on Unauthorized Migration and Development*, n. 21 above, 236.

[23] Estimated by Russell and Teitelbaum to be no more than between 10 to 25%. S. S. Russell and M. S. Teitelbaum, *International Migration and International Trade* (World Bank Discussion Papers No. 160) (Washington, DC: The World Bank, 1992) 6. Even this estimate seems to be over-extensive. Segal, n. 3 above, 127–8, has produced a short list of countries where emigrants abroad constitute 10% or more of the population. Most of these states have small populations and special relationships with receiving countries.

[24] Appleyard (1991), n. 11 above, 29.

[25] Martin (1994), n. 3 above, 243, observes succinctly with reference to both voluntary and involuntary migration: 'The determinants of migration pressure are familiar—economic inequality and conflicts push migrants out; jobs that pay relatively high wages and safe havens pull migrants in; and communication and network factors link migrants and destinations'.

Poverty, economic underdevelopment, and demographic growth

Most international labour migration movements are linked to poverty and economic underdevelopment in countries of origin[26] and the existence of considerable discrepancies in standards of living and wages[27] between these countries and countries of employment.[28] These movements are also assisted in developing countries by significant population growth, discussed earlier, with the subsequent increase in economically-active persons and chronic underemployment, in contrast with the relative demographic stability in Western Europe and North America.[29] Therefore, the combination of poverty and underemployment in underdeveloped and developing countries with large populations compels persons to leave their homeland, in many instances unwillingly and without their families, to seek a better and more dignified existence elsewhere. For some migrants, the decision to leave the country of origin for the purpose of employment is more about survival itself.[30]

[26] According to Papademetriou and Martin, severe migration pressures have also been created in some African countries by a combination of 'economic mismanagement and ecological deterioration'. D. G. Papademetriou and P. L. Martin, 'Labor Migration and Development: Research and Policy Issues' in *The Unsettled Relationship: Labour Migration and Economic Development*, n. 14 above, 3, 15.

[27] At the beginning of the 1990s, the average annual per capita income stood at US$17,000 in 'high-income countries' compared with US$750 in most developing countries and US$320 in Sub-Saharan Africa or South Asia. Ghosh, n. 21 above, 49. Such discrepancies are further illustrated by comparing wage ratios between specific receiving and sending countries which can be up to 10:1 between the USA and Mexico and as much as 80:1 between Japan and Bangladesh. See P. Stalker, *The Work of Strangers: A Survey of International Labour Migration* (Geneva: International Labour Office, 1994) 155.

[28] These countries need not necessarily fall neatly into the developing/developed dichotomy. For example the wealthy oil-exporting countries of the Arab Gulf States are significant labour importers while the former communist countries of central and eastern Europe increasingly export labour. See also Russell and Teitelbaum, n. 23 above, 6, para. 2.14. Segal, n. 3 above, 113, also observes that most voluntary migration takes place regionally between developing countries, and that 'extra-regional' migration probably accounts for less than 25% of the total world-wide.

[29] *Warzazi Preliminary Report*, n. 2 above, 9, para. 21; cf. Russell and Teitelbaum, n. 23 above, 6, para. 2.14.

[30] A useful distinction is the one made between 'survival' and 'mobility' migrants. The former mainly come from Asia, Africa, and the Latin American and Caribbean region and are generally low-skilled with little education. They are 'pushed' into migration (usually without authorization) by structural poverty reflecting household decisions about survival, and are often employed abroad in marginal jobs. The latter tend to be officially recruited from abroad, in Europe, the Middle East, South Africa, and South Asia, and are usually better educated and more skilled than the former. They are 'pulled away from home by better economic and social opportunities', and are more likely to hold better jobs abroad than survival migrants. Papademetriou and Martin, 'Labor Migration and Development: Research and Policy Issues', n. 26 above, 5–6. This distinction is taken from R. Urzua, *Population Redistribution Mechanisms as Related to Various Forms of Development in Population Redistribution Policies in Development Planning* (New York: UN, 1981), and illustrates further the difficulties in clearly distinguishing between voluntary and involuntary migrants. See also n. 3 above. Although survival migrants are not *physically* forced to leave their country of origin, it is arguable that their need to escape from abject poverty constitutes a form of 'coercion'.

Demand for labour

Pressure to migrate is exacerbated further by the demand for cheap labour, which is caused either by labour shortages in natural resource-based economies[31] or by the existence of socially undesirable (to nationals) jobs in the developed industrialized world, particularly in Western Europe and North America.[32] Unfortunately, this demand for labour, coupled with the fear migrant workers have of returning to unemployment and poverty in their own countries, creates a situation 'conducive . . . to all kinds of abusive practices which constitute a violation of human rights'.[33] The demand for foreign labour does not have to be officially sanctioned by the authorities of the receiving country and may still exist despite strict immigration controls, which invariably results in an increase in the entry of irregular migrants.[34]

Communications and transportation

Scientific and technical improvements in communication systems and readily available transportation have undoubtedly facilitated and contributed to the growth of international labour migration.[35] Mass communication systems, making people (usually city dwellers) in sending countries more aware of living standards in developed receiving countries, undoubtedly play a part in encouraging them to risk emigration.[36] Modern modes of travel also assist in migrations which would not have been possible some decades earlier. For example, Asian labour migration to the oil-rich Arab Gulf States could not have taken place on such a grand scale without the availability of air travel.[37]

Migration 'networks'

It should not be overlooked that migration generally (including international labour migration) is a dynamic process usually taking place between countries

[31] For example, most major oil exporting economies such as the Gulf States and also, to some extent, South-east Asian countries such as Malaysia. Cf. 'Labor Migration and Development: Research and Policy Issues', n. 26 above, 13.

[32] See Leary, n. 12 above, 4: 'The juxtaposition of rich, developed countries in need of workers willing to do work that nationals refuse or at a wage level unacceptable to nationals and the corresponding high level of poverty and unemployment in other countries creates the demand for labour'. Such low-paid, socially undesirable work, need not only encompass the traditional dirty industrial jobs, but also includes temporary and seasonal employment and work in the growing labour-intensive private and public service sectors. Cf. 'Labor Migration and Development: Research and Policy Issues' n. 26 above.

[33] *Warzazi Preliminary Report*, n. 2 above, 10, para. 22.

[34] However, as Appleyard astutely notes, governments may 'do little to prevent such flows if the workers fill a need and can be expelled if and when that need no longer exists'. R. Appleyard, 'Migration and Development: A Critical Relationship' (1992) 1 *Asian and Pacific Migration Journal*, 1, 9. See also Papademetriou and Martin, 'Labor Migration and Development: Research and Policy Issues', n. 26 above, 14.

[35] Appleyard (1991), n. 11 above, 2.

[36] Cf. Segal, n. 3 above, 113; cf. Ghosh, n. 21 above, 49.

[37] Russell and Teitelbaum, n. 23 above, 2.

with close historic, colonial, economic, and cultural ties which constitute 'migration systems'.[38] Contributing to this process are, *inter alia*, migrant social and ethnic 'networks' of family and friends which have been established over time,[39] and which link cities or villages to labour markets in receiving countries.[40] Migration assisted by such networks eventually becomes self-perpetuating 'because it creates the social structure needed to sustain it',[41] and its character changes to accommodate the entry of groups which were not necessarily planned in the selective immigration policies of states of employment.[42] The existence of family reunion programmes in traditional receiving countries is an example of this aspect of the migration phenomenon.

1.4 CAUSES OF IRREGULAR LABOUR MIGRATION

Many of the causes of labour migration considered above constitute equally powerful incentives for potential migrant workers to enter a country through clandestine means in order to find employment.[43] This desperate decision is accentuated by the hurdles migrant workers face in order to enter and work in a country legally. Indeed, studies suggest that there is a correlation between stringent and restrictive immigration regulations and an increase in the illicit traffic of migrant workers where appropriate preventive measures have not yet been taken.[44] Restrictive

[38] See generally M. M. Kritz and H. Zlotnik, 'Global Interactions: Migration Systems, Processes, and Policies' in M. M. Kritz, L. L. Lim and H. Zlotnik, (eds.), *International Migration Systems: A Global Approach* (1992) 1. A modern example of historical and cultural similarities influencing the migration process is the free movement of workers regime within the EC: *ibid.* 13.

[39] Cf. *ibid.* 1.

[40] P. L. Martin, 'Labor Migration: Theory and Reality' in *The Unsettled Relationship: Labor Migration and Economic Development*, n. 14 above, 24, 37.

[41] Appleyard (1992:1), n. 13 above, 255, citing from D. S. Massey, 'International Migration in Comparative Perspective', Working Papers, Commission for the Study of International Migration and Cooperative Economic Development, No. 3, Feb. 1989, Washington, DC, 396–7. Martin, n. 14 above, 28, writes: 'Most labor migration has its genesis in recruitment by employers or their agents from receiving nations. This recruitment creates information networks and economic dependencies that soon become institutionalized, a process which yields the aphorism that migration streams are much easier to start than to stop'.

[42] Appleyard, n. 13 above. Papademetriou observes: 'The occasional dissonance between the needs of a receiving country's labor market and the behavior of migration flows usually means that the receiving society, but not capital itself, has lost control over the migration process and that ethnic networks have developed and matured to the point where they are able to frustrate the host society's official immigration policies and in effect act as independent migration forces': D. G. Papademetriou, 'Migration and Development: The Unsettled Relationship' in *The Unsettled Relationship: Labour Migration and Economic Development*, n. 14 above, 213, 217.

[43] *Warzazi Preliminary Report*, n. 2 above, 16, para. 38. See also the *Report of the International Conference on Population and Development*, n. 20 above, 74, para. 10.15, which notes: 'Given that the pressures for migration are growing in a number of developing countries, especially since their labour force continues to increase, undocumented or irregular migration is expected to rise'.

[44] See also UN Commission on Human Rights, Sub-Commission on Prevention of Discrimination and Protection of Minorities, 28th Session, *Exploitation of Labour Through Illicit And Clandestine Trafficking* (Study prepared by Ms. H. E. Warzazi, Special Rapporteur) UN Doc. E/CN.4/Sub.2/

immigration policies apart, migrant workers come up against a number of specific obstacles which may tempt them to migrate illegally. The length and complexity of immigration and recruitment procedures common to many public administrations have a discouraging effect. Would-be immigrants are also likely to have a general mistrust of these bodies, a reaction possibly attributable to past colonialism[45] or to a fear of repressive governments and corrupt public officials in their home countries. Furthermore, most receiving states require newly-arrived migrant workers to fulfil certain residence and housing conditions before their families are permitted to join them. Often, migrant workers consider these requirements too harsh or impossible to meet and are willing to arrange for the entry of their families without adhering to the proper regulations.[46] Illegal migration is also exacerbated by misleading publicity by traffickers in clandestine labour[47] and the willingness of employers, eager for easily available and cheap labour, to recruit workers without regard to their nationality or status.[48]

1.5 THE IMPACT OF INTERNATIONAL MIGRATION ON RECEIVING AND SENDING COUNTRIES

In addition to the obvious economic benefits which accrue to individual migrant workers and their families,[49] it has been argued that international labour migration should be economically beneficial to both receiving and sending countries because 'scarce resources [such as labour] are reallocated to a more efficient or higher wage use',[50] but there are also considerable disadvantages which are experienced by both sets of countries, and in particular by the usually poorer countries of origin. The benefits and disadvantages, however, must be viewed in the light of one of the key challenges facing the international community, namely the successful development of the South. If this task is neglected, the economic gap between developed and developing nations will only widen further still and the international migration of labour, particularly that which is regulated by receiving countries, will continue merely to be a 'subsidy to the rich from the poor'.[51]

L.629 (4 July 1975) (hereinafter *Warzazi Final Report*) 10, para. 24, citing ILO Report No. VII (1), *Migrant Workers*, 8 and UN Doc E/CN.5/515, paras. 18–19. The above Warzazi report can also be found in the consolidated report.

45 *Warzazi Preliminary Report*, n. 2 above, 16, paras. 39–40.

46 *Ibid.* 17, para. 43.

47 *Warzazi Final Report*, n. 44 above, 9, para. 20.

48 *Warzazi Preliminary Report*, n. 2 above, 16, para. 41.

49 Papademetriou and Martin write: 'Migration has . . . accomplished at least one important goal: it has significantly improved the economic fortunes of many of the families of those who emigrated, and in some instances, of their communities': 'Labor Migration and Development: Research and Policy Issues', n. 26 above, 21.

50 Appleyard (1992:1), n. 13 above, 260; Martin, 'Labor Migration: Theory and Reality', n. 40 above, 29.

51 Papademetriou, 'Migration and Development: The Unsettled Relationship', n. 42 above, 219.

Receiving countries

Receiving countries, especially affluent countries, 'benefit' from foreign migrant labour in a number of ways. These 'benefits' are more ascertainable from a purely economic perspective and certainly less justifiable in human and moral terms. From the economic standpoint, immigrant workers constitute a source of cheap, easily available, effective and youthful labour willing to take on the most unpleasant and arduous of tasks which nationals seldom are prepared to perform. This labour has two 'advantages' for employers. First, it is arguably instrumental in reducing the strain on labour relations. So long as migrant workers are in the worst jobs, there is less cause for national workers to complain about work and employment conditions. Moreover, few migrant workers are unionized and therefore less in a position to protest, while migrant workers in an irregular situation are also less likely to complain. Secondly, resort to foreign labour initially halts the upward wage spiral, and should facilitate future salary increases to national workers.[52] For domestic consumers, lower labour costs also translate into cheaper goods and services.[53] The combination of convenience and economics adopted in many receiving countries is illustrated aptly by Walzer with reference to the situation of migrant workers in Western Europe in the early 1970s:

The managers of the economy [of a capitalist democracy and welfare State, with strong trade unions and a fairly affluent population] find it increasingly difficult to attract workers to a set of jobs that have come to be regarded as exhausting, dangerous and degrading. But these jobs are also socially necessary; someone must be found to do them. Domestically, there are only two alternatives, neither of them palatable. The constraints imposed on the labour market by the unions and the welfare State might be broken, and then the most

[52] Cf. UN Commission on Human Rights, Sub-Commission on Prevention of Discrimination and Protection of Minorities, 27th Session, *Exploitation of Labour Through Illicit and Clandestine Trafficking: Introductory Statement Concerning the Study on Illicit Trafficking in Labour and on the Present Problem of Migrant Workers* (made by Ms. H. E. Warzazi in introducing her preliminary report on the same topic, n. 2 above), UN Doc. E/CN.4/Sub.2/352 (14 Aug. 1974) (hereinafter *Warzazi Introductory Statement to Preliminary Report*) 5. This statement is also found in the Consolidated Report. It is not altogether clear whether the employment of migrant workers will actually result in eventual salary increases for national workers. Labour groups might contend that such workers facilitate the ability of employers to keep wages low for everyone. I am indebted to Bill Black for this observation. Indeed, it has been argued that the presence of low-paid immigrant workers clearly disadvantages lower-skilled national workers because it augments competition and, more importantly, contributes to the retardation of real wage growth in that sector of the economy. Cf. Martin and Richards, n. 14 above, 6; Papademetriou and Martin, 'Labor Migration and Development: Research and Policy Issues', n. 26 above, 4 (n. 5). Reliance on migrant workers may also lead to the preservation of small and inefficient establishments in which such workers are employed and which might otherwise fail in the face of foreign and domestic competition. Martin and Richards, n. 14 above. In this sense, therefore, immigrant labour may actually benefit some national workers by helping them to retain their jobs. Martin, 'Labor Migration: Theory and Reality', n. 40 above, 29 (n. 3). Warzazi also notes that the employment of immigrant labour contributes to 'technical conservatism' with the result that certain sectors of the economy, usually those comprised of old-fashioned, small and mid-size businesses, are kept in a state of under-development without any effects being felt in the economy as a whole. *Warzazi Introductory Statement to Preliminary Report*, *ibid.* 10.

[53] Martin and Richards, n. 14 above, 4.

vulnerable segment of the local working class driven to accept jobs hitherto thought undesirable. But this would require a difficult and dangerous political campaign. Or, the wages and working conditions of the undesirable jobs might be dramatically improved so as to attract workers even within the constraints of the local market. But this would raise costs throughout the economy and, what is probably more important, challenge the existing social hierarchy. Rather than adopt either of these drastic measures, the economic managers, with the help of their government, shift the jobs from the domestic to the international labour market, making them available to workers in poorer countries who find them less undesirable.[54]

The need to employ foreign workers in order to fill labour shortages or to cut labour costs might also be avoided if managers decided to shift their operations to 'capital intensive high technology industries' or to 'export capital to low-wage countries or regions for the production of labour-intensive manufactures', the latter approach having been adopted by Hong Kong and Japan in east and south-east Asia.[55]

Migrant workers also cost nothing to receiving countries in social terms, nor in terms of education and training prior to their employment,[56] although such social costs are likely to increase if migrants settle permanently in the country of employment with their children.[57] In human and moral terms, these 'benefits' to the host country are tantamount to forms of 'exploitation' not only of the immigrant workers themselves, but also of their countries of origin. This exploitative situation is exacerbated when the negative effects of labour migration on sending countries are considered.

One of the principal 'disadvantages' labour migration poses for receiving countries, especially when it becomes a vehicle for *de facto* permanent immigration, concerns the social problems that often arise as a result of the existence of a second-class, economically and socially vulnerable, and culturally distinct population in the midst of the host community. These social problems may become particularly acute in times of economic recession when immigrants are wrongly perceived as taking away jobs from nationals. Hostility towards migrants manifests itself in the form of intolerance, xenophobia, and racism. Another perceived disadvantage of labour migration for receiving countries is when an uncontrolled influx of migrant workers and their families (as illustrated by the phenomenon of illegal migration) becomes so significant that it threatens to stretch the economic

54 M. Walzer, *Spheres of Justice: A Defense of Pluralism and Equality* (New York: Basic Books, 1983) 56.

55 Skeldon, n. 18 above, 44. This approach has also been adopted by the Republic of Korea, Singapore, and Taiwan. See ILO, *World Labour Report 1992* (Geneva: International Labour Office, 1992) 48. Between 1980 and 1989, Japan alone invested US$16 billion in this region. See Appleyard, 'Migration and Development: A Critical Relationship', n. 34 above, 13. Böhning and Schloeter-Paredes observe that the use of foreign direct investment (FDI) by Japan has resulted in accelerated economic growth and democratization in east and south-east Asia, but they also point out that it has not saved Japan from migration pressures. W. R. Böhning and M. Schloeter-Paredes, 'Introduction' in *Aid in Place of Migration?*, n. 3 above, 1, 5. See below on the further pitfalls of FDI in this respect.

56 *Warzazi Introductory Statement to Preliminary Report*, n. 52 above, 11.

57 Martin and Richards, n. 14 above, 7.

and social entitlements available to members of the national community.[58] An example of a draconian measure to counter such a perceived effect is Proposition 187, the controversial 'Save Our State' (SOS) initiative, approved on 8 November 1994 by the voters of California in order to deny illegal aliens the enjoyment of education, non-emergency health care services, and other social benefits. Proposition 187 also requires service-providers to report illegal migrants to immigration authorities. However, on 20 November 1995, in *League of United Latin American Citizens* v. *Wilson* (Case No. CV94–7569), a federal judge in Los Angeles ruled that most of this new law was unconstitutional on the ground that the authority to regulate immigration belongs exclusively to the federal government with the result that only those services that are completely state-funded, such as post-secondary education, can be denied to illegal aliens.[59]

Sending countries

For poor countries, international labour migration supposedly alleviates unemployment and the resulting social turmoil created by poverty.[60] It is unlikely, however, that there are any positive long-term effects.[61] In reviewing the literature on this subject, Miller observes that labour migration has probably only a short-term stabilizing effect on sending societies and that, in the long-term, it represents a threat to the political stability of those states. Economic downturns may result in massive return migration to the countries of origin at times when they can least afford to re-integrate returning nationals.[62]

[58] Cf. P. H. Schuck, 'Immigration Law and the Problem of Community' in N. Glazer, (ed.), *Clamour at the Gates: The New American Immigration* (San Francisco: Institute for Contemporary Studies (ICS) Press, 1985) 285, 289 and 304. This 'threat' to the welfare state, however, is to some extent offset by the additional taxation income attributable to irregular migrant workers.

[59] See M. Kurfis, 'Constitutionality of California's Proposition 187: An Equal Protection Analysis' (1995) 32 *California Western L. Rev.* 129. 'Parts of Proposition 187 Unconstitutional' (1995) 2 MN No. 12 (Dec.). See also P. Martin, 'Proposition 187 in California' (1995) 29 IMR 255.

[60] Cf. Leary, n. 12 above, 4. Indeed, in some cases, international labour migration may *create* unemployment in poorer countries instead of reducing it, especially if emigration results in vacancies that cannot be filled because they require particular skills which are unavailable. According to Martin and Richards, n. 14 above, 6, when such a scenario arises in developing sending countries, its effect is to slow down socio-economic development.

[61] Cf. D. G. Papademetriou, 'Confronting the Challenge of Transnational Migration: Domestic and International Responses' in OECD, *The Changing Course of International Migration* (Paris: OECD, 1993) 207, 214.

[62] M. J. Miller, 'Introduction' (in Temporary Worker Programs: Mechanisms, Conditions, Consequences) (1986) 20 IMR 740, 749. Massive return migration may also occur as a result of war and social turmoil in the state of employment. An exemplar of this phenomenon was the huge exodus of migrant workers from Kuwait and Iraq at the beginning of the Gulf Crisis in 1990. See International Labour Organization, Governing Body, 249th Session, Geneva, 27 Feb.–2 March 1991, Report of the Director-General (Third Supplementary Report), *Migrant Workers affected by the Gulf Crisis*, ILO Doc. GB.249/15/7; and Canada, Immigration and Refugee Board Documentation Centre, Question and Answer Series, *The Persian Gulf: The Situation of Foreign Workers* (Ottawa, May 1991). Other longer-term negative effects on sending countries are agricultural decline, because of an exodus of workers from rural regions, and an 'artificial' urbanization process caused by the relocation of migrants' families unsupported by any increase in domestic productivity. Martin and Richards, n. 14 above, 8.

(a) Remittances

Remittances, mainly composed of transfers of funds from migrant workers to their families, have been described as the '*raison d'être* for migration'.[63] Without doubt, they benefit economically individual migrant workers and their families in a number of ways.[64] However, the benefit of remittances to the economies of sending countries is not so clear-cut.

On its face, migration for employment ensures the influx of a significant amount of much-needed hard currency. Globally, the total value of remittances amounted to US$60.9 billion in 1989, greater than the total value of Official Development Assistance (ODA) which amounted to US$51 billion in 1988.[65] It must be emphasized that these are *official* figures and do not include those (possibly sizeable) funds which have been transferred through informal channels.[66] Not all of the migrants' hard-earned money, however, finds its way into these economies. In actual fact, only a small portion may be transferred to sending countries.[67] Moreover, remittance capital when transferred is not always utilized in a manner conducive to the economic development of the country concerned.[68] There are differing views on the purpose for which remittances are used (for example, whether they are used for productive investment or simply for consumption) and, indeed, on the significance of the relevant usage for develop-

[63] Martin, 'Labor Migration: Theory and Reality', n. 40 above, 39.

[64] Martin, *ibid.*, writes: 'Initially, remittances provide money for daily living and debt repayment, then consumer durables, and finally funds to invest in better housing, land, or even a small business. Remittance levels are often maintained over time because the settlement abroad which encourages migrants to remit less is offset partially by their ever-higher earnings which permit migrants to remit more'.

[65] Russell and Teitelbaum, n. 23 above, 1, para. 1.3, citing from World Bank, *World Development Report 1990* (Washington, DC: The World Bank, 1990) 127. The figure of US$60.9 billion is the revised figure from the original US$65.6 billion cited in the above report. S. S. Russell, 'Migrant Remittances and Development' (1992) 30 IM 267, 269.

[66] Russell, n. 65 above, 268; cf. Russell and Teitelbaum, n. 23 above, 29, para. 3.2. Appleyard notes that about 80% of remittances are returned through official channels with the remainder coming back through non-banking institutions. R. Appleyard, 'Migration and Development: Myths and Reality' (1989) 23 IMR 486, 493, citing from I. S. Gilani, *Citizens, Slaves, Guest-Workers* (Islamabad: Institute of Policy Studies, 1985).

[67] UN Commission on Human Rights, Sub-Commission on Prevention of Discrimination and Protection of Minorities, 28th Session, *Exploitation of Labour Through Illicit and Clandestine Trafficking: Statement Concerning the Study on Illicit Trafficking in Labour and on the Present Problem of Migrant Workers* (made by Ms. H. E. Warzazi in introducing her final report on the same topic, n. 44 above), UN Doc. E/CN.4/Sub.2/L.640 (20 Nov. 1975) (hereinafter *Warzazi Introductory Statement to Final Report*) 26. This document is also part of the Consolidated Report.

[68] Papademetriou and Martin have identified a number of possible disadvantages resulting from the use of remittances in sending countries: speculative investment in real estate and farmland may artificially inflate market prices and consequently create social inequalities between migrant and non-migrant households; the purchase of consumer goods may also fuel inflation in some countries; and the subsequent increased demand and reliance on luxury imported goods may lead to the use of foreign currency reserves in order to import such products. 'Labor Migration and Development: Research and Policy Issues', n. 26 above, 19.

ment.[69] What is evident, however, is that the size of the remittance inflow does have a very significant and striking effect upon the economic picture in a certain group of developing countries when compared, for example, with their import and export flows.[70] Clearly, if the source of remittances were to suddenly dry up, this would undoubtedly have important repercussions on development strategies in countries which budget for such payments in the calculation of their estimated export earnings.[71] The mass exodus of migrant workers during the Gulf War is an example of such a sudden disruption to the flow of remittances and an indication of the volatile and vulnerable nature of these earnings.[72] In summary, therefore, it is difficult to gauge precisely the extent to which remittances contribute to a country's development,[73] or to the reduction of emigration pressures,[74] but they are clearly central to any links that are established between migration and development.[75]

(b) International trade

The relationship between international labour migration and international trade has been the subject of few studies, but there is some evidence to suggest that the presence of migrant workers and their families in the country of employment may have a substantial effect upon international trade between that country and the migrants' country of origin. Consequently, the economic development of the latter is likely to be assisted by, *inter alia*, the greater demand for transport, banking and communication services, the increase in business and tourist travel, and the promotion of the export of particular goods and products from the sending country.[76]

[69] For a summary of this debate, see Russell (1992), n. 65 above, 270–3. Papademetriou (1993), n. 61 above, 214, observes that any possible contribution which remittances may make towards development is thwarted by the lack of measures to stimulate investment opportunities: 'the most important deficiency . . . may be the frequent inability of domestic capital markets to offer the necessary incentives to direct remittance capital towards productive activities, and the concomitant failure of the public sector to provide the necessary direction for such incentives'. A positive use of remittances is their investment in the education of relatives remaining in the sending country. See Russell, n. 65 above, 271; Segal, n. 3 above, 150.

[70] For example, remittances to Egypt in 1989 constituted 94.1% of the value of merchandise exports and 30.9% of the value of merchandise imports: Russell and Teitelbaum, n. 23 above, 54–5 (Tables 5 and 6). The figures in the same year for Morocco were 43.9 and 29.1% respectively and for Bangladesh 59.1 and 23.4%. *Ibid.*

[71] Cf. Appleyard (1991), n. 11 above, 71, with reference to the supply of labour to the Middle East.

[72] See also Russell (1992), n. 65 above, 269 and Segal, n. 3 above, 150. The disruption, however, need not be so sudden and may occur more gradually because of recession in countries of employment. Cf. Martin and Richards, n. 14 above, 8.

[73] Cf. Appleyard (1992:1), n. 13 above, 261; Russell (1992), n. 65 above, 273.

[74] Martin writes: 'Remittances do make individual migrants and their families better off, but they are rarely the spark which creates enough economic activity to make emigration unnecessary': 'Labor Migration: Theory and Reality', n. 40 above, 39.

[75] Russell (1992), n. 65 above, 267.

[76] Cf. *ibid.* 274–5. For a comprehensive study examining the relationship between international migration and international trade, see Russell and Teitelbaum, n. 23 above.

(c) Skills and other contributions

The expectation that migrant workers will contribute to the development of their own country on their return is seldom realized.[77] Because migrant workers are mainly hired for mundane and repetitive tasks, they do not acquire opportunities to develop new skills or to participate in vocational training.[78] Those migrant workers who return with newly acquired skills, moreover, are rarely able, for two principal reasons, to put them to good use in the home country. First, these skills, together with the industrial experience gained, are likely to be irrelevant in countries of origin which generally have less technologically-advanced industry than the richer countries of employment, and are therefore unable to make use of such skills.[79] Secondly, returning migrants are usually reluctant to work in the domestic industrial sector (provided there are jobs available), and instead prefer to become self-employed in the service sector,[80] or may simply decide to retire on their earnings.[81] A preference for employment in the service sector, however, may lead to industrial distortion. It has been argued that the 'artificial' leap from an agriculturally-based to a service-oriented economy is detrimental to the sending country's efforts to develop the necessary industrial base, thus increasing dependence on industrially-advanced societies.[82] A contrary school of thought is that involvement in the informal service sector actually stimulates entrepreneurial activity and can be the catalyst for further development.[83]

(d) Social effects

Migration undoubtedly causes strains on family structures in sending societies: '[F]amilies left behind have to adjust to the sharply restricted interactions and

[77] According to Papademetriou, 'the possibility of return migration having a positive developmental impact . . . is tied directly to two processes: first, the permanent return of successful migrants and, second, the success of sending societies in taking at least the first tentative steps toward making the structural social and economic adjustments which are the *sine qua non* of sustained development. Only then will return migration stand a chance of making a positive impact beyond the migrant household and the immediate community': 'Migration and Development: The Unsettled Relationship', n. 42 above, 215.

[78] Papademetriou and Martin, 'Labor Migration and Development: Research and Policy Issues', n. 26 above, 17–18. If they are given such opportunities, they are more likely to integrate into the host society and less likely to want to return home: 'Migrants who acquire skills usually achieve occupational advancement, increased economic rewards, and social acceptance'. *Ibid.* 18.

[79] *Ibid.* One way to utilise acquired skills in sending countries is for receiving countries to support industrial initiatives by returning migrant workers. Papademetriou (1993), n. 61 above, 214 (n. 21), refers to a number of programmes in Europe where such schemes have been undertaken.

[80] For example, by investing their earnings in a delivery service, taxi, or shop. Martin, 'Labor Migration: Theory and Reality', n. 40 above, 32.

[81] Cf. Papademetriou and Martin, 'Labor Migration and Development: Research and Policy Issues', n. 26 above, 18; Martin, 'Labor Migration: Theory and Reality', n. 40 above.

[82] Martin and Richards, n. 14 above, 8.

[83] Papademetriou, 'Migration and Development: The Unsettled Relationship', n. 42 above, 216, citing from: A. Portes and J. Walton, *Labor, Class and the International System* (New York: Academic Press, 1981); D. Massey *et al.*, *Return to Aztlan: The Social Process of International Migration from Western Mexico* (Berkeley: University of California Press, 1987); and S. Diaz-Briquets, 'The Effects of International Migration on Latin America' in *The Unsettled Relationship: Labour Migration and Economic Development*, n. 14 above, 183.

the social and psychological problems attendant to the breadwinner's prolonged and repeated absence. As a result, family bonds and solidarity erode . . .'.[84] These strains on family life and, consequently, on the social structure of the society of origin caused by the outflow of migrant workers can be particularly acute if a significant proportion (for example, over 10 per cent) of that country's population is abroad.[85]

The return of migrants may also have negative social effects. During their stay in host countries, migrant workers acquire new lifestyles, different consumption habits and new forms of behaviour, which, when introduced into countries of origin, may threaten and disturb social harmony.[86] On the other hand, 'new socio-political attitudes' acquired in the country of employment might be employed in a positive manner and contribute to development in their country of origin.[87]

(e) 'Brain drain'

Those most likely to migrate from developing countries fall into a particular category of persons. Not only are they 'young, healthy and dynamic; their very selection by the household for emigration suggests that they will accept risk and are more likely to have the human capital characteristics that will serve them well abroad'.[88] They are also usually the better-off in those countries.[89] Although many have few skills, there is a certain proportion of highly skilled individuals among them resulting in a 'brain drain'[90] from developing countries which can be quite substantial.[91] The migration of these skilled workers, mainly to the developed world, disadvantages developing countries in a number of ways:

[84] Papademetriou, 'Migration and Development: The Unsettled Relationship', n. 42 above, 213–14. For another view, see Appleyard (1989), n. 66 above, 496–7, who observes that the separation of migrant workers from their families may foster a new appreciation of family ties and may sometimes strengthen family relationships. He refers to research which suggests that, in countries with the extended family system, the absence of the breadwinner may lead to the distribution of the latter's duties among family members with the result that the extended family as a social institution may actually be strengthened. *Ibid.* citing from M. I Abella and Y. Atal, *Middle East Interlude, Asian Workers Abroad. A Comparative Study of Four Countries* (Bangkok: UNESCO, 1986).

[85] Segal, n. 3 above, 114, 127.

[86] Cf. *Warzazi Introductory Statement to Final Report*, n. 67 above, 26.

[87] Appleyard (1992:1), n. 13 above, 254.

[88] Papademetriou and Martin, 'Labor Migration and Development: Research and Policy Issues', n. 26 above, 14–15.

[89] Russell (1992), n. 65 above, 273, observes that it is usually the better-off in developing countries who emigrate and not the poorest who seldom have the means to do so. However, when this latter group does migrate, there is nonetheless evidence to suggest that the earnings which they send back have a positive effect on poverty in the regions from which they have come.

[90] Also referred to somewhat euphemistically as 'reverse transfer of technology and transfer of talent'. Segal, n. 3 above, 166 (Glossary).

[91] For example, it was estimated that in 1987 approximately 80,000 high-level Africans from the sub-Sahara region were working abroad, many permanently. This amounted to 30% of the high-level labour stock of sub-Saharan Africa. *Ibid.* 156. Globally, it has been estimated that 1 million skilled workers migrated from developing to developed countries between 1960 and 1985. If the estimated cost of each emigrant is calculated at US$60,000, this movement represents a loss of US$60 billion

The objections to the emigration of high-level manpower are several. There is the cost to the sending society of their education at home and sometimes for overseas study. There is the opportunity cost of their lost talent, incalculable but significant. There are the psychological effects on a society of some of its most talented members leaving, usually permanently. There are concerns of national pride, of domestic scientific and technological capabilities, of malaise among those who stay behind, of the setbacks to local universities and research centres . . .[92]

Although there are also some benefits to be gained from the 'brain drain' by both the migrants themselves and their countries of origin,[93] such migration is likely to have an overall negative impact on economic development in the sending country.[94] The real beneficiaries of the 'brain drain', therefore, can only be receiving countries.[95] According to a UN Conference on Trade and Development (UNCTAD) study, the contribution of foreign skilled workers to the economy of the USA in 1970 amounted to $3.7 billion. In contrast, the total assistance that year provided by the USA to developing countries totalled $3.1 billion.[96] These admittedly dated but nonetheless staggering figures place the provision of foreign aid by developed countries to developing countries into its true perspective.[97]

There is another irony to this situation, however. While the skilled cadre of sending countries is working abroad, usually in positions which, in many cases, fall short of their aspirations, these countries need to resort to foreign technical

to developing countries. P. L. Martin, 'Migration and Development: Conference Report (Tenth IOM Seminar on Migration, Geneva, 15–17 Sept. 1992)' (1992) 30 IM 457, 461.

[92] Segal, n. 3 above, 153.

[93] Segal, n. 3 above, also refers to opposing arguments demonstrating that individuals involved in the 'brain drain' benefit themselves because they are able to fully develop their potential abroad and that the country of origin also benefits from remittances, the prestige these individuals bring, and the part they play as role models for future generations.

[94] Martin writes: 'Labor recruitment tends to attract skilled, ambitious, and often employed workers so that, instead of recruiting persons whose economic contributions will not be missed, recruitment attracts the workers needed to make an area take off economically. The vacancies created by emigrants are not always filled by the unemployed who remain behind, so economic development may slow down': 'Labor Migration: Theory and Reality', n. 40 above, 32. A secondary negative effect of the emigration of particularly talented individuals from a particular area is that it may make migration 'cumulative and self-perpetuating': *ibid.* 32, citing from N. Abadan-Unat, 'Turkish Migration to Europe and the Middle East: Its Impact on the Social Structure and Social Legislation' in L. Michalak and J. Salacuse, (eds.), *Social Legislation in the Contemporary Middle East* (Berkeley: Institute of International Studies, 1976) 325, 384.

[95] Moreover, the selective immigration policies of many receiving countries attract 'the very people most likely to bring about economic and political transformation' in less developed countries. Papademetriou (1993), n. 61 above, 215.

[96] Cited in *Warzazi Introductory Statement to Final Report*, n. 67 above, 27.

[97] Papademetriou and Martin conclude that the 'brain drain' can only widen the gap between rich and poor nations: 'While some speak of opportunity costs, surplus brain power, and the right to emigrate as a basic human right, the emigration of high level manpower from the less-developed to the advanced industrial countries clearly constitutes a drain of scarce and expensive human resources. Brain drain migrants are a subsidy to the rich from the poor, and such a subsidy can only increase the asymmetry between the two types of countries': 'Labor Migration and Development: Research and Policy Issues', n. 26 above, 16.

assistance at a cost twice or three times to that of their nationals.[98] Although some blame has been directed at sending countries for failing to appreciate the true value of their trained personnel and for not ensuring them sufficiently promising futures, the profound problem lies with 'the lack of means which prevents countries from equipping themselves with the institutes, professors and technology needed in order to train and re-adapt their own technicians locally'.[99] It is this lack of means, therefore, whether embodied in a shortage of adequate facilities, poverty or unemployment, which causes all workers, whether highly skilled or unskilled and illiterate, to migrate from developing countries. The only feasible solution to arresting the 'brain drain', and, indeed, to preventing significant labour migration from developing to developed countries, lies in the creation of employment, with international assistance and redistribution, which will help keep potential migrant workers at home.[100]

This solution to the 'brain drain' constitutes part of an overall solution to alleviating the greater inequities suffered by developing sending countries as a result of international migration for employment. Given that the prevention of migration altogether is in reality an impossible task, this inequality may be tempered somewhat by international redistribution or financial compensation to sending countries for their outflows of labour.[101]

1.6 MIGRATION AND THE RIGHT TO DEVELOPMENT

The effective protection of the rights of migrant workers and their families while in the country of employment can only be a partial solution to the human rights problems generated by international labour migration. Stemming labour migration flows altogether is not feasible and probably undesirable given the benefits of such movements which have been identified above, but improvements in conditions in sending countries can do much to reduce these movements, especially

[98] *Warzazi Introductory Statement to Final Report*, n. 67 above, 27.

[99] *Ibid.* 27–8. If the only way to keep trained personnel at home in developing countries is to compete with the remuneration of industrialized countries, such an approach would require very steep social stratification and a very large disparity in income. I am grateful to Bill Black for this observation. Developing countries have resorted to other more direct means of attempting to stem the outflow of skilled cadre. These have included: regulations restricting study abroad and imposing financial sanctions on those failing to return; 'delinking' local education from overseas norms; incentive policies involving certain benefits, such as tax benefits, to encourage return; and schemes to invite back emigrants to participate in short-term local projects. See Segal, n. 3 above, 156.

[100] *Warzazi Introductory Statement to Final Report*, n. 67 above, 27.

[101] Böhning, n. 1 above, 13–14. Segal, n. 3 above, 156, observes that receiving countries have rejected the idea of compensation and appear to pay only lip-service to the 'brain drain' problem. Some have invested modestly in cooperative research with developing country scientists whereas others have enacted restrictions to discourage developing country students from staying on permanently after their studies. This latter measure, however, should also be considered in the context of increased immigration quotas in developed countries for certain professional categories.

those of the most desperate kind such as irregular migration. In the long-term, pressures to migrate will only dissipate within a framework of human rights guarantees and successful and sustainable socio-economic development in sending countries.[102]

The adherence to, and successful implementation of, a human right to development, such as that articulated by the Declaration of the UN General Assembly in December 1986,[103] can result in a permanent reduction of international labour migration. 'Development' is defined in the second recital of the Preamble to the Declaration as:

> a comprehensive economic, social, cultural and political process, which aims at the constant improvement of the well-being of the entire population and of all individuals on the basis of their active, free and meaningful participation in the development and in the fair distribution of benefits resulting therefrom.[104]

The Declaration regards the right to development as both a collective and individual right: 'an inalienable human right' belonging to 'every human person and all peoples' (Art. 1). The human person is clearly at the core of this right: 'The human person is the central subject of development and should be the active participant and beneficiary of the right to development' (Art. 2(1)). States have a duty 'to co-operate with each other in ensuring development and eliminating obstacles to development',[105] and are also placed under an individual and collective obligation 'to formulate international development policies with a view to facilitating the full realization of the right to development' (Art. 4(1)). In this context, Art. 4(2) of the Declaration calls upon 'sustained action . . . to promote more rapid development of developing countries . . . [a]s a complement to the efforts [of those countries]'.

The Declaration on the Right to Development received broad agreement, but it was not adopted unanimously, with objections being raised by notable

[102] Cf. Appleyard (1991), n. 11 above, 2. In addition to the necessary economic measures discussed below, the *US Study on Unauthorized Migration and Development*, n. 21 above, 236, considered that 'raising educational levels is essential to socio-economic development and reduction of migratory pressure' and viewed vocational education as a 'prime necessity'.

[103] Declaration on the Right to Development, UN GA Res. 41/128 of 4 Dec. 1986, adopted by a vote of 146 to 1 against (USA) with 18 abstentions.

[104] Another definition relevant to the present discussion, which unpacks some of the elements of this process, is provided by Papademetriou: 'Development is a multidimensional process that relies on the growth and interaction of such attributes as a country's human and material resources, social and physical structure, capital, political stability, government efficacy and *migration*': Papademetriou (1993), n. 61 above, 214 (emphasis added). See also Papademeriou and Martin, 'Labor Migration and Development: Research and Policy Issues', n. 26 above, 5. Clearly, what 'development' does *not* mean is mere economic growth, such as the increases in GDP which are brought about by income from remittances. *Ibid.*

[105] Art. 3(3). Examples of such obstacles are the 'failure to observe civil and political rights as well as economic, social and cultural rights' (Art. 6(3)). The Declaration also emphasizes that these rights are 'indivisible and interdependent' (Art. 6(2)).

development aid donors. The largest international donor in monetary terms, the USA, was the only country which voted against it.[106] Moreover, eight industrialized nations abstained because they considered that priority had not been given in the Declaration to individual human rights as opposed to the concept of the human right of peoples, and that the provision of development aid should not be construed as an obligation in international law.[107] Given such dissent, it is arguable that the *human right* of individuals and peoples to development has not yet been fully recognized in international law, although the adoption of this Declaration appears to be an irrevocable step in that direction.[108] No concrete action has yet been taken by the international community to implement the right to development as set out in the Declaration, although the process to articulate this right more clearly has continued. For example, in 1990, the Global Consultation on the Right to Development as a Human Right,[109] a forum that included many experts and non-governmental organizations (NGOs) from the South, identified democratic participation, on both national and international levels, as a critical element in the realization of this right: 'the right to development is not so much a right to the improvement of material conditions, but the right to have a voice in, and share control over, the economic environment'.[110] The Global Consultation recommended that progress in realizing development should not be assessed by universal criteria, but by a UN programme that involves the organizations representing the people and groups affected by the development process.[111]

[106] See also R. Rich, 'The Right to Development: A Right of Peoples?' in J. Crawford, (ed.), *The Rights of Peoples* (Oxford: Clarendon Press, 1988) 39, 52. The reasons for this dissent were the alleged ambiguity of the Declaration, the reference to the link between disarmament and development (Art. 7) and the view that development was essentially dependent on the transfer of resources from North to South: *ibid.*, citing from UN Doc. A/C.3/41/SR.61 (1986) 32. However, Rich observes that the latter view was *not* elaborated in the Declaration.

[107] Rich, n. 106 above, citing from UN Doc A/C.3/41/SR.61 (1986) and A/41/PV.97 (1986). However, Rich, *ibid.*, also observes that such an obligation is not readily identifiable from the text of the Declaration. The eight industrialized countries were Denmark, Finland, Germany, Iceland, Israel, Japan, Sweden, and the UK.

[108] Rich, *ibid.* 53–4, outlines the following advantages of an internationally recognized right to development: it would place the practice of affirmative action in favour of developing countries 'in the framework of international human rights law'; it would link the acceptance of the benefit of development assistance 'with a corresponding obligation on developing countries to respect and advance the human rights of their people'; it would give substance to the claim that all rights are 'indivisible and interdependent' (Art. 6(2)) ensuring that no set of rights, for example, economic rights, have priority over another set such as civil and political rights; it would insist that the development of the individual 'is the ultimate objective of all development projects' and hence would correct such maldevelopment as 'the forced removal of indigenous or agrarian populations, or even unacceptable environmental damage'; it would ensure 'quality' development aid; and finally, the right to development 'would be a positive force in involving Third World countries in human rights'.

[109] UN Doc. E/CN.4/1990/9/Rev.1. For an interesting account of this meeting, see R. L. Barsh, 'The Right to Development as a Human Right: Results of the Global Consultation' (1991) 13 HRQ 322.

[110] Barsh, n. 109 above, 329. See also the second recital of the Preamble to the UN Declaration, n. 104 above, and accompanying text, which links the development process to the 'active, free and meaningful participation [of all individuals] in the development and in the fair distribution of benefits resulting therefrom'.

[111] Barsh, n. 109 above, 332.

A comprehensive development agenda, specifically tailored to the reduction of migration pressures in developing countries, should therefore be initiated by the North and be based upon the following components: 'a strengthened and extended multilateral trading system' improving access to the markets of developed countries; 'rescheduling and selected forgiveness of accumulated debt (which in turn would attract foreign direct investment (FDI))'; and 'carefully devised co-operative aid programmes'.[112]

In line with Article 4(2) of the UN Declaration, the 1990 US Study on Unauthorized Migration and Development considered that, ultimately, 'primary responsibility for their own development rests with the sending countries themselves'.[113] One of its salient conclusions, however, was that 'expanded access by sending-countries to U.S. and other markets through increasingly free trade is the most promising stimulus to their future economic growth'.[114] The emphasis on trade liberalization as a means of promoting development and hence reducing emigration pressures is promising in theory, but, according to Böhning and Schloeter-Paredes, susceptible to state protectionism in practice:

> The problem with trade is not that rich governments lack means of influencing it, but that their trade policies often reduce employment prospects in poor countries. For example, much of the trade in goods that would be most directly beneficial to migrant-sending countries involves labour-intensive products. Rich countries protect most strongly the sectors that produce competing labour-intensive goods. Electoral pressures favour protectionism, irrespective of whether the goods are imported from poor countries or from other rich countries . . .[115]

The authors are of the view that Official Development Assistance (ODA), which is entirely under government control, targeted at regions of high emigration and with the collaboration of the sending countries concerned, is likely to

[112] Appleyard (1991), n. 11 above, 2. See also Martin (1994), n. 3 above, 246. An example of positive action in respect of the first requirement is the North American Free Trade Agreement (NAFTA) between Canada, Mexico, and the USA, and the reduction of trade barriers achieved by the Uruguay Round of the GATT multilateral trade negotiations. See Papademetriou (1993), n. 61 above, 215 (n. 24). Moreover, as a necessary condition for economic growth, developing countries should 'try and create stable macro-economic environments'. Appleyard (1991), *ibid.* 9, 78–81. To this might be added 'assistance with small-business creation' and 'advising countries how best to pursue policies that stimulate and expedite economic growth'. Papademetriou (1993), *ibid.* 215. The impact of such a development agenda, however, would also have to be carefully planned with sustainable management of natural resources to take account of environmental concerns. Cf. Appleyard (1991), *ibid.* 9–10, 83; *US Study on Unauthorized Migration and Development*, n. 21 above, 237.

[113] *US Study on Unauthorized Migration and Development*, n. 21 above, 241. Stalker, n. 27 above, 165, also concludes: '[U]ltimately, the answers lie within the developing countries themselves. Unless they have the will and the incentive to pursue development strategies which keep more of their citizens at home, the flows are likely to continue unabated'.

[114] *US Study on Unauthorized Migration and Development*, n. 21 above.

[115] Böhning and Schloeter-Paredes, n. 55 above, 5. See also Stalker, n. 27 above, 156–7 and J. Niessen and R. Zegers de Beijl, *International Migration, Economic Development and Human Rights*, CCME Briefing Paper No. 18 (Brussels: Churches Commission for Migrants in Europe, Dec. 1994) 11–12.

be more successful in reducing unemployment, raising incomes, or achieving political stability in the country of origin than trade liberalization. ODA is also preferred to foreign direct investment (FDI), which is subject to the decisions of private and often transnational actors who are unwilling to invest in poor sending countries because of a less favourable return on their investment.[116] A concrete example of ODA tailored to migration is an ILO programme, which aims, through collaboration between donor and recipient countries, to make better use of international assistance in order to reduce emigration pressures in the Mahgreb region.[117] However, whatever the perceived advantages of one method over another, all the components of the development agenda have a valid role to play in reducing emigration from sending countries.[118] In this respect, Niessen and Zegers de Beijl write:

> Without under-estimating the significance of ODA, it is a moderate instrument to bring about development compared with the amounts (and the potential effects on migration) involved in FDI and trade liberalization. Therefore a comprehensive approach to development policies is needed.[119]

The European Union is developing such a comprehensive approach. In its Declaration on principles of governing external aspects of migration policy at its summit meeting in Edinburgh on 11–12 December 1992, the European Council recognized, *inter alia*, that the following principles should guide and inform the approach of the EC and member states:

> [T]hey will further encourage liberal trade and economic cooperation with countries of emigration, thereby promoting economic development and increasing prosperity in those countries, and so reducing economic motives for migration; [and] to the same end, they will ensure the appropriate volume of development aid is effectively used to encourage sustainable social and economic development, in particular to contribute to job creation

[116] Böhning and Schloeter-Paredes, n. 55 above, 4–6, 9, 10. Stalker, n. 27 above, 161, also argues that multinationals are more likely today to invest in manufacturing closer to home as a result of advances in technology and higher skill levels in the industrialized countries. Moreover, he contends, *ibid.*, that FDI can only be a viable alternative to migration if it takes place at much higher levels than at present.

[117] For further details of this programme, see International Labour Conference, 81st Session, 1994, *Report of the Director-General. Part II: Activities of the ILO, 1992–93* (Geneva: International Labour Office, 1994) 85; Böhning and Schloeter-Paredes, n. 55 above, 10 and Niessen and Zegers de Beijl, n. 115 above, 17–19. See also Stalker, n. 27 above, 164–5. In addition to ILO efforts, a number of 'cooperation' agreements have also been agreed on the bilateral level between sending and receiving countries with a view to the provision of investment and development aid in order to stem emigration. For an overview of such agreements between Greece and Albania, Netherlands and Morocco, and between Luxembourg and a number of African countries, see Commission of the European Communities, Directorate General, Employment, Industrial Relations and Social Affairs, *The EC Member States and Immigration in 1993. Closed Borders, Stringent Attitudes*, Working Document, Synthesis Report of the Information Network on Migration from Third Countries (Rimet) by C.-V. Marie (Luxembourg: OOPEC, 1995) 12, 17 and 111.

[118] Cf. Martin (1994), n. 3 above, 243.

[119] Niessen and Zegers de Beijl, n. 115 above, 15.

and the alleviation of poverty in the countries of origin, so further contributing in the longer term to a reduction of migration pressure.[120]

Ultimately, therefore, a comprehensive programme of development is the sole answer to reducing the flow of labour migrants and preventing future and potentially damaging mass exoduses. This approach can only lie in the 'enlightened self-interest' of developed countries. Without such a programme, it is arguable that the growing populations of the developing world are not sustainable, a situation with potentially negative repercussions for regional stability in political and social terms.[121] According to the US Study on Unauthorized Migration and Development: 'Development and the availability of new and better jobs at home . . . is the only way to diminish migratory pressures over time'.[122] If developing countries cannot export goods and services to create sufficient employment at home, they face no other alternative but to export people.[123] The Report of the International Conference on Population and Development comes to a similar conclusion as constituting a basis for action: 'The long-term manageability of international migration hinges on making the option to remain in one's country a viable one for all people. Sustainable economic growth with equity and development strategies consistent with this aim are a necessary means to that end'.[124] The Report recognizes, however, that:

the economic situation in . . . [developing] countries is likely to improve only gradually and, therefore, migration flows from those countries are likely to decline only in the long

[120] *EC Bulletin* 12-1992, 23. This policy has taken concrete shape in the Euro-Mediterranean Conference, which was held in Barcelona, Spain on 27–28 Nov. 1995. The Conference adopted a Declaration and Work Programme. The Declaration establishes a Euro-Mediterranean partnership comprising three components: a political and security partnership; an economic and financial partnership based on the introduction of a free trade area; and a partnership with a social, cultural, and human dimension. The latter identifies migration as one of the cooperation priorities: '[The participants] . . . acknowledge the importance of the role played by migration in their relationships; they agree to strengthen their cooperation to reduce migratory pressures, among other things through vocational training programmes and programmes of assistance for job creation . . .'. See respectively *EU Bulletin* 11-1995, 78 (Point 1.4.56) and 140. The Work Programme's entry on migration reads: 'Given the importance of the issue of migration for Euro-Mediterranean relations, meetings will be encouraged in order to make proposals concerning migration flows and pressures': *EU Bulletin* 11-1995, 145. This policy is also highlighted in the drafting of new Euro-Mediterranean Association agreements between the EC and its member states and Morocco and Tunisia, which will replace the earlier cooperation agreements. See COM(95) 740 final and COM(95) 235 final respectively. Draft Art. 7(1)(a) of both agreements, which is located in Chapter 3 on Cooperation in the Social Field, states that priority will be afforded to, *inter alia*, 'reducing migratory pressure, notably by improving living conditions, creating jobs and developing training in areas from which emigrants come'.

[121] Papademetriou (1993), n. 61 above, 215; Cf. *US Study on Unauthorized Migration and Development*, n. 21 above, 224.

[122] *Ibid.* 222. The Study, *ibid.* 241, recognized, however, in the context of unauthorized migration, that the development solution 'is measured in decades—even generations'.

[123] *Ibid.* 224.

[124] *Report of the International Conference on Population and Development*, n. 20 above, 70, para. 10.1.

term; in the interim, the acute problems currently observed will cause migration flows to continue for the short-to-medium term . . .[125]

Although the continuation of migration flows for a considerable period of time after the introduction of such a development strategy may result in diminishing public support for such a policy in countries of employment,[126] a short- to medium-term increase in migration is surely preferable to the disruption that would be caused by the inevitable mass exodus if development were neglected altogether.[127] While working for development in sending countries, alternatives to international labour migration can continue to be sought by the provision of employment opportunities in those countries.[128] More realistically perhaps, steps can be taken to ensure that the labour migration which is still occurring is factored into development policy or becomes 'an instrument of development'.[129] It

[125] *Ibid.* 71, para. 10.3. Similarly, the *US Study on Unauthorized Migration and Development*, n. 21 above, 221–2, observes that in the short-to-medium terms 'the economic development process itself tends . . . to stimulate migration by raising expectations and enhancing people's ability to migrate'. See also Russell and Teitelbaum, n. 23 above, 34, para. 4.7. This is because, 'in the short-term (30 to 40 years), rapid and successful economic development has a profoundly destabilizing effect on developing countries': Appleyard (1991), n. 11 above, 82: 'Rapid economic development also causes greater mobility and an acceleration of the urbanization process which, in turn, augments migration potential'. Appleyard (1991), *ibid.* 78, citing from a report of the Swedish Study Group on Migration: Sweden, Ministry of Labour, *A Comprehensive Refugee and Immigration Policy* (Stockholm: Swedish Government Printing Office, 1990). The temporary increase in migratory flows is most likely to occur between 'countries with large differences in capital–labour ratios and size, [where] a decrease in employment in the protected sectors of the labour-abundant country cannot be counteracted in the short run by an increase in production and employment in those sectors which are expanding as a consequence of trade liberalization and its dynamic effects. Consequently, emigration is bound to increase initially. Only in the very long run and assuming convergence should the incentive to migrate diminish': G. P. Tapinos, 'International Migration and Development' (1994) *Population Bulletin of the United Nations* No. 36, 1, 12, writing with reference to NAFTA and migration from Mexico to the USA.

[126] Tapinos, n. 125 above, 14–15, cautions that development assistance earmarked for containing migration may lead to perverse results: 'It is one thing to implement a development assistance policy for improving the general well-being in developing countries, thereby indirectly lowering, in the long run, the incentive to migrate. It is quite another matter to explicitly earmark development assistance for curtailing migration. First of all, the transition period necessary to bring about significant changes in income could take decades. At the same time and following a well-observed pattern, the adjustments resulting from the development process are prone to increase the propensity to migrate for some segments of the population. The continuation of migration flows could possibly lead to a hostile public opinion reaction in donor countries and be interpreted as a failure of development assistance policies, causing their support to wane'.

[127] Cf. Appleyard (1991), n. 11 above, 9.

[128] For example, through 'relocating production, creating joint ventures and investing in labour-surplus countries'. *Ibid.* 82–3. Such measures may also be adopted in order to encourage migrants to return home and to reintegrate them into the economy of the country of origin. Cf. *Report of the International Conference on Population and Development*, n. 20 above, 71, para. 10.5.

[129] See respectively Appleyard, 'Migration and Development: A Critical Relationship', n. 34 above, 14, citing from M. S. Teitelbaum, 'The Effects of Economic Development on Out-Migration Pressures in Sending Countries', Paper presented at the OECD International Conference on Migration, Rome, 1991; and J. N. Purcell Jr. (Director General, IOM), Foreword to *International Migration: Challenge for the Nineties*, n. 11 above, 8.

is clear, however, that the environment necessary for development must first be created before migration can facilitate development.[130] The former objective might then be achieved through the following measures: 'short-term and project-related migration' or 'migration for training', where migrants from developing countries travel to developed countries in order to gain or to improve skills which they can then use when employed in their own countries;[131] a 'strategic' and 'optimal' use of remittances;[132] and 'the concerted avoidance of "brain drain".'[133]

What is needed is an *active* policy with respect to international migration and not just a passive *ad hoc* reaction to events as they materialise. A comprehensive development strategy in which international migration is assigned a specific role, represents the most promising direction.[134]

[130] Appleyard (1992:1), n. 13 above, 263. With reference to Italy as an example, Papademetriou and Martin identify the following basic ingredients which should be in place before development can occur: 'a large and diverse economy, a large and relatively modern agricultural sector which would not be starved for labor as a result of emigration, an already socially and politically mobilized population, a relatively effective system of private and public administration, a large and relatively modern infrastructure, and a financial system capable of channelling remittances to the private sector efficiently': Papademetriou and Martin, 'Labor Migration and Development: Research and Policy Issues', n. 26 above, 21. Migration alone cannot stimulate development: 'Migration is neither capable of correcting the underlying weaknesses of the socio-economic structure of receiving societies nor can it provide a *substantial* and *sustained* impetus for the socio-economic transformation of emigration countries': Papademetriou and Martin, *ibid.* 20. Martin's analysis of empirical studies in the migration and development area concludes that 'there is no law which automatically converts emigration, remittances, and returns into economic development': 'Labor Migration: Theory and Reality', n. 40 above, 33.

[131] *Report of the International Conference on Population and Development*, n. 20 above, 71, para. 10.5; Appleyard (1991), n. 11 above, 81–2, citing from W. R. Böhning, 'International Migration to Western Europe: What to do?', a paper presented to the Seminar on International Security, The Graduate Institute of International Studies, Geneva, 15–20 July 1991, 13.

[132] See respectively Note, 'The Holy See's Perspective on Migration and Development' (1993) 21:2–3 *Migrationworld Magazine* 45, 46 (paper presented at the Tenth IOM Seminar on Migration, Geneva, 15–17 Sept. 1992); and Papademetriou (1993), n. 61 above, 214. Martin argues: 'If remittances are to be the external pump which primes an area for an economic take-off, they need to be coordinated to provide the infrastructure necessary for development . . .': 'Labor Migration: Theory and Reality', n. 40 above, 39.

[133] 'The Holy See's Perspective on Migration and Development', n. 132 above.

[134] Appleyard (1991), n. 11 above, 83. The *US Study on Unauthorized Migration and Development*, n. 21 above, 240–1, supports a similarly comprehensive approach and recommended, as a matter of urgency, re-organization of the current structure within the US Executive Branch in the form of a federal Agency for Migration Affairs 'to ensure that migration be given a high priority on the US domestic and foreign policy agendas, and that migration consequences be carefully considered by policy-makers involved in trade, *development* and international economic matters' (emphasis added). The relationship between migration and development is now also on the agenda of the UN General Assembly, which, in Res. 49/127 of 19 Dec. 1994 on international migration and development, requested the Secretary-General to prepare a report with a view to the convening of a UN conference on this subject. The report was presented to ECOSOC in June 1995. The Secretary-General canvassed the views of governments and received a fairly poor response. Many governments that did reply were rather sceptical about the need to hold a major UN conference on international migration and development. Nineteen governments (including EC member states) considered that a decision to convene a conference was premature and that it was first necessary to look at other mechanisms for addressing issues relating to international migration and development. Only fifteen governments were in favour of convening a conference. See UN, ECOSOC, Substantive Session of 1995,

1.7 CONCLUSION

In the interim, it is arguable that the degree to which receiving societies make a genuine and serious attempt to respect and promote the human rights of those migrant workers and their families living and working within their borders will also serve as a useful indicator of a developed country's commitment to the development agenda described above. If members of this vulnerable group of human beings experience maltreatment and exploitation in the country of employment, it is unlikely that their countries of origin will fare much better in the international arena of inter-state relations.

International Migration and Development, Report of the Secretary General, UN Doc. E/1995/69 (14 June 1995) 14, paras. 42–3.

2

Migrant Workers and their Families as Aliens: Development of International Law and Applicability of Universal and Regional Human Rights Instruments

The situation of aliens or foreigners seems . . . to be one of the most serious, and at the same time most widespread, departures from the principle of the universality of human rights and one of the most manifest signs of intolerance and discrimination in our age.[1]

2.1 INTRODUCTION

The position of migrant workers and their families in international law is inextricably connected to their status as aliens. Any established international legal rules concerned with the protection of aliens are therefore relevant when endeavouring to gauge the degree of protection migrants may expect to receive. Rudimentary standards regarding the treatment of aliens have developed over time and have become part of the international law of state responsibility. More recently, these standards have been reinforced, elaborated, and effectively superseded by the international community's recognition of rights pertaining to all human beings.

2.2 THE TREATMENT OF ALIENS: A SHORT HISTORICAL SURVEY

Throughout history aliens have always been treated differently from citizens. Traditional deprivations upon aliens have their roots 'deep in primitive suspicions and fears of the outsider'.[2] Indeed, 'stranger' and 'enemy' were once labelled by the same word in a number of ancient languages, including Latin.[3] The first historical records concerning differences in treatment between aliens and citizens may be traced to Ancient Greece and Rome.

[1] P. Leuprecht, 'Reflections on Human Rights' (Lecture, University of Gdansk, Poland, 25 April 1988) (1988) 9 HRLJ 163, 166.

[2] M. S. McDougal, H. D. Lasswell, and L. Chen, 'Protection of Aliens from Discrimination and World Public Order: Responsibility of States conjoined with Human Rights' (1976) 70 AJIL 432, 433. See also R. B. Lillich, *The Human Rights of Aliens in Contemporary International Law* (Manchester: Manchester University Press, 1984) 5.

[3] M. Walzer, *Spheres of Justice: A Defense of Pluralism and Equality* (1983) 32.

Roots of alienage

The Greek city-states made a very rigid distinction between citizens and aliens, much to the detriment of the latter. The city-states were not political entities like the nation-states of today, but more akin to religious and tribal associations. They excluded aliens, or *metics*[4] as they were known, almost completely from their affairs.[5] Walzer, writing on the Athenian polis, asserts that the only justification for this position 'lies in the concept of citizenship as something that the Athenians literally could not distribute given what they thought it was. All they could offer to aliens was fair treatment, and that was all the aliens could think to ask of them'.[6] Indeed, 'fair treatment' by today's standard did not amount to a great deal. Aliens were denied basic civil and political rights. They were not permitted to marry citizens or to own property, nor could they participate in the political affairs of the state. Since they were unable to swear oaths in the name of the host state's gods, access to legal machinery was also barred.[7] In addition, *metics* were unable to share in the most basic of welfare rights, such as the distribution of corn.[8] Gradually, these harsh restrictions were lifted. In order to encourage craftsmen to settle in the city, aliens were granted more rights,[9] including even grants of citizenship.[10] Later, treaties known as *isopolites* evolved between various city-states providing for the mutual granting of privileges to each others' citizens.[11]

In Roman law, the *jus civile* applied only to citizens. Foreigners were considered to be outlaws and in a position of legal inferiority.[12] With the expansion of the Roman Empire, however, aliens were gradually afforded protection under *jus gentium*, a law applicable to them alone.[13]

The Middle Ages and beyond

At the beginning of the Middle Ages, few people lived and worked outside of their home countries. Those who did had few rights and were treated, in some places, as serfs. Almost everywhere, for example, aliens were unable to transfer

[4] *Ibid.* 53.

[5] Lillich, n. 2 above, 5–6, citing generally from C. Phillipson, *The International Law and Custom of Ancient Greece and Rome* (1911) 122–209.

[6] Walzer, n. 3 above, 55. Lillich, n. 2 above, 5, also maintains that this position was not so much a result of fear or hatred of aliens, but of the inherent logic of the prevailing political and legal order.

[7] Lillich, n. 2 above, 6. [8] Walzer, n. 3 above, 53. [9] Lillich, n. 2 above, 6.

[10] UN Commission on Human Rights, Sub-Commission on Prevention of Discrimination and Protection of Minorities, *International Provisions Protecting the Human Rights of Non-Citizens*, Study prepared by Baroness Elles, Special Rapporteur, UN Doc. E/CN.4/Sub.2/392/Rev.1 (1980) 1, para. 10. For example, at the time of Solon, foreign craftsmen were encouraged to settle in Attica with the promise of Athenian citizenship. *Ibid.*

[11] Lillich, n. 2 above, 6, citing from A. Nussbaum, *A Concise History of the Law of Nations* (1947) 13.

[12] *International Provisions Protecting the Human Rights of Non-Citizens*, n. 10 above, 2, para. 11.

[13] McDougal, Lasswell, and Chen, n. 2 above, 440.

property by inheritance. However, with the expansion of trade and commerce, the position of aliens improved.[14]

In the feudal era, the precarious lot of those who did not have land tenure is illustrated by the situation of travelling merchants. Most likely to carry all their wealth with them, they were a prime target for robbers. Access to the ordinary public courts was limited to those merchants holding free tenure of land and travelling merchants could only resort to the local courts of the various manors.[15] As the advantages of trade became more evident, merchants were increasingly granted greater privileges. One of the most notable privileges was the right to hold a fair. The fair became a law unto itself and gave rise to a number of juridical immunities and informal legal rules, which today are enshrined in many legal systems.[16]

With time, merchants became more organized. Whole cities and mercantile communities (for example, the Venetian, Genoese, and Hanseatic merchants) negotiated privileges from governments, which amounted to the creation in the host country of merchant community enclaves where merchants were permitted to live under their own laws administered by their own courts and according to their national customs.[17]

The granting of privileges to aliens, as described above, constituted a collective form of protection. On a more individual level, aliens who suffered injury at the hands of the host country's subjects could request a letter of reprisal from their prince or ruler, which usually authorized them to take action against any subject of the country of the alleged wrongdoer.[18] This had significant ramifications for the development of the international law of State responsibility, crystallizing into the institution of the diplomatic protection of nationals abroad.[19]

With the development of the modern nation-state system, a more humanitarian attitude towards aliens developed. The fathers of contemporary international law, Grotius and Francisco de Vitoria, advocated fair treatment for aliens on an equal footing with nationals.[20] The doctrine expounded by Vattel, identifying concerns affecting aliens with the interests of the state, influenced the development of international customary law rules of state responsibility in this area. Because

[14] *Ibid.*, citing from F. Dawson and I. Head, *International Law, National Tribunals and the Rights of Aliens* (1971) 1.

[15] Lillich, n. 2 above, 6 (and n. 6), citing generally from M. Bloch, *Feudal Society*, trans. L. Manyon (1961). The travelling merchant's precarious legal position was exacerbated by the hopelessly underdeveloped state of the law of contract at this time. Lillich, n. 2 above, 6.

[16] Lillich, n. 2 above, 6–7, citing from H. Pirenne, *Economic and Social History of Medieval Europe* (1933) 96–102 and from W. Ferguson, *Europe in Transition 1300–1520* (1973) 153–73.

[17] Lillich, n. 2 above, 7, citing from J. Mundy, *Europe in the High Middle Ages 1150–1309* (1973). See also *International Provisions Protecting the Human Rights of Non-Citizens*, n. 10 above, 2, para. 16.

[18] Lillich, n. 2 above, 8, citing from E. Aréchaga, 'International Responsibility' in M. Sorenson, (ed.), *Manual of Public International Law* (1968) 531, 533.

[19] *Ibid.*

[20] McDougal, Lasswell, and Chen, n. 2 above, 440, citing from A. Roth, *The Minimum Standard of International Law Applied to Aliens* (1949) 27.

states generally regard people as important bases of power, Vattel's doctrine remains closest to the social reality of today.[21]

2.3 STATE RESPONSIBILITY TOWARDS ALIENS: TWO CONFLICTING APPROACHES

The level of protection which a state is obliged to afford aliens under international law was for many years (and still remains to some extent) the subject of a protracted debate between those claiming that a state need only afford aliens the same treatment provided to nationals, and those advocating that a state's treatment of aliens is subject to regulation by a superior international 'minimum standard'.

Equal treatment with nationals

The chief proponent of this approach was the Argentine jurist Calvo. His position comprises two separate lines of thought. First, he argued, that as an aspect of state sovereignty, a state should enjoy, on the basis of equality, freedom from interference by other states and that it should not be bound by international law unless it consents to be bound. The second line of thought pertains specifically to diplomatic protection and contends that an alien who suffers an alleged injury may only seek redress in the local courts.[22]

The Calvo doctrine was adopted by the first International Conference of American States in Washington in 1899–1900 and by Article 9 of the Convention on Rights and Duties of States at the seventh Conference in Montevideo in 1933.[23] This doctrine, however, has been criticized because, *inter alia*, it leaves aliens to the mercy of the state in which they are residing and affords them no outside protection: '[W]hat logically follows from this doctrine . . . is that there can be no universal standard of treatment of aliens; there can only be individual national standards which each state sets unilaterally'.[24] As eloquently articulated

[21] McDougal, Lasswell, and Chen, n. 2 above, 441–2.

[22] Lillich, n. 2 above, 16. In fact, Calvo did allow in his doctrine for resort to international means of assistance, but only if the alien was denied justice in the host country. He defined 'denial of justice' very narrowly as the denial of access to the local courts. *Ibid.* 16 (and n. 60).

[23] Convention on Rights and Duties of States, 1933, 165 LNTS 19. See McDougal, Lasswell, and Chen, n. 2 above, 445, citing from J. Scott, (ed.), *The International Conferences of American States, 1889 to 1928*, 45 and Carnegie Endowment for International Peace, (ed.), *The International Conferences of American States, First Supplement, 1933–1940*, 122; *International Provisions Protecting the Human Rights of Non-Citizens*, n. 10 above, 3, para. 22.

[24] Lillich, n. 2 above, 17. Borchard asserts: 'The doctrine of equality has . . . little or no relation to the minimum, which practice has established. If it delimited the international minimum, as it does the local maximum, municipal law would replace international law as the test of international responsibility': E. Borchard, 'The "Minimum Standard" of the Treatment of Aliens' (1940) 38 *Mich. L. Rev.* 445, 452. Moreover, aliens are also denied a political remedy on account of their status. Citing from John Bassett Moore's brief in the *Constanscia Sugar* case before the Spanish Treaty Claims Commission (Library of Congress, Briefs and Records, Spanish Treaty Claims Commission, JX 238), Borchard, *ibid.* 453 (and n. 14), adds: '[N]ationals are presumed to have a political remedy, whereas the alien's inability to exercise political rights deprives him of the principal safeguards against oppression'.

by McDougal, Lasswell, and Chen: 'In a world in which many states are tyrannical or totalitarian or otherwise oppressive such an outcome is not to be desired nor lightly accepted'.[25]

The international minimum standard

The opposing approach to the national treatment doctrine contends that there are fundamental international standards of justice by which municipal law is to be measured. An authoritative definition of the international minimum standard was given in 1910 by the US Secretary of State, Elihu Root:

> There is a standard of justice, very simple, very fundamental, and of such general acceptance by all civilized countries as to form a part of the international law of the world. The condition upon which any country is entitled to measure the justice due from it to an alien by the justice which it accords to its own citizens is that its system of law and administration shall conform to this general standard. If any country's system of law and administration does not conform to that standard, although the people of that country may be content or compelled to live under it, no other country can be compelled to accept it as furnishing a satisfactory measure of treatment to its citizens.[26]

It is arguable that numerous treaties, particularly friendship, commerce, and navigation treaties, as well as international arbitration decisions[27] and national judgments have now given international customary law status to the minimum standard for the treatment of aliens.[28]

The international minimum standard, however, contains two weaknesses. First, it is a nebulous concept, with no defined parameters, and therefore highly vague and general.[29] In 1940, Borchard attempted to fashion a conceptual framework by outlining the standard's substantive and procedural contents. The former encompassed 'certain elementary privileges of human existence . . . mainly rights to life and the elementary liberties connected with the earning of a living', whereas

[25] See n. 2 above, 445.

[26] E. Root, 'The Basis of Protection to Citizens Residing Abroad' (1910) 4 AJIL 517, 521–2, cited by Lillich, n. 2 above, 17. Lillich, *ibid.*, exposes succinctly the *raison d'être* of this doctrine: 'This doctrine takes into account the possibility that the standards prevailing in a given State may be so low that, even if nationals and aliens are treated (or oppressed) alike, the norms of international law will have been violated'.

[27] See for example the following statement in *Roberts (U.S.)* v. *Mexico*, 1 Op. Comm. 100, 105, cited by Borchard, n. 24 above, 454 (and n. 17): 'Roberts was accorded the same treatment as that given to all other persons . . . Facts with respect to equality of treatment of aliens and nationals may be important in determining the merits of a complaint of mistreatment of an alien. But such equality is not the ultimate test of the propriety of the acts of authorities in the light of international law. That test is, broadly speaking, whether aliens are treated in accordance with ordinary standards of civilization'.

[28] In accordance with the general principles of law recognized by civilized nations under Art. 38 of the Statute of the International Court of Justice 1945. See also *International Provisions Protecting the Human Rights of Non-Citizens*, n. 10 above, 3, para. 23 and McDougal, Lasswell, and Chen, n. 2 above, 447–9.

[29] Borchard, n. 24 above, 448; McDougal, Lasswell, and Chen, n. 2 above, 450; G. S. Goodwin-Gill, *International Law and the Movement of Persons Between States* (Oxford: Oxford University Press, 1978) 62.

the latter was defined by 'fair courts, readily open to aliens, administering justice honestly, impartially, without bias or political control'.[30] Although this framework continues to suffer from ambiguity, the minimum standard, in its substantive dimension at least, may be associated with the provision of certain basic rights to non-citizens.

The second weakness is that, as a creature of the international law doctrine of state responsibility and diplomatic protection, the international minimum standard may only be 'activated' by the state on behalf of its nationals residing in another country. The individual's injury is attributed to the state which alone may pursue redress for the injury in international fora.[31] Furthermore, the state is not obliged to transfer or distribute any recoverable compensation or reparations to the injured party.[32] In general, therefore, the rights which flow from the minimum standard accrue to the state and not to the individual, who in the eyes of traditional international law has no legal status.[33]

The minimum standard for the protection of aliens, as a rule of international customary law, has faced serious challenges since the end of the Second World War. The number of new independent states, which have not been part of international custom, has grown substantially.[34] Coupled with the recent lack of international practice in this area and the tendency of the new and developing states to move towards the national treatment approach, particularly in respect of economic matters,[35] the international minimum standard is no longer a secure institution of customary international law.

The international minimum standard offers aliens the possibility of an objective and guaranteed level of protection potentially superior to that afforded by inadequate national laws. Indeed, if these laws are woefully deficient, it may also provide aliens with greater protection than that accorded to nationals.[36] Today, however, when states provide nationals with comprehensive safeguards, particularly in the fields of economic and social welfare, it is arguable that the standard of equal treatment with nationals would provide greater protection in some countries if it were rigorously applied.[37]

[30] Borchard, n. 24 above, 458 and 460 respectively.

[31] Lillich, n. 2 above, 11–12; *International Provisions Protecting the Human Rights of Non-Citizens*, n. 10 above, 5, para. 31.

[32] Lillich, n. 2 above, 12.

[33] *Ibid.* This approach is particularly inept, if, as is frequently the case with migrant workers (especially illegal migrant workers), the group comes from sections of society that have little political influence in their country of origin. I am grateful to Bill Black for bringing this point to my notice.

[34] McDougal, Lasswell, and Chen, n. 2 above, 452.

[35] R. B. Lillich, 'The Current Status of the Law of State Responsibility for Injuries to Aliens' in J. F. Murphey *et al.*, 'State Responsibility, Self Help and International Law' (1979) 73 Am. Soc. Int'l L. Prcdgs 242, 245–6. The views of new and developing states prevailed in Art. 2(2)(c) of the Charter of Economic Rights and Duties of States, UN GA Res. 3281 (XXIX) of 1974, which adopts the national treatment standard. Lillich, above, 246 .

[36] Cf. W. McKean, *Equality and Discrimination under International Law* (Oxford: Clarendon Press, 1983) c. XI, 'Equality in the Treatment of Aliens' 194, 197. See also nn. 24 and 25 above and accompanying text.

[37] I am once more indebted to Bill Black for bringing this argument to my attention.

International human rights norms: new standards

With the advent of express international protections for the rights of all human beings, the debate between advocates of the standard of equal treatment of aliens with nationals and the international minimum standard has been, to some extent, rendered defunct. Towards the end of the 1950s, García-Amador, the Special Rapporteur to the International Law Commission on State responsibility, asserted that:

> the conflict and antagonism formerly existing between the 'international standard' and the principle of equality of nationals and aliens have become obsolete in consequence of the political and juridical phenomenon in the post-war world of the recognition of fundamental human rights, and hence it would be useless to continue to hope that either the 'international standard' or the principle of equality will prevail.[38]

The compromise he proposed was that aliens should enjoy the same civil rights and individual guarantees as nationals, provided that these did not fall below fundamental human rights standards.[39]

International human rights instruments have now raised the standards of protection for aliens and nationals alike to the extent that the minimum standard is arguably no longer relevant as a yardstick by which abuses are to be measured:

> The principal thrust of the contemporary human rights movement is to accord nationals the same protection formerly accorded only to aliens, while at the same time raising the standard of protection for all human beings, nationals as well as aliens, far beyond the minimum international standard under the earlier customary law.[40]

Although it might be correct to maintain that individuals, including aliens, are today subjects of modern international law and receive direct protection of their rights and freedoms through legally enforced provisions,[41] to discard the traditional state responsibility doctrine for the protection of aliens would, at the present time, be imprudent. A number of states, the USA included, are not parties to important international human rights instruments.[42] Furthermore, the enforcement procedures under these instruments dealing with individual complaints are relatively weak.[43] Given these shortcomings of the international human rights protection system, an approach synthesizing the traditional law of state responsibility

[38] G. Amador, 'Third Report' in YBILC, 1958, Vol. II, UN Doc. A/CN.4/111, para. 8, cited by Goodwin-Gill (1978), n. 29 above, 63.

[39] Draft Art. 5.1, 'Second Report' in YBILC, 1957, Vol. II, UN Doc. A/CN.4/106, 104, cited by D. J. Harris, *Cases and Materials on International Law*, 4th edn. (London: Sweet & Maxwell, 1991) 498–9.

[40] McDougal, Lasswell, and Chen, n. 2 above, 464.

[41] *International Provisions Protecting the Human Rights of Non-Citizens*, n. 10 above, 2–3, para. 20.

[42] Lillich (1979), n. 35 above, 246. It would be difficult, however, to dispute the position that many provisions in these instruments, especially the Universal Declaration of Human Rights and the two international Covenants, examined below, form part of international customary law.

[43] *Ibid.*

with this system might be more beneficial to aliens.[44] Nonetheless, it is clear that the growing plethora of human rights prescriptions and their increasing universal and regional recognition have fundamentally altered international legal precepts in relation to the protection of aliens.

2.4 THE APPLICABILITY OF UNIVERSAL AND REGIONAL INTERNATIONAL HUMAN RIGHTS INSTRUMENTS TO ALIENS

Generally-speaking, the principal universal and regional international human rights instruments protect the rights and freedoms of aliens as well as nationals.[45] Wording such as 'Everyone has the right to . . .', 'All persons . . .', and, in the negative, 'No one shall be . . .', is indicative of this all-embracing approach. The UN Charter, 'the primary source of many of the most fundamental norms of contemporary international law',[46] serves as a further example. Articles 55 and 56 specifically relate to human rights. The former provision obliges the UN to promote 'universal respect for, and observance of, human rights and fundamental freedoms for *all* without distinction as to race, sex, language or religion',[47] whereas, by virtue of the latter, UN member states 'pledge themselves to take

[44] Harris, n. 39 above, 499–500, writes: 'That the law of State responsibility for aliens is not made redundant by the emergence of international human rights law follows from the uncertainty as to the rules on the enforcement of customary human rights law and the less than perfect remedies and universal acceptance of human rights treaties. For the time being at least, the possibility of diplomatic protection by one's national State is a valuable alternative and supplement to such guarantees and procedures under international human rights law as may exist'. According to McDougal, Lasswell, and Chen, n. 2 above, 464–5, both old and new law can mutually contribute to the protection of individual human rights: '[T]he traditional channels of protection through a State, together with the newly developed procedures under the contemporary human rights program of claims by individuals, would appear to achieve a cumulative beneficent impact, each reinforcing the other, in defense and fulfilment of the human rights of the individual'.

[45] See McDougal, Lasswell, and Chen, n. 2 above, 457 (n. 100): 'It has been generally recognized that one of the major purposes of the whole panoply of human rights prescriptions has been to accord the nationals of the State the same protection previously accorded aliens and to make unnecessary, in general, any differentiation between aliens and nationals. There is nothing in the legislative history (*travaux préparatoires*) of these prescriptions to suggest any intent to exclude aliens from protection'.

[46] Lillich, n. 2 above, 41.

[47] Art. 55(c) (emphasis added). See also Art. 1(3), which includes, as one of the purposes of the UN, the achievement of international cooperation, *inter alia*, 'in promoting and encouraging respect for human rights and for fundamental freedoms for *all* without distinction as to race, sex, language, or religion' (emphasis added). However, in contrast with the open-endedness of many non-discrimination and equality provisions in international human rights law that are discussed below, the list of grounds upon which discrimination is prohibited in the UN Charter is decidedly limited. See also K. J. Partsch, 'Fundamental Principles of Human Rights: Self-Determination, Equality and Non-Discrimination' in K. Vasak and P. Alston, (eds.), *The International Dimension of Human Rights* (Westport, Connecticut: UNESCO, Greenwood Press, 1982) 61, 72–3, who argues that the four grounds specified in the Charter are more important than other grounds. For an overview of these international provisions, see A. F. Bayefsky, 'The Principle of Equality or Non-Discrimination in International Law' (1990) 11 HRLJ 1, 5–8.

joint and separate action in cooperation with the [UN] for the achievement of the purposes set forth in Article 55'.

In spite of the universality which the principal international human rights instruments embrace, they contain provisions which refer either specifically to non-citizens or which are clearly inapplicable to them. Restrictions are most prevalent with regard to those rights with which this study is concerned, namely economic, social, cultural, political, and residence rights.[48]

Universal instruments

(a) Universal Declaration of Human Rights (UDHR)[49]

The precursor to all international human rights instruments, the UDHR, is phrased in all-embracing language.[50] It contains an open-ended non-discrimination provision, found in Article 2:

> Everyone is entitled to all the rights and freedoms set forth in this Declaration, without distinction of any kind, such as race, colour, sex, language, religion, political or other opinion, national or social origin, property, birth or other status.

The *travaux préparatoires* reveal that the drafters deliberately changed the wording of a proposed text of this provision from 'without distinction as to race . . .' to 'without distinction of any kind, such as race . . .' in order to underline that the list of grounds enumerated was not exhaustive.[51] Special Rapporteur Baroness Elles agrees that the grounds specified in Article 2 are illustrative only, but also points out that this does not mean that all grounds are acceptable nor that 'nationality' may be a prohibited ground. With reference to the *travaux préparatoires*, she observes that the ground of 'national origin' was used to connote national characteristics and not citizenship.[52]

Notwithstanding its universal language, the UDHR contains some provisions that have been interpreted as excluding aliens from their protection. Articles 13 and 21 warrant particular attention. Article 13 reads:

> 1. Everyone has the right to freedom of movement and residence within the borders of each State.
> 2. Everyone has the right to leave any country, including his own, and to return to his country.

[48] See also Leuprecht, n. 1 above, 165–6.

[49] Universal Declaration of Human Rights, UN GA Res. 217A (III), adopted 10 Dec. 1948 without a dissenting vote. Seven countries abstained: Byelorussian SSR, Czechoslovakia, Poland, Saudi Arabia, Ukrainian SSR, USSR and Yugoslavia.

[50] For example, Art. 1 reads: '*All* human beings are born free and equal in dignity and rights. They are endowed with reason and conscience and should act towards one another in a spirit of brotherhood' (emphasis added).

[51] S. Skogly, 'Article 2' in A. Eide *et al.*, (eds.), *The Universal Declaration of Human Rights: A Commentary* (Oslo: Scandinavian University Press, 1992) 57, 62, citing from UN Doc. E/CN.4/52.

[52] *International Provisions Protecting the Human Rights of Non-Citizens*, n. 10 above, 15, para. 114.

Paragraphs (1) and (2) of Article 21 declare:

1. Everyone has the right to take part in the government of his country, directly or through freely chosen representatives.
2. Everyone has the right of equal access to public service in his country.

Article 13(2) grants non-citizens, including migrant workers, the right to leave the country in which they live and work and to return to their countries of origin.[53] It does not, however, unless interpreted very liberally, provide them with the right to enter a country if they do not possess the citizenship of that country. Paragraphs (1) and (2) of Article 21 appear to preclude aliens from claiming political rights in the host country.[54] Commentators on these provisions maintain that the reference to 'his country' most likely means the country of origin or nationality.[55] Lillich, however, suggests a 'freer interpretation' of Articles 13 and 21:

> It is possible to offer a more 'progressive' interpretation of Articles 13 and 21 . . . One could contend for instance, that the expression 'his country' does not refer exclusively to the state of the alien's nationality. One could argue for a more sociological, as opposed to juridical, interpretation of those words and conclude that, for any given person, 'his country' refers to the one with which he has the most substantial real connections, whether through family ties, residence, *economic activity*, or whatever. Under such an interpretation, one might then read Articles 13 and 21 to grant aliens rights in host states.[56]

But Lillich is careful not to adopt the above interpretation as his own, claiming that it would be out of place with respect to a document which, in any event, breaks new ground with its 'forcefulness—through simplicity'.[57] Nonetheless, the argument is an important one, for, as discussed below, the wording in subsequent human rights instruments does not afford non-citizens the same possibility of claiming rights of entry and political rights as that provided by Articles 13(2) and 21 of the UDHR.[58]

One of the most common restrictions imposed upon aliens and migrant workers concerns their right to work and to free choice of employment. However, Article 23(1) of the UDHR extends to *everyone* 'the right to work, to free choice of employment, to just and favourable conditions of work and to protection against unemployment'. The drafting history of this provision reveals that the word 'everyone' in this context was understood to mean that everybody ordinarily resident

[53] See also *Exploitation of Labour Through Illicit And Clandestine Trafficking* (Preliminary Study prepared by Ms. H. E. Warzazi, Special Rapporteur) (1974) (hereinafter *Warzazi Preliminary Report*) 66 and 67, paras. 246 and 268 respectively.

[54] Lillich, n. 2 above, 43.

[55] McKean, n. 36 above, 199; J. A. R. Nafziger and B. C. Bartel, 'The Migrant Workers Convention: Its Place in Human Rights Law' (1991) 25 IMR 771, 783 (n. 58).

[56] Lillich, n. 2 above, 43 (emphasis added).

[57] *Ibid.* 43–4.

[58] See also A. Rosas, 'Article 21' in *The Universal Declaration of Human Rights: A Commentary*, n. 51 above, 299, 306, with respect to the additional limitation of the right of political participation in Art. 25 of the ICCPR (discussed below) to citizens.

in the territory of the state concerned should have free access to employment outside of the public service.[59]

Another relevant provision is Article 29, which is concerned with individual duties and which also outlines the permissible limitations that may be imposed on the rights in the UDHR. Article 29(1) reads: 'Everyone has duties to the community in which alone the free and full development of his personality is possible'. Baroness Elles argues that the absence of the nexus of nationality does not mean that aliens owe no duties to the state in which they are residing.[60] She adds that in order to claim protection from the state an alien must conform to its laws, refrain from interfering in its political affairs, and contribute generally to the development of the country.[61] To read into this clause, however, a prohibition on the political activity of aliens is surely incorrect, particularly when considering Article 20(1), which grants to *everyone* 'the right to freedom of peaceful assembly and association', and the possible 'progressive' interpretation of Article 21 discussed above.[62] The second paragraph of Article 29 contains an extensive limitation clause:

> In the exercise of his rights and freedoms, everyone shall be subject only to such limitations as are determined by law solely for the purpose of securing due recognition and respect for the rights and freedoms of others and of meeting the just requirements of morality, public order and the general welfare in a democratic society.

Any restrictions upon the rights of aliens and migrants commonly imposed by states might, therefore, be justified with reference to this provision.

(b) International Covenant on Civil and Political Rights (ICCPR)[63]

The ICCPR is more precise than the UDHR regarding the applicability of its provisions to non-citizens. Article 2(1) ensures to '*all individuals*' the rights recognized in the ICCPR without distinction of any kind.[64] The Human Rights

[59] W. R. Böhning, 'Basic Rights of "Temporary" Migrant Workers: Law vs. Power' in L. F. Tomasi, (ed.), *In Defense of the Alien, Vol. VIII, Immigration Enforcement, Employment Policy, Migrant Rights and Refugee Movements*, Proceedings of the 1985 Annual National Legal Conference on Immigration and Refugee Policy (New York: Center for Migration Studies, 1986) 99, 102 (n. 7). Citing from UN Docs E/CN.4/57, E/CN.4/SR.40, E/CN.4/SR.64–66, A/C.3/SR.139–143 and A/C.3/SR.156–158.

[60] *International Provisions Protecting the Human Rights of Non-Citizens*, n. 10 above, 43, para. 321.

[61] *Ibid.* 43, para. 322.

[62] See however the reservations made by some states parties to Arts. 21 and 22 of the ICCPR, the equivalent provisions to Art. 20(1), as well as Art. 16 of the ECHR discussed below. The scope of Art. 16 is also analysed in greater detail in Ch. 8.

[63] International Covenant on Civil and Political Rights, 16 Dec. 1966; 999 UNTS 171; entered into force 23 March 1976; ratified by 133 States as at 1 Jan. 1996. See J.-B. Marie, 'International Instruments Relating to Human Rights. Classification and Status of Ratifications as of 1 January 1996' (1996) 17 HRLJ 61. Information on the ratification status of the other human rights treaties considered below and in subsequent chapters, with the exception of the Council of Europe instruments, is also taken from this source.

[64] Art. 2(1) reads: 'Each State Party to the present Covenant undertakes to respect and to ensure to *all individuals* within its territory and subject to its jurisdiction the rights recognized in the present Covenant, without distinction of any kind, such as race, colour, sex, language, religion, political or other opinion, national or social origin, property, birth or other status' (emphasis added).

Committee, the body charged with implementing the ICCPR, stated categorically in its General Comment 15/27 of 22 July 1986 on the Position of Aliens under the Covenant that 'in general, the rights set forth in the Covenant apply to everyone, irrespective of reciprocity, and *irrespective of his or her nationality* or statelessness'.[65] In addition, there is also a substantive equality clause in Article 26, which guarantees to '*all persons*' equality before the law and equal protection of the law without discrimination on the same grounds as those listed in Article 2(1).[66] Although 'nationality' is not included in the list of prohibited grounds of discrimination, the grounds in both provisions are clearly illustrative only as is evident from the words 'such as' and 'or other status'.[67] 'National origin' is specified, but it cannot be interpreted as implying the prohibition of discrimination on the grounds of nationality.[68] The general consensus which emerged from the drafting process was that states parties may discriminate against aliens so long as such distinctions are considered strictly necessary, or justified in accordance with objective and reasonable criteria.[69]

[65] UN, *Report of the Human Rights Committee*, 41 UN GAOR, Supp. No. 40, UN Doc. A/41/40, Annex VI, para. 1, cited in (1994) 1:2 IHRR 16 (emphasis added). The exceptional provisions are Art. 13 which *only* applies to aliens and the rights in Art. 25 which are restricted to citizens. *Ibid.* para. 2. See below. Although General Comments issued by the Human Rights Committee pursuant to Art. 40(4) as well as the case law on individual communications under the Optional Protocol are not legally binding in international law, these sources should nonetheless be recognized as an 'authoritative interpretation' of the ICCPR. Cf. M. Nowak, *U.N. Covenant on Civil and Political Rights. CCPR Commentary* (Kehl: Engel, 1993) xxiv, para. 21.

[66] Art. 26 proclaims: '*All persons* are equal before the law and are entitled without any discrimination to the equal protection of the law. In this respect, the law shall prohibit any discrimination and guarantee to *all persons* equal and effective protection against discrimination on any ground such as race, colour, sex, language, religion, political or other opinion, national or social origin, property, birth or other status' (emphasis added). A suggestion during drafting to replace 'persons' by 'nationals' or 'citizens' was not followed up. See B. G. Ramcharan, 'Equality and Non-discrimination' in L. Henkin, (ed.), *The International Bill of Rights: The Covenant on Civil and Political Rights* (New York: Columbia University Press, 1981) 246, 263; Nowak, n. 65 above, 479, para. 33.

[67] Nowak, n. 65 above, 45, para. 34. Indeed, in Case 196/1985, *Gueye et al.* v. *France*, cited in Nowak, n. 65 above, 51, para. 44, the Human Rights Committee confirmed that discrimination on the basis of nationality was prohibited with reference to the ground 'other status'. However, Bayefsky, n. 47 above, 7, adopts a more guarded approach, observing in relation to Art. 26 that 'the effort by the Committee to fit the ground of distinction in the case within "other status" suggests that the grounds covered by Article 26 will be limited', although she recognizes, with reference to the *travaux préparatoires*, that the inclusion of further grounds of discrimination in Art. 26 was felt to be unnecessary on the basis that any new grounds would be covered by the terms 'discrimination on any ground' and 'other status': *ibid.* 8, citing from M. J. Bossuyt, *Guide to the 'Travaux Préparatoires' of the International Covenant on Civil and Political Rights* (Dordrecht: Martinus Nijhoff, 1987) 486. The discrimination at issue in *Gueye* related to a social and economic entitlement, namely pension rights, with the result that the Committee only found a violation of Art. 26 and not Art. 2(1) which is limited to rights recognized in the ICCPR, thus illustrating that the former provision stands alone as an independent right and does not have to be activated by another right in the ICCPR. See also Nowak, n. 65 above, 473, para. 23.

[68] See n. 52 above and the accompanying text with respect to the interpretation of 'national origin' in Art. 2 of the UDHR.

[69] See respectively Ramcharan, n. 66 above, 263 and Nowak, n. 65 above, 473, para. 23 (and n. 76).

Article 4(1) of the ICCPR permits measures derogating from certain enumerated rights in time of public emergency which threatens the life of the nation provided that such measures are 'strictly required by the exigencies of the situation' and do not, *inter alia*, amount to discrimination '*solely* on the ground of race, colour, sex, language, religion or social origin'.[70] Discriminatory measures based on the ground of nationality are, therefore, permissible, thus endorsing the frequent practice of states to discriminate against nationals of enemy states who are present in their territory during wartime.[71] However, it is arguable that specific measures to the detriment of a particular class or group of aliens on the basis of one of the listed grounds in Article 4(1) would not be justified.[72]

In contrast with the UDHR, the ICCPR expressly limits the enjoyment of the right to freedom of movement in Article 12(1) to those *lawfully* within the territory of the state,[73] but, like the UDHR, it also leaves open the possibility for certain aliens to claim entry rights by virtue of Article 12(4) which reads: 'No one shall be arbitrarily deprived of the right to enter his own country'. According to Nowak, the term 'his own country' demonstrates that the protection of Article 12(4) 'extends to aliens and stateless persons who have such a strong attachment to a State that they view it as "their own country" or their home country', an interpretation confirmed by the *travaux préparatoires*.[74]

The ICCPR also excludes aliens explicitly from the enjoyment of political rights. The rights in Article 25 to take part in the conduct of public affairs, to vote and to be elected to political office, and to have access to the public service are reserved exclusively to 'citizens'.[75] There is nothing in the provision, however, which prevents states parties affording political rights to aliens or migrant

[70] Emphasis added. Art. 4(2) prohibits derogation from certain fundamental rights, for example the right to life (Art. 6) and the right not to be subjected to torture or to cruel, inhuman, or degrading treatment or punishment (Art. 7).

[71] Nowak, n. 65 above, 86, para. 28.

[72] Goodwin-Gill (1978), n. 29 above, 69; cf. McKean, n. 36 above, 200. Nowak, n. 65 above, observes, however, that the use of the word 'solely' makes it clear that 'when emergency measures primarily affect members of a certain race or a certain ethnic, religious or linguistic minority due to, e.g., their geographically limited scope of application, they are permissible as long as they do not intentionally aim at these population groups'.

[73] According to Nowak, n. 65 above, 202, paras. 9, 10, 'the term "*lawfully*" refers to the *national legal system* . . . The residency of an alien is . . . lawful when he or she has entered a State's territory in accordance with its legal system and/or is in possession of a valid residency permit (e.g., a visa)' (original emphasis). This provision, therefore, clearly would not encompass illegal aliens or irregular migrant workers.

[74] Nowak, *ibid.* 219, para. 48. Such aliens would include *inter alia*: 'above all, *children of immigrants and alien workers* who were born in the host country and no longer have a home in their country of nationality'; and '*immigrants* who have lived many years in the host country and broken all ties to their home country but have not—for whatever reason—acquired the nationality of the host country' *ibid.* 220, para. 49 (original emphasis).

[75] Nowak, *ibid.* 445, para. 20, writes: 'The fact that Art. 25 is the only provision in the Covenant that does not guarantee a universal human right but rather a *citizen's right* clearly shows that the States Parties may deny *aliens* the right to vote. The restriction to the "citizen" . . . stems from the concept of the modern nation-State, namely, that only those individuals who are attached to "their" State by the special bond of citizenship may exercise political rights' (original emphasis). See also the General Comment on the Position of Aliens under the Covenant, n. 65 above, para. 2.

workers. Indeed, if a state party has conferred political rights upon non-citizens, the shortcomings of the ICCPR in this regard do not imply that rights already granted at the national level can be taken away.[76]

Article 13 of the ICCPR is a provision which applies solely to aliens:

> An alien lawfully in the territory of a State Party to the present Covenant may be expelled therefrom only in pursuance of a decision reached in accordance with law and shall, except where compelling reasons of national security otherwise require, be allowed to submit the reasons against his expulsion and to have his case reviewed by, and be represented for the purpose before, the competent authority or a person or persons especially designated by the competent authority.

Article 13 only applies to those aliens 'lawfully'[77] in a country, affording them procedural protection or natural justice safeguards against arbitrary expulsion.[78] The expulsion decision must be taken 'in accordance with law' and aliens must be given the opportunity to challenge the decision and to have their case reviewed, with the assistance of representation, by a competent authority.[79] These procedural safeguards, however, may be overridden for 'compelling reasons of national security'. This is an extremely exceptional provision. According to commentators, 'a State can rely on national security only in serious cases of political or military threats to the entire nation', whereas the phrase 'compelling reasons' is intended to emphasize the narrowness of this exception.[80] Although Article 13 regulates only the expulsion procedure and does not restrict a state's sovereign right to determine the substantive grounds of the actual expulsion decision, it does

[76] Art. 5(2) of the ICCPR asserts: 'There shall be no restriction upon or derogation from any of the fundamental human rights recognized or existing in any State Party to the present Covenant pursuant to law, conventions, regulations or custom on the pretext that the present Covenant does not recognize such rights or that it recognizes them to a lesser extent'. See also Lillich, n. 2 above, 46.

[77] In its General Comment on the Position of Aliens under the Covenant, n. 65 above, para. 9, the Human Rights Committee confirmed that Art. 13 does not apply to 'illegal entrants and aliens who have stayed longer than the law or their permits allow', but noted that 'if the legality of an alien's entry or stay is in dispute, any decision on this point leading to his expulsion or deportation ought to be taken in accordance with Article 13'.

[78] The Human Rights Committee verified in its General Comment on the Position of Aliens under the Covenant, *ibid.* para. 10, that 'Article 13 directly regulates only the procedure and not the substantive grounds for expulsion'. See also McDougal, Lasswell, and Chen, n. 2 above, 460; Nowak, n. 65 above, 223, para. 2. Nowak, *ibid.*, 223, para. 4, observes that proposals during drafting to include an exhaustive list of substantive grounds for expulsion were not accepted.

[79] In Case 155/1983, *Hammel* v. *Madagascar*, the Human Rights Committee found a breach of Art. 13 because, *inter alia*, the applicant 'was not afforded an opportunity to challenge the expulsion order prior to his expulsion' (para. 18.2). Cited in Nowak, n. 65 above, 230, para. 17. In its General Comment on the Position of Aliens under the Covenant, n. 65 above, para. 10, the Committee stated that 'an alien must be given full facilities for pursuing his remedy against expulsion so that this right will in all the circumstances of the case be an effective one'. According to Nowak, n. 65 above, these statements imply clearly that 'States Parties must *suspend an expulsion decision pending appeal*' (original emphasis).

[80] See respectively Nowak, n. 65 above, 232, para. 20 and S. Jagerskiold, 'Freedom of Movement' in *The International Bill of Rights: The Covenant on Civil and Political Rights*, n. 66 above, 166, 184.

appear to be based on the premise that an alien lawfully in a country has a limited right to stay.[81]

Article 27 of the ICCPR is the sole provision in universal human rights treaty law with the aim of protecting the cultural, religious, and linguistic rights of persons belonging to ethnic minorities:

In those States in which ethnic, religious or linguistic minorities exist, persons belonging to such minorities shall not be denied the right, in community with the other members of their group, to enjoy their own culture, to profess and practice their own religion, or to use their own language.

Even though the text refers to 'persons', and not 'nationals' or 'citizens' as in Article 25,[82] the applicability of Article 27 to aliens is disputed.[83] The UN Special Rapporteur on Minorities, Capotorti, contends that because foreigners are able to benefit from the protection of international customary law as well as from other special rights conferred on them by treaties and various agreements, the clause should not apply to aliens.[84] In defining the term 'minority', the former Chief Justice of the Québec Superior Court, Deschênes, argues that in order to qualify as a minority the relevant group must be composed of citizens. According to Deschênes, groups of migrants or aliens, despite having resided in a country for an indefinite period of time, owe no allegiance to it: 'the first duty of the State is towards its own citizens'; to others, the state 'owes only courtesy, which does not give rise to any rights'.[85]

[81] Cf. Jagerskiold, *ibid.* Despite the promise accorded by Art. 13 to non-nationals threatened with expulsion from their country of lawful residence, a number of countries have entered reservations in respect of this provision. See Nowak, n. 65 above, 226, para. 10 (n. 22). For example, a reservation by France, a significant migrant-receiving country, asserts that Art. 13 'cannot derogate from [domestic legislation] concerning the entry into, and sojourn in, France of aliens, nor from the other instruments concerning the expulsion of aliens in force in those parts of the territory of the Republic in which the [relevant legislation] does not apply' UN Doc. CCPR/C/2/Rev.3, cited in Nowak, n. 65 above, 754–5. A provision in the ICCPR with potential to *substantively* circumscribe the State's power to expel aliens is Art. 7 which prohibits torture and the imposition of 'cruel, inhuman or degrading treatment or punishment'. The Human Rights Committee in its revised General Comment 20/44 of 3 April 1992 on the Prohibition of Torture asserted that 'States parties must not expose individuals to the danger of torture or cruel, inhuman or degrading treatment or punishment upon return to another country by way of their extradition, expulsion or refoulement' UN, *Report of the Human Rights Committee*, 47 UN GAOR Supp. No. 40, UN Doc. A/47/40, Annex VI, 193, para. 9. Also reproduced in (1994) 1:2 IHRR 27.

[82] See also Nowak, n. 65 above, 489, para. 16, who adds that the distinction between these terms was clearly recognized by most delegations during the drafting process.

[83] The discussion below is taken from R. Cholewinski, *The Positive Cultural and Linguistic Right of Ethnic Minorities* (unpublished LL.M. Thesis, College of Law, University of Saskatchewan, Saskatoon, Aug. 1988) 40 (and nn. 20 and 21).

[84] F. Capotorti, *Study of the Rights of Persons Belonging to Ethnic, Religious and Linguistic Minorities*, UN Doc. E/CN.4/Sub.2/384/Rev.1 (1979) 12, para. 57.

[85] UN Commission on Human Rights, Sub-Commission on Prevention of Discrimination and Protection of Minorities, *Proposal Concerning a Definition of the Term 'Minority'*, (by J. Deschênes), UN Doc. E/CN.4/Sub.2/1985/31 (Geneva: UN, 1985) 7–8, paras. 39–44.

Both of these arguments are unconvincing. First, international customary law, as discussed earlier, cannot afford the same extensive protection to aliens as might be provided by international human rights instruments, whereas regional or bilateral agreements aimed at protecting aliens, and particularly migrant workers, do not apply to all groups of non-citizens. Secondly, an interpretation of Article 27 excluding aliens from the scope of protection might encourage states to deny nationality to certain groups residing within their borders in order to keep them under the 'discipline' of aliens legislation.[86] In its General Comment on the Position of Aliens under the Covenant, the Human Rights Committee clearly preferred the broader interpretation of Article 27.[87]

Certain provisions in the ICCPR allow the rights in question to be restricted for a number of specified reasons. For example, Article 22(1) recognizes the right of everyone to 'freedom of association with others, including the right to form and join trade unions'. Article 22(2), however, permits restrictions on the exercise of this right:

> which are prescribed by law and which are necessary in a democratic society in the interests of national security or public safety, public order (*ordre public*), the protection of public health or morals or the protection of the rights and freedoms of others.[88]

These 'limitation clauses', therefore, present states parties with the possibility of further restricting aliens' and migrant workers' rights: 'Invoking these clauses, and provided such measures do not amount to the "destruction" of the rights at stake (Article 5), governments can suspend or limit the exercise by aliens of certain rights'.[89]

[86] C. Tomuschat, 'Protection of Minorities under Article 27 of the International Covenant on Civil and Political Rights' in *Mosler Collection*, Völkerrecht als Rechtsordnung—International Gerichtsbarkeit-Menschenrechte; Festschrift für Hermann Mosler (Berlin: Springer Verlag, 1983) 949, 960–1.

[87] See n. 65 above, para. 7: 'In those cases where aliens constitute a minority within the meaning of article 27, they shall not be denied the right, in community with other members of their group, to enjoy their own culture, to profess and practise their own religion and to use their own language': Nowak, n. 65 above, 489–90, paras. 17–18, notes, however, that the application of the provision to minority groups of non-citizens is limited in practice because (numerical) minorities must also display a certain stability, as indicated by the word 'exist', in order to come within the terms of Art. 27. He refers, *ibid.* 490, paras. 19 and 20 respectively, to the *travaux préparatoires*, which reveal that 'the strong emphasis on stability as a definitional feature of minorities was intended to prevent *immigrants*, migrant workers or other forms of "new minorities" from being recognised too rapidly' (original emphasis). However, this does not 'preclude immigrants, including migrant workers, from being able to claim the protection of this provision after a certain (longer) period of residency in their new home country when they fulfil the remaining definitional criteria'.

[88] Similar restrictions may be imposed upon the right to freedom of movement (Art. 12), the right to freedom of expression (Art. 19), and the right of peaceful assembly (Art. 21).

[89] M. Tardou, 'Migrant Workers' in R. Bernhadt, (ed.), *Encyclopaedia of Public International Law* (Amsterdam: North Holland, 1981) Instalment 8, 372–3. Indeed, the rights of irregular migrants are particularly vulnerable under the 'national security' and 'public order' grounds in these limitation clauses: *ibid.* 377.

(c) International Covenant on Economic, Social and Cultural Rights (ICESCR)[90]

The ICESCR affords less protection to aliens in comparison with the UDHR and the ICCPR. Two reasons may be advanced for this, both stemming from the nature of the rights to be found in the ICESCR. The first is that it asserts expressly, in Article 2(1), that the standards therein are to be achieved progressively, with the result that neither aliens nor nationals can always expect to benefit in full from the rights set out in the document.[91] However, the body mandated with the supervision of the ICESCR, the Committee on Economic, Social and Cultural Rights, has recognized that states should assume, as a priority, the satisfaction of a minimum core content of the enumerated rights.[92] The second reason is that the rights in the ICESCR involve state affirmative measures and

[90] International Covenant on Economic, Social and Cultural Rights, 16 Dec. 1966; 993 UNTS 3; entry into force 3 Jan. 1976; ratified by 134 states as at 1 Jan. 1996.

[91] Art. 2(1) of the ICESCR reads: 'Each State Party to the present Covenant undertakes to take steps, individually and through international assistance and cooperation, especially economic and technical, to the maximum of its available resources, *with a view to achieving progressively the full realization of the rights recognized in the present Covenant* by all appropriate means, including particularly the adoption of legislative measures' (emphasis added). According to Baroness Elles, such an approach may permit discriminatory treatment against aliens in favour of nationals: 'With the present wide disparities in economic and social development there is no reason to suppose that the progressive achievement of these standards implies equal and simultaneous progress for all individuals within the jurisdiction of the member State, including aliens': *International Provisions Protecting the Human Rights of Non-Citizens*, n. 10 above, 7, para. 43.

[92] The Committee on Economic, Social and Cultural Rights has cast more light on this obligation in its General Comment No. 3 on The Nature of States Parties' Obligations, adopted at its Fifth Session in 1990. While observing that the concept of 'progressive realization' in Art. 2(1) constitutes 'a recognition of the fact that full realization of all economic, social and cultural rights will generally not be able to be achieved in a short period of time', the Committee has nevertheless emphasized that the *raison d'être* of the ICESCR was to establish 'clear obligations for States parties in respect of the full realization of the rights in question', thus imposing 'an obligation to move as expeditiously and effectively as possible towards that goal'. The Committee asserted, furthermore, that the ICESCR imposes 'a minimum core obligation' upon states parties 'to ensure the satisfaction of, at the very least, minimum essential levels of each of the rights'. Although the ICESCR in Art. 2(1) takes account of the resource constraints existing in some countries by limiting the necessary steps to be taken by each state party 'to the maximum of its available resources', any failure to meet its minimum core obligations under this head would only be justified if the state party could demonstrate that 'every effort has been made to use all resources that are at its disposition in an effort to satisfy, as a matter of priority, those minimum obligations'. Finally, the obligation requires states parties 'to take steps, individually and *through international assistance and cooperation, especially economic and technical* . . .'. Therefore, the phrase 'to the maximum of its available resources' refers to both 'the resources existing within a State and those available from the international community through international cooperation and assistance', a view confirmed by the *travaux préparatoires*: UN Doc. E/1991/23, paras. 9, 10 and 13, reproduced in (1994) 1:1 IHRR 8–9. See also the Limburg Principles on the Implementation of the International Covenant on Economic, Social and Cultural Rights, UN Doc. E/CN.4/1987/17, Annex, reproduced in (1987) HRQ 122–135, paras. 21, 25–6. These principles were drafted by a group of international law experts, including some members of the Committee on Economic, Social and Cultural Rights. According to these principles, *ibid.* paras. 22 and 35, some of the obligations in the ICESCR must be applied immediately, such as the non-discrimination provision, Art. 2(2), which is considered below. See also General Comment No. 3, above, para. 1.

when resources are scarce, especially in developing countries, it is not surprising that states prefer to favour their own nationals.[93] Such an approach, however, should not detract from the conviction that the human rights protections in the ICESCR are designed for *all* human beings irrespective of nationality.[94] This conviction, however, is challenged by the other provisions in Article 2, which clearly reduce even further the protection accorded to aliens.

The principle of non-discrimination is found in Article 2(2):

> The States Parties to the present Covenant undertake to guarantee that the rights enunciated in the present Covenant will be exercised without discrimination of any kind as to race, colour, sex, language, religion, political or other opinion, national or social origin, property, birth or other status.

Commentators are unable to reach any firm conclusion whether this provision is open to the admission of any further grounds of discrimination, including that of nationality. Lillich suggests that the list of enumerated grounds in Article 2(2) is not stated expressly to be exhaustive, although he concludes that, on balance, the ICESCR does not have a general norm of non-discrimination against aliens as compared with the ICCPR.[95] Goodwin-Gill contends that the provision is sufficiently broad to limit the circumstances in which discrimination against aliens is justified, but he notes that Article 2(3), discussed below, may undermine this argument.[96] From a strictly textual point of view, Klerk states that the use of the words 'as to' instead of 'such as' does not necessarily mean that the list of grounds of discrimination in Article 2(2) was intended to be exhaustive given the absence of any discussion on this point during drafting. Furthermore, she observes that the drafters were of the view that the inclusion of additional grounds, such as 'association with minority groups', were unnecessary because they were adequately covered in the provision by the terms 'without discrimination of any kind' and 'other status'.[97] Warzazi observes, however, that the majority of drafters believed that the word 'discrimination' in Article 2(2) gave states sufficient leeway to make distinctions between aliens and nationals with respect to certain rights, in particular the right to work and social benefits which governments considered should continue to be restricted to nationals.[98] An examination of the practice of the Committee on Economic, Social and Cultural Rights under the ICESCR indicates that the Committee is prepared to consider the possibility of including additional grounds of discrimination in Article 2(2), such

[93] Lillich, n. 2 above, 47.

[94] McDougal, Lasswell, and Chen, n. 2 above, 460.

[95] Lillich, n. 2 above, 47–8. See also McDougal, Lasswell, and Chen, n. 2 above, 457–8 (n. 100). In contrast, the Limburg Principles, n. 92 above, para. 36, assert categorically that 'the grounds of discrimination mentioned in Article 2(2) are not exhaustive'.

[96] Goodwin-Gill (1978), n. 29 above, 68,

[97] Y. Klerk, 'Working Paper on Article 2(2) and Article 3 of the International Covenant on Economic, Social and Cultural Rights' (1987) 9 HRQ 250, 256. In another context, however, she also concedes, *ibid.* 262, that Art. 2(3) may permit discriminatory treatment against non-nationals in the progressive implementation of certain rights under the ICESCR.

[98] *Warzazi Preliminary Report*, n. 53 above, 30, para. 93.

as health, disability, age, sexual orientation, poverty, and *nationality*.[99] Thus far, however, the Committee has not clearly endorsed the full application of the principle of non-discrimination to aliens. The present position appears to be that non-nationals are entitled to equal treatment to some extent, and that they have a right to the enjoyment of the minimum core content of the rights guaranteed by the ICESCR.[100]

In contrast with the doubts that surround the extent of the application of Article 2(2) to aliens, the very next clause, Article 2(3), constitutes an unequivocal limitation on the rights of non-nationals:

> Developing countries, with due regard to human rights and their national economy, may determine to what extent they would guarantee the economic rights recognized in the present Covenant to non-nationals.[101]

Article 2(3) constitutes a *carte blanche* to developing countries permitting them to give priority to their nationals with regard to the guarantee of economic rights.[102] The aim of the clause was to enable developing countries to rectify the legacy of the post-colonial era which left certain groups of non-citizens with an undue influence over their economies.[103] Article 2(3) has met with wide criticism. Indeed, at the drafting stage, many delegates viewed it as 'contrary to the spirit of universality and equality underlying the draft Covenant and likely to give rise to all kinds of discrimination alien to the intention of the sponsors'.[104] The provision suffers from ambiguity. Developing countries may only limit the application of '*economic rights*' to non-nationals. 'Economic rights' refer to those economic rights enunciated in the ICESCR, but it is not entirely clear what these

[99] M. C. Craven, *The International Covenant on Economic, Social and Cultural Rights: A Perspective on its Development* (Oxford: Clarendon Press, 1995) 170.

[100] *Ibid.* 173–4. Distinctions between different groups of non-citizens, in line with the present approach taken under international human rights law to the norm of non-discrimination, are permissible if they pursue a legitimate aim and are proportionate to that aim. On this basis, for example, more favourable treatment in the economic, social, and cultural rights field of EC nationals by EC member states or of persons who have become aliens as a result of territorial changes by their new countries of residence might be justifiable. On the latter point and its relevance to the inhabitants of Baltic and other states, which formed part of the former Soviet Union, or to the inhabitants of those states created out of the former Yugoslavia, see A. Eide, 'Economic, Social and Cultural Rights as Human Rights' in A. Eide, C. Krause, and A. Rosas, (eds.), *Economic, Social and Cultural Rights: A Textbook* (Dordrecht: Martinus Nijhoff, 1995) 21, 34–5.

[101] Goodwin-Gill (1978), n. 29 above, 68, explains that this provision is in line with a number of UN General Assembly Resolutions, e.g. GA Res. 1803 (XVII) of 1962 on Permanent Sovereignty over Natural Resources and GA Res. 3281 (XXIX) of 1974 adopting the Charter of Economic Rights and Duties of States.

[102] Lillich, n. 2 above, 47.

[103] McKean, n. 36 above, 201 (n. 37); Limburg Principles, n. 92 above, para. 43. The provision was narrowly adopted by 41 votes in favour to 38 against with 12 abstentions: McKean, n. 36 above.

[104] L. Sohn, 'Supplementary Paper: A Short History of United Nations Documents on Human Rights' in Commission to Study the Organization of Peace, *The United Nations and Human Rights* (1968) 38, 116, cited by McDougal, Lasswell, and Chen, n. 2 above, 458 (n. 100). McKean, n. 36 above, 201, maintains that Art. 2(3) must be regarded 'as an unfortunate inclusion in a covenant of this nature and likely to cause invidious and unreasonable distinctions to be made against aliens on the ground of their foreign nationality'.

rights are. If they are defined as 'rights that enable a person to earn a living or that relate to that process',[105] the right to work in Article 6 is clearly affected by Article 2(3), although it may also be considered a 'social right'.[106] The guarantee in Article 7 to 'just and favourable conditions of work' may also fall into the 'economic rights' category.[107] It would be very difficult, however, to justify restrictions on the rights in Article 7. Although states appear to be under no obligation to grant aliens the right of access to employment on the same terms as nationals,[108] once aliens have been afforded this right, they should have the equal right to enjoy 'just and favourable conditions of work'.[109]

The meaning of the term 'developing country' in Article 2(3) is far from clear. Although no precise definition is provided, it is understood to refer to economically weak countries, especially those which have experienced colonial rule.[110] Presumably, once a country's economy achieves a certain level of improvement, it will at some point no longer fall into the 'developing' category.[111] The term 'non-nationals' is also not defined. Although doubts have been raised whether illegal immigrants may even benefit from the economic, social, and cultural rights prescribed in the ICESCR,[112] the enjoyment of these rights is clearly not restricted in the text to persons lawfully resident in the country concerned. It is important to avoid such a narrow construction of these rights if their universal nature is to be maintained.

It must be emphasized that Article 2(3) does not impose any *obligation* upon developing countries to circumscribe the economic rights of non-nationals. They are only given the discretion, as conveyed by the word 'may', to determine 'the extent' to which these rights might be guaranteed to aliens. This also means that the economic rights of non-citizens can only be limited and not taken away altogether.[113] In exercising their power under the provision, developing countries are to give 'due regard' to 'human rights', understood to encompass all those rights other than economic rights which are enumerated in international human rights instruments, and to the 'national economy', which means that this power may only be exercised if the condition of the national economy so warrants.[114]

Despite the criticism levelled at Article 2(3), in particular that it undermines

[105] E. V. O. Dankwa, 'Working Paper on Article 2(3) of the International Covenant on Economic, Social and Cultural Rights' (1987) 9 HRQ 230, 240.

[106] *Ibid.* 239–40. Art. 6 reads: 'The State Parties to the present Covenant recognize the right to work, which includes the right of *everyone* to the opportunity to gain his living by work which he freely chooses or accepts, and will take appropriate steps to safeguard this right' (emphasis added).

[107] Dankwa, n. 105 above, 240.

[108] Craven, n. 99 above, 215–16.

[109] See G. S. Goodwin-Gill, 'Immigration, Nationality and the Standards of International Law' in A. Dummett, (ed.), *Towards a Just Immigration Policy* (London: Cobden Trust, 1986) 3, 14; and G. S. Goodwin-Gill, R. K. Jenny, and R. Perruchoud, 'Basic Humanitarian Principles Applicable to Non-Nationals' (1985) 10 IMR 556, 558.

[110] Dankwa, n. 105 above, 236, 238.

[111] Cf. *International Provisions Protecting the Human Rights of Non-Citizens*, n. 10 above, 8, para. 51. In this regard, see the distinction made by the World Bank between low-income or middle-income economies and high-income economies, referred to in the introduction to this study.

[112] Dankwa, n. 105 above, 242.

[113] *Ibid.* 244–5.

[114] *Ibid.* 238, 242.

the concept of the universality of human rights, the provision arguably provides developing countries with no more than that which developed countries already enjoy. In practice, the latter have always been able to protect the economic rights of their nationals by imposing strict residence requirements upon non-citizens and, in general, by remaining in control of their economies.[115] Nonetheless, Article 2(3) also implies that developed countries cannot blatantly exclude non-nationals from economic protection.

Apart from Article 2(3) and the uncertainty surrounding the application of Article 2(2), there are no other specific limitations on the rights of aliens in the ICESCR. As discussed above, the rights to work and to the 'enjoyment of just and favourable conditions of work' are guaranteed to 'everyone'.[116] Another example is the right to education in Article 13 of the ICESCR, which is also directed to everyone. There are no qualifications preventing aliens from benefiting from this right.[117] The principle that a country's education should be available to all regardless of nationality is also clearly expressed in Article 3(1)(e) of the UNESCO Convention Against Discrimination in Education,[118] by which state parties undertake 'to give foreign nationals resident within their territory the same access to education as that given to their own nationals'. It would appear, however, that this right does not encompass equality of treatment between nationals and aliens in respect of educational scholarships and grants.[119] The ICESCR also guarantees to everyone in Article 8 the right to form and to join trade unions, and thus resembles Article 22 of the ICCPR.[120] Both provisions, however, are subject to similar restrictions.[121] The provisions concerned with granting rights to social security, health and culture, of critical importance to migrant workers while in the country of employment, make no distinctions between nationals and non-citizens.[122] Of particular interest is the right to adequate housing which is found in Article 11(1). States parties are obliged to 'recognize the right of

[115] *Ibid.* 247. [116] See also Goodwin-Gill (1986), n. 109 above, 14.

[117] Similarly, the freedom 'to establish direct educational institutions' is a right of everyone, including foreigners. See Art. 13(4) and M. Nowak, 'The Right to Education' in *Economic, Social and Cultural Rights: A Textbook*, n. 100 above, 189, 206–7.

[118] *UNESCO Convention Against Discrimination in Education*, 14 Dec. 1960; 429 UNTS 93; entry into force 22 May 1962; ratified by 85 states as at 1 Jan. 1996.

[119] Art. 3(1)(c) obliges states parties to undertake 'not to allow any differences of treatment by the public authorities *between nationals*, except on the basis of merit or need, in the matter of school fees and the grant of scholarship or other forms of assistance to pupils . . .' (emphasis added). Therefore, this non-discrimination clause seems to be confined to nationals only.

[120] Nowak, n. 65 above, 386, para. 3, identifies the right to form and to join trade unions mainly as an economic right, observing, however, that it was included in the ICCPR to emphasize that it is also a civil right.

[121] ICESCR, Art. 8(2) and ICCPR, Art. 22(2). However, the Committee on Economic, Social and Cultural Rights has expressed its 'concern' over restrictions placed upon the rights of aliens to participate in trade union activities. See Craven, n. 99 above, 265–6, 274, citing from the Committee's concluding observations on the report of Senegal, UN Doc. E/CN.12/1993/18, 2, para. 8.

[122] The relevant provisions read that 'States Parties . . . recognize the right of *everyone*': 'to social security, including social insurance' (Art. 9); 'to the enjoyment of the highest attainable standard of physical and mental health' (Art. 12(1)); and 'to take part in cultural life' (Art. 15(1)(a)).

everyone to an adequate standard of living for himself and his family, including adequate food, clothing and housing, and to the continuous improvement of living conditions'. Although the Committee on Economic, Social and Cultural Rights reiterated, during its Sixth session in 1991, that the right to adequate housing applies to 'everyone', adding that 'individuals, as well as families, are entitled to adequate housing regardless of age, economic status, group or other affiliation or status and other such factors', it did not specifically refer to 'nationality' as a prohibited ground of discrimination in this respect.[123]

Like the UDHR in Article 29(2), the ICESCR also contains a general limitation clause in Article 4:

> The States Parties to the present Covenant recognize that, in the enjoyment of those rights provided by the State in conformity with the present Covenant, the State may subject such rights only to such limitations as are determined by law only in so far as this may be compatible with the nature of these rights and solely for the purpose of promoting the general welfare in a democratic society.

The provision is clearly broader than its predecessor in the UDHR. Once again, therefore, the temptation exists for states to justify discrimination against non-nationals or migrant workers on the basis of this generally-worded clause.[124] However, Klerk rightly observes that 'the introduction or the continuation of discriminatory practices can never be "compatible with the nature of these rights"' and that 'the promotion of the general welfare can never be achieved at the expense of one section of society' even in 'a declining economy'.[125]

[123] General Comment No. 4 on the Right to Adequate Housing, UN Doc. E/1992/23, para. 6, reproduced in (1994) 1:1 IHRR 10–11. The Committee also stressed that 'States Parties must give due priority to those social groups living in unfavourable conditions by giving them particular consideration' and referred to its revised guidelines regarding the form and contents of state reports (UN Doc. E/C.12/1991/1) which emphasize the need to 'provide detailed information about those groups within . . . society that are vulnerable and disadvantaged with regard to housing'. The Committee made no specific reference to aliens in its list of such groups which includes 'homeless persons and families, those inadequately housed and without ready access to basic amenities, those living in "illegal" settlements, those subject to forced evictions and low-income groups': *ibid.* paras. 11 and 13. Without doubt, however, migrant workers and their families, and especially undocumented migrants, would clearly fall into one or more of the specified categories. However, the Committee also observed that the enjoyment of the right to adequate housing must not be subject to any form of discrimination '*in accordance with Article 2(2)*': *ibid.* para. 6 (emphasis added). Therefore, if it is accepted that the enumerated prohibited grounds of discrimination in this provision cannot be extended to include nationality, this would mean that states would find it easier to justify discrimination against non-nationals with regard to the housing guarantee.

[124] Tardou, n. 89 above, 374, contends that the effect of the non-discrimination provision, Art. 2(2), which is framed in restrictive terms, as combined with Art. 4, 'implicitly allows distinctions between nationals and foreigners'. Goodwin-Gill (1978), n. 29 above, 68, criticizes the ambiguity of Art. 4: 'Permissible grounds for derogation of this nature are so vague as to be nearly meaningless'.

[125] Klerk, n. 97 above, 263–4. The Limburg Principles, n. 92 above, paras. 46 and 47, limit the application of Art. 4 by stating that it was 'primarily intended to be protective of the rights of individuals rather than permissive of the imposition of limitations by the State' and that the provision was 'not meant to introduce limitations on rights affecting the subsistence or survival of the individual or integrity of the person'.

(d) International Convention on the Elimination of All Forms of Racial Discrimination (ICERD)[126]

In common with the other international human rights instruments discussed, the ICERD is universal in coverage, applying to both citizens and non-citizens. 'Racial discrimination' is defined in Article 1(1) of the ICERD as:

> any distinction, exclusion, restriction or preference based on race, colour, descent, or national or ethnic origin which has the purpose or effect of nullifying or impairing the recognition, enjoyment or exercise, on an equal footing, of human rights and fundamental freedoms in the political, economic, social, cultural or any other field of public life.[127]

However, the most pertinent provision in the ICERD relating to aliens, similar to Article 2(3) of the ICESCR, is a clause concerned with the restriction of rights. Article 1(2) of the ICERD declares: 'This Convention shall not apply to distinctions, exclusions, restrictions or preferences made by a State Party to this Convention between citizens and non-citizens'.

It must be emphasized that this prescription does not exclude aliens from the protection of the instrument altogether. Nor is it a new norm permitting general discrimination on the basis of alienage. The ICERD clearly operates to protect the rights of non-citizens. The body charged with the implementation of the ICERD, the Committee on the Elimination of Racial Discrimination, has stressed that Article 1(2) does not absolve states parties from any obligation to report on matters relating to legislation on foreigners and that it 'must not be interpreted to detract in any way from the rights and freedoms recognized in other instruments'. The Committee made particular reference in this regard to the UDHR, the ICESCR and the ICCPR.[128] Article 1(2) was introduced to encourage governments to accept the instrument, which they would otherwise have been reluctant to agree to if they had been unable to withhold certain entitlements from aliens, such as political rights and the right to work. It has been maintained,

[126] *International Convention on the Elimination of All Forms of Racial Discrimination*, 21 Dec. 1965; 660 UNTS 195; entry into force 4 Jan. 1969; ratified by 146 states as at 1 Jan. 1996.

[127] In para. 2 of its General Recommendation XIV (42) on Article 1, Paragraph 1 of the Convention, adopted at its 981st meeting on 17 March 1993, the Committee for the Elimination of Racial Discrimination observed that 'a differentiation of treatment will not constitute discrimination if the criteria for such differentiation, judged against the objectives and purposes of the Convention, are legitimate or fall within the scope of article 1, paragraph 4': UN, *Report of the Committee on the Elimination of Racial Discrimination*, 48 UN GAOR Supp. No. 18, UN Doc. A/48/18, 114. Article 1(4) permits special measures to secure 'adequate advancement of certain racial or ethnic groups or individuals' (affirmative action) and deems such measures not to constitute racial discrimination provided that they do not 'lead to the maintenance of separate rights for different racial groups and that they shall not be continued after the objectives for which they were taken have been achieved'.

[128] General Recommendation XI (42) on Non-Citizens, adopted at the Committee's 969th meeting on 9 March 1993, paras. 2 and 3. *Ibid.* 112–13. The current Chairman of the Committee writes that Art. 1(2) 'shuts out any consideration of whether or not a State's immigration laws are "racist", though it leaves open the possibility of considering whether such laws are implemented in a racially discriminatory manner'. See M. Banton, *International Action Against Racial Discrimination* (Oxford: Clarendon Press, 1996) 193. The German Government, however, insists that there is no obligation in the ICERD to report on legislation relating to foreigners and its implementation. *Ibid.* 193–4.

however, that the provision is drafted in an unfortunate manner. The *travaux préparatoires* reveal that the drafters intended that the ICERD, as one of its main objectives, protect both citizens and aliens from racial discrimination. Indeed, the practice of the Committee on the Elimination of Racial Discrimination and of states parties reporting under the ICERD indicates that distinctions between citizens and aliens are prohibited if there exists the slightest hint of racial discrimination.[129] For example, in the first individual communication considered by the Committee, *Yilmaz-Dogan* v. *the Netherlands*,[130] a Turkish woman was dismissed from her employment after a request from her employer to the local court to terminate her contract was accepted. She alleged that the employer's request contained racially discriminatory remarks. The Committee found that the Netherlands had failed to guarantee the applicant equality before the law in respect of the right to work and protection against unemployment, as required by Article 5(e)(i), because the court which had issued the final decision as regards the applicant's dismissal had not addressed all the circumstances of the case, including the allegation of racial discrimination.

According to McDougal, Lasswell, and Chen, Article 1(2) only reserves to states the competence to continue to make such historic differentiations between aliens and nationals as are reasonable under international customary law.[131] For example, Article 5(c) guarantees political rights to everyone without distinction as to 'race, colour or national or ethnic origin'. Traditionally, these rights have been withheld from non-nationals and Article 1(2) would justify a similar approach.[132] It would be more difficult, however, to defend, with reference to Article 1(2), differences in treatment between nationals and aliens in respect of, for example, the right to security of the person in Article 5(b) and the right to education and training in Article 5(e)(v). Moreover, by virtue of Article 6 of the ICERD, states parties are obliged to afford everyone within their jurisdiction effective legal protection against racial discrimination and access to adequate remedies. A situation whereby a state grants such protection and remedies to its citizens but fails to provide them to non-nationals, who are arguably more likely to be subject to racial discrimination, is surely an infringement of Article 6. Any

[129] D. Mahalic and J. G. Mahalic, 'The Limitation Provisions of the International Convention on the Elimination of All Forms of Racial Discrimination' (1987) 9 HRQ 74, 75–6. A study of Committee and State practice reveals that the protection of the cultural rights of migrant workers is clearly a concern of the ICERD. See R. Cholewinski, 'The Racial Discrimination Convention and the Protection of Cultural and Linguistic Ethnic Minorities' (1991) *Revue de Droit International* 157, 185–7.

[130] Communication 1/1984, *Yilmaz-Dogan* v. *The Netherlands* in UN, *Report of the Committee on the Elimination of Racial Discrimination*, 43 UN GAOR Supp. No. 18, UN Doc. A/43/18, Annex IV, 59–64.

[131] McDougal, Lasswell, and Chen, n. 2 above, 461.

[132] *Ibid.*; Goodwin-Gill (1978), n. 29 above, 67. See also *Diop* v. *France*, where the Committee on the Elimination of Racial Discrimination applied this provision in allowing the French authorities to refuse to admit the applicant, a Senegalese national, to the Lyon bar on the ground that he was not a French national. Communication 2/1989, *Demba Talike Diop* v. *France* in UN, *Report of the Committee on the Elimination of Racial Discrimination*, 46 UN GAOR Supp. No. 18, UN Doc. A/46/18, Annex VIII, 124–30.

other interpretation would be contrary to the spirit of the ICERD.[133] In a recent communication under the ICERD, the Committee on the Elimination of Racial Discrimination confirmed this approach when it found, *inter alia*, a violation of Article 6 by the Dutch authorities who had failed to exercise due diligence when conducting an investigation in respect of racial remarks and threats (constituting 'incitement to racial discrimination and to acts of violence against persons of another colour or ethnic origin' contrary to Article 4(a) of the ICERD) directed at a Moroccan citizen residing in the Netherlands.[134]

Another provision in the ICERD which refers specifically to nationality is Article 1(3):

> Nothing in this Convention may be interpreted as affecting in any way the legal provisions of States parties concerning nationality, citizenship or naturalization, provided that such provisions do not discriminate against any particular nationality.

The Committee on the Elimination of Racial Discrimination has pointed out that the aim of Article 1(3) is to qualify Article 1(2)[135] by declaring that, among non-citizens, States parties may not discriminate against any particular nationality.[136]

Regional instruments

(a) European Convention for the Protection of Human Rights and Fundamental Freedoms (ECHR)[137]

The ECHR was adopted in 1950 under the auspices of the Council of Europe. Because its application to alien migrant workers is examined in some depth in the European case study in Part Three, only a very brief overview of the relevant provisions is given here. Like the other instruments considered above, the ECHR is phrased in all-embracing language.[138] It also contains an open-ended non-discrimination clause and is therefore similar in this respect to the UDHR and the ICCPR.[139]

The provisions in the ECHR relating specifically to aliens concern procedural

[133] See also Goodwin-Gill, n. 29 above.

[134] Communication 4/1991, *L.K.* v. *The Netherlands* in *Report of the Committee on the Elimination of Racial Discrimination*, UN Doc. A/48/18, n. 127 above, Annex IV, 130–6. For a brief commentary on this case, see (1993) 11 NQHR 470–1.

[135] In the fields outlined.

[136] General Recommendation XI (42) on Non-Citizens, n. 128 above, para. 1. See also *International Provisions Protecting the Human Rights of Non-Citizens*, n. 10 above, 26, para. 182.

[137] European Convention for the Protection of Human Rights and Fundamental Freedoms, 4 Nov. 1950, Council of Europe ETS No. 5; entry into force 3 Sept. 1953; ratified by 33 states as at 1 July 1996.

[138] For example, Art. 1 proclaims: 'The High Contracting Parties shall secure to *everyone* within their jurisdiction the rights and freedoms defined in Section 1 of this Convention' (emphasis added).

[139] Art. 14 of the ECHR reads: 'The enjoyment of the rights and freedoms set forth in this Convention shall be secured without discrimination on any ground such as sex, race, colour, language,

safeguards against the arbitrary expulsion of lawfully resident aliens,[140] freedom of movement[141] and the arrest and detention of illegal immigrants.[142] However, the most significant provision relating to non-nationals is a limitation clause, Article 16, which declares: 'Nothing in Articles 10, 11 and 14 shall be regarded as preventing the High Contracting Parties from imposing restrictions on the political activity of aliens'. The provisions specified in this clause concern, respectively, the right to freedom of expression, 'the right to freedom of peaceful assembly and to association with others, including the right to form and to join trade unions' and non-discrimination. Although the instruments examined above, in particular the ICCPR, limit the enjoyment of political rights to citizens, the ambit of Article 16 is clearly broader. The corresponding provisions in the ICCPR, namely Article 19 (right to freedom of expression), Article 21 (right of peaceful assembly) and Article 22 (right to freedom of association) apply to nationals and aliens equally, although a number of significant European migrant-receiving countries have issued reservations in respect of these provisions permitting themselves to restrict the political activity of aliens in accordance with Article 16 of the ECHR.[143]

In addition to Article 16, many of the rights in the ECHR are also subject to limitations, such as the right to respect for family and private life (Article 8), the right to freedom of expression (Article 10) and the right to freedom of assembly and association (Article 11). These limitations are separately written into each provision.

(b) American Convention on Human Rights (ACHR)[144]

The Preamble to the ACHR contains a 'unique proclamation'[145] in the second paragraph:

> Recognizing that the essential rights of man are not derived from one's being a national of a certain State but are based upon attributes of the human personality, and that they therefore justify international protection in the form of a Convention reinforcing or complementing the protection provided by the domestic law of the American States.

religion, political or other opinion, national or social origin, association with a national minority, property, birth or other status'. This provision, however, is not a substantive equality clause in the same vein as Art. 26 of the ICCPR.

[140] Protocol No. 7 to the ECHR, Art. 1. Under Art. 4 of Protocol No. 4 to the ECHR, the collective expulsion of all aliens is strictly prohibited.

[141] Art. 2(1) of Protocol No. 4 to the ECHR, like Art. 12(1) of the ICCPR, also confines the right of freedom of movement within the territory of a state party to nationals and to aliens in a regular situation.

[142] Art. 5(1)(f) of the ECHR prescribes an exception to the right to liberty and security of person by permitting the arrest and detention of illegal immigrants with a view to expulsion.

[143] UN Doc. CCPR/C/2/Rev.3 (reservations of Austria, France and Germany), cited by Nowak, n. 65 above, 751, 755.

[144] American Convention on Human Rights, 22 Nov. 1969; OAS Treaty Series No. 36; entry into force 18 July 1978; ratified by 25 states as at 1 Jan. 1996.

[145] McDougal, Lasswell, and Chen, n. 2 above, 463.

This principle is also found in the second recital of the Preamble to the American Declaration of the Rights and Duties of Man,[146] the forerunner to the ACHR.

Despite these positive assertions, the grounds of prohibited discrimination in Article 1(1) of the ACHR appear to be exhaustive, thereby precluding the prescription of additional grounds based on nationality.[147] The very next clause, however, tempers this restrictive interpretation somewhat by returning to the universal spirit of the above-cited recital of the Preamble: 'For the purposes of this Convention, "person" means *every* human being'.[148] Another interesting provision is Article 22(8) which effectively recognizes the right of asylum by explicitly affording aliens protection against deportation or return to countries where their rights to life and personal liberty are in danger of violation because of 'race, nationality, religion, social status or political opinions'.[149]

Apart from these innovative provisions, the position of aliens under the ACHR is similar to that under other international human rights instruments: freedom of movement is restricted to those persons 'lawfully in the territory of a State party'; a legal alien may only be expelled 'pursuant to a decision reached in accordance with law'; and 'the collective expulsion of aliens is prohibited'.[150] Article 23(1) of the ACHR expressly reserves political rights for citizens with the addendum in Article 23(2) that these rights may be regulated by law exclusively on the basis of, *inter alia*, 'nationality'. Article XX of the American Declaration of the Rights and Duties of Man proclaims that 'every person having legal capacity is entitled to participate in the government of his country' and 'to take part in popular elections'. It is clear, however, that in this context 'person' means 'citizen' because the Declaration, in its second chapter concerning duties, proclaims in Article XXXVIII that: 'It is the duty of every person to refrain from taking part in political activities that, according to law, are reserved exclusively to the citizens of the State in which he is an alien'.

Special note should also be taken of Article 32 of the ACHR under the heading 'Chapter V—Personal Responsibilities'. Article 32(1) is similar to Article 29(1) of the UDHR in that it recognizes that 'every person has responsibilities to his family, his community and mankind'. Article 32(2) contains a general limitation clause, which is rather similar in ambiguity to Article 4 of the ICESCR: 'The rights of each person are limited by the rights of others, by the security of all, and by the just demands of the general welfare, in a democratic society'.

[146] American Declaration of the Rights and Duties of Man, OAS Res. XXX, adopted by the 9th International Conference of American States, Bogotá, 1948. The text of the Declaration is reproduced in I. Brownlie, (ed.), *Basic Documents on Human Rights*, 3rd edn. (Oxford: Clarendon Press, 1992) 488–94.

[147] Art. 1(1) reads: 'The States Parties to this Convention undertake to respect the rights and freedoms recognized therein and to ensure to all persons subject to their jurisdiction the free and full exercise of those rights and freedoms, without any discrimination for reasons of race, colour, sex, language, religion, political or other opinion, national or social origin, economic status, birth, or any other social condition'.

[148] Art. 1(2) (emphasis added).

[149] In this respect, see also Art. 14(1) of the UDHR: 'Everyone has the right to seek and to enjoy in other countries asylum from persecution'.

[150] Arts. 22(1), 22(6) and 22(9) respectively.

This provision repeats, almost word for word, Article XXVIII of the earlier American Declaration.

The ACHR is mainly concerned with civil and political rights in contrast with the American Declaration of the Rights and Duties of Man, which devotes considerable space to economic, social, and cultural rights.[151] The ACHR only contains a passing reference to economic, social, and cultural rights.[152] In November 1988, however, states parties to the ACHR adopted the Additional Protocol to the ACHR in the Area of Economic, Social and Cultural Rights, which has not yet come into force.[153] The Additional Protocol reiterates in the third recital of its Preamble the proclamation in the Preamble to the ACHR that essential human rights are not derived from citizenship ties to a particular state, 'but are based upon attributes of the human person'. Although Article 1 of the Additional Protocol asserts, like Article 2(1) of the ICESCR, that the economic, social, and cultural rights recognized therein are to be achieved progressively, these rights in the Protocol are assigned to 'everyone' without any exceptions based on nationality.[154] As with Article 32(2) of the ACHR, the Additional Protocol contains a general limitation clause in Article 4, which empowers states parties to restrict the rights enumerated in the Protocol 'by means of laws promulgated for the purpose of preserving the general welfare in a democratic society', but subject to the proviso that these laws 'are not incompatible with the purpose and reason underlying those rights'.

[151] For example, see Art. VII (right of women and children to special protection and care); Art. XI (right to preservation of health); Art. XII (right to education); Art. XIII (right to take part in the cultural life of the community); Art. XIV (right to work); Art. XV (right to leisure time); Art. XVI (right to social security).

[152] Chapter III of the ACHR, entitled Economic, Social and Cultural Rights, contains only one provision, Art. 26, which is labelled 'Progressive development': 'The States Parties undertake to adopt measures, both internally and through international co-operation, especially those of an economic and technical nature, with a view to achieving progressively by legislation or other appropriate means, the full realization of the rights implicit in the economic, social, educational, scientific and cultural standards set forth in the Charter of the Organisation of American States [OAS] as amended by the Protocol of Buenos Aires'. LeBlanc comments on this provision as follows: 'The content of this article reflects the lack of enthusiasm of the American States at the time the American Convention on Human Rights was adopted for taking a clear stand on economic, social and cultural rights. It fails to recognize that such rights are proclaimed in the American Declaration *as* human rights, and it recognizes the rights as being only *implicit* in the economic, social and cultural standards of the OAS Charter under the terms of the Protocol of Buenos Aires': L. LeBlanc, 'The Economic, Social and Cultural Rights Protocol to the American Convention and its Background' (1992) 10 NQHR 130, 137–8 (author's emphasis).

[153] Additional Protocol to the American Convention on Human Rights in the Area of Economic, Social and Cultural Rights, 17 Nov. 1988; OAS Treaty Series No. 69; not in force; ratified by 5 states (Ecuador, El Salvador, Panama, Peru, and Surinam) as at 1 Jan. 1996. The Protocol requires 11 ratifications in order to come into force (Art. 21(3)).

[154] The following economic, social, and cultural rights are protected in the Additional Protocol to the ACHR: right to work (Art. 6); right to just, equitable, and satisfactory conditions of work (Art. 7); trade union rights (Art. 8); right to social security (Art. 9); right to health (Art. 10); right to a healthy environment (Art. 11); right to food (Art. 12); right to education (Art. 13); right to benefits of culture (Art. 14). The Additional Protocol also guarantees: the right to formation and the protection of families (Art. 15); the rights of children (Art. 16); the protection of the elderly (Art. 17); and the protection of disabled persons (Art. 18).

(c) African Charter on Human and Peoples' Rights (ACHPR)[155]

The ACHPR is a unique document because it emphasizes the rights of peoples and individual duties in addition to the protection of individual rights. Nonetheless, the ACHPR's provisions relating to non-nationals are unexceptional and similar to many of the provisions already considered in other international human rights instruments: the prohibited grounds of discrimination in the general non-discrimination clause are clearly illustrative;[156] freedom of movement, however, is restricted more broadly to 'law-abiding' individuals; a legally admitted non-national may only be expelled from a state party's territory by virtue of a decision taken in accordance with the law; and the mass expulsion of aliens, defined as that aimed at 'national, racial, ethnic or religious groups', is prohibited.[157] Given, however, the many instances of mass expulsions of aliens (including migrant workers) in Africa's recent history,[158] the existence of the latter clause is of great importance in deterring future reoccurrences.

Individual duties are extensively outlined in Chapter II of the ACHPR (Articles 27 to 29) and include, *inter alia*, the duty of the individual 'not to compromise the security of the State whose national or resident he is' (Article 29(3)). This clause does not appear strong enough to sanction restrictions on aliens' political activities, unless a very broad interpretation of the term 'security' is adopted or the activities seriously threaten the stability of the state. Although there is no explicit general limitation clause, like in the ACHR, Article 27(2) asserts that individual rights and freedoms are to be exercised 'with due regard to the rights of others, collective security, morality and common interest'.

2.5 THE PROTECTION OF THE FAMILY

This work is concerned with the protection of the rights of migrant workers and *their families*. Widespread protection is given to families in universal and

[155] African Charter on Human and Peoples' Rights, 26 June 1981: OAU Doc. CAB/LEG/67/3/Rev. 5; entry into force 21 Oct. 1986; ratified by 50 states as at 1 Jan. 1996.

[156] Art. 2 of the ACHPR reads: 'Every individual shall be entitled to the enjoyment of the rights and freedoms recognized and guaranteed in the present Charter without distinction of any kind such as race, ethnic group, colour, sex, language, religion, political or other opinion, national and social origin, fortune, birth or other status'.

[157] Arts 12(1), (4) and (5) respectively.

[158] For an overview of the mass expulsions of migrant workers from Ghana in 1969, from Nigeria in 1983 and 1985, and other expulsions of migrant workers in Africa, see J.-M. Henckaerts, *Mass Expulsion in Modern International Law and Practice* (The Hague: Martinus Nijhoff, 1995) 63–72. On the first mass expulsion of an estimated 1.2 to 1.5 million irregular migrants from Nigeria in January 1983, see A. Adepoju, 'Illegals and Expulsion in Africa: The Nigerian Experience' (1984) 18 IMR 426. The threat of expulsion continues to hang over many foreigners and migrant workers in African countries. Most recently, in Oct. 1995, Libya threatened to expel over one million African foreign workers in addition to the thousands of Palestinians which it had already expelled from the country. See I. Black, 'Angry Gadafy threatens to deport 1m Workers' *Guardian*, 19 Oct. 1995, 16.

regional human rights instruments. Indeed, the family is considered to be sacrosanct. Article 16 of the UDHR declares: 'The family is the natural and fundamental group unit of society and is entitled to protection by society and the State'. This clause is repeated, word for word, in Article 23(1) of the ICCPR[159] and Article 17 of the ACHR. The wording in the ICESCR and the Additional Protocol to the ACHR is even more forceful. Article 10(1) of the ICESCR maintains that 'the *widest possible* protection and assistance should be accorded to the family, which is the natural and fundamental group unit of society, particularly for its establishment and while it is responsible for the care and education of dependent children'.[160] Article 15(1) of the Additional Protocol to the ACHR stipulates that 'the family is the natural and fundamental element of society and ought to be protected by the State, which should see to the improvement of its spiritual and material conditions'. The family also occupies a special place in African society and this is brought out in the first two paragraphs of Article 18 of the ACHPR:

(1) The family shall be the natural unit and basis of society. It shall be protected by the State which shall take care of its physical health and moral.
(2) The State shall have the duty to assist the family which is the custodian of morals and traditional values recognized by the community.

The protection of the family in European human rights instruments is more the object of the European Social Charter, which imposes positive obligations upon states parties towards families,[161] than of the ECHR. Article 8(1) of the ECHR, however, guarantees the right of everyone 'to respect for his private and family life, his home and correspondence'. These provisions are discussed in greater detail in the European case study.

The clauses protecting the family and family life must be borne in mind when considering the particular problems faced by the families of migrant workers. One problem, which merits particular attention, concerns family reunification. Given the extensive protection afforded families by the aforementioned provisions, measures to ensure or to facilitate the reunion of families with migrant workers

[159] Art. 23(1) is buttressed by Art. 17(1): 'No one shall be subjected to arbitrary or unlawful interference with his privacy, *family*, home or correspondence, nor to unlawful attacks on his honour and reputation' (emphasis added).

[160] Emphasis added. See also the fifth recital of the Preamble to the UN Convention on the Rights of the Child: '*Convinced* that the family, as the fundamental group of society and the natural environment for the growth and well-being of all its members and particularly children, should be afforded the necessary protection and assistance so that it can fully assume its responsibilities within the community . . .'. Convention on the Rights of the Child, 20 Nov. 1989; UN GA Res. 44/25; entry into force 2 Sept. 1990; ratified by 185 states as at 1 Jan. 1996.

[161] Art. 16 of the European Social Charter, entitled 'The right of the family to social, legal and economic protection', reads: 'With a view to ensuring the necessary conditions for the full development of the family, which is a fundamental unit of society, the Contracting Parties undertake to promote the economic, legal and social protection of family life by such means as social and family benefits, fiscal arrangements, provision of family housing, benefits for the newly married, and other appropriate means'.

would appear to be a logical attribute of such protection. However, this is one area where rights clash with state sovereign interests in the immigration field, with the result that these grand and noble phrases concerning the protection of families have effectively been little more than hortatory statements which seem to have had minimal practical effect.[162]

2.6 SUPERVISION AND ENFORCEMENT

All the universal and regional human rights instruments examined in this chapter, with the exception of the legally non-binding UDHR, provide for control machinery with the aim of supervising and enforcing the rights therein.

The ICCPR, the ICESCR and the ICERD oblige states parties to submit periodic reports to special bodies set up under each treaty on the measures which they have adopted to give effect to the provisions of the instrument in question.[163] In addition, both the ICCPR and the ICERD allow for the right of individual petition. A state party which has ratified the Optional Protocol to the ICCPR[164] or which has made a declaration under Article 14 of the ICERD[165] recognizes

[162] Art. 8(1) of the ECHR, discussed in Ch. 8, and the relevant provisions of the ICCPR constitute exceptions largely because of the extensive practice under these instruments. The Human Rights Committee asserted in its General Comment 19/39 of 24 June 1990 on Marriage and Family: 'The right to found a family implies, in principle, the possibility to procreate and live together . . . [T]he possibility to live together implies the adoption of appropriate measures, both at the internal level and as the case may be, in co-operation with other States, *to ensure the unity or reunification of families*, particularly when their members are separated for political, *economic* or similar reasons' (para. 5) (emphasis added): UN, *Report of the Human Rights Committee*, 41 UN GAOR Supp. No. 40, UN Doc. A/41/40, Annex VI, cited in (1994) 1:2 IHRR 24–6. In Case 35/1978, *Mauritian Women*, the Committee found an infringement of Art. 23(1) in respect of legislative measures that placed the foreign husbands of Mauritian women in a worse position than the foreign wives of Mauritian men: UN, *Report of the Human Rights Committee*, 36 UN GAOR Supp. No. 40, UN. Doc. A/36/40, paras. 9.2(b)2(i)3 and 9.2(b)2(ii)1–4, cited by Nowak, n. 65 above, 406, para. 9. It also found a violation of Art. 17(1) on the basis that the exclusion of persons from a country where close members of their family are living is an interference with their family life: *ibid.* para. 9.2(b)2(i)(2) cited by Nowak, n. 65 above, 300, para. 28. Moreover, this legislation infringed Arts 2(1), 3 (equality between men and women to the enjoyment of all civil and political rights set forth in the ICCPR), and 26 in conjunction with Art. 17(1). Nowak, n. 65 above, 293, para. 14.

[163] Art. 40 of the ICCPR (Human Rights Committee), Art. 16 of the ICESCR (Committee on Economic, Social and Cultural Rights) and Art. 9 of the ICERD (Committee on the Elimination of Racial Discrimination). Although Art. 16 of the ICESCR stipulates that reports are to be submitted to the UN Secretary-General for transmission to ECOSOC, there is now a Committee on Economic, Social and Cultural Rights which was set up by the Council to oversee the implementation of the ICESCR in the same way as the Human Rights Committee monitors the implementation of the ICCPR. The Committee on Economic, Social and Cultural Rights began its work in 1987. For an overview of the Committee's role in supervising the ICESCR, see Craven, n. 99 above, Ch. 2, and P. Alston, 'The Committee on Economic, Social and Cultural Rights' in P. Alston, (ed.), *The United Nations and Human Rights: A Critical Appraisal* (Oxford: Clarendon Press, 1992) 473.

[164] Optional Protocol to the International Covenant on Civil and Political Rights, 16 Dec. 1976; 999 UNTS 171; entry into force 23 March 1976; ratified by 87 states as at 1 Jan. 1996.

[165] Declaration regarding Art. 14 of the International Convention on the Elimination of All Forms of Racial Discrimination (competence of the Committee on the Elimination of Racial Discrimination

the competence of the Human Rights Committee and the Committee on the Elimination of Racial Discrimination 'to receive and consider communications from *individuals [individuals or groups of individuals] subject to [within] its jurisdiction*' who claim a violation by that state party of their rights.[166] Both citizens and aliens, therefore, may lodge a complaint against that state party provided that the relevant admissibility criteria are complied with, including, in particular, the exhaustion by the petitioner of all available domestic remedies.

Individual communications are also permitted by the ECHR, the ACHR, and the ACHPR. Under Article 25 of the ECHR, the European Commission of Human Rights may receive petitions 'from any person, non-governmental organization or group of individuals' claiming a violation of their rights by a state party. As with the right of individual complaint under the ICCPR and the ICERD, only complaints against states parties which have made declarations under Article 25 of the ECHR are valid.[167] Article 44 of the ACHR provides that petitions, containing denunciations or complaints of violation of the ACHR by a state party, may be lodged with the Inter-American Commission on Human Rights by 'any person or group of persons, or any non-governmental entity legally recognized in one or more member States of the Organization [of American States]'. This generous right of individual petition under the ACHR is automatic and does not depend on any separate state declarations.

The ACHPR makes provision under Article 55 for communications 'other than those of States parties to the present Charter' to be considered by the African Commission on Human and Peoples' Rights. This procedure, however, is more limited than those described above, since the Commission is only obliged to take the matter further by drawing the attention of the OAU Assembly of Heads of State and Government if one or more communications 'apparently relate to special cases which reveal the existence of a series of serious or massive violations of human and peoples' rights'.[168]

to receive communications from individuals); entry into force 3 Dec. 1982; 21 declarations as at 1 Jan. 1996. The Committee has only issued four opinions under the individual communications procedure: UN, *Report of the Committee on the Elimination of Racial Discrimination*, 49 UN GAOR Supp. No. 18, UN Doc. A/49/18, 88, para. 576. This situation essentially reflects the small number of states parties which have issued a declaration regarding Art. 14 of the ICERD in comparison with the substantially larger number which have ratified the Optional Protocol to the ICCPR.

[166] See Art. 1 of the Optional Protocol to the ICCPR and Art. 14 of the ICERD respectively (emphasis added). The wording in parentheses refers to the additional and slightly different terminology found in the latter provision.

[167] Declaration regarding Art. 25 of the European Convention on Human Rights (right of individual petition); entry into force 5 July 1955; 33 declarations as at 1 July 1996. All the states parties to the ECHR have therefore recognized the right of individual petition. The Commission and the Court of Human Rights will be merged into one single control mechanism once all the states parties to the ECHR have ratified the eleventh Protocol to the ECHR. For a brief overview of the proposed merger, see Ch. 5.

[168] Art. 58(1). In the event of such violations, the Commission is obliged to draw them to the attention of the Assembly of Heads of State and Government of the Organization of African Unity (OAU). The Assembly may then instruct the Commission to undertake an in-depth study of these cases and to prepare a factual report, accompanied by its finding and recommendations (Art. 58(2)).

2.7 THE UNITED NATIONS DECLARATION ON THE HUMAN RIGHTS OF INDIVIDUALS WHO ARE NOT NATIONALS OF THE COUNTRY IN WHICH THEY LIVE

Background: United Nations action[169]

Moves in the UN to establish distinct international principles for the protection of the human rights of aliens began earnestly in 1972 after the mass expulsion of Asians from Uganda.[170] Although it was acknowledged in discussions in the UN Commission on Human Rights that legal doctrine and judicial practice afforded states the right to expel aliens, it was also asserted that this right was not wholly discretionary and contained defined limits.[171]

In 1973, acting on a draft resolution of the UN Commission for Human Rights, ECOSOC requested the Commission and the Sub-Commission on Prevention of Discrimination and Protection of Minorities, *inter alia*, to consider, as a matter of priority, the application of international human rights provisions for the protection of non-citizens and to consider what human rights measures, including the possibility of a declaration, would be desirable.[172] One year later, the Sub-Commission appointed one of its members, Baroness Elles, as Special Rapporteur, to prepare a report to supplement the survey on the subject by the UN Secretary-General.[173] Baroness Elles submitted her full report in 1976 together with a draft declaration.[174] This report was considered the following year by the Sub-Commission at its 30th Session. The Sub-Commission requested the Secretary-General to submit the draft declaration to governments for their comments and invited the Special Rapporteur to take into account their replies so that she could present a new draft declaration to the Sub-Commission at its next session.[175] At its 31st Session in 1978, the Sub-Commission sent the Special Rapporteur's study and revised declaration to the Commission on Human Rights.[176] After consideration by the Commission, these documents, together with comments submitted by governments, were sent via ECOSOC to the General Assembly. At its 35th Session, the General Assembly set up an open working group entrusted with the elaboration of a final version of the draft declaration.[177] The Declaration on the Human Rights of Individuals who are not Nationals of the Country in which

[169] The summary below is largely taken from UN Centre for Human Rights, *United Nations Action in the Field of Human Rights* (New York and Geneva: UN, 1994) 239–40, paras. 1972–1981.

[170] Lillich, n. 2 above, 51. For a critical account of this expulsion and of the response of the international community, see Henckaerts, n. 158 above, 23–7.

[171] UN Centre for Human Rights, *United Nations Action in the Field of Human Rights* (New York: UN, 1988) 249.

[172] Res. 1790 (LIV) of 18 May 1973.

[173] See Res. 10 (XXVII) of 21 Aug. 1974 and UN Doc. E/CN.4/Sub.2/335 respectively.

[174] UN Doc. E/CN.4/Sub.2/392 and Annex I.

[175] Res. 4 (XXX) of 31 Aug. 1977.

[176] Res. 9 (XXXI) of 13 Sept. 1978.

[177] UN GA Res. 35/199 of 15 Dec. 1980. Similar working groups were established at the next four sessions of the General Assembly.

They Live was eventually adopted by the UN General Assembly by consensus in 1985.[178]

The contents of the Declaration

The UN Declaration on the Human Rights of Individuals who are not Nationals of the Country in which They Live commences by reiterating in the Preamble the non-discrimination provisions of the UN Charter, the UDHR, the ICCPR and the ICESCR, and by recognizing, in the seventh recital of the Preamble, that 'the protection of human rights and fundamental freedoms provided for in international instruments should also be ensured for individuals who are not nationals of the country in which they live'.

By and large, the Declaration applies to both legal and illegal aliens, which was not the original intention of the draft declaration submitted by Baroness Elles. Article 1 of the Declaration reads: 'For the purposes of this Declaration, the term "alien" shall apply, with due regard to qualifications made in subsequent articles, to any individual who is not a national of the State in which he or she is *present*'. In contrast, Article 1 of the draft Declaration stated: 'For the purposes of this Declaration, the term "non-citizen" shall apply to any individual who *lawfully* resides in a State of which he is not a national'.[179] Indeed, the application of the Declaration to undocumented aliens was only agreed upon after a number of years of divisive debate.[180] Extensive qualifications upon its application to illegal immigrants, however, were placed in the text. Article 2(1) emphasizes that the Declaration does not condone illegal immigration nor that it operates to restrict the right of states to regulate the entry and stay of aliens unless these laws are contrary to their international legal obligations. Moreover, although many essential civil and political rights[181] are guaranteed, by virtue of Article 5(1) of the Declaration, to *all* aliens, the enjoyment of economic and social rights is restricted to aliens '*lawfully residing* in the territory of a State',[182] a position which clearly detracts from the recognized universality of these rights.

In many respects, the Declaration's provisions are similar in content to those in other international human rights instruments. For example, Article 5(3) grants lawfully resident aliens 'the right to liberty of movement and freedom to choose

[178] UN GA Res. 40/144 on 13 Dec. 1985.

[179] Emphasis added. For the text of the draft Declaration, see *International Provisions Protecting the Human Rights of Non-Citizens*, n. 10 above, 53.

[180] See L. S. Bosniak, 'Human Rights, State Sovereignty and the Protection of Undocumented Migrants under the International Migrant Workers Convention' (1991) 25 IMR 737, and G. S. Goodwin-Gill, 'International Law and Human Rights: Trends Concerning International Migrants and Refugees' (1989) 23 IMR 536, 539. For example, Mexico supported the 'simple presence' of aliens as a sufficient criterion for the application of the Declaration, whereas Canada, Germany and the USA wanted to retain the lawful residence requirement: Goodwin-Gill, *ibid.* 540, citing from *Report of the Open-ended Working Group* (Dec. 1985), UN Doc. A/C.3/40/12, paras. 61–88.

[181] There is no mention in the Declaration of 'political rights' in the strict sense, namely the right to participate in public affairs, including the right to vote, and the right to employment in the public service.

[182] Art. 8(1) (emphasis added).

their residence within the borders of the State', and Article 7 affords them procedural safeguards against expulsion. The individual or collective expulsion of lawfully resident aliens on grounds of 'race, colour, religion, culture, descent or national or ethnic origin' is also prohibited by the same provision. The prohibition on collective expulsion is narrower than all other international provisions on this subject which apply regardless of an alien's legal status in the country of employment or residence.

With regard to the protection of economic and social rights, Article 8(1)(a) guarantees lawfully resident aliens just and favourable conditions of work, but *not* the right to work.[183] Under Article 8(1)(b), aliens in a regular situation are also entitled to join trade unions and other organizations and associations and to participate in their activities,[184] but there is no right to form trade unions. Nor may such a right be inferred from any other provision in the Declaration. There is no clause explicitly guaranteeing a general right to freedom of association, but only the right of peaceful assembly in Article 5(2)(c). In contrast, Article 22 of the ICCPR treats non-nationals and nationals equally in this respect. Finally, under Article 8(1)(c), lawfully resident aliens are granted the right to health protection, medical care, social security, social services, education, and rest and leisure. In order to benefit from this right, however, they must 'fulfil the requirements under the relevant regulations for participation'. Consequently, any state may limit the enjoyment of these rights by setting stringent qualifying conditions. In the case of social security, for example, many countries require a certain duration of residence and participation in public funds before non-nationals may enjoy social security benefits. Alien migrant workers often find it hard to meet these conditions and are therefore disadvantaged as compared with national workers.[185] A further restriction on the right in Article 8(1)(c) is that 'undue strain is not placed on the resources of the State'. A state may, therefore, plead poverty in order to avoid its obligations towards aliens under the provision. Although this qualification rings similar to Article 2(3) of the ICESCR, its scope is potentially broader, because it covers not only economic rights, but also certain social entitlements. Furthermore, it is applicable to all states and not just to developing countries.

With regard to cultural rights, Article 5(1)(f) confers upon all aliens the right

[183] See also Lillich, n. 2 above, 53, referring to a similar provision in the Elles draft declaration, and Eide, n. 100 above, 34.

[184] This right, however, is subject tc legal limitations necessary in a democratic society 'in the interests of national security or public order or for the protection of the rights and freedoms of others'.

[185] *Exploitation of Labour Through Illicit And Clandestine Trafficking* (1975) (Study prepared by Ms. H. E. Warzazi, Special Rapporteur) 25, para. 80, citing from the *Report of the ILO Symposium on Equality of Opportunity and Treatment in Employment in the European Region*, Geneva, 21–29 April 1975, ILO Doc. CECTE 1975/R, para. 32. It is arguable that qualifying conditions based on participation, if too stringent, risk infringing the norm of non-discrimination with regard to aliens. In contrast, the provision concerned with social security in the ICESCR (Art. 9) reads forcefully: 'The States Parties to the present Covenant recognize the right of *everyone* to social security, including social insurance' (emphasis added).

'to retain their own language, culture and tradition'. One commentator has suggested that this clause may grant aliens 'the legal right to resist integration into the life of the host country'.[186] A more positive justification for this provision, however, is that the right of aliens to retain their own language, culture, and tradition is an essential element of integration itself. Forced assimilation, incompatible with genuine integration, is an affront to human dignity and a negation of cultural diversity.[187]

The right to family reunification is recognized in Article 5(4) of the Declaration, which imposes the duty upon the state to admit the spouse and minor or dependent children in order to accompany, join, and stay with the alien residing lawfully in its territory. State authorities, however, appear to retain considerable discretion, if not complete discretion, as to whom to admit and under what conditions, because the obligation is subject to 'national legislation and due authorization'.[188]

The Declaration is not a legally binding document in contrast with the universal and regional human rights treaties and arguably the UDHR, which, though a declaration itself, is widely considered to be part of international customary law. Although it contains a number of novel provisions,[189] there is nothing to suggest that the Declaration will revolutionize the treatment of aliens in many parts of the world. On the contrary, as inferred above, it constitutes a step backwards in respect of the protection of a number of rights accorded to *all* persons by previous human rights instruments, particularly economic and social rights.

2.8 CONCLUSION

Migrant workers and their families as aliens might be considered to be in a rather vulnerable position as far as the international protection of their economic,

[186] Lillich, n. 2 above, 55. Lillich, *ibid.*, observes, however, that the Declaration, in Art. 4, also imposes the duty upon aliens to 'respect the customs and traditions' of the people of the state in which they reside.

[187] The participants of the 1975 UN Seminar on the Human Rights of Migrant Workers stressed that the fundamental aims of policy in the area of cultural rights should be 'to preserve at all costs the migrant worker's own cultural identity' and that 'assimilation should never be attempted': *Report of the Seminar on the Human Rights of Migrant Workers* (1976), 16, para. 58.

[188] The need to defer to state sovereignty was underlined during the drafting of the Declaration by the US representative, who noted that the references in the text to domestic law did not necessarily impose an obligation to legislate and although the right of family reunion existed, it was subject to the right of sovereign states to enact laws on entry and immigration. See Goodwin-Gill (1989), n. 180 above, 541, citing from UN Doc. A/C.3/39/9, para. 41.

[189] Two novel provisions include the right of *any* alien to communicate with the consulate or diplomatic mission of his or her home state (Art. 10) and a clause particularly applicable to migrant workers, namely Art. 5(1)(g), which accords to all aliens 'the right to transfer abroad earnings, savings or other personal monetary assets, subject to domestic currency regulations'. The final phrase of this latter provision, maintains Lillich, n. 2 above, 54, commenting on similar wording in the draft Declaration, 'has a ring of tautology about it . . . [and] is tantamount to saying that States must allow the repatriation of earnings provided that their laws allow it'.

social, cultural, political, and residence rights is concerned. Universal and regional human rights instruments are full of promise in terms of the protection of these rights, but on closer examination, deliver substantially less.

Although international human rights norms possess an 'all-embracing' approach with the objective of protecting *all* human beings, expectations that they would greatly raise the protection of aliens above that afforded by the vague and rudimentary minimum standard of traditional international law have not been fulfilled. Nowhere is 'nationality' an expressly prohibited ground of discrimination, although many of the human rights instruments examined contain open-ended non-discrimination clauses. Considerable discretion is provided to states to impose restrictions on the economic and social rights of non-citizens. Their rights to freedom of assembly and association, including the right to form and join trade unions, may also be limited on a number of grounds, especially in the European context if these activities are perceived as 'political' by host countries. Aliens are denied political rights regardless of their length of residence in a country. Finally, safeguards against their expulsion are procedural only and may be overridden, even if they are lawfully present in a country. For undocumented migrants, there is minimal protection against expulsion.

Although the UN Declaration on the Human Rights of Individuals who are not Nationals of the Country in which They Live introduces new concepts with respect to the protection of the human rights of aliens, it is a legally non-binding document and hardly comprehensive in its coverage. Indeed, it even retrogresses from some of the human rights protections in the universal and regional instruments. The examination of these instruments has revealed that new conventions tailored to the needs of aliens and migrant workers were clearly required. Such specific conventions have been adopted under the auspices of the ILO, the UN and the Council of Europe, and are examined in the remaining chapters of this study. Nonetheless, the universal and regional international human rights instruments, despite their shortcomings, remain a valuable tool for the protection of the rights of aliens and especially migrant workers, largely because of the familiarity that they exude and their wide ratification by states from all regions of the globe.

PART II

Universal Standards Specifically Relating to the Protection of Migrant Workers and their Families

3

The Protection of the Rights of Migrant Workers and their Families by the ILO With Particular Reference to the Migrant Workers Instruments of 1949 and 1975

3.1 INTRODUCTION

This chapter examines the International Labour Organization's contribution to the protection of the economic, social, cultural, political, and residence rights of migrant workers and their families, the first of a series of chapters dealing with international approaches to this question. It is fitting to begin with the International Labour Organization (ILO), which has a long-standing tradition of the protection of people in their working environment. Moreover, ILO Conventions relating to the protection of migrant workers and their families are the only universal set of standards concerned with this group currently *in force* at the international level.[1] Before undertaking an examination of these standards, it is proposed to set the discussion within the framework of ILO standard-setting activities in the field of human rights and the unique ILO supervisory procedures and mechanisms concerned with their protection and promotion.

3.2 THE ILO AND HUMAN RIGHTS

Origins and the Constitution

The ILO was founded in 1919 by the Peace Treaty of Versailles to regulate international labour concerns. International regulation was seen as essential to respond to demands for better working conditions prevalent in many countries since the end of the nineteenth century, and to offset any economic and competitive disadvantages which might accrue to those states that sought to combat these problems alone.[2] The ILO was the only significant intergovernmental organization

[1] The UN International Convention on the Protection of the Rights of All Migrant Workers and Members of Their Families is not yet in force. See Ch. 4.

[2] V. A. Leary, *International Labour Conventions and National Law: The Effectiveness of the Automatic Incorporation of Treaties in National Legal Systems* (The Hague: Martinus Nijhoff, 1982) 6; L. Betten, 'At its 75th Anniversary, the International Labour Organization Prepares itself for an Active Future' (1994) 12 NQHR 425, 429.

to survive the demise of the League of Nations and continued to exist after the Second World War as a specialized agency of the UN.[3]

Human rights have been described as being at the very heart of the ILO's mission.[4] The constitutional documents of the ILO reveal a clear commitment to the protection and promotion of human rights. The fundamental principles and objectives of the Organization are located in Part XIII of the Treaty of Versailles (Articles 387–427), which incorporates the original ILO Constitution of 1919 (Articles 1–49), and in the Declaration of Philadelphia concerning the Aims and Purposes of the ILO adopted by the International Labour Conference (the ILO's 'legislative assembly') in 1944 and incorporated as an annex into the revised Constitution of 1946.[5] Section II(a) of the Declaration contains the following principle:

[*A*]*ll* human beings, irrespective of race, creed or sex, have the *right* to pursue both their material well-being and their spiritual development in conditions of freedom and dignity, of economic security and equal opportunity.[6]

From a human rights perspective, this particular phrase is valued very highly:

In brevity and scope, this sentence ranks as one of the finest succinct statements of the rights of the individual. It avoids problems of distinctions and priorities among different types of rights, and gives equal value to material well-being, economic security, freedom, and non-discrimination. The ILO approach to human rights has been to place them within the broader concept of social justice.[7]

Although all human rights constitute an integral aspect of the ILO programme, the protection and advancement of economic and social rights, by virtue of the

[3] V. A. Leary, 'Lessons from the Experience of the International Labour Organisation' in P. Alston, (ed.), *The United Nations and Human Rights: A Critical Appraisal* (Oxford: Clarendon Press, 1992) 580, 582.

[4] F. Wolf, 'Human Rights and the International Labour Organisation' in T. Meron, (ed.), *Human Rights in International Law: Legal and Policy Issues* (Clarendon Press: Oxford, 1984) 273. However, the ILO's commitment to human rights work was not clearly articulated in human rights language until after the Second World War: Leary, n. 3 above, 583; Betten, n. 2 above, 425.

[5] See also N. Valticos, 'The International Labour Organisation' in K. Vasak, (ed.), *The International Dimensions of Human Rights*, vol. 1, revised and edited for the English edition by P. Alston (Westport, Connecticut: Greenwood Press, 1982) 363–4. The amended ILO Constitution and the Declaration of Philadelphia are reproduced in *International Organization and Integration: Annotated Basic Documents and Descriptive Directory of International Organizations and Arrangements*, Vol. I.B, 2nd rev. edn. (The Hague: Martinus Nijhoff, 1982) I.B.1.2.a and I.B.1.2.a.i.

[6] The non-discrimination element in this principle should be underlined. Jenks observes astutely that the principle that human rights transcend differences of race, creed, and sex, which has now become the keynote of the UDHR and the two UN human rights covenants, was first formulated in the Declaration of Philadelphia: C. W. Jenks, 'Human Rights, Social Justice and Peace—The Broader Significance of the ILO Experience' in A. Eide and A. Schou, (eds.), *International Protection of Human Rights*, Proceedings of the 7th Nobel Symposium, Oslo, 25–27 Sept. 1967 (Stockholm: Almquist and Wiksell, 1968) 227, 244.

[7] Leary (1992), n. 3 above, 591. In this context, Leary, *ibid.* 590, observes that the ILO has adopted an integrated or 'holistic' approach to human rights and has not discriminated between civil and political rights and economic and social rights, as has occurred within the UN and as is reflected in the adoption of two separate Covenants on these sets of rights.

ILO's primary concern with labour, constitute its thrust: 'Economic and social rights, which are usually stated in general terms, have been given a more precise and concrete definition by the ILO'.[8] Indeed, the ILO's emphasis on general areas of economic and social policy has become more prominent with time.[9]

Human Rights Standards

The ILO's principal means of promoting and protecting human rights is through standard-setting.[10] Arguably, *all* ILO standards deal with the protection and promotion of human rights in a broad sense. Even the most technical ILO instruments can be contemplated as measures for the implementation of the right to 'just and favourable conditions of work' proclaimed by Article 23(1) of the UDHR and recognized by Article 7 of the ICESCR.[11] Some ILO standards, however, are more specifically human-rights oriented; for example, those concerned with fundamental freedoms and rights, such as freedom of association, freedom from forced labour, and the right to equal opportunity and treatment in employment,[12] and those which direct their attention to the protection of social groups, such as women, children, and certain categories of workers, including foreign and migrant workers.[13]

Although ILO instruments have in-built flexibility, permitting states to accede to them in accordance with their level of economic and social development,[14] the standards themselves are strictly of universal application. A former Assistant Director-General of the ILO has stressed the importance of universality in this regard:

> One of the main effects of the standards adopted by the ILO has been to underline the universal validity of human rights. There has sometimes been a tendency to voice doubts as to the possibility of having universal standards in view of the diversity which exists between countries in the economic, social and political fields. Nothing could be more dangerous for the protection of human rights than this sceptical relativism.[15]

[8] Leary, n. 3 above, 587. See also K. Kaplansky, 'The International Labour Organization' in R. Matthews and C. Pratt, (eds.), *Human Rights in Canadian Foreign Policy* (McGill-Queen's University Press: Kingston and Montreal, 1988) 115 and Jenks, n. 6 above, 228–9.

[9] Leary (1982), n. 2 above, 7.

[10] Leary (1992), n. 3 above, 583. Other means include technical cooperation, research, and diplomatic contacts. *Ibid.* Indeed, these 'other means' are also used to help states maintain labour standards: 'The ILO provides technical assistance to member States to assist them in drafting legislation which will ensure conformity with conventions they have ratified, maintains a system of regional advisers on labour standards, organizes regional seminars on standards, and, through direct contacts, assists States in overcoming difficulties in implementing conventions': *ibid.* 589. For an elaboration of direct contacts, see below.

[11] Jenks, n. 6 above, 235–6. See also Wolf, n. 4 above, 274 and Valticos (1982), n. 5 above, 365.

[12] Jenks, n. 6 above, 236; Wolf. n. 4 above.

[13] Cf. Valticos (1982), n. 5 above, 365.

[14] Leary (1982), n. 2 above, 23.

[15] N. Valticos, 'The Role of the ILO: Present Action and Future Perspectives' in B. G. Ramcharan, (ed.), *Human Rights: Thirty Years after the Universal Declaration*, Commemorative Volume on the Occasion of the Thirtieth Anniversary of the Universal Declaration of Human Rights (The Hague: Martinus Nijhoff, 1979) 211, 213. Indeed, the universality of international labour standards has been

However, there is a significant functional distinction regarding ILO standards in that some are binding while others are merely promotional or explanatory. The international labour code consists of conventions or recommendations.[16] The former are formal legally binding standards that, once ratified, impose obligations upon states in international law. The latter are informal, non-binding principles, which deal with questions that do not lend themselves easily to precise obligations, often because diverse national conditions prevent the establishment of universal rules, but where it is nonetheless helpful to have a set of guidelines.[17] Recommendations frequently accompany conventions. In such cases, they either provide further detailed definition of the standards in the corresponding Convention or set higher or more advanced standards.[18] The significance of the distinction between these two kinds of ILO instrument becomes more apparent on consideration of the standards relating to the protection of migrant workers.

ILO standards have unquestionably influenced, directly or indirectly, provisions in other international human rights instruments. For example, the European Social Charter was drawn up on the basis of ILO standards and with the participation of the ILO.[19] Moreover, the ILO also contributed to the drafting, implementation, and revision of a number of EC regulations governing the social security of migrant workers.[20]

National laws, regulations and practice, however, are the primary target of ILO standard-setting efforts. International labour standards lose significance and vitality if they are not effectively implemented and incorporated into law at the domestic level.[21] Conventions impose binding obligations upon ratifying states, but unratified conventions and recommendations, as shown above, may also substantially influence state legislation and practice. The latter legally non-binding standards 'spell out the targets to which countries should aspire in law

stressed by the ILO Committee of Experts on the Application of Conventions and Recommendations and by the International Labour Conference Committee, which have stated that their function is to determine whether standards are being met regardless of the economic and social situation in a given country. Cf. Valticos (1979:1), *ibid.* 226; Wolf, n. 4 above, 283. See below for a description of the functions of these two ILO bodies.

[16] The texts of all the ILO conventions and recommendations, up to and including all those adopted by the International Labour Conference in 1991, are reproduced in ILO, *International Labour Conventions and Recommendations 1919–1991*, Vols I and II (Geneva: International Labour Office, 1992).

[17] Wolf, n. 4 above, 273–4.

[18] Wolf, *ibid.* 274; Leary (1982), n. 2 above, 12; Valticos (1982), n. 5 above, 364; H. Kellerson, 'International Labour Conventions and Recommendations on Migrant Workers' in A. Dummett, (ed.), *Towards a Just Immigration Policy* (London: Cobden Trust, 1986) 33, 34.

[19] Valticos (1982), n. 5 above, 377; Jenks, n. 6 above, 254; International Labour Conference, 52nd Session, 1968, Report of the Director General (Part I), *The ILO and Human Rights* (Geneva: International Labour Office, 1968) Ch. IV, 'Equality' 51, 55.

[20] UN Commission for Social Development, 24th Session, 6–24 Jan. 1975, Note by the Secretary-General, *ILO Action on Behalf of Foreign and Migrant Workers and their Families*, UN Doc. E/CN.5/523 (hereinafter *ILO Action on Behalf of Migrants*) 2–3, para. 7. This is an ILO report to the UN. The ILO also played a role in the preparation of the European Convention on Social Security 1972. *Ibid.* 2, para. 7 and 16, para. 47.

[21] Wolf, n. 4 above, 294; Leary (1982), n. 2 above, 1.

and practice';[22] the mere existence of these principles may establish in time 'a kind of common law'.[23] ILO supervisory procedures are an important catalyst in this regard. By virtue of Articles 19(5)(b) and 19(6)(b) of the ILO Constitution, member states are under an obligation to bring any Convention or Recommendation adopted by the International Labour Conference within one year of adoption (and no later than 18 months) before the competent authority (usually the national parliament) for enactment of legislation or other action. Any measures taken by member states to bring conventions or recommendations before the competent authorities are to be communicated to the Director-General of the International Labour Office (the ILO 'secretariat').[24] Articles 19(5)(e) and 19(6)(d) require member states to report to the Director-General on the position of their national law and practice with respect to unratified conventions and recommendations and the effect which has been given or is proposed to be given to them. Every year the Governing Body (the executive organ of the ILO) chooses the instruments for which such reports are to be requested. Instruments with a particular human rights content are often the subject of scrutiny. The receipt of the reports allows the Committee of Experts on the Application of Conventions and Recommendations (an independent body involved in the first tier of the ILO's regular system of supervision, and discussed below) to make a general survey of the situation in a particular field.[25] The effect of these general surveys is difficult to measure, but they have undoubtedly provided an opportunity for reporting a great deal of positive action in the field covered by the instruments under examination, which in the absence of such a stimulus might not have taken place.[26] In 1980, the four ILO instruments relating to the protection of migrant workers were the subject of such a survey, which was a source of valuable information on the measures being taken in member states to protect the rights of migrant workers and their families.[27]

Supervisory procedures and mechanisms

ILO procedures and bodies established for the purpose of ensuring the protection of human rights set forth in the Constitution and in conventions and

[22] W. R. Böhning, *Studies in International Labour Migration* (1984) Ch. 10, 'International Contract Migration in the Light of ILO Instruments' 233, 235.

[23] Wolf, n. 4 above, 294, citing from ILO Governing Body, 194th Session, Nov. 1974, *In-Depth Review of International Labour Standards*, ILO Doc. GB.194/PFA/12/5, 41.

[24] Arts 19(5)(c) and 19(6)(c). See also Wolf, n. 4 above, 246. The purpose of these provisions is to stimulate ratification and the adoption of legislation applying ILO Conventions: Leary (1982), n. 2 above, 12.

[25] Wolf, n. 4 above, 278–9. The object of such a survey is to describe the situation existing in various states with regard to the area covered by the instruments, to evaluate the difficulties which stand in the way of the application of the texts, and to suggest means of surmounting these difficulties. See Valticos (1982), n. 5 above, 370.

[26] Jenks, n. 6 above, 239.

[27] International Labour Conference, 66th Session, 1980, Report of the Committee of Experts on the Application of Conventions and Recommendations, *General Survey of the Reports relating to Conventions Nos. 97 and 143 and Recommendations Nos. 86 and 151 concerning Migrant Workers* (Geneva: International Labour Office, 1980) (hereinafter *General Survey*).

recommendations have a twofold objective: to ensure compliance with state obligations under ratified conventions and to promote the application of ILO standards irrespective of any formal obligation.[28] This second objective has already been illustrated in the discussion of the ILO mandate to monitor state action with respect to unratified conventions and recommendations.

This section provides a general description of the ILO supervisory system and highlights some of its essential and unique features pertinent to the protection and promotion of human rights.

(a) Tripartism

The ILO is unique among intergovernmental organizations concerned with human rights in that its policy-making organs are composed not only of government representatives, but also of workers' and employers' representatives who participate on an equal basis.

International labour standards are adopted as a result of discussions and negotiations at consecutive annual International Labour Conferences and in the Committee established by the Conference at the beginning of each Session. Both of these forums are composed on a tripartite basis, as is the ILO Governing Body, which meets regularly between the annual Conference sessions to set the agenda and to determine priorities in standard-setting. The Governing Body and the Conference Committee are also involved in the supervisory process and discuss the conclusions reached by the Committee of Experts.[29] According to the late C. Wilfred Jenks, a former Director-General of the ILO, the unique composition of the ILO Governing Body and the Conference Committee has:

> profoundly influenced their methods of work and approach to problems; it has dethroned the arrogance of sovereignty and made possible imaginative initiatives which could not have been taken in purely governmental bodies which take their tone from current official thought.[30]

[28] Valticos (1982), n. 5 above, 367–8 and 391.

[29] Kaplansky, n. 8 above, 115; Valticos (1982), n. 5 above, 392; Leary (1982), n. 2 above, 6; Leary (1992), n. 3 above, 587 (and n. 7); Kellerson, n. 18 above, 34; *ILO Action on Behalf of Migrants*, n. 20 above, 4, para. 11. An ILO Convention is adopted after two readings. On the first reading the instrument is usually adopted by a voice vote. On the second reading the Convention requires a two-thirds majority of the *whole* International Labour Conference in order to gain adoption. In practice, this means a three-quarters majority, since those who abstain or are not present at the vote count against adoption. By way of contrast, simple majorities suffice in the UN system. I am indebted to Kalmen Kaplansky, former Canadian Labour Congress delegate to the ILO, for bringing this distinction to my attention. Despite the equal division of the Conference into employers', workers', and government representatives, the latter have 50% of the vote in the plenary session because only 2 out of 4 votes are allocated to the employer and worker members of each national delegation. This is a considerable advantage to governments given that much important work, such as the adoption of conventions, recommendations, and the reports of the Conference Committee, comes to fruition in the plenary. Cf. Leary (1992), n. 3 above, 601.

[30] Jenks, n. 6 above, 231. The 'arrogance of sovereignty' remains intact, however, when employers' and workers' representatives are *not* truly independent. Leary (1992), n. 3 above, 585.

As a result, groups with a genuine interest in the subject-matter covered by the ILO may participate effectively in, and contribute substantially to, the formulation of international labour standards and the mechanisms established for their protection and implementation.[31]

(b) Reporting

Under Article 22 of the ILO Constitution, states which have ratified ILO Conventions are required to submit annual reports. However, revisions to this rule have been necessary in order to protect the reporting system from saturation in terms of the volume of work expected from the supervisory organs and the national administrations responsible for preparing the reports. The most recent revision was adopted by the Governing Body in November 1993 and took effect as at the beginning of 1995. The general rule is that two detailed reports are now required from states in the years following their ratification of a Convention. Thereafter, simplified reports will be requested every 5 years. So-called 'priority' Conventions, such as those concerned with freedom of association, forced labour, and equal treatment (but not those relating to migrant workers) will continue to demand biennial detailed reporting. However, detailed reports may still be requested at any time if problems arise.[32] Workers' and employers' organizations have rights to comment on the report during its preparation and, by virtue of Article 23(2) of the Constitution, to receive a copy of the final version.[33]

The reports are subject to a two-tier examination which is known as the 'regular system of supervision'. They are examined by the Committee of Experts on the Application of Conventions and Recommendations and also at the annual International Labour Conference by a tripartite Committee on the Application of the Conventions and Recommendations of the Conference (otherwise known as the Conference Committee on Standards).[34] As discussed earlier, reports on selected unratified Conventions and Recommendations may also be requested by the Governing Body. These reports constitute the data for general surveys carried out by the Committee of Experts on the instruments in question.

[31] Cf. Jenks, n. 6 above, 251. Despite the successful formal involvement of employers' and workers' groups in the work of the ILO, non-occupational groups, such as those non-governmental organizations (NGOs) concerned with human rights, are unable to participate in the same (informal) way as they can in the work of the UN. The failure of the ILO to integrate other NGOs into its human rights work has meant that it has missed an opportunity to gain additional support and much-needed publicity from this source: Leary (1992), n. 3 above, 585–6. The Committee of Experts, however, has recently taken note of emerging cooperation between employers' and workers' organizations and NGOs regarding the exchange of information. International Labour Conference, 81st Session, 1994, Report III (4A), *Report of the Committee of Experts on the Application of Conventions and Recommendations* (Geneva: International Labour Office, 1994) 19, para. 51.

[32] *Report of the Committee of Experts*, (n. 31 above), 15, para. 38 and 36–7, para. 115, citing from ILO, Governing Body, 258th Session, Nov. 1993, *Report of the Committee on Legal Issues*, ILO Doc. GB.258/6/19.

[33] *Report of the Committee of Expects*, 18, paras. 46–7.

[34] *Ibid.* 12, para. 25. See also Leary (1992), n. 3 above, 595–6.

(c) The Committee of Experts on the Application of Conventions and Recommendations

The Committee of Experts on the Application of Conventions and Recommendations is composed of twenty experts (prominent judges, professors, and labour law experts from selected geographic regions), appointed in their personal capacities for a renewable period of 3 years by the ILO Governing Body (on the proposal of the Director-General), who examine reports submitted by states on their application of ratified Conventions. The Committee may comment on these reports in two ways depending on the degree of the discrepancy between the Convention requirements and state law and practice. For serious discrepancies, 'observations' are published in an annual report, submitted each year to the International Labour Conference. For minor discrepancies, the Committee issues unpublished 'direct requests' to governments, a list of which, however, is included in the published report.[35] An example of the former type of comment is the recent observation directed to the United Kingdom Government in reply to a communication from the Trades Union Congress opposing, *inter alia*, the proposal of the government to denounce Convention No. 97 on Migration for Employment (Revised), 1949 (discussed below): '[The Committee] *hopes* that the Government will be in a position to ask the [International Labour] Office for technical advice before taking a final decision concerning the denunciation of that Convention'.[36] In addition, as described earlier, the Committee also undertakes general surveys, based on state reports, on unratified Conventions and Recommendations.

Generally-speaking, the Committee of Experts is the ILO's equivalent to the various independent supervisory bodies established under international and regional human rights instruments, although it arguably has a greater degree of independence.[37]

[35] Wolf, n. 4 above, 281–3; Valticos (1982), n. 5 above, 369–70; Leary (1982), n. 2 above, 19; Leary (1992), n. 3 above, 596–8.

[36] International Labour Conference, 79th Session, 1992, Report III (4A), *Report of the Committee of Experts on the Application of Conventions and Recommendations* (Geneva: International Labour Office, 1992) 264 (emphasis added). In its next report, the Committee noted with interest that 'following constructive contacts with the Office, the United Kingdom [would continue] to be bound by Convention [No. 97]': International Labour Conference, 80th Session, 1993, Report III (4A), *Report of the Committee of Experts on the Application of Conventions and Recommendations* (Geneva: International Labour Office, 1993) 251. The use of the word 'hopes' in the former comment is an example of the respectful nature of 'observations' and 'direct requests', which is a special feature of the Committee's supervisory work: 'The Committee of Experts does not "condemn" States for "violations" of human rights. Rather, it directs questions or comments to a government in the most polite terms when it finds that a convention is not being fully implemented': Leary (1992), n. 3 above, 598. This does not mean, however, that the Committee does not take its work seriously. It is capable of undertaking persistent communications with a government if it is dissatisfied with that government's response in respect of a particular discrepancy. See Leary, *ibid.*

[37] Leary (1992), n. 3 above, 596, observes that the ILO selection process of members for the Committee of Experts is less prone to government interference than, for example, the selection of individuals to work in UN human rights treaty bodies. This is because the former are chosen by the tripartite Governing Body on the nomination of the ILO Director General, whereas the latter are appointed by states which have ratified the conventions concerned. Consequently, writes Leary,

(d) Sanctions

The ILO reporting system contains only two forms of 'sanctions' to which states might be subjected. The first has already been referred to and involves the publication in the Committee of Experts' annual report of 'observations' concerning significant irregularities between state obligations under ratified conventions and national law and practice. The second 'sanction' is imposed by the tripartite Conference Committee on Standards on consideration of the Committee of Experts' report. The Conference Committee selects approximately one quarter of the latter Committee's more serious observations for public discussion. Representatives of censured governments have the opportunity to respond during these discussions.[38] The Conference Committee then submits a report to the Conference Plenary which includes 'special paragraphs' referring to states that have continually failed to fully implement conventions. This 'mobilization of shame' sanction has been described as being 'to date . . . the most substantial international sanction for human rights violations'.[39]

(e) Contentious procedures

In addition to reporting requirements, the ILO has distinct contentious procedures in place allowing representations or complaints to be made alleging that a state has not fulfilled its obligations under a Convention or Conventions that it has ratified.

(i) Representations

Representations may be made by employers' or workers' organizations to the International Labour Office, alleging that a member state has failed to implement Convention obligations. The representation is then communicated to the government in question for reply and to a tripartite committee within the Governing Body. If no reply is received within a reasonable time or the response is unsatisfactory, the Governing Body may decide to publish the representation and the government statement (in the case of an unsatisfactory response).[40]

ibid., 'the ILO method of appointment ensures the protection of the process from government pressures to a greater degree than the UN election method'.

[38] Valticos (1982), n. 5 above, 371; Leary (1982), n. 2 above, 19–20; Leary (1992), n. 3 above, 598–9. The nature and composition of the Conference Committee provide it with a more political and less technical tone than the Committee of Experts. See Leary (1982), n. 2 above, 20; Leary (1992), n. 3 above, 599.

[39] Leary (1992), n. 3 above, 600. Indeed, Betten, n. 2 above, 428, observes that 'if the vehement protests of receiving States against such a decision [to be cited in a "special paragraph"] is to be taken seriously, inclusion in a special paragraph is considered to be quite humiliating'.

[40] ILO Constitution, Arts. 24 and 25. See also *Report of the Committee of Experts* (1994), n. 31 above, 13, para. 28 and Wolf, n. 4 above, 286. If an organization withdraws a representation, the Governing Body can continue with the procedure on the understanding that the representation may have been withdrawn as a result of fear or pressure and that the proceedings are recognized to be of public interest: Valticos (1982), n. 5 above, 381. For a long time, this procedure was used very sparingly and only 8 representations were made between 1924 and 1970, although recently the number of representations has increased. See Leary (1992), n. 3 above, 610.

(ii) Complaints

The complaint procedure is the most formal and far-reaching procedure in the ILO supervisory armoury.[41] A complaint may be lodged by a state against another state for breach of its obligations under a Convention which both have ratified, or the procedure may be initiated by the Governing Body on its own motion or on receipt of a complaint from a delegate to the International Labour Conference. In the latter case, therefore, the procedure may be set in motion by employers or workers who are represented at the Conference. The Governing Body may communicate the complaint to the state concerned and invite the government to make a statement. If the response received is insufficient or if the Governing Body considers that communication of the complaint is unnecessary, it may appoint a Commission of Inquiry, composed of three independent experts, to investigate the complaint. The inquiry is conducted in a quasi-judicial fashion and includes the assembly of relevant documents, the hearing of parties and witnesses, and on-the-spot visits. On completion of the inquiry, the Director-General communicates the Commission of Inquiry's report, together with its recommendations, to the Governing Body and to the governments concerned, and arranges for its publication.[42] In contrast with other ILO supervisory procedures and mechanisms, such as the regular system of supervision and the Committee on Freedom of Association (discussed below), which have a political dimension with the participation of government representatives, the Commissions of Inquiry, according to one commentator, are 'the best guarantee of impartiality and objectivity among the various ILO implementation procedures'.[43]

The representation and complaint procedures have been used sparingly, although the tendency in past years has been to resort to them more often, especially when the implementation of basic human rights is at issue.[44] Two complaints in the 1980s alleging violations of ILO labour standards and pertaining to migrant workers are worth noting as examples. The first was set in motion by another state and was eventually settled. The second was initiated by workers' delegates to the International Labour Conference and led to the appointment of a Commission of Inquiry.

In 1985, the Government of Tunisia brought a complaint before the ILO against the Libyan Government following the expulsion of tens of thousands of Tunisian migrant workers from Libya. The complaint alleged a number of violations of ILO Conventions which both states had ratified. Matters of concern included the non-payment of wages, the question of compensation as a result of the premature

[41] Valticos (1982), n. 5 above, 377; Wolf, n. 4 above, 288.

[42] ILO Constitution, Arts. 26–29(1). See also Wolf, n. 4 above, 288–9 and Leary (1992), n. 3 above, 609–10. If a state does not accept the recommendation in the Commission of Inquiry's report, it may refer the complaint to the International Court of Justice (Art. 29(2)). The decision of the Court is final (Art. 31).

[43] Leary (1992), n. 3 above, 610–11.

[44] Wolf, n. 4 above, 286, 289. With regard to the complaint procedure, Leary (1992), n. 3 above, 609–10, observes that states have seldom brought any actions, although a number of complaints have been filed by Conference delegates in recent years.

termination of employment, and reimbursement of social security contributions. Representatives of both governments agreed to meet under the auspices of the ILO to find a solution to the dispute in the light of ILO labour standards. The matter was settled when the Libyan Government transferred a large sum of money to the Tunisian Government.[45] Earlier, in 1981, during the 67th Session of the International Labour Conference, complaints concerning the mistreatment of Haitian migrant workers employed on sugar plantations in the Dominican Republic were filed against both Haiti and the Dominican Republic by the workers' delegates of Burkina Faso, the Central African Republic, Rwanda, and Surinam. The Commission of Inquiry, established to investigate the case, concluded that the Dominican Republic and Haiti were in violation of a number of ILO Conventions which they had both ratified and which were relevant to the protection of migrant workers.[46]

(f) The special supervisory procedure on freedom of association

The principle of freedom of association is referred to in the ILO Constitution of 1919 and reaffirmed in the Declaration of Philadelphia.[47] In 1950, the ILO set up a special procedure, following an agreement with ECOSOC, to supervise the implementation of this principle and to supplement the aforementioned procedures of general application. Matters concerning the right to freedom of association are now referred to a Committee on Freedom of Association (known as the 'FAS Committee'), a tripartite organ composed of nine members of the ILO Governing Body and appointed by that Body. Although specific ILO Conventions

[45] See W. R. Böhning, 'The Protection of Migrant Workers and International Labour Standards' (1988) IM 133, 142.

[46] International Labour Office, *Report of the Commission of Inquiry appointed under Article 26 of the Constitution of the International Labour Organization to Examine the Observance of certain International Labour Conventions by the Dominican Republic and Haiti with respect to the Employment of Haitian Workers on the Sugar Plantations of the Dominican Republic* (1983) 66 *Official Bulletin*, Series B. The ILO Conventions under consideration by the Commission of Inquiry were, in the case of both countries, Convention No. 29 of 1930 concerning Forced or Compulsory Labour, Convention No. 105 of 1957 concerning the Abolition of Forced Labour, Convention No. 87 of 1948 concerning Freedom of Association and Protection of the Right to Organize and Convention No. 98 of 1949 concerning the Application of the Principles of the Right to Organize and Collective Bargaining, and, in the case of the Dominican Republic, Convention No. 95 of 1949 concerning the Protection of Wages. The 1949 and 1975 Conventions specifically relating to migrant workers (considered below) were not at issue, since neither country has ratified these instruments. See also V. Leary, 'Migrant Workers and Human Rights' *Materials for the 18th Study Session of the International Institute of Human Rights*, Strasbourg, France, July 1987 (Strasbourg: International Institute of Human Rights, 1987) 12 and M. E. Gorden, 'Haitian Forced Labor in the Dominican Republic' (1994) 15 *Comp. Lab. L.J.* 206, 216–17 and 221. The latter article is a detailed account of the institution of Haitian forced labour in the Dominican Republic. Since the Commission of Inquiry report, the Government of the Dominican Republic has invited the ILO for a number of 'direct contacts' to assess the situation. It would appear that recent efforts undertaken by the Government to regularize the status of irregular Haitian migrants have resulted in an improvement of their situation. See ILO, *World Labour Report 1993* (Geneva: International Labour Office, 1993) 14.

[47] Preamble, second recital and Section I(b) respectively. See also Leary (1992), n. 3 above, 591.

deal with the right to freedom of association,[48] workers' and employers' organizations may also complain under this special procedure against those ILO member states which have not ratified these instruments, and without the consent of these states, on the basis that this principle is found in the ILO Constitution which applies to all member states. After examining the complaint, the FAS Committee submits recommendations to the Governing Body which may then transmit them to the government concerned.[49]

The FAS Committee considered an untypical complaint concerning 'foreign' workers in the early 1950s. The complaint related to restrictions on trade union rights in Morocco. At the time, Morocco was still a French protectorate and Moroccans were treated effectively as 'foreigners' in their own land. The Committee found that only European workers residing in Morocco were permitted to form their own trade unions, while Moroccan workers were unable to do so, and that only those employed in certain industries could join existing organizations. Legislation abolishing this discrimination was noted by the Committee in 1955.[50]

The pioneering and innovative role of the ILO with respect to the protection and promotion of human rights

As the oldest functioning organization with an interest in the protection and promotion of human rights, the ILO is widely acknowledged to have a pioneering role in this field. Leary has observed that 'international labour conventions were virtually the first multilateral treaties primarily intended to improve the lot of individuals within States'.[51] Moreover, ILO standards have inspired the formulation of economic and social rights in universal and regional human rights instruments,[52] and the ILO experience has also demonstrated that these rights

[48] The principal ILO conventions on freedom of association are: Convention No. 87 of 1948 concerning Freedom of Association and Protection of the Right to Organize, adopted 9 July 1948, entry into force 4 July 1950, ratified by 114 states as at 1 Jan. 1996; and Convention No. 98 of 1949 concerning the Application of the Principles of the Right to Organize and Bargain Collectively, adopted 1 July 1949, entry into force 18 July 1951, ratified by 125 states as at 1 Jan. 1996.

[49] Wolf, n. 4 above, 290; Valticos (1982), n. 5 above, 381–2, Kaplansky, n. 8 above, 118, Leary (1992), n. 3 above, 602–4. Initially, the FAS Committee was set up to filter complaints, which were then submitted to a Fact-Finding and Conciliation Commission on Freedom of Association, a body of independent experts set up by the Governing Body to operate in a similar way to a commission of inquiry under Arts. 26 and 29 of the Constitution. However, because the consent of governments was required before complaints could be submitted to the Commission and because this consent was rarely forthcoming, the FAS Committee took on the pivotal role in this special procedure. *Report of the Committee of Experts* (1994), n. 31 above, para. 33.

[50] J. Hodges-Aeberhard, 'The Right to Organise in Article 2 of Convention No. 87. What is meant by Workers "without distinction whatsoever"?' (1989) 128 ILR 177, 191, citing from ILO, *Eighth Report of the International Labour Organization to the United Nations*, Appendix II, 12th Report of the Committee on Freedom of Association (Geneva: ILO, 1954) Case No. 16, paras. 292–446.

[51] Leary (1982), n. 2 above, 6–7.

[52] Valticos (1982), n. 5 above, 363; cf. Jenks, n. 6 above, 229.

can be precisely defined and that their implementation can be successfully monitored.[53] ILO procedures have also been in the forefront of attempts to supervise the implementation of human rights. Although the ILO supervisory machinery cannot readily be transposed as a whole into other human rights protection systems, such as those of the UN, because of the distinct milieu in which it was created,[54] it retains a number of innovative features which remain of ongoing importance. The obligation of states under the ILO Constitution to submit adopted International Labour Conference instruments to the national competent authorities has already been noted. The unique tripartite structure of ILO policy-making organs illustrates the positive role that can be played by non-governmental representatives who are permitted to participate in human rights standard-setting and monitoring activities.[55] The supervisory machinery applies uniformly to all member states and, in general, to all ILO standards.[56] Moreover, no reservations may be made to Conventions.[57] The ILO has also developed useful informal methods which supplement formal mechanisms. For example, the system of 'direct contacts' is based on short visits by ILO representatives to a country and detailed discussions between them and the government concerned, initiated by the latter, with a view to obtaining technical assistance, undertaking fact-finding, or resolving disputes (for example, by overcoming difficulties in the application of ratified conventions or obstacles in the way of ratification) between the government and an ILO supervisory body.[58]

[53] Leary (1992), n. 3 above, 617. The Committee of Experts reported in 1994, n. 31 above, 9, para. 14, that in the previous 30 years the ILO supervisory bodies had recorded over 2,000 cases where national legislation and practice had been changed, following comments by the supervisory bodies, in order to conform with the requirements of a ratified Convention.

[54] Cf. Valticos (1982), n. 5 above, 394; Jenks, n. 6 above, 253. In writing about the lessons of the ILO experience and how they can be usefully applied to the human rights work of the UN, Leary (1992), n. 3 above, 617, concludes: 'The ILO and the UN differ in aims, structure, and historical development; practices and procedures cannot easily be transposed from one to another'. Nonetheless, the ILO system might still serve as a valuable model in the development of other systems of supervision. Valticos (1982), n. 5 above.

[55] Leary (1992), n. 3 above.

[56] Kaplansky, n. 8 above, 117. Furthermore, most ILO Conventions only require two ratifications before they come into force. A. Trebilcock, 'Migrant Workers: An Overview of International Labour Standards' in Max Planck Institute for Comparative Public Law and International Law, (ed.), *The Legal Position of Aliens in National and International Law* (Berlin: Springer-Verlag, 1987) 1827, 1828 (n. 4); Leary (1982), n. 2 above, 9.

[57] Leary (1982), n. 2 above, 6; Jenks, n. 6 above, 237. Jenks, *ibid.*, observes that most Conventions permit a considerable flexibility in their application, but the result of the prohibition on reservations means that the measure of this flexibility is determined by the terms of the instruments themselves and not by unilateral action by states parties. See also Trebilcock, n. 56 above.

[58] *Report of the Committee of Experts* (1994), n. 31 above, 14–15, para. 35. See also Wolf, n. 4 above, 285–6 and Leary (1992), n. 3 above, 611–12. Leary, *ibid.* 612, has described 'direct contacts' as proving 'to be a particularly efficacious means of reaching solutions or establishing the existence of contested facts. The success of such contacts is due to the speed with which they can be arranged and the low-key discreet manner in which they are carried out. They are primarily informal means of entering into negotiations with government representatives. They have been widely used in recent years and have become an important complement to the other more formal ILO procedures'.

The ILO's long-standing tradition regarding the protection and promotion of the dignity of human labour and its concern with the rights of the worker set an ideal context in which to consider the human rights of migrant workers and their families. The plight of this group has attracted the special attention of the ILO.

3.3 THE ILO, MIGRANT WORKERS, AND MIGRATION POLICY

Background

One of the ILO's predominant concerns since its inception has been with the protection of foreign migrant workers.[59] Indeed, it has traditionally been the international organization with the greatest concern for this particular group.[60]

ILO constitutional documents are more explicit about the protection of the rights of migrant workers than about human rights in general. The second recital of the Preamble to the revised ILO Constitution includes the following statement:

> Whereas conditions of labour exist involving such injustice, hardship and privation to large numbers of persons as to produce unrest so great that the peace and harmony of the world are imperilled; and an improvement in these conditions is urgently required; as for example . . . [*inter alia* the] *protection of the interests of workers when employed in countries other than their own*.[61]

The original ILO Constitution proclaims that 'the standard set by law in each country with respect to the conditions of labour should have due regard to the equitable economic treatment of *all* workers lawfully resident therein',[62] whereas the Declaration of Philadelphia reaffirms, as one of the fundamental principles on which the ILO is based, that 'labour is not a commodity' and that 'poverty anywhere constitutes a danger to prosperity everywhere'.[63]

Throughout its long history, the ILO has added substance to the above principles by adopting standards relating to a number of subjects that affect migrant

[59] *ILO Action on Behalf of Migrants*, n. 20 above, 1, para. 3; N. Valticos, *International Labour Law* (Deventer: Kluwer, 1979) Ch. XIV, 'Foreign and Migrant Workers', 207, para. 537; Kellerson, n. 18 above, 33.

[60] Leary (1987), n. 46 above, 11. See also R. Zegers de Beijl and R. Böhning, 'Combating Discrimination against Migrant Workers: International Labour Standards and Operational Activities' in Commission on Security and Cooperation in Europe, *CSCE Human Dimension Seminar on Migrant Workers: Report, Briefing and Documentation* (1994) 87, 88.

[61] Emphasis added. References to this provision also appear in the Preambles to both 1975 ILO instruments concerning migrant workers.

[62] Art. 41, point 8 (emphasis added). See also *General Survey*, n. 27 above, 1, para. 2, and M. Hasenau, 'ILO Standards on Migrant Workers: The Fundamentals of the UN Convention and Their Genesis' (1991) 25 IMR 687, 688.

[63] Section I(a) and (c). Also cited in the third recital of the Preamble to the 1975 Migrant Workers Convention, n. 75 below and accompanying text.

workers, for example: reciprocity of treatment,[64] unemployment,[65] discrimination in employment,[66] social security,[67] housing,[68] and termination of employment.[69]

The most important ILO standards concerning migrant workers, however, are contained in the comprehensive instruments dealing with their protection as a separate group. In June 1939, the International Labour Conference adopted Convention No. 66 concerning Migration for Employment and two accompanying Recommendations.[70] The 1939 Convention never came into force because it was not ratified by a single state.[71] These instruments were revised and finally came into being as Convention No. 97 of 1949 concerning Migration for Employment (Revised) (C97) and Recommendation No. 86 of 1949 concerning Migration for Employment (Revised) (R86).[72] The next comprehensive instrument approved

[64] Recommendation No. 2 of 1919 concerning Reciprocity of Treatment. This instrument was adopted by the International Labour Conference at its First Session and requested each member state 'on condition of reciprocity' to admit 'foreign workers (together with their families) employed within its territory to the benefit of its laws and regulations for the protection of its own workers, as well as to the right of lawful organization as enjoyed by its own workers'. See International Labour Conference, 59th Session, 1974, Report VII(1), *Migrant Workers* (Geneva, International Labour Office, 1973) (hereinafter *Migrant Workers VII(1)*) 17.

[65] See Convention No. 2 of 1919 concerning Unemployment and Recommendation No. 1 of 1919 concerning Unemployment. Para. 2 of the Recommendation specifies that the recruitment of migrant workers should be promoted only by mutual agreement between the countries concerned and after consultation with workers' and employers' organizations in these countries. See also *ILO Action on Behalf of Migrants*, n. 20 above, 3, para. 9.

[66] Convention No. 111 of 1958 concerning Discrimination in respect of Employment and Occupation: adopted 25 June 1958; entry into force 15 June 1960; ratified by 121 states as at 1 Jan. 1996. See also Recommendation No. 111 of 1958 concerning Discrimination in Respect of Employment and Occupation.

[67] Convention No. 19 of 1925 concerning Equality of Treatment for National and Foreign Workers as regards Workmen's Compensation for Accidents; Convention No. 48 of 1935 concerning the Establishment of an International System for the Maintenance of Rights under Invalidity, Old-Age and Widows' and Orphans' Insurance; Convention No. 102 of 1952 concerning Minimum Standards of Social Security; Convention No. 118 of 1962 concerning Equality of Treatment of Non-Nationals and Nationals in Social Security; Convention No. 157 of 1982 concerning the Establishment of an International System for the Maintenance of Rights in Social Security. See the section on social security rights below for an account of the latter three instruments.

[68] Recommendation No. 115 of 1961 concerning Workers' Housing.

[69] See Convention No. 158 of 1982 concerning Termination of Employment at the Initiative of the Employer and Recommendation No. 166 of 1982 concerning Termination of Employment at the Initiative of the Employer.

[70] Recommendation concerning the Recruitment, Placing and Conditions of Labour of Migrants for Employment and Recommendation concerning Cooperation between States Relating to the Recruitment, Placing and Conditions of Labour of Migrants for Employment.

[71] Hasenau, n. 62 above, 692–3. See also R. Plender, *International Migration Law*, rev. 2nd edn. (Dordrecht: Martinus Nijhoff, 1988) Ch. 9, 'Migration for Employment', 295, 297 and R. B. Lillich, *The Human Rights of Aliens in Contemporary International Law* (1984) 70.

[72] For the texts, see *International Labour Conventions and Recommendations, 1919–1991*, n. 16 above, 495 and 508 respectively. C97 was adopted on 1 July 1949 and came into force on 22 Jan. 1952. It has been ratified by 40 states as at 1 Jan. 1996: Algeria, Bahamas, Barbados, Belgium, Belize, Bosnia-Herzegovina, Brazil, Burkina Faso, Cameroon, Cuba, Cyprus, Dominica, Ecuador, France, Germany, Grenada, Guatemala, Guyana, Israel, Italy, Jamaica, Kenya, Malawi, Malaysia, Mauritius, Netherlands, New Zealand, Nigeria, Norway, Portugal, Saint Lucia, Slovenia, Spain, Tanzania, Trinidad and Tobago, United Kingdom, Uruguay, Venezuela, Yugoslavia, Zambia.

by the International Labour Conference regarding migrant workers was Recommendation No. 100 of 1955 concerning the Protection of Migrant Workers in Underdeveloped Countries and Territories (R100).[73]

In the early 1970s, when many industrialized nations were undergoing the effects of a recession and a subsequent deterioration in the labour market, the ILO turned once more towards the problem of migrant workers, which was growing in urgency as a result of the unfavourable economic climate. The International Labour Conference adopted three resolutions concerning migrant workers, which led to the question being placed again on the ILO agenda.[74] Eventually, in 1975, the 1949 instruments were supplemented by Convention No. 143 concerning Migrations in Abusive Conditions and the Promotion of Equality of Opportunity and Treatment of Migrant Workers (C143) and Recommendation No. 151 concerning Migrant Workers (R151). Unfortunately, as at 1 January 1996, C143 had only been ratified by 17 ILO member states and by even fewer major countries of employment.[75]

Migration policy

Before discussing the ILO standards specifically pertaining to the economic, social, cultural, political, and residence rights of migrant workers, it is helpful to consider these standards in the light of what may be termed as 'ILO migration policy'. Essentially, this policy has ebbed and flowed with global economic fluctuations and developments. Originally, the objective of the policy was to promote organized migration for employment from labour-surplus countries to countries with labour shortages. Gradually, however, with the economic downturn in the western industrialized world and a greater understanding of the negative consequences of migration, particularly on countries of origin, the policy shifted to the support of more restrictive and controlled migration with sensitivity to the problems faced by developing countries.

The primary focus of the 1949 migrant workers' instruments concerned the organization and regulation of the movements of migrant workers in demand in

[73] For the text, see *International Labour Conventions and Recommendations, 1919–1991*, n. 16 above, 598.

[74] Resolution concerning ILO Action for Promoting the Equality of Migrant Workers in All Social and Labour Matters, adopted 22 June 1971 at the 56th Session; Resolution concerning Conditions and Equality of Treatment of Migrant Workers, adopted 27 June 1972 at the 57th Session; and Resolution concerning Future ILO Action in the Field of Migrant Workers, adopted 24 June 1974 at the 59th Session. The texts of the first two resolutions are reproduced in *Migrant Workers VII(1)*, n. 64 above, 72–5 (Appendix I).

[75] For the texts, see *International Labour Conventions and Recommendations, 1919–1991*, n. 16 above, 1091 and 1098 respectively. C143 was adopted by the International Labour Conference on 23 June 1975 by 265 votes in favour and none against with 81 abstentions. Note 'The 60th Session of the International Labour Conference, June 1975' (1975) 112 ILR 231, 236. It came into force on 9 Dec. 1978 and has been ratified by 17 states as at 1 Jan. 1996: Benin, Bosnia-Herzegovina, Burkina Faso, Cameroon, Cyprus, Guinea, Italy, Kenya, Norway, Portugal, Slovenia, San Marino, Sweden, Togo, Uganda, Venezuela, Yugoslavia.

industrialized countries.[76] The original ILO policy on migration is clearly outlined in paragraph 4(1) of R86:

It should be the general policy of Members to develop and utilize all possibilities of employment and for this purpose to facilitate the international distribution of manpower and in particular the movement of manpower from countries which have a surplus of manpower to those countries that have a deficiency.[77]

According to Böhning, this policy was in line with the neo-liberal international economic order that existed at the time:

The *leitmotif* of the neo-liberal order . . . was that economic growth should not be held up in one country for lack of labour so long as there was suitable labour available elsewhere, irrespective of the skills involved and quite irrespective of the short-term or long-term interests of the emigration countries involved. The objectives and the instruments were clearly biased in favour of the immigration countries.[78]

A shift in ILO migration policy was detectable in 1955 in R100. Part III of R100 is concerned with measures to discourage migration of workers when considered undesirable in the interests of those workers and of the communities and countries of origin; the object being to improve the conditions of life and to raise living standards in countries of emigration.[79] The policy proposes, *inter alia*, the adoption in emigration areas of economic development and vocational training programmes in order to make fuller use of available manpower resources as well as the establishment of job-creation schemes.[80] The effect of this purported shift in ILO migration policy in R100, however, is questionable due to the relative weakness of an ILO Recommendation which 'stands alone' without the normative validity which an accompanying Convention provides.[81] The approach taken by the ILO to migration was essentially reiterated in Recommendation No. 122 of 1964 concerning Employment Policy, although, here too, there was a suggestion that employment migration is damaging to developing countries.[82]

Moves to develop and implement the changes hinted at in R100 were made during the drafting of the 1975 instruments on migrant workers. The ILO was urged to refer to the following matters: the need to create employment in countries from which migrants originate, particularly by international cooperation

[76] Kellerson, n. 18 above, 41.

[77] See also Böhning (1984), n. 22 above, Ch. 1, 'International Migration and the International Economic Order' 3, 7. Böhning, *ibid.*, refers to para. 14(1) of R86 and Art. 5(3) of the Model Agreement on Temporary and Permanent Migration for Employment annexed to R86, which advocate the speedy technical selection of qualified migrants.

[78] Böhning (1984), n. 22 above.

[79] Para. 16. See also Böhning (1984), *ibid.* 7 (n. 8); Plender, n. 71 above, 307–8; *Migrant Workers VII(1)*, n. 64 above, 11.

[80] Para. 17(a).

[81] Cf. Böhning (1984), n. 22 above, Ch. 1, 7.

[82] Para. 33 of the Recommendation reads: 'International migration of workers for employment which is *consistent with the economic needs of the countries of emigration* and immigration, including migration from developing countries to industrialized countries, should be facilitated . . .' (emphasis added).

and investment in industrialization in those countries;[83] the danger of giving priority to short-term economic requirements without examining the long-term consequences of migration;[84] and the need to undertake efforts to secure full employment in the host country before recruiting foreign labour.[85] A coherent international migration policy, taking into account all the elements referred to, was advocated by the ILO.[86] Eventually, a new policy approach on migration crystallized in paragraph 1 of R151:

> Members should apply the provision of this Recommendation within the framework of a coherent policy on international migration for employment. That policy should be based upon the economic and social needs of both countries of origin and countries of employment; it should take account not only of short-term manpower needs and resources but also of the long-term social and economic consequences of migration for migrants as well as for the communities concerned.

This provision should be read together with the fourth recital of the Preamble to C143:

> [I]n order to overcome underdevelopment and structural and chronic unemployment, the governments of many countries increasingly stress the desirability of encouraging the transfer of capital and technology rather than the transfer of workers in accordance with the needs and requests of these countries in the reciprocal interest of the countries of origin and the countries of employment . . .[87]

In addition to the desirability of economic investment in developing countries, another limb of the migration policy, in the preceding recital of the Preamble to C143, also stresses the 'need to avoid the excessive and uncontrolled or unassisted increase of migratory movements because of their negative social and human consequences'. Therefore, there is an implicit recognition of a clear link between the lack of economic opportunities in the country of origin and the migration of illegal labour.[88]

[83] International Labour Conference, 59th Session, 1974, Report VII(2), *Migrant Workers* (Geneva: International Labour Office, 1974) (hereinafter *Migrant Workers VII(2)*) 28 (opinion of Finland). Similar views were expressed during those proceedings of the 59th Session of the Conference that related to migrant workers. See International Labour Conference, 60th Session, 1975, Report V(1), *Migrant Workers* (Geneva: International Labour Office, 1974) (hereinafter *Migrant Workers V(1)*) 4 (general discussion in the Conference Committee), 40 (Mr. Vercellino, workers' advisor, Italy), and 42 (Mr. Haase, Government delegate from the Federal Republic of Germany).

[84] *Migrant Workers VII(2)*, n. 83 above, (opinions of France and Austria respectively).

[85] *Ibid.* (opinion of Finland).

[86] *Migrant Workers VII(1)*, n. 64 above, 58–9; *Migrant Workers VII(2)*, n. 83 above, 27.

[87] An approach advocating alternatives to labour emigration was also posited by the 1976 ILO World Employment Conference. See W. R. Böhning and M. Schloeter-Paredes, 'Introduction' in W. R. Böhning and M. Schloeter-Paredes, (eds.), *Aid in Place of Migration* (1994) 2, citing paras. 36–37 of the Declaration of Principles and Programme of Action adopted by the Tripartite World Conference on Employment, Income Distribution and Social Progress and the International Division of Labour, Geneva, 4–17 June 1976.

[88] In its General Survey on the four main ILO instruments relating to migrant workers, the Committee of Experts, n. 27 above, 145, para. 501, observed that the pressure to emigrate 'illegally' could only be relieved by long-term action, which calls for collaboration among the countries concerned.

It should be emphasized that this new policy approach on international migration germinated in a harsh economic climate. Whether the same concern for migrant-sending countries would have been shown if the demand for labour in industrialized nations was still substantial is a matter for debate. Nonetheless, the policy has continued to develop. Paragraph 39(a) of Recommendation No. 169 of 1984 concerning Employment Policy (Supplementary Provisions) emphasizes the creation of 'more employment opportunities and better conditions of work in countries of emigration so as to reduce the need to migrate to find employment'. The policy also encourages migrant-receiving countries to participate in the development of sending countries in order to establish an alternative to labour migration:

Members which habitually or repeatedly admit significant numbers of foreign workers with a view to employment should, when such workers come from developing countries, endeavour to cooperate more fully in the development of such countries, by appropriate intensified capital movements, the expansion of trade, the transfer of technical knowledge and assistance in the vocational training of local workers, in order to establish an effective alternative to migration for employment and to assist the countries in question in improving their economic and employment situation.[89]

Clearly, present ILO migration policy is consistent with international efforts to reduce the gap between rich and poor countries. Real progress in this regard, however, lies in fundamentally altering the present international economic order by a system of redistribution and compensation. In the field of migration, this would entail the deliberate and explicit channelling of the gains of migration in favour of the poorer emigration countries.[90] The ILO has yet to endorse expressly such an approach.[91]

Another principle of the present ILO migration policy asserts, in fairly brusque terms, that those who profit most from migration should pay for its social costs. Paragraph 11 of R151 supports this approach in relation to the obligation of host countries to formulate and apply a social policy on behalf of migrant workers and their families:

[89] Para. 40. See also Plender, n. 71 above, 308; Kellerson, n. 18 above, 41–2 and Böhning and Schloeter-Paredes, n. 87 above, 3.

[90] Böhning (1984), n. 22 above, Ch. 1, 10. Böhning, *ibid.*, argues that behind the concern with international equity lies the realization that national policy measures on the side of individual emigration countries are insufficient to tip the balance of gains significantly in their favour since the productive effects of international migration in the sending states cannot match those in the receiving states. See also W. R. Böhning, 'International Migration in Western Europe: Reflections on the Past Five Years' (1979) 118 ILR 401, 407–411, for an elaborated version of this view.

[91] According to Böhning (1979), n. 90 above, 410, the Programme of Action adopted by the World Employment Conference in 1976, n. 87 above, gives an element of recognition to the validity of the demand by poor countries for compensation with respect to the inequalities arising out of international migration. Para. 43(i) of the Programme of Action stipulates that multilateral and bilateral migration agreements should 'provide ways of limiting losses in countries of origin, particularly developing countries, which may result from the departure of skilled personnel whose education and training they have provided'.

The policy should take account of the need to spread the social cost of migration as widely and equitably as possible over the entire collectivity of the country of employment, and in particular over those who profit most from the work of migrants.

The drafting history of this provision indicates that its principal objective was to guarantee the funding of a social policy in respect of migrant workers. The ILO view was that the policy should as far as possible be financed by receiving countries and that the allocation of social costs should be determined according to national conditions.[92] In addition, the general perception was that some of these costs also ought to be borne by the employers of migrant workers.[93]

3.4 THE SCOPE OF ILO STANDARDS RELATING TO THE PROTECTION OF MIGRANT WORKERS AND THEIR FAMILIES

General standards

It is widely acknowledged that the majority of ILO labour standards, with few exceptions, apply to alien migrant workers and nationals equally.[94] In a number of more general ILO Conventions, the standards are specified to apply to 'all persons employed', to 'every person employed', or to workers 'without distinction as to nationality', or 'without distinction whatsoever'.[95] Notable exceptions to this principle are Convention No. 111 of 1958 concerning Discrimination in Respect of Employment and Occupation and the accompanying Recommendation No. 111. The non-discrimination provision in Article 1(1)(a) of Convention No. 111 does not include 'nationality' amongst the prohibited grounds of

[92] Claydon notes that the principle in this provision recognizes the benefits of migration to receiving countries: J. Claydon, 'International Protection of the Welfare of Migrant Workers' in R. S. J. Macdonald, D. M. Johnston, and G. L. Morris, (eds.), *The International Law and Policy of Human Welfare* (Alphen aan den Rijn, The Netherlands: Sijthoff & Noordhoff, 1978) 347, 357.

[93] *Migrant Workers VII(2)*, n. 83 above, 43–5. Not surprisingly, this provision was opposed by employers. See *Migrant Workers VI(1)*, n. 83 above, 28–9 and International Labour Conference, 60th Session, Geneva, 1975, *Record of Proceedings* (Geneva: International Labour Office, 1976) 650, para. 119.

[94] *General Survey*, n. 27 above, 3, para. 7; *ILO Action on Behalf of Migrants*, n. 20 above, 3, para. 8; Böhning (1984), n. 22 above, Ch. 10, 239; Lillich, n. 71 above, 70; Valticos (1979: 2), n. 59 above, 208, para. 537; G. S. Goodwin-Gill, 'Immigration, Nationality and the Standards of International Law' in *Towards a Just Immigration Policy*, (1986), n. 18 above, 3, 16; Trebilcock, n. 56 above, 1883. Trebilcock, *ibid.*, adds that this is notably the case for ILO instruments on general conditions of work, such as those concerning wages, hours of work, minimum age requirements, safety, and health.

[95] Valticos (1979: 2), n. 59 above, 210–11, para. 544. For example, see Art. 2 of Convention No. 87 of 1948 concerning Freedom of Association and Protection of the Right to Organize with respect to the latter term: 'Workers and employers, *without distinction whatsoever*, shall have the right to establish and, subject only to the rules of the organization concerned, to join organizations of their own choosing without previous authorization' (emphasis added). For an in-depth analysis of this provision, see Hodges-Aeberhard, n. 50 above, 39

discrimination, although Article 1(1)(b) stipulates that additional grounds may be added by ILO member states after tripartite consultation with workers' and employers' organizations and with other appropriate bodies.[96]

The Migrant Workers Instruments of 1949 and 1975

(a) Coverage and subject-matter

The most important instruments concerned with the protection and promotion of the rights of migrant workers and their families are those adopted by the International Labour Conference in 1949 and 1975. These instruments, however, cannot deal with all the rights' concerns of this group because of the limited competence of the ILO with respect to the protection of human rights generally. Strictly speaking, the ILO is primarily concerned with the economic and social rights of workers pertaining to questions of labour.[97] Questions concerned with immigration,[98] expulsion,[99] political rights,[100] and rights to education and culture[101] essentially do not fall within the ILO's jurisdiction. However, the interdependence of civil and political rights with economic and social rights makes it difficult to separate questions of labour from the broader economic, social, cultural, and political context in which migrant workers and their families find themselves. Indeed, to do so would be to treat migrants merely as objects of labour rather than as fully integrated social beings. Fortunately, as demonstrated below, the ILO interprets its protective function towards migrant workers very broadly. The measures in the migrant workers instruments cover a wide range of questions going beyond the employment situation to include general conditions of life.[102]

Although the standards laid down in the comprehensive instruments on migrant workers constitute the ILO's principal method of dealing with the protection

[96] See also H. K. Nielsen, 'The Concept of Discrimination in ILO Convention No. 111' (1994) 43 ICLQ 827, 840, 844; Goodwin-Gill (1986), n. 94 above, 16; *International Provisions Protecting the Human Rights of Non-Citizens* (1980) 23, paras. 158–9; M. Tardou, 'Migrant Workers' in *Encyclopaedia of Public International Law*, vol. 8 (1981) 374. Some of the ILO instruments, particularly those relating to the social security of migrant workers, operate on the basis of reciprocity. In other words, migrants may only benefit from the provisions in these instruments if their country of origin and the country in which they reside have both ratified the convention in question. More explicit references to these standards are made below in the section on the social security rights of migrant workers. Reciprocity is also a feature of most Council of Europe human rights instruments relevant to the protection of migrants, with the exception of the European Convention on Human Rights. See Ch. 5.

[97] Leary (1987), n. 46 above, 12.

[98] Kellerson, n. 18 above, 33.

[99] Claydon, n. 92 above, 363.

[100] *Migrant Workers V(1)*, n. 83 above, 12, para. 60 (discussions in the Committee on Migrant Workers during the 59th Session of the International Labour Conference in 1974); *General Survey*, n. 27 above, 88, para. 316.

[101] *General Survey*, *ibid.* 88, para. 315.

[102] *Ibid.* 141, para. 487. The provisions also go beyond the actual *period of employment* and cover the initial phases of recruitment, travel, and settlement in the receiving country as well as post-employment problems, such as return to the country of origin, arrangements for continued residence in host countries, and the regulation of rights arising out of employment and continuing after its termination. *Ibid.*

of this group, they are only part of a broader programme which has migrant workers' interests at heart and which includes: the collection and dissemination of information; studies and research; and the provision of technical assistance for developing countries.[103]

With regard to the subject-matter generally, the 1949 instruments are concerned with the organization of migration and equality of treatment between migrants and nationals under law and administrative practice. The 1975 instruments supplement the 1949 provisions, but are also concerned, in particular, with the suppression of clandestine migration and the illegal employment of migrants and with the promotion of equality of opportunity and treatment.[104]

(b) Form and structure

The form and structure of the migrant workers instruments, and the two Conventions in particular, are rather complicated. C97 consists of a general treaty of core provisions and three Annexes, some or all of which may be excluded by ratifying states.[105] Annexed to R86 is a Model Agreement on Temporary and Permanent Migration for Employment. The object of this Model Agreement was to serve as inspiration for bilateral agreements,[106] but, according to one commentator, it has had little impact on state treaty practice.[107] C143 is divided into two parts dealing with migrations in abusive conditions and with equality of opportunity and treatment. States parties are free to exclude either of these parts on ratification.[108] As a result, the structure of C143 is controversial, for it effectively enables ratifying states to avoid substantial obligations towards migrant workers. The drafting history of the document reveals the reasons for this approach and also provides a valuable insight into the position of ILO member states and employers' and workers' organizations with respect to the tenet of equality of opportunity and treatment underlying Part II of the instrument. Part by part ratification of C143 was introduced by the International Labour Conference Committee on Migrant Workers as 'a compromise solution'.[109] The aim of this

[103] *ILO Action on Behalf of Migrants*, n. 20 above, 20, para. 59. See also the ILO's Mahgreb Programme, discussed in Ch. 1.

[104] See also *General Survey*, n. 27 above, 3, para. 10.

[105] See also Plender, n. 71 above, 299 and Lillich, n. 71 above, 70. Annexes I and II deal with recruitment and conditions for migrants recruited by private groups and under government-sponsored arrangements respectively, whereas Annex III is concerned with the import of migrants' personal effects into countries of employment.

[106] Plender, n. 71 above, 301.

[107] Lillich, n. 71 above, 72.

[108] C143, Art. 16(1). However, by virtue of Art. 16(3), the exclusion of either part of C143 does not enable ratifying states, when reporting on C143, to avoid their reporting obligations in respect of the excluded part.

[109] *Record of Proceedings*, n. 93 above, 792 (Mr. Yllanes Ramos, Employers' delegate, Mexico, and Vice-Chairman of the Conference Committee on Migrant Workers). See also F. Russo, 'Migrant Workers: Existing and Proposed International Action on their Rights' (1975) *The Review of the International Commission of Jurists*, No. 15, 51. Russo, *ibid*. 56, observes that delegates were concerned that if states were otherwise forced to choose between ratifying all or none of the Convention's provisions, the more controversial elements of Part II would doom the whole Convention to a low number of ratifications. Even so, C143 has still only received 17 ratifications as at 1 Jan. 1996.

approach was to appease those (mainly states and employers) who wanted either to exclude the question of equality of opportunity and treatment altogether,[110] to impose conditions and restrictions upon it,[111] or to deal with the matter in a recommendation,[112] and also to accommodate those (mainly workers' representatives) who argued that Part II of the instrument was complementary to the first section dealing with the suppression of migrations in abusive conditions, if not essential to the success of Part I.[113]

Definition of 'Migrant Worker'

The definition of 'migrant worker' for the purposes of C97 and C143 is similar:

> a person who migrates from one country to another [or who has migrated from one country to another] with a view to being employed otherwise than on his own account and includes any person regularly admitted as a migrant for employment [migrant worker].[114]

This definition, therefore, excludes self-employed persons and illegal or irregular migrant workers. In C143, it pertains solely to Part II (provisions concerning equality of opportunity and treatment), which applies only to legal migrants.[115] The definition also goes on to explicitly exclude other categories of persons, namely: frontier workers; members of the liberal professions and artists entering a country on a short-term basis; seafarers; those who enter specifically for the purposes of education and training; and workers who are employed in the

[110] *Migrant Workers VII(2)*, n. 83 above, 19 (opinion of France).

[111] The kinds of conditions and restrictions proposed included: requirements of residence for a certain period of time before equality of opportunity and treatment could be enjoyed by migrant workers, *ibid.* 20 and 30 (opinion of Switzerland) and International Labour Conference, 60th Session, 1975, Report V(2), *Migrant Workers* (Geneva: International Labour Office, 1975) (hereinafter *Migrant Workers V(2)*) 16 (opinion of Denmark); and restrictions on their access to employment in the receiving country, for example, by according priority to nationals, *Record of Proceedings*, n. 93 above, 644, para. 54.

[112] *Migrant Workers V(2)*, n. 111 above, 4, 6 and 16 (opinions of Finland, the United Kingdom, and the Norwegian Employers' Confederation). See also 'The 60th Session of the International Labour Conference, June 1975', n. 75 above, 235.

[113] *Record of Proceedings*, n. 93 above, 639, para. 17. The latter point was made by Mr. Vercellino, the Workers' advisor from Italy, during the 59th Session of the International Labour Conference, who argued that illicit traffic in manpower and the guarantee of genuine equality of treatment and rights 'were, in fact, two inseparable and interrelated aspects of the same problem. Without eliminating limitations and discrimination (whether in law or in practice) it was impossible to take effective action against the black market in manpower which stemmed from this discrimination': *Migrant Workers V(1)*, n. 83 above, 40.

[114] Art. 11(1) in both C97 and C143. The wording in parentheses refers, respectively, to the additional and alternate wording used in Art. 11(1) of C143. Refugees and displaced persons who are also migrant workers are included within the ambit of the definition by para. 2 of R86. See also Plender, n. 71 above, 301.

[115] *General Survey*, n. 27 above, 10, para. 36. The equality provision in C97, Art. 6(1), is also restricted in its application to 'immigrants lawfully within its territory'. The drafting history of Art. 11 of C143 indicates that efforts were made to exclude illegal migrant workers *expressly* from the definition. *Migrant Workers V(2)*, n. 111 above, 19 (opinion of the Netherlands).

receiving country for a specific period of time to complete a particular job.[116] This last category does not exclude all workers admitted to a country to work for a specific length of time or who are recruited collectively to do so.[117] It is the nature of the employment which seems to determine this question. A distinction may be made between workers who enter a country to undertake employment not limited in time, but who hold a work permit of limited duration, and those who are admitted for the purpose of specific employment or a specific project that will be completed after a certain period.[118]

The migrant workers instruments apply by implication to 'seasonal workers' in spite of a number of attempts to exclude this group from the definition.[119] Seasonal workers, however, suffer from an inherent disadvantage regarding measures concerned with affording them equal opportunity and treatment with nationals because their stay in the receiving country is often short in duration.[120]

Finally, the definition of 'migrant worker' does not refer to the family of the migrant worker, although members of the worker's family are clearly at the core of many of the instruments' protective provisions. Measures concerned with equality of opportunity and treatment, family reunification and health are but a few significant examples,[121] and these are discussed in greater detail below.

3.5 THE RIGHTS OF MIGRANT WORKERS AND THEIR FAMILIES

This part of the chapter focuses on the protection of the economic, social, cultural, political and residence rights of migrant workers and their families by ILO

[116] C143, Art. 11(2)(a)–(e). The last two categories were added by C143. The exclusion of 'frontier workers' from the definition was opposed by some workers' and government delegates to the Conference during the drafting of C143. *Migrant Workers V(1)*, n. 83 above, 41 (Mr. Vercellino, Workers' advisor, Italy, during discussions at the 59th Session of the International Labour Conference); *Migrant Workers V(2)*, n. 111 above, 18–19 (opinions of Italy and Yugoslavia). However, an amendment to include frontier workers was also opposed by a number of state members and employers' representatives on the basis that many of the provisions in the proposed Convention could not be applied to frontier workers because of their special situation. Consequently, the amendment was rejected by the Conference. *Record of Proceedings*, n. 93 above, 645, para. 64. There is no definition at all of 'frontier workers' in the ILO instruments on migrant workers.

[117] *General Survey*, n. 27 above, 10, para. 35; Zegers de Beijl and Böhning, n. 60 above, 89.

[118] Böhning (1984), n. 22 above, Ch. 10, 238. Böhning labels the latter 'project-tied' migrants as opposed to 'individual contract' migrants. Although excluded from the protection of the migrant workers instruments, this group is nonetheless protected by most of the other ILO standards on the basis that these standards apply to all workers irrespective of their nationality. *Ibid.* 239.

[119] *Migrant Workers V(1)*, n. 83 above, 13 (opinion of Switzerland during discussions of the proposed C143 at the 59th Session of the International Labour Conference); *Migrant Workers V(2)*, n. 111 above, 18 (opinion of Denmark).

[120] *General Survey*, n. 27 above, 83, para. 290. See also *Migrant Workers V(2)*, n. 111 above, 19. Moreover, because the right of migrant workers to free choice of employment can be restricted for up to 2 years under Art. 14 of C143 (discussed in the section on employment rights below), the possibility of seasonal workers benefiting, for example, from vocational training is limited in practice. *General Survey*, n. 27 above.

[121] *General Survey*, n. 27 above, 10–11, para. 37.

instruments. A separate section is also devoted to a discussion of protection by the ILO of the rights of undocumented migrants. The standards reviewed are mainly those found in the four migrant workers instruments, with a particular emphasis on the 1975 Convention and Recommendation, although references are also made to other relevant standards. Many provisions of C97 and the accompanying R86 are concerned with the recruitment, introduction, and placing of migrant workers and Part I of C143 deals chiefly with the suppression of migrations in abusive conditions. In general, these matters are not the object of detailed discussion, with the exception of the application of Part I of C143 to the protection of illegal migrants.

Rights specifically covered by ILO Instruments

(a) Basic rights

Article 1 of C143 reads: 'Each Member for which this Convention is in force undertakes to respect the basic human rights of all migrant workers'. Article 1 was a late addition to C143 and was only introduced at the 60th Session of the International Labour Conference at which the 1975 instruments were adopted.[122] The provision lays down a general obligation to respect the basic rights of all migrant workers irrespective of their legal status in the country of employment.[123] It was stressed during the drafting discussions, however, that this obligation did not affect the state's right to control migratory movements.[124]

In spite of its promise as a broad state obligation for the protection of migrant workers' rights, Article 1 is fairly limited in scope. According to the Committee of Experts on the Application of Conventions and Recommendations, the obligation in Article 1 is restricted to 'basic' rights or only to those rights considered to be most 'fundamental'.[125] Moreover, the provision is located in Part I of C143 which deals with migrations in abusive conditions. It encompasses *all* migrant workers, including those in an irregular situation, but it does not extend to the rights found in Part II of C143, which apply solely to lawfully admitted migrants.[126]

[122] The provision was originally introduced as a result of an amendment submitted by the government members of Algeria and Mexico, which was later sub-amended by the workers' members. *Record of Proceedings*, n. 93 above, 641, para. 29.

[123] *General Survey*, n. 27 above, 69, para. 257. See also Trebilcock, n. 56 above, 1830 and Lillich, n. 71 above, 73.

[124] *Record of Proceedings*, n. 93 above, 641, para. 29 and 791 (Mr. Yllanes Ramos, Employers' delegate, Mexico, and Vice-Chairman of the Conference Committee on Migrant Workers).

[125] *General Survey*, n. 27 above, 69, para. 256. For example, these rights would include: the right to life; the right to protection against torture, cruel, inhuman, degrading treatment or punishment; the right to liberty and security of the person and protection against arbitrary arrest; and the right to a fair trial (Arts 6, 7, 9 and 14 of the ICCPR). *Ibid.* 69, para. 257.

[126] *Ibid.* 69, para. 258. The Committee of Experts, *ibid.*, also underlined that Art. 1 does *not* cover those rights in the ICCPR and the ICESCR whose exercise presupposes lawful residence as a member of a given society.

(b) Equality of opportunity and treatment

The principle of equality of opportunity and treatment is at the centre of the protection of the rights of migrant workers by the ILO;[127] the objective is to ensure that migrant workers and their families are afforded equal treatment with nationals not only in respect of those matters pertaining to their labour, but in respect of other conditions of life as well.

(i) Proscription of discrimination in law and administration
The principle of equality of treatment for *all* workers residing in a country is enshrined in the earliest ILO constitutional documents.[128] The ILO applied this principle to migrant workers in Article 6(1) of C97 in respect of, *inter alia*, the employment situation (including equality of remuneration), trade union rights, accommodation, and social security. The weakness of this provision, however, is that it only proscribes inequality of treatment in respect of the first three areas if these are 'regulated by law or regulations, or are subject to the control of administrative authorities' (Article 6(1)(a)). Moreover, there is no obligation upon states to promote equality and eliminate discrimination in practice.[129]

(ii) Promotion of equality and elimination of discrimination in practice
Standards to promote equality of opportunity and treatment are to be found in Convention No. 111 of 1958 concerning Discrimination in respect of Employment and Occupation and in Recommendation No. 111,[130] but discrimination based on nationality is not enumerated.[131] Indeed, the Preamble to C143, in the

[127] In recent Memorandums submitted to the UN Sub-Commission on Prevention of Discrimination and Protection of Minorities, the International Labour Office observed that 'the key concern of [ILO standards concerning migrant workers] is non-discrimination and equality of opportunity and treatment': UN Doc. E/CN.4/Sub.2/1993/3 (30 July 1993) 8, para. 26; UN Doc. E/CN.4/Sub.2/1994/5 (17 June 1994) 10, para. 27.

[128] Art. 41 of the original ILO Constitution, point 8; Section II(a) of the Declaration of Philadelphia. See also n. 62 above, and accompanying text.

[129] See also *Migrant Workers VII(1)*, n. 64 above, 17–18 and *General Survey*, n. 27 above, 81, para. 281. Art. 17 of the Model Agreement annexed to R86 is a similar provision to Art. 6(1) of C97, but extends equal treatment to a broader range of matters, such as, *inter alia*, access to education and hygiene, safety and medical assistance.

[130] Art. 2 of Convention No. 111 reads: 'Each Member for which this Convention is in force undertakes to declare and pursue a national policy designed to promote, by methods appropriate to national conditions and practice, equality of opportunity and treatment in respect of employment and occupation, with a view to eliminating any discrimination in respect thereof'. Art. 3 outlines what the requirements of such a policy entail. See also *Migrant Workers VII(1)*, n. 64 above, 21–2.

[131] See n. 96 above and accompanying text. See also *Migrant Workers VII(1)*, n. 64 above, 22. Article 1(1)(a) of Convention No. 111 prohibits discrimination on the ground of 'national extraction', but this term was deliberately used to ensure that 'nationality' was not covered. See Nielsen, n. 96 above, 840, citing from International Labour Conference, 1957, *Report VII(2)* (Geneva: International Labour Office, 1957) 104–5. Nielsen, *ibid.* 843, also observes that both the Committee of Experts and a Committee of the Governing Body have adopted the view that distinctions made by states parties among non-nationals from different countries solely on the basis of nationality are beyond the scope of Art. 1(1)(a). With respect to the latter body, see the Report of the Governing

tenth recital, takes note of this omission and calls for further standards 'to promote equality of opportunity and treatment of migrant workers'.

During the drafting of the 1975 migrant workers instruments, voices were raised in support of widening the ambit of the equality provision to include the promotion of equality of opportunity and treatment and the elimination of discrimination in practice. Formal equality before the law was regarded as insufficient protection for migrant workers and their families.[132] The need for promotional measures and positive programmes to secure real equality in practice was therefore underlined.[133] It was recognized that migrant workers are more likely to be victims of prejudice and other unfavourable attitudes in their workplace and where they live than as a result of discriminatory laws.[134] Furthermore, their opportunities for seeking redress are limited.[135] These concerns are largely tackled in Part II of C143 and the accompanying R151.

Article 10 in Part II of C143 is the principal equality provision in the 1975 ILO instruments on migrant workers:

> Each Member for which the Convention is in force undertakes to declare and pursue a national policy to promote and guarantee, by methods appropriate to national conditions and practice, equality of opportunity and treatment in respect of employment and occupation, of social security, of trade union and cultural rights and of individual and collective freedoms for persons who as migrant workers or as members of their families are lawfully within its territory.

Although the provision omits to specify whether equality in the enumerated areas is to be sought with nationals, paragraph 2 of the accompanying Recommendation, which is an elaboration of this policy, confirms that this is the case.[136] With regard to the implementation of the national policy in Article 10, the Committee of Experts has stated that it may take any form (not necessarily that of legislation)

Body Committee, appointed under Art. 24 of the ILO Constitution, to examine a representation against Iraq regarding its treatment of Egyptian workers in Iraq and Kuwait, ILO Doc. GB.250/15/25, paras. 42–3. However, distinctions between national and foreign workers, based on any of the other grounds in Art. 1(1)(a), are outlawed. Nielsen, *ibid.* 854. See also Zegers de Beijl and Böhning, n. 60 above, 93, with reference to the prohibition of discrimination under Convention No. 111 on the ground of 'national extraction'.

132 *Migrant Workers V(1)*, n. 83 above, 35 (opinion of Mr. Öberg, Government advisor, Sweden, and Reporter of the Conference Committee on Migrant Workers during the discussions at the 59th Session of the International Labour Conference).

133 *Migrant Workers V(1)*, n. 83 above, 5, para. 15 (consensus reached during the general discussion at the 59th Session of the International Labour Conference). See also *General Survey*, n. 27 above, 100, para. 375.

134 *General Survey*, *ibid.* 82, para. 285. For a good account of the manifestation of such discrimination against migrant workers in practice, particularly in relation to the workplace and access to the labour market, and for recent ILO efforts to combat such discrimination, see Zegers de Beijl and Böhning, n. 60 above, 94–7.

135 Migrant workers are frequently unable to avail themselves of their rights because of a lack of information and knowledge compounded by linguistic difficulties. *General Survey*, n. 27 above.

136 See also Plender, n. 71 above, 304 and Lillich, n. 71 above, 74.

and be formulated progressively under a coordinated programme of positive measures.[137] Such a programme is outlined in Article 12 of C143.[138]

The broad ambit of the principle of equality of opportunity and treatment in the 1975 instruments is further reflected in R151, which elaborates on some of the provisions in C143, particularly those concerned with employment and cultural rights, and which advocates the formulation of a national social policy in the areas of family reunification and health and social services to ensure that migrant workers not only benefit from the same advantages enjoyed by nationals, but also that their particular needs are catered for.[139] Such an approach subscribes to the thesis that the realization of genuine equality between migrants and nationals requires special measures to enable the former group to adapt to the society of the country of employment.

The concern in C143 with the promotion of equality of opportunity and treatment in law and in practice was underlined by the Committee of Experts in an observation to the Government of Italy in 1988. In response to a direct request from the Committee, the Italian Government submitted information on new legislation (Law No. 943 of 30 December 1986), which provided, *inter alia*, for equality of treatment between nationals and migrant workers from outside of the European Community. The Committee requested further information on the practical measures taken by the Italian Government to promote and ensure the observance of this legislation.[140]

(iii) Problems with the application of the equality principle

A number of problems exist with the application of the equality principle in respect of migrant workers. The need, at times, to accord migrant workers special measures in order to guarantee genuine equality with nationals might be problematic. Paragraph 9 of R151 concerned with social policy stresses that special measures for migrant workers should not adversely affect the principle of equality of opportunity and treatment. In this connection, the International Labour Office has stated that a distinction is to be drawn between special measures that promote the effective equality of migrants with nationals and measures that grant rights and guarantees to migrants which nationals do not enjoy.[141]

137 *General Survey*, n. 27 above, 82–3, paras. 287–8 and 148, para. 519.

138 This programme involves: co-operation between employers' and workers' organizations in the promotion of the acceptance and observance of the policy; the enactment of legislation and the promotion of educational programmes, including programmes which inform and assist migrant workers with respect to their rights and obligations; the repeal of statutory or administrative practices inconsistent with the policy; the formulation of a social policy which takes account of the special needs of migrant workers in consultation with employers' and workers' organizations; the promotion of the cultural rights of migrant workers and their children; and the guarantee of equality of treatment with regard to the working conditions of migrant workers.

139 R151, para. 9. The areas covered by the social policy in R151 are discussed in greater detail below.

140 International Labour Conference, 75th Session, 1988, Report III(4A), *Report of the Committee of Experts on the Application of Conventions and Recommendations* (Geneva: International Labour Office, 1988) 363–4.

141 *Migrant Workers VII(2)*, n. 83 above, 31.

Since the equality sought is that with nationals, a problem arises if the treatment that nationals themselves receive is hardly adequate, especially if the economic and social conditions are poor as is frequently the case in developing countries. Although other ILO and human rights instruments are also a relevant yardstick in outlining minimum standards, little progress in this regard may seriously undermine the rights of migrant workers and their families, particularly as discriminatory provision in favour of nationals might be implemented to a greater extent by countries which possess scarce resources.

A further difficulty concerns the absence of a comparison on the basis of which to measure equal treatment of migrants with nationals, particularly in respect of employment conditions. In many countries, migrant workers perform work not performed by nationals. Although there are usually some standards of comparison among Western countries in the form of legislation, judicial decisions, or collective agreements, these are largely absent, for example, in the Arab Gulf States where migrant workers are sometimes employed in occupations or sectors which contain few local workers and where there are no labour institutions or social legislation of the kind found in industrialized countries.[142]

The problem of the application of the equality provisions in the migrant workers instruments to short-term migrants has already been referred to in relation to seasonal workers. This problem is exacerbated by Article 14(a) of C143, which effectively places a two-year restriction on migrant workers' free choice of employment.[143] The Committee of Experts has noted that some countries find it difficult to apply a policy of equality of opportunity and treatment to migrant workers whose access to employment is subject to restrictions for a specified period.[144] However, it is difficult to see how such restrictions might justify denying to them equal opportunity and treatment with nationals generally. Böhning argues that discrimination, like equality, is indivisible. If some rights are granted to migrant workers and others refused, discrimination subsists. Therefore, if the grant of rights is effectively made subject to a qualifying period, there can be no genuine equality.[145]

Finally, it has already been noted that Part II of C143, including Articles 10 and 12, does not apply to illegal migrants. There are, however, provisions which cater specifically for this group; for example, Article 9(1) in Part I of C143, which articulates the principle of equal treatment between irregular and regular migrant workers in respect of rights arising out of past employment. There is a strong argument to be made, with the support of the ILO, for affording illegal migrants equal treatment with regular migrants and nationals in other areas. This question is discussed further in the section on illegal migrants below.

[142] Böhning (1984), n. 22 above, Ch. 10, 243.

[143] The importance of this controversial provision and its potentially wide-ranging effects are discussed below.

[144] *General Survey*, n. 27 above, 83, para. 290 and 148, para. 520.

[145] Böhning (1984), n. 77 above, Ch. 1, 14.

(c) Employment rights

(i) Employment and work conditions

The principle that all migrant workers should receive the same treatment as nationals in respect of employment and work conditions is well recognized in the four main ILO instruments on migrant workers. Article 10 of C143 imposes the obligation on ratifying states to promote and guarantee equal opportunity and treatment between migrant workers and nationals in respect of, *inter alia*, 'employment and occupation'. From the migrant workers instruments, rights to employment and occupation include the following rights: equal remuneration for work of equal value; equal work conditions; access to vocational training, promotion, or advancement; security of employment, including the provision of alternative employment, relief work, and retraining; and rest periods and leisure.[146] Equal treatment between migrant workers and nationals in respect of employment and work conditions is relatively uncontroversial, although some problems exist with its application.[147]

States have contended that absolute security of employment for migrant workers is not feasible because, in market economies, no such guarantees are provided to nationals either.[148] Although such a position may seem obvious in difficult economic times, a tendency may still exist to accord priority to nationals and to terminate the employment of migrants first.[149] The objective of ILO provisions in this regard is to ensure that migrant workers enjoy job security on the *same terms* as nationals.[150] If the employment of lawfully resident migrant workers is terminated, Article 8(1) of Part I of C143 provides that this shall not mean that they are to be regarded as in an irregular situation or imply in itself the withdrawal of their residence or work permits.

(ii) The right to free choice of employment

The right of migrant workers to 'free choice of employment' is problematic for migrant-receiving countries. Without doubt, the more this right is recognized and respected, the greater is the likelihood that migrant workers and their families will stay indefinitely in the country of employment.

Both the 1949 and 1975 instruments concerning migrant workers provide that migrant workers should have the right to free choice of employment after a

[146] See respectively Art. 6(1)(a)(i) of C97, Art. 17(2)(a)(i) of Annex I to R86 and para. 2(e) of R151; Art. 12(g) of C143 and para. 2(f) of R151; Arts. 9 and 17(2)(a)(iii) of Annex I to R86 and paras. 2(b) and (c) of R151; Art. 8(2) of C143 and para. 2(d) of R151; Art. 17(2)(a)(i) and (iv) of Annex I to R86 and para. 2(f) of R151. Rights to employment and occupation also comprise the right of free access to employment (Art. 14(a) of C143, para. 6 of R151 and para. 2(b) of R151), considered below, which includes access to employment services. See *General Survey*, n. 27 above, 95, para. 351.

[147] For example, granting migrant workers, whose stay in a country is of a short duration, equal treatment with nationals in respect of access to vocational training.

[148] *Migrant Workers VII(2)*, n. 83 above, 29 and 31 (opinions of Austria and Switzerland).

[149] *General Survey*, n. 27 above, 91 and 149, paras. 334 and 524 respectively.

[150] *Ibid.* 149, para. 524.

specified period of work and residence in the country of employment. The general principle enunciated in paragraph 16(1) of R86 is that 'migrants for employment authorized to reside in a territory and the members of their families authorized to accompany or join them should as far as possible be admitted to employment in the same conditions as nationals'. But where any restrictions on the free choice of employment for migrant workers and their families exist, these are to be lifted after 5 years of regular and lawful residence in the host country (paragraphs 16(2)(a) and (b)). The right to free choice of employment is elevated to a Convention obligation in Article 14(a) of C143 (this clause is repeated in paragraph 6 of the accompanying R151). The time period at the expiration of which limitations on this right are to be removed is also reduced considerably. Under this provision, a member state may:

> make the free choice of employment, while assuring migrant workers the right to geographical mobility, subject to the conditions that the migrant worker has resided lawfully within its territory for the purpose of employment for a prescribed period not exceeding two years or, if its laws or regulations provide for contracts for a fixed term of less than two years, that the worker has completed his first work contract.

Two years is the *maximum* period for which restrictions may be imposed on free choice of employment. Under Article 14(a), migrant workers may acquire free choice of employment within 2 years if their work contracts are less than 2 years in duration. Free choice of employment is absolute, with the exception of access to the public service (see the section on political rights below), and is not dependent on the discretion of the state.[151] Further, any restriction must not limit the geographic mobility of migrant workers, although mobility might be indirectly affected as a result of the issue of work permits which have certain occupational conditions attached to them.[152]

The adoption of Article 14(a) was very controversial and involved heated debate during drafting. Originally, the prescribed period of residence, during which restrictions on free choice of employment could be imposed, was to be 5 years, as laid down in paragraph 16(2) of R86. A number of countries, however,

[151] See also *General Survey*, n. 27 above, 92–3, para. 339. The Committee of Experts has clarified this last point by confirming that the position of the Kenyan Government, which insisted on retaining discretion in this regard in the framework of its localization policy, was in conflict with Art. 14(a) of C143. International Labour Conference, 78th Session, 1991, Report III(4A), *Report of the Committee of Experts on the Application of Conventions and Recommendations* (Geneva: International Labour Office, 1991) 453–4. See also the Committee's report issued at the 79th Session in 1992, n. 36 above, 499.

[152] *General Survey*, n. 27 above, 95–6, paras. 354–5. The Committee of Experts provided examples of such work permits, which are issued to migrant workers in France and Germany for a given post or employer or for a given region. A further permissible restriction on access to employment is found in Art. 14(b) of C143, which stipulates that a state may make regulations, after consultation with representative organizations of employers and workers, concerning recognition of occupational qualifications acquired outside its territory.

were of the opinion that the 5-year residence qualification was too long.[153] A second draft proposal for Article 14(a) eliminated reference to a specified time period altogether and merely asserted that migrant workers should have free choice of employment after the completion of their first work contract.[154] After receiving requests from a number of countries to impose a prescribed waiting-period,[155] the International Labour Office recommended that restrictions on free choice of employment should only be permitted for a maximum of 2 years.[156] Some countries, however, continued to press for the retention of the 5-year waiting-period or opposed the provision altogether.[157]

Article 14(a) is a remarkable achievement which, at least on its face, greatly decreases state control over the employment of migrant workers and contributes to an overall reduction in their exploitation. According to Russo, this provision, if implemented, would 'free migrants from working exclusively in the least desirable and lowest paid jobs, promote their equality with nationals, and enable them to compete for other occupations based on their ability and effort'.[158] Old habits die hard, however, and state practice shows that restrictions on migrants' free choice of employment go beyond limitations based on the 2-year waiting-period. In its General Survey of 1980, the Committee of Experts found the following additional restrictions: in many countries, the waiting-period is longer

[153] *Migrant Workers VII(2)*, n. 83 above, 23–4 (opinions of Finland, Norway, and Sweden). On the other hand, some countries insisted that it should be left entirely up to the state of employment to decide how long restrictions on free choice of employment for migrant workers should last. *Ibid.* 22–4 (opinions of Bangladesh, Denmark, Egypt, Iran, Malaysia, Morocco and Sudan).

[154] *Migrant Workers V(2)*, n. 111 above, 21.

[155] Finland and Sweden recommended a waiting-period of 2 years, whereas Norway advised that the waiting-period should be one year only: *ibid.* 21–2.

[156] *Ibid.* 23. This time-period was finalized at the 60th Session of the International Labour Conference in 1975. *Record of Proceedings*, n. 93 above, 646, para. 77.

[157] *Migrant Workers V(2)*, n. 111 above, 21–2 (opinions of France and the Netherlands respectively). This provision was unacceptable to the USA because short-term migrant workers are not granted any free choice of employment in that country: *Record of Proceedings*, n. 93 above, 792 (Mr. Sehgal, US Government advisor) and 796 (Mr. Sorn, Employers' advisor). At the 60th Session of the International Labour Conference, an amendment by Germany to add a further qualification to the proposed Art. 14(a) in order to take into account the situation of the labour market was rejected. *Ibid.* 646, para. 78. The views of this government were reiterated by its delegate, Mr. Haase, *ibid.* 795, during the discussions of the Report of the Conference Committee on Migrant Workers: '[H]ost countries are asked to relinquish any possibility of regulation if the foreign worker has completed his first—and perhaps very short—contract of employment. Such a provision would cause my Government great difficulty. We have had an extremely liberal policy for the employment of foreigners, thus, reducing, the employment market difficulties of many other countries . . . But the Federal Republic of Germany, with its high density of population, is not a country of immigration in the classical sense. It must therefore reserve some possibility of control for a certain period—at present five years—during which it can ensure the indispensable priority of employment for national workers'.

[158] Russo, n. 109 above, 57. Russo, *ibid.*, adds that when read with Art. 8(1) of C143, which stipulates that loss of employment by legally resident migrants does not place them in an irregular situation, Art. 14 'enables migrants of two years residence to refuse to accept exploitative conditions in the occupations they were restricted to in their original work permits, and should provide an incentive for improvements to be made by employers of those migrants'.

than 2 years; priority in employment is frequently given to nationals; in certain states, migrant workers cannot change jobs without applying for a new work permit irrespective of the duration of their stay; and the prohibition on access by foreigners to employment services in some countries severely compromises any free choice of employment they may have. Finally, these restrictions are also applicable to the families of migrant workers.[159]

Not surprisingly, Article 14(a) has been the most serious obstacle to the ratification of Part II of C143.[160] It has been labelled as 'probably the most problematical provision of the Convention', even though it cannot support a right to stay.[161] Nonetheless, Article 14(a) unquestionably encroaches upon the realm of state sovereignty in the traditionally secure fields of employment and immigration.[162] Its application, though not immediately evident, may well be far-reaching.

(d) Trade Union rights

'Trade union rights' are described by Trebilcock as embodying two aspects: that of the individual worker and that of the trade union organization to act effectively in defence of its members' interests. If a trade union cannot defend its foreign members to the same extent as its national members working in the same enterprise then it will itself be weakened as an institution.[163] It is arguable that *all* workers suffer when employers are able to tap a labour force that accepts low wages and poor conditions and when one part of their class is treated without regard to standards established to protect workers as a single group.[164]

Trade union rights encompass the right to freedom of association and collective bargaining, which constitute fundamental tenets of the ILO.[165] As discussed earlier, the principle of freedom of association was first enshrined in the ILO Constitution and is endowed with a special procedure devoted to its implementation. Furthermore, Convention No. 87 of 1948 concerning Freedom of Association and the Protection of the Right to Organize prohibits discrimination on the basis of nationality in respect of the formation and membership of trade unions.

[159] *General Survey*, n. 27 above, 149, para. 523. For specific country references in respect of these restrictions on migrants' free choice of employment, see *ibid*. 94–5, paras. 346–53.

[160] *Ibid*. 149, para. 523.

[161] Kellerson, n. 18 above, 38. The provision does not preclude a state from withdrawing migrants' residence rights even if they have resided and worked in a country for over 2 years and are entitled to free choice of employment. Nor does Art. 14(a) affect the state's right to admit or to refuse to admit the entry of a foreigner to its territory. *General Survey*, n. 27 above, 92, para. 338. See also Trebilcock, n. 56 above, 1841.

[162] These broader implications of the provision have been recognized by the Committee of Experts: 'The question of free choice of employment for migrant workers is a . . . complex one, involving as it does national policy in the fields of immigration and employment generally and the concern to protect the employment position of a country's own citizens': *General Survey*, n. 27 above, 151, para. 532.

[163] See n. 56 above, 1837–8.

[164] L. S. Bosniak, 'Exclusion and Membership: The Dual Identity of the Undocumented Worker under United States Law' (1988) *Wisconsin L. Rev.* 955, 1005. This argument is especially forceful in the case of illegal migrant workers who are frequently subjected to exploitation as workers in the country of employment.

[165] Böhning (1984), n. 22 above, Ch. 10, 244.

C97 provides for equal treatment between migrant workers and nationals in respect of 'membership of trade unions and enjoyment of the benefits of collective bargaining'.[166] Article 10 of Part II of C143 uses the broader term 'trade union rights'.[167] These are defined in paragraph 2(g) of R151 to also encompass 'eligibility for office in trade unions and in labour-management relations bodies, including bodies representing workers in undertakings'.

In its General Surveys, the Committee of Experts has found that migrant workers are permitted to join trade unions on the same terms as nationals in most countries, but that their eligibility for trade union office is more likely to be the subject of restrictions.[168] The Committee has stated that legislation in this area should be flexible in order to allow trade union organizations to choose their leaders without hindrance and also to permit foreign migrant workers to hold trade union office, at least after a reasonable period of residence in the country of employment.[169] The drafting history of the 1975 instruments reveals that states have justified these restrictions on the basis of non-interference in union affairs or national sovereignty.[170] The existence of these restrictions on the trade union rights of migrant workers is unfortunate. Broader participation by migrant workers in trade unions not only gives migrants a say in labour matters that affect them,[171] but is also an important aspect of an active programme to increase co-operation between minority and immigrant groups and the majority population.[172] Moreover, the exercise of trade union rights by migrant workers constitutes an important aspect of their broader social participation in society, which is essential to their acquisition of further rights.

Article 10 of C143 also guarantees equal treatment between migrant workers and nationals in respect of 'individual and collective freedoms'. The Committee of Experts has noted that this text is intended to cover freedoms, such as freedoms

[166] Art. 6(1)(a)(ii). The same provision is included in Art. 17(2)(a)(ii) of the Model Agreement in Annex I to R86.

[167] See also Böhning (1984), n. 22 above, Ch. 10, 245. Although Art. 10 does not apply to illegal migrant workers, para. 8(3) of R151 maintains that these workers ought to receive equal treatment with nationals in respect of trade union membership and the exercise of trade union rights.

[168] See *General Survey*, n. 27 above, 91, paras. 328–31 and 149, para. 525 and International Labour Conference, 69th Session, 1983, Report of the Committee of Experts on the Application of Conventions and Recommendations, Pt III(4B), *General Survey on the Application of the Conventions on Freedom of Association, the Right to Organize and Collective Bargaining and the Convention and Recommendation concerning Rural Workers' Organizations* (Geneva: International Labour Office, 1983) (hereinafter *General Survey on Freedom of Association*) 31, para. 96 and 53, para. 159.

[169] *General Survey on Freedom of Association*, n. 168 above, 53, para. 160.

[170] *Migrant Workers VII(2)*, n. 83 above, 29 and 30 (opinions of Austria and Libya, and Malaysia respectively).

[171] The Committee of Experts has observed that restrictions based on nationality may prevent migrant workers from playing an active role in the defence of their interests, especially in sectors where they constitute the major source of labour. *General Survey on Freedom of Association*, n. 168 above, 31, para. 97.

[172] *General Survey*, n. 27 above, 119, para. 417, referring to the Swedish policy aimed at assisting immigrants in retaining their cultural identity.

of information, expression, and assembly, upon which the full exercise of trade union rights depends.[173]

(e) Social Security Rights

The protection of the social security rights of migrant workers and their families is one of the main areas in which the standard-setting activities of the ILO regarding migrant workers have been concentrated. The object of these activities has been to establish the right to equal treatment between nationals and aliens in respect of social security and to set up a system for the maintenance of acquired rights and rights in the course of acquisition for workers who move from one country to another.[174]

The principle of equal treatment between migrant workers and nationals in respect of social security appears in Article 6(1)(b) of C97 which also defines social security.[175] Social security benefits, which are financed out of public funds on a non-contributory basis, may, however, be restricted to nationals.[176] C143 restates the fundamental principle of equal treatment in Article 10, which in contrast with the 1949 provision, applies to both contributory and non-contributory forms of social security.[177] Reciprocity is not required under both C97 and C143. So long as the country of employment has ratified the Convention in question, the social security rights of migrants are to be respected, regardless of whether the migrant worker's home country has ratified the instrument.[178]

References to social security were not included in the draft 1975 Convention prepared by the International Labour Office because this matter was considered to have been adequately articulated elsewhere.[179] A reference to social security was eventually added in Article 10 on the understanding that it constituted

[173] *Ibid.* 89, para. 317. This observation was made in connection with the assertion that, for the purpose of Art. 10 of C143, 'individual and collective freedoms' do not encompass 'political rights'. See also the commentary by the International Labour Office in *Migrant Workers V(2)*, n. 111 above, 17.

[174] *General Survey*, n. 27 above, 3, paras. 8–9. See also Böhning (1984), n. 22 above, Ch. 10, 250.

[175] Social security is defined as: 'legal provision in respect of employment injury, maternity, sickness, invalidity, old age, death, unemployment and family responsibilities, and any other contingency which, according to national laws or regulations, is covered by a social security scheme'. R100, in paras. 45 to 47, also refers to the need for appropriate arrangements in order to guarantee the social security of migrant workers and their families, particularly in the field of health care (paras. 46(a), (b) and (j)) and in the event of employment injury (para. 46(d)).

[176] Art. 6(1)(b)(ii) of C97. See also *The ILO and Human Rights*, n. 19 above, 54.

[177] *General Survey*, n. 27 above, 86, para. 306. The 1975 instruments make other references to social security rights. Provisions of note are Art. 9(1) of C143, which protects the social security rights of irregular migrant workers arising out of 'past employment' and para. 2(f) of R151, which provides that all migrant workers should be accorded equal treatment with nationals in respect of 'conditions of work, including . . . social security measures and welfare facilities and benefits provided in connection with employment'. R151 also stipulates, in para. 34(1)(c)(ii), that *all* migrant workers, who leave the country of employment, should be entitled to 'reimbursement of any social security contributions which have not given and will not give rise to rights under national laws or regulations or international arrangements'.

[178] *General Survey*, n. 27 above, 86, para. 303.

[179] *Ibid.* 85–6, para. 302. See the specific social security instruments discussed below.

merely a restatement of a fundamental principle and that it would not contradict other more technically-oriented conventions in this area.[180] This strategy is in line with the ILO approach to the question of social security rights generally. Although bilateral or specific regional multilateral treaties are arguably the best method of dealing with the technical matters arising in this complex and diverse field, the affirmation and maintenance of fundamental principles and general guidelines are better ensured at the universal multilateral level.[181]

Social security is the object of a number of specific ILO Conventions and Recommendations. These standards have evolved considerably since 1919:

> Great strides have been made since the ILO started to be active in this field. These can be seen especially in the gradual extension of the range of application of instruments of co-ordination to all branches and schemes, whether contributory or not, as well as to all workers, whether employees or self-employed, and even to beneficiaries who do not form part of the economically active population. They can also be seen in the widening of the advantages to which the various categories of persons covered by these instruments are entitled, including in particular entitlements to short- or long-term benefits outside the country whose legislation is applicable.[182]

The Committee of Experts has observed that the social security provisions in the migrant workers instruments should be read in the context of other ILO standards concerned with social security.[183] There are three relevant ILO social security conventions, the contours of which warrant description.[184] Convention No. 102 of 1952 concerning Minimum Standards of Social Security[185] enunciates, in Article 68(2), the principle of equality of treatment between national and non-national workers in respect of *contributory* social security schemes subject to any conditions of reciprocity provided for in bilateral and multilateral agreements. The next two conventions are specifically concerned with equal treatment between nationals and non-nationals in the social security field. Convention No. 118 of 1962 concerning Equality of Treatment of Nationals and Non-Nationals in Social Security[186] focuses on domestic law and provides for equal treatment between nationals and non-nationals from other states parties in respect of the

[180] *Ibid.* 86, paras. 302 and 150, para. 527. See also *Migrant Workers* I (2), n. 111 above, 16 (opinions of Finland and Italy) and 17–18 (commentary by the International Labour Office), and *Record of Proceedings*, n. 93 above, 644, para. 53 (opinion of Spain).

[181] Cf. Böhning (1984), n. 22 above, Ch. 10, 250. [182] Böhning (1988), n. 45 above, 135.

[183] *General Survey*, n. 27 above, 86, para. 303.

[184] See generally the following observations: Trebilcock, n. 56 above, 1848–9; Böhning (1984), n. 22 above, Ch. 10, 250–2; Böhning (1988), n. 45 above, 134–6; and Plender, n. 71 above, 307.

[185] Convention No. 102 of 1952 concerning Minimum Standards of Social Security; adopted 28 June 1952; entry into force 27 April 1955, ratified by 39 states as at 1 Jan. 1996. For the text, see *International Labour Conventions and Recommendations, 1919–1991*, n. 16 above, 544.

[186] Convention No. 118 of 1962 concerning Equality of Treatment of Nationals and Non-Nationals in Social Security; adopted 28 June 1962, entry into force 25 April 1964; ratified by 38 states as at 31 Dec. 1994. For the text, see *International Labour Conventions and Recommendations, 1919–1991*, n. 16 above, 753.

accepted branches of social security.[187] Benefits are to be awarded without any condition of residence, although non-contributory benefits, with the exception of medical care, sickness benefit, employment injury benefit, and family benefit, may be subject to conditions of residence of a prescribed duration.[188] Convention No. 157 of 1982 concerning the Establishment of an International System for the Maintenance of Social Security Rights[189] deals with the maintenance of rights in the course of acquisition (Part III) and the maintenance of acquired rights and provisions of benefits abroad (Part IV), and also applies to all branches of social security. The Convention permits states parties to give effect to their obligations by concluding bilateral and multilateral agreements. However, these agreements need not cover all branches of social security, nor apply to all categories of persons.[190]

The principal difference, however, between the provisions which refer to social security in the 1949 and 1975 migrant workers instruments and the ILO social security Conventions is that equal treatment with nationals is only accorded by the latter texts to migrants (and their survivors) on the basis of reciprocity, in other words, to nationals of member states which have ratified these Conventions.

(f) Cultural rights

Because questions of cultural and linguistic identity are generally separable from those relating to employment and the workplace, it is therefore arguable that they should, strictly-speaking, fall outside of the competence of the ILO. Nonetheless, the 1975 migrant workers instruments *are* concerned with these questions, which were included towards the end of the drafting process largely as a result of concerns expressed by certain countries and workers' members.[191]

[187] The principle of equal treatment is enunciated in Arts. 3–6 of the Convention. The branches of social security are listed in Art. 2(1): medical care, sickness benefit, maternity benefit, invalidity benefit, old-age benefit, survivors' benefit, employment injury benefit, unemployment benefit, and family benefit. Medical care is not included in the definition of social security in Art. 6(1)(b) of C97. However, the third recital of the Preamble to Recommendation No. 69 of 1944 concerning Medical Care declares that the availability of adequate medical care is 'an essential element in social security'. Furthermore, para. 12 of R86 provides that migrants under Government-sponsored arrangements for group transfer should benefit from medical assistance on the same terms as nationals and Art. 17(2)(d) of the Model Agreement annexed to R86 extends the equality principle to include medical assistance for migrant workers and their families. R151 also maintains that migrant workers and their families should enjoy effective equality of opportunity and treatment with nationals in respect of, *inter alia*, 'the benefits of . . . health facilities' (para. 2(i)).

[188] Arts. 4(1) and 4(2) respectively.

[189] Convention No. 157 of 1982 concerning the Establishment of an International System for the Maintenance of Social Security Rights; adopted 21 June 1982; entry into force 11 Sept. 1986; ratified by three states, Philippines, Spain and Sweden, as at 31 Dec. 1994. For the text see *International Labour Conventions and Recommendations, 1919–1991*, n. 16 above, 1255.

[190] The branches of social security must, however, apply to invalidity, old-age and survivors' benefits and employment injury pensions, including death grants (Art. 4(3)(a)), and the categories of persons must at least comprise employees, including frontier and seasonal workers, and members of their families as well as their survivors (Art. 4(3)(b)).

[191] On the need for special measures to maintain and develop the cultural identity of migrant workers, see *Migrant Workers VII(2)*, n. 83 above, 29–30 and 36 (opinion of Finland) and *Migrant*

Article 10 of C143 refers to 'cultural rights' as one of the objectives of the national policy which states are under an obligation to declare and pursue in order to promote and guarantee equality of opportunity and treatment. According to the Committee of Experts, the rationale for the inclusion of cultural rights in Article 10 is 'to give express recognition to the right of migrant workers to participate in the cultural life of the country and to maintain and develop their own cultural heritage in the same condition as nationals'.[192] It is difficult to gauge the exact scope of this reference to cultural rights in Article 10. The Committee of Experts has observed that cultural rights do not encompass a right to education in general on the basis that education does not lie within the competence of the ILO, although it acknowledged that an amendment regarding equality of opportunity in respect of general education was withdrawn as pursuing similar objectives.[193] In any case, it is difficult to see how the maintenance and development of the cultural identity of migrants might proceed without some provision for the teaching to their children of the mother tongue and culture of the country of origin. Indeed, this proposition is supported by Article 12(f) of C143 which imposes an obligation upon states to:

> take all steps to assist and encourage the efforts of migrant workers and their families to preserve their national and ethnic identity and their cultural ties with their country of origin, including the possibility for children to be given some knowledge of their mother tongue.[194]

The Committee of Experts has noted that states only have to 'assist and encourage' the efforts of migrant workers to preserve their cultural identity. The onus, therefore, is on the migrants themselves to take the initiative.[195] Examples of state measures to teach the mother tongue to the children of migrant workers include the adoption of bilateral arrangements between the home country and the country of employment, assistance to schools run by immigrant associations,

Workers V(2), n. 111 above, 20 (opinion of the former Yugoslavia); on the need for migrants to maintain ties with their own countries, see *Migrant Workers V(1)*, n. 83 above, 6, para. 18 (view of workers' members and some government members during the proceedings of the 59th Session of the International Labour Conference) and *Migrant Workers V(2)*, *ibid.* 20 (opinion of the former Yugoslavia); and on the need to teach the native language to children of migrant workers, see *Migrant Workers VII(2)*, *ibid.* 9 and 37 (opinion of Sweden) and *Migrant Workers V(2)*, *ibid.* 27 (opinion of Finland).

[192] *General Survey*, n. 27 above, 88, para. 313.

[193] *Ibid.* 88, para. 315. The Committee, *ibid.*, added that the inclusion of cultural rights cannot be considered as anything more than a statement of principle whose purpose is not to regulate all questions resulting from its application, particularly those concerned with educational assistance.

[194] This provision arose as a result of an amendment introduced by workers' members and the government members of Algeria, Greece, and the former Yugoslavia during the 60th Session of the International Labour Conference in 1975. *Record of Proceedings*, n. 93 above, 646, para. 72.

[195] *General Survey*, n. 27 above, 107, para. 405. This approach is based on the premise that adaptation by migrant workers to the living and working conditions of the country of employment involves continuing efforts on the part of states as well as of the immigrants themselves. *Ibid.* 151, para. 533. For further discussion of the questions of adaptation and integration, see below.

and the placing of school premises at the disposal of the consular authorities of the country of emigration.[196] More general measures aimed at the preservation of the cultural identity of migrant workers and their families and the maintenance of cultural ties with their countries of origin consist of radio and television broadcasts in the native language, assistance to immigrant associations, and special arrangements enabling migrant workers to take leave from their employment for the celebration of their principal national or religious holidays.[197]

The terms of Article 12(f) of C143 are repeated in paragraph 7(1) of the accompanying R151 as part of a broader programme to enable migrant workers and their families to take full advantage of their rights and opportunities in employment and occupation and as a means of promoting their adaptation to the society of the country of employment. The Committee of Experts has stressed that adaptation and integration (as opposed to assimilation) of migrant workers into the society of the country of employment and the preservation of their national identity is the keystone of ILO social policy. The dual objective of special measures aimed at the integration of migrants and the preservation of their identity should be considered within the broad framework of equality of opportunity and treatment with nationals.[198] This approach is valid regardless of whether migrant workers and their families stay in a country indefinitely or go back home within a short space of time.[199] In the latter case, measures aimed at the preservation of the cultural identity of migrants facilitate their reintegration into the country of origin on their return.[200]

(g) Family reunification

In a preliminary report entitled *Migrant Workers*, issued by the International Labour Office in 1973, the problem of family reunification was described as follows:

> Uniting migrant workers with their families living in the countries of origin is recognized to be essential for the migrants' well-being and their social adaptation to the receiving country. Prolonged separation and isolation lead to hardships and stress situations affecting both the migrants and the families left behind and prevent them from leading a normal life. The large numbers of migrant workers cut off from social relations and living on the fringe of the receiving community create many well known social and psychological problems that, in turn, largely determine community attitudes towards migrant workers.[201]

[196] *Ibid.* 107, paras. 406–8. [197] *Ibid.* 107–8, paras. 409–12.

[198] *Ibid.* 118, para. 413. Special measures are also necessary in other areas, such as health and housing (see below) and not just in relation to culture, in order to assist the integration of migrant workers and their families into the host society.

[199] An interesting 'independent' approach to integration noted by the Committee of Experts is that adopted in Sweden. The emphasis in Sweden is upon the need for immigrants to retain their cultural identity, with the assistance of the state, but only to the extent that they wish to do so: *ibid.* 119, para. 417. See also the discussion in the section on cultural rights in Ch. 8.

[200] *Ibid.* 118, para. 414. In addition to this latter objective, the preservation of the cultural identity of migrants arguably contributes to the enrichment of contacts between the country of origin and country of employment. *Ibid.*

[201] *Migrant Workers VII(1)*, n. 64 above, 27.

Given the social importance of the matter and the prominence given to respect for family life in other international human rights instruments, it is surprising that there is no firm state obligation in ILO instruments to reunite migrant workers with their families. Whereas the 1949 migrant workers instruments are limited in scope, with R86 only concerning itself with family reunion from the standpoint of permanent migration and subject to agreement between the states concerned,[202] the 1975 instruments have a broader application. Article 13(1) of C143 reads:

> A Member may take all necessary measures which fall within its competence and collaborate with other Members to facilitate the reunification of the families of all migrant workers legally residing in its territory.

This provision leaves to states a discretion whether to facilitate family reunification. The drafting history indicates that Article 13(1) was introduced as an amendment at the 60th Session of the International Labour Conference by the workers' members and the Italian Government delegation, but was not couched in terms of a strict obligation.[203] Consequently, C143 has been described as being 'weak on family reunification'.[204]

R151 uses stronger language with regard to family reunion. Paragraph 13(1) of R151 reads: 'All possible measures *should* be taken both by countries of employment and by countries of origin to facilitate the reunification of families of migrant workers *as rapidly as possible*. These measures should include, as necessary, national laws or regulations and bilateral and multilateral arrangements'.[205]

For the purpose of family reunification, 'the family' in C143 and R151 is defined as 'the spouse and dependent children, father and mother'.[206] The Committee of Experts noted from state practice that the spouse and unmarried minor children of migrant workers are usually permitted to enter the country of employment but difficulties exist in a number of countries with regard to the admission of dependent adult children and parents.[207] These problems are especially acute in the case of adult disabled children, students in full-time education, and those

[202] Para. 15(1) of R86 reads: 'Provision should be made by agreement for authorisation to be granted for a migrant for employment introduced on a permanent basis to be accompanied or joined by the members of his family'

[203] *Record of Proceedings*, n. 93 above, 647, para. 81.

[204] Russo, n. 109 above, 57.

[205] Emphasis added. See also Lillich, n. 71 above, 74 and Kellerson, n. 18 above, 39.

[206] Art. 13(2) and para. 15 respectively. This definition is broader than that found in para. 15(3) of R86, which is limited to the migrant worker's wife and minor children with favourable consideration to be given to other dependent family members.

[207] *General Survey*, n. 27 above, 121, paras. 421–2. The extension of the definition of 'family' to dependent adult children and parents was opposed at the drafting stage by a number of governments which preferred to retain as much discretion as possible with regard to the admission of adult or married children and other relatives: *Migrant Workers V(2)*, n. 111 above, 30 (opinions of New Zealand and the United Kingdom). The United Kingdom justified its position with the claim that it is impossible to ascertain the degree of dependence and precise relationships in the case of those migrants who are members of extended families. *Ibid.*

children unable to find work in the country of origin because of the lack of employment opportunities.[208]

In addition to the tendency of states not to admit some family members as provided for in the C143 definition, the Committee of Experts also found that the entry of migrant workers' families was normally subject to a number of prerequisites, for example, a proscribed period of residence, health requirements, the possession of sufficient resources, or adequate housing.[209] This approach is not surprising given the views of states during the drafting of the 1975 instruments, particularly with regard to the prerequisite of adequate housing.[210] Consequently, paragraph 13(2) of R151 provides that the migrant worker should have 'appropriate accommodation' which meets the standards normally applicable to nationals. This requirement is tempered somewhat by paragraph 16 which asserts that states should take full account of the needs of migrant workers and their families, *inter alia*, in particular in their policy 'regarding the construction of family housing [and] assistance in obtaining this housing . . .'.[211]

During the drafting of the 1975 instruments, concerns were expressed by states with regard to the difficulties of encouraging the reunification of short-term migrant workers with their families.[212] These have been recognized by the Committee of Experts, which has conceded that family reunification in the case of short-term or seasonal workers might not be possible. The fact that workers are required to find suitable accommodation before their families are permitted to join them indicates that the provisions in R151 were not drawn up with short-term stays in mind.[213] For those workers, however, who cannot have their families join them, R151 does provide for some measures in mitigation by allowing them to visit their families after one year of residence without the loss of their employment or residence rights, or to be visited by their families.[214] But these measures are not watertight and provide no additional protection to migrant workers in relation to nationals against the termination of their employment while on leave if their dismissal is otherwise valid.[215]

The ILO approach to family reunification in C143 and R151 was criticized during the 60th Session of the International Labour Conference for failing to

[208] *General Survey*, n. 27 above, 120, para. 422. [209] *Ibid*. 121, para. 426.

[210] *Migrant Workers VII(2)*, n. 83 above, 46, 49 and 61 (opinions of Germany, the United Kingdom, and Norway respectively).

[211] This provision was proposed by the USA delegation during the 60th Session of the International Labour Conference. *Record of Proceedings*, n. 93 above, 650, para. 126. In the *General Survey*, n. 27 above, 49, 121, para. 429, the Committee of Experts commended the Norwegian Government's policy of issuing grants to local authorities for housing immigrants and its establishment of a government-financed society to acquire and make available housing for this group.

[212] *Migrant Workers VII(2)*, n. 83 above, 46 and 59 and 61 (opinions of the Netherlands and France respectively). [213] *General Survey*, n. 27 above, 122, para. 431.

[214] See paras. 17(a), (b) respectively. Para. 18 of R151 adds that 'consideration should be given to the possibility of giving the migrant worker financial assistance towards the cost of travel envisaged in [para. 17] . . . or a reduction in the normal cost of transport, for instance by the arrangement of group travel'. [215] *General Survey*, n. 27 above, 123, para. 433.

recognize explicitly that the migrant worker has an inalienable right to a normal family life which cannot be refused or restricted by the state.[216] Undoubtedly, this approach is influenced by the perception that family reunification is a decisive stage in the migration process which may lead to the indefinite residence of migrant workers and their families, a situation unacceptable to those countries which do not consider themselves to be countries of immigration.[217]

(h) Health

Concern for the health of migrants in the country of employment is embodied in two objectives: to provide adequate health care for migrant workers and their families on the same basis as that provided for nationals and to ensure that migrant workers are protected in their work environment from special health risks.[218]

(i) The right to health care

There is no explicit provision in the ILO migrant workers instruments dealing with the right of migrant workers and their families to health care. As noted earlier, the definition of social security in C97 does not include medical care, although references to equal treatment between migrant workers and nationals in respect of medical assistance are made in R86, the Model Agreement annexed to R86 and in R100.[219] The equality provision in C143 does not specifically mention medical care, although it includes social security, which is defined under Recommendation No. 69 of 1944 concerning Medical Care and the latter two ILO Social Security Conventions (Nos. 118 and 157) to include medical care.[220] The strongest support for the above right is paragraph 2(i) of R151 which asserts that migrant workers and their families should enjoy effective equal opportunity and treatment with nationals in respect of 'conditions of life, including . . . the benefits of . . . health facilities'.[221]

Genuine equal treatment between migrants and nationals in respect of health or medical care requires a particular sensitivity to the special health problems of the former group. Paragraph 20 of R151 provides that all appropriate measures should be taken to prevent any special health risks to which migrant workers might be exposed. Three types of special health risk were identified by the preparatory work of the ILO on the 1975 instruments: conditions already suffered

[216] *Record of Proceedings*, n. 93 above, 794 (opinion of Mr. Stark, representative of the International Catholic Migration Commission).

[217] *Migrant Workers VII(2)*, n. 83 above, 47 (opinion of Germany).

[218] Art. 5 of C97 provides for measures protecting the health of migrants at the time of recruitment, travel, and arrival in the country of employment, but because the principal object of this chapter is to analyse the protection by the ILO of the rights of migrant workers while resident in the host country, these measures are not discussed here.

[219] Para. 12, Art. 17(2)(d) and paras. 46(a), (b) and (j) respectively.

[220] See nn. 187–190 above and accompanying text.

[221] Plender, n. 71 above, 305–6, observes that this clause is probably a satisfactory statement of the principle of equal treatment between migrants and nationals in respect of access to health care. Nonetheless, it is only to be found in a Recommendation, which has no legal force.

from by migrants in their countries of origin; disorders contracted in host countries where migrants may have inadequate immunity to certain diseases; and physical and psychological disorders peculiar to the process of adaptation to a new environment.[222] In addition, the health concerns of migrant women and children may be especially acute.[223] The health problems of migrant workers and their families are exacerbated by their linguistic and financial difficulties, their unfamiliarity with the health care system, the different cultural attitudes they may have towards this system, and by the generally poor socio-economic conditions in which they live.[224] Clearly, special measures are required to identify the disorders to which migrants are vulnerable and to assist them in obtaining the health care to suit their particular needs. Specially adapted social services may play an important role in providing such assistance.[225]

(ii) Occupational health and safety

Measures dealing with the occupational health and safety of migrant workers are located in paragraphs 21 to 22 of R151. Employment training should include instruction in occupational safety and hygiene. Migrants should be informed, in their own language if necessary and during paid working hours, of the laws, regulations and collective agreements concerned with the protection of workers. Finally, employers should ensure that migrant workers understand all the warnings, symbols and other signs relating to safety and health hazards at work. The training and instruction given to nationals may be inadequate for migrant workers and special measures are necessary to counteract their particular problems, which place them at a substantially greater risk of suffering industrial accidents than nationals.[226]

(i) Housing

The ILO report on *Migrant Workers* in 1973 observed that housing migrant workers and their families is one of the major problems faced by countries of

[222] *Migrant Workers VII(1)*, n. 64 above, 33; also cited by the Committee of Experts in its *General Survey*, n. 27 above, 123, para. 436.

[223] Report of the UN Secretary-General to the UN Commission for Social Development, 28th Session, Vienna, 7–16 Feb. 1983, *Social Integration. Pertinent Regulations concerning the Welfare of Migrant Workers and their Families*, UN Doc. E/CN.5/1983/10 (hereinafter *Welfare of Migrant Workers and their Families*), 16. Migrant women face particular health problems during pregnancy. Moreover, delivery is complicated by language problems, attachment to a particular tradition, and unfamiliarity with the hospital environment. *Ibid.* Migrant women, if married and not working, are also more likely to suffer from isolation in the host country in which their husbands are employed. See also *Migrant Workers VII(2)*, n. 83 above, 69 (opinion of Sweden).

[224] *Welfare of Migrant Workers and their Families*, n. 223 above, 16–17. See also *General Survey*, n. 27 above, 123–4, para. 437.

[225] R151 asserts that social services in the country of employment should give migrant workers and their families every assistance in adapting to the economic, social, and cultural environment of the country of employment (para. 24(a)) and should help them make full use of, *inter alia*, health services (para. 24(b)).

[226] Para. 22(2) of R151 emphasizes the need for special measures to ensure that migrant workers fully understand their training and instruction. See also *General Survey*, n. 27 above, 124, para. 440.

employment. The housing that migrant workers often seek is of the low- to medium-rent variety in urban industrial areas, which is likely to be in short supply. Such accommodation is chiefly to be found within the public housing sector and long waiting-lists make it difficult for newcomers to obtain it. In the private housing market, migrants encounter excessive rents, poor living conditions, and face a greater risk of exploitation, especially if they are in an irregular situation.[227] The provision of adequate housing to all migrant workers and their families residing in the country of employment has particular social significance, for it plays a vital role in assisting their integration into the society of that country.[228]

ILO instruments contain a number of explicit provisions concerned with the entitlement of migrant workers and their families to suitable housing. The equality provision in C97 maintains that migrant workers are to be treated equally with nationals in respect of accommodation. R86 requires states to ensure that migrant workers 'are provided in case of necessity with adequate accommodation, food and clothing on arrival in the country of immigration' and the Model Agreement annexed to R86 imposes an obligation on the host country to provide, subject to availability, suitable and hygienic housing to migrants and their families.[229] In R100, housing for migrant workers, which conforms with approved standards, is to be provided either at the expense of the employer or by the provision of appropriate financial aid. The competent local authority is responsible for ensuring the establishment of satisfactory housing conditions and for defining and enforcing minimum housing standards and the rights of workers with respect to accommodation.[230] Recommendation No. 115 of 1961 concerning Workers' Housing is the only ILO instrument devoted entirely to the question of workers' accommodation. Paragraph 2 of Part II of the Recommendation, which is concerned with the objectives of a national housing policy and which is found in the section on 'General Principles', stipulates:

> It should be an objective of national policy to promote, within the framework of general housing policy, the construction of housing and related community facilities with a view

[227] *Migrant Workers VII(1)*, n. 64 above, 43.

[228] *Welfare of Migrant Workers and their Families*, n. 223 above, 12, para. 39. The right to adequate housing is perhaps more important for migrants than the enjoyment of other rights, because the existence of suitable housing for migrant workers and their families establishes a social and materially secure base upon which these other rights can flourish.

[229] See respectively Art. 6(1)(a)(iii) of C97, para. 10(a) of R86 and Art. 20 of the Model Agreement. The reference to hygienic accommodation in the Model Agreement annexed to R86 is not repeated in Art. 6 of C97. Although the International Labour Conference was concerned with this question, it was excluded from C97 because it might have been interpreted as granting more favourable treatment to foreigners than to nationals: *General Survey*, n. 27 above, 89, para. 319.

[230] Paras. 21 and 22. Although employers should provide, or assist with the finding of, accommodation for migrant workers recruited through official channels (see *Migrant Workers VII(1)*, n. 64 above, 46), the provisions in R100 appear to be the only measures specifically referring to such an obligation. Böhning (1984), n. 22 above, Ch. 10, 249, observes that the Recommendation concerning Workers' Housing (see below) does not concern itself with this question.

to ensuring that adequate and decent housing accommodation and a suitable living environment are made available to *all workers and their families. A degree of priority should be accorded to those whose needs are most urgent.*[231]

In the section of the Recommendation which deals with suggestions concerning methods of application of the general principles, special attention is to be given to the problem of housing migrant workers and their families 'with a view to achieving as rapidly as possible equality of treatment between migrant workers and national workers in this respect' (Part I, paragraph 5). Unfortunately, this Recommendation is not accompanied by a legally binding Convention and its effectiveness, like R100, is therefore substantially reduced.

The only references to housing in the 1975 migrant workers instruments are in R151. Paragraph 2(i) states that migrant workers and their families should enjoy effective equality of opportunity and treatment with nationals in respect of, *inter alia*, 'conditions of life, including housing . . .'. The other references to housing in R151 are concerned with the question of accommodation as a prerequisite for family reunification and the requirement that states take the needs of migrant workers and their families into account in their housing construction and assistance policies. These were discussed earlier in the section on family reunification.

The drafting documents relating to the 1975 instruments on migrant workers and the General Survey carried out by the Committee of Experts in 1980 identify a number of problems which states encounter in their attempts to provide adequate accommodation for migrant workers and their families. Given that there is a shortage of accommodation in the public housing sector, short-term migrants face a struggle in obtaining this sort of accommodation for themselves and their families. Countries of employment may therefore have difficulty in providing for this particular group when there are long lists of nationals waiting for public housing.[232]

In addition to the existence of such long waiting-lists which disadvantage new applicants, some states have expressly discriminated in favour of nationals with regard to the allocation of public housing. In an observation in 1988, the Committee of Experts noted the position in Spain, where regulations accorded priority to Spaniards in the allocation of accommodation built under the auspices of the National Accommodation Institute, adding that these regulations were contrary to the principle of equal treatment in respect of accommodation laid down in Article 6(1)(a)(iii) of C97, which had been ratified by Spain. Accordingly, the Spanish Government changed its laws to ensure equal treatment between foreigners and nationals in respect of subsidized housing.[233] The existence of local autonomy, particularly in respect of the allocation of public housing, is another

[231] Emphasis added.

[232] Cf. *Migrant Workers VII(2)*, n. 83 above, 31 (opinion of the United Kingdom).

[233] *Report of the Committee of Experts* (1988), n. 140 above, 191–2.

factor which may limit the extent to which states are able to fulfil their housing obligations towards migrant workers and their families.[234]

Another problem arises if migrant workers' accommodation is connected to their employment and if that employment is terminated. Although there are measures preventing the establishment of a direct link between loss of job and the expulsion of migrant workers from the host country, no equivalent provision exists protecting migrants from the loss of accommodation tied to their previous employment. Efforts to include such a clause in R151[235] were regarded by the tripartite working party, set up by the Committee on Migrant Workers at the 60th Session of the International Labour Conference, as too specific for inclusion in a Recommendation dealing with general policy.[236]

In a number of countries, access to home ownership by foreigners is restricted. The Committee of Experts, however, has stated that this question does not come within the scope of the migrant workers instruments and that the equality provision in C97 in respect of accommodation cannot be taken to refer to access to home ownership or to the various forms of public assistance which may be granted to facilitate home ownership.[237]

Finally, the discussion of the problems faced by countries in housing migrant workers and their families would be incomplete without referring to the realities which exist in developing countries, particularly those of Latin America and Africa, to which migrants come to work. In these countries, the availability of adequate accommodation for both nationals and migrants leaves much to be desired, to the extent that it is difficult to isolate the problems of migrant workers and their families or to envisage special programmes for them. Such problems are particularly acute in urban centres, which attract national migrants from rural areas and international migrants seeking employment. These two groups mingle and congregate in large shanty-towns where conditions of housing and life in general are extremely poor indeed.[238]

Rights not specifically covered by ILO Instruments

Throughout this chapter, references have been made to matters that arguably fall outside the ILO's mandate in relation to the protection of migrant workers and their families, although the parameters of this mandate are admittedly nebulous and the rights necessary to protect people in their working environment clearly encompass a broader spectrum than merely those rights relating to adequate work and employment conditions. Earlier, it was maintained that economic and

[234] *Migrant Workers VII(2)*, n. 83 above, 83 (opinion of the United Kingdom). This is a problem which applies equally to other areas, such as education, and is particularly an issue in federal countries where the constituent units possess exclusive spheres of jurisdiction.

[235] *Migrant Workers V(2)*, n. 111 above, 35 (proposal of the former Yugoslavia).

[236] *Record of Proceedings*, n. 93 above, 650, para. 145.

[237] *General Survey*, n. 27 above, 89, paras. 319–20.

[238] *Migrant Workers V(1)*, n. 83 above, 50.

social rights constitute the ILO's basic thrust, and yet, as has already been discussed, the protection of the cultural rights of migrant workers and their families is also a specific concern of ILO instruments. Furthermore, it is by no means self-evident why the Committee of Experts considers the obligation 'to respect the basic human rights of all migrant workers' in Article 1 of C143 to apply only to certain so-called fundamental rights and not to others; for example, economic and social rights that are not specifically provided for in the migrant workers instruments, such as the right to food, education, and political rights. The only feasible explanation that might be offered for this very constrained approach is that to extend the concept of 'fundamental rights' to such matters would risk incurring disapproval from those governments that do not consider these rights to be so fundamental or at all applicable to migrant workers and their families, especially to those who reside and work in a country illegally.[239] This section examines those rights claimed by migrants in countries of employment which are not central to the ILO's remit, but which nonetheless find some support in the ILO instruments concerned with the protection of migrant workers and their families.

(a) Education

In its General Survey on the 1949 and 1975 migrant workers instruments, the Committee of Experts maintained, in assessing the scope of 'cultural rights' in Article 10 of C143, that education did not in principle lie within the ILO's field of competence.[240] Educational rights, however, are referred to both expressly and by implication in the migrant workers instruments. Arguably, the very objective to secure effective equality of opportunity and treatment between migrants and nationals is severely compromised without some provision for the education of the former. Indeed, paragraph 2(i) of R151 seeks to realize this objective in respect of 'conditions of life, including . . . the benefits of . . . educational . . . facilities'.[241] Similarly, education is a crucial component in the general programme aimed at the adaptation and integration of migrant workers into the society of the receiving country.[242] The education of migrant workers and their families has essentially two facets: workers' education and the education of migrant children. The former, which is clearly relevant to ILO responsibilities to

[239] See also n. 126 above, for the possible explanation that Art. 1, because it applies to both regular and irregular migrants, may only cover those 'fundamental rights' whose exercise does not presuppose lawful residence in the country of employment.

[240] *General Survey*, n. 27 above, 88, para. 315.

[241] Art. 17(2)(a)(iii) of the Model Agreement in the Annex to R86 expands the equality provision in Art. 6 of C97 with respect to the question of education. The clause obliges the country of employment to secure equal treatment between migrant workers and nationals in respect of 'admission to schools, to apprenticeship and to courses or schools for vocational or technical training'. However, this positive wording is severely compromised by the following phrase which reads: 'provided that this does not prejudice nationals of the country of immigration'.

[242] *Migrant Workers VII(1)*, n. 64 above, 41.

people in their working environment, is considered in this section, in recognition of the intrinsic link between these two kinds of education and also to ensure consistency with the consideration of these matters elsewhere in this study.

(i) Workers' education: vocational training and language instruction

Clearly, workers' education can serve as a catalyst for improving the working environment and is therefore most relevant to the ILO's realm of responsibility. It must not be considered in isolation but within a more comprehensive context which includes language training, pre-vocational and vocational training, and basic civic and political instruction.[243] These different aspects of workers' training can all be detected in the migrant workers instruments. Article 6(1)(a)(i) of C97 ensures to migrant workers equal treatment with nationals in respect of 'apprenticeship and training'. Further to the obligation in Article 10 of C143 to declare and pursue a national policy to promote and guarantee equality of opportunity and treatment in respect of, *inter alia*, 'employment and occupation', which encompasses vocational training, Article 12(c) imposes a broad educational duty on member states to inform migrant workers of this policy:

> Each Member State shall, by methods appropriate to national conditions and practice,
>
> . . .
>
> take measures, encourage educational programmes and develop other activities aimed at acquainting migrant workers as fully as possible with the policy, with their rights and obligations and with activities designed to give effective assistance to migrant workers in the exercise of their rights and for their protection.

This provision must also be viewed within the context of a general social policy which, in addition to enabling migrants to share in the advantages enjoyed by nationals, takes into account the special needs which migrants might have during their adaptation to the society of the country of employment.[244] Measures to familiarize migrants with the language or languages of the latter country play an important role in this process. Paragraph 7(1)(b) of R151 provides for the teaching of such languages to migrant workers during working hours. There are also analogous provisions enabling migrants to receive information and instruction in their own language about their rights in the host country.[245] Equal access by migrant workers with national workers to vocational training is also ensured in paragraph 2(b) of R151. The difficulties, however, of making such training

[243] *ILO Action on Behalf of Migrants*, n. 20 above, 11–12, para. 29, citing from *Symposium on the Workers' Education Needs of Migrant Workers*, Report ILO/WEP/S28/D4, para. 4 (Annex to the Report on the Symposium presented to the Governing Body, 194th Session, ILO Doc. GB.194/10/34).

[244] *General Survey*, n. 27 above, 104, para. 390 with reference to Art. 12(e) of C143. See also the section on social policy in R151 (Pt II).

[245] See para. 7(1)(a) generally and para. 21(2) with regard to occupational health and safety.

available to 'seasonal' or short-term workers given the restrictions imposed on free choice of employment have already been noted.

(ii) Education of migrant children

The education of migrant children involves general instruction in the host country and teaching in their native language and culture. The latter question has already been discussed in the section on cultural rights together with examples on the ways teaching the native language and culture to the children of migrant workers is carried out in a number of countries.

As far as general educational instruction to the children of migrant workers is concerned, special measures are necessary to tackle a number of problems which arise largely because of the enrolment of significant numbers of these children in the educational system of the host country. Practical problems concerning lack of classroom space, shortage of teachers, and difficulties in matching by age group the educational level of migrant children to local children in schools are exacerbated by largely xenophobic public fears that the enrolment of migrant children lowers the level of education generally, thus affecting the welfare of local children. In addition, the children of migrant workers face the personal struggle of adapting to life in two cultures.[246] One way of attempting to deal with some of these problems is the establishment of special adaptation classes for the children of migrant workers with a view to integrating them into the regular educational system.[247] Although there are no explicit provisions in the ILO migrant workers instruments concerned with special educational measures for the children of migrant workers, this question should be considered together with the broader objective of the adaptation and integration of migrant workers and their families into the society of the receiving country, as outlined in paragraph 7(1)(b) and in the social policy in R151.

Two other matters are worth noting briefly with regard to the education of the children of migrant workers. First, claims to equal treatment with nationals in respect of the granting of scholarships and educational assistance, a question of particular relevance to the pursuit of higher education, are weak under ILO instruments.[248] Secondly, as has already been observed with reference to migrant workers' housing, the chronic shortage of educational facilities in developing

[246] *Migrant Workers VII(1)*, n. 64 above, 41.

[247] *Ibid.*; *General Survey*, n. 27 above, 105, para. 395. Collaboration between countries of origin and countries of employment with regard to the education of the children of migrant workers should also be encouraged: *Migrant Workers VII(2)*, n. 83 above, 83 (opinion of Turkey).

[248] The Committee of Experts maintained in its *General Survey*, n. 27 above, 88, para. 315, with reference to 'cultural rights' in Art. 10 of C143, that this general principle cannot regulate all questions resulting from its application, particularly those concerned with the granting of scholarships and other forms of educational assistance. The Committee also noted that the 1960 UNESCO Convention against Discrimination in Education, discussed in Ch. 2, only prohibits expressly different treatment *as between nationals* with regard to scholarships and other forms of educational assistance (Art. 3(1)(c)).

countries is bound to affect adversely both the children of foreign migrant workers and nationals alike.[249]

(b) Political rights

Political rights are defined in Article 25 of the ICCPR as the right to take part in the conduct of public affairs, the right of equal access to the public service, and the right to vote and to be elected to political office. The ILO instruments relating to migrant workers only contain references to the first two rights.

The International Labour Conference Committee on Migrant Workers and the Committee of Experts have explicitly stated that political rights, in particular the right to participation in public affairs, are not included in the expression 'individual and collective freedoms' in Article 10 of C143.[250] The drafting history of C143 reveals a disagreement between states that wanted to exclude questions of political participation from the instrument and those states and workers' members that insisted on granting a degree of political participation to migrant workers. One government delegation argued that political rights should be outside the scope of the proposed C143 and that reference to voting rights in particular was inappropriate for an international labour instrument.[251] Proponents of affording migrant workers some form of political participation viewed it as a necessary aspect of their integration into the country of employment: '[I]t was not only possible but desirable, in order to promote genuine integration of the workers in the host country, to seek to have them enter into certain commitments at the level of the local community'.[252] In the end, the International Labour Conference Committee on Migrant Workers decided not to expressly exclude political rights from C143 in order to avoid the negative effects that might have resulted from such express exclusion in view of the changing attitudes in a number of countries to granting migrant workers rights to political participation at the local level.[253] Such participation is arguably necessary in order to guarantee to migrant workers the enjoyment of their rights in C143:

[249] *Migrant Workers VII(1)*, n. 64 above, 42.

[250] *General Survey*, n. 27 above, 88, para. 316.

[251] *Migrant Workers VII(2)*, n. 83 above, 24 (opinion of the United Kingdom); *Migrant Workers V(1)*, n. 83 above, 42 (Miss Green, Government delegate, United Kingdom).

[252] *Migrant Workers V(1)*, *ibid.* 46 (Mr. Cavazutti, Workers' advisor, Italy and Vice-Chairman of the Committee on Migrant Workers at the 59th Session of the International Labour Conference).

[253] *Migrant Workers V(1)*, *ibid.* 12, para. 60; *General Survey*, n. 27 above, 89, para. 316. During the 60th Session of the International Labour Conference, the French Government wanted to add the words 'within the competence of the ILO' after the expression 'individual and collective freedoms' in the draft Art. 10 of C143. Although this amendment was supported by employers' members, it was opposed by workers' members on the grounds that public opinion was evolving in many countries *vis-à-vis* freedoms and civic rights for migrant workers. *Record of Proceedings*, n. 93 above, 644, para. 57. See also *Migrant Workers V(2)*, n. 111 above, 16, citing the opinion of Finland supporting the political participation of migrant workers at the local level. For examples where migrants have voting rights at the municipal level in European countries of employment, see the section on political rights in Ch. 8.

In order to fully implement the spirit and letter of the [1975] ILO Convention and to secure equal economic, social and cultural rights for migrants, their participation in politics, at least on a local level, is imperative . . . Political parties are more likely to pay attention to the needs of migrants if their success at the polls is determined, in part, on the votes of migrant workers . . . It seems only reasonable that, since migrants contribute to the development of the countries they are in by undertaking those tasks citizens are not willing to perform and by paying taxes, they should have some say in how these funds are spent.[254]

The question whether migrant workers may hold public office or work in the public service is considered implicitly by Article 14(c) of C143 which permits states to 'restrict access to limited categories of employment or functions where this is necessary in the interests of the state'. An identical provision is found in paragraph 6(c) of R151. In preparatory work on the 1975 instruments, the International Labour Office noted that foreigners are often excluded in many countries from certain sectors of employment, such as the public service or certain occupations that are regarded as being better reserved, in the public interest, for nationals.[255] The Committee of Experts has observed that the concept of 'public service' may cover a very wide range of activities which vary from country to country. With this point in mind, the Committee has drawn the attention of governments to the conditions which they must fulfil in Article 14(c) before restricting the access of foreign migrant workers to the public service. The exceptions which states parties make must only apply to *limited categories of employment or functions* and must also be necessary *in the interests of the state*.[256] Once these conditions are satisfied, however, it is significant that access to the specified employment may be restricted indefinitely, in contrast with Article 14(a) which only permits restrictions on the access of migrant workers to other kinds of employment for a period not exceeding 2 years.[257]

(c) Residence rights, protection from expulsion and the right to stay

The ILO instruments relating to migrant workers make no explicit reference to a right to stay or to permanent residence in the state of employment, or to naturalization. Provisions exist, however, providing a limited right of residence to migrant workers, such as those protecting them against unfair expulsion from the host country on termination of their employment. Article 8 of C97 prohibits the expulsion of migrant workers and their families admitted to the territory of

254 Russo, n. 109 above, 57–8. 255 *Migrant Workers VII(1)*, n. 64 above, 19.

256 *General Survey*, n. 27 above, 96, para. 359. The Committee, *ibid.* 96, para. 359 (n. 87), referred to an interesting development in Australia where the Royal Commission on Australian Government Administration recommended the abolition of the requirement of Australian citizenship as a general condition of entry into the Australian civil service and that it should only be retained as a condition of qualification for certain special posts, for example, in national security and diplomatic services. In Canada, the Supreme Court has rejected the claim that lawyers need to be citizens because of the public functions they perform. See *Andrews* v. *Law Society of British Columbia* [1989] 1 SCR 143, 56 DLR (4th) 1. 257 *General Survey*, n. 27 above, 96, para. 357.

a member state on a permanent basis because of loss of occupation on account of illness or injury arising after entry to the country of employment. Paragraph 18(1) of R86 is a similar provision, but applies to all lawfully admitted migrant workers and urges member states to refrain 'as far as possible' from expelling migrants on account of their lack of means or the condition of the employment market unless there is an agreement to this effect between the countries of emigration and immigration. Paragraph 18(2)(a) maintains, however, that such an agreement should take into account the length of a migrant's stay in the country of employment and that, in principle, no migrant is to be removed after 5 years of residence.[258] C143 contains more forceful provisions against unfair removal. Article 8(1) provides that legally resident migrants are not to be regarded as being in an irregular situation simply because of their loss of employment, which should not in itself imply the withdrawal of a work or residence permit.[259] Such measures are necessary to prevent potential exploitation by employers, who, by terminating the employment of migrant workers, might also effectively determine their stay in the host country.[260] Despite the manifest fairness of Article 8(1) of C143, the drafting history of the clause indicates, nonetheless, that some countries were opposed to it on the basis that the expulsion of migrants upon termination of their employment might be deemed necessary in order to safeguard the interests of national workers in a declining labour market.[261] Such an attitude still persists despite these promising ILO provisions. According to Goodwin-Gill, these standards:

> have not been noticeably followed in many of the labour-importing countries in Western Europe, where the unemployment of the migrant labour force has been viewed as a social and economic burden that is best re-exported to the home State. Studies also have confirmed, for example, that ethnic minorities in Western Europe, which is what the migrant

[258] The Committee invoked para. 18 in a recent observation to Nigeria in connection with massive expulsion measures taken against Chadian migrant workers: International Labour Conference, 82nd Session, 1995, Report III(4A), *Report of the Committee of Experts on the Application of Conventions and Recommendations* (Geneva: International Labour Office, 1995) 236.

[259] See also Plender, n. 71 above, 302 and 306 and Goodwin-Gill (1986), n. 94 above, 17–18. The Committee of Experts underlined in its General Survey, n. 27 above, 146, para. 511, that this provision does not require the renewal or extension of the residence permits of migrant workers. Paras. 30–34 of R151, however, elaborate somewhat on Art. 8 of C143 and also appear to be more generous in their application to this question. Para. 31 provides that migrants who lose their employment should be given sufficient time to find alternative employment at least for a period corresponding to that during which they may be entitled to unemployment benefit. Moreover, the residence permit should be extended accordingly.

[260] *Migrant Workers VII(1)*, n. 64 above, 51. These provisions, however, are not watertight. Even if migrants are permitted to stay in the host country in order to seek alternative employment, they might effectively be prevented from doing so by the restrictions on their free choice of employment in Art. 14(a) of C143. See also *General Survey*, n. 27 above, 65, para. 234.

[261] *Migrant Workers VII(2)*, n. 83 above, 74 (opinion of Austria). It is noteworthy that Art. 8 of C143, introduced as a result of an amendment by the workers' members of Finland and Sweden, was opposed by the government members of France, Germany, and the USA. *Record of Proceedings*, n. 93 above, 642, para. 45.

labour force has become, remain vulnerable to dismissal during recession and generally have high rates of unemployment.[262]

In the debate during drafting on the right to free choice of employment for migrant workers in C143, some government delegations, workers' members and NGOs called for a 'right to stay' to be included in the 1975 instruments. An argument was advanced by one government delegation to accord the right to stay to those migrant workers who have been accepted for residence.[263] Another argued that no limits should be imposed on the residence of migrants in the country of employment with the exception of skilled workers.[264] Though not going so far as to propose an explicit right to stay for migrant workers, one government was of the opinion that the length of employment and residence of workers as well as other relevant social factors should be taken into consideration before a state decides *not* to renew a residence permit.[265]

The workers' members, however, were most vociferous in advocating the inclusion of a right to stay in the 1975 ILO instruments. Indeed, in the debate in the Conference Committee during the 59th Session of the International Labour Conference, the workers' members proposed that the following provision be included in R151: 'The migrant workers who have regularly occupied a job in a country will be authorized to reside in this country as long as they desire and to obtain employment there'. This amendment was strongly opposed by the employers' members and several government members and was subsequently withdrawn.[266] According to one workers' member, a blind deferment to sovereignty by states in this regard was unjustified and merely relegated the labour performed by migrant workers to that of a commodity.[267] During the 60th Session of the International Labour Conference, the proposal to insert in R151 a clear definition of a right to stay was advanced on the basis that the country of employment had a duty to grant this right to migrant workers within its territory:

> The host country should assume an obligation towards a worker whom it has encouraged to come and contribute to its economic development and, in exchange, should give him a veritable permanent right to reside there and to renew his employment contract.[268]

In spite of these powerful moral pleas, however, there is no right to stay, to permanent residence, or to naturalization in the ILO instruments on migrant workers.

[262] G. S. Goodwin-Gill, 'International Law and Human Rights: Trends Concerning International Migrants and Refugees' (1989) 23 IMR 526, 535 (footnote omitted).

[263] *Migrant Workers VII(2)*, n. 83 above, 5 (opinion of Sweden). Otherwise, benefits guaranteed by laws and international agreements are rendered illusory if residence is subject to a time-limit. *Ibid.*

[264] *Migrant Workers V(2)*, n. 111 above, 83 (opinion of Turkey).

[265] *Ibid.* 75 (opinion of Iran).

[266] *Migrant Workers V(1)*, n. 83 above, 24, para. 153.

[267] *Ibid.* 38 (opinion of Mr. Cavazutti, Italy and Vice-Chairman of the Conference Committee). Mr. Cavazutti, *ibid.*, added: 'It would be inhuman to prevent migrant workers, who had legally occupied a job in a country, from staying there if they so wished or from obtaining employment there'.

[268] *Record of Proceedings*, n. 93 above, 794 (Mr. Stark, International Catholic Migration Commission).

Irregular migrant workers

This chapter has thus far mainly considered the protection by the ILO of those migrant workers and their families who are lawfully resident and legally employed in the host country. Although the protection of irregular migrants by the ILO would appear to be inconsistent with one of its objectives as set out in its original Constitution, namely the 'equitable economic treatment of all workers *lawfully resident*' in member states,[269] the plight of those who have entered the country in a clandestine fashion to work, or those who have entered legally but who have taken up employment without authorization, cannot be ignored by the ILO. Indeed, to do so would be to neglect a problem affecting a considerable number of workers in the world today.

In its preparatory work for the 1975 instruments, the International Labour Office acknowledged that undocumented migrant workers are particularly vulnerable to exploitation in the host country, for example: in employment, they are unlikely to complain about unfavourable conditions and forego certain rights to which they are entitled for fear of losing their job or being deported;[270] in housing, their situation is especially severe, since they rarely have access to accommodation provided by the employer or subsidized by the state;[271] and, if their families are with them, similar problems arise in respect of their education, health, and welfare, because these families, of course, have not arrived legally under normal family reunification arrangements and, therefore, also acquire an irregular status in the country of employment.[272]

References to illegal migration in the 1949 migrant workers instruments are minimal, probably because this question was not considered as much of a problem as it is today. It is worth recalling in this context that the promotion of migration for employment from countries with a surplus of labour to those with a deficiency received official ILO backing in 1949.[273] The only explicit reference in the 1949 instruments to illegal migration concerns the state obligation to penalize, by way of 'appropriate penalties', those promoting clandestine or illegal immigration.[274]

The 1975 migrant workers instruments were largely influenced by the growth in clandestine migration during the 1960s and early 1970s.[275] Indeed, Part I of C143 is devoted entirely to the suppression of migrations in abusive conditions. Although the focus of the study is on the situation of both legal and illegal migrants and their families already in the country of employment and the provisions relating to their protection, it is clear that the effectiveness of the measures in much of Part I of C143, designed to prevent clandestine migrations, will determine the number of undocumented workers who enter the host country in

[269] Art. 41, point 8 (emphasis added). See also n. 62 above and accompanying text.
[270] *Migrant Workers VII(1)*, n. 64 above, 24 and 51. [271] *Ibid.* 43. [272] *Ibid.* 32.
[273] Para. 4(1) of R86. [274] Art. 8 of Annex I and Art. 13 of Annex II to C97.
[275] *ILO Action on Behalf of Migrants*, n. 20 above, 6, para. 17.

the first place. The importance of these measures, therefore, should not be minimized. Although the state duty in Article 1 of C143 to respect the basic human rights of *all* migrant workers extends to illegal migrants,[276] the rights to be protected under this provision are 'fundamental' rights only and do not include the right to equal opportunity and treatment with nationals.[277] Illegal migrants are excluded from the protectional scope of this right in both C97 and C143.[278] In spite of these restrictions, the 1975 instruments still contain greater protection for the rights of illegal workers than those of 1949. Article 2 of C143 obliges member states to seek systematically to determine whether there are illegally employed migrant workers in their territories and whether, *inter alia*, the conditions to which they are subject during their period of residence and employment contravene relevant international multilateral or bilateral instruments or agreements, or national laws or regulations. It is noteworthy that the terms of Article 2 cover not only employment conditions but also living conditions such as housing standards, which are governed by relevant international agreements or national laws.[279]

In addition to this general duty to be aware of the conditions in which illegal migrants work and reside, states are also under an obligation, by virtue of Article 6(1) of C143, to define and apply sanctions in respect of the illegal employment and trafficking of migrant workers.[280] Although the provision provides member states with the discretion to define the offence of 'illegal employment',[281] this should not mean that the imposition of punishments is to be transferred from employers to migrant workers themselves. Article 6 presupposes that national law renders unlawful the employer's act and not the alien's presence.[282] In examining state practice, however, the Committee of Experts found that under the laws of some countries only the worker is guilty of an offence.[283]

[276] *Record of Proceedings*, n. 93 above, 641, para. 29; *General Survey*, n. 27 above, 69, para. 257; Lillich, n. 71 above, 73.

[277] See nn. 125–6 above and accompanying text.

[278] Art. 6 of C97 and Pt II of C143. Both Art. 6 of C97 and Art. 10 of C143 apply to those migrant workers 'lawfully' within the territory of the country of employment. It should be recalled that the division of C143 into two separate parts was criticized during the drafting on the basis that providing equality of treatment to *all* workers, regular and irregular alike, would greatly contribute to discouraging illicit trafficking in migrant labour. See n. 113 above. See also *Record of Proceedings*, n. 93 above, 638, para. 15.

[279] *General Survey*, n. 27 above, 65, para. 234.

[280] These are to be 'administrative, civil and penal sanctions, which include imprisonment in their range'. Art. 6(2) of C143, however, enables employers, in the event of prosecution for hiring an illegal worker, to furnish proof of their good faith, presumably on the basis that they were unaware of the worker's undocumented status.

[281] *General Survey*, n. 27 above, 66, para. 241.

[282] See also Plender, n. 71 above, 304 and J. Niessen, 'Immigrants and Migrant Workers' in A. Eide, C. Krause, and A. Rosas, (eds.), *Economic, Social and Cultural Rights: A Textbook* (1995) 323, 327.

[283] *General Survey*, n. 27 above, 66, para. 239. In its preparatory work on the 1975 instruments, the International Labour Office found that undocumented workers in a number of countries were not only subject to deportation, but also to fines. *Migrant Workers VII(1)*, n. 64 above, 12–16. Art. 9(3) of C143 provides that migrant workers and their families are not to bear the cost of their expulsion from the country of employment. Para. 8(5) of R151 contains an identical provision. The Committee of Experts has emphasized, however, that migrants are only exempt from payment of the

Although the equality provisions in Part II of C143 are inapplicable to migrants in an irregular situation, Article 9(1) provides that illegal migrant workers should enjoy, together with their families, equality of treatment 'in respect of rights arising out of past employment as regards remuneration, social security and other benefits'. Equal treatment, in this case, is with regular migrant workers and not with nationals.[284] The purpose of this clause is to ensure that illegal migrant workers receive wages and other benefits for the work which they have actually performed,[285] and to prevent employers from claiming that the illegality of the employment precludes them from paying the worker or from making the appropriate social security contributions resulting from the employment.[286] The application of equal treatment between illegal migrants and regular migrants in respect of social security rights is limited in scope and also gives rise to a number of problems. The Committee of Experts has emphasized that equal treatment only applies in respect of social security rights *arising out of past employment* and does not extend to benefits which are not dependent on a period of work. In addition, illegal migrants must complete other qualifying conditions required in the case of legally employed migrants. Problems arise, however, when, as the Committee discovered, countries make benefits conditional upon legal residence or upon the possession of a valid work permit.[287]

The 1975 instruments also contain two provisions referring to the regularization of undocumented migrant workers. Article 9(4) of C143 asserts that 'nothing in this Convention shall prevent Members from giving persons who are illegally residing or working within the country the right to stay and to take up legal employment'. This clause is declaratory only and does not constitute an obligation.[288] Furthermore, paragraph 8(1) of R151 urges member states to decide speedily whether or not an undocumented migrant's situation may be regularized.

In its General Survey, the Committee of Experts concluded that the existence

administrative or judicial costs (or both) of the expulsion proceedings and not from payment for travel to the country of origin. *General Survey*, n. 27 above, 72, para. 274 and 147, para. 516. See also Kellerson, n. 18 above, 37. This may, therefore, constitute a form of financial penalty for those migrants who are apprehended and who have sufficient funds to cover the cost of their journey home.

[284] *General Survey*, n. 27 above, 69, para. 260; Goodwin-Gill (1986), n. 94 above, 18.

[285] *General Survey*, n. 27 above; Kellerson, n. 18 above, 37. States were concerned during the drafting process that Art. 9(1) should not have too broad a coverage and that it should be restricted strictly to employment matters. *Migrant Workers VI(2)*, n. 83 above, 39–40 (opinions of Belgium, the former Czechoslovakia, Germany, Sweden, and the USA). Para. 8(3) of R151, a similar provision to Art. 9(1) of C143, extends equal treatment between illegal migrants and lawful migrants to 'trade union membership and exercise of trade union rights'.

[286] Kellerson, n. 18 above.

[287] *General Survey*, n. 27 above, 71, paras. 265–6. Para. 34(1) of R151 provides that *all* migrant workers 'irrespective of the legality of [their] stay', on leaving the country of employment, are entitled to the following benefits in addition to any outstanding remuneration for work performed: severance pay normally due; employment injury benefit in respect of any employment injury suffered; compensation in lieu of holiday entitlement acquired but not used; and reimbursement of any social security contributions which have not accorded and will not accord rights under national laws or regulations or international arrangements.

[288] *General Survey*, n. 27 above, 73, para. 277.

of provisions relating to illegal migrant workers in Part I of C143 constitute further obstacles to the ratification of the instrument. Practical problems such as lack of administrative machinery and length of land frontiers make enforcement of these provisions difficult in some countries. Furthermore, the provision concerning employer sanctions is not acceptable in those countries where it is not an offence for employers to hire illegal migrants or where imprisonment is not included among the penalties.[289] Despite these obstacles, the 1975 migrant workers instruments, particularly C143, are to be commended because they acknowledge, at least, that the problem of illegal migration exists and endeavour to deal with this problem by not only drawing up measures to suppress this kind of migration altogether, but also by providing limited protection for those irregular workers already in the country of employment. These protective measures are far from comprehensive, but they are a step in the right direction. They should be seen, however, not as an end in themselves, but only as a means to achieving real solutions to the problem of illegal migration, which, as the Committee of Experts has pointed out, will only be resolved through collaboration between countries of immigration and emigration as well as long-term action to alleviate the lack of economic opportunities existing in the latter.[290]

3.6 CONCLUSION

This chapter has provided a comprehensive analysis of the protection of the economic, social, cultural, political, and residence rights of migrant workers and their families under the auspices of the ILO. The standards applicable to migrants under ILO instruments represent only the minimum required for their protection,[291] but they are also innovative, rich in detail and break new ground, particularly with respect to the question of free choice of employment, and economic and social rights, such as rights to social security, housing, and the education of migrant children. Furthermore, C143 is the first international convention to expressly afford rights to migrants in an irregular situation.

Unfortunately, the ILO instruments concerning migrant workers seem to have been generally ignored by the international community, particularly by countries to which migrant workers and their families tend to migrate. The latest instruments were adopted in 1975 and yet C143 had received only 17 ratifications as at the beginning of 1996, with only a handful from migrant-receiving countries. This is perhaps not surprising given the admission by the Committee of Experts in 1980 that the ratification prospects for C143 were not very encouraging in view of the numerous problems which both of its parts give rise to in a number of member states.[292]

289 *Ibid.* 145 and 146, paras. 501 and 508 respectively.

290 *Ibid.* 145, para. 501.

291 *Welfare of Migrant Workers and their Families*, n. 223 above, 22, para. 64.

292 *General Survey*, n. 27 above, 150, para. 528.

Have ILO efforts, therefore, to protect this vulnerable and frequently exploited group of workers and human beings been in vain? It is easy to succumb to cynicism and point to the perceived ineffectiveness of international human rights instruments to breach the walls of state sovereignty, especially in areas such as immigration and access to employment which countries hold as cornerstones of national self-interest and which they are loath to submit to even the slightest outside tinkering. Nonetheless, ILO standards for the protection of migrant workers and their families, though effectively dormant in practice, continue to be important in theory. In many respects, they are superior to the provisions of the more recent UN Convention, which are examined in the next chapter, and to many of the standards devised in Europe for the protection of migrants. In contrast with other international human rights instruments, over whose design states have greater if not exclusive control, the unique tripartite contribution by governments, employers, and workers to the content of ILO standards make them a worthy foundation on which to build further safeguards for migrant workers and their families.

In times of substantial employment instability in western industrialized countries, a corresponding increase in migration pressures caused by political, economic, and social uncertainty in central and eastern Europe, and continuing and ever deepening poverty in the developing world, the principles proclaimed by these standards must remain a constant and welcome reminder of our moral obligation to choose the dignity of human labour over the pursuit of a blind economic expediency.

4

The United Nations International Convention on the Protection of the Rights of All Migrant Workers and Members of their Families

4.1 INTRODUCTION

The International Convention on the Protection of the Rights of All Migrant Workers and Members of Their Families (ICMW) was adopted by the UN General Assembly without a vote on 18 December 1990.[1] It is said to be the 'culmination of [an] evolutionary process' which has seen the development of universal standards protecting the rights of non-nationals.[2] This process began, as examined in Chapter 2, with the endorsement of international human rights standards applicable to all human beings, the adoption of the UDHR and its 'codification' in the two UN Covenants. As observed in the previous chapter, the adoption by the ILO of international labour standards pertaining specifically to migrant workers, particularly Convention No. 143 of 1975, was a further step in this process.

The question which begs an answer is whether the ICMW is indeed the culmination of this 'evolutionary process', or whether it falls short of affording adequate protection for migrant workers and their families. In gauging the extent to which it safeguards the economic, social, cultural, political, and residence rights of migrants, this chapter also seeks to answer the above question by comparing the standards in the ICMW with those of other international instruments examined earlier. References are also made, where appropriate, to some of the European instruments which are the focus of the European case study. Because the ICMW is only a recent addition to the plethora of international human rights instruments, any attempt to provide an authoritative interpretation of its provisions risks being rather a speculative exercise. Consequently, by resorting extensively to the *travaux préparatoires*, some of this speculation concerning the interpretation of the ICMW may be avoided.

The text of the ICMW and the *travaux préparatoires* reflect numerous tensions and compromises. In their attempt to cover, almost without exception, *all* the human rights of *all* migrant workers and their families, the drafters of the

[1] GA Res. 45/158. The text of the ICMW can be found in (1991) 30 ILM 1517 and in I. Brownlie, (ed.), *Basic Documents on Human Rights*, 3rd edn. (1992) 203.

[2] See A. Helton, 'The New Convention from the Perspective of a Country of Employment: The US Case' (1991) 25 IMR 848, 849.

ICMW embarked on a thorough definition of 'migrant worker' and chose to distinguish between those migrants with legal status from those in an irregular or non-documented situation by providing the former with more rights. This division is the clearest illustration of the schism between the protection of migrants' rights and the principle of state sovereignty underlying the whole text. Protection of national interests is further evident in the debate between developed and developing countries that took place during the drafting process. The ICMW also reveals a jurisdictional conflict between the UN and the ILO. This conflict came to the fore when the decision was taken to draft a convention concerning migrant workers and their families under the auspices of the UN and not the ILO.

The tensions and compromises in the ICMW give rise to a complex instrument. The intention is not to unravel the intricacies of this document completely, but to concentrate on the following question: does the ICMW indeed advance the rights of migrant workers and their families? This question must also be considered in the light of the startling fact that only seven states had ratified the ICMW as at 1 November 1996. In contrast, the Convention on the Rights of the Child, which was adopted by the UN General Assembly just one year earlier, had already received 185 ratifications.

4.2 UN CONCERN FOR THE PROTECTION OF THE RIGHTS OF MIGRANT WORKERS AND THEIR FAMILIES

The early Resolutions

The UN's concern for the protection of migrant workers and their families commenced in earnest in 1972 with ECOSOC Resolution 1706 (LIII) of 28 July 1972, which noted with alarm and indignation incidents involving the illegal transportation and exploitation of workers. The Resolution condemned this exploitation, appealed to governments, *inter alia*, to combat and prevent the malpractices in question and instructed the UN Commission on Human Rights to consider the matter and to recommend further action.[3]

The belated entry of the UN into the migration debate was probably the result of a 1947 agreement between the UN and the ILO. This agreement set out the competencies of both organizations with respect to migration. The ILO was to be concerned with migrants as workers and the UN was to be concerned with their status as aliens.[4] The work of the UN with respect to the protection of the

[3] The Resolution took note of the steps taken by the ILO to reinforce its actions for the protection of migrant workers and also invited the ILO to undertake an energetic examination of the problem. The ILO's investigation led to the adoption of Convention No. 143 and Recommendation No. 151, considered in the previous chapter.

[4] 'Co-ordination of International Responsibility in the Field of Migration' (1947) 30 *ILO Official Bulletin* 417, cited by M. Hasenau, 'ILO Standards on Migrant Workers: The Fundamentals of the UN Convention and Their Genesis' (1991) 25 IMR 687, 693.

rights of aliens or non-citizens, culminating in the 1985 Declaration, has been examined in Chapter 2. It would appear, however, that this agreement between the UN and the ILO has lost much, if not all, of its validity as a result of the adoption of the ICMW.

The UN General Assembly expressed its concern for migrants in a series of resolutions in the 1970s.[5] This was a period of great flux for migrants everywhere. In Europe, for example, the soaring economic growth of the 1960s and early 1970s ended with the oil crisis of 1973–4 and the deep recession which followed. Official migration to certain European countries of employment came to rather an abrupt halt,[6] but few migrant workers returned home. Instead, the number of migrants in countries of employment actually increased because of family reunion.[7] Restrictions on immigration also resulted in an increase in clandestine movements.[8]

The General Assembly resolutions focused on a number of questions of concern in the migration field. The first Resolution in 1972 considered the exploitation of labour through illicit and clandestine trafficking and also expressed alarm at the discriminatory treatment meted out to foreign workers, particularly in Europe.[9] Subsequent resolutions called for efforts to be undertaken by states to combat the problems that existed. In particular, these resolutions advocated the promotion of bilateral agreements to reduce the illicit traffic in foreign workers as well as measures to ensure equal treatment between legal migrants and nationals in the country of employment. They also appealed to states to respect the human rights of those workers who succeeded in breaching the barriers of national sovereignty by entering illegally and finding unauthorized employment.[10] The equality principle was elaborated in Resolution 32/120 of 1977, which invited states, in paragraph 2(a), to accord to regular migrants equal opportunity and treatment with nationals in respect of employment, social security, trade union and cultural rights, and individual and collective freedoms. The Resolution called for state policies relating to training, health, social services, housing, and educational and cultural development for migrant workers and their families (paragraph 3). It also emphasized the need to normalize family life through family reunion (paragraph 8). Lastly, the later General Assembly resolutions urged states to ratify existing ILO instruments protecting migrant workers, especially Convention No. 143 of 1975.

[5] GA Res. 2920 (XXVII) of 15 Nov. 1972; GA Res. 3224 (XXIX) of 6 Nov. 1974; GA Res. 3449 (XXX) of 9 Dec. 1975; GA Res. 31/127 of 16 Dec. 1976; GA Res. 32/120 of 16 Dec. 1977; GA Res. 33/163 of 20 Dec. 1978.

[6] Cf. T. Hammar, 'Introduction' in T. Hammar, (ed.), *European Immigration Policy: A Comparative Study* (Cambridge: Cambridge University Press, 1985) 1, 6.

[7] See the section on family reunion in Ch. 8.

[8] International Confederation of Free Trade Unions (ICFTU), European Trade Union Confederation (ETUC), Union Syndicale des Travailleurs du Mahgreb Arabe (USTMA), *Report to the Conference on Migrant Workers from the Mahgreb in the European Community*, Tunis, 18–20 April 1991, 23, para. 3.17.

[9] See GA Res. 2920 (XXVII).

[10] See especially GA Res. 3224 (XXIX) and GA Res. 31/127.

The dawning of a Convention

In 1973, ECOSOC requested, *inter alia*, the Sub-Commission on Prevention of Discrimination and Protection of Minorities to study the migrant workers' question in depth, on the basis of information submitted by member states, and to recommend what further action was necessary for the protection of migrant workers.[11] The Sub-Commission appointed one of its members, Ms. Halima Warzazi from Morocco, as Special Rapporteur, and instructed her to prepare a preliminary study on the exploitation of labour through illicit and clandestine trafficking.[12] The Special Rapporteur submitted a series of draft recommendations in 1975. In them, she expressed the view that the elaboration of future international instruments relating to migrant workers should involve the UN in order 'to ensure that all humanitarian aspects of the problem are covered' and noted that the ILO had acknowledged that its competence to deal with human rights in general was limited.[13] The recommendations of the Special Rapporteur, together with her introductory remarks and her preliminary and final reports, were consolidated in one report[14] and examined by the Sub-Commission in 1976, after which the consolidated report was forwarded to the Commission on Human Rights.[15] The Special Rapporteur's study has been recognized as being the 'catalyst' for the ICMW.[16]

Moves to elaborate an international convention on the protection of the human rights of all migrant workers and their families gathered momentum in the late 1970s. The World Conference to Combat Racism, held in August 1978, adopted a Programme of Action, which recommended, *inter alia*, 'that States consider the possibility of adopting an international convention on the protection of all migrant workers'.[17] Later that same year, General Assembly Resolution 33/163 of 20 December 1978 requested the UN Secretary-General to explore, with member states and particularly with the cooperation of the ILO, the possibility of

[11] Res. 1789 (LIV) of 18 May 1973. See also *UN Action in the Field of Human Rights* (1994) 241, para. 1985.

[12] Res. 6 (XXVI) of 19 Sept. 1973. See also *UN Action in the Field of Human Rights*, n. 11 above, 241, para. 1986.

[13] UN, ECOSOC, Commission on Human Rights, Sub-Commission on Prevention of Discrimination and Protection of Minorities, 28th Session, *Exploitation of Labour Through Illicit and Clandestine Trafficking (Draft Recommendations submitted by Mrs. Halima Embarek Warzazi, Rapporteur)*, UN Doc. E/CN.4.Sub.2/L.636 (9 Sept. 1975) 1.

[14] *Exploitation of Labour Through Illicit and Clandestine Trafficking*, UN Doc. E/CN.4/Sub.2/1986/6.

[15] *UN Action in the Field of Human Rights*, n. 11 above, 241, para. 1987.

[16] S. Hune, 'Equality of Treatment and the International Convention on the Protection of the Rights of All Migrant Workers and Members of Their Families' in J. Cator and J. Niessen, (eds.), *The Use of International Conventions to Protect the Rights of Migrants and Ethnic Minorities* (Strasbourg, 1994) 79, 82.

[17] *Report of the World Conference to Combat Racism and Racial Discrimination*, Geneva, 14–25 Aug. 1978, UN Doc. A/CONF.92/40 (New York: UN, 1979) 19, para. 13(x). See also M. Cissé, 'The "Right to Live" and the Protection of Migrant Workers at the International Level' in D. Prémont, (ed.), *Essays on the Concept of A 'Right to Live' in Memory of Yougindra Khushalani* (Bruylant: Brussels, 1988) 133, 141–2.

drawing up such a convention. In Resolution 34/172 of 17 December 1979, the General Assembly decided to create, at its 35th Session in 1980, an open-ended Working Group to elaborate an international convention on the protection of the rights of all migrant workers and their families.

The jurisdictional conflict: why the UN and not the ILO?

The adoption of Resolution 34/172 was by no means a formality. A division arose mainly between developed countries who wanted to elaborate a convention within the framework of the ILO and a number of developing countries who insisted on the project taking place under the auspices of the UN. The ILO itself claimed competence in this area:

> [W]ith a view to concentration of resources and the avoidance of duplication or conflict, it would be preferable for standard-setting for the protection of migrant workers to continue to be entrusted to the ILO, as the agency with specific constitutional responsibility for this question, in collaboration, where appropriate, with the other organizations concerned.[18]

An amendment to the draft resolution submitted by Sweden would have given the ILO time to arrive at proposals for revising or expanding existing instruments before proceeding with a new convention in the UN. This amendment, however, was rejected by the developing nations.[19]

Böhning, the Chief of the International Migration for Employment Branch at the ILO, has put forward a number of reasons why developing countries preferred the UN as a forum for drafting the new convention. These reasons are based largely upon their dissatisfaction with Convention No. 143 and with the ILO system of working and supervision. First, the emphasis in Convention No. 143 on the suppression of migrations in abusive conditions threatened to reduce remittances to developing countries from those migrants illegally employed in developed countries. Secondly, the ILO is not solely a 'state forum' like the UN and the position of developing countries on issues such as migration is subject to challenge, not only from developed nations but also from employers' and workers' representatives. This trade union voice, in particular, is less acceptable to developing nations. Thirdly, the 'automatic majority' of developing countries in the UN system is not guaranteed in the ILO.[20]

[18] ILO, Governing Body, 212th Session, Geneva, Feb.–March 1980, *Role and Place of the ILO in the Restructured United Nations System*, ILO Doc. GB.212/IO/1/8, 5, para. 17, citing from ILO Doc. GB.211/IO/3/6, para. 9.

[19] The amendment was rejected by 65 votes to 12, with 34 abstentions: *Role and Place of the ILO*, n. 18 above, 5–6, paras. 18–19. See also W. R. Böhning, 'The ILO and the New UN Convention on Migrant Workers: The Past and Future' (1991) 25 IMR 698, 700–1. Although Resolution 34/172 was adopted by a majority of 118 in favour to 0 against, 19 delegations, including the Nordic countries and many other developed countries, abstained. See J. Lönnroth, 'The International Convention on the Rights of All Migrant Workers and Members of their Families in the Context of International Migration Policies: An Analysis of Ten Years of Negotiation' (1991) 25 IMR 710, 726.

[20] Böhning, n. 19 above, 699–700. See also S. Hune and J. Niessen, 'The First UN Convention on Migrant Workers' (1991) 9 NQHR 131, 133, with regard to the second point.

More generally, the prevailing view that the competence of the ILO is limited to labour rights, as pointed out by Special Rapporteur Warzazi in her report, and the small number of states that have ratified ILO Convention No. 143, were two further reasons why the UN appeared to be the most appropriate organization within which further standard-setting action in the field of human rights and migration ought to take place. In addition, arguments were advanced that a UN convention would not only cover a broader range of rights, but was also more likely to gain greater international support than an analogous ILO instrument.[21]

On the other hand, opponents of a UN convention, in addition to insisting that any new instrument be drafted within the ILO framework, were also of the opinion that a new instrument was unnecessary in the light of existing international standards applicable to migrants. Fears were expressed that the rights in the convention would not only overlap with ILO and regional standards, but might even undermine these standards to the extent of weakening the international protection already enjoyed by migrant workers and their families.[22] The ILO advised that duplication or conflict with existing standards would be avoided if the drafting focused on laying down general standards in accordance with human rights principles, in contrast with the detailed and technical ILO provisions, and dealt with those aspects which are not considered, or only considered partially, in existing international instruments. In the event of duplication, however, the ILO emphasized the need to exercise special care to ensure the greatest possible consistency among the relevant international instruments.[23]

4.3 DRAFTING HISTORY

Political and economic context

The drafting of the ICMW lasted 10 years, from 1980 to 1990.[24] During this period, a number of political and economic developments took place which had a considerable effect upon migration for employment and the way migrants were

[21] Hune and Niessen (1991), n. 20 above, 132. See also S. Hune, 'Drafting an International Convention on the Protection of the Rights of All Migrant Workers and their Families' (1985) 19 IMR 570, 571, with regard to the latter point. Lönnroth n. 19 above, 726–7, argues that the question of migrants' rights was more likely to receive greater attention in the international community if the new convention was drafted under the guidance of 'the world's political conscience', namely the UN General Assembly.

[22] Cf. J. A. R. Nafziger and B. C. Bartel, 'The Migrant Workers Convention: Its Place in Human Rights Law' (1991) 25 IMR 771, 779–80, citing from UN Docs A/34/535 (1979) and A/36/378 (1981).

[23] *Report of the Open Working Group*, UN Doc A/C.3/35/13 (25 Nov. 1980) (hereinafter *Working Group Report (Nov. 1980)*), Annex II, 'Possible Contents of a United Nations Convention on Protection of the Rights of All Migrant Workers and Their Families', paper prepared by the International Labour Organization', UN Doc. A/C.3/35/WG 1/CRP.2 (7 Oct. 1980) 1–2, para. 3. See also *Role and Place of the ILO in the Restructured UN System*, n. 18 above, 6, para. 20.

[24] The mandate of the Working Group was renewed on a regular basis by the UN General Assembly: *UN Action in the Field of Human Rights*, n. 11 above, 242, para. 1993.

perceived in countries of employment. The 1980s in Western Europe were characterized by a tightening of immigration controls, which severely restricted the further admission of migrant workers, and by the gradual transformation of migrant workers and their families from temporary immigrants into permanent ethnic minorities in the receiving country. The latter process also led to an escalation of racism and xenophobia directed at migrants by certain sections of the host population.[25] The end of the 1980s, however, saw a dramatic shift in political power, especially in the European context, which threatened to augment East-West migration. Moreover, the further development of the single internal market in the EC was also expected to result in a general increase in international labour migration.

The actual drafting of the ICMW occurred in the 1980s, but the impetus for the instrument dates back to the migration concerns of the 1960s and 1970s, which heavily influenced the initial debate in the UN Working Group. Issues such as South-North migration, the situation of migrants in industrialized Europe, and undocumented labour migration to the USA pervade this debate.[26]

Working method

The Working Group was open to all UN member states and not just restricted to selected countries. Although such an open and flexible approach to the drafting of the ICMW gave the work a somewhat haphazard nature because of the continuous change in the number of participants, it also allowed for the participation of a broad range of countries which was vital to the universality of the exercise.[27]

The principal working method of the Working Group was based upon consensus rather than majority voting. Consensus was the natural outgrowth of the lengthy negotiation process, which began in an atmosphere of mistrust and hostility.[28] This method of work also avoided friction between the developed or industrialized countries and the majority of developing countries, which would have undoubtedly ensued if proposed provisions were put to a vote. The main disadvantage of the consensus approach, however, was that it inevitably bred compromise to the extent that certain proposals with a strong 'rights' content at the beginning of the drafting process were diluted to mere recommendations by the end.[29]

[25] Cf. J. Niessen and P. Taran, 'Using the New Migrant Workers' Convention' (1991) 25 IMR 859–60.

[26] Lönnroth, n. 19 above, 716.

[27] *Ibid.* 724–5. It is estimated that approximately one half of UN member states took part in the drafting process. *Ibid.*

[28] *Ibid.* 715. The consensus approach was also suited to the open-endedness of the Working Group, since it avoided the unpredictability that would have resulted from majority voting in a forum with ever-changing participation. *Ibid.* 724.

[29] *Ibid.* Indeed, it is noteworthy that despite the numerous compromises in the ICMW, the consensus approach has not resulted in a spate of ratifications.

The drafting of the ICMW was divided into two readings. The first was largely an exploratory exercise in which state delegates were freer to express their own visions and opinions. The second reading involved the finalization of the text and was therefore subject far more to the attention of states and, consequently, to the demands of national sovereign interests. It is at this stage that many of the 'rights' in the ICMW were whittled down to less binding obligations.[30]

Country participation and groupings

Commentators on the drafting history of the ICMW have identified four loose country groupings which made substantial contributions to the final outcome. The most influential grouping was the European MESCA group, mainly composed of seven Mediterranean and Scandinavian states.[31] These countries endeavoured to ensure that the ICMW would be as universal an instrument as possible, which would adequately protect individual rights and move into those areas not previously covered. These objectives were in line with their interests, as medium-sized states, to preserve a structured and well-functioning international order without which their influence would be minimal.[32]

MESCA was firmly against illegal migration and was formed largely as a response to Group 77, the authors of an early draft of the ICMW in 1981, which, according to MESCA members, actually encouraged this form of migration, or, at least, made it very difficult for states to prevent it.[33] Group 77 was composed of various sending countries, mostly from Africa, Asia, and Latin America.[34] The countries in this grouping were plainly allied by their concern to ensure the protection of their nationals in states of employment.[35]

The former socialist countries of central and eastern Europe also formed their own grouping, but their influence appears to have been relatively nominal. Their principal aims were to ensure that the ICMW would not deviate from the human rights language of the international covenants and that persons travelling between them for the purpose of employment (for example, Poles to the former German Democratic Republic) would not be classified as 'migrant workers', but rather as 'socialist exchange of labour'.[36] This grouping now is of historical interest

[30] *Ibid.* 721–3.

[31] MESCA was composed of the following countries: Finland, Greece, Italy, Norway, Portugal, Spain, and Sweden. France also participated in the deliberations of this group, but retained an independent position. More country delegations took part in MESCA meetings as the drafting of the ICMW progressed. *Ibid.* 731; Hune and Niessen (1991), n. 20 above, 133–4.

[32] Lönnroth, n. 19 above, 733–4.

[33] Böhning (1991), n. 19 above, 702.

[34] Group 77 consisted of the following countries: Algeria, Barbados, Egypt, Mexico, Pakistan, Turkey, and the former Yugoslavia. India and Morocco belonged to Group 77, but also pursued independent policies: Lönnroth, n. 19 above, 731.

[35] *Ibid.* 733. Lönnroth, *ibid.*, contends that the approach of Group 77 states was motivated largely by collective or political interests in their position as countries of origin rather than by their concern for individual human rights. Indeed, in some quarters, the aim may have been to use the negotiations and the drafting of the ICMW as a tool to condemn some states of employment for their discriminatory use of migrant labour.

[36] *Ibid.* 723 and 732 respectively.

only, since many of the opinions expressed by these countries are unlikely to constitute their approach today.

The final grouping consisted of those industrialized nations outside of MESCA,[37] who shared three common concerns. First, they wanted to retain sovereign control over crucial matters of immigration policy, such as admission of immigrants and regularization of illegal migrants. Secondly, they showed a special interest in those provisions involving positive obligations and hence social cost. Thirdly, they were intent on ensuring that the ICMW was sufficiently flexible to accommodate different political, legal, and administrative systems.[38]

This alignment of state interests during the drafting debate, though hardly precise, is illuminating. Many of the controversial provisions of the ICMW came about as a result of compromises between the different country groupings. Rights were watered down to recommendations or non-binding obligations when no other solution was possible using the consensus approach. The position of a particular country or countries during the drafting process also serves as an indicator as to whether ratification of the ICMW will follow.

Participation by the ILO

Officially, ILO participation in drafting the ICMW was minimal. It consisted of papers submitted to the General Assembly and the dispatch of a representative to the meetings of the Working Group.[39] Unofficially, the ILO contribution was quite considerable, largely as a result of its special relationship with MESCA. The MESCA countries even requested the ILO to formulate draft articles, although its influence in the role as draftsperson for MESCA, as noted by one commentator, was in fact fairly limited because the proposals were closely scrutinized by MESCA members.[40]

4.4 RATIONALES FOR THE CONVENTION

A number of rationales for the ICMW may clearly be identified from the Preamble: to improve the situation of migrant workers and their families by building upon existing international standards and by recognizing the contribution of other international organizations in the migration field; to underline the link between the importance and extent of the migration phenomenon, and the hardships it

[37] These countries included Australia, Canada, Denmark, Germany, Japan, the Netherlands, and the USA: *ibid.* 731. Denmark was aligned with this grouping rather than with MESCA, because of its shift towards a more restrictive immigration policy at the beginning of the 1980s. Immigration pressures in Japan persuaded that country to support the arguments of the western states of employment: *ibid.* 719.

[38] *Ibid.* 733–4.

[39] See respectively n. 23 above and Böhning (1991), n. 19 above, 704. An ILO supplementary paper was submitted to the General Assembly in 1981: UN Doc. A/36/378 (1981), Annex II, cited by Böhning, *ibid.*

[40] Böhning, n. 19 above.

causes to those human beings involved; and to prevent clandestine migration, but at the same time to recognize the fundamental human rights of illegal migrants.

Not all the rationales, however, are conspicuously outlined in the Preamble. For example, as mentioned earlier, the ICMW constitutes a delicate balance between the protection of migrants' rights and the principle of state sovereignty. This principle finds no place in the Preamble,[41] although it pervades the entire document, and is explicitly outlined in Article 79 of the ICMW, which is analysed towards the end of this chapter.

Improvement of the situation of migrant workers and their families

(a) Building upon existing international standards

The ICMW builds on other international human rights instruments, but it does not necessarily incorporate them. This was made clear during the drafting of the first recital of the Preamble, which 'takes into account' the principles embodied in general international human rights instruments. These words were preferred to the term 'reaffirming', which according to the representatives of France, Germany, and the USA, would have implied that the previous instruments are tied to the ICMW even though several states were not parties to them.[42] The second recital of the Preamble refers to the 'principles and standards' set forth in ILO Conventions.[43]

In addition to referring to the above Conventions and other international instruments, including regional and bilateral treaties (Preamble, recital 7), the *raison d'être* for the ICMW is proclaimed in recital 11 of the Preamble: '*Convinced* that the rights of migrant workers and members of their families have not been sufficiently recognized everywhere and therefore require appropriate international protection'.

(b) Recognition of the contribution of international organizations in the migration field

The Preamble to the ICMW recognizes the work of numerous other organizations in the UN system, particularly the ILO, in advancing the rights of migrant

[41] The USA, however, supported by the Netherlands, urged the Working Group to take into account, in a further examination of the text of the Preamble, the following considerations: (i) the obligation of migrants to comply with the laws and regulations of both receiving and sending countries and (ii) the 'sovereign right' of every state to determine and apply its own immigration law and policies concerning admission to its territory: *Report of the Open-ended Working Group*, UN Doc. A/C.3/36/10 (23 Nov. 1981) (hereinafter *Working Group Report (Nov. 1981)*) 8, para. 29.

[42] *Report of the Open-ended Working Group on the Elaboration of an International Convention on the Protection of the Rights of All Migrant Workers and Their Families*, UN Doc. A/C.3/40/1 (20 June 1985) (hereinafter *Working Group Report (June 1985)*) 17, para. 68.

[43] It is interesting to observe that the US delegation found difficulty in accepting the word 'standards': *ibid.* 18, para. 74. This attitude is not surprising considering that the USA has not ratified either of the two major ILO conventions concerning migrant workers. However, it does appear to contradict the efforts of that same country to underline the importance of the ILO's work in the field of migration (see below).

workers and their families. Separate reference is made to the ILO in the fifth recital:

Recalling also that one of the objectives of the International Labour Organization, as stated in its Constitution, is the protection of the interests of workers when employed in countries other than their own, as well as the expertise and experience of the said Organization in matters related to migrant workers and members of their families.

The wording of this paragraph represents a compromise between countries, such as the USA, who wanted to recognize the ILO's 'unique competence, expertise, and experience in migrant worker matters' and those states who preferred to down play the ILO's influence in the ICMW by including less assertive terms.[44]

The link between migration and hardships

The link between the migration phenomenon and the hardships it causes for those that participate most in its dynamics, namely the migrants themselves, is reflected in recitals 8 to 10 and 12 of the Preamble. These recitals refer respectively to the importance and the extent of the migration phenomenon, the impact of migration upon the countries and people concerned, the vulnerability of migrant workers and their families and the disruptive effect of migration upon families *per se*. It is this link which constitutes another rationale for the ICMW.

Prevention of clandestine migration and recognition of the fundamental human rights of illegal migrants

The specific problems of migrants in an irregular situation and the way the ICMW attempts to deal with them are analysed later in the chapter. The Preamble sets out in recitals 13 to 15 the general policy *vis-à-vis* this exploited group. The ICMW approaches this question on the basis that irregular migrant workers and their families face greater human hardships than regular migrants, generally as well as in the employment context, and hence advocates action to prevent and eliminate illegal labour migration. It takes care, however, to ensure that the fundamental human rights of irregular migrants are secured at the same time. Through the broader protection of the fundamental rights of *all* migrants, the ICMW hopes to discourage the employment of illegal migrant workers.

4.5 STRUCTURE AND SCOPE

The ICMW is divided into the following nine parts: scope and definitions; non-discrimination with respect to rights; human rights of all migrants; other rights

[44] *Working Group Report (Nov. 1981)*, n. 41 above, 4–5, paras. 15–17. The latter consisted of the following migrant-sending countries: Jamaica, Morocco, and the former Yugoslavia. See also *Working Group Report (June 1985)*, *ibid.* 20–1, paras. 82–3.

of migrants who are in a regular situation; provisions applicable to particular categories of migrants; the promotion of sound, equitable, humane, and lawful conditions in connection with international migration; application of the Convention (which contains the control machinery); general provisions; and final provisions (which contains the provision on reservations).

Prohibition on excluding certain parts of the convention and categories of migrant workers

The ICMW applies to *all* migrant workers and their families without distinction of any kind (Article 1). States parties are prohibited by Article 88 of the ICMW from excluding certain categories of migrants. Moreover, Article 88 stipulates that all parts of the ICMW must be accepted by states parties *in toto*, unlike, for example, ILO Convention No. 143 and the European Social Charter (ESC) which permit the selective ratification by states of certain provisions.

Attempts were made during the drafting process to enable states to specify certain parts of the ICMW that would only apply to nationals of states parties on the basis of reciprocity or to completely exclude certain parts of the ICMW or categories of migrants on ratification of the instrument.[45] These efforts, however, were unsuccessful. Reciprocity for certain parts of the ICMW was rejected primarily on the basis that the concept 'was inconsistent with the universality of human rights and could lead to discrimination in the treatment by host countries of migrant workers depending upon which country they came from'.[46] Blanket exclusion by states of parts of the ICMW or categories of migrant workers was also considered to be unacceptable. Consequently, the insertion of draft Article

[45] A broad proposal on reciprocity potentially applicable to the whole of the ICMW (later amended to Parts III and IV only) was originally submitted by Italy and supported by France, Germany, and Japan. The proposal was opposed by the MESCA countries (apart from Italy) and by Algeria, Australia, Canada, China, Colombia, Morocco, Mexico, the Netherlands, and the former Yugoslavia. The second proposal on exclusion of certain parts of the ICMW or categories of migrant workers was originally submitted by Denmark (later withdrawn), but opposed by the former Byelorussian SSR, Cameroon, Finland, Greece, Spain, and Tunisia. See respectively *Report of the Open-ended Working Group on the Elaboration of an International Convention on the Protection of the Rights of All Migrant Workers and Their Families*, UN Doc. A/C.3/39/4 (11 Oct. 1984) (hereinafter *Working Group Report (Oct. 1984)*) 24–6, paras. 72–8 and *Report of the Open-ended Working Group on the Drafting of an International Convention on the Protection of the Rights of All Migrant Workers and Their Families*, UN Docs A/C.3/44/1 (19 June 1989) (hereinafter *Working Group Report (June 1989)*) 41–2, paras. 239–47 and A/C.3/45/1 (21 June 1990) (hereinafter *Working Group Report (June 1990)*) 14–17, paras. 52–71.

[46] *Working Group Report (June 1989)*, n. 45 above, 42, para. 242. States in support of reciprocity contended that not all the provisions in the ICMW related strictly to human rights (France, Germany, and Italy) and that, from a practical perspective, reciprocity would have the effect of attracting more ratifications (Italy). *Working Group Report (June 1989)*, *ibid.* 42, para. 243; *Working Group Report (June 1990)* n. 45 above, 16–17, para. 68; and *Working Group Report (Oct. 1984)*, n. 45 above, 24, para. 74.

88 was proposed by Finland to expressly preclude such an eventuality and to emphasize the 'indivisibility' of the ICMW.[47]

Reservations

As with most international human rights instruments, the ICMW, in Article 91, allows for reservations to specific provisions. States were concerned about reservations which are contrary to the spirit of the ICMW.[48] Hence, Article 91(2) precludes reservations that are 'incompatible with the object and purpose of the present Convention'. An example of a prohibited reservation provided in the drafting debate is one which aims to exclude a whole category of migrant workers,[49] which is now expressly disallowed by Article 88. There is nothing in the ICMW, however, which would prevent states from submitting reservations to specific articles that deal, for example, with the rights of illegal migrants, nor from subjecting particular provisions to reciprocity.[50]

4.6 DEFINITION

Part I of the ICMW contains the most comprehensive definition of 'migrant worker' found in any international instrument concerned with migrants. This, in itself, has been described as a 'major accomplishment'.[51] The definition strives to be inclusive rather than exclusive. It therefore encompasses many of the groups of migrant workers excluded from other international conventions. For example, the definition of 'migrant worker' is considerably broader than those found in the European Convention on the Legal Status of Migrant Workers (EMW) and ILO Conventions No. 97 and No. 143.[52]

Part I of the ICMW also defines what persons constitute the 'members of the

[47] *Working Group Report (June 1990)*, n. 45 above, 14, para. 53. Draft Art. 88 (as amended) eventually received the support of Australia, China, France, India, Italy, Mexico, Morocco, the Netherlands, Sweden, the USA, and the former USSR. *Ibid.* 15–16, paras. 55–64.

[48] *Working Group Report (June 1989)*, n. 45 above, 50, para. 283 (Morocco); *Report of the Open-ended Working Group on the Drafting of an International Convention on the Protection of the Rights of All Migrant Workers and Their Families*, UN Doc. A/C.3/44/4 (17 Oct. 1989) (hereinafter *Working Group Report (Oct. 1989)*) 67, para. 324 (Germany and Mexico).

[49] *Working Group Report (Oct. 1989)*, n. 48 above, 67, paras. 328–9 (declaration of Finland, supported by Italy, Mexico, and the former Yugoslavia).

[50] See respectively L. S. Bosniak, 'Human Rights, State Sovereignty and the Protection of Undocumented Migrants under the International Migrant Workers Convention' (1991) 763–4 and *Working Group Report (June 1990)*, n. 45 above, 17, para. 71 (Italy). See also Nafziger and Bartel, n. 22 above, 786, with regard to the latter point.

[51] S. Hune, 'Drafting an International Convention on the Protection of the Rights of All Migrant Workers and their Families' (1987) 21 IMR 123, 124.

[52] Despite the tensions that existed between the ILO and the UN with regard to the drafting of the ICMW, Böhning (1991), n. 19 above, 705, observes that the ILO Secretariat and members of the Governing Body are satisfied with the extended definition of 'migrant worker' found in the ICMW.

family' of a migrant worker and when migrants are considered to be in a regular or irregular situation. These definitions are considered separately in this chapter under the sections relating to family reunion and illegal migrants.

General definition

As mentioned earlier, the ICMW is applicable to *all* migrant workers and members of their families (Article 1). It also applies to all migrant workers residing and working in the territory of a state party regardless of whether the country from which they came has ratified it.[53] Therefore, the ICMW avoids the inequality which migrants face from the start under the EC regime and Council of Europe instruments, which, with the exception of the European Convention on Human Rights (ECHR), operate on the basis of reciprocity by extending protection only to those migrants whose countries are members of the EC or have ratified the Council of Europe convention in question. Moreover, in accordance with a major objective of the ICMW, 'all migrant workers and members of their families' refers to migrants in an irregular situation, in spite of attempts by some states to confine the definition solely to regular migrants.[54]

The term 'migrant worker' is defined in Article 2(1) as 'a person who is to be engaged, is engaged, or has been engaged in a remunerated activity in a State of which he or she is not a national'.[55] The drafting debate sheds more light on this definition. The term 'to be engaged' refers to potential migrant workers who hold a work contract, even if they have not yet left the country of origin to take up employment in the host country. Such a contract or a similar document constitutes the 'starting-point' for the recognition of a person as a migrant worker. The words 'has been engaged' were included to protect the rights of migrant workers under the ICMW and to maintain their quality as 'migrant workers' after completing employment, for whatever reason, in the host state.[56] It was also made clear that this provision did not cover someone who was 'seeking employment'

[53] As discussed above, attempts to enable states parties to apply certain provisions on a systematic basis solely to nationals from other states parties were unsuccessful. See nn. 45–6 above.

[54] *Report of the Open-ended Working Group on the Elaboration of an International Convention on the Protection of the Rights of All Migrant Workers and Their Families*, UN Doc. A/C.3/38/5 (11 Oct. 1983) (hereinafter *Working Group Report (Oct. 1983)*) 24, para. 78 and *Report of the Open-ended Working Group on the Elaboration of an International Convention on the Protection of the Rights of All Migrant Workers and Their Families*, UN Doc. A/C.3/39/1 (14 June 1984) (hereinafter *Working Group Report (June 1984)*) 33, para. 105 (USA); *Working Group Report (June 1985)*, n. 42 above, 28, para. 122 (Germany).

[55] Penna makes the interesting observation that recent territorial changes, such as those in the newly-independent republics of the former Soviet Union, have now resulted in the creation of migrant workers employed in countries of which they are *no longer* nationals: L. R. Penna, 'Some Salient Human Rights in the UN Convention on Migrant Workers' (1993) 2 *Asian and Pacific Migration Journal* 179, 183.

[56] *Working Group Report (June 1985)*, n. 42 above, para. 168. For example, the term 'has been engaged' would include: persons who have contracted an occupational disease which only manifests itself after they have left the country of employment; unemployed migrant workers seeking re-employment; those who have been victims of work accidents and remain in the country of employment

for the first time.[57] Finally, although the term 'remunerated activity' was not defined, it was understood that it did not refer to an activity regarded by state laws as contrary to the rules of *ordre public*.[58]

Included categories

As noted above, the comprehensive definition of 'migrant worker' in the ICMW covers many categories of migrant workers excluded from other international conventions. Seasonal workers are expressly included,[59] although certain rights, such as the right to vocational training or family reunion which some states of employment would contend require a longer period of residence, might not apply to them because, by virtue of Article 59 in Part V of the ICMW, they are only entitled to those rights (in Part IV) that, *inter alia*, are 'compatible with their status in [the State of employment] as seasonal workers, taking into account that they are present in that State for only part of the year'. Moreover, frontier and self-employed workers, excluded under the two major ILO Conventions specifically concerned with migrant workers are covered by the ICMW.[60] A self-employed worker is defined in Article 2(2)(h) as:

to collect invalidity benefits; and those who depart from the host country on temporary leave: *ibid.* 37, paras. 168–9. This term also suggests that once a person has been employed in a remunerated activity at some point, he or she is *always* a migrant worker: Nafziger and Bartel, n. 22 above, 786. One of the concerns which the US delegation had with this broad definition of 'migrant worker' was based on the term 'has been engaged'. For example, a person who once worked in a state of which he or she is not a national might return there as a tourist and might still be classified as a migrant worker under the definition because he or she has 'been engaged' there in a remunerated activity: *Working Group Report (June 1985)*, *ibid.* 35, para. 153.

[57] The inclusion in the definition of an additional term, such as 'seek to engage', was opposed by a number of state representatives who were of the view that the application of the ICMW 'should not be extended to persons having the mere intent to migrate': *Working Group Report (June 1985)*, n. 42 above, 32, para. 141 (Cape Verde, Finland, Greece, Italy, Morocco, and Sweden). Under EC law, the definition of 'worker' includes those 'seeking employment'. See Case C-292/89, *R* v. *Immigration Appeal Tribunal, ex parte Antonissen* [1991] ECR I-745, [1991] 2 CMLR 373, discussed in Ch. 6.

[58] *Working Group Report (June 1985)*, n. 42 above, 38, para. 174. Penna, n. 55 above, 183, contends that 'remunerated activity' must be understood as meaning 'gainful employment'.

[59] Art. 2(2)(b) defines 'seasonal workers' as those migrant workers 'whose work by its character is dependent on seasonal conditions and is performed only during part of the year'. Seasonal workers are only implicitly included in the ILO conventions concerning migrant workers and expressly excluded from the EMW. Indeed, a proposal by Denmark (later withdrawn) to transpose the definition of 'migrant worker' in Art. 1 of the latter instrument to that of the ICMW was rejected as 'too restrictive and unacceptable' by a number of countries on the grounds that the mandate of the Working Group was to draft a global convention for the protection of all migrant workers and members of their families. See the *Working Group Report (Oct. 1984)*, n. 45 above, 6, para. 15 (Greece, Finland, Spain, Sweden, and the former Yugoslavia).

[60] Art. 2(2)(a) defines 'frontier worker' as a migrant worker 'who retains his or her habitual residence in a neighbouring State to which he or she normally returns every day or at least once a week'. Indeed, according to the Chairman of the Working Group, the proposal to include frontier workers under the ICMW was prompted by their exclusion from the application of other international conventions concerning migrant workers. *Working Group Report (June 1985)*, n. 42 above, 41, para. 195. Frontier and self-employed workers are explicitly excluded under the EMW, although self-employed workers are covered by the ESC, unless excluded separately by states parties under the selective ratification procedure.

a migrant worker who is engaged in a remunerated activity otherwise than under a contract of employment and who earns his or her living through this activity normally working alone or together with members of his or her family, and to any other migrant worker recognized as self-employed by applicable legislation of the State of employment or bilateral or multilateral agreements.

This rather restrictive interpretation of a 'self-employed' worker was the result of a compromise between those states who wanted to exclude the category altogether[61] and those who strove to ensure that they were included, but on condition that coverage would be confined to 'poor' or 'underprivileged' persons employed on their own account and not to 'highly privileged' categories of self-employed migrants.[62] The provision was clarified somewhat towards the end of the drafting process by the Vice-Chairman of the Working Group. It covers only self-employed workers who earn a living through their own means or with the help of their families. The inclusion of self-employed workers who employ others would only be permitted if consistent with applicable legislation of the state of employment, or with bilateral or multilateral agreements.[63]

The ICMW also creates, in Article 2(2)(g), a special category of migrant workers, namely 'specified-employment workers', which essentially refers to those workers who enter a country to take up employment for a 'restricted and defined period of time'. By virtue of Article 62 in Part V of the ICMW, the provisions concerned with equal treatment between migrant workers and nationals in respect of vocational training, free access to employment after a defined period of time, and access to alternative employment in the event of loss of work, are inapplicable to specified-employment workers. These two clauses were part of another compromise in order to satisfy the demands of those non-European countries of immigration, such as Australia, Canada, and the USA, which do not permit migrant workers the right to free choice of employment after a period of work and residence.[64]

[61] *Working Group Report (Oct. 1983)*, n. 54 above, 23, para. 76 (Morocco) and 23–4, para. 78 (Netherlands); *Working Group Report (June 1985)*, n. 42 above, 32, para. 141 (Germany); and *Working Group Report (Oct. 1989)*, n. 48 above, 8, para. 28 (Germany), 9, para. 29 (Australia) and 9, para. 31 (Japan).

[62] *Working Group Report (Oct. 1983)*, n. 54 above, 23, para. 76; *Working Group Report (June 1984)*, n. 54 above, 33, para. 108; *Report of the Open-ended Working Group on the Drafting of an International Convention on the Protection of the Rights of All Migrant Workers and Their Families*, UN Doc. A/C.3/40/6 (15 Oct. 1985) (hereinafter *Working Group Report (Oct. 1985)*) 7–8, paras. 17–19 (Argentina, Finland, Greece, India, Italy, Norway, Portugal, Spain, and Sweden). This piecemeal approach was criticized by the ILO in observations on the text provisionally agreed at the first reading: 'The exclusion of self-employed persons (*or of any particular categories of self-employed persons*) would result in the introduction of an arbitrary distinction, inconsistent with the protection already provided for in UN human rights instruments and in a number of important international labour conventions': ILO, Governing Body, 229th Session, Geneva, Feb.–March 1985, *International Convention on the Protection of the Rights of All Migrant Workers and Their Families*, ILO Doc. GB.229/IO/1/6, Appendix, para. 2 (emphasis added).

[63] *Working Group Report (Oct. 1989)*, n. 48 above, 8, para. 26.

[64] See also Lönnroth, n. 19 above, 730–1. The representative of Australia justified the inclusion of Art. 62 as follows: 'Australia's views on this category of worker [specified-employment worker]

Excluded categories

The categories of persons excluded from the ICMW's coverage are listed in Article 3. Employees of international organizations, government officials, and 'persons sent or employed by a State or on its behalf outside its territory who participate in development programmes and other co-operation programmes' are excluded.[65]

Article 3 also excludes investors, refugees and stateless persons, students and trainees, and non-national non-resident seafarers and workers on an offshore installation. To exclude investors was largely the concern of developing countries who wanted to confine the ICMW to the protection of the most vulnerable migrants.[66] It is essentially this group of countries which was also interested in a restrictive interpretation of the definition of 'self-employed' worker. Refugees and stateless persons were excluded on the basis that they are protected under other international instruments and that they possess a 'specific international status'.[67] Nonetheless, their exclusion creates the anomalous situation in which persons claiming asylum are defined as 'migrant workers' if they are permitted to work in a country, but lose their 'migrant worker' status under the ICMW once they are granted refugee status.[68] Although students and trainees are not covered by any other international instrument relating to migrant workers, their exclusion from the ICMW's application was by no means automatic. One of the rationales for excluding this category is to discourage the effects of the 'brain drain' from developing to developed countries.[69] Efforts undertaken to extend protection to those students who are granted a work permit appear to have been

proceeded from the basis that it was a country of immigration. Australia made a basic distinction between those accepted as permanent members of its society and those admitted on a temporary basis. As a legitimate exercise of its sovereignty, Australia limited the right freely to choose employment to the former': *Report of the Open-ended Working Group on the Drafting of an International Convention on the Protection of the Rights of All Migrant Workers and Their Families*, UN Doc. A/C.3/43/1 (20 June 1988) (hereinafter *Working Group Report (June 1988)*) 59–60, para. 317.

65 Arts. 3(a) and (b). Art. 3(b) was inserted at the request of the grouping of socialist countries in order to exclude the so-called 'socialist exchange of labour' between these states from the application of the ICMW. This reasoning is unlikely to hold much significance today. See Lönnroth, n. 19 above, 714, 732.

66 The proposal to exclude investors was originally put forward by the Mexican delegation: *Working Group Report (June 1984)*, n. 54 above, 34, para. 110. Lönnroth, n. 19 above, 716, also observes that, in formulating a definition of 'migrant worker', the focus during drafting was initially upon the traditional industrial migrant as opposed to the modern mobile professional.

67 *Working Group Report (Oct. 1985)*, n. 62 above, 25, para. 112. However, the representative of Italy, supported by France and Germany, observed that such instruments said very little on the subject of employment and that this group of persons should neither be expressly included nor expressly excluded from the application of the ICMW: *ibid.* 25–6, para. 113. Indeed, refugees and stateless persons, as migrant workers, are not expressly excluded from the application of the two ILO conventions concerning migrant workers, nor from the EMW. Moreover, the Appendix to the ESC urges states parties to grant refugee migrant workers the most favourable treatment possible.

68 Böhning (1991), n. 19 above, 707–8.

69 *Working Group Report (Oct. 1985)*, n. 62 above, 28, para. 126 (Germany and Morocco).

unsuccessful,[70] although one commentator has argued for such a broader interpretation on the basis that the spirit of the provision was meant to be as inclusive as possible and that it would discourage countries from exploiting cheap student and trainee labour.[71] It is noteworthy that the ILO in its observations strongly urged the drafters to ensure the protection of 'all persons working in a country other than their own, whatever the nature of their activity or contractual status, including refugees, stateless persons, students and trainees *whenever they are economically active*'.[72]

Finally, the ICMW excludes non-national *non-resident* seafarers and workers on offshore installations. Indeed, in contrast with other conventions relating to migrants, the original intention of the ICMW was to provide comprehensive protection for this category of workers, despite the opposition of certain states.[73] The ICMW protects non-national *resident* seafarers and offshore installation workers (Articles 2(2)(c) and (d)), but the exclusion of *non-residents* was introduced in the final stages of drafting in order to conform to the policies of those Western countries which pay differential wages to seafarers on the basis of their nationality. This provision was introduced despite the ILO observation that such a practice was contrary to general ILO international labour standards concerning discrimination in employment.[74]

4.7 RIGHTS

Parts III and IV of the ICMW are devoted to the protection of the rights of migrant workers and their families. Part III (Articles 8 to 35) concerns the protection of the 'human rights of *all* migrant workers and members of their families' and hence applies to irregular migrants, whereas Part IV (Articles 36 to 56) is restricted to those migrant workers and their families 'who are *documented or in a regular situation*'.[75] The rights covered in Part IV are more extensive and

[70] *Ibid.* 28, para. 127 (Greece). The representative of Finland proposed that students be classified as 'migrant workers' if they engage in a remunerated activity that is not considered as part of their course of studies: *ibid.* 30, para. 145.

[71] Cf. Y. Kitamura, 'Recent Developments in Japanese Immigration Policy and the United Nations Convention on Migrant Workers' (1993) 27 *UBC Law Rev.* 113, 126–8 and 130.

[72] International Labour Organisation, Governing Body, 235th Session, Geneva, Feb.–March 1987 *Recent Events in the United Nations System (Draft International Convention on the Protection of the Rights of All Migrant Workers and their Families)* ILO Doc. GB.235/IO/1/3, 2; ILO Doc. GB.229/IO/1/6, n. 62 above, Appendix, para. 3 (emphasis added).

[73] *Working Group Report (Oct. 1989)*, n. 48 above, 10, paras. 41–2 (Germany and Japan).

[74] *Working Group Report (Oct. 1989)*, *ibid.* 10–11, para. 43. For example, see ILO Convention No. 111 of 1958 concerning Discrimination in respect of Employment and Occupation. See also M. Hasenau, 'Setting Norms in the United Nations System: The Draft Convention on the Protection of the Rights of All Migrant Workers and their Families in Relation to ILO in Standards on Migrant Workers' (1990) 28 IMR 133, 135.

[75] Emphasis added. Variations on these rights as they apply to particular categories of migrant workers are found in Part V (Arts 57–63).

specific than those in Part III. Article 33(1)(a) imposes an obligation upon all states in the labour migration process (states of origin, transit, and employment) to inform migrant workers and their families of their rights under the ICMW.

This section examines both Parts III and IV under the relevant rights' headings, although a separate section also considers specific issues concerning irregular migrants, such as the prevention of clandestine migration, employer sanctions, and regularization, which are mainly dealt with in Part VI (Articles 64 to 71) of the ICMW.

Non-discrimination and equality

(a) Non-discrimination with respect to rights in the Convention

Article 7 of the ICMW (Part II) places an obligation upon states parties to guarantee the rights of migrant workers and their families provided for therein 'without distinction of any kind such as sex, race, colour, language, religion or conviction, political or other opinion, national, ethnic or social origin, nationality, age, economic position, property, marital status, birth or other status'. This is not a substantive anti-discrimination clause, because it only refers to rights enumerated in the ICMW.[76] As such, it resembles Article 14 of the ECHR which also ties non-discrimination to the rights enumerated therein. The list of prohibited grounds of discrimination is illustrative only, but it expressly refers to a broader range of grounds than that found in comparable provisions in other instruments, such as Article 2(1) of the ICCPR.[77]

In addition to Article 7, Article 1(1) of the ICMW contains a general provision underlining its applicability to all migrant workers and their families 'without distinction of any kind' and lists the same prohibited grounds of discrimination as enumerated in Article 7. The difference between these two provisions is that Article 7 is an obligation specifically imposed upon states, whereas Article 1(1) is more general and may also encompass companies and employers in the private sector.[78] Both provisions, however, only prohibit distinctions between different groups of migrant workers and their families. This interpretation would, therefore, preclude the reference to 'nationality' as a prohibited ground of discrimination in Article 7 from affording migrants *general* equal treatment with nationals in respect of the rights covered by the ICMW. However, if states are under an obligation in Article 7 to treat all migrant workers within their territory

[76] Hune and Niessen (1991), n. 20 above, 135. The Chairman of the Working Group pointed out that 'the essence of the provision was the obligation of every State to apply every article of the Convention, without distinction of any sort': *Report of the Open-ended Working Group on the Drafting of an International Convention on the Protection of the Rights of All Migrant Workers and Their Families*, UN Doc. A/C.3/41/3 (10 Oct. 1986) (hereinafter *Working Group Report (Oct. 1986)*) 18, para. 106.

[77] See also A. Eggers, 'The International Convention on the Protection of the Rights of All Migrant Workers and Members of Their Families' (1991) 34 *German YBIL* 429, 431.

[78] *Working Group Report (Oct. 1986)*, n. 76 above, para. 108 (Chairman of the Working Group).

equally in respect of the rights provided in the ICMW, does this mean that the free movement regime established by the EC, which grants preferential treatment to EC nationals, is discriminatory *vis-à-vis* non-EC nationals on the ground of nationality? By virtue of Article 81 of the ICMW, domestic laws or practices or bilateral and multilateral treaties which grant more favourable rights or freedoms to migrant workers and their families are not affected by the ICMW. Although this provision does not automatically sanction discriminatory treatment between different groups of migrants residing within the territory of a state party, it is arguable that so long as the minimum standards prescribed in the ICMW are upheld in respect of *all* migrant workers, it would seem that more favourable treatment by EC member states for nationals from other EC member states would be permissible under the ICMW.[79] Such an interpretation would have been more difficult to justify had the ICMW contained a substantive equality clause.

(b) Equality of treatment between migrants and nationals and regular and irregular migrants

The ICMW has been recognized as containing three implicit categories of equality of treatment: between nationals and non-nationals, between documented and undocumented migrants, and between women and men.[80] The first two categories are considered below, while the position of women migrants is discussed in a separate section.

As with other international instruments concerning migrant workers, the ICMW strives to realize equal treatment between migrant workers and nationals, but this equality is by no means complete. The very fact that the rights in the ICMW are divided into two categories, those applying to *all* migrants and those confined to regular migrants, means that the degree of equal treatment enjoyed by migrant workers and their families with other migrants and with nationals depends on their legal status in the country.

Part III of the ICMW enumerates rights applicable to all migrant workers and their families. Many are civil and political rights and the majority may be classified as 'fundamental' or 'basic' rights. Indeed, the wording in these provisions repeats textually much of that found in the ICCPR. The repetition in a subsidiary human rights instrument of human rights principles also found in the ICCPR and the ICESCR risks a divergent interpretation of these standards by different supervisory bodies. Such a conflict is most likely to occur with regard to the interpretation of limitation clauses.[81]

Equality in respect of 'fundamental' rights is absolute except for any limitation provision applicable to both nationals and migrant workers. The approach

[79] See also the discussion in S. Hune and J. Niessen, 'Ratifying the UN Migrant Workers Convention: Current Difficulties and Prospects' (1994) 12 NQHR 393, 403.

[80] Hune (1994), n. 16 above, 83–4.

[81] Hasenau (1990), n. 74 above, 137.

in Part III is consistent with the principle of non-discrimination with respect to the rights of nationals and aliens (regardless of the status of the latter) found in general international human rights treaties and with Article 1 of ILO Convention No. 143 which guarantees for *all* migrant workers equal treatment with nationals in respect of 'basic human rights'. In Convention No. 143, however, these rights are not specified as they are in Part III of the ICMW.[82]

With regard to economic, social, and cultural rights, Part III specifically provides for equal treatment between all migrant workers and nationals in respect of remuneration, work, and employment conditions (Article 25), social security (Article 27), emergency medical care (Article 28), and access to education (Article 30). These rights are discussed in more detail below under the relevant headings.

In addition to extending some of the Part III rights in respect of regular migrant workers and their families, especially in the field of employment (Articles 54 and 55), Part IV also contains, in Articles 43 and 45, two general equality provisions which resemble those found in the two ILO Conventions concerning migrant workers.[83] Article 43(1) accords to migrant workers equal treatment with nationals in respect of access to educational institutions and services, vocational guidance and training, housing, social and health services, co-operatives and self-managed enterprises, and access to and participation in cultural life. Article 43(2) imposes an obligation upon states parties to:

> promote conditions to ensure effective equality of treatment to enable migrant workers to enjoy the rights mentioned in paragraph 1 of this Article whenever the terms of their stay, as authorized by the State of employment, meet the appropriate requirements.

This provision resembles Article 10 of ILO Convention No. 143, which also obliges states parties to '*promote* and guarantee' the rights enumerated in the provision. Such an approach recognizes that to eliminate discrimination between migrant workers and nationals, the prohibition of discriminatory laws and measures is insufficient. A positive effort has to be undertaken to ensure equality in practice.[84]

Article 45(1) accords to the *family* of migrant workers who are in a regular situation in the country of employment equal treatment with nationals in respect of practically the same rights as those found in Article 43(1). However, there is no equivalent provision to Article 43(2) promoting effective equality of treatment

[82] According to Hasenau, *ibid.*, however, the ILO approach to the protection of the 'basic' or 'fundamental' rights of all migrant workers is better, because it avoids misunderstandings based on conflicting interpretation. Hasenau, *ibid.* 137–8, contends that only *additional* civil and political rights should have been elaborated in the ICMW. The ICMW contains few such rights, such as the right to have recourse to the protection of consular and diplomatic authorities (Art. 23) and protection against collective and arbitrary expulsion (Arts 22 and 56).

[83] Art. 6(1)(a) of ILO Convention No. 97 and Art. 10 of ILO Convention No. 143. See also Art. 19(4) of the ESC, discussed in Ch. 7.

[84] By way of contrast, see Art. 6(1)(a) of ILO Convention No. 97 and Art. 19(4) of the ESC (largely modelled on the latter), which, on their face, confine the state obligation to the proscription of discriminatory legislation and administrative measures.

with respect to the enumerated rights.[85] The contents of these provisions are examined in greater detail under the relevant headings below.

The drafting history of Articles 43 and 45 reveals an endeavour by states to down play the effect of both provisions. Attempts to make equal treatment in Articles 43(1) and 45(1) subject to the 'national legislation of the State of employment' were rejected on the basis that such an approach would 'open doors for the State of employment not to allow migrant workers to enjoy equality of treatment with nationals'.[86] The French representative, for example, was generally opposed to Article 45 on the basis that families of migrants were admitted to the state of employment on humanitarian grounds and consequently were not entitled to all the rights enumerated in the provision.[87]

Article 43(1) can best be compared with Article 10 of ILO Convention No. 143, but it does not encompass all the rights specified in that provision, even though these rights are found elsewhere in the ICMW. Article 43(1) was to include an express reference to equal treatment in respect of 'trade union rights', but this was deleted during drafting leading to criticism from some delegations.[88] Even though these 'omitted' rights are found elsewhere in the ICMW, they are not subject to the broader policy of 'promotion' in Article 43(2), which is expressly confined to the rights enumerated in Article 43(1).[89] Furthermore, Article 10 of ILO Convention No. 143 is also buttressed by Article 12, which outlines a coordinated programme of measures through which such a policy is to be pursued.[90]

(c) Protection against violence

In addition to securing non-discrimination between all migrant workers with respect to rights in the ICMW as well as general equality of treatment and opportunity between nationals and migrants (in certain defined areas), the ICMW also ensures, in Article 16(2), that all migrant workers and their families have the right to 'effective protection by the State against violence, physical injury, threats

[85] See also Hasenau (1990), n. 74 above, 146.

[86] *Report of the Open-ended Working Group on the Drafting of an International Convention on the Protection of the Rights of All Migrant Workers and Their Families*, UN Doc. A/C.3/42/6 (9 Oct. 1987) (hereinafter *Working Group Report (Oct. 1987)*) 27, para. 134 with respect to Art. 43(1). This proposal was supported by Australia, France, Germany, the USA and specifically opposed by Finland, Greece, the Netherlands, and the former Yugoslavia. *Ibid.* Similarly, both the German and US delegations advocated that equal treatment in Art. 45(1) be made subject to the 'national legislation of the State of employment': *ibid.* 45, para. 237. The ILO representative, however, emphasized earlier in the drafting process that international conventions, rather than merely recording national legislation, should constitute 'a means of promoting social justice throughout the world'. See the *Report of the Open-ended Working Group on the Elaboration of an International Convention on the Protection of the Rights of All Migrant Workers and Their Families*, UN Doc. A/C.3/37/7 (19 Nov. 1982) (hereinafter *Working Group Report (Nov. 1982)*) 19, para. 71.

[87] *Working Group Report (Oct. 1987)*, n. 86 above, para. 236; in particular, the right to access to vocational guidance and training facilities which might imply the right to work.

[88] *Ibid.* 30, para. 150 (Finland and the Netherlands).

[89] See also Hasenau (1990), n. 74 above, 145–6.

[90] Cf. *ibid.* 146.

and intimidation, whether by public officials or by private individuals, groups, or institutions'. This provision is located in the context of ensuring migrants the right to 'liberty and security of the person' (Article 16(1)), and thus extends, in this respect, the protection accorded to them by comparable provisions in other international human rights instruments, such as Article 9 of the ICCPR. It may also be considered as part of a broader concept of non-discrimination that is specifically alert to the pervading atmosphere of xenophobia and racial hatred directed at migrants in Western Europe and in many other parts of the world, often resulting in violence and sometimes even fatalities.[91]

Employment rights

(a) Equal work and employment conditions

Article 25(1) in Part III of the ICMW guarantees equal treatment between all migrant workers and nationals in respect of remuneration, 'other conditions of work' and 'other terms of employment' which are enumerated in the provision. 'Other conditions of work' include overtime, hours of work, weekly rest, holidays with pay, safety, health, and termination of the employment relationship (Article 25(1)(a)), while 'other terms of employment' encompass minimum age of employment and restriction on home work (Article 25(1)(b)). Both are open in that they may be 'extended' by national law and practice.[92] Article 25(2) prohibits derogation from the equal treatment principle in private contracts of employment.[93] Because Article 25 is situated in Part III of the ICMW, it applies to irregular as well as to regular migrant workers, which is emphasized in Article 25(3):

> States parties shall take all appropriate measures to ensure that migrant workers are not deprived of any rights derived from this principle [of equality of treatment] by reason of any irregularity in their stay or employment. In particular, employers shall not be relieved of any legal or contractual obligations, nor shall their obligations be limited in any manner by reason of any such irregularity.

The application of the broad list of rights in Article 25 to irregular as well as regular migrants met with some opposition during drafting. The German representative claimed that placing all migrant workers, including illegal migrant workers, on an equal footing with national workers in respect of social conditions

[91] Cf. Penna, n. 55 above, 190; cf. Eggers, n. 77 above, 431.

[92] The debate during drafting questioned whether it was necessary to have a list defining work conditions. In the end, an illustrative list was agreed upon, permitting variations according to national law: *Report of the Open-ended Working Group on the Elaboration of an International Convention on the Protection of the Rights of All Migrant Workers and Their Families*, UN Doc. A/C.3/37/1 (11 June 1982) (hereinafter *Working Group Report (June 1982)*) 5, para. 14.

[93] See also Art. 82 which prohibits, *inter alia*, derogation by contract from any of the rights recognized in the ICMW.

and working life 'would prove increasingly impracticable'.[94] The Austrian delegation recorded a reservation to Article 25(3) on the grounds that Austrian labour legislation does not entitle foreign workers, if they are employed without a work permit, to claims arising in connection with a notice of dismissal or termination of employment.[95]

Further rights with respect to work and employment conditions are granted to regular migrant workers in Part IV under Articles 54 and 55. Article 54(1) ensures equal treatment between these workers and nationals in respect of protection against dismissal, unemployment benefits, access to public work schemes intended to combat unemployment, and access to alternative employment in the event of loss of work or termination of other remunerated activity.[96] Many of these rights, however, are also guaranteed in Part III of the ICMW, which applies to all workers, and do not necessarily 'augment or modify' those afforded migrant workers in Art. 25(1) or in Art. 27 concerning social security.[97] For example, equal treatment with regard to protection against dismissal from work is already safeguarded in Article 25(1)(a) under 'termination of the employment relationship', whereas equality in respect of the receipt of unemployment benefits is implicitly covered by Article 27(1) on social security.[98] Rights of equal access to public work schemes and to alternative employment in the event of loss of work are also safeguarded by Articles 49 and 51, which regulate in greater detail the rights of migrant workers in the event of loss of employment (see the section on residence rights below).[99]

Article 55 guarantees equal treatment with nationals in the exercise of a remunerated activity to those migrant workers granted permission to engage in that activity. Although this provision, on its face, appears to be covered by the content of Article 25, the drafting history reveals that those migrant workers who exercise activities or professions on an independent basis do not come within the ambit of Article 25, which applies only to employees.[100] In this sense, therefore, Article 55 supplements the provisions in Article 25.

[94] *Report of the Open-ended Working Group on the Drafting of an International Convention on the Protection of the Rights of All Migrant Workers and Their Families*, UN Doc. A/C.3/42/1 (22 June 1987) (hereinafter *Working Group Report (June 1987)*) 40, para. 196. The whole of the provision, however, was expressly supported by Finland, India, Italy, the Netherlands, and the former Soviet Union: *ibid.* 40, para. 197.

[95] *Ibid.* 41, para. 208.

[96] Art. 54(2) entitles migrant workers to bring a claim before the competent authorities if the terms of their work contract have been violated by the employer.

[97] *Working Group Report (June 1988)*, n. 64 above, 31, para. 151 (Australia).

[98] See also Hasenau (1990), n. 74 above, 143. Indeed, a number of state delegations contended that Art. 54(1)(b) concerning equal treatment between regular migrant workers and nationals in respect of unemployment benefits could only apply if these benefits were not part of the national social security system to which Art. 27(1) is applicable. *Working Group Report (June 1988)*, n. 64 above, 31, para. 153 (France, Germany, the Netherlands, Norway, and the USA).

[99] See also Hasenau (1990), n. 74 above.

[100] *Working Group Report (June 1988)*, n. 64 above, 34, para. 176 (Chairman of the Working Group). Indeed, an earlier draft version of Art. 55 submitted by the MESCA grouping of countries referred to migrant workers who have been granted permission to work 'in a defined profession or occupation': *ibid.* 32, para. 157.

The ICMW provisions governing equal work and employment conditions are quite advanced compared with other international standards in this area. They have a wider coverage than equivalent ILO standards because they guarantee rights to migrant workers directly as against their employers as well as against the state. Rights, therefore, are paramount, in contrast with state duties to prevent the discriminatory practices of public authorities or to promote equal opportunity with regard to work and employment conditions found in ILO provisions.[101] As far as detail is concerned, the ICMW provisions most resemble EC standards, although their scope is significantly broader because they encompass, in Part III, *all* migrant workers resident in the territory of a state party regardless of legal status.[102]

(b) Free choice of employment

The tension in the ICMW between the protection of the rights of migrant workers and their families and the preservation of the principle of state sovereignty is very evident in Articles 52 and 53, which are concerned with their right to free choice of employment.[103] Not surprisingly, this right is confined to legal migrants. In contrast with the comprehensive rights' protections provided by the ICMW in respect of work and employment conditions, the right to free choice of employment is subject to a number of significant restrictions reflecting the interest of states to retain sovereign control in a sensitive area with important economic implications.

Article 52(1) of the ICMW enunciates the principle that 'migrant workers in the State of employment shall have the right freely to choose their remunerated activity . . .'. The remainder of Article 52 lists a number of restrictions or conditions on this principle. The first two limitations apply to 'any migrant worker'. By virtue of Article 52(2)(a), a state of employment may restrict the access of migrant workers 'to limited categories of employment, functions, services or activities where this is necessary in the interests of this State and provided for by national legislation'. Although this restriction is chiefly aimed at confining public service positions to nationals,[104] its wording appears sufficiently broad to

[101] See also Hasenau (1990), n. 74 above, 139. In this regard, it is interesting to observe that the US representative preferred to have the opening phrase of Art. 25(1) commence with the following words: 'States parties to the Convention shall ensure that . . .': *Working Group Report (June 1987)*, n. 94 above, 40, para. 201.

[102] Hasenau (1990), n. 74 above, 140, notes that the employment of illegal migrant workers becomes a less economically attractive proposition when their rights as against employers are secured in law. The enforcement of these rights, however, is more problematic. This question is considered in greater detail below in the section on illegal migrants.

[103] By virtue of Art. 62, neither Arts 52 nor 53 apply to specified-employment workers and their families. However, the ICMW makes a special, though limited, concession to seasonal workers with regard to access to employment. By virtue of Art. 59(2), a country of employment is obliged 'to consider granting seasonal workers who have been employed in its territory for a significant period of time the possibility of taking up other remunerated activities and giving them priority over other workers who seek admission to that State, subject to applicable bilateral and multilateral agreements'.

[104] Hasenau (1990), n. 74 above, 140.

cover other categories of employment. Under Article 52(2)(b), a state may also limit free access to employment 'in accordance with its legislation concerning recognition of occupational qualifications acquired outside its territory'.[105]

Further restrictions may be imposed in respect of 'migrant workers whose permission to work is limited in time'. The reason for the distinction in Article 52 between these workers and others was to distinguish between temporary workers admitted to a country for a limited period of time and permanent immigrants, such as those admitted to the USA and Australia, who are given free access to employment, with certain minor exceptions, from the moment of entry.[106] With respect to the former category of migrant workers, a state of employment may also make free choice of employment subject to the condition that migrant workers have been lawfully resident and employed in its territory for a period not exceeding 2 years (Article 52(3)(a)). The 2-year period was the subject of extensive discussions during drafting. A number of states wanted to specify a longer time-period, others preferred no defined time-period, while the ILO representative was concerned that any period of time over 2 years would deviate from Article 14(a) of ILO Convention No. 143.[107]

Access to employment may be limited further in respect of temporary migrant workers in accordance with a policy granting priority in employment to nationals and to those persons who are 'assimilated' to nationals for this purpose by virtue of national legislation, or bilateral or multilateral agreements; for example, regional free movement of labour regimes such as those operating within the EC or the Nordic Labour Market. Such a limitation must be removed, however, if migrant workers have been lawfully resident and employed in the host country for 5 years (Article 52(3)(b)).

The time-periods in these provisions are only recommendatory.[108] Consequently, the state of employment has discretion whether to increase these limits without necessarily infringing the ICMW. This approach was criticized by some states on the basis that it weakened existing international norms, especially ILO standards.[109] With regard to self-employed migrant workers, the state of employment is free to determine the conditions under which such persons may work within its territory, although the period of lawful residence is to be taken into account in prescribing such conditions (Article 52(4)).

[105] States parties are also obliged under this clause to 'endeavour to provide for recognition of such qualifications'.

[106] Hasenau (1990), n. 74 above, 140.

[107] See respectively: *Working Group Report (June 1988)*, n. 64 above, 21, paras. 92 and 93 (the Netherlands and Norway); 20, para. 90, 23, para. 105 and 21, para. 95 (Australia and Germany); and 21–2, para. 98 (International Labour Office representative).

[108] However, these periods must be prescribed in the national legislation of the state of employment.

[109] *Working Group Report (June 1988)*, n. 64 above, 22–3, para. 104 (Finland and Greece). These countries, *ibid.*, underlined the need to ensure that any restrictions imposed upon the free choice of employment for migrant workers are not indefinite in duration. Hasenau (1990), n. 74 above, 141, also argues that the formulation of mere recommendations in Art. 52(3) is a considerable step backwards in comparison with existing ILO standards because it enables states to restrict access to employment without limitation.

Article 53 concerns the question of free choice of employment for members of the migrant worker's family. A similar distinction to that in Article 52 is made between members of a migrant worker's family 'who have themselves an authorization of residence or admission that is without limit of time or is automatically renewable' (Article 53(1)) and those who 'are not permitted freely to choose their remunerated activity' (Article 53(2)). The former have the same rights to free choice of employment as those accorded to their working relatives under Article 52, while states of employment need only give favourable consideration to granting the latter priority in obtaining permission to work over other workers who seek admission to the state of employment.[110] It was suggested during drafting that Article 53 should include those family members who were born and had remained in the territory of the host country at the requisite age in addition to those who already had authorization of residence, as members of the migrant worker's family, on entering the state of employment.[111]

The free choice of employment provisions in the ICMW hardly advance the economic and social situation of migrant workers and their families in the host country. Indeed, they significantly undermine the progress made in this area by Article 14(a) of ILO Convention No. 143, which grants migrant workers free access to most categories of work after 2 years of residence and employment, regardless of whether they are admitted indefinitely or temporarily into the state of employment. Unfortunately, the importance of the ILO Convention was greatly minimized by a number of state delegations during the drafting of the ICMW.[112] As a result, the restrictions on access to employment found in Articles 52 and 53 of the ICMW resemble more the convoluted approach taken by some Council of Europe instruments, such as the European Convention on Establishment (ECE), rather than an evolution of the forceful simplicity manifested by Article 14(a) of ILO Convention No. 143.[113] In conclusion, therefore, the ICMW provisions concerning the right to free choice of employment reflect a marked deference to state sovereignty, and considerably weaken the ICMW as a rights-oriented instrument.

[110] Concern was expressed during drafting by some state representatives that this provision might require states parties to give priority to family members of migrant workers coming to the state of employment to work temporarily over migrant workers entering the state for the purpose of permanent settlement: *Working Group Report (June 1988)*, n. 64 above, 26, paras. 122–3 (Australia, Canada, and the USA).

[111] *Ibid.* 28, para. 138 (France).

[112] The representative of the Netherlands opined that the ILO Convention has only been ratified by a small number of states and therefore cannot be regarded as part of accepted international human rights law. The representatives of Germany and Australia, while recognizing the contribution of the ILO Convention to the ICMW, stressed that states parties which had not ratified ILO instruments could not be considered bound by them and that, in any event, within the network of international human rights standards, the instruments comprising the International Bill of Rights, namely the UDHR, the ICCPR, and the ICESCR, were regarded as 'paramount': *Working Group Report (June 1988)*, n. 64 above, 22, paras. 99 and 100 respectively.

[113] The Moroccan representative remarked that the series of restrictions in Art. 52 effectively rendered the phrase 'the right freely to choose their remunerated activity' in Art. 52(1) redundant: *ibid.* 20, para. 84. For a description of the free choice of employment provisions of the ECE, see the section on employment rights in Ch. 8.

Trade union rights

The ICMW introduces two-tier protection in respect of the trade union rights of migrant workers and their families. The two provisions dealing with trade union rights are Article 26 and Article 40, located in Parts III and IV of the ICMW respectively. The former provides migrant workers with the following rights: 'to take part in meetings and activities of trade unions and of any other associations established in accordance with law, with a view to protecting their economic, social, cultural and other interests . . .' (Article 26(1)(a)); 'to join freely any trade union . . .' (Article 26(1)(b)); and 'to seek the aid and assistance of any trade union . . .' (Article 26(1)(c)). Since Article 26 is located in Part III of the ICMW, it applies to *all* migrant workers and their families, including those with an irregular status, despite the opposition of some states to extending trade union rights to illegal migrants.[114] Article 40(1) provides to migrant workers and their families in a regular situation 'the right to form associations and trade unions in the State of employment for the promotion and protection of their economic, social, cultural and other interests'.[115] Both provisions also permit identical limitations on the rights expressed therein.[116]

This two-tier protection in the ICMW has been criticized as departing from existing international standards in the ICCPR, the ICESCR and ILO instruments, especially with regard to the protection of the trade union rights of migrant workers and their families in an irregular situation. Both Article 22 of the ICCPR and Article 8 of the ICESCR provide for the right to freedom of association to *all* persons, including the right to *form* and join trade unions. On their face, therefore, these general international human rights instruments grant illegal migrant workers the right to form trade unions for the protection of their interests, notwithstanding that this right might be difficult to exercise in practice. Furthermore, both provisions also assert that they do not impair the obligations of states parties to ILO Convention No. 87 of 1948 on Freedom of Association and the Protection of the Right to Organize, which proscribes, in Article 2, discrimination on the basis of nationality with respect to the *formation* and membership of trade unions.[117]

[114] *Working Group Report (June 1982)*, n. 92 above, 6, para. 18; *Working Group Report (June 1987)*, n. 94 above, 43, para. 211 (Germany).

[115] A number of state delegations expressed their opposition to this provision because they 'could not support the establishment of unions based on the national origin of their members in the State of employment, which would compete with existing national trade unions and would thus exclusively serve the interests of foreign nationals' (Argentina, Malaysia, and Venezuela), *Working Group Report (Nov. 1982)*, n. 86 above, 12, para. 43. It is also noteworthy that Art. 40(1) speaks of the 'promotion and protection' of the specified interests of migrant workers, whereas Art. 26(1) speaks merely of 'protecting' those interests.

[116] Under Arts 26(2) and 40(2) restrictions may be imposed on the exercise of trade union rights in the interests of national security, public order (*ordre public*), or the protection of the rights and freedoms of others. These restrictions must be prescribed by law and necessary in a democratic society.

[117] See also Eggers, n. 77 above, 433 and cf. Hasenau (1990), n. 74 above, 138–9. Hasenau, *ibid.* 139, observes that these deviations from the International Covenants and ILO Convention No. 87

The trade union rights protected by the ICMW appear not to include the right of migrant workers to electoral participation in trade unions or work councils. It is unlikely that the words 'to take part in meetings and activities of trade unions . . .' in Article 26(1)(a) would cover this right, especially as this term is located in Part III of the ICMW and is not elaborated upon in Article 40 in the context of regular migrants, where such a right would most likely be found. Indeed, the deleted provision in draft Article 43, referring to equal treatment between regular migrant workers and nationals in respect of trade union rights, went on to define extensively these rights as including 'eligibility for office in trade unions, in bodies of an occupational, economic or social character, and in labour-management relations bodies, including bodies representing workers in undertakings'.[118] Consequently, the ICMW provisions depart from ILO standards, where 'trade union rights' in Article 10 of ILO Convention No. 143 have been effectively defined by paragraph 2(g) of Recommendation No. 151 as encompassing 'eligibility for office in trade unions and in labour-management relations bodies, including bodies representing workers in undertakings'.[119]

Social security rights

The approach to the protection of social security rights in the ICMW resembles that taken to this question by ILO Convention No. 143 and the Council of Europe instruments (the ESC and the EMW) examined in the European case study, in that it is confined to a statement of general principle rather than being concerned with the details of this complex subject. Article 27 of the ICMW deals with two separate matters. Article 27(1) guarantees equal treatment between migrants and nationals in the state of employment in respect of social security 'in so far as they fulfil the requirements provided for by the applicable legislation of that State and the applicable bilateral and multilateral treaties'. Article 27(2) obliges states parties 'to examine the possibility of reimbursing contributions' made by migrant workers and their families on an equal basis with nationals who are in similar circumstances in the event that the applicable legislation does not provide for a right to receive the benefit concerned.

Although Article 27 is situated in Part III of the ICMW, it is not entirely clear from the drafting history whether it applies to illegal migrants to the same extent as it does to regular migrants. A clause in the draft text of Article 27 explicitly

have to be considered as 'a considerable depreciation of trade union rights of migrant workers in an irregular situation'. Indeed, the representative of the Netherlands only agreed to the consensus of the Working Group on Art. 26 on the understanding that the provision in no way limited the rights of migrant workers and their families in the ICCPR and the ICESCR: *Working Group Report (June 1987)*, n. 94 above, 46, para. 244.

[118] *Working Group Report (Oct. 1987)*, n. 86 above, 26, para. 133.

[119] As observed in the European case study, there is no express reference to such a right in Council of Europe instruments either, although EC law explicitly provides for this right in Art. 8 of Regulation 1612/68/EEC.

limiting the application of the equality principle in respect of undocumented migrants to those social security benefits to which they have contributed was shelved during the second reading.[120] Earlier during this reading some state delegations wanted to transfer the whole of Article 27 to Part IV of the ICMW.[121] Other states, however, together with the Chairman of the Working Group, contended that illegal migrant workers should have the right to at least some social security benefits, especially to those benefits to which they have contributed.[122] It would appear, therefore, that because of its location in Part III, Article 27 sets a minimum standard concerning social security applicable to *all* migrant workers and their families. However, one commentator argues that, in practice, Article 27(1) merely contains a minimum standard for the protection of the social security rights of regular migrant workers and their families. By virtue of the proviso in Article 27(1), which makes equal treatment with respect to social security benefits subject to 'the requirements provided for by the applicable legislation of [the] State and the applicable bilateral and multilateral agreements', it would be possible for states parties to adopt 'different provisions according to the regularity of the migrant worker's situation'.[123]

Article 27(2) applies to migrant workers' rights in the course of acquisition, the rights of those migrant workers who have already left the state of employment and have acquired rights in that state but not the right to receive benefits abroad, as well as to those migrants who are in an irregular situation.[124] States, however, need only 'examine the possibility' of reimbursing the contributions of migrant workers and their families in cases where the applicable legislation does not permit them to receive benefits. Hence this provision only constitutes a 'weakly worded' recommendation to reimburse such contributions.[125] This limited protection of social security rights, in the course of acquisition and acquired rights, by the ICMW is in stark contrast with ILO standards in this area.

Article 27, as a statement of general principle, differs somewhat from other similar general international standards by its lack of a specific reference point. The equality principle with respect to social security rights in Article 27(1) is

[120] *Working Group Report (Oct. 1987)*, n. 86 above, 8–9, paras. 27, 30.

[121] *Working Group Report (June 1987)*, n. 94 above, 50, para. 261 (Germany and Italy).

[122] *Ibid.* 50–1, paras. 262 (Chairman of the Working Group), 263 (Morocco), 266 (the former Soviet Union) and 267 (Greece).

[123] Cf. Hasenau (1990), n. 74 above, 143.

[124] *Ibid.* 144.

[125] *Ibid.* Hasenau, *ibid.*, concludes that this provision might, therefore, be meaningless because it is not a known practice for states to reimburse nationals either for rights in the course of acquisition or for acquired rights. During the drafting of the ICMW, for example, the Swedish representative observed that in Sweden there was no provision for the reimbursement of social security, even for Swedish citizens who had left the country and were living abroad: *Working Group Report (June 1987)*, n. 94 above, 50, para. 259. Similarly, Austrian legislation does not provide for the reimbursement of contributions because the social security system in that country is based on the 'insurance principle': *Working Group Report (June 1987)*, *ibid.* 50, para. 258 and *Working Group Report (Oct. 1987)*, n. 86 above, 9, para. 33. France and the USA also noted their concern regarding the possibility of reimbursing the social security contributions of migrant workers: *Working Group Report (Oct. 1987)*, *ibid.* 10, para. 35.

subject to migrant workers fulfilling the requirements provided by the applicable legislation of the state and 'applicable bilateral and multilateral treaties'. However, no specific multilateral treaty is mentioned. In contrast, Article 10 of ILO Convention No. 143, which provides for, *inter alia*, equality in respect of social security rights, may quite readily be supplemented by more precise ILO standards concerning social security. Similarly, Article 12 of the ESC refers specifically to ILO Convention No. 102 of 1952 concerning Minimum Standards of Social Security.[126] Consequently, the level of social security that migrant workers might expect is only ascertainable from the international social security treaties, if any, which a state party has agreed to, or from national legislation. One advantage of the ICMW, however, is that it does not require reciprocity for the social security provision to take effect and hence applies to those migrants who are nationals of states that have not ratified it.

Because Article 27 is a statement of general principle, the scope of social security is not defined, although at least two branches of social security seem to be covered by other ICMW provisions.[127] This problem of definition is exacerbated by the lack of a reference in Article 27 to a specific international social security instrument. Similarly, the lack of a definition of 'social security' raises doubts whether the term includes non-contributory benefits, which are not provided to migrant workers in some countries.[128] During the drafting of Article 27, some State delegations pointed out the need for a definition of 'social security'.[129] The Working Group Chairman, however, underlined the practical difficulties and complexities involved in finding a universally acceptable definition, and suggested that the Working Group would be better advised to adopt a very general provision.[130]

Right to health

The ICMW covers the rights of migrant workers and their families to equal treatment with nationals in respect of access to health care and occupational health

[126] Indeed, Art. 27(1) of the ICMW appears similar, in its generality, to Art. 18(1) of the EMW, which grants migrant workers equal treatment with nationals in respect of social security, 'subject to conditions required by national legislation and by bilateral or multilateral agreements already concluded or to be concluded between the Contracting Parties concerned'.

[127] Art. 25(1) would arguably cover the right to employment injury benefit and Art. 28 provides for the right to emergency medical care (see below). Arts 43(1)(e) and 45(1)(c) provide for equal treatment between regular migrants and nationals in respect of 'access to social and health services, provided that the requirements for participation in the respective schemes are met'. The *travaux préparatoires* shed little light on the meaning of this phrase. The German representative, however, stressed the need to distinguish between 'social security' and 'social services': *Working Group Report (Oct. 1987)*, n. 86 above, 29–30, para. 148.

[128] *Working Group Report (June 1987)*, n. 94 above, 50, para. 258 and *Working Group Report (Oct. 1987)*, n. 86 above, 9, para. 32 (Austria).

[129] *Working Group Report (June 1982)*, n. 92 above, 9, paras. 24–6 (the Netherlands, the United Kingdom, and the USA).

[130] *Working Group Report (June 1987)*, n. 94 above, 49, para. 256.

and safety, but in somewhat qualified and fleeting terms. Article 28, situated in Part III of the ICMW, reads as follows:

Migrant workers and members of their families shall have the right to receive any medical care that is urgently required for the preservation of their life or the avoidance of irreparable harm to their health on the basis of equality of treatment with nationals of the State concerned. Such emergency medical care shall not be refused to them by reason of any irregularity with regard to stay or employment.

Although this provision clearly applies to both regular and irregular migrant workers and their families, as emphasized by the final sentence, an attempt was made by the US delegation during the first reading to transfer Article 28 to Part IV of the ICMW on the basis that this Part alone dealt with social welfare rights.[131] Furthermore, Article 28 merely guarantees to migrant workers and their families the right to receive *emergency* medical care necessary 'for the preservation of their life or the avoidance of irreparable harm to their health'. In an earlier draft of Article 28, the latter part of this phrase was broader, reading 'or the restoration of their health', which again was opposed by the US delegation because it failed to distinguish adequately between emergency medical care actually required for the preservation of life and other forms of less urgent medical care.[132] Under Part IV of the ICMW, migrant workers and their families in a regular situation are also granted equal treatment with nationals of the state of employment in respect of 'access to . . . health services' (Articles 43(1)(e) and 45(1)(c)). The *travaux préparatoires* provide no clues as to the possible interpretation of this text. The special health problems which migrants face in the country of employment (and which were highlighted in Chapter 3) are not specifically addressed by the Convention.[133]

As far as equality between migrant workers and nationals in respect of occupational health and safety is concerned, the ICMW only contains brief references to this question in Article 25(1)(a) concerning equal treatment in respect of remuneration and, *inter alia*, other conditions of work, and in Article 70, considered in greater detail below in relation to the right to housing. Under the former, 'other conditions of work' are defined expressly to include 'safety' and 'health'. The latter provision, which only applies to migrant workers and their families who are in a regular situation, obliges states parties to adopt measures which are not less favourable than those applied to nationals to ensure that

[131] *Working Group Report (June 1982)*, n. 92 above, 11, para. 32.

[132] *Ibid.* The phrase 'or the avoidance of irreparable harm to their health' was introduced in an amendment proposed by the German delegation and supported by the US representative: *Working Group Report (June 1987)*, n. 94 above, 54, paras. 281–2. The latter also wanted to 'downgrade' the principle of 'equal' emergency medical care with nationals to 'equivalent' care: *ibid.* 54, para. 282. This proposal was opposed by the representative of the former Yugoslavia who argued that the situation of migrant workers was very different to that of nationals and that 'real equivalence could not exist': *ibid.* 54, para. 283. In the end, the German delegation was still unable to accept Art. 28 because of the word 'any' before 'medical care': *ibid.* 54, para. 287.

[133] See also Eggers, n. 77 above, 433.

migrants' working and living conditions 'are in keeping with the standards of fitness, *safety, health* and principles of human dignity'.[134] These passing references in the ICMW to the occupational health and safety rights of migrant workers should be contrasted with the more detailed and comprehensive provisions found in ILO Recommendation No. 151.

Right to housing

Chapter 3 underlined the importance of adequate housing for migrant workers for facilitating family reunion, as a prerequisite for the enjoyment by migrant workers and their families of other important rights, and for their successful integration in the state of employment. However, the ICMW only contains fleeting references to the housing rights of regular migrant workers. Illegal migrant workers are not entitled to any express housing rights.[135] Under Article 43(1)(d) of the ICMW, migrant workers in a regular situation are afforded equality of treatment with nationals in respect of 'access to housing, including social housing schemes, and protection against exploitation in respect of rents'. The reference to 'social housing schemes' was retained on the insistence of some state delegations,[136] and includes, therefore, public rental accommodation. Furthermore, because Article 43 supports the 'general equality' of migrant workers and nationals in various fields that do not first have to be the subject of regulation by the state, it would seem that Article 43(1)(d) also operates to protect migrant workers against discrimination by private landlords. Under Article 43(3), states of employment are prohibited from preventing an employer of migrant workers from establishing '*housing* or social or cultural facilities for them'. It was understood during drafting, however, that this provision did not impose a *positive* obligation upon employers to build the aforesaid facilities.[137]

There are no other direct references in the ICMW to the housing of migrant workers and their families. Contrary to most other international and regional standards, the family reunification provision in the ICMW imposes no express condition upon migrant workers to possess suitable family housing before family reunion may take place. This is probably because, as observed below, the provision is phrased in weak language, granting broad discretion to states parties in deciding whether to permit the entry of family members. There are also no express obligations to take into account the needs of migrants in housing construction

[134] Emphasis added. On one interpretation, these standards include standards of environmental hygiene that preclude, in relation to migrant farm workers, exposure to dangerous pesticides and insanitary conditions: UN, ECOSOC, Commission on Human Rights, 49th Session, *Summary Record of the 64th Meeting*, UN Doc. E/CN.4/1992/SR.64 (16 March 1993) 8, para. 30 (Mrs. Adams, Sierra Club Legal Defense Fund, Inc.).

[135] Note, however, the general obligation imposed upon states by Part VI of the ICMW in Art. 64 to 'consult and co-operate with a view to promoting sound, equitable and humane conditions in connection with international migration of workers and members of their families'.

[136] *Working Group Report (Oct. 1987)*, n. 86 above, 29, para. 145 (Algeria and Finland).

[137] *Working Group Report (Oct. 1989)*, n. 48 above, 11, para. 47 (Germany).

policies, as found in ILO Recommendation No. 115 of 1961 concerning Workers' Housing and Recommendation No. 151 concerning Migrant Workers, nor to promote the housing conditions of migrants. The latter obligation, however, may be implied in respect of regular migrants from Article 70 of the ICMW, which imposes a duty upon states parties to:

> take measures not less favourable than those applied to nationals to ensure that working and living conditions of migrant workers and members of their families in a regular situation are in keeping with the standards of fitness, safety, health and principles of human dignity.

A draft version of Article 70 was more explicit with regard to the housing of migrant workers and their families. The relevant measures to be taken by states parties were to include 'inspection of the working and living premises of migrant workers and members of their families by . . . competent authorities'. The authorities were also to be empowered to 'make recommendations for the improvement in the quality of these conditions'.[138] Originally, the provision was also to apply to *all* migrant workers and their families, but its ambit was eventually restricted to those persons in a regular situation.[139] It was also emphasized by two state representatives during drafting that Article 70 did not mean that states parties were under an obligation to 'establish for migrant workers conditions that were more favourable than those of nationals'.[140]

The ICMW contains no provision expressly guaranteeing the right to acquisition of private property, although it is arguable that equal treatment accorded by Article 43(1)(d) to regular migrant workers with nationals in respect of 'access to housing' should include access to the purchase of private accommodation. Moreover, both the applicability of the ICMW as a whole and the rights guaranteed therein to all migrant workers and members of their families are to be secured without distinction of any kind such as, *inter alia*, 'property' (Articles 1 and 7 respectively). By virtue of Article 15 of the ICMW, *all* migrant workers and their families are also protected against the arbitrary deprivation of their property. If such property or assets, however, are expropriated under the legislation of the state of employment, migrants have 'the right to fair and adequate compensation'.

[138] *Report of the Open-ended Working Group on the Drafting of an International Convention on the Protection of the Rights of All Migrant Workers and Their Families*, UN Doc. A/C.3/43/7 (17 Oct. 1988) (hereinafter *Working Group Report (Oct. 1988)*) 30, para. 139. Opposition to the inclusion of this provision came from Finland, Italy, Morocco, the former Soviet Union, and the USA, and was based on the arguments that the ICMW already provided for equal treatment in respect of working conditions (Art. 25) and that equal treatment in respect of living conditions would be difficult to assess and 'might require control which might infringe upon the right to privacy of migrant workers': *ibid.* 30, para. 140. The need, however, to make some statement in the ICMW on the subject of the living standards of migrants, which were deplorable in certain parts of the world, was stressed by a number of state delegations (China, India, and the former Yugoslavia): *ibid.* 30, para. 141.

[139] *Ibid.* 32, paras. 151–2 (Australia, China, Denmark, Norway, Sweden, and the USA).

[140] *Ibid.* 31, para. 149 (Germany and Norway).

Right to family reunification

The concept of 'family' under the ICMW has two different connotations. For the purpose of the *whole* of the ICMW, Article 4 defines the 'members of the family' of a migrant worker as those:

persons married to migrant workers or having with them a relationship that, according to applicable law, produces effects equivalent to marriage, as well as their dependent children and other dependent persons who are recognized as members of the family by applicable legislation or applicable bilateral and multilateral agreements between the States concerned.

A similar definition of the family is provided under Article 44(2) concerned solely with family reunification, with the exception that this provision specifically refers to 'minor dependent unmarried children' and omits the reference to 'other dependent persons'. These definitions constituted a compromise between western and developing countries, particularly those developing countries with Islamic roots.[141] The former, being essentially countries of employment, wanted to restrict the definition to the 'nuclear' family,[142] whereas the latter preferred that the definition encompass a broader group of persons in order to account for the 'extended' family.[143] Muslim countries were also opposed to a definition of the family which included relationships that produce 'effects equivalent to marriage' on the basis that this definition was incompatible with the concept of the family as defined by legislation in those countries, and consequently recorded their formal reservation to the provision.[144] Although such relationships encompass common law marriages, it is by no means clear what other relationships might be covered.[145]

In essence, however, the general definition in Article 4 is extremely flexible since relationships producing 'effects equivalent to marriage' and 'dependent children and other dependent members of the family' are to be determined in accordance with the 'applicable law', and also in the latter case, by applicable bilateral and multilateral agreements. This flexibility favours western countries of employment. Given that the laws of these countries are based on the 'nuclear family' concept, they may effectively decide who is a member of the migrant

[141] See also Hune (1987), n. 51 above, 124 and Lönnroth, n. 19 above, 730.

[142] *Working Group Report (June 1985)*, n. 42 above, 32, paras. 152–3 (Australia, Denmark, and Sweden). In addition, the German representative argued for a restricted definition of the family of a migrant worker on the basis that 'migration for remunerated activity was conceived only as a transitory phenomenon and not a permanent one': *Working Group Report (Oct. 1986)*, n. 76 above, 8, para. 37.

[143] *Working Group Report (June 1985)*, n. 42 above 32, para. 155 (Algeria, Morocco, and Tunisia).

[144] *Working Group Report (Oct. 1986)*, n. 76 above, 10, para. 51; *Working Group Report (Oct. 1987)*, n. 86 above, 41–2, para. 217 (Algeria, Bahrain, Egypt, Ghana, Iraq, Ivory Coast, Jordan, the Libyan Arab Jamahiriya, Mauritania, Morocco, Oman, Pakistan, Saudi Arabia, Senegal, Somalia, the Sudan, Syrian Arab Republic, and the United Arab Emirates).

[145] Cf. Nafziger and Bartel, n. 22 above, 786–7. Penna, n. 55 above, 184, reasons that if a restrictive interpretation were given to the word 'effects' in Art. 4, so as to refer to the biological capability of a relationship to produce offspring, common law marriages might be recognized, but not gay or lesbian relationships.

worker's family for the purpose of family reunion and for according rights under the ICMW.[146]

The provision concerning family reunification is Article 44 which is located in Part IV of the ICMW and therefore only applicable to regular migrants. To extend the right of family reunion to migrants in an irregular situation seems highly impractical because it could encourage a substantial inflow of other persons into the country of employment. Such an approach is consistent with the argument from the position of national sovereignty that limitations upon uncontrolled immigration are justified if such immigration threatens the physical security of the state. It has been contended, however, that confining the right to family reunification to legal migrants conflicts with the basic human right tenet outlined in Article 44(1):[147]

> States Parties, recognizing that the family is the natural and fundamental group unit of society and is entitled to protection by society and the state, shall take measures to ensure the protection of the unity of the families of migrant workers.

Unfortunately, the principle espoused in Article 44(1) appears to have been 'abandoned' in Article 44(2), which deals with family reunification *per se*. Under Article 44(2), states parties are under an obligation 'to take measures that they deem appropriate and that fall within their competence to facilitate the reunification of migrant workers with their [families as defined above]'. This provision is phrased in terms of a 'mere recommendation'[148] and can only be considered as 'guidance'[149] to states parties when exercising their discretion in deciding which members of the migrant worker's family to admit. The broad discretion accorded to states parties by Article 44(2) would also appear to permit the imposition of a number of conditions on family reunification, such as the possession of appropriate accommodation and resources to maintain the family.[150] Indeed, such conditions were expressly referred to in an earlier draft, although this draft also provided for family reunion as a qualified *right* of the migrant worker.[151] As the drafting progressed, however, this right was eroded. Finally, Article 44(3) imposes the duty upon states parties to 'favourably consider' facilitating the reunification of migrant workers with *other* family members 'on humanitarian grounds'. Even this weak obligation was opposed during drafting by some states of employment which wanted to delete the word 'favourably'.[152]

[146] See also Lönnroth, n. 19 above, 730. The countries of the Mahgreb, however, argued that the 'applicable law' should be the 'personal law' of the migrants concerned: *Working Group Report (June 1985)*, n. 42 above, 32–3, paras. 155, 157 (Algeria, Morocco, and Tunisia).

[147] Cf. Bosniak, n. 50 above, 759 (n. 38).

[148] Hasenau (1990), n. 74 above, 149.

[149] *Working Group Report (Oct. 1987)*, n. 86 above, 42, para. 219 (Norway).

[150] The French delegation interpreted the provision as permitting the state to set conditions on family reunification, in terms of migrant workers' duration of stay before the arrival of their families, and in terms of housing and resources: *ibid.* 42, para. 222.

[151] *Working Group Report (June 1982)*, n. 92 above, 21, para. 74.

[152] *Working Group Report (Oct. 1987)*, n. 86 above, 43, para. 229 (Australia, France, and the USA). However, the delegations of Algeria, Denmark, Ghana, Morocco, and the Netherlands insisted on retaining the term 'favourably': *ibid.* 43, para. 227.

Clearly, to speak of a *right* to family reunification in the ICMW is a misnomer. In line with other international instruments in this area, with the exception of the EC regime, states parties are given ample discretion to regulate the entry of the members of a migrant worker's family. What is most troubling about the family reunion provisions in the ICMW, however, is that this discretion is accorded to states to an extraordinary degree.[153] Article 44 is a significant step backwards in efforts to realize this important right of migrants. At this stage in the development of international human rights standards protecting migrant workers and their families, the more progressive approach would have been to grant migrant workers the *right* to family reunion and to subject this right to regulation. Instead, Article 44 constitutes a *carte blanche* provision, effectively permitting states parties to control and restrict at will the entry of migrant workers' families.

Right to education

(a) Vocational guidance and training

Equality between migrant workers and nationals in respect of access to vocational guidance and placement services, vocational training and retraining facilities and institutions is guaranteed under Articles 43(1)(b) and (c).[154] Because of their location in Part IV of the ICMW, these provisions in Article 43 apply only to regular migrant workers. Under Article 25, however, *all* migrant workers are afforded equal treatment with national workers in respect of, *inter alia*, other conditions of work and employment. Vocational guidance or training are not specifically enumerated in this provision, but the list in Article 25 is not exhaustive and room is made for additional conditions of work and employment in accordance with 'national law and practice'. If a state party, therefore, considers vocational guidance and training as a necessary component of its labour laws, illegal migrant workers might be encompassed by such legislation, although it is improbable that they would be able to benefit from it in practice.

Article 45(1)(b) extends the equality principle in respect of 'access to vocational guidance and training institutions and services' to members of the family of regular migrant workers. The express application of equality in this area to migrant workers' families is a welcome addition at a time when migrant youth,

[153] Art. 12 of the EMW also accords to states parties' considerable discretion in applying the principle of family reunion, but this discretion is circumscribed and also subject to a number of safeguards. State discretion in this area is also limited to some extent under the ICCPR and the ECHR by provisions prohibiting arbitrary and unlawful interference with, *inter alia*, family and private life (Arts. 17 and 8 respectively). Art. 14 is the equivalent provision in Part III of the ICMW.

[154] The US delegation objected to the application of equal treatment of migrant workers with nationals to 'placement services' because workers temporarily admitted to the USA for a specific job are unable to benefit from such services: *Working Group Report (Oct. 1987)*, n. 86 above, 29, para. 146. This concern is reflected in Art. 62, which excludes the application of Arts. 43(1)(b) and (c) from the rights to be enjoyed by specified-employment workers.

particularly second- and third-generation migrants in Western Europe, face considerable difficulties in ascending the occupational ladder.[155] The extension of vocational guidance and training rights to members of the families of migrant workers was opposed, however, by the representative of France on the grounds that such entitlements might imply a right to work.[156] Article 45(1)(b) is qualified by the phrase 'provided that requirements for participation are met', which was submitted by the US delegation in order to exclude the application of the provision to the family members of those migrant workers admitted temporarily to the USA, on the grounds that they might not possess authorizations to work.[157]

(b) Education of migrant children

Article 30 in Part III of the ICMW guarantees to each child of the migrant worker 'the basic right of access to education on the basis of equality of treatment with nationals'. This right applies to *all* such children, irrespective of whether they or their parents are in an irregular situation. The provision specifies that 'access to public pre-school educational institutions or schools shall not be refused or limited by reason of the irregular situation with respect to stay or employment of either parent or by reason of the irregularity of the child's stay in the State of employment'.[158] Although there was widespread support for the inclusion of a basic right to education in the ICMW, several states of employment were of the opinion that this right should have been confined to those in a regular situation and preferred to see the provision in Part IV.[159] In practice, however, the extensive exercise of the right to education by the children of irregular migrants is unlikely, because of the dangers involved for these migrants when they come into contact with public authorities.[160]

Under Articles 43(1)(a) and 45(1)(b) in Part IV of the ICMW, the right to 'access to educational institutions and services' on an equal footing with nationals is extended in general (and not just to children) to migrant workers and members of their families in a regular situation 'subject to the admission requirements and

[155] Only EC provisions and the EMW explicitly refer to a right of migrant workers' children to equal treatment with nationals in respect of vocational guidance and training. See respectively Art. 12 of Regulation 1612/68/EEC and Art. 14(1) of the EMW. Such a right is also available to migrant children by virtue of Arts. 9 and 10 of the ESC and is implicit in Art 6(1)(a)(i) of ILO Convention No. 97 and Arts 10 and 12(c) of ILO Convention No. 143.

[156] *Working Group Report (Oct. 1987)*, n. 86 above, 45, para. 239. See also n. 87 above and accompanying text.

[157] *Working Group Report (Oct. 1987)*, n. 86 above, 46, para. 244. There are no express references in the ICMW to the provision of local language instruction to migrant workers, such as those found in ILO Recommendation No. 151 and the EMW, nor to equal treatment between migrants and nationals in respect of financial assistance for vocational training.

[158] The restriction to 'public' educational institutions was inserted as a result of a proposal by the US representative: *Working Group Report (June 1987)*, n. 94 above, 55, para. 292.

[159] *Working Group Report (June 1982)*, n. 92 above, 12, para. 36 (USA) and *Working Group Report (June 1987)*, n. 94 above, 55, paras. 289 (Germany), 290 (Australia), and 293 (France).

[160] Hasenau (1990), n. 74 above, 146.

other regulations of the institutions and services concerned'.[161] It was emphasized by the US representative during drafting that equality in respect of 'educational services' does not include financial assistance for education.[162] Such an interpretation is in line with other international instruments, with the exception of the EC regime, where the grant of scholarships and government assistance to foreigners in the sphere of education is left to the discretion of states.

Finally, the ICMW obliges states of employment under Article 45(2) to:

> pursue a policy, where appropriate in collaboration with the States of origin, aimed at facilitating the integration of children of migrant workers in the local school system, particularly in respect of teaching them the local language.

The importance of integrating the children of migrant workers into the local school system was stressed during drafting.[163] It was also understood that the phrase 'where appropriate in collaboration with the States of origin' did not imply an obligation to collaborate, but left the initiative for any kind of collaboration to the discretion of the state of employment.[164] This provision resembles similar clauses in the EMW and in EC law, which seek to integrate the children of migrant workers into the local educational system through emphasis on teaching them the language or languages of the host state.

Cultural rights

Under Article 31(1) in Part III of the ICMW, states parties are under a duty to 'ensure respect for the cultural identity of migrant workers and members of their families'. The corresponding duty not to prevent migrants from 'maintaining their cultural links with their State of origin' is also included in this provision. Article 31 applies to *all* migrant workers and their families, but as with the basic right to education, there was opposition from those states which preferred to see this provision transferred to Part IV of the ICMW.[165] In the opinion of the US delegation, the approach in Article 31(1) placed a 'positive obligation on States parties to protect the cultural rights of all migrant workers'.[166] Any implication of the existence of a positive state duty in Article 31(1), however, was tempered considerably by the subsequent introduction of a second paragraph (Article 31(2)), which reads: 'States Parties may take appropriate measures to assist and encourage efforts in this respect [namely, in preserving the cultural identity of migrant workers and their families and maintaining their ties with their country of origin]'.

[161] This provision only applies to those migrant workers, who continue to be migrant workers and does not enable them to change their status: *Working Group Report (Oct. 1987)*, n. 86 above, 28, para. 141 (Norway). Furthermore, it was stressed by the Algerian and Finnish delegations that the inclusion of the criterion of 'admission requirements' concerning access to educational institutions 'must not authorize discrimination against migrant workers as regards [these] requirements': *ibid.* 29, para. 144.

[162] *Ibid.* 28, para. 139.

[163] *Ibid.* 47, para. 251 (Morocco).

[164] *Ibid.* 47, para. 252 (Norway).

[165] *Working Group Report (June 1982)*, n. 92 above, 13, para. 42 (USA).

[166] *Ibid.*

The original draft proposal contained the word 'shall' instead of 'may',[167] but the 'watering-down' of the obligation in this paragraph reflected the position that 'it was the sovereign right of each State to decide whether to encourage and assist in the cultural activities of the migrant workers'.[168]

The cultural rights of regular migrant workers and their families are reinforced by Parts IV and VI of the ICMW. In Part IV, Articles 43(1)(g) and 45(1)(d) guarantee them equal treatment with nationals in respect of 'access to and participation in cultural life'. In Part VI, under Article 67(2), which concerns the return of regular migrants to their country of origin, the states parties are required to 'co-operate as appropriate, on terms agreed upon by those States, with a view to promoting adequate economic conditions for [their] resettlement and to facilitating their durable social and *cultural* reintegration in the State of origin'.[169]

As discussed in Chapter 3, the enjoyment of cultural rights by migrant workers and their families is incomplete in the absence of measures assisting children in the maintenance and development of their mother tongue and culture. This concern is addressed in Articles 45(3) and 45(4). Under the former provision, states of employment are under a duty to 'endeavour to facilitate for the children of migrant workers the teaching of their mother tongue and culture'. Under the latter, these states 'may provide special schemes of education in the mother tongue of children of migrant workers'. In both cases, collaboration with the states of origin is advocated.[170] Neither provision appears to impose a positive obligation on states parties because both effectively constitute recommendations.[171] With regard to Article 45(3), this interpretation is supported by the cumbersome phrasing of the duty to 'endeavour to facilitate',[172] while Article 45(4) is clearly worded in terms of a recommendation, as indicated by the use of the word 'may' instead of 'shall'.[173]

[167] This proposal was submitted by 5 sending countries: *Working Group Report (Oct. 1987)*, n. 86 above, 56–7, para. 302 (Algeria, Morocco, Senegal, Turkey, and the former Yugoslavia).

[168] *Ibid.* 57, para. 306 (Finland). See also Hasenau (1990), n. 74 above, 148, who observes that Art. 31(2) does *not* oblige states parties to take any 'concrete' measures.

[169] Emphasis added. The text of this provision was originally proposed by the Algerian representative: *Working Group Report (Oct. 1983)*, n. 54 above, 7, para. 20.

[170] As with the obligation in Art. 45(2) to 'facilitate the integration of children of migrant workers in the local school system' and to teach them the local language, collaboration with states of origin appears to be optional only: *Working Group Report (Oct. 1987)*, n. 86 above, 47, paras. 258–9 (Norway and Finland with respect to Art. 45(3)).

[171] See also Hasenau (1990), n. 74 above, 148.

[172] According to the representative of the USA, Art. 45(3) does not impose an affirmative obligation on states parties to teach other languages, 'but only to endeavour to make the teaching of such languages possible': *Working Group Report (Oct. 1987)*, n. 86 above, 48, para. 264. This view was supported by the German delegation, which asserted that states of employment could not be required to provide the teaching of the mother tongue in all cases: *ibid.* 48, para. 265.

[173] The original draft proposal submitted by the Yugoslav delegation contained the word 'shall', but this was changed to 'may' on a proposal of the Italian representative specifically to ensure that the introduction of special educational schemes in the mother tongue of migrant children was in the form of a recommendation rather than an obligation on states of employment: *ibid.* 48, para. 261.

Despite the weaknesses in the text, general opposition to the concept of obliging states of employment to provide teaching of the mother tongue and culture, as well as some instruction in that language, to the children of migrants, was also voiced by some delegations. The French representative observed that many children of migrant workers were provided with the teaching of their culture and mother tongue in France, but insisted that such instruction 'was not a matter for States of employment to initiate, but rather it was exclusively for countries of origin to promote, often in co-operation with countries of employment'.[174] Moreover, the German delegation was unable to accept Article 45(4) on the basis that 'it would open the door to the principle of national classes in educational establishments, a principle which was at variance with the concept of integration'.[175] Nonetheless, Articles 45(3) and 45(4) are a considerable improvement on other international standards existing in this area, particularly those found in Article 15 of the EMW and Directive 77/486/EEC, which are discussed in the European case study.

Political rights

In contrast with other international standards concerned with the protection of migrant workers and their families, the political rights of migrant workers are relatively well defined in the ICMW. In principle, all migrant workers and their families, by virtue of Articles 26 and 40, considered earlier in the section on trade union rights, have a right to participate in political activities in the state of employment. Article 26(1) recognizes the right of migrant workers and members of their families 'to take part in meetings and activities of trade unions and of any other associations established in accordance with law, with a view to protecting their economic, social, cultural and other interests'. With regard to migrants in a regular situation, Article 40(1) grants the further right 'to form associations and trade unions in the State of employment for the promotion and the protection' of those same interests. The reference to 'other interests' in both provisions can be interpreted to encompass 'political activities', although the drafting debate reveals that many countries, including both sending and receiving states, preferred to exclude migrants from participating in political activities in the host country.[176] Indeed, the original draft text of Article 26 expressly excluded participation in 'political parties and organizations'.[177] In the light of this debate, therefore, an interpretation of the ICMW provisions which favours a right to general political activity for all migrants is hardly watertight. Moreover, states are also permitted to restrict the rights of migrants in both Articles

[174] *Ibid.* 48, para. 266. [175] *Ibid.* 49, para. 268.

[176] *Working Group Report (June 1982)*, n. 92 above, 6, para. 19; *Working Group Report (June 1987)*, n. 94 above, 43, para. 213 (Venezuela), 43, para. 216 (India, Morocco, and the former Yugoslavia) and 44, para. 220 (Ghana). This approach resembles the somewhat outdated philosophy enshrined in Art. 16 of the ECHR, which is discussed in the section on political rights in Ch. 8.

[177] *Working Group Report (June 1982)*, n. 92 above, 6, para. 20.

26(1) and 40(1) on the grounds of, *inter alia*, 'national security' and 'public order' or '*ordre public*' (Articles 26(2) and 40(2) respectively).

To restrict the political activity of migrants would arguably be inconsistent with the limited rights to political participation granted to them by Articles 41 and 42 of the ICMW. These rights are located in Part IV and are therefore confined to migrants in a regular situation. Article 41(1) guarantees migrant workers and members of their families 'the right to participate in public affairs of their State of origin and to vote and to be elected at elections of that State, in accordance with its legislation'.[178] As far as political participation by migrants in the state of employment is concerned, Article 42 outlines two state obligations. Article 42(1) urges states parties to:

> consider the establishment of procedures or institutions through which account may be taken, both in States of origin and in States of employment, of special needs, aspirations and obligations of migrant workers and members of their families and shall envisage, as appropriate, the possibility for migrant workers and members of their families to have their freely chosen representatives in those institutions.

Article 42(2) imposes a duty on states of employment to 'facilitate, in accordance with their national legislation, the consultation or participation of migrant workers and their families in decisions concerning the life and administration of local communities'. The first obligation concerns the establishment of participatory mechanisms enabling migrants to articulate their interests to the state authorities in question. The second obligation is actually more substantial and may possibly entail granting to migrants a right of electoral participation in the state of employment at the municipal level, despite the opposition of some countries to such a notion.[179] Any obligation to 'facilitate' the participation of migrants in local elections, however, is subject to the 'national legislation' of host states. The reference to 'national legislation' provides those countries opposed to affording migrants electoral rights with the discretion to continue such policies.[180] The extent of these two obligations is confused somewhat by Article 42(3) which declares that 'migrant workers may enjoy political rights in the State of employment if that State, in the exercise of its sovereignty, grants them such rights'. It

[178] Art. 41(2) imposes an obligation on the 'States concerned . . . to facilitate the exercise of these rights' as appropriate and in accordance with their legislation. It is not clear whether a positive duty is implied by this provision requiring the state of employment to take active measures, such as the setting up voting booths within its territory. Both the USA and Norway disputed such an interpretation at the drafting stage: *Working Group Report (Oct. 1987)*, n. 86 above, 34, para. 172.

[179] For example, the representative of the United Kingdom expressed her reservation to Art. 42(2) if it were to be interpreted to mean granting migrant workers and their families the right to vote in local affairs in the state of employment: *Working Group Report (Nov. 1982)*, n. 86 above, 15, para. 59.

[180] The delegation of the Netherlands, however, a country which grants migrant workers the right to vote in local elections, did not deem it necessary to include any reference to 'national legislation' in Art. 42(2): *Working Group Report (Oct. 1987)*, n. 86 above, 36–7, paras. 185, 191. Whether the reference to 'national legislation' would permit limitations on the political rights of migrants by lesser laws, such as municipal by-laws, is a moot point.

is not clear whether this provision leaves the granting of *further* political rights to the discretion of states of employment or whether it constitutes an additional restriction to the rights already accorded to migrants in the preceding two paragraphs.[181] Despite their limitations, the *potential* political rights which Article 42 of the ICMW offers migrants in a regular situation 'represent the highest standard reached in international instruments'.[182]

In line with other international instruments relating to the protection of migrant workers, the ICMW also restricts, in Article 52, their access to employment in the public service. By virtue of Article 52(2)(a), a state of employment may restrict for any migrant worker in a regular situation 'access to limited categories of employment, functions, services or activities where this is necessary in the interests of this State and provided for by national legislation'.[183] This provision is very similar to Article 14(c) of ILO Convention No. 143, with the exception that the latter does not refer to 'services' and 'activities' nor to the added safeguard that the restriction must be 'provided for by national legislation'. All that can be ascertained from the text of Article 52(2)(a) is that the restriction must be prescribed by law, apply to limited categories of employment, and be necessary in the 'interests of [that] State'. There are few further clues provided in the drafting process as to the possible interpretation of this clause. It is noteworthy, however, that the representative of the Netherlands suggested more specific wording during drafting, replacing the terms 'necessary in the interests of this State' with the words 'necessary in the interests of national security or public safety and public order (*ordre public*)'. But this proposal was withdrawn for lack of sufficient support.[184]

Residence rights

(a) The right of residence

As with ILO and European standards relating to the protection of migrant workers and members of their families, the ICMW ties the right of residence to the employment of the migrant worker. This is clearly reflected in Article 49(1), which

[181] For example, the representative of the Netherlands agreed to this provision, but only on the understanding that it did not limit the scope of Art. 42(2). On the other hand, the US delegation understood the limitations on political rights of migrant workers in the state of employment provided by Art. 42(3) as applying to any political rights that might arise out of the previous paragraphs: *ibid.* 37, paras. 191 and 192 respectively.

[182] G. Kojanec, 'The UN Convention and the European Instruments for the Protection of Migrants' (1991) 25 IMR 818, 826. But see now the rights granted by the Treaty on European Union to EC nationals who are resident in another EC member state enabling them to vote and to stand as candidates in municipal elections and in elections to the European Parliament. The applicable EC law is discussed in Ch. 8.

[183] Under Art. 53(1), members of a migrant worker's family, in possession of an authorization of residence or admission that is without time limit or is automatically renewable, are subject to the same conditions as are applicable to the migrant worker in respect of free access to employment in accordance with Art. 52.

[184] *Working Group Report (June 1988)*, n. 64 above, 20, para. 83.

obliges those states of employment that operate a dual-permit system to align authorizations of residence with work permits by stating that the former are to be issued for at least the same period of time as the latter.[185]

The ICMW also provides protection for migrant workers in a regular situation whose employment is terminated prior to the expiration of their work permits. This protection differs slightly depending on whether these migrant workers have the right to free choice of employment. In either case, however, migrant workers are not to be regarded as being in an irregular situation nor are they to lose their residence authorizations if their employment is terminated (Articles 49(2) and 51 respectively).[186]

With respect to migrant workers who have the right to free choice of employment, Article 49(3) provides them with the right to stay in the state of employment 'at least for a period corresponding to that during which they may be entitled to unemployment benefits' in order to enable them to find alternative work. The provision does not place an upper ceiling on the time migrant workers may stay in the state of employment under these circumstances, despite proposals from some state delegations to limit their period of residence to a maximum of 5 months, as in Article 9(4) of the EMW, or to ensure that this period does not exceed the duration of the work permit.[187]

Migrant workers in the state of employment who are not permitted to freely choose their remunerated activity are also provided, under Article 51, with the right to seek alternative employment as well as 'participation in public work schemes and retraining'. This right, however, may only be exercised 'during the remaining period of their authorization to work, subject to such conditions and limitations as are specified in the authorization to work'.[188]

The rights accorded to migrant workers in Articles 49 and 51 in respect of the termination of their employment should be read with Article 52 regulating the free access of migrant workers to employment in the host country. The opportunities open to migrant workers to find alternative employment are restricted by the operation of this provision. In contrast, ILO standards, in particular Article 8 of Convention No. 143, offer migrant workers in the host country greater opportunities to find alternative work because, in accordance with Article 14(a)

[185] This provision, therefore, is broader in scope than Art. 9(2) of the EMW, which, in the case of work permits of an indefinite duration, only requires states parties to issue residence permits for at least one year.

[186] Except, in the case of migrant workers who are not permitted freely to choose their remunerated activity in the state of employment, where 'the authorization of residence is expressly dependent upon the specific remunerated activity for which they are admitted' (Art. 51).

[187] *Working Group Report (Oct. 1987)*, n. 86 above, 63, paras. 348–9 (Sweden and Norway). For a discussion of Art. 9(4) of the EMW, see the section on residence rights in Ch. 8.

[188] Hasenau (1990), n. 74 above, 142, observes that the migrant worker must be given a reasonable period of time within the duration of the work permit in order to make effective use of the right granted in Art. 51. Any other interpretation would render the provision meaningless. He suggests that a period of 6 months or the length of time during which a migrant worker is entitled to unemployment benefit might be sufficient.

of the Convention, restrictions on their right to free choice of employment must be lifted after 2 years of residence or on completion of the first employment contract, if shorter in duration.[189]

Finally, residence must not be 'forced'. In accordance with other international human rights instruments, Article 8 of the ICMW grants migrant workers and their families the right to leave 'any State including the State of origin' and the right to enter and remain in the state of origin subject to certain specified restrictions.[190] Practices which require migrant workers to submit their passports or other travel documents to their employers in order to ensure that they remain in the specified employment for the duration of their contract are therefore unlawful under the ICMW.[191]

(b) Right to remain and to naturalization

The ICMW accords no right to remain to migrant workers and members of their families. Nor is there any right to acquire naturalization or citizenship in the host country. An interesting provision, however, is Article 50. Article 50(1) imposes an obligation on states parties, 'in the case of death of a migrant worker or dissolution of marriage, . . . [to] favourably consider granting family members of that migrant worker residing in that State on the basis of family reunion an authorization to stay'. In considering whether to grant such an authorization, the state of employment is to take into account 'the length of time [family members] have already resided in that State'. The principal objective of this provision is to ensure that family members of a migrant worker do not find themselves in an irregular situation in the event of his or her death or because of divorce.[192] The extent of Article 50(1) is ambiguous, however. No time-limit is provided specifying how long members of the migrant worker's family may stay in the host country. The drafting process reveals that the aim of the provision is not to grant an 'absolute right' to family members of a migrant worker to remain in the state of employment, but rather to encourage states 'to consider granting such permission taking into account humanitarian grounds'.[193] Article 50(2) grants to those

[189] See also Hasenau (1990), *ibid*. Consequently, ILO standards guarantee a considerable degree of security and stability to migrant workers and their families. *Ibid*.

[190] Art. 8, however, is less ambiguous and therefore more restrictive than its predecessors, Arts 12(1) and (4) of the ICCPR and Art. 13 of the UDHR, because the 'State of origin' is clearly defined in Art. 6(a) of the ICMW as 'the State of which the person concerned is a national'. Consequently, a migrant worker who is permanently resident in a country, but not a national, has no express right to enter and remain in that country. The *travaux préparatoires* reveal that the definition of 'State of origin' in Art. 6(a) was adopted in the light of discussions which had taken place on Art. 8. See *Working Group Report (Nov. 1981)*, n. 41 above, 10–11, para. 36; *Working Group Report (Oct. 1986)*, n. 76 above, 15, para. 76.

[191] See also Penna, n. 55 above, 187.

[192] *Working Group Report (June 1988)*, n. 64 above, 7, para. 24 (the Netherlands).

[193] *Ibid*. 9, para. 39 (the Canadian delegation supported by the representatives of Australia and Norway). The Finnish delegation expressed the view that the state of employment was under no duty to consider favourably granting dependants their own right to remain in that state beyond the period allowed to the migrant worker: *ibid*. 10, para. 41. The location of Art. 50 between Arts 49 and 51, considered above, would support such an interpretation.

members of a migrant worker's family, who are not granted an authorization to stay, a 'reasonable period of time' before departure 'to enable them to settle their affairs in the State of employment'.

(c) Expulsion and protection against expulsion

The provisions in the ICMW protecting migrant workers and their families against unfair and arbitrary expulsion are extensive. Article 22 in Part III enumerates a number of procedural safeguards to be followed before an expulsion decision may be valid and before it may actually be enforced. Because it applies to both regular and irregular migrants, Article 22 is broader than corresponding procedural safeguards against the expulsion of aliens found in Article 13 of the ICCPR and in Article 1 of Protocol No. 7 to the ECHR, which apply only to aliens *lawfully* resident within the territory of states parties.

Article 22(1) prohibits collective expulsion adding that each case of expulsion is to be examined and decided individually. Article 22(2) asserts that a decision to expel must be taken 'by the competent authority in accordance with law'. Article 22(3) requires that the migrants in question receive notification of the decision in a language that they understand. Where this is not mandatory, and if they so request, such a decision must be communicated to them in writing together with the reasons for the decision.[194] The requirement to give reasons may be waived in exceptional circumstances on account of national security.

Article 22(4) provides migrants facing expulsion with the right to submit reasons against their expulsion and to have the case reviewed by a competent authority, unless the decision is a final one pronounced by a judicial authority or unless compelling reasons of national security require otherwise. This right is not, strictly-speaking, a right of appeal because it does not entitle migrants access to an administrative authority of higher instance or to a judicial body.[195] Article 22(4) also specifically provides migrants facing expulsion with the right to seek a stay of the decision pending review. Although the guarantee is only to 'seek' a stay of expulsion, the provision offers migrants the opportunity to remain in the country while the decision is being reviewed and hence is phrased in stronger language than other international instruments concerned with this question.[196]

[194] During drafting, the US delegation questioned whether this requirement constituted 'a fundamental human right': *Working Group Report (June 1987)*, n. 94 above, 26, para. 107.

[195] Hasenau (1990), n. 74 above, 150. The original draft version of Art. 22(4) expressly granted migrants the right to 'appeal' a decision of expulsion. The word 'appeal' was substituted by 'review' on the insistence of a number of state delegations: *Working Group Report (June 1987)*, n. 94 above, 27, paras. 117 and 120 (China and Norway). The Tunisian delegation, however, strongly supported the concept of a right of all migrant workers and their families to have an opportunity to appeal against a decision of expulsion to higher (administrative or judicial) authorities: *ibid.* 27, para. 119.

[196] For example, Council of Europe and EC standards, which provide aliens and migrant workers procedural protection against expulsion, do not explicitly provide for the suspension of the expulsion decision pending its review. See Ch. 8 for a discussion of these standards.

If an expulsion decision, which has already been executed, is subsequently annulled, Article 22(5) gives the person concerned the right to seek compensation and underlines that the earlier decision is not to be used to prevent that person from re-entering the state from which he or she was originally expelled.[197]

Article 22(7) permits migrant workers and their families subject to a decision of expulsion to seek entry into a state other than their state of origin and Article 22(8) exempts migrants who are being expelled from 'the costs of expulsion', with the exception of travel expenses. The costs in question relate to the costs of administrative and judicial procedures leading up to the expulsion order and the expense of ensuring that migrants leave the country.[198]

Finally, Articles 22(6) and 22(9) were included to protect rights which migrant workers and their families acquire out of past employment. Under the former provision, a person facing expulsion is given 'a reasonable opportunity before or after departure to settle any claims for wages and other entitlements due to him or her and any pending liabilities'.[199] The latter assures migrants that expulsion from the state of employment does not prejudice their acquired rights, including the right to receive wages and any other entitlements due to them.

Article 22 is only concerned with procedural safeguards protecting migrant workers and their families from *arbitrary* or *unfair* expulsion. So long as the correct procedures are followed, states parties may expel migrants from their territory quite liberally. There are no provisions specifying the grounds upon which expulsion must be based.[200]

Article 56 in Part IV of the ICMW provides additional safeguards against the expulsion of migrant workers and their families in a regular situation. Article 56(1) maintains that migrants 'may not be expelled from a State of employment, except for reasons defined in the national legislation of that State'. These reasons, however, are not elaborated. An earlier draft of Article 56(1) stipulated that migrants in a regular situation could only be expelled for reasons of 'national security, public order (*ordre public*), or morals', but no agreement could be reached regarding the inclusion of these grounds. It was agreed, however, that Article 56(1) should go beyond Article 13 of the ICCPR, which is limited to procedural

[197] The need for such a provision may be justified in the light of the remarks made during drafting by the Swedish representative, who noted that although compensation was possible under Swedish law in the event of wrongful expulsion, there was no general right of compensation: *Working Group Report (June 1987)*, n. 94 above, 28, para. 127.

[198] Hasenau (1990), n. 74 above, 151. This provision corresponds to Art. 9(3) of ILO Convention No. 143. During the drafting of Art. 22(8), however, the Austrian and Norwegian representatives wished to place on record that, under their respective laws, the costs of physical removal from the country and the detention costs prior to departure constituted the responsibility of the persons concerned: *Working Group Report (June 1987)*, n. 74 above, 32–3, para. 153.

[199] The French delegation claimed that the words 'after departure' in Art. 22(6) might be interpreted as giving the right to migrants to re-enter the territory of the state concerned in order to settle their affairs. According to the delegation, 'such readmissions were within the exclusive sovereignty of States and should not be covered in an international instrument': *Working Group Report (Oct. 1987)*, n. 86 above, 6, para. 19.

[200] *Working Group Report (June 1988)*, n. 64 above, 36, para. 188.

protection only. Hence the wording, 'for reasons defined in the national legislation of the State', which implies the need to stipulate substantive grounds for expulsion.[201]

Article 56(2) provides that expulsion cannot be resorted to in order to deprive regular migrants 'of the rights arising out of the authorization of residence and the work permit'. According to a number of state delegations, the objective of this provision is to ensure that expulsion is not motivated by the desire to deprive the migrant workers of their rights 'as a result of the employment situation or other economic considerations'.[202] This intention to prevent expulsion on economic grounds, however, is not defined clearly in the text.[203] Finally, Article 56(3) urges states parties to take account of 'humanitarian considerations and of the length of time that the person concerned has already resided in the State of employment' in determining whether to expel a migrant worker or a member of his or her family.

Omissions: migrant women and youth

Although the ICMW is a comprehensive document, it arguably fails to give adequate attention to the protection of two particularly important groups of migrants, namely migrant women, who comprise nearly half of the migrant worker population, and migrant youth.[204] This is because the ICMW is not laid out in a manner suited to address coherently a number of specific problems raised by the international labour migration phenomenon.[205]

The ICMW clearly protects women, as migrant workers and as members of the family of the migrant worker. It uses inclusive language throughout, and its provisions apply equally to both male and female migrant workers.[206] The ICMW also contains specific provisions protecting women as family members, notably Article 45 relating to equality rights and Article 50 which provides for

[201] *Ibid.* 42, para. 219. See also Hasenau (1990), n. 74 above, 150. In addition, there is no reference in Art. 56(1) to 'compelling reasons of national security', such as there is in Art. 13 of the ICCPR, permitting states to waive some of the prescribed procedural safeguards against the unfair expulsion of migrants. Hasenau, *ibid.*

[202] *Working Group Report (June 1989)*, n. 45 above, 6, para. 17 (Australia, Finland, Germany, Italy, Mexico, Morocco, Sweden, and the former Yugoslavia).

[203] The Algerian representative claimed that if the sponsors of the text of Art. 56(2) really wanted to give effective protection to migrant workers threatened with arbitrary expulsion for economic reasons, the provision should have been 'worded more clearly so as to avoid any ambiguity': *ibid.* 7, para. 20.

[204] See V. P. Nanda, 'The Protection of the Rights of Migrant Workers: Unfinished Business' (1993) 2 *Asian and Pacific Migration Journal* 161, 172–3 and S. Hune, 'Migrant Women in the Context of the International Convention on the Protection of the Rights of All Migrant Workers and Members of Their Families' (1991) 25 IMR 800, 802.

[205] Cf. Nanda, n. 204 above, 170.

[206] Moreover, Art. 1 declares that the ICMW is applicable to all migrant workers and their families 'without distinction of any kind' such as, *inter alia*, sex, while Art. 7 prohibits discrimination on the ground of, *inter alia*, sex with respect to rights provided for in the ICMW. Hune (1991), n. 204 above, 809, observes, however, that the Working Group only agreed to use inclusive language throughout the ICMW, namely 'he or she' and 'his or her', towards the end of the drafting process. Originally, such language was only to be included in the provision concerned with definitions.

the possibility for women as family members to stay in the state of employment if the migrant worker dies or in the event of dissolution of marriage.[207]

The specific problems faced by migrant women, particularly by those from the developing world, were eloquently described by an NGO representative at the 48th Session of the Commission on Human Rights in March 1992:

> [W]hile the problems faced by migrant women could not be isolated from the problems facing all migrant workers, it was nevertheless true that their situation was considerably harder than that of men. They were living in a male-dominated industrial society and came from societies where man was the absolute master. They were alienated, exploited and oppressed in many ways. As migrants, they shared the conditions suffered by all migrant workers. As the wives of migrant workers, they had in most cases been obliged to leave their homes and follow their husbands. As women workers, they worked for the lowest wages in the hardest and most exhausting conditions and were subject to discrimination and pettiness of all kinds. As foreign women, they had to be the guardians and defenders of the traditions of their own countries while going through the cultural shock of adapting to new ways of life. As mothers, their traditional role was to transmit the language, customs and religion of their country to their children, while the children attended school where only the values, language and way of life of the receiving country were taught. Lastly, as women, they were vulnerable to sexual abuse and rape.[208]

The ICMW does not explicitly address many of these specific concerns.[209] It fails to expressly protect migrant women's particular vulnerability as victims of prostitution and of sexual as well as other forms of physical abuse.[210] Nor does

[207] See generally Hune (1991), n. 204 above, 812.

[208] UN, ECOSOC, Commission on Human Rights, 48th Session, *Summary Record of the 51st Meeting*, UN Doc. E/CN.4/1992/SR.51 (6 March 1992) 16, para. 91 (Ms. de Asis, Third World Movement Against the Exploitation of Women). See also UN, ECOSOC, Commission on Human Rights, 51st Session, *Summary Record of the 21st Meeting*, UN Doc. E/CN.4/1995/SR.21 (17 Feb. 1995) 12, para. 63 (Ms. Lochbihler, Women's International League for Peace and Freedom): 'Migrant women faced a triple discrimination as foreigners, economically underprivileged and subject to gender-specific oppression. Undocumented migrant women were especially vulnerable to violations of their basic human rights, including rape and other forms of sexual exploitation. The situation was exacerbated by the disintegration of traditional support structures and by the lack of culturally and linguistically appropriate services'.

[209] The discussion below is largely taken from Hune (1991), n. 204 above, 810–13 and Hune (1994), n. 16 above, 87–8.

[210] Hune (1994), *ibid.* 87, argues that some of the provisions in Part III of the ICMW, such as Art. 10 (protection against torture or cruel, inhuman, or degrading treatment or punishment), Art. 11 (protection against slavery or servitude) and Art. 16(2) (effective protection by the state against violence, physical injury, threats, and intimidation) should be interpreted 'to directly address the exceptional vulnerability of women in the areas of sexual exploitation, physical abuse and forced prostitution and illicit trafficking'. Some of the provisions in Part VI of the Convention on the 'promotion of sound, equitable, human and lawful conditions in connection with international migration of workers and members of their families' also provide, according to Hune, *ibid.*, 'opportunities to protect women in their special situation'. Despite the existence of these provisions, Hune, *ibid.*, concludes: 'the Convention does not adopt specific language that addresses the situation of women who are recruited without their knowledge for the purposes of prostitution and sexual entertainment and who are subject to sexual abuses such as rape and other forms of violence and harassment as part of their work conditions. If the above articles are gendered, that is, interpreted from the experiences of men, then women migrant workers remain at risk. In other words, the universality of men does not necessarily incorporate women's perspectives'. The problem of violence against women

the ICMW recognize that women's and men's work may not be the same and that women, as migrant workers, are more likely to experience occupational segregation by finding themselves in employment, such as light manufacturing and 'home' or 'domestic' work, where there are generally no organized trade unions and no records to measure entitlements to social benefits. Because women nationals of the state of employment also tend to find work in large numbers in similar activities, formal guarantees of equal treatment between nationals and migrant workers will not alleviate the situation of women migrant workers. Finally, the ICMW does not address the fact that women are the primary care-givers for children. The lack of child care facilities results in migrant women moving in and out of the paid labour force to care for their children, leaving them in a vulnerable position. The absence of guarantees in the ICMW for teaching the local language to adult migrants is especially detrimental to women, because women, as family members in particular, tend to be more isolated than their male counterparts, and therefore have fewer opportunities to learn the language of the host state, which would greatly assist their integration into the host society.

The ICMW also neglects to give specific attention to the situation of migrant youth, or second- and third-generation migrants. The primary social problem facing migrants as a whole in Western Europe largely concerns this group.[211] Although they might be either migrant workers themselves or fall into the category of 'members of the family' of the migrant worker, the ICMW does not refer specifically to migrant youth, particularly in those areas which are most important to them, such as employment, education, and naturalization.[212]

4.8 ILLEGAL MIGRANTS

Definition

The ICMW applies to *all* migrant workers and their families, including those who are in an irregular situation. For the purposes of the ICMW, Article 5(a)

migrant workers is now receiving the specific attention of the UN General Assembly. See GA Res. 47/96 of 16 Dec. 1992, GA Res. 48/110 of 20 Dec. 1993, GA Res. 49/165 of 23 Dec. 1994, and GA Res. 50/168 of 22 Dec. 1995. See also Commission on Human Rights Resolutions 1995/20 of 24 Feb. 1995 and 1996/17 of 11 April 1996 on the same topic and the Declaration on the Elimination of Violence against Women (GA Res. 48/104 of 20 Dec. 1993). At the Fourth World Conference on Women, held at Beijing in Sept. 1995, the Platform for Action called upon governments, *inter alia*, to 'ensure the full realization of the human rights of all women migrants, including women migrant workers, and their protection against violence and exploitation . . .': UN, *Report of the Fourth World Conference on Women*, Beijing, 4–15 Sept. 1995, UN Doc. A/CONF.177/20 (17 Oct. 1995), Annex II, Platform for Action, para. 58(k).

[211] See generally J. Widgren, 'The Position of "Second-Generation" Migrants in Western Europe' (1986) 23 *Studi Emigrazione/Etudes Migrations* 7, 16–18 and J. Gundara, 'Racism and the National Question in Europe' (1988) NQHR (SIM Special No. 7) 30, 42–3.

[212] See also Hune (1991), n. 204 above, 813. For example, as noted earlier, the ICMW contains no provisions facilitating naturalization for migrants in the state of employment.

considers migrant workers and members of their families to be documented or in a regular situation 'if they are authorized to enter, to stay and to engage in a remunerated activity in the State of employment pursuant to the law of that State and to international agreements to which that State is a Party'. By virtue of Article 5(b), migrant workers and members of their families are expressly considered as 'non-documented or in an irregular situation if they do not comply with the conditions provided for in subparagraph (a)'. The text provides a 'subjective' definition, leaving it up to the law of the state of employment to determine whether migrant workers and members of their families are non-documented or in an irregular situation. The provisions defining migrant workers and their families in Articles 2 to 4 are all applicable to illegal migrants. Consequently, illegal migrants who have been engaged in any remunerated activity *at any time* in the host country are encompassed by the appropriate ICMW provisions (Article 2(1)) and the persons most closely related to the irregular migrant worker are also protected (Article 4).[213] Illegal non-resident migrant seafarers, however, are not protected (Article 3(f)). The ICMW actually protects most illegal immigrants in the territory of a state party, with the exception of those who have overstayed their visa authorizations but are not employed, and those who do not meet a state's definition of 'members of the family'.[214]

The drafting debate

Throughout the drafting debate, various views were expressed regarding the extent of protection that should be afforded illegal migrants. These views have been succinctly analysed and summarized by Bosniak.[215]

There were those countries which considered according substantial rights to irregular migrants as extremely 'problematic' on the basis that providing more rights for this group encourages and even rewards violating a country's borders.[216] The opposite approach was taken by those states which viewed the protection of the human rights of illegal migrants as a question of universal values; an example of the recent movement within the international community of conferring special protection upon vulnerable groups. Another argument for according more rights to illegal migrants was based on instrumental as opposed to normative reasoning. It was contended that extending rights to illegal migrant workers would discourage employers from hiring such workers and improve conditions for national workers. Indeed, this reasoning is reiterated by recital 15 of the Preamble to the ICMW which maintains that 'recourse to the employment of migrant workers who are in an irregular situation will be discouraged if the fundamental human rights of all migrant workers are more widely recognized'.[217]

[213] See also Bosniak, n. 50 above, 740 (n. 7). [214] *Ibid.* [215] *Ibid.* 747–51.

[216] This view was shared by Germany and the USA, which wanted to limit the definition of 'migrant worker' only to those migrant workers in a regular situation. See n. 54 above and accompanying text.

[217] See also Bosniak, n. 50 above, 750.

These arguments for according rights to illegal migrant workers and members of their families may be buttressed by further justifications, which partly shift the responsibility for irregular migration to host countries: their insatiable demand for cheap migrant labour; the history of political and economic exploitation of illegal migrants' countries of origin; and the economic contribution of illegal migrants to the national community. Finally, the argument was advanced that strict controls on entry combined with effective enforcement measures to penalize those who exploit and hire non-documented migrants constitutes the best method of preventing the phenomenon of clandestine labour. This approach, however, has to be combined with the protection of the human rights of those who have already entered the state of employment without authorization. It is this policy which the ICMW seems to have adopted *vis-à-vis* illegal migrants.

Convention policy: rights for illegal migrants versus prevention of illegal migration: two irreconcilable principles?

The ICMW's dual objective to protect the human rights of illegal migrants and, at the same time, to prevent clandestine movements and trafficking in migrant labour is evident throughout the instrument. It has been argued, however, that this policy leads to a great deal of ambivalence regarding the protection of this vulnerable group because it attempts to achieve a compromise between two essentially irreconcilable principles.[218]

Part III of the ICMW contains a list of rights that is applicable to *all* migrant workers and members of their families. As outlined earlier, non-documented migrants receive express protection with respect to the following rights of concern in this study: rights to equal conditions of employment and work, trade union rights, social security rights, rights to health care, and rights to education and culture.[219] They are also entitled to certain specific safeguards when threatened with expulsion. Some of the protections afforded illegal migrants in Part III, however, fall below generally recognized international human rights standards. For example, the trade union rights guaranteed to non-documented migrant workers fall into this category, because these workers are not guaranteed the right to *form* trade unions. All of these rights, however, are augmented and strengthened in Part IV of the ICMW in relation to migrants in a regular situation. Moreover, Part IV accords rights to regular migrants, namely free choice of employment, family reunion, and political participation, which are denied to those in an irregular situation, mainly because these entitlements are inextricably connected with the sovereign interests of the state of employment.

218 See also Bosniak, *ibid.* 741 and Nafziger and Bartel, n. 22 above, 784.

219 Although non-documented migrants have no express right to housing under the ICMW, it is arguable that they are afforded some protection in this respect by the obligation of states parties to 'consult and co-operate with a view to promoting *sound, equitable and humane conditions* in connection with international migration of workers and members of their families' (Art. 64) (emphasis added). See n. 135 above and accompanying text.

The objective of preventing illegal migration is largely the concern of Part VI of the ICMW, entitled, 'Promotion of sound, equitable, humane and lawful conditions in connection with international migration of workers and members of their families'.[220] Under Article 68(1), states parties, including states of transit, are obliged to 'collaborate with a view to preventing and eliminating illegal or clandestine movements and employment of migrant workers in an irregular situation'. The measures to be taken to this end by states of employment are to include, in Article 68(2), the imposition of employer sanctions in order to 'eliminate the employment in their territory of migrant workers in an irregular situation'.[221] Article 68(2) further provides that the 'rights of migrant workers *vis-à-vis* their employer arising from employment shall not be impaired by these measures'. This provision came about as a result of proposals from the delegations of India and Italy, which were concerned that employers should not be able to escape their responsibilities with respect to the protection of the employment rights of illegal migrant workers on account of the existence of measures imposing employer sanctions.[222] It was emphasized during the drafting of Article 68(2), however, that the rights protected were only those that had 'already accrued at the point the employment was terminated owing to its illegality'.[223] Article 68(2) does not define the extent of the employer sanctions to be imposed in contrast with Article 6(1) of ILO Convention No. 143, which asserts that the sanctions to be applied are to consist of 'administrative, civil and penal sanctions, which include imprisonment in their range'.

Bosniak contends that the provision concerned with employer sanctions and the exercise of ICMW rights by illegal migrants are in conflict, and provides the following example:

> [A]n employer might fire a particular migrant worker who had begun to participate in a trade union (an activity protected by the Convention under Article 26(1)), claiming that he wished to comply with the sanctions laws. If, under that state's law, discharge of nationals is prohibited on grounds of trade union participation, then the employer's discharge of the undocumented employee could constitute *both* a violation of Article 25(1)(a) of the Convention (which mandates equality of treatment with nationals for all migrant workers with respect to laws regarding 'termination of the employment relationship') *and* a compliance with state sanction laws. Under the circumstances, it might be difficult to

[220] See also Art. 64, *ibid.*

[221] Opposition to a provision relating to employer sanctions was voiced by the representative of the USA, who argued that 'the question of imposing sanctions on employers of undocumented workers was a matter exclusively within the jurisdiction of the State of employment and should not be discussed in [Art. 68]': *Report of the Open-ended Working Group on the Elaboration of an International Convention on the Protection of the Rights of All Migrant Workers and Their Families*, UN Doc. A/C.3/38/1 (16 June 1983) 34, para. 109.

[222] *Working Group Report (Oct. 1983)*, n. 54 above, 9, para. 27.

[223] *Working Group Report (Oct. 1988)*, n. 138 above, 25, para. 112. On this interpretation, the provision resembles Art. 9(1) of ILO Convention No. 143, which guarantees illegal migrant workers equal treatment with regular migrant workers in respect of 'rights arising out of past employment as regards remuneration, social security and other benefits'.

ensure that sanctions do not 'impair' undocumented migrant workers' rights with respect to their employer. Even if the employer was found to have violated the undocumented worker's rights by 'pretextual' use of sanctions against the employee, sanctions against hiring irregular migrants would insulate the employer from ever having to reinstate the worker.[224]

The ICMW does not provide an answer to such difficulties. This example also illustrates the problems which illegal migrants face with respect to the exercise of their ICMW rights, a question that is considered in more detail below.

Problem of the exercise of convention rights

Expressly granting rights to illegal migrants in a universal multilateral instrument is a considerable step forward in the international protection of this vulnerable group, but it does little to alleviate the practical problems which exist in respect of the exercise of their ICMW rights. This chapter has already referred to some of the obstacles illegal migrants might face if they attempt to enforce, for example, claims to rights to equal work and employment conditions and to the right of their children to education.[225] Attempts by illegal migrants to exercise their Part III rights may be thwarted if they are subject to detection, prosecution, and punishment as a result and, ultimately, expulsion. Indeed, the threat of detection and expulsion is usually sufficient to prevent them from seeking redress for any violations.[226] There is no provision in the ICMW which would guarantee any protection, for example some form of immunity for violating immigration law, to illegal migrants who approach state authorities to complain about infringement of their rights under the ICMW.[227] Indeed, other ICMW provisions seem to preclude such protection. For example, Article 79, examined below, reaffirms state sovereign rights in respect of the admission of migrant workers and their families. Furthermore, Article 34, strategically placed in Part III of the ICMW, also asserts, *inter alia*, that nothing in that Part operates to relieve migrants from 'the obligation to comply with the laws and regulations of any State of transit and the State of employment . . .'.

[224] Bosniak, n. 50 above, 761–2 (n. 43) (original emphasis).

[225] A good practical example of such obstacles is the legal situation in Japan, described by Kitamura, n. 71 above, 121–2, 125. On their face, Japanese labour standards apply equally to all workers regardless of nationality or legality of visa status. However, Japanese immigration law imposes an obligation on civil servants to report the whereabouts of illegal migrant workers to the Immigration Control Bureau (Art. 62 of the Immigration Control and Refugee Recognition Act 1990). Therefore, any allegations of labour standards' violations which undocumented workers make against their employers risk leading to their detection and expulsion.

[226] See also Bosniak, n. 50 above, 759. According to Bosniak, this is essentially the experience of many non-documented migrant workers in those states of employment which formally extend rights to them. *Ibid.* 759–60.

[227] Bosniak, *ibid.* 760, observes that such provisions do exist in national legislation. For example, the US Immigration Reform and Control Act 1986 contains a 'confidentiality clause', which maintains that information provided in an application for regularization of status by non-documented immigrants shall not be used for any other purpose than to make a determination on the application. Failure to apply this clause may result in criminal prosecution.

Regularization

There is no obligation in the ICMW to regularize the status of illegal migrants. Article 69(1) in Part VI imposes a duty on states parties to take appropriate measures to ensure that a situation whereby illegal migrants are present within their territory does not persist. Juxtaposed to this provision is Article 69(2) which provides that whenever states parties are considering the possibility of regularizing the situation of such persons they should take into account 'the circumstances of their entry, the duration of their stay in the States of employment and other relevant considerations, in particular those relating to their family situation'. During drafting, some state delegations were of the opinion that this provision might imply an obligation to regularize irregular migrant workers.[228] Clearly, however, no such strict obligation is intended. The provision only requires that certain matters be taken into account once a state has decided to proceed with regularization or an amnesty programme for illegal migrants.

The only other international measures that deal with the question of regularization are Article 9(4) of ILO Convention No. 143 and paragraph 8(1) of ILO Recommendation No. 151. The former declares that nothing in the Convention shall prevent states parties from affording illegal migrant workers the right to stay and to take up employment, whereas the latter urges member states to arrive at a speedy decision whether the non-documented status of the migrant may be regularized or not. Neither of these provisions implies an obligation to regularize the situation of illegal migrants and are therefore similar to Article 69(2) of the ICMW. Article 69(2) should also be read with Article 35 in Part III of the ICMW, which provides that nothing in that Part is to be interpreted as implying:

> the regularization of the situation of migrant workers or members of their families who are non-documented or in an irregular situation or any right to such regularization of their situation, nor shall it prejudice the measures intended to ensure sound and equitable conditions for international migration as provided in Part VI.

The reference in this Article to Part VI makes it clear that the provision does not conflict in any way with Article 69(2).

The lack of a clear obligation in the ICMW to regularize the illegal status of migrant workers, particularly if they have resided in and contributed to the economy of the country of employment for some considerable time, or at least to move towards some gradual redefinition of their situation, further undermines their exercise of ICMW rights in the absence of provisions providing them with protection against detection if they attempt to avail themselves of these rights.[229]

[228] *Working Group Report (Oct. 1988)*, n. 138 above, 27–8, paras. 122, 127 (Canada and Germany). Indeed, the representative of Germany argued that Art. 69(2) *explicitly* assumed that 'regularization was an appropriate method of combating irregular migration', whereas the first paragraph *implicitly* assumed the same.

[229] Cf. Bosniak, n. 50 above, 763. Bosniak, *ibid.* (and n. 45), argues that such an approach threatens 'to take away with one hand what has been offered by the other', although she also concedes

This schism is a direct result of the compromise in the ICMW between the protection of human rights and the principle of state sovereignty, which is most prevalent in the area of illegal immigration. Nonetheless, the ICMW constitutes a significant advance in the protection of the human rights of irregular migrant workers and their families in contrast with, for example, European instruments which do not refer to this question.[230] Indeed, it represents a meaningful effort, although by no means an entirely successful one given the constraints of state sovereignty, to implement the universal principles of human rights protection:

> The inclusion of undocumented migrants within the protective framework of the international human rights regime is . . . significant for what it reveals about the development of human rights law more generally. In an international society in which State sovereignty remains the paramount ordering principle, undocumented migrants present human rights law with an especially hard case. By promulgating this Convention, and by including the breadth of protections for undocumented immigrants that it has, the United Nations has demonstrated a notable, albeit partial, willingness to rise to the challenge of universality which the international law of human rights has posed.[231]

4.9 STATE SOVEREIGNTY

As stated at the beginning of this chapter, the ICMW constitutes a delicate balance between the protection of migrants' rights and the principle of state sovereignty, notwithstanding that the latter finds no place in the Preamble from which the other essential rationales for the ICMW can be identified. The principle of state sovereignty, however, in the specific context of immigration, is clearly underlined in Article 79 in Part VIII of the ICMW on General Provisions:

> Nothing in the present Convention shall affect the right of each State Party to establish the criteria governing admission of migrant workers and members of their families. Concerning other matters related to their legal situation and treatment as migrant workers and members of their families, States Parties shall be subject to the limitations set forth in the present Convention.

It is difficult to assess how this provision is likely to affect the ICMW as a vehicle for promoting the rights of migrant workers and their families, although some clues as to its possible interpretation can be gauged from debates during drafting leading up to the inclusion of this controversial clause in the ICMW. According to the US representative, the purpose of this provision is to reaffirm 'the well-recognized principle that all States have the sovereign right to adopt

that, in practice, resorting constantly to amnesties is a self-defeating exercise because it encourages further illegal entry and stay in the country, in expectation of yet further regularization.

[230] Nanda, n. 204 above, 170, also writes that the 'two-tiered structure notwithstanding, the Convention is a promising step forward toward extending protection to undocumented workers'.

[231] Bosniak, n. 50 above, 765.

and enforce their own immigration policies'.[232] The insertion of Article 79, however, was opposed by a number of state delegations on the basis that it was not indispensable to the ICMW.[233] The Swedish representative added that Article 79 may undermine the other provisions of the ICMW, and this was of particular concern given the need to ensure the protection of the fundamental human rights laid down in the ICMW which 'always have to be respected by all States'.[234] The scope of Article 79 is ambiguous as is evident from the debate over the interpretation of the word 'admission' during drafting. Some state representatives from 'immigration countries' argued for a broad interpretation of 'admission', claiming that the state's sovereign rights in respect of the 'admission' of migrant workers and their families are not only concerned with border controls, but also extend to questions of residence and expulsion.[235] Although the second sentence of Article 79 appears to preclude such an interpretation, the Swedish concern, according to Bosniak, 'attests to the enormous, almost talismanic power that assertions of state sovereignty have had often in the area of human rights for aliens'.[236]

4.10 SUPERVISION AND ENFORCEMENT

Supervision

The application of the ICMW is the subject of Part VII. The body that is to be set up for the purpose of reviewing the application of the ICMW is the Committee on the Protection of the Rights of All Migrant Workers and Members of Their Families (Article 72). The Committee will consist of 10 experts at the time of the entry into force of the ICMW, and of 14 experts after its ratification by 41 states.[237] These experts are to be of 'high moral standing, impartiality and recognized competence in the field covered by the present Convention'. They

[232] *Working Group Report (June 1988)*, n. 64 above, 5, para. 13.

[233] *Working Group Report (Nov. 1982)*, n. 86 above, 5, para. 17; *Working Group Report (Oct. 1987)*, n. 86 above, 19, para. 94; *Working Group Report (June 1988)*, n. 64 above, 5, para. 10.

[234] *Working Group Report (June 1988)*, *ibid.* 6, para. 20.

[235] *Ibid.* 5–6, paras. 13, 14, 15 and 17 (USA, France, Canada, and Germany respectively). See also Bosniak, n. 50 above, 756–7. Kitamura, n. 71 above, 25, contends that such an interpretation of Art. 79 is unacceptable if the word 'admission' is to be interpreted in the context of the object and purpose of the Convention. Kitamura argues that the word 'admission' in Art. 79 'refers to the power of the State to admit or deny a foreigner at the entry stage, and does not include the discretionary power of the State to deport or expel'.

[236] Bosniak, n. 50 above, 757.

[237] The size of the Committee was a bone of contention during drafting. Some state delegations, largely for financial reasons but also to ensure effective implementation of the ICMW, preferred a small Committee consisting of a maximum of 10 or 12 experts. Indeed, this approach was in line with the present preference in the UN for smaller supervisory committees. Under both the Convention on the Rights of the Child and the Convention Against Torture and Other Forms of Cruel, Inhuman and Degrading Treatment or Punishment 1984 (GA Res. 39/46), 10-member monitoring committees have been established. Other delegations were of the view that a larger Committee would do greater justice to the complexity of the ICMW and better ensure equitable geographical representation, including the maintenance of a balance between migrant-sending and -receiving countries. The 10- to 14-member Committee constituted a compromise solution between these two approaches. See the *Working Group Report (Oct. 1988)*, n. 138 above, 36–40, paras. 172–5, 179, 181–8 and 42–3, paras. 196–202.

are to be nominated and elected by states parties to the ICMW to serve in their personal capacities for a 4-year term.

The Committee's supervisory functions are threefold. It is to examine reports on the application of the ICMW submitted by states parties and it may also receive complaints from states and individuals. These functions are therefore similar to those established under other UN human rights instruments.

(a) State reporting

Under Article 73, states parties are under an obligation to submit reports on the 'legislative, judicial, administrative and other measures they have taken to give effect to the provisions of the Convention'. Initially, these reports must be submitted one year after the entry into force of the ICMW and thereafter every 5 years and whenever the Committee so requests.

Under Article 74(1), the Committee is to examine these reports and may transmit appropriate comments to the state party concerned. It may also request supplementary information when considering the reports and receive observations from state parties on any comments made.

(b) Inter-state complaints

Article 76 provides for an inter-state complaints procedure involving the Committee. Under this provision, a state party may, if it considers that another state party is not fulfilling its obligations under the ICMW, bring the matter, in writing, to the attention of the latter. If the matter is not resolved within 6 months of the initial communication, either state may refer it to the Committee. The Committee is to make its good offices available to the states parties concerned with a view to reaching a friendly settlement. The inter-state complaints procedure is optional and only becomes operational if both states concerned have made a declaration accepting it and if 10 states parties in total have made such a declaration. During drafting, the view of those state delegations who wanted to make this procedure optional prevailed over those who preferred a mandatory inter-state complaints mechanism.[238] The former considered a mandatory procedure as inappropriate because of the complexity of the ICMW and also because it would discourage potential states parties from ratifying it.[239] The latter were of the opinion that such a procedure would ensure the ICMW's effective implementation.[240] This debate is another example of the conflict between the principle of state sovereignty and the international protection of human rights that permeates the ICMW and its whole drafting process.[241]

(c) Individual complaints

Article 77 of the ICMW provides for an individual complaints procedure. The Committee is empowered to receive communications from or on behalf

[238] *Working Group Report (June 1989)*, n. 45 above, 18–22, paras. 81–109.

[239] *Ibid.* 19, para. 85 (Germany) and *ibid.* 20, para. 89 (USA) regarding the latter point.

[240] *Ibid.* 20, para. 87 (Algeria and China).

[241] Bosniak, n. 50 above, 752 (n. 27).

of individuals who allege that their rights as established by the ICMW have been violated by a State party. Communications must meet a set of admissibility requirements in order to be accepted, including the exhaustion by the petitioner of all available domestic remedies.[242] The Committee is required to bring any communications before it to the attention of the state party concerned, which is obliged, within 6 months, to submit to the Committee 'written explanations or statements clarifying the matter and the remedy, if any, that may have been taken by the State'. The Committee shall then forward its views to the state party concerned and to the individual. As with state complaints, this procedure is optional. It applies only to those states parties that have made a declaration to this effect under Article 77 and comes into force when 10 states parties have made this declaration.

A proposal to include an individual complaints mechanism in the ICMW was introduced by the Dutch delegation during the drafting process in the latter stages of the second reading in order to complement the inter-state complaints procedure.[243] Further justification for a provision allowing individual communications was based on the practice established under other international human rights instruments, which had shown that individual complaints mechanisms had proved to be relatively efficient in contrast with inter-state grievance machinery which was rarely used.[244] Opposition to such a provision, however, was voiced by a number of states of employment.[245] Although the Canadian delegation supported the inclusion of a procedure allowing for the communication of individual complaints, it expressed concern that such a provision would apply to a broad range of rights, 'including those of an economic, social and cultural nature', which might give rise to problems of interpretation for the Committee and result in the Committee being 'burdened with an overwhelming number of unsubstantiated, frivolous complaints'. Nevertheless, since most state delegations supported the inclusion of an individual complaints mechanism in the ICMW and because

[242] A communication is also inadmissible if, according to the Committee, it is anonymous, an abuse of the right of submission of such communications, or incompatible with the provisions of the ICMW (Art. 77(2)). The Committee will not consider communications that have been or are being examined under another procedure of international investigation or settlement (Art. 77(3)(a)). The Committee may waive the need to exhaust all domestic remedies by the petitioner if it considers that the application of the remedies is 'unreasonably prolonged or is unlikely to bring effective relief to that individual' (Art. 77(3)(b)).

[243] *Working Group Report (June 1989)*, n. 45 above, 18 and 19, paras. 82, 92.

[244] *Working Group Report (Oct. 1989)*, n. 48 above, 58, para. 274.

[245] *Ibid.* 59, paras. 278–9 (France, Germany, and the USA). The objections of the German representative were similar to those made in respect of the inter-state complaints mechanism: *ibid.* 57, para. 267 and n. 239 above and accompanying text. Originally, the MESCA grouping of countries was also opposed to an optional individual complaints procedure 'in view of the broad range of the Convention's stipulations and having regard to the state of the law in the field'. See 'Reflections on a System for Supervision of the Application of the Convention', Working Paper submitted by Finland, Greece, Italy, Norway, Portugal, Spain, and Sweden: Further Suggestions Relating to Proposals presented in Document A/C.3.35/WG.1/CRP.15 and Corr.1 and 2 (Part VI) on the Draft International Convention on the Protection of the Rights of All Migrant Workers and Their Families (para. 8). This document is annexed to *Working Group Report (Oct. 1983)*, n. 54 above.

its opponents were unwilling to block the consensus, Article 77 was added to the final draft.[246]

(d) Participation of the ILO

The question of ILO participation in the ICMW's supervision was the topic of a lively debate.[247] The opinions in this debate ranged from those of state delegations who wanted to transfer the whole supervision process to the ILO Committee of Experts on the Application of Conventions and Recommendations[248] to those who preferred that the ILO have no or very little say in the application of the ICMW.[249] In between, were the MESCA countries which advocated a substantive role for the ILO within a distinct supervisory mechanism. Initially, this grouping of countries proposed that the Governing Body of the ILO be empowered to appoint 6 independent experts to an 18-member Committee. The rationale for this proposal was based on the special competence and experience of the ILO in the field of labour migration.[250] Because of the opposition to this proposal by those states who preferred a greatly reduced role for the ILO,[251] the MESCA countries submitted a compromise proposal which was eventually accepted. Article 74(5) stipulates that the International Labour Office 'shall be invited by the Committee to appoint representatives to participate, in a consultative capacity, in the meetings of the Committee'. The Working Group interpreted the words 'consultative capacity' to have the same meaning as the words 'without the right to vote'.[252] Hasenau argues that the presence of non-voting ILO representatives in the Committee is unlikely to have much influence on that body's work. Indeed, he observes that a similar advisory role given to the ILO during the meetings of the Working Group did not prevent the adoption of watered-down provisions which jeopardize existing international labour standards.[253]

[246] The delegations of Algeria, Australia, Canada, Finland, Mexico, Morocco, the Netherlands, and Sweden provided their express support for this mechanism: *Working Group Report (Oct. 1989)*, n. 48 above, 57–60, paras. 270–1, 273–5, 281–2. The Moroccan representative even advocated the adoption of a mandatory individual complaints procedure: *Working Group Report (Oct. 1989)*, *ibid.* 59, para. 275.

[247] See also Hasenau (1990), n. 74 above, 152–3.

[248] *Working Group Report (June 1984)*, n. 54 above, 14, para. 47 and 17, para. 60 (USA).

[249] *Ibid.* 15, para. 48 and 17, para. 56 (Algeria, India, Morocco, and Tunisia).

[250] 'Reflections on a System for Supervision of the Application of the Convention', n. 245 above, 34, paras. 10–11.

[251] Arguments during drafting, which were submitted against the participation of the ILO Governing Body in the appointment of a number of experts to the UN Committee, can be summarized as follows: the ICMW was to cover many matters considered outside the competence of the ILO; the ILO would be placed in a privileged position with respect to states as far as participation is concerned because states would only be permitted to appoint one expert each, whereas the ILO would be able to appoint several; the proposal for ILO participation constituted a departure from established practice in the supervision of a UN instrument; and the proposal might result in the appointment of persons from states which are not parties to the ICMW. See *Working Group Report (June 1984)*, n. 54 above, 15, para. 50. See also *Working Group Report (Oct. 1988)*, n. 138 above, 34, para. 167.

[252] *Working Group Report (Oct. 1988)*, n. 138 above, 62, para. 330.

[253] Hasenau (1990), n. 74 above, 153. Böhning (1991), n. 19 above, 704–5, maintains that the task of the ILO representatives will be to persuade the UN Committee that provisions in the ICMW, which are similar to ILO standards, should be interpreted and applied on the lines already drawn by the ILO Committee of Experts.

Further to its participation in the deliberations of the Committee, the ILO is provided with additional but less significant status with respect to the ICMW's application. Article 74(2) instructs the UN Secretary-General to transmit to the Director-General of the International Labour Office copies of reports submitted by states parties and information relevant to the consideration of these reports in order to enable the Office to assist the Committee with any expertise relevant to the matters falling within ILO competence. Under Article 74(8), the UN Secretary-General is also specifically required to transmit the Committee's annual report to, *inter alia*, the International Labour Office.

Enforcement

The ICMW contains no formal enforcement mechanism beyond the inter-state and individual complaint procedures examined above. If a state party is found to have infringed the ICMW, there are no binding sanctions available to the Committee to enforce against that state party. This lack of a binding enforcement mechanism is a feature of UN human rights conventions.

The only specific instructions with regard to enforcement are directed to states parties by Articles 83 and 84 in Part VIII. The former provision obliges states parties to ensure the following: that any person whose rights have been violated under the ICMW has an effective remedy; that the person seeking a remedy is entitled to a review of his or her claim and to a decision by competent judicial, administrative, or legislative authorities; and enforcement of remedies by the competent authorities when such remedies are granted. Under the latter provision, states parties undertake to adopt the legislative and other measures necessary to implement the provisions of the ICMW. Otherwise, those wishing to 'enforce' the ICMW must rely on informal mechanisms, which are essentially limited to publicity and action by NGOs. NGOs may play a significant role, not only in obtaining acceptance of the ICMW but also, once the ICMW has been accepted, in making use of the supervisory procedures in order to put pressure upon states parties to comply with its provisions.

(a) Publicity

Once states have ratified ICMW, Article 73(4) obliges states parties to make their reports 'widely available to the public in their own countries'. This provision was introduced by Sweden late into the drafting process and received widespread support.[254] The clause, however, was opposed by the German delegation on the grounds that it dealt with a 'politically sensitive' matter. A requirement, therefore, that states give broader dissemination to reports submitted under Article 73 of the ICMW was unacceptable to this delegation.[255]

In order to encourage states to ratify the ICMW, the UN General Assembly

[254] *Working Group Report (June 1990)*, n. 45 above, 13, para. 49. See also T. Ansay, 'The New UN Convention in Light of the German and Turkish Experience' (1991) 25 IMR 831, 844.

[255] *Working Group Report (June 1990)*, n. 45 above, 13–14, para. 50.

and Commission on Human Rights have called upon the Secretary-General to provide all the facilities and assistance necessary for the promotion of the ICMW, and have urged UN organizations and agencies, as well as intergovernmental organizations and NGOs, to intensify their efforts with a view to disseminating information on and promoting understanding of the ICMW.[256]

(b) Action by NGOs

NGOs may play a vital role in ensuring that states accept and comply effectively with the ICMW.[257] Their role in publicizing the Convention is crucial.[258] The first strategic priority for NGOs should be to urge states to ratify the ICMW so that the minimum of 20 ratifications necessary for its entry into force are obtained as quickly as possible. Strategies for realizing this objective may focus on convincing those states of employment, which presently secure some rights to migrants, that their laws are already more or less in conformity with the ICMW, or on encouraging sending countries, which are concerned with the living and working conditions of their nationals resident in receiving countries, to ratify the ICMW.[259]

Once the ICMW comes into force, NGOs may also play a considerable role in its supervision. Under Article 77(1), NGOs may assist individuals alleging a violation of the ICMW's provisions by submitting communications to the Committee on their behalf.[260] Because fewer states have accepted the right of individual complaint under international human rights instruments,[261] the NGO role in the ICMW supervisory system is more likely to be confined to action on the submission of state reports and the Committee's examination of these reports. NGOs may involve themselves in the former process by requesting governments to organize public hearings before finalizing their reports and then by stimulating political and public debate once these reports have been issued and publicized.[262]

[256] For example, see GA Res. 49/175 of 23 Dec. 1994 and Commission on Human Rights Res. 1995/21 of 24 Feb. 1995. It has also been suggested that 'sufficient resources should be allocated (to the UN and the UN Centre for Human Rights) to ensure production and wide distribution of materials, including a briefing paper on the Convention for government officials, parliamentarians and legislatures involved in ratification procedures': UN, ECOSOC, Commission on Human Rights, 49th Session, *Summary Record of the 64th Meeting*, n. 134 above, 5, para. 15 (Ms. Grange, Commission of the Churches on International Affairs of the World Council of Churches).

[257] The potential role of NGOs in this regard is considered more extensively by Hune and Niessen (1991), n. 20 above, 140–1 and Niessen and Taran, n. 25 above.

[258] An example of such publicity is a briefing paper, available in four languages, produced by the Churches' Committee for Migrants in Europe (CCME) under the title *Proclaiming Migrants' Rights. The New International Convention on the Protection of the Rights of All Migrant Workers and Members of Their Families*, Briefing Paper No. 3 (CCME, March 1991). To date, however, NGOs, with few exceptions, have not publicized the ICMW nor placed sufficient pressure on governments to sign and ratify it. See Hune and Niessen (1994), n. 79 above, 399.

[259] Niessen and Taran, n. 25 above, 861.

[260] See also Niessen and Taran, *ibid.* 862–3.

[261] As at 1 Jan. 1996, out of 146 states parties to ICERD only 21 have made a declaration under Art. 14 recognizing the right of individual complaint. Under the ICCPR, however, 87 out of 133 states parties have ratified the Optional Protocol to the Covenant which permits individuals to submit complaints to the Human Rights Committee.

[262] Niessen and Taran, n. 25 above, 863–4. See also Art. 73(4) above on the question of publicity.

Article 74(4) also gives NGOs a 'quasi-formal' role in the Committee's examination of state reports. Under this provision, the Committee may invite, *inter alia*, 'other concerned bodies to submit, for consideration by the Committee, written information on such matters dealt with in the Convention as fall within the scope of their activities'. The Working Group understood the words 'other concerned bodies' to include NGOs in consultative status with ECOSOC.[263] The response to this inclusion of NGOs was rather mixed. The German delegation preferred to explicitly exclude NGOs as a source of information arguing that many NGOs, whose activities centred on the international migration of workers, 'were often inspired more by their partisan alignment than by their competence and objectivity and it was difficult to distinguish between such organizations'. The Swedish representative, on the other hand, supported an explicit reference to NGOs in Article 74(4) on the basis that NGOs carried out important work in the field of human rights all over the world and that the ICMW should include an express recognition of this contribution.[264] Irrespective of Article 74(4), which requires an invitation from the Committee, NGOs may also submit their own informal 'reports' to the Committee to complement those of states, as occurs before other international human rights supervisory bodies.[265]

The ICMW supervisory mechanism is arguably weaker than that found within the ILO tripartite structure, a consideration that may yet eventually stimulate its wider ratification[266] in contrast with the poor record of ratifications under corresponding ILO instruments. Any potential for the widespread ratification of the ICMW, however, will not hide the fact that it contains no binding enforcement mechanism, which is a weakness suffered by UN human rights instruments. In this respect, therefore, the ICMW cannot compare with the comprehensive enforcement machinery available under the ECHR and the EC regime.

4.11 Conclusion: Success, Failure, or Merely a 'White Elephant'?: Prospects for Ratification

The reaction to the ICMW has been mixed. The ICMW contains a number of innovative features, which take it beyond what is already offered elsewhere with respect to the international protection of the economic, social, cultural, political, and residence rights of migrant workers and their families. It constitutes the first comprehensive universal codification of migrants' rights. The only other universal approach is found within the ILO, which has limited competence to deal with such concerns as culture, education, and political participation. The ICMW also contains the most comprehensive definition of 'migrant worker' formulated to date

263 *Working Group Report (Oct. 1988)*, n. 138 above, 62, para. 330.

264 *Ibid.* 61–2, paras. 323 and 324 respectively.

265 Niessen and Taran, n. 25 above, 864.

266 Cf. W. R. Böhning, 'The Protection of Migrant Workers and International Labour Standards' (1988) 26 IMR 133, 143.

and clearly applies to *all* migrant workers and their families, including those in an irregular situation. It extends and strengthens a number of rights applicable to migrants in other international human rights instruments, such as the right to equal treatment with nationals in respect of work and employment conditions and the right to protection against arbitrary and unfair expulsion. It also creates new rights, such as limited political rights for documented migrants.[267]

Another valuable characteristic is the participation of the ILO in the meetings of the supervisory body, which although less extensive and active than some states would have wished for, is nevertheless a concrete step towards the realization of productive cooperation between the UN and the ILO in the field of international migration.[268] It is true that the ICMW has encroached upon a sphere of competence which was the traditional reserve of the ILO. This does not necessarily mean, however, that the rights of migrants are any poorer. Although ILO standards for the protection of migrant workers and their families are in general stronger, the UN is more 'visible', especially in the present international political climate. The ICMW, therefore, regardless of whether it receives rapid ratification, is more likely, as a UN instrument, to remain in the limelight longer.

The ICMW has the potential to become a 'standard norm among the major human rights instruments' for the protection of migrants.[269] It can constitute a framework for the adoption of other international instruments in this area, particularly bilateral agreements between labour-sending and labour-receiving countries.[270] In the European context, it may also serve as a minimum standard of treatment for migrant workers and their families from central and eastern Europe and from the developing world who, as indicated in the European case study, are generally not protected under the EC regime and by other Council of Europe instruments, with the exception of the ECHR.[271] More importantly, the ICMW offers a minimum standard of treatment for illegal migrants in Europe, who are presently ignored by analogous European standards.

[267] The ICMW also assists in ensuring the economic security of the families of migrant workers left behind in the country of origin, or in another state, by providing for the 'right [of migrant workers] to transfer their earnings and savings, in particular those funds necessary for the support of their families . . .' (Art. 47). This provision, however, is located in Part IV of the ICMW and thus only applies to documented workers. It should be contrasted with Art. 5(1)(g) of the Declaration on the Human Rights of Individuals who are not Nationals of the Country in which They Live, considered in Ch. 2, which grants to *all* aliens, 'the right to transfer abroad earnings, savings or other personal monetary assets'. See also the equivalent provisions in Art. 9 of ILO Convention No. 97 and para. 9(c) of Recommendation No. 86, which are identical and by virtue of which states parties undertake 'to permit, taking into account the limits allowed by national laws and regulations concerning export and import of currency, the transfer of such part of the earnings and savings of the migrant for employment as the migrant may desire'.

[268] See generally Lönnroth, n. 19 above, 735–6.

[269] Cf. *ibid.* 734. Although Penna, n. 55 above, 197, accepts that the drafters of the ICMW did not realistically expect it to attract prompt ratification and incorporation into domestic law by major countries of employment, he claims that the ICMW nonetheless 'illustrates the awareness by the international community of the hazards and hardship encountered by migrant workers and its aspirations to find effective solutions'.

[270] Cf. Lönnroth, n. 19 above, 735.

[271] See also cf. Kojanec, n. 182 above, 818 and 829.

The innovations that the ICMW affords with respect to the international protection of the rights of migrant workers and their families should not eclipse its failings. The tension between the principle of national sovereignty and the protection of human rights, evident in the text and pervasive throughout the drafting debate, is clearly resolved in favour of states with respect to certain crucial matters of concern to migrants that affect their living and working conditions in the host country. In particular, the 'rights' to free choice of employment and family reunification are effectively reduced to mere recommendations. The extent of protection offered with regard to these 'rights' also falls below that found in other international instruments pertaining to migrants, particularly those of the ILO. Other notable 'rights' omissions' from the ICMW are the right of *all* migrant workers to *form* trade unions and the lack of a transparent provision concerned with the right of migrant workers and their families to adequate accommodation. Any conflict between standards constitutes an impediment to the establishment of a uniform law on the international protection of migrants' rights.[272] Furthermore, there are no rights to stay or to naturalization in the ICMW, which, taken together with the weak protections offered in terms of access to employment and family reunification, prevent migrant workers from planning a secure life in the state of employment.[273] The ICMW also pays insufficient attention to specific problems caused by labour migration, for example by neglecting to address the special health problems of migrants, and by failing adequately to protect migrant women, as workers and as family members, and second- and third-generation migrants who constitute a 'sociological time-bomb' in many states of employment.[274] Finally, the ICMW, like many other UN human rights instruments, does not contain any binding enforcement machinery. Enforcement is dependent on national action and NGO pressure.

Clearly, the success of the ICMW very much depends on action at the national level.[275] The more states that ratify it, the more likely it is that the ICMW will become a recognized and authoritative statement of the protection of migrants' rights. A number of obstacles to ratification, however, can be identified. First, the ICMW is a complex and detailed instrument, and contains new wording, which in many cases departs from established human rights language.[276] Secondly, the

[272] Hasenau (1990), n. 74 above, 153, writes on the subject of the co-existence of ICMW and ILO standards: 'The elaboration of the United Nations Convention has led to the existence of two distinct sets of standards on the rights of migrant workers and their family members, subject to separate supervisory mechanisms. Some provisions of the UN Convention fall below ILO standards, while others are more progressive and thus erode existing international labour standards'. Even if some standards are essentially similar, different interpretations by different supervisory bodies may lead to conflict. The ICMW offers no solution as to what is to be done in the event of such conflict. See Nafziger and Bartel, n. 22 above, 784–5.

[273] Cf. Ansay, n. 254 above, 842.

[274] Hune (1991), n. 204 above, 813, citing from International Labour Office, *World Report*, vols 1–2 (Oxford: Oxford University Press, 1987) 74.

[275] See also Hune, *ibid.* 814.

[276] Nafziger and Bartel, n. 22 above, 787. These authors, *ibid.* 786–7, also point out that ambiguous drafting might 'haunt' the future of the ICMW, particularly the drafting of Art. 2 (definition of 'migrant worker') and Art. 4 (definition of 'members of the family' of a migrant worker).

recent proliferation of specific human rights conventions hardly facilitates the acceptance of the ICMW's sizeable text.[277] Technical questions alone, therefore, may prevent many states from speedily accepting its provisions.[278] Thirdly, the lack of publicity about the ICMW has also contributed to misconceptions about the purpose of the instrument.[279] But there are also more serious substantive obstacles to widespread ratification of the ICMW. Provisions explicitly granting rights to illegal migrants are likely to hinder ratification,[280] despite the fact that the ultimate aim of this approach is to end irregular migration altogether.[281] Throughout the drafting process, as discussed earlier, both Germany and the USA opposed granting rights to migrants in an irregular situation. Such states are prevented by Article 88 of the ICMW from excluding this group of migrants on ratification and are therefore more likely to consider not ratifying the ICMW at all. More generally, the present international political and economic situation is hardly conducive to the protection of the rights of migrant workers and their families. The end of the Cold War, the political instability in central and eastern Europe, the large refugee flows from former Yugoslavia and the Caucusus, as well as the continuing uncertainty in the global economy, the deepening gulf between poor and wealthy nations, and the growth of permanent migrant populations with different racial and cultural backgrounds, have resulted in less sympathy for the condition of migrant workers and their families resident in developed countries of employment.[282] From the perspective of the developing nations, the 'new wind of liberalism' sweeping the world endangers the already precarious situation of certain vulnerable groups, such as migrant workers and their families, by failing to cater for their fundamental needs.[283]

The ICMW will enter into force 3 months after 20 states have ratified it (Article 87). A second landmark is 41 ratifications, after which the Committee on the Protection of the Rights of All Migrant Workers and Members of Their Families will commence operating to its full 14-member capacity. Early UN projections were that 20 states would ratify the ICMW in 1991 or 1992 and that it

[277] Cf. A. Boudahrain, 'The New International Convention: A Moroccan Perspective' (1991) 25 IMR 866, 867.

[278] Hune and Niessen (1994), n. 79 above, 402, write: 'The great number of articles of the Convention covering many aspects of the situation of migrant workers necessitate that many governmental departments must be consulted before the ratification process can be started. This explains why it will take a long time before States can actually ratify'.

[279] Cf. Hune (1994), n. 16 above, 89. Hune, *ibid.*, argues that 'many believe that an international convention that provides such forms of human rights protection to migrant workers will only encourage more migration, especially irregular migration'. One of the principal aims of the ICMW, however, is 'to *reduce* irregular migration and its exploitation' (emphasis added). See also Hune and Niessen (1994), n. 79 above, 400.

[280] Hune (1994), n. 16 above; Hune and Niessen (1994), n. 79 above, 402; R. B. Lillich, *The Human Rights of Aliens in Contemporary International Law* (1984) 76 with regard to a draft version of the ICMW.

[281] See also Hune and Niessen (1994), n. 79 above, 403.

[282] Hune (1991), n. 204 above, 814; Hune and Niessen (1994), n. 79 above, 396–8.

[283] Boudahrain, n. 277 above, 814.

would receive 41 ratifications by 1993.[284] In retrospect, these estimates were very optimistic given the present state of affairs. In addition to the obstacles mentioned above, a number of major countries of employment asserted at the time of drafting that they were unlikely to ratify the ICMW.[285] On the other hand, it is expected that the smaller MESCA countries, other states of employment and many labour-sending countries will ratify it.[286] The ICMW, however, will be considerably weakened if it is not endorsed by some major countries of employment.[287] At present, its entry into force in the near future is rather wishful thinking. As at 1 November 1996, nearly 6 years after the ICMW was adopted by the UN General Assembly, only 7 states (Colombia, Egypt, Kuwait, Morocco, the Philippines, the Seychelles, Sri Lanka, and Si Leone) had ratified it,[288] despite frequent calls for ratification by the UN General Assembly and the Commission on Human Rights.[289] This very low figure speaks volumes and is a clear reflection

[284] Böhning (1991), n. 19 above, 706 (n. 5), citing from UN General Assembly, *Programme Budget Implications of Draft Decision A/C.3/45/L.62*, UN Doc. A/C.5/45/60 (New York: UN, 1990). See also Hune and Niessen (1991), n. 20 above, 139.

[285] It would appear from the deliberations in the Working Group that Australia, Germany, the Gulf States, Japan, and the USA are unlikely to ratify the ICMW. See Böhning (1991), n. 19 above; Hune and Niessen (1991), n. 20 above, and Kitamura, n. 71 above, 129 regarding the position of Japan. Indeed, the German representative made this categorically clear in the following statement: '[The German] delegation maintained its substantive reservations with respect to the need for the adoption of a new convention on the protection of the rights of migrant workers, since, in its view, such protection was already amply afforded by the Universal Declaration of Human Rights and the International Covenants on Human Rights, which should not be diminished through the elevation of supplementary rights to the rank of human rights. As regards rights relating to employment, social security and the stay of migrant workers, the International Labour Organization was the competent organization. Apart from such substantive reservations, . . . [the] delegation had objections to a great many provisions adopted on second reading. The most important of these objections related to the fact that migrant workers in an irregular situation should become subjects of an international convention, that such a convention should accord them too many rights and that Article 2, paragraph 2, included within the scope of the [draft] Convention categories of persons which . . . were not truly migrant workers. In the light of all those objections, it seemed highly unlikely that . . . Germany would ratify the Convention': *Working Group Report (Oct. 1987)*, n. 86 above, 66, para. 376.

[286] According to Hune and Niessen (1991), n. 20 above, in addition to MESCA countries, Algeria, Argentina, Canada, Mexico, Morocco, the Netherlands, Tunisia, and Venezuela are likely to ratify the ICMW eventually. Hune (1994), n. 16 above, 89, contends that the size of the ICMW and the resulting need to conduct extensive national consultations is the principal reason why it has not yet been ratified by those countries which were closely involved in the drafting process and which expressed their support for it.

[287] Hune and Niessen (1994), n. 79 above, 404, argue that 'if only sending countries ratify, the Convention would lose its practical meaning'.

[288] Two states, Chile and Mexico, have signed the ICMW. See UN Doc. E/CN.4/1997/65, para. 4.

[289] GA Res. 46/114 of 17 Dec. 1991, GA Res. 47/110 of 16 Dec. 1992, GA Res. 48/148 of 20 Dec. 1993, GA Res. 49/175 of 23 Dec. 1994, GA Res. 50/169 of 22 Dec. 1995; Commission on Human Rights (CHR) Res. 1991/60 of 6 March 1991, CHR Res. 1992/81 of 6 March 1992, CHR Res. 1993/89 of 10 March 1993, CHR Res. 1994/17 of 25 Feb. 1994, CHR Res. 1995/21 of 24 Feb. 1995, CHR Res. 1996/18 of 11 April 1996. Res. 1994/17, adopted by the Commission on Human Rights, uses stronger language than before and 'calls upon all Member States to sign and ratify . . .' the ICMW rather that the words: 'calls upon all Member States to consider the possibility of signing and ratifying . . .'. It is noteworthy that this resolution, which was proposed by the representative of Mexico, was not adopted by consensus, as is the normal practice, but by a vote, on the initiative of

that, for the moment at least, the political will required to protect migrant workers and their families is lacking. The application and implementation of the ICMW will require a Herculean effort on behalf of individual states, NGOs, and the international community at large.

the US representative. The resolution was adopted by 39 votes to none against with 13 abstentions. See UN, ECOSOC, Commission on Human Rights, 50th Session, *Summary Record of the 41st Meeting*, 25th Feb. 1994, UN Doc. E/CN.4/1994/SR.41, 14–15, paras. 85–91. See also Hune and Niessen (1994), n. 79 above, 403. However, Res. 1995/21 and Res. 1996/18 revert back to the less forthright language. The Vienna Declaration and Programme of Action, adopted by the World Conference on Human Rights on 25 June 1993, also calls for (in Pt II) the ratification of the ICMW, but in very mild terms: 'The World Conference on Human Rights invites States to consider the possibility of signing and ratifying, at the earliest possible time, the [ICMW]': UN Doc. A/CONF.157/24 (Pt I), 36, para. 35.

PART III

Case Study of the Regional Protection of the Rights of Migrant Workers and their Families in Europe

5

Council of Europe Human Rights Conventions and European Community Law: A Comprehensive Framework for Protecting the Rights of Migrants in Europe?

5.1 INTRODUCTION

The international protection of the economic, social, cultural, political, and residence rights of migrant workers and their families in Europe is discernible on a number of levels, and it is necessary to distinguish the different regimes, organizations, and multilateral instruments which play a part in the protection of this vulnerable group.

The European Community (EC), consisting of 15 member states,[1] is the most advanced international regime applicable to migrant workers and their families. Free movement of labour within EC countries is a reality and brings with it a plethora of elaborate provisions aimed at the realization of full equality between nationals of member states. The recent Treaty on European Union (TEU),[2] which amends the Treaty Establishing the European Economic Community (EEC),[3] (the principal instrument concerned with the free movement of workers), also establishes the European Union (EU) with the result that a range of new provisions and mechanisms has been introduced which will have a profound effect on

[1] Austria, Belgium, Denmark, Finland, France, Germany, Greece, Ireland, Italy, Luxembourg, Netherlands, Portugal, Spain, Sweden, and the United Kingdom. Austria, Finland, and Sweden became full EC members as at 1 Jan. 1995, although these countries had effectively been incorporated, together with Iceland and Norway (all European Free Trade Association (EFTA) states), into the free movement of workers rubric since 1 Jan. 1994 because of their ratification of the Agreement on the European Economic Area (EEA), OJ 1994, L 1/1 (Pt III, Free Movement of Persons, Services and Capital). The provisions in the EEA Agreement concerning free movement of persons are also applicable to Liechtenstein, but will not come into effect for that country until 1 Jan. 1998. See Groupe d'information et de soutein des travailleurs immigrés (GISTI) and Immigration Law Practitioners' Association (ILPA), *The Movement of Aliens in the European Area* (GISTI, ILPA, May 1995) 23. For a comprehensive assessment of the operation of the EEA freedom of movement provisions, see I. Borgerud, 'Application of the Right of Free Movement for Workers under the European Economic Area Agreement' in J. Kenner, (ed.), *Trends in European Social Policy: Essays in Memory of Malcolm Mead* (Aldershot: Dartmouth, 1995) 189. For a summary of these provisions, see *The Movement of Aliens in the European Area, ibid.* 23–6.

[2] OJ 1992, C 191.

[3] Rome, 25 March 1957, 298 UNTS 11. The EEC Treaty is renamed the Treaty Establishing the European Community (hereinafter EC Treaty). See Art. G(1) TEU. The text of the EC Treaty, as amended, is reproduced in *European Union: Selected Instruments Taken from the Treaties*, Book I, Vol. 1 (Luxembourg: OOPEC, 1993) 91–669.

migrant workers and their families in Europe, both upon those who possess the nationality of an EC country and those who do not. It should not be forgotten, however, that there are also other free movement of labour regimes in Europe, namely those operating between the five Nordic countries[4] and the three countries of the Benelux region.[5]

All EC member states are also members of the Council of Europe (COE) which has been enlarged to 39 states with the admission of the former communist countries of central and eastern Europe and a number of countries which were formerly republics of the old Soviet Union.[6] The COE is the principal organization on the continent concerned with the protection of human rights. It has sponsored a number of human rights conventions which are relevant to the protection of migrant workers and their families.

The different regimes and instruments in Europe concerned with freedom of movement and the protection of migrant workers and their families overlap substantially. However, their common denominator is that they benefit those specifically defined to come within the ambit of their protection, with the exception of the COE's European Convention on Human Rights (ECHR) which applies to all persons residing within the territories of states parties, regardless of whether their country of origin has ratified it or whether this country is even a member of the COE. The other COE agreements, however, operate on the basis of reciprocity and apply exclusively to nationals of states parties.[7] Similarly, the free movement of labour regimes operate only between member states. The degree

[4] Denmark, Finland, Iceland, Norway, and Sweden. All these countries are members of the Council of Europe (see n. 6 below). Denmark, Finland, and Sweden belong to the EC, and Iceland and Norway are also parties to the EEA Agreement (see n. 1 above). Free movement of labour between the Nordic countries first came into operation in 1954. It is now regulated by the Agreement of 6 March 1982 concerning a Common Labour Market: entry into force 1 Aug. 1983. The first recital of the Preamble to this Agreement declares that 'liberty to take up employment and settle anywhere in the Nordic countries is a fundamental right of nationals of the Nordic countries'. An English version of the agreement is reproduced in (1983:6) Överenskommelser mellan de nordiska länderna inom arbetsmarknadsområdet 143. For an overview, see N. O. Andersen, 'Free Movement of Labour within the Nordic Countries and within the European Communities' (1988) 57 *Nordic J. Int'l L.* 384.

[5] See the Treaty Establishing the Economic Benelux Union 1959, 381 UNTS 165, and the Benelux Convention on Establishment 1960, (1960) VIII *European Yearbook* 169; ratified by Belgium, Luxembourg, and the Netherlands on 1 Nov. 1960 and 1 July 1960 respectively. Excerpts from these two instruments are reproduced in R. Plender, (ed.), *Basic Documents on International Migration Law* (Dordrecht: Martinus Nijhoff, 1988) 395 and 398 respectively. All three countries also belong to the EC and the Council of Europe. See also E. D. J. Kruijtbosch, 'Benelux Experiences in the Abolition of Border Controls' in H. G. Schermers *et al.* (eds.), *Free Movement of Persons in Europe: Legal Problems and Experiences* (Dordrecht: Martinus Nijhoff, 1993) 31.

[6] Statute of the Council of Europe, 5 May 1949; Council of Europe ETS No. 1, 87 UNTS 103; entry into force 3 Aug. 1949. As at 1 July 1996, the member countries of the COE were: Albania, Andorra, Austria, Belgium, Bulgaria, Cyprus, Czech Republic, Denmark, Estonia, Finland, France, Germany, Greece, Hungary, Iceland, Ireland, Italy, Latvia, Liechtenstein, Lithuania, Luxembourg, Macedonia, Malta, Moldova, Netherlands, Norway, Poland, Portugal, Romania, Russia, San Marino, Slovakia, Slovenia, Spain, Sweden, Switzerland, Turkey, Ukraine, United Kingdom.

[7] See also A. H. J. Swart, 'The Legal Status of Aliens: Clauses in Council of Europe Instruments Relating to the Rights of Aliens' (1980) *Netherlands YBIL* 3, 47.

of protection, therefore, that migrants might expect to receive depends on the country from which they come. For example, Italian migrant workers are able to benefit from both EC provisions and those COE instruments that Italy has ratified. Turkish migrant workers, however, may only benefit from the weaker provisions of COE instruments unless provisions of the Association Agreement which their country has entered into with the EC, or decisions taken thereunder by the Association Council, are deemed to apply directly in national laws. In the great majority of cases, only the ECHR is applicable to nationals from non-EC or non-COE member countries, such as those of the developing world, who reside and work in a country which has ratified the ECHR. It is this group of migrants which is likely to face the most serious exploitation in Europe today.

5.2 COUNCIL OF EUROPE CONVENTIONS

According to Article 1(a) of the Statute of the COE, the aim of the Organization is 'to achieve a greater unity between its Members for the purpose of safeguarding and realizing the ideals and principles which are their common heritage and facilitating their economic and social progress'. This aim is to be pursued through the organs of the COE by, *inter alia*, agreements and common action in 'the maintenance and further realization of human rights and fundamental freedoms' (Article 1(b)). Indeed, by virtue of Article 3, acceptance of the principles of the rule of law and of the enjoyment by all persons within the jurisdiction of human rights and fundamental freedoms, together with collaboration in this venture, constitutes a prerequisite to membership. Because of this emphasis in the COE's role upon the protection of human rights, which arguably is only reinforced with the admission of new countries,[8] it is in a strong position to pay special attention to the plight of aliens and migrant workers.[9]

The Committee of Ministers (the COE's executive body), on its own initiative or on the recommendation of the Parliamentary Assembly (the COE's deliberative organ), is obliged to consider the action required to further the aim of the COE, including the adoption of conventions or agreements (Article 15(a)). In line with the aim of the 'maintenance and further realization of human rights and fundamental freedoms', a number of human rights conventions have been drafted under the auspices of the COE which have either a direct or indirect bearing on aliens and migrant workers and their families. It has been suggested in this context that the protection of the human rights of aliens has a greater chance of success at the multilateral level than at the national level where the interests of sovereignty hold sway.[10] The principal COE conventions of importance to the

[8] Cf. A. Clapham, 'The Role of the European Community' (1991) 1 AEHRYB 63, 65.

[9] Swart, n. 7 above, 50.

[10] P. R. Hammond, 'International Agreements—New Convention Aimed at Improving Condition of Migrant Workers in Council of Europe Nations' (1977–78) 13 *Texas Int'l L. J.* 353, 359.

protection of migrant workers and their families are the ECHR, the European Convention on Establishment (ECE), the European Social Charter (ESC), and the European Convention on the Legal Status of Migrant Workers (EMW). A general appraisal of this protection is presented below, together with a brief analysis of the effectiveness of the supervisory and enforcement mechanisms concerned with the implementation of each instrument. Other pertinent COE instruments are considered in Chapter 8 under the relevant headings.

The Committee of Ministers and the Parliamentary Assembly may also issue recommendations and resolutions to member states proposing common courses of action. Recommendations and resolutions are not legally binding. According to one commentator, they proclaim 'far-reaching and general lofty principles', which member states are unlikely to accept as legally binding rules in the near future. This gulf between word and deed, therefore, makes their usefulness questionable.[11] When binding legal provisions are sparse or absent in a particular area, references are also made to recommendations and resolutions which directly concern migrant workers and their families.

European Convention on Human Rights (ECHR)[12]

The applicability of the ECHR to the protection of the rights of aliens was briefly outlined in Chapter 2. This section offers a fuller exposition, but with specific reference to the protection of the rights of migrant workers and their families.

The ECHR is the only COE instrument which is generally applicable to all individuals residing in those countries which have ratified it and not merely to nationals of other states parties. This is reflected in the all-embracing language used in the instrument such as 'everyone' and 'no person'.[13] Despite the use of these inclusive terms, the ECHR's relevance to the protection of the economic, social, and cultural rights of migrant workers and their families is rather minimal, because, with few exceptions, it is predominantly concerned with safeguarding civil and political rights.

[11] Swart, n. 7 above, 48. Swart, *ibid.* 48–9, reasons that resolutions would take on more importance if continuous deliberations were to take place between COE member states as to whether it is time to convert a resolution into a convention.

[12] European Convention for the Protection of Human Rights and Fundamental Freedoms, 4 Nov. 1950; Council of Europe ETS No. 5; entry into force 3 Sept. 1953; ratified by 33 states as at 1 July 1996: Andorra, Austria, Belgium, Bulgaria, Cyprus, Czech Republic, Denmark, Estonia, Finland, France, Germany, Greece, Hungary, Iceland, Ireland, Italy, Liechtenstein, Lithuania, Luxembourg, Malta, Netherlands, Norway, Poland, Portugal, Romania, San Marino, Slovakia, Slovenia, Spain, Sweden, Switzerland, Turkey, United Kingdom.

[13] See also A. Drzemczewski, 'The Position of Aliens in Relation to the European Convention on Human Rights: A General Survey' in Council of Europe, Directorate of Human Rights, *Human Rights of Aliens in Europe*, Proceedings of the Colloquy on Human Rights of Aliens in Europe, Funchal, Madeira, Portugal, 17–19 Oct. 1983 (Dordrecht: Martinus Nijhoff, 1985) 349, 395. For example, Art. 1 of the ECHR proclaims: 'The High Contracting Parties shall secure to *everyone within their jurisdiction* the rights and freedoms defined in Section 1 of this Convention' (emphasis added).

It is not disputed that the ECHR affords aliens and nationals equal treatment with respect to 'absolute rights', defined as those rights from which no derogation is permissible, such as the right to life (Article 2) and the right to be free from torture (Article 3).[14] The only 'explicit' exception[15] to the general applicability of the ECHR to alien migrant workers is Article 16: 'Nothing in Articles 10, 11 and 14 shall be regarded as preventing the High Contracting Parties from imposing restrictions on the political activity of aliens'. The possible implications of Article 16 are considered in Chapter 8 in the section on Political Rights.

Aliens are specifically mentioned in a number of other ECHR provisions. Article 1 of Protocol No. 7 to the ECHR[16] provides procedural safeguards against the arbitrary expulsion of legally resident aliens. Furthermore, there is a blanket prohibition on the collective expulsion of *all* aliens in Article 4 of Protocol No. 4 to the ECHR.[17] The ECHR and its Protocols also contain provisions explicitly restricting the rights of illegal migrants. Article 5(1) of the ECHR guarantees the right to liberty and security of the person, but permits the lawful arrest or detention of those who attempt to enter the country without authorization (Article 5(1)(f)), and Article 2(1) of Protocol No. 4 limits the right to freedom of movement within the territory of a state party to those *lawfully* within that territory. The applicability of these provisions, as well as the remainder of the ECHR and its Protocols, to migrants is examined in more detail under the relevant sections in Chapters 7 and 8.

Therefore, despite the all-embracing language of the ECHR, the classical distinction between aliens and citizens is still apparent.[18] Nevertheless, the very fact that states agree to this instrument limits their sovereignty with respect to the treatment of foreigners, particularly in matters of immigration:

[14] According to Drzemczewski, n. 13 above, 359, human rights guarantees in the ECHR may be divided into three categories: 'absolute' rights, referred to above; 'qualified' rights, specifying rights and freedoms which may be limited provided that the restrictions are prescribed by law and necessary in a democratic society and that the aims of these restrictions are deemed legitimate; and 'minimum' rights which are considered to be an acceptable common denominator found to exist within COE member states and relatively easy to determine, such as the right to a fair trial (Art. 6).

[15] See also G. S. Goodwin-Gill, *International Law and the Movement of Persons Between States* (1978) 79.

[16] Protocol No. 7 to the European Convention on Human Rights, 22 Nov. 1984; Council of Europe ETS No. 117; entry into force 1 Nov. 1988; ratified by 19 states as at 1 July 1996: Austria, Czech Republic, Denmark, Estonia, Finland, France, Greece, Hungary, Iceland, Italy, Lithuania, Luxembourg, Norway, Romania, San Marino, Slovakia, Slovenia, Sweden, Switzerland.

[17] Protocol No. 4 to the European Convention on Human Rights, securing certain rights and freedoms other than those already included in the Convention and in the first Protocol thereto, 16 Sept. 1963; Council of Europe ETS No. 46; entry into force 2 May 1968; ratified by 24 states as at 1 July 1996: Austria, Belgium, Cyprus, Czech Republic, Denmark, Estonia, Finland, France, Germany, Hungary, Iceland, Ireland, Italy, Lithuania, Luxembourg, Netherlands, Norway, Poland, Portugal, Romania, San Marino, Slovakia, Slovenia, Sweden.

[18] K. Oellers-Frahm, 'The Contribution of the Council of Europe to the Legal Position of Aliens' in Max Planck Institute of Comparative Law, (ed.), *The Legal Position of Aliens in National and International Law*, vol. 2 (1987) (hereinafter *The Legal Position of Aliens*) 1725, 1728; Drzemczewski, n. 13 above, 395.

[A] State which signs and ratifies the European Convention on Human Rights must be understood as agreeing to restrict the free exercise of its rights under general international law, including the right to control the entry and exit of foreigners to the extent and within the limits of the obligations which it has accepted under that Convention.[19]

Restrictions on state sovereignty are further manifested in the supervisory and enforcement mechanism of the ECHR. The ECHR contains the most developed, effective, and successful control machinery found in all the COE conventions. It is unique among COE conventions concerned with human rights in that Article 25 of the ECHR allows a direct right of petition to the European Commission of Human Rights 'from any person, non-governmental organization or group of individuals claiming to be the victim of a violation by one of the High Contracting Parties of the rights set forth in this Convention'. Inter-state actions are also permissible.[20] The Commission is charged with determining the admissibility of the petition,[21] and is also available as conciliator for the parties in order to assist them in securing a friendly settlement.[22] If a petition is found admissible, the Commission proceeds to establish the facts and issues a report, expressing its opinion on the alleged violation or violations.[23] The case may then be referred by the Commission or the state party or parties concerned to the European Court of Human Rights, which rules on the matter.[24] If no referral is made to the Court within 3 months, the Committee of Ministers decides by a two-thirds majority, on the basis of the Commission's report, whether there has

[19] Application 434/58, *X* v. *Sweden* (1958/59) 2 YBECHR 354, 372–3 (European Commission of Human Rights). See also Drzemczewski, n. 13 above, 368 and R. Plender, *International Migration Law* (1988) 227. It should be emphasized that the ECHR, by virtue of Art. 60, does not preclude a more favourable regime operating in respect of aliens. Art. 60 provides that the rights and freedoms in the ECHR cannot be construed 'as limiting or derogating' from those already ensured by the domestic law of states parties or by other international agreements by which states parties are bound. See also Drzemczewski, n. 13 above, 353.

[20] Art. 24.

[21] Arts. 27 and 29. Art. 26 contains two important admissibility criteria. The Commission will only consider a petition after all domestic remedies have been exhausted and if it has been submitted within 6 months from the date on which the final domestic decision was taken.

[22] Art. 28(b).

[23] Art. 31(1). The report is then transmitted to the Committee of Ministers and the state party or parties concerned (Art. 31(2)).

[24] Arts. 44 and 48. Arts. 3 and 5 of Protocol No. 9 to the ECHR revise, *inter alia*, Arts. 44 and 48 by extending this right of reference to 'the person, non-governmental organization or group of individuals having lodged the complaint with the Commission' (revised Art. 48(1)(e)). If such a reference is made, and it is the only reference, revised Art. 48(2) provides for a filter mechanism whereby a panel of 3 Court judges may decide unanimously not to consider the application 'if the case does not raise a serious question affecting the interpretation or application of the Convention and does not for any other reason warrant consideration by the Court': Protocol No. 9 to the European Convention on Human Rights, 6 Nov. 1990; Council of Europe ETS No. 140; entry into force 1 Oct. 1994; ratified by 23 states as at 1 July 1996: Austria, Belgium, Cyprus, Czech Republic, Denmark, Estonia, Finland, Germany, Hungary, Ireland, Italy, Liechtenstein, Luxembourg, Netherlands, Norway, Poland, Portugal, Romania, San Marino, Slovakia, Slovenia, Sweden, Switzerland. However, once the new supervisory mechanism comes into operation (see below), Protocol No. 9 will be repealed (Art. 2(8) of Protocol No. 11).

been a violation of the ECHR.[25] All the states parties to the ECHR have made the relevant declarations under Articles 25 and 46 recognizing the right of individual petition and the jurisdiction of the European Court of Human Rights. This supervisory mechanism will be changed fundamentally when Protocol No. 11 to the ECHR comes into force.[26] This Protocol establishes a single supervisory body, replacing the existing Commission and Court by a permanent European Court of Human Rights, which will both assess the admissibility of applications and rule on their merits. Because it is an amending instrument, Protocol No. 11 will only come into force one year after all the states parties to the ECHR have ratified it.[27]

European Convention on Establishment (ECE)[28]

The broadly defined COE goal of achieving greater unity among its members was the predominant driving force behind the adoption of the ECE.[29] During the drafting process, it was recognized that the ECE's 'governing principle should be that of equality of treatment as between nationals of one Party and those of other Parties'.[30] Therefore, the personal scope of the ECE is narrower than that of the ECHR because it applies only to nationals of those COE member states that have ratified it. The ECE facilitates temporary visits and prolonged or permanent residence in states parties.[31] It contains clauses on entry, residence, and

[25] Art. 32(1). Protocol No. 10 to the ECHR establishes that a simple majority is sufficient for the adoption of this decision: Protocol No. 10 to the European Convention on Human Rights, 25 March 1992; Council of Europe ETS No. 146; not in force; ratified by 23 states as at 1 July 1996: Austria, Belgium, Cyprus, Czech Republic, Estonia, Finland, Germany, Ireland, Italy, Liechtenstein, Luxembourg, Malta, Netherlands, Norway, Poland, Portugal, Romania, San Marino, Slovakia, Slovenia, Sweden, Switzerland, United Kingdom. Protocol No. 10 requires ratification by all states parties to the ECHR in order to enter into force (Art. 3).

[26] Protocol No. 11 to the European Convention on Human Rights, restructuring the control machinery established thereby, 11 May 1994; Council of Europe ETS No. 155; not in force; ratified by 21 states as at 1 July 1996: Andorra, Austria, Bulgaria, Cyprus, Czech Republic, Estonia, Finland, France, Germany, Hungary, Iceland, Liechtenstein, Lithuania, Malta, Norway, Romania, Slovakia, Slovenia, Sweden, Switzerland, United Kingdom.

[27] Art. 4 of Protocol No. 11. For commentaries on this reform, see R. Bernhardt, 'Reform of the Control Machinery under the European Convention on Human Rights: Protocol No. 11' (1995) 89 AJIL 145; A. Drzemczewski and J. Meyer-Ladewig, 'Principal Characteristics of the New ECHR Control Mechanism, as established by Protocol No. 11, signed on 11 May 1994' (1994) 15 HRLJ 81; and H. Schermers, 'The European Court of Human Rights after the Merger' (1993) 18 *EL Rev*. 493.

[28] European Convention on Establishment, 13 Dec. 1955; Council of Europe ETS No. 19; entry into force 23 Feb. 1965; ratified by 12 states as at 1 July 1996: Belgium, Denmark, Germany, Greece, Ireland, Italy, Luxembourg, Netherlands, Norway, Sweden, Turkey, United Kingdom.

[29] Council of Europe, *Commentary on the European Convention on Establishment (adopted by the Standing Committee)* (Strasbourg: Council of Europe, 1980) 5, para. 1; Goodwin-Gill, n. 15 above, 227.

[30] *Commentary on the European Convention on Establishment*, n. 29 above, 8, para. 12.

[31] Arts. 1 and 2. See also Lillich, who contends that the ECE functions more as a charter of rights for persons *already settled* in other countries: R. B. Lillich, *The Human Rights of Aliens in*

expulsion as well as extensive provisions concerning equal treatment between nationals of member states in respect of gainful employment. There are also equality provisions dealing with rights in the workplace, participation in economic and professional organizations, and education rights, including rights to vocational training.

Implementation of the ECE is supervised by the Standing Committee, composed of representatives drawn from, and appointed by, each state party. The Committee is charged with several dynamic functions: it is to make proposals 'designed to improve the practical implementation of the Convention and, if necessary, to amend or supplement its provisions'; it is to attempt to settle differences of opinion between the contracting parties over the interpretation of certain provisions of the ECE; and it is to arrange for the publication of periodic reports on the compliance of the current laws and regulations of each state party with the ECE's provisions.[32] The Committee's opinions or recommendations are also submitted to the Committee of Ministers.[33]

This supervisory machinery is limited in comparison with the complaint procedures provided for by the ECHR. Moreover, any practical value the ECE might have is further reduced given that all of the countries which have ratified it, with the exception of Turkey, are either members of the EC or, as in the case of Norway, a party to the EEA Agreement, with their far more liberal free movement regimes.[34] In spite of its secondary status to the EC regime, the ECE has played a significant role as precedent for many EC provisions, especially those concerned with restrictions on free movement of labour on the grounds of '*ordre public*', national security, and public health.[35] The ECE has also served as a catalyst for the development of other COE norms regarding the treatment of foreign workers residing in member states, most notably those standards found in the two conventions discussed below.[36]

Contemporary International Law (1984) 85. With regard to temporary visits, reference should also be made to the European Agreement on Regulations governing the Movement of Persons between Member States of the Council of Europe, 13 Dec. 1957; Council of Europe ETS No. 25; entry into force 1 Jan. 1958; ratified by 13 states as at 1 July 1996: Austria, Belgium, France, Germany, Greece, Italy, Luxembourg, Malta, Netherlands, Portugal, Spain, Switzerland, and Turkey. This agreement, *inter alia*, permits nationals from one state party to enter the territory of another state party for visits of not more than 3 months' duration without the need to obtain an entry visa (Art. 1). For a brief overview of this agreement, see F. W. Hondius, 'Legal Aspects of the Movement of Persons in Greater Europe' (1990) 10 YBEL 291, 293–4.

[32] Arts. 24(1), (2) and (3) respectively. See also *Commentary on the European Convention on Establishment*, n. 29 above, 11, paras. 27, 29 and 23–4, paras. 78–80.

[33] Art. 24(6).

[34] See also cf. Goodwin-Gill, n. 15 above, 227.

[35] Plender, n. 19 above, 238. The *Commentary on the European Convention on Establishment*, n. 29 above, 9, para. 19, observes: 'A comparison with the international conventions which have been concluded since the signature of the European Convention on Establishment—notably, the Treaty of Rome [EEC Treaty], the aims of which are far more ambitious, since it sets out to establish a genuine union—suggests that those who drafted the Council of Europe's Convention were pioneers in the establishment field at the international level'.

[36] Cf. Goodwin-Gill, n. 15 above, 227.

European Social Charter (ESC)[37]

The ESC was adopted in accordance with the aim of the COE to achieve greater unity between member states for the purpose, *inter alia*, of 'facilitating their *economic* and *social* progress, in particular by the maintenance and further realization of human rights and fundamental freedoms'.[38] With its concern for economic and social rights, including social policy and labour relations, the ESC is the companion instrument to, or counterpart of, the ECHR.[39] As with the ECE, the ESC only protects the rights of nationals of COE member states that are parties to the agreement.[40] This inapplicability to migrants who are not nationals of states parties, residing and working within the territory of another state party, must, however, put into question the fundamental nature of the economic and social rights contained in the instrument:

[37] European Social Charter, 18 Oct. 1961; Council of Europe ETS No. 35; entry into force 26 Feb. 1965; ratified by 20 states as at 1 July 1996: Austria, Belgium, Cyprus, Denmark, Finland, France, Germany, Greece, Iceland, Ireland, Italy, Luxembourg, Malta, Netherlands, Norway, Portugal, Spain, Sweden, Turkey, United Kingdom. The ESC has been *signed* by 8 other COE member states: the Czech Republic, Hungary, Liechtenstein, Poland, Romania, Slovakia, Switzerland, Ukraine.

[38] Preamble, first recital (emphasis added).

[39] D. Gomien, D. Harris, and L. Zwaak, *Law and Practice of the European Convention on Human Rights and the European Social Charter* (Strasbourg: Council of Europe, 1996) (hereinafter *Law and Practice of the ECHR and the ESC*) 377; D. Harris, *The European Social Charter* (Charlottesville, Virginia: University Press of Virginia, 1984) 8–9; O. Kahn-Freund, 'The European Social Charter' in F. G. Jacobs, (ed.), *European Law and the Individual* (Amsterdam: North-Holland, 1976) 181, 182; Lillich, n. 31 above, 88.

[40] The Appendix to the ESC, which is described in Art. 38 as 'an integral part of it', is concerned in para. 1 with the scope of the ESC in terms of the persons protected: 'Without prejudice to Article 12, paragraph 4 and Article 13, paragraph 4, the persons covered by Articles 1 to 17 include foreigners *only insofar as they are nationals of other Contracting Parties lawfully resident or working regularly within the territory of the Contracting Party concerned*, subject to the understanding that these Articles are to be interpreted in the light of the provisions of Articles 18 and 19' (emphasis added). Arts. 18 and 19 are specifically concerned with migrant workers and their scope is also limited to migrant workers from other contracting parties by wording to this effect in paras. 18 and 19 of Pt I to the ESC. See below. The Appendix declares that 'this interpretation would not prejudice the extension of similar facilities to other persons by any of the Contracting Parties', although this statement cannot be regarded as an obligation. See also Council of Europe, *The European Social Charter. Origin, Operation and Results* (Strasbourg: Council of Europe Press, 1991) 24. In October 1994, the Committee on the European Social Charter (Charte-Rel), an *ad hoc* body set up towards the end of 1990 by the Committee of Ministers' Deputies with a mandate to 'revitalize' the ESC by making proposals for improving the effectiveness of the ESC, and particularly its supervisory mechanism, completed a draft version of a revised ESC. See Council of Europe, Parliamentary Assembly, *Request for an Opinion from the Committee of Ministers to the Assembly on the Draft Revised European Social Charter*, Doc. 7242, 10 Feb. 1995 (hereinafter *Request for an Opinion on the Draft Revised ESC*) 57 (Draft Explanatory Report, paras. 2 and 4). The Charte-Rel Committee agreed to extend the scope of the revised ESC to 'all persons whatever their nationality, while keeping however the conditions that they must be lawfully resident or working regularly within the territory of a Party'. Because of the importance of this proposal, however, the Committee decided to leave the final decision on this matter to the Committee of Ministers: *ibid.* paras. 148–9. The European Social Charter (Revised), Council of Europe ETS No. 163, was adopted on 3 May 1996 and had been signed by 9 states as at 1 July 1996: Belgium, Cyprus, Denmark, Finland, France, Greece, Italy, Portugal, Sweden. However, the scope of the revised ESC in terms of persons protected remains unchanged.

[O]ne cannot escape the conclusion that the possibility of discrimination specifically contemplated by the Social Charter must lead to serious hesitations as to how far the rights enumerated therein may be considered fundamental, and virtually deprives of all meaning the description of the Charter as being 'complementary to the Human Rights Convention'.[41]

The ESC is divided into two parts. Part I is a list of rights, considered to be a declaration of aims by states parties (Article 21(1)(a)), and Part II translates these rights into precise legal obligations.[42] Ratifying states, however, do not have to accept all the provisions in Part II, provided that they accept 5 out of 7 specified 'core' articles and not less than 10 of the total number of articles or 45 numbered paragraphs.[43] The obligations in Part II are themselves essentially divided into two groups: those necessitating immediate action by states parties

[41] See M. Evans, 'The European Social Charter' in J. Bridge, D. Lasok, and R. D. Plender, (eds.), *Fundamental Rights: A Volume of Essays to Commemorate the 50th Anniversary of the Founding of the Law School in Exeter, 1923–1973* (London: Sweet & Maxwell, 1973) 278, 284. This observation has been repeated elsewhere: 'The Charter does not . . . protect the nationals of non-contracting parties at all which seems a curious omission if it purports to set a standard of fundamental social rights which no State should fall below. To exclude a section of those legally resident on the territories of the States parties from the protection of those rights is contrary to the spirit of other major human rights instruments, which protect without discrimination': see N. Mole, 'Freedom of Movement in a Wider Europe: A Comparison of International Instruments' (1991) 1 AEHRYB 199, 204. See also *Law and Practice of the ECHR and the ESC*, n. 39 above, 433: 'Part II [of the ESC—see below] does not protect the nationals of non-Contracting Parties at all. This is so whether they are nationals of member states of the Council of Europe or not. This is a limitation that smacks more of the reciprocal arrangements found in bilateral treaties of friendship than a human rights guarantee and that compares most unfavourably with similar instruments [such as the ICESCR, most ILO instruments and the ECHR] . . . The more restrictive rule in the Charter, which stems from economic and political considerations, is particularly open to criticism because the Charter does not limit a state's power to control entry into its territory. If a Contracting Party allows an alien to take up residence or work within its territory, it is difficult to justify excluding that person from the rights guaranteed in the Charter solely on the basis of nationality'. Evans, *ibid.*, provides a possible justification for this approach in the observation that the preparation of the ESC began in 1954 when concern for the social problems of migrant workers was not as acute as in the early 1970s and before the principle of equality of treatment of migrants with nationals had begun to gain acceptance.

[42] Four additional rights are found in the Additional Protocol to the European Social Charter, 5 May 1988; Council of Europe ETS No. 128; entry into force 4 Sept. 1992; ratified by 5 states as at 1 July 1996: Finland, Italy, Netherlands, Norway, Sweden. These rights are: the right to equal opportunity and treatment in matters of employment and occupation regardless of sex; the right of workers to be informed and to be consulted within the undertaking; the right of workers to participate in the determination and improvement of working conditions and working environment within the undertaking; and the right of elderly persons to social protection. The Additional Protocol follows the same format as the ESC. See generally L. Betten, 'The Protocol to the European Social Charter: More Rights; A Better Impact?' (1988) 6 NQHR 9. The revised ESC also introduces new rights, such as more elaborate employment rights, the right to protection against poverty and social exclusion (Art. 30), and the right to housing (Art. 31).

[43] Arts. 20(1)(b) and (c). The seven specified articles are: Art. 1 (right to work), Art. 5 (right to organize), Art. 6 (right to bargain collectively), Art. 12 (right to social security), Art. 13 (right to social and medical assistance), Art. 16 (right of the family to social, legal, and economic protection) and Art. 19 (right of migrant workers and their families to protection and assistance). The ESC's principal supervisory organ, the Committee of Independent Experts, has asserted clearly that states parties must comply with all those obligations which they have accepted in respect of nationals from other states parties even though the latter have not accepted the same obligations. In other words, the lack of reciprocity in respect of certain provisions does not preclude the ESC's application. *Conclusions VII*, 77, cited by H. Wiebringhaus, 'Introduction' in A. Ph. C. M. Jaspers and L. Betten, (eds.), *25 Years of the European Social Charter* (Deventer: Kluwer, 1988) 9, 15.

and those requiring a state party to embark on a course of action with a view to achieving a result.[44] Although the whole of the ESC applies to migrant workers, there are two provisions in the ESC which relate specifically to this group: Article 18 (the right to engage in a gainful occupation in the territory of other contracting parties)[45] and Article 19 (the right of migrant workers and their families to protection and assistance). Article 19 also constitutes one of the seven specified 'core' articles of the ESC.[46]

The ESC's provisions are largely modelled on ILO conventions and recommendations.[47] For example, Article 19 was based on ILO Convention No. 97 of 1949.[48] However, despite this cooperation between the ILO and the COE in the drafting of the ESC, a clear distinction should be drawn between the ESC and ILO instruments. Although ESC provisions are less detailed and precise than some of the analogous ILO clauses, the ESC is formulated more in terms of human rights and embodies in a single document many of the provisions dispersed throughout numerous ILO instruments.[49]

The ILO has also significantly influenced the ESC's supervisory machinery[50] and continues to play a role in the instrument's implementation. The supervisory mechanism is presently undergoing radical transformation as a result of amendments to the ESC, some of which are already operating despite the fact that these amendments have not yet formally entered into force. An overview of the original mode of supervision is first presented, together with some of the pertinent criticisms, before proceeding to consider the recent changes that have been introduced.

The first part of the supervisory mechanism essentially remains unchanged. It is based on the consideration of reports, which states parties submit every 2 years on the application of the provisions they have accepted.[51] The reports are

[44] Kahn-Freund (1976), n. 39 above, 187. Examples of the former are the duty to issue safety and health regulations regarding working conditions (Art. 3(1)) and the right of men and women workers to equal pay for work of equal value (Art. 4(3)). Examples of the latter are obligations to *aim* at a high and stable level of employment (Art. 1(1)) and to *progressively* reduce working hours (Art. 2(1)).

[45] Certain parts of Art. 18 are also framed in terms of a 'progressive' obligation. See the discussion on the right of access to employment in Ch. 8.

[46] Out of the 20 states that have ratified the ESC, Denmark, Iceland, and Malta have not accepted Art. 19 *in toto*.

[47] O. Kahn-Freund, 'Labour Relations and International Standards—Some Reflections on the European Social Charter' in *Miscellanea W. J. Ganshof Van der Meersch*, vol. 1 (Brussels: Emile, 1972) 131, 132; F. Vandamme, 'The Revision of the European Social Charter' (1994) 133 ILR 635, citing from H. Wiebringhaus, 'The European Social Charter and International Labour Standards' (1961) 84 ILR 354.

[48] Plender, n. 19 above, 244.

[49] Cf. Harris (1984), n. 39 above, 11; cf. Kahn-Freund (1976), n. 39 above, 198.

[50] Kahn-Freund (1972), n. 47 above, 132.

[51] Art. 21. A new system for reporting was adopted for a trial period of 4 years at the 479th meeting of the Ministers' Deputies on 17 Sept. 1992. This system applies to all states parties, with the exception of Germany, which refused to participate in the new procedure, and those states parties which have recently ratified the ESC. Under the new system, states parties are to continue to submit biennial reports on the core provisions of the ESC. Reports on other provisions only have to be submitted once every 4 years, unless such provisions were the subject of a negative or adjourned conclusion from the Committee of Independent Experts in the previous cycle of supervision. See

first scrutinized by the Committee of Independent Experts, (composed of not more than 7 experts 'of recognized competence in international social questions' and appointed by the Committee of Ministers from a list of experts nominated by the states parties), which issues conclusions. A representative of the International Labour Office participates in a consultative capacity at the meetings of the Committee. Together with the national reports, the conclusions of the Committee of Independent Experts are submitted to a Governmental Committee, (composed of one representative of each of the state parties).[52] The conclusions of the Committee constitute a valuable source of 'case law' for the interpretation of various provisions of the ESC. This 'case law' has expanded significantly the protection afforded migrant workers and their families under the ESC.

The main changes to the supervisory mechanism have been introduced in respect of the following procedures. Originally, on receipt of the conclusions of the Committee of Independent Experts, the Governmental Committee would produce a separate report. The Parliamentary Assembly would then express its views on this documentation before it was communicated to the Committee of Ministers, which could decide by a two-thirds majority of all COE member states to make any necessary recommendations to states parties.[53] This latter part of the supervisory procedure was criticized on a number of grounds.[54] First, the governmental element in the process was said to be too influential. The conclusions of the Committee of Independent Experts were 'diluted' somewhat by the 'official' observations which followed. Secondly, the ESC failed to integrate the tripartite ideal, which has worked so successfully in the procedures of the ILO. No more than 2 representatives of employers and trade unions were permitted to participate as observers 'in a consultative capacity' during the deliberations of the Governmental Committee. One commentator remarked that 'this is the marginal, one might say the vestigial, role the tripartite idea is allowed to play in the control mechanism of the Council of Europe'.[55] Thirdly, recommendations

Law and Practice of the ECHR and the ESC, n. 39 above, 416. It would seem, however, that the system of full biennial reporting will be re-introduced for the 14th cycle of supervision: *ibid.* 417. By virtue of Article 22, states parties are also obliged to report on the ESC provisions which they have not accepted. This obligation, however, depends on a further decision of the Committee of Ministers 'in respect of which provisions such reports shall be requested and the form of the reports to be provided'. A similar obligation exists under Art. 19 of the ILO Constitution in respect of unratified conventions and recommendations.

[52] Arts. 24–7(1). [53] Arts. 27(3)–9.

[54] See L. Betten, 'European Social Charter' (1988) 6 NQHR 69, 71–4; Kahn-Freund (1976), n. 39 above, 201–2; and Lillich, n. 31 above, 88.

[55] Kahn-Freund, *ibid.* Another modest tripartite element in the enforcement procedure is found in Art. 23 of the ESC, which requires states parties to provide copies of their reports to those national organizations which are members of international organizations of employers and workers invited, in accordance with Art. 27(2), to be represented as observers in a consultative capacity at the meetings of the Governmental Committee. Art. 27(2) also provides the Committee with the discretion to consult no more than 2 representatives of international NGOs having consultative status with the COE. It has been observed that the Governmental Committee has not exercised its power to consult such NGOs: *Law and Practice of the ECHR and the ESC*, n. 39 above, 421.

could only be adopted by the Committee of Ministers by a two-thirds majority of *all* COE member states, including those that were not parties to the ESC.[56] Finally, there was no right of individual complaint and no adjudication body, like the Commission and Court under the ECHR.

Most of the above criticisms are no longer valid in practice because of the significant changes that have been introduced by the Protocol Amending the European Social Charter.[57] The Committee of Independent Experts is to consist of at least 9 members, who will be elected by the Parliamentary Assembly from candidates nominated by the states parties (Article 3). The Governmental Committee is no longer able to disagree with the legal interpretation given to the ESC's provisions by the Committee of Independent Experts. Instead, it has been given the function of preparing decisions for the Committee of Ministers and of selecting, 'on the basis of social, economic and other policy considerations the situations which should, in its view, be the subjects of recommendations to each Contracting Party concerned' (Article 4). Moreover, the Parliamentary Assembly is no longer to give its views on the Conclusions of the Committee of Independent Experts, but only to hold periodical plenary debates on matters arising from the supervisory process (Article 6). The Protocol also changes the voting system at the stage of the Committee of Ministers. The Committee is able to adopt resolutions containing recommendations to individual states parties by a two-thirds majority of states parties to the ESC rather than by a two-thirds majority of all COE member states (Article 5).[58] Finally, though it is still not possible to bring *individual* complaints under the ESC, a new Additional Protocol was recently adopted providing for a system of *collective* complaints.[59]

[56] Betten (1988: 2), n. 54 above, 72, underlined the absurdity of this process. About one-third of the countries represented in the Committee of Ministers had still to ratify the ESC, which made it then very difficult for this group to judge those COE member states that had ratified the instrument. Indeed, no recommendations were adopted under the original supervisory mechanism: *Law and Practice of the ECHR and the ESC*, *ibid*. 425.

[57] Protocol Amending the European Social Charter; 21 Oct. 1991; Council of Europe ETS No. 142; not in force; ratified by 10 states as at 1 July 1996: Austria, Cyprus, Finland, France, Italy, Malta, Netherlands, Norway, Portugal, Sweden. For an appraisal of the changes introduced by the Amending Protocol, see D. Harris, 'A Fresh Impetus for the European Social Charter' (1992) 41 ICLQ 659, 662–72; M. Mohr, 'The Turin Protocol of 22 October 1991: A Major Contribution to Revitalizing the European Social Charter' (1992) 3 EJIL 362; J. G. C. Schokkenbroek, 'The Results of the Ministerial Conference on the European Social Charter' (1992) 13 HRLJ 177, and Vandamme, n. 47 above, 651–2.

[58] The information base from which the supervisory organs may draw to ensure state party compliance with the ESC is also broadened to allow for comments from national employers' and workers' organizations, which are to be sent directly to the COE Secretary-General (Art. 1), and by measures enabling the Committee of Independent Experts to request further information from states parties, a process which may include, if necessary, the holding of meetings with state party representatives (Art. 2). Furthermore, the Governmental Committee will be able to consult an unlimited number of international NGOs which have consultative status with the COE and a particular competence in the matters governed by the ESC (Art. 4).

[59] Additional Protocol to the European Social Charter providing for a System of Collective Complaints, 9 Nov. 1995, Council of Europe ETS No. 158; not in force; no ratifications as at 1 July 1996. The Protocol has been signed by 8 states: Belgium, Cyprus, Denmark, Finland, France, Italy,

These changes will arguably lead to a more balanced and objective judgement on the compliance of states parties with the ESC.

Although the Amending Protocol still remains a long way from coming into force, because it requires ratification by *all* the Contracting parties to the ESC (Article 8), the Committee of Ministers, in a decision on 11 December 1991, requested contracting parties and the supervisory bodies of the ESC 'to envisage the application of certain of the measures provided for in [the] Protocol, before its entry into force, in so far as the text of the Charter will allow'.[60] The membership of the Committee of Independent Experts has already been increased from 7 to 9.[61] During the 12th cycle of supervision, the Governmental Committee decided to adopt its new role under the Amending Protocol,[62] and the Parliamentary Assembly informed the Committee of Ministers that it would no longer exercise its right to give its views on the Conclusions of the Committee

Portugal, Sweden. The Protocol enables, in Art. 1, the following categories of organizations to submit complaints against states parties for failing to apply ESC provisions in a satisfactory manner: international organizations of employers and trades unions referred to in Art. 27(2) of the ESC; other international NGOs which have consultative status with the COE and have been put on a list established for this purpose by the Governmental Committee; and representative national organizations of employers and trade unions within the jurisdiction of the contracting party against which they have lodged a complaint. Under Art. 2, a state party may also issue a declaration recognizing the right of any other representative national NGO within its jurisdiction to complain against it. A complaint by such a NGO as well as by an international NGO possessing consultative status with the COE (Arts. 2(1) and 3) can only be brought if the NGO has a particular competence in areas covered by the ESC. The complaint is to be submitted, via the COE Secretary General, to the Committee of Independent Experts (Art. 5), which has a mandate to examine the matter by contacting the state party concerned and the complaining organization (Art. 7) and to draw up a report to be transmitted to the latter and the Committee of Ministers (Art. 8). If the Committee of Independent Experts finds that the ESC has not been applied in an adequate manner, the Committee of Ministers has the power to adopt a recommendation to the state party concerned on a majority vote of those states parties voting (Art. 9(1)). The Protocol will enter into force one month after 5 COE member states have ratified it (Art. 14(1)). For short commentaries on this reform, see *Law and Practice of the ECHR and the ESC*, n. 39 above, 426–9, Documentation and Comment, 'Council of Europe. The Introduction of a System of Collective Complaints' (1995) 3 IJCLLIR 270–1, and Vandamme, n. 47 above, 652–3.

[60] Cited in the sixth recital of Resolution ChS (93)1 on the implementation of the ESC during the period 1988–89, adopted by the Committee of Ministers on 7 Sept. 1993 at the 497th meeting of the Ministers' Deputies. This Resolution is reproduced in (1994) 1:1 IHRR 264.

[61] Decision taken at the 509th meeting of the Committee of Ministers' Deputies in March 1994. See Council of Europe, Committee of Independent Experts of the European Social Charter, *Conclusions XIII-2* (Strasbourg: Council of Europe Press, 1995) 21.

[62] Council of Europe, European Social Charter, Governmental Committee, *12th Report (I) (1988–89)* (Strasbourg: Council of Europe Press, 1993) 13–14, para. 16. The Committee continued with this new approach during the 13th cycle of supervision. See Council of Europe, European Social Charter, Governmental Committee, *13th Report (I)* (Strasbourg: Council of Europe Press, 1995) 13, para. 19. The Committee has also adopted a practice not provided for in the Amending Protocol by issuing 'warnings' to states parties in cases where the Committee of Independent Experts has adopted a negative conclusion or where adequate information has not been submitted. A proposal for a recommendation follows a warning in the next cycle of supervision if the appropriate actions are not taken: *13th Report (I)*, *ibid.* 14, para. 20. See also *Law and Practice of the ECHR and the ESC*, n. 39 above, 423.

of Independent Experts.[63] The composition of the Committee of Ministers was also restricted for the first time to ESC states parties, with the result that it has already adopted a number of recommendations to individual states parties concerning the implementation of the ESC.[64]

It will become evident in the following chapters that the substantive provisions in the ESC applicable to migrant workers and their families and the means of implementing them fall considerably short of the standards and enforcement mechanisms found in the EC regime. However, this is probably less the result of the weakness of the ESC and more the consequence of the strength and greater integration of the EC.[65] Nonetheless, the ESC probably remains the most promising COE instrument concerned with the protection of the rights of migrant workers and their families.

European Convention on the Legal Status of Migrant Workers (EMW)[66]

The EMW is the culmination of COE efforts to produce a specific instrument for the protection of migrant workers and their families. In 1966, a committee of experts was established to draw up a draft convention on migrant workers with the intention of outlining the minimum obligations that COE member states would accept regarding the legal status of this group. These experts were supported by a committee of observers consisting of persons from a number of international organizations, including the International Labour Office. International employer and trade union organizations were also consulted.[67]

Despite this diverse input, the contents of the EMW, on the whole, are disappointing. The EMW was drafted during a period of great fluctuation with regard to migration for employment in Europe, which undoubtedly had a negative influence on the drafting work. International labour migration was no longer viewed favourably in the light of the oil crisis of 1973–4, which had a damaging

[63] Council of Europe, Committee of Independent Experts of the European Social Charter, *Conclusions XII-2 (1989–90)* (Strasbourg: Council of Europe, 1993) 13.

[64] See L. Betten, 'Committee of Ministers of the Council of Europe—Call for Contracting States to Account for Violations of the European Social Charter' (1994) 10 IJCLLIR 147. These recommendations, like the conclusions of the Committee of Independent Experts, are not legally binding. See Harris (1992), n. 57 above, 661.

[65] Kahn-Freund (1976), n. 39 above, 195–6, writes: 'The great actual and even greater potential importance of the European Communities for the development of a European labour law and a European body of social legislation does not stem from the powers of the Communities to make new law. It does stem from the fact of European symbiosis and from the vastly increased incentive by voluntary action to arrive at a harmonisation of labour law and social legislation'.

[66] European Convention on the Legal Status of Migrant Workers, 24 Nov. 1977; Council of Europe ETS No. 93; entry into force 1 May 1983; ratified by 8 states as at 1 July 1996: France, Italy, Netherlands, Norway, Portugal, Spain, Sweden, Turkey. There are 4 signatories: Belgium, Germany, Greece, and Luxembourg.

[67] H. Golsong, 'La convention européenne relative au statut juridique du travailleur migrant' in Société française pour le droit international, (ed.), *Les travailleurs étrangers et le droit international* (Paris: Éditions A. Pedone, 1978) 226, 230.

effect on the large foreign workforce present in Western Europe during this period. Many migrant workers lost their jobs, and a number of host countries reacted to the changing economic climate by halting further labour migration.[68] The EMW, therefore, could not have been adopted at a less opportune time.[69]

As with the ECE and the ESC, the EMW operates on the basis of reciprocity and applies only between COE member states that are parties to the agreement. As a result, migrant workers from the Mahgreb region, for example, residing and working in state parties, are unable to benefit from the EMW's provisions. The purpose of the EMW, as outlined in the Preamble, is 'to ensure that as far as possible they [migrant workers] are treated no less favourably than workers who are nationals of the receiving state in all aspects of living and working conditions' and 'to facilitate the social advancement of migrant workers and members of their families'.[70] The phrase 'in all aspects of living and working conditions' is a reflection of the concern of the EMW for migrant workers as workers, and more generally, as human beings.[71] The Preamble to the EMW, in the first recital, also reiterates the COE's aim to facilitate the 'economic and social progress (of member states) while respecting human rights and fundamental freedoms'. Despite this emphasis on human rights, few provisions in the EMW are phrased in terms of the rights of migrant workers.[72] The provisions are more concerned with inter-state obligations than with the conferment of rights upon individuals that are to be applicable in national law.[73] Consequently, the EMW is weaker in terms of the direct protection of the rights of migrant workers and their families than may appear to be the case at first reading. This conclusion

[68] Cf. *ibid.* 231.

[69] Cf. J. Niessen and H. de Lary de Latour, 'Equality of Treatment: The European Social Charter and the European Convention on the Legal Status of Migrant Workers' in J. Cator and J. Niessen, (eds.), *The Use of International Conventions to Protect the Rights of Migrants and Ethnic Minorities* (1994) 93, 97. See also Council of Europe, *Fourth Report on the Application of the European Convention on the Legal Status of Migrant Workers* (Reference period: 1 January 1989–30 June 1990) (Strasbourg: Council of Europe, 1991) (hereinafter *Fourth Report on the Application of the EMW*) 12, para. 91.

[70] Preamble, second, and third recitals respectively. See also Council of Europe, *Explanatory Report on the European Convention on the Legal Status of Migrant Workers* (Strasbourg: Council of Europe, 1978) (hereinafter *Explanatory Report on the EMW*) 6, para. 7.

[71] In 1984, Lillich, n. 31 above, 89, observed optimistically that the EMW is 'the furthest progression of international human rights law with respect to migrant workers' because it 'concerns itself with the life of migrant workers *in toto* and not just with respect to the employment relationship'. See also Hammond, n. 10 above, 362. However, the UN Convention now goes further in this respect.

[72] These are the right to leave and the right to enter subject to the necessary authorization (Art. 4(1)); equal rights with nationals regarding the prevention of industrial accidents and occupational diseases (Art. 20); the right of access to courts and administrative authorities in the receiving state (Art. 26); the exercise of the right to organize (Art. 28); and the clause conserving rights acquired under other multilateral and bilateral instruments as well as under national legislation (Art. 31). See also Plender, n. 19 above, 252, who argues consequently that the title of the EMW is 'more ambitious than its content' and that it should be characterized as a treaty of establishment rather than as the basis for a system of regulating migrant labour.

[73] Plender, *ibid.*; Golsong, n. 67 above, 240.

is further supported by the assertion that the EMW is a 'framework' instrument which does not purport to regulate in detail all aspects of the legal status of migrant workers, but refers instead to other relevant multilateral and bilateral instruments as well as to national legislation.[74]

The organ charged with implementing the EMW is the Consultative Committee, comprised of representatives from each state party to the agreement.[75] The function of the Committee is to 'examine proposals submitted to it by one of the Contracting Parties with a view to facilitating or improving the application of the Convention, as well as any proposal to amend it'. The Committee adopts opinions and recommendations by a majority of its members, although unanimous consent is necessary for the adoption of proposals to amend the EMW. Any Consultative Committee opinions, recommendations, and proposals are submitted to the Committee of Ministers, which decides upon the action to be taken.[76] The Consultative Committee is also required to prepare a periodic report for the Committee of Ministers containing information on the laws and regulations in force in states parties in respect of the EMW's provisions.[77] This report is drawn up on the basis of national reports which the Committee invites states parties to submit on the application of the EMW.[78] Unlike under the ESC, however, there is no formal state reporting requirement under the EMW.[79] The *travaux préparatoires* reveal that, in the absence of another body within the COE capable of undertaking this task, the purpose of the Consultative Committee is to respond to the rapid economic and social developments that may affect migrant workers.[80] In theory, therefore, the Consultative Committee provides for an 'evolutionary' and 'fluid' element in the EMW enabling appropriate responses to be made to the ever-changing conditions affecting migrant workers and their families.[81] In practice, however, the Consultative Committee remains under the control of the politically-oriented Committee of Ministers.[82]

The EMW offers more promise than it can ever hope to translate into practice. Given that a mere 8 countries have ratified the instrument, including only two *long-standing* labour-receiving countries (France and the Netherlands), its practical usefulness is questionable. The EMW has also been ratified by 3 southern

[74] *Explanatory Report on the EMW*, n. 70 above, 6, para. 8; Golsong, n. 67 above, 232.

[75] Art. 33(2). Any COE member state may also be represented on the Committee by an observer with the right to speak.

[76] See Art. 33(3), (4) and (5) respectively. Any revision to the EMW would be effected by means of a Protocol adopted by the Committee of Ministers and opened for signature to COE member states: *Explanatory Report on the EMW*, n. 70 above, 29, para. 105.

[77] Art. 33(7).

[78] *Fourth Report on the Application of the EMW*, n. 69 above, 3, paras. 10–11. The Consultative Committee also has a role to play in the implementation of Art. 12 of the EMW with respect to family reunification. See Ch. 8.

[79] See also Niessen and de Lary de Latour, n. 69 above, 100.

[80] Golsong, n. 67 above, 248.

[81] Cf., *ibid.* 232, 247.

[82] Cf. *Explanatory Report on the EMW*, n. 70 above, 29, para. 105. This is mainly the result of the ineffective supervisory machinery. Two commentators have observed rather bluntly: 'The whole supervisory mechanism of the Legal Status Convention is extremely weak. There is no report writing obligation and no place at all for NGOs': Niessen and de Lary de Latour, n. 69 above, 101.

European countries, Italy, Portugal, and Spain, which have become significant receiving countries in recent years, and by Norway, Sweden, and Turkey. With the exception of Turkey, free movement of labour between the other state parties is a reality by virtue of the EC or the EEA. For the moment, therefore, the practical value of the EMW concerns its application in respect of inter-state relations between Turkey, (which is a major provider of migrant workers in Western Europe), and the remaining states parties to the EMW.[83]

5.3 THE EUROPEAN COMMUNITY

EC norms relating to free movement of workers are the most advanced provisions concerning the protection of migrant workers and their families. Although the relevance of these standards, outside of the uniquely integrated context of the EC and beyond the example of the operation of a liberal regime in this area, is debatable,[84] the recent expansion of the EC, the clamour for accession, particularly from the countries of central and eastern Europe, and the development of regional trading blocs elsewhere in the world mean that these standards are taking on an additional significance.[85]

The EC's concern with labour migration has been primarily economic,[86] within the context of the free movement of goods and services, but it has also increasingly paid attention to the social and human rights' aspects of this migration. For example, EC provisions extend to protect migrant workers outside of their immediate employment context in such fields as social security, family reunification, the education of migrant workers' children, including the teaching of their culture and language, and electoral participation. This approach is in line with the EC philosophy that the creation of a single internal market cannot take place without concomitant progress in the social field.[87] An important part of this philosophy is the protection of the social rights of persons residing and working within the EC, which is the aim of the Charter of the Fundamental Social Rights of Workers of 1989.[88] The Charter is only a 'statement of intent'[89] and imposes

[83] Cf. Golsong, n. 67 above, 251.

[84] Cf. T. Stein and S. Thomsen, 'The Status of the Member States' Nationals under the Law of the European Communities' in *The Legal Position of Aliens*, n. 18 above, 1775, 1776.

[85] Cf. Clapham, n. 8 above, 68.

[86] Stein and Thomsen, n. 84 above, 1785.

[87] L. Betten, 'Towards a Community Charter of Fundamental Social Rights' (1989) 7 NQHR 77, 78, 83–4; *Report to the Conference on Migrant Workers from the Mahgreb in the European Community* (1991) 13, para. 2.12.

[88] *Community Charter of the Fundamental Social Rights of Workers*, adopted by the Heads of State or Government of the Member States of the European Community, Strasbourg, 9 Dec. 1989; reprinted in Commission of the European Communities, Directorate-General for Employment, Industrial Relations and Social Affairs, *Social Europe 1/90* (Luxembourg: OOPEC, 1990) 46–50. The second recital of the Preamble to the Charter asserts that 'in the context of the single European market, the same importance must be attached to the social aspects as to the economic aspects and . . . therefore, they must be developed in a balanced manner'. For a comprehensive analysis of the contents of the Charter, see B. Bercusson, 'The European Community's Charter of Fundamental Social Rights of Workers' (1990) 53 MLR 624 and P. Watson, 'The Community Social Charter' (1991) 28 *CML Rev.* 37.

[89] Note (EEC), 'Charter on Fundamental Social Rights' (July 1989) EIRR 11.

no legally binding obligations upon member states. It also finds expression in the Protocol on Social Policy annexed to the EC Treaty. In this Protocol, member states have expressed the wish 'to continue along the path laid down in the 1989 Social Charter', and have adopted an agreement to this end known as the Agreement on Social Policy. All member states, with the exception of the United Kingdom, have accepted the Charter, Protocol, and the Agreement.[90]

The elimination of obstacles to the principles of free movement of labour and non-discrimination constitute obligations under Articles 3(c), 6 (formerly Article 7 EEC) and 48 EC. These principles are mainly implemented by Regulation 1612/68/EEC.[91] The Regulation contains provisions concerning equal treatment between workers who are nationals of member states in respect of access to employment, employment and work conditions, social and tax advantages, trade union rights, accommodation, vocational training, and education. It also determines which family members may join the worker in the country of employment and under what conditions. Freedom of movement and residence within the EC, irrespective of any exercise of economic activity, has now been confirmed, by virtue of amendments introduced by the TEU, as an integral component of European citizenship and extends to all nationals of EC member states subject to certain conditions.[92]

Initiatives in the labour migration field have also been the subject of EC policy developments. The EC Commission is the author of a number of policy documents on migration.[93] These documents also constitute an important part of the EC's concern regarding the protection of migrant workers and their families from countries beyond the EC, who reside and work in the EC. Presently, this group is only subject to the protective framework of EC law in limited circumstances. Proposals to provide workers and members of their families from third countries protection on equal terms with EC nationals are examined in the next chapter.

The system of implementation of EC law is the most extensive and developed of those examined thus far.[94] It is a supranational as opposed to an intergovernmental scheme of law. EC institutions comprise the Council of Ministers, the

[90] In the Agreement, member states confirm their wish 'to implement the 1989 Social Charter on the basis of the "*acquis communautaire*"' (Preamble). The Agreement, *inter alia*, foresees action in the social field by the Council and, to a lesser extent, by the EC Commission and European Parliament.

[91] Council Regulation 1612/68/EEC of 15 Oct. 1968 on freedom of movement for workers within the Community, as amended, OJ Sp. Ed. 1968–69, 475, JO 1968, L 257/2.

[92] Art. 8(a)(1) EC.

[93] See in particular: Commission of the European Communities, Communication to the Council, *Action Programme in Favour of Migrant Workers and Their Families*, COM (74) 2250 of 18 Dec. 1974; Commission of the European Communities, Communication to the Council, *Guidelines for a Community Policy on Migration*, COM (85) 48 final of 7 March 1985; and Commission of the European Communities, Communication to the Council and the European Parliament, *Immigration and Asylum Policies*, COM (94) 23 final of 23 Feb. 1994.

[94] The brief overview below is largely taken from D. Wyatt and A. Dashwood, *European Community Law*, 3rd edn. (London: Sweet & Maxwell, 1993).

Commission, the European Parliament, and the Court of Justice. The Council[95] is composed of Ministers and political representatives from each member state and enacts legislation to ensure coordination of the economic policies of the member states. The Commission is an independent body which initiates and enacts decisions and oversees their implementation. The European Parliament, a body consisting of 626 members directly elected to 5-year terms, plays an important role in determining the EC budget. It is also an actor in the EC law-making process and exercises detailed political supervision over the Commission. Finally, the Court of Justice, assisted by the Court of First Instance, is the principal institution responsible for the adjudication of disputes and for the clarification and interpretation of EC law. In its role as 'guardian of the Treaties', the Commission may bring an action before the Court of Justice under Article 169 EC against any member state that it believes has failed to fulfil an obligation under EC law. A direct action for the annulment of EC acts can also be brought before the Court under Article 173 EC by any natural or legal person, provided the *locus standi* rules are complied with. EC rules are enforceable in the national courts of all member states and take precedence over domestic law. Any conflict between domestic law and EC law is to be resolved in favour of EC law.[96] If the application of EC law is unclear, a national court may refer the question to the Court of Justice for clarification under Article 177 EC. On the whole, the Court has given a broad interpretation to EC provisions implementing free movement of labour, and has viewed the permissible limitations on this principle in a very restrictive light.[97]

5.4 CONCLUSION

The European framework protecting the rights of migrant workers and their families in Europe is truly unique. No other region in the world can boast such an elaborate mosaic of overlapping standards, some of which are subject to effective enforcement. Even so, as the forthcoming chapters reveal, this framework is hardly comprehensive given that a large group of migrants find themselves outside of the protective web; hence raising the spectre of an unjust Europe concerned with the narrow interests of a few affluent nations at the expense of the developing world.

[95] This body is to be distinguished from the European Council, which holds meetings at the highest political level (heads of state or government of the member states and the President of the EC Commission, assisted by the ministers for foreign affairs of the member states and by a member of the Commission) and is charged with the responsibility of providing the European Union 'with the necessary impetus for its development and . . . [defining] the general political guidelines thereof' (Art. D TEU).

[96] See Case 6/64, *Costa* v. *ENEL* [1964] ECR 585, [1964] CMLR 425.

[97] C. Greenwood, 'Nationality and the Limits of the Free Movement of Persons in Community Law' (1987) 7 YBEL 185.

6

Who is a 'Migrant Worker' in Europe?

6.1 INTRODUCTION

The question—'who is a migrant worker?'—is given a broad interpretation by universal instruments specifically concerned with the protection of the rights of migrant workers and their families. Although some categories of migrant workers are not always covered, such as self-employed workers, students, trainees, and seafarers, what is significant about these instruments is that states parties are obliged to afford protection to *all* migrants within their territories regardless of ratification by the country from which these persons originate. The principle of reciprocity, however, is dominant in European arrangements for the protection of migrant workers and their families and is evidenced by the narrower personal scope of the relevant COE conventions and the free movement regimes, such as the EC. Migrant workers and their families from non-European countries and in particular from the developing world as well as illegal migrants, who are legitimate subjects of protection under the ILO and UN conventions, are especially at risk from exploitation and abuse in a continent which is becoming increasingly anxious about their presence.

6.2 COUNCIL OF EUROPE INSTRUMENTS

From the COE instruments applicable to migrant workers and their families, only the ESC and the EMW contain specific provisions on migrant workers and only the latter has a comprehensive definition of 'migrant worker'. A definition may be 'implied' from the provisions of the ESC, particularly from Article 19, but there is no definition of 'migrant worker' in the ECHR or the ECE.

With the exception of the ECHR, the other COE conventions only apply to migrant workers who are nationals of other states parties.[1] From the text of Article 19 of the ESC, it is clear that illegal migrant nationals from other states

[1] The application of Arts. 1 and 2 of the ECE, obliging states parties to facilitate temporary entry and prolonged or permanent residence, is specifically restricted to 'nationals of the other Parties'. Although there is no explicit provision in Art. 19 of the ESC circumscribing its operation to nationals of states parties, such an interpretation is maintained by the Committee of Independent Experts: *Conclusions I*, 81, cited by D. Harris, *The European Social Charter* (1984) 158. This interpretation is consistent with the remainder of the ESC. For example, para. 19 of Pt. I, the 'declaratory' parallel provision to Art. 19, limits the right of migrant workers and their families to protection and assistance to those who are 'nationals of a Contracting Party'. Furthermore, the Appendix to the ESC clearly maintains that Arts. 1 to 17 are only applicable to foreigners in so far as they are 'nationals of other Contracting Parties'. See also Harris, *ibid*. Finally, Art. 1(1) of the EMW defines 'migrant worker' for the purpose of the EMW as a 'national of a Contracting Party'.

parties are excluded. A number of paragraphs in this provision refer to workers 'lawfully within' or 'lawfully residing within' the territories of states parties.[2] The ESC also specifically obliges contracting parties 'to extend the protection and assistance provided for [in Article 19] to self-employed migrants in so far as such measures apply'.[3] This provision only operates in those states parties that have accepted it under the selective ratification procedure of the ESC.[4] Some measures, however, appear to be inapplicable to self-employed migrants, namely those in Article 19(4) concerning equal treatment with nationals in respect of employment and trade union rights.[5] As for refugee migrant workers, the Appendix to the ESC obliges states parties to grant them the most favourable treatment possible.

Article 1(1) of the EMW defines 'migrant worker' as 'a national of a Contracting Party who has been authorized by another contracting Party to reside in its territory in order to take up paid employment'. Therefore, the reference to the need for 'authorization' in the definition excludes migrant workers from other contracting parties who are in an irregular situation. Furthermore, the EMW only applies to persons taking up 'paid employment' and hence excludes the self-employed as well as those who are not economically active.[6] In addition to this definition of 'migrant worker', Article 1(2) lists the categories of migrants to which the EMW does not apply: frontier workers; artists and other entertainers and sports persons who are engaged for a short period; members of a liberal profession; seafarers; those undergoing training; seasonal workers; and workers carrying out specific employment in a contracting party on behalf of an undertaking with its registered office outside the territory of that country.[7]

[2] The Appendix to the ESC also requires lawful residence and regular employment for the application of Arts. 1 to 17 of the ESC to foreigners.

[3] Art. 19(10). Compare this provision with Art. 11 in both ILO Conventions No. 97 of 1949 and No. 143 of 1975, which excludes self-employed migrants from the ambit of its protection by defining 'migrant worker' as a person who migrates for employment to another country 'with a view to being employed *otherwise than on his own account*' (emphasis added).

[4] Austria and Finland have not accepted Art. 19(10) of the ESC and Art. 19 has not been accepted *in toto* by Denmark, Iceland, and Malta.

[5] Harris, n. 1 above, 188; R. Plender, *International Migration Law* (1988) 247. Art. 19(4), however, also provides for equal treatment with nationals in respect of accommodation and this provision should clearly be applicable to self-employed migrants: Plender, *ibid*. 247–8. The Committee of Independent Experts has confirmed this view: '[C]ertain paragraphs of Article 19 relating, for instance, to free assistance services, family reunion, equal treatment as regards taxation, dues, access to courts, housing, etc. must also be applied to self-employed migrant workers and their families': *Conclusions IX-2*, 102, cited in Council of Europe, *Case Law on the European Social Charter—Supplement No. 2* (Strasbourg: Council of Europe, 1987) 31.

[6] See also Plender, n. 5 above, 253, who includes students, tourists, and retired persons in this category. Foreign students who have completed their studies and are now seeking work in the same country are not covered by the definition, unless they have been authorized to reside in that country in order to take up paid employment: *Explanatory Report on the EMW* (1978) 8, para. 13.

[7] This list resembles the list of excluded categories of migrants in Art. 11 of ILO Convention No. 143, the only differences being that the EMW provision excludes seasonal workers and that the exclusion with respect to migrants carrying out specific work contracts is drawn more broadly and precisely than its counterpart in Art. 11(2)(e). See H. Golsong, 'La convention européenne relative au statut juridique du travailleur migrant' (1978) 234 regarding this last point.

The exclusion of seasonal workers from the application of the EMW has been justified on the grounds that these workers were treated as a separate category from the very beginning of the drafting process and that it therefore seemed preferable to treat the problems of seasonal migrant workers outside of the framework of the EMW.[8] Article 1(2)(e) of the EMW defines seasonal migrant workers as those 'in an activity dependent on the rhythm of the seasons, on the basis of a contract for a specified period or for specified employment'. Arguably, therefore, the EMW would be applicable to those migrants, such as the '*faux saisonniers*' in Switzerland, who are employed on seasonal contracts, but whose activities constitute *de facto* year-round jobs[9] and are hardly 'dependent on the rhythm of the seasons'. Such a group of workers should not be excluded from the application of the EMW.[10]

Although the definition in Article 1 of EMW does not expressly refer to the families of migrant workers, they are clearly covered by virtue of the numerous references made to them throughout the instrument. Article 19 of the ESC also covers migrant workers' families. Indeed, the provision is entitled The Right of Migrant Workers *and Their Families* to Protection and Assistance.[11]

6.3 WHO IS A 'MIGRANT WORKER' UNDER EC LAW?

The definition of 'migrant worker' under EC law is much broader than the definition in the EMW and that which may be ascertained from the provisions of the ESC. The EC regime functions on a different level to that of COE conventions because the concept of 'alien' under EC law is not the same as that found in general international law. EC law strives to break down the barriers of state sovereignty by seeking complete equality between member state nationals in

[8] Golsong, *ibid.* 234. The Consultative Committee recognized that traditional migratory movements, which effectively resulted in settlement in host countries, have been overtaken by new forms of temporary migration. The Committee resolved that a Protocol should be drafted in order to extend protection to temporary migrants and decided to study this question with the assistance of a consultant: *Fourth Report on the Application of the EMW* (1991) 12, paras. 92–4, 96. The consultant produced a report in 1992 proposing the adoption of an Additional Protocol which would extend the protection of the EMW to frontier, seasonal, project, and specified-employment workers: Council of Europe, Consultative Committee on the European Convention on the Legal Status of Migrant Workers, 9th Meeting, 9–10 Sept. 1992, *Draft Explanatory Memorandum on the Additional Protocol to the European Convention on the Legal Status of Migrant Workers* (prepared by H. de Lary de Latour), COE Doc. T-MG (92) 7 rev. See also J. Niessen and H. de Lary de Latour, *Equality of Treatment: The European Social Charter and the European Convention on the Legal Status of Migrant Workers* (1994) 97.

[9] See R. Rogers, 'Western Europe in the 1980s: The End of Immigration?' in *Guests Come to Stay: The Effects of European Labour Migration on Sending and Receiving Countries* (Boulder, Colorado: Westview Press, 1985) (hereinafter *Guests Come to Stay*) 285, 290.

[10] A specific argument in relation to Switzerland, of course, is academic because Switzerland has not ratified the EMW.

[11] Emphasis added.

employment and related matters. Indeed, the advent of 'European Citizenship' in the TEU is testimony to this approach. In contrast, COE instruments can only hope to improve the treatment of migrant workers with respect to nationals and to achieve equality in certain areas.[12] As with the ECE, ESC, and EMW, however, the EC free movement regime operates on the basis of reciprocity and only applies as between member state nationals.[13]

The workers to which the protection of EC law extends constitute a broad group.[14] The Court of Justice has stated that the fundamental principle of the free movement of workers requires that the term 'worker' in Article 48 EC is broadly interpreted and given an objective EC definition as opposed to one subjectively determined by member states.[15] The Court has ruled that so long as migrants perform services for and under the direction of another in return for remuneration, they are 'workers' for the purpose of EC law.[16] The worker's activities, however, must be economic, effective, and genuine.[17] Small-scale activities, if they are

[12] T. Stein and S. Thomsen, 'The Status of the Member States' Nationals under the Law of the European Communities' (1987) 1777.

[13] Nationality is to be determined exclusively by each state party. See C. Closa, 'Citizenship of the Union and Nationality of Member States' (1995) 32 *CML Rev.* 487, 510. See also the interesting discussion in A. Rosas, 'Nationality and Citizenship in a Changing European and World Order' in M. Suksi, (ed.), *Law under Exogenous Influences*, Publications of Turku Law School, Vol. 1, No. 1/1994 (Kirjapairo Grafia OY: Turku, 1994) 30, 43–50. A Declaration on Nationality of a Member State attached to the Final Act of the TEU confirms this position: 'The Conference declares that, wherever in the Treaty establishing the European Community reference is made to nationals of the Member States, the question whether an individual possesses the nationality of a Member State shall be settled solely by reference to the national law of the Member State concerned. Member States may declare, for information, who are to be considered their nationals for Community purposes by way of declaration lodged with the Presidency and may amend any such declarations when necessary'. A ruling by the Court of Justice has also confirmed the absolute discretion of EC member states to determine nationality: Case C-369/90, *Micheletti and others* v. *Delegación del Gobierno en Catabria* [1992] ECR I-4239. However, because this doctrine is based on due regard for EC law (*ibid.* para. 10), some commentators have argued that the Court would be within its powers to limit this principle in the event of abuse. See Closa, *ibid.* 513–14.

[14] For a useful short commentary on the meaning of 'worker' under EC law and an exposition of recent case law, see E. Johnson and D. O'Keeffe, 'From Discrimination to Obstacles to Free Movement: Recent Developments concerning the Free Movement of Workers 1989–1994' (1994) 31 *CML Rev.* 1313, 1315–19.

[15] Case 75/63, *Hoekstra (née Unger)* v. *Bestuur der Bedrijfsvereniging voor Detailhandel en Anbachten* [1964] ECR 177, [1964] CMLR 319; Case 53/81, *Levin* v. *Staatssecretaris van Justitie* [1982] ECR 1035, [1982] 2 CMLR 454.

[16] Case 66/85, *Lawrie-Blum* v. *Land Baden-Württemberg* [1986] ECR 2121, [1987] 3 CMLR 389; Case 344/87, *Bettray* v. *Staatssecretaris van Justitie* [1989] ECR 1621, [1991] 1 CMLR 389; Case 197/86, *Brown* v. *Secretary of State for Scotland* [1988] ECR 3205, [1988] 3 CMLR 403.

[17] *Levin*, n. 15 above, and *Bettray*, n. 16 above. Effective and genuine activities include part-time employment, even when a person's income is supplemented by financial assistance from state funds. Case 139/85, *Kempf* v. *Staatssecretaris van Justitie* [1986] ECR 1741, [1987] 1 CMLR 764. Effective and genuine activities may also encompass work as a trainee. *Levin*, *ibid.*; *Lawrie-Blum*, n. 16 above; Case C-3/90, *Bernini* v. *Minister van Onderwijs en Wetenschappen* [1992] ECR 1071. In relation to a person employed as a trainee, however, the Court of Justice has recognized in *Bernini*, *ibid.* para. 16, that national courts can legitimately inquire into the length of time spent in employment in order to determine whether the trainee has acquired adequate occupational aptitude to perform the job in question.

regarded as marginal and ancillary, are excluded from the definition.[18] Migrant workers who become unemployed, but who are capable of taking another job,[19] and those who are seeking employment[20] are also covered by Article 48 EC. Furthermore, self-employed workers are encompassed by Articles 52 to 66 EC which are concerned with the right of establishment and the freedom to provide services.[21]

Since 1990, freedom of movement and residence within the EC is no longer confined to economic activity. All EC nationals now have the right to move and reside freely within the territory of EC member states. This freedom, however, is not absolute and is subject to conditions.[22]

6.4 NON-EC MIGRANT WORKERS AND THEIR FAMILIES[23]

Background

There were approximately 12 million non-EC nationals *legally* resident in the fifteen EC member states at the beginning of 1993,[24] with about half originating in Turkey, the former Yugoslavia, and the Mahgreb region of North Africa.[25]

[18] In *Bettray*, n. 16 above, the Court of Justice ruled that work under a social integration scheme with the principal aim of rehabilitating and integrating a person into the labour market was not an effective and genuine economic activity.

[19] *Hoekstra (née Unger)*, n. 15 above.

[20] Case C-292/89, *R* v. *Immigration Appeal Tribunal, ex parte Antonissen* [1991] ECR I-745, [1991] 2 CMLR 373. In this case, a Belgian national was made subject to a deportation order for failing to find employment 6 months after entering the United Kingdom. The Court of Justice stated that, in the absence of EC rules on the question, it was reasonable for national law to provide a time limit within which migrants from other member states may seek employment and that the period of 6 months imposed by the United Kingdom authorities was sufficient time for such employment to be found. EC migrants, however, cannot be required to leave the country after the expiry of such a time limit if they are able to produce evidence that they are continuing to seek work and that they have a genuine chance of obtaining it. For a commentary on this decision, see C. Fox, 'European Community Migrant Workers: The Right to Remain and Look for Work' [1992] *Journal of Social Welfare and Family Law* 85.

[21] Arts. 52–8 and 59–66 EC respectively. EC law on freedom of movement does not apply to stateless persons and refugees. EC member states, however, have agreed to treat as favourably as possible recognized refugees who reside in the territory of another member state, if they seek entry for the purpose of employment. See the Declaration of Intent of 25 March 1964, JO 1964, 1225. See also P. Oliver, 'Non-Community Nationals and the Treaty of Rome' (1985) 5 YBEL 57, 58; Stein and Thomsen, n. 12 above, 1778, and Plender (1988), n. 5, 201.

[22] See Ch. 8 and the section on residence rights.

[23] The discussion in this section is based on a paper by the author entitled 'The Rights of Non-EC Immigrant Workers and Their Families in European Community Countries of Employment: A Case for Integration' in J. Dine and R. Watt, (eds.), *Discrimination Law: Concepts, Limitations and Justifications* (London: Longman, 1996) 134.

[24] Eurostat, 'Non-nationals make up less than 5% of the Population of the European Union on 1.1.93' (1996) *Statistics in Focus. Population and Social Conditions* No. 2, 1.

[25] There were over 2.5 million nationals from Turkey, 1.4 million from the former Yugoslavia, and more than 2 million nationals from Algeria, Morocco, and Tunisia legally resident in EC countries at the beginning of 1993. A significant majority of nationals from the Mahgreb (approximately 1.4 million) were living in France: *ibid.* 6 (Table 4).

Over 70 per cent of the non-EC population is resident in just four EC countries, namely France, Germany, the Netherlands, and the United Kingdom.[26] Non-EC migrant workers and their families have outnumbered their EC counterparts for many years;[27] the 1994 EC Labour Force Survey revealed that there were nearly twice as many non-EC migrants as EC migrants in member states of employment.[28] Given these figures, it is probably no exaggeration to refer to non-EC migrants as constituting the EC's 'sixteenth member State';[29] the 'cushion of a relatively cheap and flexible workforce during times of labour shortage'.[30]

Freedom of movement for workers within the EC does not, however, apply to non-EC nationals. At its inception, it seems that the intention of the drafters of the EEC Treaty was to leave open the possibility of accommodating all workers lawfully resident in member states regardless of their nationality. This is evident from the wording of Articles 6 and 48 EC. For example, Article 48(2) EC speaks of 'the abolition of any discrimination based on nationality *between workers of the member States* as regards employment, remuneration and other conditions of work and employment'.[31] As observed by a number of commentators, neither provision is expressly limited to nationals of EC member states.[32] As EC law

[26] Eurostat, *Labour Force Survey Results 1994* (Luxembourg: OOPEC, 1996) 42–3 (Table 012). The three most recent EC member states are not included in the calculation of these figures. In the four specified states, non-EC migrants account for considerably more that half of the total foreign population: France (63% in 1990), Germany (78% in 1993), the Netherlands (76% in 1993), and the United Kingdom (64% in 1993). See *SOPEMI 1994*, 201, 202, 206 and 211 respectively (percentages worked out by calculation).

[27] Free movement of labour within the EC has not resulted in an increase in migration for employment across the borders of member states. On the contrary: in 1959, when freedom of movement for workers was in its infancy, 75% of migrant workers in the original six EC member states originated from the other member states, mainly from Italy. In 1973, however, when the free movement principle was beginning to be fully implemented, 75% of migrant workers within the EC, which had been by then enlarged to 9 member states, came from third countries. See Commission of the European Communities, *Action Programme in Favour of Migrant Workers and Their Families* (1974) 1 and Plender (1988), n. 5 above, 215.

[28] There were over 10.2 million non-EC migrants compared with approximately 4.8 million EC migrants in the EC at the beginning of 1993. *Labour Force Survey Results 1994*, n. 26 above, 42–3 (Table 012). The proportion of non-EC migrants to EC migrants in the labour force is comparable: 4.6 to 2.7 million respectively. *Ibid.* 50–1 (Table 016). Again, these statistics exclude the three new EC member states.

[29] A. Geddes, 'Immigrant and Ethnic Minorities and the EU's "Democratic Deficit"' (1995) 33 JCMS 197, 204.

[30] Note (EEC), 'Migrant Workers: A Two-tier Labour Market' (Aug. 1990) EIRR 12.

[31] Emphasis added.

[32] S. O'Leary, 'Nationality Law and Community Citizenship: A Tale of Two Uneasy Bedfellows' (1992) 12 YEL 353, 357; T. Hoogenboom, 'Integration into Society and Free Movement of Non-EC Nationals' (1992) 3 EJIL 36, 41. See also R. Plender, 'Competence, European Community Law and Nationals of Non-Member States' (1990) 39 ICLQ 599, 604; A. Evans, 'Third Country Nationals and the Treaty on European Union' (1994) 5 EJIL 199, 200, and R. Fernhout, '"The United States of Europe have Commenced", but for whom?' (1993) 11 NQHR 249, 255–6 with respect to Art. 48 EC. However, the Court of Justice seems now to have adopted the position that the reference to 'workers' in Art. 48 EC only applies to EC nationals. See O'Leary, *ibid.*; K. Hailbronner and J. Polakiewicz, 'Non-EC Nationals in the European Community: The Need for a Coordinated Approach' (1992) 3 *Duke J. Int'l & Comp. L.* 49, 66. See also S. Peers, 'Towards Equality: Actual

developed, however, the extensive rights it conferred were generally limited to EC nationals, and most secondary legislation, such as Regulation 1612/68/EEC, is clearly limited to nationals of member states.[33] This legislation, together with the largely unsuccessful initiatives of the EC Commission and European Parliament, and subsequent developments, such as the adoption of the Single European Act, the Charter of the Fundamental Social Rights of Workers and the 'Third Pillar' of the TEU, have all served to underline that the position of non-EC immigrant workers and their families is inferior to that of EC nationals in EC countries of employment.

Positive initiatives of the Commission and European Parliament

The Commission and the European Parliament have frequently urged member states to improve the legal and social status of lawfully resident non-EC nationals. The Commission's work in this regard has consisted of a number of policy documents, which advocate the integration of this group into the host society by moving towards the realization of equality with EC nationals. These efforts, however, have not resulted thus far in any fundamental changes to the *status quo*.

In 1974, the Commission presented an Action Programme in Favour of Migrant Workers and Their Families, which it submitted to the Council. The Commission gave equal attention in this document to the position of EC migrants and lawfully resident non-EC migrants. It identified 'an urgent need—both now and in the foreseeable future—for specific social and educational measures to improve the conditions of migrant workers and their families', and in particular the social conditions of third country migrants.[34] Consequently, the Commission was of the view that:

and Potential Rights of Third-Country Nationals in the European Union' (1996) 33 *CML Rev*. 7, 19 and M. Cremona, 'Citizens of Third Countries: Movement and Employment of Migrant Workers within the European Union' (1995) LIEI No. 2, 87, citing Case 238/83, *Caisse d'Allocations Familiales* v. *Meade* [1984] ECR 2631 and Case C-355/93, *Eroglu* v. *Land Baden-Württemberg* [1994] ECR I-5113, para. 21 respectively. In *Meade, ibid.* 2641, Advocate General Mancini was in no doubt as to the scope of Art. 48 EC: '[T]he workers referred to in Article 48 must be Community citizens. That article itself confirms it. In any event, there is no doubt that the authors of the Treaties . . . intended to limit freedom of movement to citizens of the Member States . . .'.

[33] Not all EC law, however, bears this characteristic. Art. 119 EC, which proclaims that men and women are to receive equal pay for equal work, and legislation implementing this provision as well as other secondary legislation protecting workers, such as that concerned with health and safety at work, apply to non-EC nationals. See Hailbronner and Polakiewicz, n. 32 above, 65, 70–2. EC social security legislation is also applicable to refugees and stateless persons from non-EC member states, and to members of their families and their survivors. See Art. 2 of Council Regulation 1408/71/EEC of 14 June 1971 on the application of social security schemes to employed persons, to self-employed persons, and to members of their families moving within the Community, JO Sp. Ed. 1971, 416, JO 1971, L 149/2, as amended and updated.

[34] *Action Programme in Favour of Migrant Workers and Their Families*, n. 27 above, 4: '[T]he social conditions of the migrant do . . . give cause for serious concern—especially in the case of Third Country nationals, who have no Community protection and rely solely on often restrictive national legislation, for example in regard to the type of job they can take, where they may live, and the right to be joined by their families': *ibid.* 4–5.

one of the basic objectives of an action programme for migrants must be *the progressive elimination of all discrimination against them in living and working conditions, once, in the case of Third Country migrants, they have been legally admitted to employment in the Community.*[35]

In spite of this concern with the situation of migrants in EC countries of employment, the Commission also made it clear that the problem of migration required a comprehensive strategy, and recognized that:

A *long-term* programme for migrants cannot, therefore, confine itself to the social problems caused by migration for the migrants themselves and the communities within which they settle. It must embrace the whole range of economic, regional, industrial, and development policies which affect the phenomenon of migration. It is necessary to examine the effects of migration not only on the Community but also on the Third Countries concerned. Within this context, it is necessary . . . to establish coordination at Community level of the national policies of Member States towards migration and migrants, as well as taking the problem of migration into account in drawing up Community policies in other areas.[36]

In response to the Commission's initiative, the Council of Ministers emphasized the need:

to improve the circumstances of workers who are nationals of third countries and members of their families who are allowed into Member States, by aiming at equality between their living and working conditions, wages and economic rights and those of workers who are nationals of the Member States and members of their families.[37]

In the same resolution, the Council also considered it important to 'undertake appropriate consultation on migration policies *vis-à-vis* third countries'.[38]

In 1985, the Commission renewed its initiatives on behalf of migrants from third countries with its Guidelines for a Community Policy on Migration, a document also communicated to the Council. The Commission emphasized that EC action in this area should aim at equal treatment in living and working conditions for all migrants, including non-EC nationals:

[M]igrant communities, whether of Community or non-Community origin, face much the same problems in their social and working life. It is a constant factor of the Community approach to these problems that the aim should be equality of treatment in living and working conditions for all migrants, whatever their origin, and workers who are nationals.[39]

[35] *Ibid.* 5–6 (original emphasis). [36] *Ibid.* 3–4 (original emphasis).

[37] Council Resolution of 9 Feb. 1976 on an action programme for migrant workers and members of their families, OJ 1976, C 34, Preamble, recital 5 and Art. 2(c).

[38] Preamble, recital 6 and Art. 5(a). The Council reiterated this proposal in a Resolution of 27 June 1980 on guidelines for a Community labour market policy, OJ 1980, C 168.

[39] *Guidelines for a Community Policy on Migration* (1985), 1, para. 1. On the basis of 'the assumption that a migration policy at European level may gradually take shape as an integral part of the move towards European citizenship' the Commission also considered it fundamental that, *inter alia*, 'the legal status of immigrants from Third Countries should be adapted with the aim of consolidating foreign communities which have acquired the characteristics of permanence, by reason of their length of stay and above all through the existence of the second and third generations': *ibid.* 5, para. 10 (footnote omitted).

The Commission also proposed, as one of the priority actions, the development of consultation aimed primarily at migrants from non-EC countries.[40] In a subsequent resolution, the Council recognized the desirability of promoting 'co-operation and consultation between the Member States and the Commission as regards migration policy, including *vis-à-vis* third countries'. The Council also emphasized, however, that EC member states were to retain their sovereignty in respect of the access, residence, and employment of migrant workers from third countries.[41]

The Commission adopted a binding decision, on the basis of Article 118 EC, setting up a prior communication and consultation procedure on migration policies in relation to non-member countries.[42] The decision required member states to inform the Commission and other member states in advance of draft measures and agreements pertaining to third country migrants with particular reference to such matters as entry, residence, employment, equality of treatment in living and working conditions, wages and economic rights, and the integration of migrants and their families into the labour force, society, and cultural life of the host state.[43] The decision also provided for a consultation procedure, the objective of which was, *inter alia*, to adopt a common EC position on migration from non-EC countries and to ensure that individual state draft measures and agreements were in conformity with EC policy in this field.[44] In *Germany and others* v. *EC Commission*,[45] five countries challenged the decision mainly on the grounds that the issue of migration from outside the EC was beyond the scope of Article 118 EC. The Court of Justice did not agree that the policies of member states relating to non-EC workers fell outside the reach of this provision because these policies were bound to affect the employment and working conditions of EC nationals, but it considered the part of the decision dealing with the cultural integration of migrant workers as exceeding the scope of EC social policy. The Court also declared the decision void on the basis that the powers afforded the Commission

[40] The consultation was to be particularly concerned with, *inter alia*, the following matters: safeguarding the rights of migrant workers, and, particularly, ratification by EC member states of the EMW; clandestine migration and the illegal employment of migrant workers; social and educational insertion of migrants; continuing priority activities to help second generation immigrants; providing information on housing standards and on procedures for obtaining financial support; and implementing social security provisions in Association and Cooperation agreements and gradually extending to third country migrants the principles governing EC rules relating to EC migrants: *ibid*. 27, para. 44.

[41] Council Resolution of 16 July 1985 on guidelines for a Community policy on migration, OJ 1985, C 186, Art. 3 and recital 12 of the Preamble respectively.

[42] Commission Decision 85/381/EEC of 8 July 1985 setting up a prior communication and consultation procedure on migration policies in respect of non-member countries, OJ 1985, L 217/25. Under Art. 118 EC, the Commission is required to promote close cooperation between the member states in the social field.

[43] Art. 1(1).

[44] Art. 3.

[45] Cases 281/85, 283–285/85 and 287/85, *Re the Immigration of Non-Community Workers: Germany, France, Netherlands, Denmark and the United Kingdom* v. *EC Commission* [1987] ECR 3203, [1988] 1 CMLR 11. For commentaries on this case, see K. R. Simmonds, 'The Concertation of Community Migration Policy' (1988) 25 *CML Rev*. 177 and C. Greenwood, 'Nationality and the Limits of the Free Movement of Persons in Community Law' (1987) 7 YBEL 185, 269.

under Article 118 EC were purely procedural. The Commission could only initiate the consultation procedure and not pre-determine its outcome. Without doubt, this judgment has played a significant role in stalling the Commission's efforts to promote the rights of migrant workers from non-EC countries:

> Whilst, therefore, a welcome must be given to the Court's ruling that Article 118 EEC does indeed extend to migration policy in relation to non-member countries, and that it bestows a power upon the Commission to adopt binding decisions with a view to the arrangement of consultations, there are other aspects of the judgment which give rise to considerable disappointment. Since the somewhat uncertain start made with the action programme of 1974, it had appeared that the Community, at the highest level, had committed itself to the development of a policy which aimed to provide, at least, a concertation of migration policy in three priority areas—those of employment policy, social security and the integration of migrants into the host society. It had appeared, to judge from the official announcements, that the social advancement of migrants was accepted as necessary for social justice, economic efficiency and to counter racial and ethnic tensions. Against the background of an increasingly uncertain social and economic climate, the promotion of migrants' rights—whatever their country of origin—had come to be regarded as one of the principal social objectives of the Community . . . The belated attention paid in recent years to the position of migrants from non-member countries has received a major setback with this judgment—and from an unexpected source.[46]

In 1988, the Commission revised its decision in compliance with the Court's ruling, but this amended decision has borne little fruit.[47]

The most recent policy statement by the Commission is its 1994 communication to the Council and the European Parliament on Immigration and Asylum Policies. Unlike the communications of 1974 and 1985, the 1994 communication is specifically confined to 'immigration and integration of third country nationals'.[48] It builds on two earlier communications submitted by the Commission in October 1991,[49] and stresses the need for a comprehensive approach to the immigration question based on three separate but interrelated elements: 'action on migration pressure, particularly through co-operation with the main countries of would-be immigration to Europe'; 'action on controlling immigration in order to keep it within manageable structures'; and 'action to strengthen

[46] Simmonds, *ibid.* 200. In his opinion on the case, Advocate General Mancini, *ibid.* 3223 and 19 respectively, described the attitude of member states towards any measure relating to non-EC immigration as one of 'dissension, but above all coldness, distrust and vigorous defence of national sovereignty'.

[47] Commission Decision 88/384/EEC of 8 June 1988 setting up a prior communication and consultation procedure on migration policies in relation to non-member countries, OJ 1988, L 183/35. See also T. Hoogenboom, 'The Position of Those who are not Nationals of a Community Member State' in A. Cassesse, A. Clapham, and J. Weiler, (eds.), *Human Rights and the European Community: Methods of Protection* (Baden-Baden: Verlagsgesellschaft, 1991) 351, 402–3.

[48] Commission of the European Communities, *Immigration and Asylum Policies* (1994) 3, para. 6.

[49] Commission of the European Communities, Communications to the Council and to the Parliament on the *Right of Asylum* and *Immigration*, SEC(91) 1855 final of 11 Oct. 1991 and SEC(91) 1857 final of 11 Oct. 1991.

policies for legal immigrants'.[50] With regard to the last element, the communication calls for the strengthening of integration policies for the benefit of legal immigrants by, *inter alia*, improving the situation of third country nationals legally resident within the EC and by the creation of appropriate economic and socio-cultural conditions for successful integration.[51] The proposed components of such a strengthened policy include: 'security of stay and permanent residence for all those satisfying stability criteria', including some security of residence for the family members of migrant workers;[52] free movement within the EC, including the gradual implementation of free movement for the purpose of exercising an economic activity;[53] equality of treatment with nationals in respect of remuneration, working conditions, and social security;[54] liberalization of naturalization and nationality laws;[55] and the improvement of conditions for migrants in areas such as employment, housing, access to health services, and the education of their children.[56]

In addition to the work of the Commission, the European Parliament has often advocated the social integration of non-EC immigrant workers.[57] For example, paragraph A of its Resolution of 14 June 1990 on migrant workers from third countries[58] echoes the premise that the completion of the single market implies the speedy implementation of a parallel social dimension and notes that arrangements in this respect cannot possibly exclude a group of 8 million (now nearly 12 million) non-EC migrants working and living lawfully within the EC. In support of such integration, the European Parliament advocates the gradual extension of Regulation 1612/68/EEC to non-EC migrants,[59] a position reiterated in a Resolution on European immigration policy adopted in 1992.[60]

[50] *Immigration and Asylum Policies*, n. 48 above, Foreword and 11, para. 38.

[51] *Ibid.* 33, para. 123.

[52] *Ibid.* 33, paras. 124–5.

[53] *Ibid.* 34, paras. 127–9.

[54] *Ibid.* 35, paras. 130–1. In this regard, the Commission urges member states to ratify the UN Convention on Migrant Workers: 'Ratification of this Convention by the Member States would constitute the expression of the value attached by the Union to improving the position of migrant workers and their families resident in the Union and ensure that the rights accorded to them correspond to the highest international norms': *ibid.* 35, para. 132.

[55] *Ibid.* 35, para. 133.

[56] *Ibid.* 36–7, paras. 134–5, 138–9.

[57] For an interesting and informative overview of the recent activity of the European Parliament in the immigration field and the prospects for further action, see J. Monar, 'The European Parliament and Immigration Policy: Its Positions and Possibilities of Control' in G. D. Korella and P. M. Twomey, (eds.), *Towards a European Immigration Policy* (Brussels: European Interuniversity Press, 1995) 123.

[58] OJ 1990, C 175/180.

[59] *Ibid.* point 1. See also the European Parliament's amendments of 14 Feb. 1990 to the Commission Proposal for a regulation amending Council Regulation (EEC) 1612/68 on freedom of movement for workers within the Community (COM (88) 815 final), OJ 1990, C 68/88 advocating the extension of free movement rights to refugees and stateless persons resident in EC member states.

[60] Resolution of 18 Nov. 1992 on European immigration policy, OJ 1992, C 337/94, point 30. However, a 1993 resolution does not call for extending EC freedom of movement to third country nationals, but emphasizes instead the need to ensure unimpeded access to citizenship after a reasonable period of legal residence, equal treatment in respect of economic and social rights, and the right to vote in local elections after 5 or more years of legal residence. See Resolution of 15 July 1993 on European immigration policy, OJ 1993, C 255/184, point 13.

The Single European Act, the internal market and the elimination of internal frontiers

The purpose of the Single European Act (SEA),[61] adopted on 29 June 1987, was to realize an internal market without internal frontiers by the end of 1992, an objective which is now outlined in Article 7a EC.[62] The internal market is defined as 'an area without internal frontiers in which the free movement of goods, persons, services and capital is ensured . . .'.[63] At the time of the SEA's adoption, two declarations were attached, reserving the right of member states to take measures in respect of, *inter alia*, the control of immigration from third countries, but also confirming the powers of the Commission 'as regards the entry, movement and residence of nationals of third countries'.[64] The legal significance of these declarations is not clear.[65] The United Kingdom Government has relied upon them to support its position that freedom of movement is limited to EC nationals,[66] but the Commission has since clearly asserted that 'free movement of persons' within the internal market refers to:

[61] OJ 1987, L 169/1.

[62] Art. 7a EC provides that 'the Community shall adopt measures with the aim of progressively establishing the internal market over a period expiring on 31 December 1992'.

[63] Art. 7a EC, second para. See also Art. 3(c) EC asserting that the activities of the Community shall include 'an internal market characterized by the abolition, as between Member States, of obstacles to the free movement of goods, persons, services and capital'. Art. 7a EC constitutes a progression from Art. 3(c) EC (which was in the EEC Treaty) because it defines what the obstacles to free movement of persons are, namely internal frontiers, and sets a deadline (31 Dec. 1992) by which the objective is to be achieved. See W. de Lobkowicz, 'Intergovernmental Cooperation in the Field of Migration—From the Single European Act to Maastricht' in J. Monar and R. Morgan, (eds.), *The Third Pillar of the European Union* (Brussels: European Interuniversity Press, 1994) 99, 101–2.

[64] The first was a General Declaration on Arts. 13–19 of the SEA (the provisions concerned with the internal market): 'Nothing in these provisions shall affect the right of the Member States to take such measures as they consider necessary for the purpose of controlling immigration from third countries, and to combat terrorism, crime, the traffic in drugs and illicit trading in works of art and antiques'. A Political Declaration on the free movement of persons was also attached to the SEA as a whole and reads as follows: 'In order to promote free movement of persons, the Member States shall co-operate *without prejudice to the powers of the Commission, in particular as regards the entry, movement and residence of nationals of third countries*. They shall also co-operate in the combating of terrorism, crime, the traffic in drugs and illicit trading in works of art and antiques' (emphasis added). See also Hoogenboom (1992) n. 32 above, 49–50 and K. Hailbronner, 'Third Country Nationals and EC Law' in A. Rosas and E. Antola, (eds.), *A Citizen's Europe: In Search of a New Order* (London: SAGE, 1995) 182, 185–6. Hailbronner, *ibid.* 185, argues that the reference to the powers of the Community 'must be understood as referring to *the powers explicitly transferred* to the Community' (emphasis added). See also Hailbronner and Polakiewicz, n. 32 above, 53.

[65] Hailbronner & Polakiewicz, *ibid.*, contend, basing their arguments on Art. 31(2)(a) of the Vienna Convention on the Law of Treaties (23 May 1969; 1155 UNTS 331, (1969) 8 ILM 679), that the General Declaration is an 'agreement relating to the treaty which was made between all the parties in connexion with the conclusion of the Treaty' and therefore must be taken into account when interpreting the relevant SEA provisions.

[66] The United Kingdom Government has stated that it will retain internal border controls in order to supervise the movement of non-EC nationals. Cf. Hailbronner and Polakiewicz, n. 32 above, 62–3 and cf. D. O'Keeffe, 'The Free Movement of Persons and the Single European Act' (1992) 17 *EL Rev.* 3, 8. Of course, such controls can only be effective if all entrants are examined. Consequently, the Immigration (EEA) Order 1994 (S.I. 1994 No. 1895), which came into force in July 1994,

all persons, whether or not they are economically active and irrespective of their nationality. The internal market could not operate under conditions equivalent to those in a national market if the movement of individuals within this market were hindered by controls at internal frontiers.[67]

The Commission has emphasized, however, that 'free movement of persons' in this context does not give rise to the same rights as those conferred by the free movement provisions of the EC Treaty:

free movement of persons in the common market must not be confused with the rights which flow directly from Articles 48 to 66, and in particular the taking-up of economic activities as self-employed or employed persons and hence the right of residence, and which . . . apply only to nationals of Member States.[68]

Firm proposals to implement Article 7a EC were presented by the Commission in July 1995 concerning the elimination of controls on persons crossing internal frontiers and the right of third country nationals to travel in the EC, together with a 'flanking' or 'ancillary' measure to bring EC law into line with the proposal to abolish internal frontier controls.[69]

However, these proposals to realize the single internal market do nothing to enhance the conditions of access to employment and residence for non-EC nationals.[70] Any potential development towards a greater role for EC organs in

preserves the power of UK immigration officers to carry out full checks on all EC or EEA nationals and their families (Art. 20(2)(e)). See C. Vincenzi, 'European Citizenship and Free Movement Rights in the United Kingdom' (1995) *Public Law* 259, 264–5.

[67] Commission of the European Communities, Communication to the Council and to the Parliament, *Abolition of Border Controls*, SEC (92) 877 final of 8 May 1992, Annex I, 10, para. 6 (original emphasis). This position is supported by the European Parliament. See the Resolution of 19 Nov. 1992 on the abolition of controls at internal borders and free movement of persons within the European Community, OJ 1992, C 337/211, point 18. Indeed, the European Parliament instructed its President to institute proceedings against the Commission under Art. 175 EC for failing to act to implement the internal market in respect of free movement of persons pursuant to Art. 7a EC. See the Resolution of 15 July 1993 on free movement of persons pursuant to Article 8a of the EEC Treaty (now Art. 7a of the EC Treaty), OJ 1993, C 255/183, point 3. The case is now pending before the Court of Justice (Case C-455/93, *Parliament* v. *Commission*, OJ 1994, C 1/12), but may well be withdrawn as a result of the recent Commission proposals, n. 69 below and accompanying text. See Peers (1996), n. 32 above, 11–12 (n. 12).

[68] *Abolition of Border Controls*, n. 67 above.

[69] Commission of the European Communities, *Proposal for a Council Directive on the Elimination of Controls on Persons Crossing Internal Frontiers*, COM (95) 347 final of 12 July 1995; *Proposal for a Council Directive on the Right of Third-country Nationals to Travel in the Community*, COM (95) 346 final of 12 July 1995; *Proposal for a European Parliament and Council Directive amending Directive 68/360/EEC and Directive 73/148/EEC*, COM (95) 348 final of 12 July 1995. For commentaries on these measures, see: Editorial, 'Legislating Free Movement: An Over-ambitious Commission Package' (1996) 33 *CML Rev.* 1; Cremona, n. 32 above, 97–9; Peers (1996), n. 32 above, 17; and ILPA, *Update: October 1995*, 1–5. It is understood that the first and third Commission proposals can only be adopted once the harmonization of controls at external borders, (discussed below in relation to illegal migration), is complete. See Cremona, *ibid.* 97 and ILPA, *Update: October 1995*, *ibid.* 5.

[70] Indeed, this position is confirmed by Art. 1(3) of the proposed Directive on the Rights of Third-country Nationals to Travel in the Community, n. 69 above, 21, which states clearly that it will not affect provisions of EC or domestic law applicable to third-country nationals concerning 'stays other than for a short time, and access to employment and the taking-up of activities as a self-employed person'.

this field seems now to have given way to member state action on the intergovernmental level as a result of the TEU.[71]

EC Charter of the Fundamental Social Rights of Workers and the Agreement on Social Policy

The provisions of the Charter of the Fundamental Social Rights of Workers relating to 'living and working conditions' are all-inclusive embracing 'every worker', and therefore would seem to apply to workers from third countries.[72] Any uncertainty in this regard has been dispelled by subsequent reports of the Commission.[73] However, a reference to *comparable* treatment in the eighth recital to the Preamble of the Charter would appear to indicate that member states need not strive for complete equality between EC and non-EC nationals:[74]

> *Whereas* it is for Member States to guarantee that workers from non-member countries and members of their families who are legally resident in a Member State of the European Community are able to enjoy, as regards their living and working conditions, treatment comparable to that enjoyed by workers who are nationals of the Member State concerned.

The Charter's significance, however, is questionable given that it is merely a statement of intent and therefore not legally binding.

An important provision for non-EC nationals is Article 2(3) of the Agreement on Social Policy, annexed to the Protocol on Social Policy (opted out of by the United Kingdom) which is itself annexed to the TEU. By virtue of Article 2(3), the Council is obliged to act unanimously on a proposal from the Commission, after consulting the European Parliament and the Economic and Social Committee (an advisory body to the Council and the Commission), in the area of, *inter alia*, 'conditions of employment for third-country nationals legally residing in Community territory'. It is too early to say whether this provision will lead to the augmentation of the rights of non-EC nationals. Although it brings these rights into the domain of EC competence, the area of action is limited to 'conditions of employment' and, consequently, any measures flowing from Article 2(3) are unlikely to assist significantly with the fuller integration of non-EC migrant workers and their families in EC countries of employment.

[71] Fernhout, n. 32 above, 257–8.

[72] Bercusson notes that the final draft of the Charter replaced the word 'citizens' with 'workers'. The all-embracing nature of the term 'workers', therefore, may apply to workers from third countries. B. Bercusson, 'The European Community's Charter of Fundamental Social Rights of Workers' (1990) 53 MLR 624, 626–7. See also Hailbronner and Polakiewicz, n. 32 above, 73.

[73] Watson reluctantly conceded that because of, *inter alia*, the lack of a reference to third country nationals in the main text, 'they are . . . plainly excluded from the Charter': P. Watson, 'The Community Social Charter' (1991) 28 CML Rev. 37, 65. But see now Commission of the European Communities, *Second Report from the Commission to the Council on the Application of the Community Charter of Fundamental Social Rights*, COM (92) 562 final of 23 Dec. 1992, 12–13, para. 21, in which the Commission refers to EC action in respect of third country nationals under the section of the Charter entitled Improvement of Living and Working Conditions.

[74] See also Hailbronner and Polakiewicz, n. 32 above, 73–4.

Treaty on European Union (TEU)

The TEU is the final affirmation of the non-applicability of fundamental EC principles to non-EC nationals. In essence, it assigns their fate to the results of inter-governmental cooperation among EC member states. The concept of European citizenship is restricted to nationals from those countries.[75] Policy regarding non-EC or third country nationals constitutes a matter of 'common interest' in Title VI of the TEU, the so-called 'Third Pillar', which commits member states to cooperate in the fields of justice and home affairs.[76] Non-EC nationals, therefore, are to be the subject of an obligation to cooperate at the inter-governmental level.[77] The roles of the Commission, the European Parliament, and the Court of Justice under the Third Pillar are limited.[78] The Commission is only given a right of initiative,[79] which may result in the Council unanimously adopting joint positions and joint actions,[80] or in the drawing up of conventions and their

[75] Art. 8(1) EC: 'Citizenship of the Union is hereby established. Every person holding the nationality of a Member State shall be a citizen of the Union'.

[76] Art. K.1(3) TEU. For a critique of the workings of the Third Pillar, see the collection of essays in *The Third Pillar of the European Union*, n. 63 above and R. Bieber and J. Monar, (eds.), *Justice and Home Affairs in the European Union* (Brussels: European Interuniversity Press, 1995). See also D. O'Keeffe, 'Recasting the Third Pillar' (1995) 32 *CML Rev*. 893.

[77] In its communication on Immigration and Asylum Policies, n. 48 above, 5–6, para. 17, the Commission recognizes that inter-governmental cooperation in this area was already taking place on an *ad hoc* basis. However, it views the obligation to cooperate in the TEU as a step forward: 'The move from ad hoc intergovernmental cooperation, theoretically reversible at any moment, to a Treaty commitment to cooperate on a permanent basis nevertheless constitutes a considerable political signal both to political opinion in Member States and to the outside world'. In a similar vein, O'Keeffe observes: 'To some extent, this formal commitment [to cooperate] consolidates and codifies the ad hoc intergovernmental cooperation which had grown up in the 1980s . . . However, it marks a significant step forward in that it institutionalizes that cooperation, provides for "*passarelles*" to Community competence and enshrines an obligation to cooperate, albeit intergovernmentally, on a permanent basis': D. O'Keeffe, 'The Emergence of a European Immigration Policy' (1995) 20 *EL Rev*. 20, 25. Consequently, the inter-governmental cooperation under the Third Pillar cannot be regarded as 'pure' inter-governmentalism. See D. O'Keeffe, 'From Maastricht to the 1996 Intergovernmental Conference: The Challenges Facing the Union' (1994) LIEI No. 2, 135, 137–8.

[78] For a rather sceptical view of inter-governmental cooperation under the Third Pillar and for an assessment of the limited role of EC institutions, see H. U. J. D'Oliveira, 'Expanding External and Shrinking Internal Borders: Europe's Defence Mechanisms in the Areas of Free Movement, Immigration and Asylum' in D. O'Keeffe and P. M. Twomey, (eds.), *Legal Issues of the Maastricht Treaty* (London: Wiley Chancery Law, 1994) 261, 263–5. For a far more positive assessment, see de Lobkowicz, n. 63 above, 118–20.

[79] The Commission also has a limited role to play in the work of the Coordinating Committee, a body comprising senior officials with a complex structure and supported by a number of steering committees (O'Keeffe (1995:1), n. 76 above, 903 (n. 15)), which is set up under Art. K.4(1) TEU to coordinate, give opinions, and contribute to the preparation of the Council's discussions in the areas referred to in Art. K.1 TEU. Art. K.4(2) TEU asserts that the Commission is be 'fully associated' with this work. Practice indicates, however, that the Commission has only the status of a 'privileged observer' in relation to the work under the Third Pillar: O'Keeffe, *ibid*. 903.

[80] Art. K.3(2)(a)–(b) TEU. Whether joint positions and joint actions adopted under the Third Pillar have any binding legal effect is unclear. See the differing views of O'Keeffe (1995:1), n. 76 above, 913–14 and P.-C. Müller-Graff, 'The Legal Bases of the Third Pillar and its Position in the Framework of the Union Treaty' in *The Third Pillar of the European Union*, n. 63 above, 21, 35–6. For a view considering that measures adopted under Art. K.3 TEU are unlikely to have 'legally

recommendation to member states for adoption.[81] The European Parliament has a right to be informed and consulted, and may also ask questions of the Council and make recommendations to it.[82] The Court of Justice has no official role assigned to it, but any of the conventions adopted by member states may stipulate that the interpretation of their provisions and the settlement of disputes regarding their application are to be the responsibility of the Court.[83] Because the adoption of joint positions and joint actions requires unanimity (unless an option under Article K.3(2)(b) is exercised deciding that measures implementing joint actions are to be adopted by a qualified majority), most decisions relating to third country nationals and immigration taken by the Justice and Home Affairs Council have been in the form of conclusions, resolutions, and recommendations, which clearly have no binding legal effect.[84]

There is also scope for the Council, acting unanimously on the initiative of

binding force' between the member states, but nonetheless cannot be considered as 'mere declarations of common intent', see K. Hailbronner, 'Migration Law and Policy within the Third Pillar of the Union Treaty' in *Justice and Home Affairs in the European Union*, n. 76 above, 95, 106–7. The first joint action taken by the Justice and Home Affairs Council under Art. K.3(2)(b) TEU was a decision, adopted on 30 Nov. 1994, concerning travel facilities for school pupils from third countries resident in a member state, OJ 1994, L 327. The decision exempts children who are non-EC nationals residing in a EC member state from the requirement of a visa if they are travelling to another member state as members of a group on a school trip.

[81] Art. K.3(2)(c) TEU.

[82] Art. K.6 TEU. De Jong writes that Art. K.6 TEU does not contain 'a very substantive information and consultation procedure. To which extent these provisions offer more than the polite exchange of views that already took place on the intergovernmental cooperation, will depend on the generosity of Member States': C. De Jong, 'Towards a European Immigration Policy under the Treaty on European Union' in *Towards a European Immigration Policy*, n. 57 above, 45, 55–6. It would appear to date that only lip-service has been given to Art. K.6 TEU. The European Parliament has expressed its concern at the narrow interpretation afforded this provision and at the lack of openness in the decisions taken by the Council under the Third Pillar. Indeed, most decisions adopted by the Council were forwarded to the European Parliament after their adoption, a practice which the Parliament considers unacceptable. See Resolution of 14 Dec. 1995 on the progress made in the implementation of cooperation in the fields of justice and home affairs pursuant to Title VI of the Treaty on European Union, OJ 1996, C 17/17, points 4, 7, and 8 respectively. The European Parliament, *ibid.* point 4, has called on the Council and Commission to resume negotiations with it on the proper implementation of Art. K.6.

[83] Art. K.3(2)(c) TEU.

[84] O'Keeffe (1995:1), n. 76 above, 894. This practice has been criticized by the European Parliament because such measures are not provided for in Title VI of the TEU and are not normally published in the EC's Official Journal. See Resolution of 14 Dec. 1995 on the progress made in the implementation of cooperation in the fields of justice and home affairs, n. 82 above, point 9. However, this working method clearly presents a number of advantages to member state governments and is also likely to result in changes to domestic law: '[T]he technique of non-binding conclusions and resolutions by which ministers agreed to seek to ensure that their national laws are adapted by a specified date permit a more flexible proceeding for the coordination of national legislation. In general, consensus can be much easier achieved if there is still a legal possibility to deviate and if there is scope for future review and amendment. Judging from the experience with the resolutions of the immigration ministers on coordination of national asylum legislation, it can be observed that substantial principles of these resolutions have had a considerable impact on the national laws of Member States'. See Hailbronner (1995:2), n. 80 above, 104–5. Relevant conclusions, resolutions and recommendations are discussed in the section on illegal migrants in this chapter and under the pertinent headings in Chs. 7 and 8.

the Commission or a member state, to transfer Third Pillar matters, including policy on third country nationals, to Article 100c and thus to the realm of EC competence by the application of Article K.9 TEU, and at the same time to determine the relevant voting conditions relating to such matters.[85] Although the Commission and Parliament are in favour of 'communitarization' of significant aspects of the Third Pillar, including immigration and asylum policy, the Commission has decided that it is wiser to pursue this matter within the context of the 1996–97 Intergovernmental Conference (IGC) reviewing the Treaties rather than through the application of Article K.9 TEU.[86] In preparation for the IGC, the governmental Reflection Group issued a report in December 1995 in which it expressed a strong preference for the transfer of all immigration matters to EC competence.[87] Such a transfer would increase transparency in the immigration field by making it subject to control by the Court of Justice as well as by national courts.[88]

Although the reference to non-EC nationals in the Third Pillar of the TEU clearly pertains to matters which are of importance to them, such as their conditions of entry, movement, and residence (including family reunion and access to employment),[89] it is also made in the context of such 'related' concerns as combating unauthorized immigration[90] and 'police cooperation for the purpose of preventing and combating terrorism, unlawful drug trafficking and other serious

[85] See also Art. 100c(6) EC. Presently, Art. 100c EC, in its first paragraph, is concerned with one aspect of immigration policy, namely the adoption of a common EC visa policy in respect of third countries. The Council has already taken action in this area. See Council Regulation 2317/95/EC of 25 Sept. 1995 determining the third countries whose nationals must be in possession of visas when crossing the external borders of the member states, OJ 1995, L 234/1, which draws up a common list of 101 third countries in the Annex. As at 1 Jan. 1996, decisions adopted under Art. 100c(1) EC are to be taken by the Council by a qualified majority (Art. 100c(3) EC).

[86] Commission of the European Communities, Communication from the Commission to the European Parliament and the Council, *Possible Application of Article K.9 of the Treaty on European Union*, COM (95) 566 final of 22 Nov. 1995, 4–5, paras. 10–11. The European Parliament called for the 'communitarization' of all the areas in Art. K.1 of the Third Pillar in Sept. 1993. See Resolution of 20 Sept. 1993 on cooperation in the fields of justice and home affairs under the Treaty on European Union (Title VI and other provisions), OJ 1993, C 255/168, points 3 and 4. Communitarization of asylum and immigration was also advocated by the German Government in 1991 during the previous IGC that drafted the TEU, but this position was not supported by most other EC member states (with only Belgium fully in favour), which preferred to retain their sovereignty in this politically sensitive area. See de Lobkowicz, n. 63 above, 117.

[87] General Secretariat of the Council of the European Union, Information Policy, Transparency and Public Relations, *1996 Intergovernmental Conference (IGC '96): Reflection Group Report and Other References for Documentary Purposes*, Brussels, Dec. 1995 (Luxembourg: OOPEC, 1996) 23: 'Many of us take the view that, in order to act more efficiently, we need to put fully under Community competence matters concerning third country nationals, such as immigration, asylum and visa policy, as well as common rules for external border controls'. See also *ibid.* 51, para. 49.

[88] ILPA, *1996: The Intergovernmental Conference on the Re-Negotiation of the European Union Treaties: The Impact on Asylum and Immigration* (March 1996) 10. See also cf. D. O'Keeffe, 'Reflections on a European Immigration Policy' in *Towards a European Immigration Policy*, n. 57 above, 19, 31.

[89] Art. K.1(3)(a)–(b) TEU. It is noteworthy that the term 'right' does not appear in this list.

[90] Art. K.1(3)(c) TEU.

forms of international crime'.[91] The *rights* of non-EC immigrant workers and their families are unlikely to be rapidly advanced in such a context.[92] It is significant that the Third Pillar is silent on the question of what overriding objective is to be achieved through inter-governmental cooperation in 'matters of common interest'. In noting that all concrete measures taken to date have been 'restrictive', one commentator concludes that 'restriction' in matters such as asylum and immigration appears clearly to constitute 'the objective'.[93]

Limited free movement rights of non-EC nationals under EC law

(a) Derived rights

EC law caters for non-EC nationals in some respects.[94] The right to family reunion permits the EC migrant worker to be joined by his or her spouse and dependants regardless of their nationality.[95] Once in the country of employment, non-EC family members have free access to the labour market.[96] However, these are not independent rights but derived from the status of the primary rights-holder. The liberal rules on family reunion have resulted in 'reverse discrimination' against national workers, who wish to be joined by their families, because they are subject to the usually stricter national legislation on family reunion if they have not activated their EC status.[97] On the other hand, non-EC family members, who come to join an EC worker while he or she is employed in another member state, may effectively by-pass more stringent domestic immigration controls

[91] Art. K.1(9) TEU.

[92] Geddes, n. 29 above, 207, writes: 'At EU level, immigration is primarily defined as a security/crime issue . . . , not one of, for example, economic development or human rights'. In this regard, Evans, n. 32 above, 215, also writes: '[T]he principal concern seems to be with tightening controls on [third country] nationals, and this may be a natural consequence of including migration issues within the scope of Article K TEU, thereby linking them with criminal matters rather than with social policy or the freedoms entailed by the internal market'. See also the similar context of the declarations appended to the SEA, n. 64 above. To a great extent, this context mirrors the way governments in many European countries increasingly regard immigrants, as potential criminals and trouble-makers. A redeeming feature, however, is Art. K.2(1) TEU, which asserts that the matters referred to in Art. K.1 TEU are to be dealt with in compliance with the ECHR and the Geneva Convention Relating to the Status of Refugees.

[93] A. Achermann, 'Asylum and Immigration Policies: From Cooperation to Harmonization' in *Justice and Home Affairs in the European Union*, n. 76 above, 127, 130 and 134.

[94] For a fuller discussion of some of the case law referred to below, see W. Alexander, 'Free Movement of Non-EC Nationals. A Review of the Case-Law of the Court of Justice' (1992) 3 EJIL 53.

[95] Reg. 1612/68/EEC, Art. 10. The *right* to family reunion is limited to spouses, children under 21, or to children over 21 if they are still dependent on the worker, and to dependent parents and grandparents (Art. 10(1)). Member States only have an obligation *to facilitate* the reunion of other dependent relatives with the migrant worker (Art. 10(2)). These provisions are discussed in greater detail in the section on the right to family reunion in Ch. 8.

[96] Reg. 1612/68/EEC, Art. 11.

[97] See Case 35–36/82, *Morson and Jhanjan* v. *Netherlands* [1982] ECR 3723, [1983] 2 CMLR 221, in which the Court of Justice held that the provisions on free movement of workers are inapplicable to workers who have always lived and worked in their *own* country, and who want to bring in family members. Similarly, non-EC nationals cannot rely on EC law to claim a right to remain on the death of the spouse if the latter did not exercise free movement rights. Joined cases C-297/88 and C-197/89, *Dzodzi* v. *Belgian State* [1990] ECR I-3763.

on return to the worker's home country and enjoy there the rights which flow from EC law.[98]

Non-EC nationals may also acquire limited free movement rights under Articles 59 EC *et seq.*, the provisions concerned with the freedom to provide services.[99] The Court of Justice ruled in *Rush Portuguesa Lda* v. *Office National d'Immigration* that a company originating in one EC member state and providing services in another member state is not required to obtain work permits from the national immigration authority for non-EC nationals in its lawful employment.[100] The approach taken in *Rush Portuguesa* was confirmed by the Court in its decision in *Vander Elst* v. *Office des Migrations Internationales (OMI).*[101]

(b) Agreements with third countries

The EC and its member states have entered into a number of Association and Cooperation agreements[102] with non-member states, such as Turkey,[103] the Mahgreb countries,[104] and central and eastern European states,[105] which confer a range of

[98] Case C-370/90, *R* v. *Immigration Appeal Tribunal and Singh, ex parte Secretary of State for the Home Department* [1992] ECR I-4265, [1992] 3 CMLR 358. With the advent of the single internal market and European citizenship, it is arguable that the anomaly of reverse discrimination cannot be justified any longer. Cf. Johnson & O'Keeffe, n. 14 above, 1338 (and n. 71), citing from J. D'Oliveira, 'The Community Case—Is Reverse Discrimination still Permissible under the Single European Act' in *Forty Years On: The Evolution of Postwar Private International Law in Europe*, Symposium in celebration of the 40th Anniversary of the Centre of Foreign Law and Private International Law, University of Amsterdam, 27 Oct. 1981, 76; and S. Weatherill and P. Beaumont, *EC Law* (London: Penguin, 1993) 540.

[99] See also the second para. of Art. 59 EC which provides the Council with the power, by a qualified majority, to 'extend the provisions of the Chapter [on the freedom to provide services] to nationals of a third country who provide services and who are established within the Community'. To date the Council has not exercised this power. See Peers (1996), n. 32 above, 43.

[100] Case C-113/89, *Rush Portuguesa Lda* v. *Office National d'Immigration* [1990] ECR I-1417, [1991] 2 CMLR 818. The facts of *Rush Portuguesa* were unique in that they concerned a Portuguese company providing services in France through the employment of Portuguese nationals. At the time, the freedom to provide services was applicable between Portugal and other members of the EC, but free movement of workers had not yet been implemented.

[101] Case C-43/93, *Vander Elst* v. *Office des Migrations Internationales (OMI)* [1994] ECR I-3803. This decision is briefly discussed in the section on access to employment in Ch. 8.

[102] There are a number of legal bases in the EC Treaty for such agreements, including the general powers available to the Council under Arts. 100 and 235. There is also a specific power to conclude Association agreements in Art. 238: 'The Community may conclude with one or more States or international organizations agreements establishing an association involving reciprocal rights and obligations, common action and special procedure'.

[103] EEC–Turkey Association Agreement (1963) and Protocol (1970), OJ 1973, C 113/1.

[104] EEC–Morocco Cooperation Agreement, OJ 1973, L 264/1; EEC–Algeria Cooperation Agreement, OJ 1978, L 263/1; EEC–Tunisia Cooperation Agreement, OJ 1978, L 265/1. The agreements with Morocco and Tunisia will soon be replaced by new Euro-Mediterranean Association agreements. See Commission of the European Communities, *Proposal for a Decision of the Council and the Commission on the conclusion of a Euro-Mediterranean Agreement establishing an association between the European Communities and their Member States, of the one part, and the Republic of Tunisia [and the Kingdom of Morocco], of the other part*, COM (95) 235 final of 13 May 1995 and COM (95) 740 final of 20 Dec. 1995 respectively. A Euro-Mediterranean Association agreement has also been proposed with Israel (SEC (95) 1719 of 13 Nov. 1995). See Peers (1996), n. 32 above, 8 (and n. 6).

[105] Association agreements, known as 'Europe Agreements', have been concluded with the following central and eastern European countries: Bulgaria (OJ 1994, L 358/1), the Czech Republic (OJ

rights on their nationals. Generally speaking, implementation of these agreements is entrusted to Association or Cooperation Councils composed of representatives from EC institutions, EC member states, and the non-member state concerned. The Court of Justice has observed that these agreements and the decisions adopted thereunder are an integral part of the EC legal order[106] and are capable of having direct effect in member states, if they are of sufficient clarity and precision to be applied without further measures of implementation.[107] The EC has also entered into a number of agreements with African, Caribbean, and Pacific (ACP) countries, which contain provisions aimed at the protection of ACP and EC nationals who are legally resident in each others' territories.[108]

The rights which nationals of non-EC member countries that have entered into Association and Cooperation agreements may enjoy chiefly concern rights to equal work and employment conditions, access to the labour market, and social security. The scope of these rights is analysed in greater detail under the relevant headings in Chapter 8.

1994, L 360/1), Hungary (OJ 1993, L 347/1), Poland (OJ 1993, L 348/1), Romania (OJ 1994, L 357/1), and the Slovak Republic (OJ 1994, L 359/1). The Agreements with Hungary and Poland came into force on 1 Feb. 1994, whereas the remaining Agreements entered into force on 1 Feb. 1995. Similar agreements have been proposed by the Commission with the Baltic States (Estonia, Latvia, and Lithuania) and Slovenia. See respectively COM (95) 207 final of 2 June 1995 and COM (95) 341 final of 12 July 1995. Partnership and Cooperation agreements have been proposed with Russia (COM (94) 257 final of 15 June 1994) and the following former republics of the Soviet Union: Armenia (COM (95) 136 final of 27 March 1996); Azerbajan (COM (95) 137 final of 27 March 1996); Belarus (COM (95) 24 final of 22 Feb. 1995); Georgia (COM (96) 135 final of 27 March 1996); Kazakhstan (COM (94) 411 final of 5 Oct. 1994); Kyrgyz Republic (COM (94) 412 of 5 Oct. 1994); Moldova (COM (94) 477 final of 3 Nov. 1994); Ukraine (COM (94) 226 final of 1 June 1994); Uzbekistan (COM (96) 254 final of 5 June 1996).

[106] Case 12/86, *Demirel v. Stadt Schwäbisch Gmünd* [1987] ECR 3719, [1989] 1 CMLR 421; Case C-192/89, *S. Z. Sevince v. Staatssecretaris van Justitie* [1990] ECR 3461, [1992] 2 CMLR 57.

[107] In Case C-58/93, *Yousfi v. Belgium* [1994] ECR I-1353 and Case C-18/90, *Kziber v. Office National de L'Emploi* [1991] ECR I-199, Art. 41(1) of the EEC–Morocco Cooperation Agreement, which is concerned with equal treatment in the field of social security, was held to be directly effective. In *Sevince*, n. 106 above, Case C-237/91, *Kus v. Landeshauptstadt Wiesbaden* [1993] 2 CMLR 887 and *Eroglu*, n. 32 above, the access to employment provisions in decisions issued by the Association Council under the EEC–Turkey Association Agreement and Protocol were also found by the Court of Justice to confer direct effect. For a criticism of the Court's liberal interpretation of Association and Cooperation agreements, see Hailbronner (1995:1), n. 64 above, 190–1.

[108] For example, see the Fourth ACP–EC Convention, Lomé, 15 Dec. 1989, OJ 1991, L 229/3, Art. 5(2), para. 3, which calls upon EC member states and ACP States to ensure that 'migrant workers, students and other foreign nationals legally within their territory are not subjected to discrimination on the basis of racial, religious, cultural or social differences, notably in respect of housing, education, health care, other social services and employment'. Although there is no reason why the provisions of this Convention should not be directly effective in EC member states, in the same way as certain provisions in Association and Cooperation agreements, it is doubtful whether Art. 5(2), para. 3 would meet the test for direct effect because the state obligation is subject to 'legal or administrative measures which [States] have or will have adopted'. Moreover, the Joint Declaration on workers who are nationals of one of the Contracting Parties and are legally resident in a territory of a member state or an ACP state, found in Annex VI of the Final Act of the Fourth ACP–EC Lomé Convention, which advocates the equal treatment of such workers with nationals as regards working conditions, pay, and social security benefits linked to employment (paras. 1 and 2), is unlikely to confer direct effect. See Peers (1996), n. 32 above, 29.

It is arguable, however, that these agreements can only constitute stop-gap measures and that their patchwork approach is insufficient in attaining genuine equality between non-EC migrant workers and their families and EC nationals. Although those agreements that confer limited free movement rights on some non-EC migrants have undoubtedly resulted in the creation of a higher 'intermediate' status for this group,[109] this process will inevitably lead to further social stratification unless it is plainly seen as a step on the road to the full integration of *all* non-EC migrant workers and their families.[110]

A case for integration?

The integration of immigrant workers and their families, especially those who have been lawfully resident in the country of employment for a long period of time, can only be successful if they are permitted to feel that the society in which they live and work fully accepts them and offers them opportunities to fulfil their aspirations and to attain a decent standard of living. Short of citizenship entitlements, the process of integration requires the protection of important rights comparable with those held by EC nationals residing and working in other EC member states, namely the whole panoply of economic, social, cultural, political, and residence rights.[111]

Three reasons for advocating the integration of non-EC nationals can be identified: the realization of social justice; the goal of economic efficiency encompassed in the successful completion of the internal market; and as a vital precursor in the struggle to eradicate ethnic and racial discrimination.[112] First, the overriding justification is the realization of social justice. It is surely inequitable to discriminate between two groups of residents living side by side in many aspects of their working and living conditions, and to attempt to justify this discrimination

[109] N. Burrows, 'The Rights of Turkish Workers in the Member States' (1994) 19 *EL Rev.* 305 (annotation on, *inter alia*, *Kus*, n. 107 above), 307.

[110] Of course, one way of achieving this objective is to move speedily in the direction of converting the Association agreements with European countries into fully-fledged EC memberships. Although the EC is committed to expansion eastwards, it is unlikely that this will occur until the end of the century, or even later. In the interim period, as one commentator argues, the EC should move towards the acceptance of east European states into the EEA as a prelude to the acquisition of full EC membership: S. Peers, 'An Ever Closer Waiting Room?: The Case for Eastern European Accession to the European Economic Area' (1995) 32 *CML Rev.* 187, 187, 189, 213.

[111] In its 1994 communication to the Council and European Parliament on Immigration and Asylum Policies, n. 48 above, 32, para. 119, the Commission defined integration as follows: '[Integration] means offering migrants and their descendants the opportunity to live "normally" in the host country. That requires providing migrants with sufficient resources (knowledge of the local language, housing, education, vocational training, etc.) to enable them gradually to attain "parity" with the national population. From the immigrants themselves it requires the willingness to adapt to the lifestyle of the host society without losing their cultural identity and acceptance of the fact that equality of rights entails equality of obligations': O'Keeffe (1995: 2), n. 76 above, 31, observes that the Commission's view that immigrants should adapt to the lifestyle of the host society is somewhat controversial given that 'in some cases, certain aspects of the lifestyle of the host country are offensive to immigrants, and not merely for cultural reasons'.

[112] Simmonds, n. 45 above, 200; Fernhout, n. 32 above, 260–2.

on the basis that the members of one group have not acquired the citizenship of the country of employment. This argument is reinforced if non-EC nationals have lived and worked there for a considerable length of time, thus contributing significantly in economic and social terms,[113] or, indeed, if they were born in that country. Secondly, the concept of the temporary worker or 'guest worker', contrived in the 1950s and early 1960s to ensure that migrant workers would be able to make an economic contribution to the host society at minimum expense to that society, is outdated and no longer workable.[114] Today, the successful completion of the EC internal free market of goods, persons and services cannot take place when over 4.5 million economically active persons are systematically excluded from its operation.[115] Thirdly, the frequent reports in newspapers about increasing racism and xenophobia in Europe and the horrific racist attacks perpetrated against asylum-seekers as well as against long-term immigrant residents is a serious cause for concern.[116] The growth of extreme right-wing politics in Western Europe also remains a current topic of debate. For example, electoral gains by the 'Far Right' in Austria in that country's general election in October 1994, open public support for these gains from Le Pen's National Front in France, and the latter's strong performance in the recent French presidential elections, are timely reminders of the dark vein of nationalism present throughout Europe.[117]

[113] See cf. W. R. Böhning and J. Werquin, 'Some Economic, Social and Human Rights Considerations concerning the Future Status of Third-Country Nationals in the Single European Market', WEP Working Paper (International Labour Office: Geneva, 1990) 13, para. 29.

[114] This was the object of the 'rotation principle' which held an extremely narrow conception of the migrant worker: 'The rotation principle implies a uni-dimensional view of the migrant; his economic contribution is welcomed, but at the same time his needs other than that to work and earn a living remain unsatisfied, and his freedoms are abridged: the migrant's role as a family member is ignored; he may be housed in a dormitory where the concept of privacy hardly exists; opportunities for occupational or geographical mobility are restricted; his cultural needs are neglected; and as a political actor he is in limbo': R. Rogers, 'Post-World War II European Labour Migration: An Introduction to the Issues' in *Guests Come to Stay*, n. 9 above, 1, 21. However, the rotation principle could not be fully implemented because of increasing family reunification. See also R. Cholewinski, 'The Protection of the Right of Economic Migrants to Family Reunion in Europe' (1994) 43 ICLQ 568, 571.

[115] Writing in 1990, Böhning and Werquin, n. 113 above, 9, para. 19, reasoned as follows: 'In any labour market, statutorily imposed restrictions on economically active persons introduce rigidities and inefficiencies; that is to say, the market-clearing mechanism cannot work as well as it would in the absence of such restrictions. Inefficiencies incur lower output, and lower employment. As the establishment of the Single Market is, in essence, an attempt to render the member States' economies more efficient and competitive, the maintenance of 12 national policies that have the effect of confining a considerable part of the EC's labour force . . . to 12 segregated territories, conflicts with the very goals of the Single European Market'. See also Evans, n. 32 above, 207.

[116] For example, see Commission of the European Communities, *The EC Member States and Immigration in 1993. Closed Borders, Stringent Attitudes* (1995) (hereinafter *Closed Borders, Stringent Attitudes*) 78–9. See also the feature articles on racism in Europe, *Independent*, 18 June 1993, 10; *Independent*, 13 Jan. 1994, 16. For an in-depth analysis of current and historical perspectives of racism in Western Europe, see J. Wrench and J. Solomos, (eds.), *Racism and Migration in Western Europe* (Berg: Oxford, 1993).

[117] See respectively A. Bridge, 'Austria's Chancellor Determined to Hang On', 'Le Pen Hails Gains' *Independent*, 11 Oct. 1994, 10, and P. Webster, 'Le Pen Savours Influence' *Guardian*, 24 April 1995, 8. On the xenophobic stance adopted towards immigrants by the separatist Northern League in Italy, see F. Verderani, 'Battle joined over Racist Decree' *Guardian*, 15 Nov. 1995, 15.

Well-meaning and noble declarations to counter racism and xenophobia issued by EC institutions[118] are inherently flawed if one of the groups they aim to protect remains *officially* marginalized.

The EC must *itself* find an equitable solution to safeguard the rights of non-EC migrant workers and their families. This solution must make way for the integration of this neglected group into the free movement of workers system. Besides confirming in recent legislative proposals that free movement of persons in Article 7a EC must apply to all persons 'irrespective of nationality',[119] the Commission has also recognized that 'an internal market without frontiers in which the free movement of persons is ensured logically implies the free movement of all legally resident third country nationals *for the purpose of engaging in economic activities*'. The Commission argues further that 'this objective should be realized progressively', starting with a proposal urging member states 'to give priority to third-country nationals permanently and legally resident in another Member State, when job vacancies cannot be filled by EU nationals or nationals of third countries legally resident in the Member State', and eventually leading to 'the realization of full free movement rights' which will 'depend on the labour market situation'.[120]

In realistic terms, given the potential political opposition to such a radical move,[121] extension to the freedom of movement principle and the rights that follow would probably have to be implemented gradually, but the Commission's suggestion that full free movement rights ought to depend on whether the non-EC national is *permanently* resident in the country and on the labour market situation ultimately amounts to a sacrifice of human rights principles at the altar of political and economic expediency. A more just approach would be to set a

[118] For example, see the Joint Declaration against Racism and Xenophobia adopted by the European Parliament, the Council, and the Commission on 11 June 1986, OJ 1986, C 158/1. For further details on current EC action in this area, see the overview in the next chapter.

[119] For example, see *Proposal for a Council Directive on the Elimination of Controls on Persons Crossing Internal Frontiers*, n. 69 above, 4, para. 1.

[120] Commission of the European Communities, *European Social Policy—A Way Forward for the Union: A White Paper*, COM (94) 333 final of 27 July 1994, 29–30, paras. 21–2 (emphasis added). See also *Immigration and Asylum Policies*, n. 48 above, 34, para. 129. The Commission stated later that it would present a recommendation in the first half of 1996 inviting member states to realize the former proposal. See Commission of the European Communities, Communication to the Council, the European Parliament, the Economic and Social Committee and the Committee of Regions, *Medium Term Social Action Programme 1995–1997*, COM (95) 134 final of 12 April 1995, 14, para. 3.3.5.

[121] An academic version of such likely opposition is provided by Hailbronner (1995:1), n. 64 above, 197–8, who suggests a more cautious approach with regard to granting rights to non-EC nationals based on the adoption of reciprocal bilateral agreements: 'An extended application of the freedom of movement concept by Community regulations to non-EC nationals could endanger the functioning of the system. Equal treatment of non-EC nationals has to be agreed upon in bilateral agreements on the basis of the principle of reciprocity. It should be limited to particular matters like social security or employment conditions according to the different economic, social and political situation in each particular country. A global transfer of the Community's wide concept of freedom of movement to non-EC nationals risks neglecting the basic premise upon which the freedom of movement and equal treatment of EC nationals within the Community rests'.

specific timetable, such as one permitting non-EC nationals to seek employment freely in other member states after a period of between 2 and 4 years legal employment in the host country regardless of the prevalent economic conditions. Of course, this proposal would mean that equality between *established* non-EC migrants and EC migrants would have to be realized immediately,[122] but at least it would constitute a principled way forward and would signal a return to the original understanding of Articles 6 and 48 EC which arguably were never intended to be restricted to non-EC nationals.[123]

Whatever the method chosen, EC member states must find the political will to address urgently the blatant, systematic, and unjustifiable discrimination that exists between non-EC and EC migrants. Steps forward in this direction, in line with the suggestions provided above, could be taken at the 1996–97 IGC.[124] As it now stands, the TEU essentially defers the status of non-EC migrants to state sovereign interests, and contrary to popular belief, must be seen as a rather menacing step backwards in the overall process of European integration.

6.5 ILLEGAL MIGRANTS

Background

In 1978, illegal migrants in Western Europe were described as:

> inevitably the worst exploited group of migrants: as long as their situation remains illegal, they can be sent home, usually at a moment's notice, once they are discovered. So they have no legal recourse against exploitation or blackmail. Employers are often willing to hire them, because they can be put to work for lower wages and longer hours than native or legal migrant workers. They will also do jobs that regular migrants would consider beneath them. They are not eligible for unemployment or sickness benefits or for family allowances. Because of their vulnerability, they are unlikely to become organized or militant, and are ready targets for blackmail or other exploitation.[125]

[122] Fernhout, n. 32 above, 263. Fernhout disagrees with the argument that this prospect would greatly increase migration to the EC by emphasizing that 4 years *legal* employment would be required. The 2-year period (or less if the first employment contract is shorter than 2 years) laid down in Article 14(a) of ILO Convention No. 143 of 1975 is preferable from a human rights standpoint, but given the attitude of the majority of EC member states to this instrument and the restrictive policies in place in respect of immigration to Western Europe generally, the 4-year period is probably a politically more viable goal. Böhning and Werquin, n. 113 above, 11, para. 23, favour the 2-year limit as set down in Art. 14(a) of the ILO Convention.

[123] Cf. Fernhout, n. 32 above, 264.

[124] The Report of the Reflection Group preparing the IGC, n. 87 above, 51, para. 55, reveals a lack of any clear direction regarding the legal status of non-EC nationals: 'As regards the arrangements for aliens, some members . . . would like to see the Union introduce a common status for legally resident third country nationals, whilst others point out that this would require the precondition of an overall common immigration policy'. See also, *ibid.* 46, para. 38.

[125] J. Power, *Western Europe's Migrant Workers*, Minority Rights Group Report No. 28, rev'd edn. (London: Minority Rights Group, 1978) 24. Furthermore, the situation of the children of illegal migrants in the country of employment is particularly harsh. They rarely attend school, because their detection might result in the expulsion of the whole family: *ibid.* 35 with respect to the situation of illegal migrants in Switzerland.

This description still holds true today. If legal migrant workers are considered to be at the inferior end of a dual labour market in Western Europe, then those workers in an irregular situation must form an even lower third labour market.[126]

There are a large number of migrants in Europe who find themselves in an irregular situation in the country of employment. It is very difficult to provide any accurate figures because of their undocumented status and reluctance to make themselves known for fear of expulsion. The ILO estimated that there were approximately 2.6 million non-nationals in an irregular or undocumented situation residing in Western Europe in 1991. This figure comprises migrant workers and their families, including seasonal workers, and asylum-seekers who have not succeeded in obtaining refugee status and whose presence is not tolerated officially.[127]

Illegal labour migration has become a particular problem in southern Europe. The former labour-sending countries of the Mediterranean region have now become significant importers of labour.[128] The influx of immigrant workers, particularly into Greece, Italy, and Spain, began in the early 1970s. Most of these workers came from North Africa and other developing countries and were employed illegally.[129] This trend continued sharply upwards. For example, between 1975 and 1981, the *officially* registered alien population in Italy and Greece grew by 67.6 and 61.7 per cent respectively.[130] If undocumented migrant workers were included in this calculation, this would represent quite a staggering increase in the rate of migration for employment to these countries. Estimates of the number of illegal immigrants in Greece in 1993 ranged from 100,000 to 500,000.[131] Most of these migrants work in agriculture, construction, tourism, and commercial shipping, and in the informal or 'underground' economy which is estimated

[126] T. Hammar, 'Immigrant Policy' in T. Hammar, (ed.), *European Immigration Policy: A Comparative Study* (1985) 263, 267.

[127] W. R. Böhning, 'Integration and Immigration Pressures in Western Europe' (1991) 130 ILR 445, 449. Clearly, this is a conservative estimate.

[128] See generally Commission of the European Communities, Directorate-General for Employment, Industrial Relations and Social Affairs, *Immigration of Citizens from Third Countries into the Southern Member States of the European Community: A Comparative Survey of the Situation in Greece, Italy, Spain and Portugal*, Social Europe, Supplement 1/91 (Luxembourg: OOPEC, 1991).

[129] International Labour Organization, Second European Regional Conference, Report II, Geneva, Jan. 1974, *Some Growing Employment Problems in Europe: Manpower Aspects of Recent Economic Developments in Europe* (Geneva: International Labour Office, 1973) Ch. IV, 'Migration of Workers as an Element in Employment Policy' 81, 83; Power, n. 125 above, 23. Over 70% of non-EC nationals resident in Italy on 31 Dec. 1991 were from developing countries (excluding the countries of eastern Europe): OECD, *Continuous Reporting System on Migration—SOPEMI 1990* (Paris: OECD, 1991) 23, Table 9 (worked out by calculation from Table 9).

[130] R. Penninx, 'International Migration in Western Europe since 1973: Developments, Mechanisms and Controls' (1986) 20 IMR 951, 955.

[131] See *Closed Borders, Stringent Attitudes*, n. 116 above, 19. See also N. Sitaropoulos, 'The New Legal Framework of Alien Immigration in Greece: A Draconian Contribution to Europe's Unification' (1992) 6 INLP 89 (and n. 10), who cites estimates for 1991 of between 150,000 (Greek Ministry of Public Order) and 400,000 (unofficial sources): *ibid.* These figures are considerably higher than the number of work permits issued by the Greek authorities. In Dec. 1993, there were about 30,000 legally recognized immigrant workers in Greece and 62,000 legal foreign residents. See *SOPEMI 1994*, n. 26 above, 92 and *Closed Borders, Stringent Attitudes*, *ibid.* respectively.

to constitute 30 per cent of the total Greek labour market.[132] In Italy, before the introduction of regularization programmes, there were between 700,000 and one million illegal migrants. These numbers have since fallen, but estimates continue to range erratically from 250,000 to 670,000.[133] Many of these migrants had come to Italy spontaneously, initially to work in the service sector and then seasonally in agriculture and industry and in various activities within the informal sector, particularly in the southern and central parts of the country.[134] Estimates of illegal migrants in Spain and Portugal vary considerably. In 1989, there were between 170,000 and 260,000 illegal migrants resident in Spain, although the most recent figures, taking into account the regularization process carried out in 1991, point to there being at least 70,000 foreigners without residence permits.[135] Estimates for 1992 indicate there were about 80,000 illegal immigrants in Portugal.[136]

The countries of southern Europe have started to adopt harsh measures aimed at curbing the flow of illegal migrants. Italian legislation introduced in 1986 and 1990[137] defines the status of illegal immigrants already living in Italy and facilitates their regularization, but it also imposes stricter restrictions on future inflows and proposes firmer measures to combat illegal immigration.[138] The expulsion of approximately 20,000 Albanian 'refugees' in August 1991 is an example of the new uncompromising Italian attitude towards illegal immigration.[139] Similarly, the Greek Government has adopted new measures to restrict irregular

[132] *SOPEMI 1990*, n. 129 above, 50; *SOPEMI 1994*, n. 26 above, 93.

[133] For the pre-regularization estimate, see G. Simon, 'Migration in Southern Europe: An Overview' in OECD, *The Future of Migration* (Paris: OECD, 1987) 258, 284. The regularization process indicates that the average proportion of illegal migrants in Italy is about 25% of the legally resident foreign population. Since there were almost one million legally resident foreigners in Italy in January 1996, this would mean that there are about 250,000 illegal immigrants: MNS No. 159/96 (June 1996) 5. However, a recent report published by the Italian National Institute of Statistics in Nov. 1995 estimated that there were still some 670,000 irregular migrants in Italy: MNS No. 154/96 (Jan. 1996) 5. For information on the regularization programmes in Italy, see below.

[134] *SOPEMI 1990*, n. 129 above, 24. Simon, n. 133 above, 288–9, argues that illegal migration to southern European countries can only be regulated if measures to tackle the informal sector are also introduced. The informal sector in these countries is very large employing 2 to 5 million workers in Italy alone.

[135] See C. B. F. De Valderrama, 'The New Hosts: The Case of Spain' (1993) 27 IMR 169, 178 and J. Salt, A. Singleton, and J. Hogarth, *Europe's International Migrants* (London: HMSO, 1994) 191. See also MNS No. 158/96 (May 1996) 6. For the 1991 regularization process, see below.

[136] *Europe's International Migrants*, n. 135 above, 192. It is estimated that there are as many as 50,000 illegal immigrants from Portugal's African colonies. See M. Eaton, 'Foreign Residents and Illegal Immigrants: *os Negros em Portugal*' (1993) 16 *Ethnic and Racial Studies* 536, 537.

[137] Law No. 943 of 30 Dec. 1986 (effective 27 Jan. 1987); Law No. 39 of 28 Feb. 1990 (known as the 'Martelli law').

[138] M. Biagi, 'Non-EEC Nationals and the Italian Labour Market: The Institutional Framework' (1992) 8 IJCLLIR 154; G. Campani, 'Immigration and Racism in Southern Europe: The Italian Case' (1993) 16 *Ethnic and Racial Studies* 507, 522–6; *SOPEMI 1990*, n. 129 above, 36; F. Isgro, 'Italy Enacts Law to Protect Basic Human Rights of Foreign Workers' (1986) 1 *Georgetown Immigration L.J.* 693 (on the 1986 legislation). It is noteworthy that Law No. 943 was passed to give effect to ILO Convention No. 143 which the Italian Parliament ratified in 1981: Isgro, *ibid.* 694.

[139] Campani, n. 138 above, 526, writes: '[T]he expulsion of [the] Albanians . . . has shown that Italy is not a "gateway" into western Europe for people originating from the Third World and eastern Europe. Rather, it shows that the Italian state will play its part in building the high wall necessary to defend "Fortress Europe". The time of "tolerance and generosity", if it ever existed, is undoubtedly over'.

immigration.[140] In the summer of 1993, the Greek authorities signalled their determination to enforce these laws by expelling *en masse* approximately 26,000 illegal Albanian migrants from their territory in just 2 weeks.[141]

One of the consequences of the process of democratization in the countries of central and eastern Europe and the former Soviet Union has been the recognition of the right to leave and the right to travel abroad. This development, together with the expected widespread and long-term hardships that are likely to result from the changes being implemented to move this region from centrally-planned to market economies, means that economic migration has become an attractive option for the unemployed and underemployed in these countries.[142] Although east–west migration has increased, the anticipated substantial movements from the former Soviet Union and central and eastern Europe, with the exception of refugee flows from the former Yugoslavia, have not materialized.[143] It has been suggested, however, that if 'outlets' are not provided for some of the migration pressure in this region, many people may increasingly seek to make an illicit living in Western Europe.[144] Moreover, growing economic disparities between the countries of this region[145] have also resulted in a significant flow of illegal migrant labour, particularly from the former Soviet Union to central and eastern European states.[146]

The many forms of illegal labour migration as well as the principal motivations

[140] Law 1975/1991. Arts. 3–5 of this legislation enable the authorities to set in motion procedures leading to the immediate removal of illegal immigrants. See Sitaropoulos, n. 131 above, 91.

[141] T. Barber, 'Albanians go Barefoot to their Barren Land' *Independent on Sunday*, 11 July 1993, 16. The same article reports that Greek authorities expelled 379,000 illegal Albanian immigrants in 1992. See also *Closed Borders, Stringent Attitudes*, n. 116 above, 68. According to the OECD, from Jan. 1991 to Aug. 1994, 764,000 illegal entrants were deported from Greece of which 96% were Albanians. It must be emphasized, however, that these figures probably included many deportees who had crossed the border on several occasions: *SOPEMI 1994*, n. 26 above, 93.

[142] Cf. Refugee Policy Group (RPG), The North American-European Dialogue on Politics and Migration, *Changing Migration in and from Eastern Europe and the Soviet Union*, Summary of the Third Meeting in Vienna, 16–17 July 1990 (Washington/Geneva: RPG, 1990) 4–5; B. Ghosh, 'The Future of East–West Migration' in S. Ardittis, (ed.), *The Politics of East–West Migration* (New York: St. Martin's Press, 1994) 217. The effect of economic restructuring on unemployment in central and eastern European countries has been very significant. For example, in Poland unemployment rose from 55,000 to approximately 2.5 million between Jan. 1990 and Sept. 1992. See M. Okolski, 'Poland' in *The Politics of East–West Migration, ibid.* 51, 58.

[143] Ghosh, n. 142 above; *SOPEMI 1994*, n. 26 above, 58; OECD, *Trends in International Migration—Continuous Reporting System on Migration—SOPEMI 1993* (Paris: OECD, 1994) 14; OECD, *Trends in International Migration—Continuous Reporting System on Migration—SOPEMI 1992* (Paris: OECD, 1993) 12 and 98; *SOPEMI 1990*, n. 129 above, 7.

[144] V. Grecic, 'East–West Migration and its Possible Influence on South–North Migration' (1991) 29 IM 241, 245, 246; *Changing Migration in and from Eastern Europe and the Soviet Union*, n. 142 above, 9; *SOPEMI 1992*, n. 143 above, 12; cf. J.-C. Chesnais, 'By Way of Introduction' in Council of Europe, *People on the Move. New Migration Flows in Europe* (Strasbourg: Council of Europe, 1992) 13, 32.

[145] For example, the SOPEMI 1994 report, n. 26 above, 137, observes in relation to the Czech Republic: 'The low level of unemployment along with real wages that are among the highest in Central and Eastern Europe has served as a pull-factor for migrant workers from neighbouring countries'.

[146] In Poland, estimates of irregular migrants range from 55,000 (official) to 200,000 (unofficial). See respectively *SOPEMI 1994*, n. 26 above, 148 and P. Korcelli, 'International Migrations in Europe: Polish Perspectives for the 1990s' (1992) 26 IMR 292, 302–3. In the middle of 1992, it was

for entering a country without proper authorization have already been described in Chapter 1 and apply equally to the European situation. One important group of undocumented migrants in Europe are women who are more likely to take up irregular employment than their male counterparts. Many women obtain this kind of work after joining their husbands or parents in the country of employment without permission. If they enter lawfully, they may seek unauthorized employment once in the country in order to supplement the normally low family income.[147] Restrictive regulations in some European countries limiting access to employment for members of migrant workers' families exarcebate this situation. In addition to being in an irregular situation, many migrant women perform unskilled labour, for example as domestic servants. Most domestic female workers originate from developing countries and constitute the great majority of female migrant workers from those countries.[148] They are frequently employed in an irregular situation and suffer from deplorable working and living conditions, which are characterized by extremely low wages, long hours and little rest, the absence of written contracts and social security coverage, minimal protection against dismissal, and verbal and physical abuse, including sexual harassment.[149]

Combating illegal migration

Although the employment of illegal migrant workers may serve the economic interests of some employers and private landlords[150] (who put these workers up

estimated that between 50,000 and 70,000 workers from the former Soviet Union were illegally resident in Poland. See Okolski, n. 142 above, 55. In Hungary, estimates of illegal migrants range from between 40,000 and 70,000 to 250,000. See respectively *Europe's International Migrants*, n. 135 above, 198 and L. Szoke, 'Hungarian Perspectives on Emigration and Immigration in the New European Architecture' (1992) 26 IMR 305, 317. The former Czechoslovakia is home to about 100,000 'false tourists' (those who extend their stay beyond the 30 days permitted without applying for legal status). See Z. Pavlik and J. Maresova, 'Former Czechoslovakia' in *The Politics of East-West Migration*, n. 142 above, 111, 121–2.

[147] A 1980 study suggested that many migrant workers working illegally at the time in Europe were in fact women. With a spouse in Europe, it is easier for wives to obtain resident permits than work permits. The documentation of this illegal employment, however, is difficult because of the dependent status of these women. See A. Kudat and M. Sabuncouglu, 'The Changing Composition of Europe's Guestworker Population' (1980) 103 *Monthly Labour Review* 10, 13–14.

[148] For example, in Italy and Spain respectively, 90 and 95% of migrant Filipino women are employed as domestic servants. Note (International), 'Foreign Women in Domestic Service' (1991) ILO SLB 361. In 1993, there were 46,000 Filipinos resident in Italy and over 8,000 in Spain: *SOPEMI 1994*, n. 26 above, 55, 203 and 208 (Table B.1). According to one estimate, 90% of the 30,000 Filipinos living in Greece were also employed in the domestic service. See *Closed Borders, Stringent Attitudes*, n. 116 above, 83 (n. 211). For an overview of Filipino economic migration generally, including numerous examples highlighting the difficult conditions of Filipino domestic workers, see Catholic Institute for International Relations, *The Labour Trade* (London: CIIR, 1987). For an insight into the plight of domestic workers in one European country, see B. Anderson, *Britain's Secret Slaves: An Investigation into the Plight of Overseas Domestic Workers in the United Kingdom* (London: Anti-Slavery International, 1993).

[149] 'Foreign Women in Domestic Service', n. 148 above, 361–2.

[150] T. Hammar, 'Towards Convergence' in *European Immigration Policy: A Comparative Study*, n. 126 above, 292, 304.

in sub-standard and expensive accommodation), it is clear that their existence subverts the entire labour migration system, since 'though victims themselves, [illegal migrants] are the enemies of both indigenous and legal workers'.[151] The EC Commission has outlined succinctly the disadvantages of illegal migration and the need to combat the phenomenon:

Illegal forms of migration undermine the effect of admission policies, are detrimental to policies aimed at the integration of legal immigrants and put the people concerned in a vulnerable position. The [European] Union therefore requires an active policy to prevent and combat illegal migratory movements.[152]

Combating illegal migration takes a number of forms, involving internal measures aimed at the present illegal immigrant population and at deterring future flows, and external preventive measures. A positive and comprehensive approach that has been proposed to combat irregular migration would be first to regularize the status of illegal immigrants already in the country and then to enforce effectively stricter controls on future illegal entrants as well as adopt severe sanctions against labour traffickers and employers.[153]

(a) Regularization

Regularization programmes for illegal migrants have been instituted in the past in a number of European countries. The largest schemes have been in France, where an estimated 1.4 million illegal aliens were regularized between 1948 and 1981,[154] and more recently, in Italy, where over 320,000 non-EC immigrants were regularized between 1986 and the end of 1990,[155] and in Spain, where over

[151] D. G. Papademetriou, 'International Migration in North America and Western Europe: Trends and Consequences' in R. T. Appleyard, (ed.), *International Migration Today—Vol. 1: Trends and Prospects* (Paris; Nedlands, Western Australia, The Centre for Migration and Development Studies: UNESCO, 1988) 311, 366. See also *Some Growing Employment Problems in Europe*, n. 129 above, 100. In the same vein, Castles writes that 'the rightless illegal migrant is the dream-worker of many employers and the nightmare of the labor movement': S. Castles, 'The Guest-Worker in Western Europe—An Obituary' (1986) 20 IMR 761, 762.

[152] *Immigration and Asylum Policies*, n. 48 above, 27, para. 102.

[153] Power (1978), n. 125 above, 27.

[154] Plender (1988), n. 5 above, 317, citing from Service des Etudes et de la Statistique, Ministre des Affairs Sociales et de la Solidarité Nationale, *Immigration Clandestine, La Régularisation des travailleurs 'Sans Papiers'*, Supp. No. 106 (1983) 9. Further regularization was initiated after the 1981 elections (won by the French Socialist party) and encompassed illegal foreign workers who had entered the country before Jan. 1981 and who had 'stable employment': Plender, *ibid.*, citing from the above Report, 10.

[155] *SOPEMI 1990*, n. 129 above, 24. The relatively low number of applications for regularization, in comparison with the projected number of illegal immigrants in the country, is probably due to the fact that many illegal migrant workers feared losing their jobs if regularized, since the employer would then have to pay minimum wages and social fund contributions, and might well decide to take on other irregular migrant workers in their place: *Report to the Conference on Migrant Workers from the Mahgreb in the European Community* (1991) 4, para. 1.7. A further exceptional regularization programme was undertaken between Nov. 1995 and the end of March 1996 when about 250,000 applications for regularization were received: MNS No. 159/96 (June 1996) 5.

100,000 irregular migrants were legalized in 1991.[156] In addition to pre-empting harsher control mechanisms aimed at preventing future irregular migration, regularization programmes have also been independently justified on the basis that they prevent the creation of a permanent under-class of exploited workers unable to protect themselves legally against their employers.[157]

(b) Employer sanctions

Another method of internal control aimed at deterring the employment of undocumented migrant labour concerns the imposition of penalties on employers. Employer sanctions have been adopted by most Western European countries.[158] A good example is that of France, where uncompromising employer sanctions were introduced in 1981, with the result that the employer faced, for a second offence, imprisonment of up to 4 years and a fine not exceeding FF 40,000 for every illegal alien hired.[159] These sanctions were strengthened at the end of 1991

[156] *SOPEMI 1993*, n. 143 above, 91–2, Table II.22; *SOPEMI 1992*, n. 143 above, 33 and 76. Another regularization scheme, lasting 5 months, took place between 23 April and 23 Aug. 1996. See MNS No. 158/96 (May 1996) 6 and MNS No. 162/96 (Sept. 1996) 6–7. In Portugal, over 38,000 people took advantage of a regularization programme held between Oct. 1992 and March 1993: *SOPEMI 1994*, n. 26 above, 115; MNS No. 154/96 (Jan. 1996) 6. A further 6-month regularization programme took effect in June 1996. See MNS No. 159/96 (June 1996) 5. An amnesty for illegal immigrants was also introduced by the Dutch Government. As from 1 Jan. 1995, illegal immigrants in the Netherlands, who can show they have held legal work (paying both their taxes and social contributions) for a continuous period of at least 6 years, are entitled to an official residence permit. This programme is to continue until 1 Jan. 1999: 'Dutch Amnesty' MN Vol. 2, No. 2 (Feb. 1995).

[157] Cf. *Report to the Conference on Migrant Workers from the Mahgreb in the European Community*, n. 155 above, 21, para. 3.11. The Report proposes, *ibid.*, that European countries should consider adopting an amnesty regularizing illegal workers, following the above French and Italian examples, and coordinated perhaps at the level of the EC. As noted in Ch. 4, however, frequent recourse to regularization policies or amnesties may defeat the object of the exercise because it ultimately encourages further illegal entry.

[158] M. J. Miller, 'Towards Understanding State Capacity to Prevent Unwanted Migration: Employer Sanctions Enforcement in France, 1975–1990' (1994) 17 *West European Politics* (Special Issue on The Politics of Immigration in Western Europe) 140, 142–5 and Table 1. For an overview of measures applying employer sanctions in EC member states, see Commission of the European Communities, *Member States' National Legislation Applicable to Non-Community Citizens (reference date: 31 Dec. 1990)*, Working Paper No. V/1685/90 (hereinafter Commission Working Paper) 110–12. Until recently, there were no employer sanctions for hiring an illegal immigrant in the United Kingdom. Employers were in the same position as anyone else in that they commited an offence if they knowingly harboured an illegal entrant or a person who had committed an offence relating to immigration control: Immigration Act 1971, s. 25. The Asylum and Immigration Act 1996 (c. 49) now makes it a criminal offence to employ someone over the age of 16 subject to immigration control. Those convicted of the offence will be liable to a fine of up to £5,000 (s. 8). This provision has not yet been brought into force, but is expected to come into force in Jan. 1997. See The Refugee Council, Refugee Advisers Support Unit, 'The Asylum and Immigration Act 1996. What it means—Related Measures—Timetable' *Bulletin* (Sept. 1996) 5. The Justice and Home Affairs Council under the Third Pillar of the TEU has recommended that 'any person who is considered, under the national law of the Member State concerned, to be employing a foreign national who does not have authorization should be made subject to appropriate penalties'. See Council Recommendation of 22 Dec. 1995 on harmonizing means of combating illegal immigration and illegal employment and improving the relevant means of control, OJ 1996, C 5/1, point 6.

[159] Labour Code Law of 17 Oct. 1981. For a first offence, the term of imprisonment was not less than 2 months and not more than 2 years and the fine ranged from FF 2,000 to 20,000 for the employment of every illegal immigrant. See Commission Working Paper, n. 158 above, 110 and 111 and Miller, n. 158 above, 144 (Table 1).

and 1993. Under the Act of 31 December 1991, employers of undocumented labour risked a range of new penalties, such as confiscation of goods, debarment from the exercise of the business activity in question and exclusion from public contracts, and if they were foreigners, expulsion from France.[160] Similar harsh punishments for hiring illegal migrant labour exist in Germany and Italy.[161] The effectiveness of employer sanctions, however, is questionable especially if insufficient resources are allocated to the detection of the employment of illegal migrants. At best, the policies in labour-receiving European countries have been ambivalent towards this practice.[162]

(c) Harmonization

One of the most recent and wide-ranging initiatives taken to prevent illegal migration is concerted action at the inter-governmental level towards this objective, which inevitably involves the 'harmonization' of state laws and policies. Although the EC Commission proposed such a course of action in the 1970s,[163] developments in this area have only begun to take concrete shape since 1990 and have largely taken place outside of EC control. The scope of the following

[160] The 1991 law also introduced provisions to close a loophole in the law, whereby employer sanctions could be evaded through a succession or 'cascade' of sub-contracts. Anyone resorting to the services of an undocumented foreign worker, even if through an intermediary, is now also liable to penalties: *SOPEMI 1992*, n. 143 above, 32; *SOPEMI 1993*, n. 143 above, 46. See also *Closed Borders, Stringent Attitudes*, n. 116 above, 46 and 115, regarding the Act of 20 Dec. 1993 (Arts. 34 and 35–1), which imposes harsher penalties for those found guilty of recruiting and introducing foreign workers.

[161] Imprisonment for employers in Germany may range from one year, up to (for particularly serious offences), 5 years with respect to the employment of migrants. Fines can be up to 100,000 DM (Temporary Employment Act to Combat Illegal Employment 1981). See Commission Working Paper, n. 158 above, 111–12 and Miller, n. 158 above, 144 (Table 1). In Italy, an employer recruiting foreign workers who have entered the country illegally may be imprisoned for up to one year and face a fine of up to two million lire. Harsher penalties are imposed for providing illegal conditions of employment: a maximum fine of 10 million lire and a maximum period of imprisonment of 5 years: Law No. 943 of 30 Dec. 1986, Art. 12. See Isgro, n. 138 above, 697 and Commission Working Paper, *ibid.* 110–11.

[162] R. Rogers, 'Western Europe in the 1980s: The End of Immigration?' (1985), n. 9 above, 295. Miller, n. 144 above, 165, notes the pessimism in some circles over the question of enforcement, but he also argues that employer sanctions have a limited deterrent effect even though they are unlikely to significantly restrict illegal immigration. For information on the enforcement of employer sanctions in Belgium, France, the Netherlands, Portugal, and Spain, see *Closed Borders, Stringent Attitudes*, n. 116 above, 46–7.

[163] See *Action Programme in Favour of Migrant Workers and Their Families*, n. 27 above, 24: 'In view of the growth of . . . [the] problem of illegal immigration, it is urgently necessary for the Member States to adopt a common approach to deterrent measures'. In 1978, the Commission issued a revised proposal for a Council Directive with the intention of approximating the legislation of Member States in respect of, *inter alia*, 'the prevention and suppression of illegal migration and illegal employment' (Art. 1(2)). Commission of the European Communities, *Proposal for a Council Directive concerning the approximation of the legislation of Member States, in order to combat illegal migration and illegal employment*, COM (78) final of 3 April 1978, Annex I, 4. The rationale for this approach can be found in the third recital of the Preamble to this draft Directive: 'Whereas . . . in view of the growing interdependence and integration of national labour markets, measures taken by Member States individually against migration for the purpose of illegal employment, or the absence of such measures, inevitably impinge on the effectiveness of measures taken by the other Member States; whereas in addition to measures within the sphere of competence of the Member States themselves, Community action is needed to combat the illegal employment of non-Community workers'.

discussion is confined to an examination of these developments as they specifically relate to controls on illegal immigration.

(i) The Schengen Agreement and the implementing Convention[164]

In June 1990, in anticipation of the lifting of internal borders in the EC by the end of 1992, five EC countries (Belgium, France, Germany, Luxembourg, and the Netherlands) adopted a Convention with the aim of implementing an earlier framework agreement signed at Schengen, Luxembourg in 1985.[165] Five more EC countries (Austria, Greece, Italy, Portugal, and Spain) have since acceded to this instrument.[166] The control system established under the Convention was delayed for technical reasons connected with the establishment of the Schengen Information System (SIS),[167] and only came into operation for 7 of the signatories (except Austria, Greece, and Italy) on 26 March 1995.[168] At the end of June 1995, however, the French Government, largely concerned at the ease with which 'soft drugs' were entering the country from the Netherlands as well as at the reluctance of other Schengen states to take back asylum-seekers who had crossed into France illegally, announced a 6-month delay in implementing the Agreement.[169] This period was extended, but the French Government finally lifted

[164] A detailed analysis of the Schengen Agreement and the implementing Convention is undertaken in the following literature: H. Meijers *et al.*, (eds.), *Schengen: Internationalization of Central Chapters of the Law on Aliens, Refugees, Privacy, Security and the Police*, 2nd rev. edn. (Leiden: Stichting NJCM—Boekerij, 1992); K.-P. Nanz, 'The Schengen Agreement: Preparing the Free Movement of Persons in the European Union' in *Justice and Home Affairs in the European Union*, n. 76 above, 29; D. O'Keeffe, 'The Schengen Convention: A Suitable Model for European Integration?' (1991) 11 YBEL 185; E. Whitaker, 'The Schengen Agreement and its Portent for the Freedom of Personal Movement in Europe' (1992) 6 *Georgetown Immigration L.J.* 191.

[165] Convention applying the Schengen Agreement of 14 June 1985 between the Governments of the States of the Benelux Economic Union, the Federal Republic of Germany and the French Republic on the Gradual Abolition of Checks at their Common Borders, 19 June 1990; (1991) 30 ILM 84; entry into force 1 Sept. 1993 (Belgium, France, Germany, Luxembourg, and the Netherlands). The 1985 agreement is reproduced in (1991) 30 ILM 68.

[166] Italy acceded to the Agreement and the Convention in Nov. 1990, Portugal and Spain joined the Schengen process in June 1991 and Greece in Nov. 1992. The most recent state signatory is Austria (April 1995). See Nanz (1995), n. 164 above, 31.

[167] The SIS is the computer database underpinning the control mechanism (Title IV of the Schengen Implementing Convention). See also Hailbronner (1995:1), n. 64 above, 192. For a critical assessment of the SIS, see S. Mahmood, 'The Schengen Information System: An Inequitable Data Protection Regime' (1995) 7 IJRL 179.

[168] 'Convention is Finally Applied' MNS No. 145/95 (April 1995) 1–2; I. Traynor, 'The Brave New World of a Europe without Frontiers' *Guardian*, 27 March 1995, 20; 'Schengen Free Movement Begins' MN Vol. 2, No. 4 (April 1995). Five EC countries, Denmark, Finland, Ireland, Sweden, and the United Kingdom, remain outside the Schengen system, but only the latter does not envisage eventually lifting its internal frontier controls. See Nanz (1995), n. 164 above, 46; cf. United Kingdom, Commission for Racial Equality, *Citizens, Minorities and Foreigners* (London: Commission for Racial Equality, 1994) 18. In April 1996, Denmark, Finland, and Sweden, together with the other member states of the Nordic Union, Iceland and Norway, were admitted to the Schengen process as observers with a view to obtaining full membership in the future. Cf. Nanz, *ibid.* 31 and 46 and MNS No. 158/96 (May 1996) 2.

[169] M. Dejevsky, 'France Stalls on Border Deal' *Independent*, 29 June 1995, 11; T. Barber, 'EU's Border-free Zone Hobbles into Place' *Independent*, 1 July 1995, 9.

checks at its land borders with Germany and Spain in April 1996, although it decided to maintain checks at its borders with Belgium and Luxembourg.[170]

The Preamble to the Schengen Implementing Convention declares that the purpose of the instrument is to realize, in keeping with the objective of the EC Treaty, the abolition of internal border controls between the countries concerned.[171] In principle, all those lawfully present in the Schengen area are permitted to move freely within this enlarged territory, although free movement for the 'alien', defined in Article 1 as 'any person other than a national of a Member State of the European Communities', is subject to a number of conditions. Non-EC nationals are permitted to cross internal borders unchecked subject to the possession of the correct documentation[172] and provided that they report to the competent authorities of the country visited, either on entry or within 3 working days of entry.[173]

In order to stem illegal migration between Schengen states, which is a foreseeable consequence of the elimination of internal frontier checks, the external borders of the countries in question are tightened by the more effective enforcement of controls and the imposition of common visa requirements. Entry to 'aliens' for visits for up to 3 months may be granted provided that certain conditions are fulfilled. Non-EC nationals who are not in possession of the relevant documentation, including a valid visa if required, or who cannot provide evidence of possessing 'sufficient means of support' for the visit, will not be permitted to enter the Schengen area.[174] Moreover, contracting parties must also refuse entry to an alien who has 'been reported as a person not to be permitted entry' or who is deemed 'to be a threat to the public policy, national security, or the international relations of *any* of the Contracting parties'.[175] Although these terms are not given a uniform and objective definition, and therefore it may be assumed that they are subject to national determination, some elaboration is provided in Article 96 of the Convention which outlines the circumstances that may lead to a report prohibiting entry. Article 96 stipulates that a report is to result from

[170] See MNS No. 154/96 (Jan. 1996) 1, MNS No. 156/96 (March 1996) 1 and MNS No. 157/96 (April 1996) 1.

[171] Preamble, Recitals 3–5. O'Keeffe (1992), n. 66 above, 12, has criticized the incoherency of this approach: 'The peculiarity of this approach is that it is inter-governmental, and is outside the Community framework, whereas it is responding to a Community imperative, fixed by an instrument of Community law . . . Such an approach is to be deplored. A dual system whereby the Community's competence is limited and Member States retain competence in areas which are crucial for the development of the internal market is clearly unsatisfactory'. See also O'Keeffe (1995:2), n. 77 above, 21. Title II of the Convention is entitled Abolition of Checks at Internal Borders and Movement of Persons. Art. 2(1) asserts succinctly: 'Internal borders may be crossed at any point without any checks on persons being carried out'. Art. 2(2), however, permits contracting parties, provided that they consult with the other parties, to re-introduce internal border controls for a limited period 'where public policy or national security so require'.

[172] If aliens possess a valid uniform visa, they will be able to move freely within the Schengen territory throughout the period of validity of their visas (Art. 19(1)). Aliens can also move freely within this area for up to 3 months if they hold a valid residence permit issued by one of the contracting parties as well as a valid travel document (Art. 21(1)).

[173] Art. 22(1).

[174] Art. 5(1)(a)–(c).

[175] Art. 5(1)(d)–(e) (emphasis added).

decisions taken, in accordance with procedural rules laid down by national legislation, the administrative authorities, or courts responsible, and may be premised 'on a threat to public order or national security and safety which the presence of an alien in national territory may pose'. The provision provides some examples when this might be the case. Decisions leading to a report may also be based on the fact that the aliens concerned have been subject to expulsion measures, which are still in force, or to a prohibition on entry or residence 'based on non-compliance with national legislation on the entry or residence of aliens'. Consequently, if one state party adopts a policy to report all migrants who have been found to have breached its external frontier controls without authorization, regardless of the seriousness of the infraction, these persons would normally have to be refused entry at the external border of another state party, even if, in the future, they were to present themselves at that border with the correct documentation.[176] Therefore, a harsher approach to illegal migration taken by one state party is decisive. The danger is that a similar approach will be gradually adopted by the other states parties with a view to 'harmonizing' their laws and policies accordingly. This is an example of 'the risk of downwards spiralling' which has been recognized in relation to the Convention's approach towards the examination of asylum applications.[177] Although the Convention makes provision for persons to bring actions before the courts or the competent authority under national law to 'correct, delete or provide information or obtain compensation' in respect of reports that have been made concerning them,[178] the proportionality of the reporting decision, according to one commentator, cannot be challenged. Consequently, this might constitute a possible infringement of Article 13 of the ECHR which guarantees the right to an 'effective remedy before a national authority'.[179]

The Convention possesses an entirely executive character.[180] It fails to provide

[176] Art. 5(2) allows a state party to admit aliens who do not satisfy all the conditions in Art. 5(1) by derogating from these requirements 'on humanitarian grounds or in the national interest or because of international obligations'. However, permission to enter, in such cases, is to be restricted to the territory of the state party concerned, which must inform the other states parties accordingly.

[177] H. Meijers 'Schengen: Introduction' in Meijers *et al.* (1992), n. 164 above, 1, 3. For the provisions concerning responsibility for the processing of applications for asylum, see Title II, Ch. 7. These are essentially reproduced in another instrument drafted by the Ad Hoc Group on Immigration. See Convention determining the state responsible for examining Applications for Asylum lodged in one of the Member States of the European Communities, 15 June 1990 (Dublin); (1991) 30 ILM 425; not in force; ratified by 10 states parties as at 31 July 1996: Belgium, Denmark, France, Germany, Greece, Italy, Luxembourg, Portugal, Spain, United Kingdom. The Convention still requires the ratifications of Ireland and the Netherlands before it can enter into force. See MNS No. 161/96 (Aug. 1996) 7, MNS No. 158/96 (May 1996) 15 and MNS No. 156/96 (March 1996) 6.

[178] Art. 111(1). Art. 110 enables a person to have 'factually inaccurate data relating to him corrected or have legally inaccurate data related to him deleted'. O'Keeffe (1991), n. 164 above, 190–1, observes, however, that under the Convention 'the alien is not informed that there is data concerning him in the [Schengen Information] System, so a discussion of remedies may be moot'.

[179] P. Boeles, 'Schengen and the Rule of Law' in Meijers *et al.* (1992), n. 164 above, 135, 142–3.

[180] J. J. Bolten 'From Schengen to Dublin: The New Frontiers of Refugee Law' in Meijers *et al.* (1992), *ibid.* 8, 9. According to Bolten, *ibid.*, the 1985 Schengen Agreement was only 'uncovered' by the French press in May 1989. Indeed, the whole Schengen process has been secretive, although

for an independent control mechanism to supervise its implementation, a function which is entrusted to an Executive Committee, composed of ministers, one from each contracting party.[181] The Convention's provisions are made subject to the Geneva Convention relating to the Status of Refugees and its Protocol,[182] but there are no references to their compatibility with other international human rights instruments, particularly the ECHR.[183]

(ii) The draft Convention on the crossing of external frontiers

The Convention implementing the Schengen Agreement has been recognized as a 'laboratory', or as having a 'pilot function',[184] to EC initiatives in this area. It is subordinate to EC law by virtue of Article 134, which categorically asserts that 'the provisions of this Convention shall apply only in so far as they are compatible with Community law'.[185] The Convention also explicitly obliges states parties to agree on a procedure making way for the replacement or amendment of its provisions in the event of comparable instruments being concluded among EC member states.[186] At the end of 1993, the EC Commission submitted a revised draft Convention on Controls on Persons Crossing External Frontiers, which contains provisions that mirror many of the measures in the Schengen Implementing

the EC Commission was present in the capacity of an observer during the negotiations leading to the adoption of the Implementing Convention. See O'Keeffe (1991), n. 164 above, 188. Secrecy as well as lack of transparency also constitute criticisms of decision-making under the Third Pillar of the TEU. See O'Keeffe (1995:1), n. 76 above, 916–17. See also n. 82 above.

181 Arts. 131–2. The decisions of the Committee are to be taken unanimously. See also Meijers, n. 177 above, 5. In its first decision on 18 Oct. 1993, the Committee adopted its Rules of Procedure. It has also issued a series of other decisions on Title VII of the Convention, which relates to the Committee. For an overview of the Committee's work, with a particular focus on the need for openness, see D. Curtin and H. Meijers, 'The Principle of Open Government in Schengen and the European Union: Democratic Retrogression?' (1995) 32 *CML Rev*. 391, 403–16. For the proposal to attach a protocol to the Schengen Convention in order to allow the Court of Justice to give preliminary rulings on its interpretation, see Mahmood, n. 167 above, 191 and C. A. Groenendijk, 'The Competence of the EC Court of Justice' in H. Meijers *et al*, (eds.), *A New Immigration Law for Europe? The 1992 London and 1993 Copenhagen Rules on Immigration* (Utrecht: Dutch Centre for Immigrants, 1993) 45, 51.

182 Art. 135.

183 See also Meijers, n. 177 above, 5. In a Resolution of 21 Dec. 1992 on the entry into force of the Schengen Agreements, OJ 1992, C 337/214, point 9, the European Parliament regretted that the Implementing Convention made no reference whatsoever to the ECHR.

184 See respectively O'Keeffe (1995:2), n. 77 above, 23 and Nanz (1995), n. 164 above, 29 and 44, and Hailbronner (1995:1), n. 64 above, 192 and Hailbronner & Polakiewicz, n. 32 above, 60.

185 O'Keeffe (1991), n. 164 above, 210, observes, *inter alia*, that the provisions in the Convention relating to border checks appear to be too onerous and thus incompatible with EC law, although he doubts whether the Commission would challenge the controls given its opinion of the Convention as experimental in nature and as a testing ground for its own activities with a view to the completion of the single market. Moreover, the Convention's potential incompatibility with international human rights law might also cause problems given that the EC considers itself to be bound by such law.

186 Art. 142(1). However, this provision also places contracting parties under the obligation to take account of the fact that the Schengen provisions may provide for 'more extensive cooperation' than that resulting from the Conventions adopted under the auspices of the EC. Consequently, these clauses may lead to tension between the two systems, in respect of determining which Schengen provisions conflict with the EC provisions and which result in the 'more extensive cooperation': Bolten, n. 180 above, 13.

Convention that are concerned with external border controls. The Commission proposed that the Council issue a decision, based on Article K.3 TEU, recommending adoption of the Convention by member states.[187]

In contrast with the equivalent provisions of the Convention implementing the Schengen agreement, the Commission's version of the draft treaty on Crossing External Frontiers is a more liberal document. It applies 'primarily to persons not entitled under Community law'.[188] The definition of 'persons entitled under Community law' is broadly drawn, not merely encompassing EC citizens, but also third country nationals who have rights of entry and residence in an EC member state, as family members of an EC citizen or by virtue of agreements concluded between the EC and their countries of origin.[189] Third country nationals who fall into this category, therefore, are exempt from control arrangements at external frontiers, although they may be required to hold a visa in accordance with measures enacted under Art. 100c EC.[190]

The draft Treaty on Crossing External Frontiers introduces a number of safeguards which are absent from the Schengen Implementing Convention. Most importantly, it recognizes the primacy of the ECHR and envisages a role for the Court of Justice, in accordance with Article K.3 TEU.[191] It also introduces

[187] In the same document, the Commission included a separate but related proposal for a Council decision, in accordance with Article 100c EC, to determine the third countries whose nationals must be in possession of a visa when crossing the external frontiers of the EC. See Commission of the European Communities, Communication from the Commission to the Council and the European Parliament, *(1) Proposal for a Decision based on Article K.3 of the Treaty on European Union establishing the Convention on the Crossing of the External Frontiers of the Member States; (2) Proposal for a Regulation based on Article 100c of the Treaty Establishing the European Community Determining the Third Countries whose Nationals must be in Possession of a Visa when crossing the External Borders of the Member States*, COM (93) 684 final of 10 Dec. 1993: 'These proposals . . . will provide the legislative base for establishing the agreed rules for crossing the external borders in which all Member States can have confidence . . . , [which] is an essential element in the creation of an area without internal frontiers', as provided for in Art. 7a EC. *Ibid.* para. 5. The proposal on visas was recently adopted by Council Regulation 2317/95/EC, n. 85 above. The Commission's proposal for a Convention on the Crossing of External Frontiers supersedes an earlier draft (Ad Hoc Working Group on Immigration, Brussels, 24 June 1991, Doc. SN 2528/91 WGI 822), discussed on the inter-governmental plane, which has not been adopted by EC member states because of an ongoing dispute between the United Kingdom and Spain over its application to Gibraltar. See Hailbronner and Polakiewicz, n. 32 above, 62; Hailbronner (1995:1), n. 64 above, 194 and Evans, n. 32 above, 212. For an examination of both of these proposals, see D. O'Keeffe, 'The New Draft External Frontiers Convention and the Draft Visa Regulation' in *The Third Pillar of the European Union*, n. 63 above, 135.

[188] Explanatory Memorandum to the Proposal for a Council Decision establishing a Convention on Controls on Persons Crossing External Frontiers in COM (93) 684, n. 187 above, 11, para. 21.

[189] Art. 1(1).

[190] See Arts. 5(2) and 7(1)(b). Moreover, by virtue of Art. 8(1), visas are not required of those non-EC nationals not entitled under EC law who hold a residence permit issued by another member state and which, at the time of entry, will be valid for at least a further 4 months. The conditions for refusing entry into the territory of a member state are set in Art. 7(1) and mirror those found in Art. 5(1)(a)–(e) of the Schengen Implementing Convention.

[191] See Arts. 27 and 29 respectively. Under Art. 29, the Court of Justice is provided with jurisdiction, on the application by a member state or the Commission, to give preliminary rulings concerning the interpretation of the Convention and to adjudicate disputes with regard to its implementation.

additional safeguards in the provisions relating to illegal migration. The decision of the national authorities to put a person on a joint list *must* be based on 'the threat which that person may represent to the public policy or national security of a member State' *and* on a ruling of an administrative or judicial authority, taken with due regard for the proper national procedures, on account of a number of grounds, including, *inter alia*, 'a *serious* offence or *repeated* offences against the law relating to the entry and residence of foreigners'.[192] Therefore, an isolated offence against a member state's immigration controls would be insufficient to activate a decision to put an illegal migrant on the joint list, unless that offence is deemed to be '*serious*'. Consequently, illegal migrants should only find themselves placed on this list if they have *repeatedly* flouted national immigration laws. It is to be hoped that the Court of Justice will give a uniform interpretation to the vague concepts of 'serious' and 'repeated' offences as well as 'public policy' and 'national security'.[193] Article 15(1) of the draft Convention stipulates that persons who are present in a member state without authorization are required to leave the territory without delay, unless their stay is regularized. Article 15(2) provides for the expulsion of illegal migrants, in accordance with national legislation, if they do not leave voluntarily, or if their immediate departure is required for reasons of national security or public policy.

(iii) Intergovernmental cooperation

In the shadow of the Schengen Convention and the more liberal initiatives of the Commission, ministerial discussions relating to immigration in the EC continue on the inter-governmental level. As noted earlier, these discussions have now crystallized into a formal obligation to cooperate in the fields of justice and home affairs under the Third Pillar of the TEU. 'Combating unauthorized immigration, residence and work by nationals of third countries on the territory of Member States' is recognized specifically in Article K.1(3)(c) TEU as a matter of common interest. In this context, EC Immigration Ministers and the Justice and Home Affairs Council have already adopted a number of resolutions and recommendations with a view to establishing a common policy to curb the flow of illegal migrants. These include, *inter alia*, proposals to facilitate the expulsion

In the Explanatory Memorandum to its Proposal, n. 188 above, 12, para. 23, the Commission considered that this provision was warranted 'both to ensure the uniform interpretation of the Convention, given the link between the subject of the Convention and matters falling under the EC Treaty, and to resolve any differences that may arise over its implementation. Such a provision also serves to meet the concerns of the European Parliament and non-governmental organizations'. In addition to the deadlock over the status of Gibraltar, it is noteworthy that the adoption of the draft Convention, as prepared by the Commission, has also been delayed because of opposition by some EC member states to the role envisaged for the Court of Justice. See O'Keeffe (1995:1), n. 76 above, 910 and Hailbronner (1995:2), n. 80 above, 124. According to Hailbronner, *ibid.* 105, this opposition is based on the assumption that the Court is ill-equipped to deal with immigration issues submitted by national courts.

[192] Art. 10(3) (emphasis added). [193] See also O'Keeffe (1994), n. 187 above, 145.

of illegal immigrants, which also call for the introduction of laws to permit the fingerprinting of those expelled, and to conduct internal checks.[194]

(d) Readmission agreements

A so-called 'buffer zone' or *cordon sanitaire* against illegal immigration is also being constructed around the Schengen area by the adoption of 'readmission agreements' with third states. For example, on 29 March 1991, the Schengen states concluded an agreement with Poland requiring the contracting parties to readmit their own nationals as well as others who have entered from their territory into the territory of another contracting party without authorization.[195] This 'buffer zone' has been extended because Poland has since concluded a separate readmission agreement with Germany and comparable agreements with countries to the east and south, such as Belarus, Bulgaria, the Czech Republic, Romania, Slovakia, and Ukraine. After the conclusion of the agreement with Germany, a significant reduction was recorded in the number of illegal migrants crossing the Polish–German border. However, the number of undocumented migrants crossing Poland's eastern border continued to rise in the first half of 1994.[196] Other

[194] See respectively Recommendation regarding practices followed by Member States on expulsion (Doc. SN 4678/92, WGI 1266), adopted by EC Immigration Ministers on 30 Nov. 1992, Ch. III, para. 2, and Recommendation concerning checks on, and expulsion of, third country nationals residing or working without authorization (Doc. SN 3017/93, WGI 1516), adopted by EC Immigration Ministers on 1 June 1993. For a brief note of the latter measure, see *EC Bulletin* 6-1993, point 1.4.18. A further Recommendation adopted by the Justice and Home Affairs Council on 2 Dec. 1995 advocates that internal identity checks on the residence status of third country nationals should also be carried out by central or local authorities responsible for dispensing benefits to foreign nationals and by employers. See Council Recommendation on harmonizing means of combating illegal immigration and illegal employment and improving the relevant means of control, n. 158 above, points 4 and 5. Internal identity checks are already carried out in France and the Netherlands. See *SOPEMI 1994*, n. 26 above, 45 and *Closed Borders, Stringent Attitudes*, n. 116 above, 58–9. It is doubtful, however, whether such checks can be effectively undertaken without adversely affecting those persons from local immigrant communities, who are either nationals of the country concerned or who have legal status in the country. See also the 1993 European Parliament Resolution on immigration policy, n. 60 above, point 1(g), with regard to the second ministerial Recommendation and cf. Böhning and Werquin, n. 113 above, 35, para. 34. The Justice and Home Affairs Council has also adopted an additional measure to facilitate and speed up the expulsion process, which, *inter alia*, calls for the cooperation of member states in the procurement of the necessary documentation and in carrying out transit for expulsion purposes. See Council Recommendation of 22 Dec. 1995 on concerted action and cooperation in carrying out expulsion measures, OJ 1996, C 5/3.

[195] Accord relatif à la réadmission des personnes en situation irregulière (Agreement on Readmission of Persons in an Irregular Situation). The French version of the text is reproduced in Meijers *et al.* (1992), n. 164 above, 215–17 (Appendix). A Joint Declaration was attached to the Agreement provisionally limiting the readmission obligations to persons coming from Poland. See also O'Keeffe (1991), n. 164 above, 186, 195 and d'Oliveira, n. 78 above, 275. The Agreement has been described as 'one of the most important prototypes of readmission agreements . . . not only due to its multilateral construction but also because it was the first agreement of a "new generation" of readmission agreements which is no longer based on illegal border crossing as the main criterion for the readmission obligation but upon illegal stay': K.-P. Nanz, 'The Harmonization of Asylum and Immigration Legislation within the Third Pillar of the Union Treaty—A Stocktaking' in *The Third Pillar of the European Union*, n. 63 above, 123, 131–2.

[196] See A. Sakson, 'Nowa Fala Migracji w Europie' (1995) *Przegląd Zachodni* (Western Review) No. 1, 75, 86. See also *SOPEMI 1994*, n. 26 above, 148.

central and eastern European countries have entered into similar agreements amongst themselves and with Western European countries.[197] Readmission agreements are also rapidly gaining support within the EC. Towards the end of 1992, EC Immigration Ministers proposed that 'insofar as re-admission agreements do not already exist, consideration should be given to establishing them with appropriate States'.[198] 'Readmission clauses' have been included in recent draft EC agreements with non-member countries. Most of the draft Partnership and Cooperation agreements with countries which were once part of the former Soviet Union contain an identical clause obliging the Cooperation Council (that is to be set up thereunder) to 'examine which joint efforts can be made to control illegal immigration taking into account the principle and the practice of readmission'.[199] The proposed new Euro-Mediterranean Agreements with Morocco and Tunisia[200] also assert that dialogue on social matters shall encompass issues connected with, *inter alia*, 'illegal immigration and the conditions governing the return of individuals who are in breach of the legislation dealing with the right to stay and the right of establishment in their host countries'.

In spite of the enforcement measures taken and envisaged to suppress illegal migration in Europe, this phenomenon is still very much alive. Indeed, it is likely to continue and increase because of the combination of very restrictive immigration policies, both on the national and inter-governmental levels, and the development of well-established migration communities in the countries of employment, which play a significant role in encouraging migrants to enter without authorization and which provide them with the necessary support once they arrive.[201] Only a controlled 'migration management' approach, as proposed by

[197] *SOPEMI 1994*, *ibid.* 60. For an accessible example of a bilateral readmission agreement, see the Agreement in Relation to the Reassimilation of German and Romanian Citizens, Budapest, 24 Sept. 1992; entry in force 1 Nov. 1992; (1992) 31 ILM 1295.

[198] Recommendation regarding practices followed by Member States on expulsion, n. 194 above, Ch. IV, para. 1. Although the Ministers preferred the conclusion of multilateral agreements, along the lines of the agreement between Poland and the Schengen States, they considered that bilateral treaties would also be acceptable: *ibid.* Indeed, at its meeting on 30 Nov.–1 Dec. 1994 under the auspices of the Third Pillar of the TEU, the Justice and Home Affairs Council issued a Recommendation concerning a specimen Bilateral Readmission Agreement between a Member State of the European Union and a Third Country (Doc. SN 10339/94). See MNS No. 141/94 (Dec. 1994) 1.

[199] For the reference to these draft agreements, see n. 105 above. Similarly, Art. 84 of the draft agreement with Russia obliges the state parties to establish cooperation aimed at preventing illegal activities such as 'illegal immigration and illegal presence of physical persons of their nationality on their respective territories, taking into account the principle and practice of readmission'.

[200] See n. 104 above, Art. 69(3) in both agreements. Morocco has also completed a bilateral agreement with Spain on the circulation of persons, transit, and readmission of illegal immigrants. See Hailbronner and Polakiewicz, n. 32 above, 85 (and n. 242). However, enforcement of this agreement, which was signed on 13 Feb. 1992, has not been very successful. Morocco has only accepted 5 out of 600 illegal immigrants, rejecting all the others on the ground that documentary evidence showing that they have passed through Morocco is lacking. See MNS No. 161/96 (Aug. 1996) 5.

[201] Cf. Rogers, 'Western Europe in the 1980s: The End of Immigration?', n. 9 above, 294.

the Commission, without attempting to halt immigration altogether, is likely to reduce illegal migration in the long-term.[202] At the same time, it is necessary to ensure that migrant workers already in an irregular situation in the host country have similar rights to those possessed by legally employed migrants,[203] especially if they have lived and worked in that country for a considerable period of time. In any event, their rights connected with the employment situation must be guaranteed. The dignity of human labour demands that *all* workers, regardless of nationality and legal status, have the right not to be exploited in the workplace.

Protection of the rights of illegal migrants

The particularly vulnerable position of illegal migrant workers and their families has already been outlined above and in preceding chapters. Their irregular status makes them especially subject to exploitation, and, consequently, to a gross violation of their rights. The ultimate objective should be the elimination of this exploited class of workers altogether by the implementation of strict enforcement mechanisms aimed at preventing illegal immigration. Such mechanisms, however, should not include fining or imprisoning illegal migrants, a practice prevalent in a number of European countries,[204] given that, as pointed out in Chapter 1, the root cause of irregular migration is economic inequality between developed countries and the developing and underdeveloped world. Genuine solutions for eradicating this phenomenon should therefore focus on alleviating this inequality. While working towards these objectives, the existence of this group cannot be ignored and measures to ensure its protection need to be put into place.

In spite of the sizeable number of illegal migrants in Europe, COE and EC standards are woefully deficient in the protection of their rights. It is indisputable that the ECHR protects the basic fundamental rights or 'absolute rights' (from which no derogation is permissible) of irregular migrant workers and their families, since it applies to all those resident in the territory of a state party.

[202] *Immigration and Asylum Policies*, n. 48 above, 20, para. 70. The Report to the Conference on Migrant Workers from the Mahgreb in the European Community, n. 155 above, 23, para. 3.17, observes that the principle of encouraging the *controlled* entry of migrant workers is generally conducive to efforts undertaken to reduce illegal migration, but attempts by some European countries since 1974 to stop immigration altogether has simply increased the number of illegal migrants. The Report, *ibid.* and Annex III, 2–3, cites paras. 6 and 7 of the Framework Declaration on Integrating Extra-European Workers into the European Labour Market, approved by the Executive Committee of the European Trade Union Confederation on 14–15 Dec. 1989: '[S]topping immigration completely actually promotes the illegal entry of labour, the black economy, conditions of work and pay which are not covered by contract, the absence of social protection, and the development of very poor living conditions in both urban centres and rural areas. Similarly, it encourages the development of an insecure economy based on the unsound practice of social dumping (para. 6) . . . [W]hat is needed is the controlled opening of national frontiers in keeping with the demand for labour (para. 7)'.

[203] Cf. Power, n. 125 above, 27.

[204] See Commission Working Paper, n. 158 above, 113–14, which lists a range of sanctions imposed on illegal migrant workers in a number of EC member states.

As observed at the beginning of this chapter, however, the rights provided for in the ECE, ESC, and EMW, exclude undocumented workers from their coverage because, with few exceptions,[205] they only apply to those migrants lawfully within or authorized to reside in the territories of states parties. The ECHR also specifically limits the application of some provisions to those 'lawfully within' or 'lawfully resident' in contracting parties.[206] The concept of 'lawful residence' has been defined by the Committee of Independent Experts, for the purpose of Article 19(8) of the ESC which is concerned with protection against expulsion, as 'the possession [by migrant workers] of all papers legally required by the country of residence, including, if need be, a residence permit and a work permit',[207] and thus is to be determined in accordance with national law.

The one provision in the ECHR, which explicitly refers to illegal migrants, concerns their expulsion. Article 5 of the ECHR guarantees the right to liberty and security of the person, but an exception is provided in Article 5(1)(f), which permits the lawful arrest or detention of persons in order to prevent their illegal entry into a country, or against whom action is being taken with a view to deportation or extradition. Detention under Article 5(1)(f), with the objective of achieving other purposes, is not permitted.[208] The clause stipulates that the detention must be 'lawful', which means that it has to be in accordance with the applicable domestic law and not arbitrary.[209] The detention will be lawful even if no actual expulsion order is in force provided that expulsion proceedings have been commenced and are being seriously pursued.[210] Moreover, these proceedings must be conducted with the 'requisite diligence'.[211]

Under EC law, EC nationals may possess an 'irregular status', but only if they

[205] Art. 12(4) of the ESC, which calls for, *inter alia*, equal treatment between nationals of states parties in respect of social security rights in accordance with bilateral and multilateral agreements, is arguably applicable to illegal migrant workers from other states parties. See the discussion in the section on social security rights in Ch. 8.

[206] See respectively Art. 2(1) of Protocol No. 4 (the right to freedom of movement within the territory of a state party) and Art. 1 of Protocol No. 7 (procedural safeguards against the arbitrary expulsion of aliens).

[207] *Conclusions II*, 97, cited in Council of Europe, *Case Law on the European Social Charter* (Council of Europe: Strasbourg, 1982) 71. Similarly, within the meaning of the European Convention on Social and Medical Assistance 1953, residence for an alien is lawful 'so long as there is in force . . . a permit or such other permission as is required by the laws and regulations of the country concerned to reside therein' (Art. 11(a)). For a discussion of this convention, see the sections on social security and the right of equal access to health care in Ch. 8.

[208] See J. L. Murdoch, *Article 5 of the European Convention on Human Rights. The Protection of Liberty and Security of Person*, Human Rights Files No. 12 (Strasbourg: Council of Europe Press, 1994) 31, para. 36.

[209] *Bozano* v. *France*, judgment of 18 Dec. 1986, Eur. Ct. H.R. 1986, Ser. A, No. 111, (1987) 9 EHRR 297.

[210] Application 6871/75, *Caprino* v. *U.K.* (1978) 21 YBECHR 284, (1978) 12 D & R 14 (admissibility decision), (1981) 22 D & R 5 (Commission report); Application 9174/80, *Zamir* v. *United Kingdom* (1985) 40 D & R 42 (Commission report).

[211] Application 7317/75, *Lynas* v. *Switzerland* (1977) 20 YBECHR 413, (1977) 6 D & R 141. See also Application 11683/85, *Farmakopoulos* v. *Belgium* (1990) 64 D & R 52. There is no precise reference, however, to the permissible duration of confinement in Art. 5(1)(f) or in the case law.

fail to comply with the proper formalities with regard to residence permits.[212] However, they cannot be expelled as a result.[213] Non-EC nationals who are illegally employed in a host EC member state cannot expect any protection under EC law. Although the declaratory Charter of the Fundamental Social Rights of Workers pertains to *all* workers employed and resident in the EC, illegal migrant workers appear to be excluded from its coverage by virtue of the ninth recital of the Preamble, which obliges member states to afford comparable treatment with national workers as regards living and working conditions to those non-EC workers and members of their families 'legally resident' in EC member states.

Illegal migrant workers and their families clearly lack legal protection under COE agreements and the EC regime. Provisions safeguarding the rights of irregular migrants arising out of past employment and measures urging states to adopt employer sanctions and to consider regularization, which are found in the 1975 ILO instruments and the UN Convention on migrant workers, are noticeably absent from the European standards. However, COE and EC institutions have attempted to make up for this omission in the area of policy.

COE Parliamentary Assembly Recommendation 990 (1984) on clandestine migration in Europe commences with the premise that all migrant workers, regardless of status, should enjoy protection of their human rights on the same terms as nationals (paragraphs 5 and 11(c)(i)). It also advocates that COE member states consider 'as a first step, regularization of the situation of migrant workers who have already settled'. Regularization, however, is viewed as 'only an exceptional and non-renewable arrangement' (paragraph 11(b)). The Recommendation also calls for 'severe administrative and penal sanctions for [*inter alia*] employers of clandestine workers' and the provision of 'equal treatment and working conditions for migrant workers' in order to 'prevent illicit migration' (paragraph 11(c)(ii)).[214] This approach is in line with that taken by the UN Convention which is based on the premise that safeguarding the basic rights of irregular migrants discourages further employment of them rather than contributing to an increase in their numbers.

The EC Commission's approach to the problem of illegal migration has centred mainly on prevention. In its 1974 Action Programme, the Commission emphasized the urgent need for member states to 'adopt a common approach to deterrent measures' and pledged to undertake preparatory work with a view to formulating proposals for 'minimum safeguards against illegal immigration . . . [which] would include strong legal sanctions against exploiters of immigrant labour'.[215] These objectives were reiterated by the Commission in 1985. Attention was also

[212] See Council Directive 64/221/EEC of 15 Feb. 1964 on the co-ordination of special measures concerning the movement and residence of foreign nationals, OJ Sp. Ed. 1963–64, 117.

[213] Case 48/75, *State* v. *Royer* [1976] ECR 497, [1977] 2 CMLR 585.

[214] Recommendation 990 (1984) of 27 Sept. 1984 on clandestine migration in Europe. Under para. 11(a) of the Recommendation, COE member states are invited to ratify ILO Convention No. 143.

[215] *Action Programme in Favour of Migrant Workers and Their Families*, n. 27 above, 24–5.

given, however, to 'the protection of workers' rights relating to the work they have already carried out' and 'the fulfilment of employers' obligations'.[216] The focus on prevention, as observed above, has now formally crystallized into a matter of common interest which is subject to inter-governmental cooperation under the Third Pillar of the TEU. The Commission's 1994 report on Immigration and Asylum Policies sanctioned the various preventive measures that have been taken to deter illegal migration and to identify illegal migrants once in the territory of the host country, but it also stressed the need to define minimum standards for their treatment.[217] In this regard, the Commission urged member states to sign and ratify the UN Convention on migrant workers.[218]

6.6 CONCLUSION

The stage has now been set for the examination of the protection of the economic, social, cultural, political, and residence rights of migrant workers and their families by COE instruments and EC law. Two preliminary conclusions with regard to the personal scope of protection may be offered at this juncture.

First, and most obviously, COE Conventions and EC law fail to protect comprehensively *all* migrant workers and members of their families. The ESC and the EMW, the two COE instruments containing explicit provisions on migrant workers, apply only to nationals of states parties. The EMW is the sole COE instrument which contains an express definition of 'migrant worker'. Even so, it excludes a number of significant categories of migrant workers, notably self-employed, seasonal, and undocumented workers. All these categories, for example, are covered by the definition of 'migrant worker' in the UN Convention. In contrast, the EC regime, thanks to a liberal interpretation by the Court of Justice, offers the broadest definition of 'migrant worker' found anywhere, but EC institutions have struggled to protect adequately non-EC nationals residing and working in EC countries of employment who remain 'disenfranchised' in respect of the free movement of labour provisions. This group is only afforded limited protection

[216] *Guidelines for a Community Policy on Migration*, n. 39 above, 14, para. 24. The views of the Commission with respect to illegal migrants in the Guidelines are taken from the objectives in a proposal for a Council Directive concerning the approximation of the legislation of the member states in order to combat illegal migration and illegal employment, n. 163 above, which was originally presented to the Council of Ministers in 1976, but never came to fruition. As indicated earlier, efforts to adopt a common approach towards the prevention of illegal migration have, until recently, developed outside of the ambit of the EC in the form of the Schengen process.

[217] 'Although a generally firm and effective action against illegal immigration is essential . . . , it should not be forgotten that the persons concerned can be subject to exploitation and be in an extremely vulnerable position. It should therefore be taken into account that they are entitled to a fair procedure ensuring full protection of the human rights and fundamental freedoms as provided by international law. To this effect, defining minimum standards will be a necessary step which will equally help ensure the credibility of restrictive policies concerning illegal immigration': *Immigration and Asylum Policies*, n. 48 above, 29, para. 109.

[218] *Ibid.* 29–30, para. 110.

under EC law: as members of an EC worker's family, as employees of EC nationals who provide services in other member states, and by virtue of Association and Cooperation agreements.

Secondly, the rights of illegal migrants are almost wholly unprotected by COE instruments and EC law. None of the COE Conventions and EC regulations, nor even the Community Charter of the Fundamental Social Rights of Workers, apply to them, with the exception of the ECHR which in essence only safeguards their fundamental rights. In contrast with the universal standards found in ILO instruments and the UN Convention, the protection afforded illegal migrants in Europe by the relevant regional standards is significantly inferior. The emphasis on the prevention of clandestine immigration appears, thus far, to have eclipsed the concern to protect the rights of this vulnerable group.

Given the lack of adequate safeguards for those in an irregular situation and for lawfully resident migrant workers and their families, who are neither nationals of states that are parties to relevant COE instruments nor nationals of EC member states, equal treatment between all migrants and nationals in Europe remains a relative concept.

7
The Right to Equal Treatment and Non-Discrimination

7.1 BACKGROUND

The extent to which equality is realized between migrants and nationals is profoundly connected to the protection of the rights outlined in the following chapter. Discrimination against migrant workers and their families manifests itself in all parts of Europe.[1] This discrimination also takes on many forms. Two distinct seams are distinguishable: 'systematic institutionalized discrimination',[2] officially sanctioned by the State, and discrimination suffered by migrants at the hands of the general host population.[3]

The first vein of discrimination is interwoven into the fabric of the temporary migration system.[4] It is particularly evident in the employment restrictions imposed

[1] Although much of the literature on this subject concerns Western Europe, migrants in central and eastern Europe, and Vietnamese contract workers in particular, have also suffered discrimination. For a description of the dismal employment conditions and treatment of Vietnamese workers in this region, see E. Greenspon, 'What can happen when Guests overstay their Welcome' *[Toronto] Globe and Mail*, 22 Oct. 1990, A12 (concerning the situation in the former East Germany); G. Ginsburg, 'The Case of Vietnamese Gastarbeiters in the Soviet Union' (1989) 35 *Osteuropa-Recht* 166; M. Fisher, 'Unhappy Vietnamese Workers corner Illegal Bulgarian Market' *[Toronto] Globe and Mail*, 5 Feb. 1990; J. Topol, 'Slavery in a Newly Free State' (1990) 3 *Uncaptive Minds* 24; and Fédération Internationale des Droits de L'Homme, *Rapport de Mission à Prague* (Paris: Fédération Internationale des Droits de L'Homme, 1990) (concerning the situation in the former Czechoslovakia). The sweeping political changes and economic restructuring that is taking place in this region have led to many of these migrants losing their jobs and returning home. For example, there were over 33,000 Vietnamese workers in the former Czechoslovakia at the end of 1990. As at 30 June 1992, this number had fallen to a mere 5,483: *SOPEMI 1993*, 125, Table III.14 and Z. Pavlik and J. Maresova, 'Former Czechoslovakia' (1994) 120 (Table 6.12). On 21 July 1995, Germany signed a readmission agreement with Vietnam to repatriate 40,000 Vietnamese nationals by the year 2000, including those who were formerly guest workers in East Germany. The implementation of this agreement, however, has been very slow to take effect. See MNS No. 160/96 (July 1996), MNS No. 159/96 (June 1996) 3, and Dateline Migration (International), 'Repatriation of Vietnamese in Germany' (1995) 23:1 *Migrationworld Magazine* 5.

[2] J. S. Gundara, 'Racism and the National Question in Western Europe' (1988) 33.

[3] Castles and Kosack write that since the curtailment of primary migration in the 1970s, the continued inferior position of migrants on the labour market can only be explained by the effect of practices of institutional and informal discrimination against migrant workers: S. Castles and G. Kosack, *Immigrant Workers and Class Structure in Western Europe*, 2nd edn. (Oxford: Oxford University Press for the Institute of Race Relations, 1985) 499.

[4] P. L. Martin and M. J. Miller, 'Guest Workers: Lessons from Western Europe' (1980) 33 *Industr. & Lab. Rel. Rev.* 315, 328, 329–30. Martin and Miller, *ibid.* 329–30, observe, in assessing the possibility of establishing a temporary worker policy in the USA, that such a policy is unlikely to ensure respect for the human dignity of migrant workers. They contend that temporary worker policy in the context of a democratic society is, by its very nature, discriminatory and stands in opposition to the principle of equal opportunity.

on migrants in terms of work permits and geographic and occupational mobility, which, when considered together with such pre-migration traits as a lack of education, and language difficulties on arrival in the host country, contribute greatly to their lowly status in the working society.[5] The consequences of such restrictions go beyond their immediate economic effects:

> When you have a work permit system which allows some freedom of choice and movement to the worker, he will be able to move about within the economy of the country, and perhaps to take a better job, and take advantage of the same opportunities that the economy is offering to nationals. The consequences are not only economic, but social and political. The immigration regulations have a direct effect upon the migrants' integration into the society of the host country.[6]

Formal constraints on other rights in the economic, social, cultural, and political spheres further marginalize migrant workers and their families.[7] Poverty, poor housing, and inadequate education are some of the more profound consequences of this marginalization process. The discrimination inherent in the migration system itself has been compared to an extension of colonialism (*'le colonialisme chez nous'*) in that many migrant workers to Western Europe originate from developing countries: 'Indeed, there is not only a similarity but also continuity between the traditional exploitation of labour under colonialism and the insertion of immigrant labour in the workforce of the industrialized countries'.[8]

Migrant workers and their families also suffer from general discrimination in the workplace, in the allocation of housing, and in other aspects of their daily lives. They are perceived as a threat to the nation's integrity and homogeneity.[9] They are portrayed in the media and by politicians as the cause of all ills and particularly as the cause of all social and economic problems in the country.[10] The increased visibility of migrants, largely because of the arrival of their families and their concentration in certain regions of the country and in inner-city areas, leads to competition for employment, housing, and social facilities with the

[5] ILO, *Some Growing Employment Problems in Europe: Manpower Aspects of Recent Economic Developments in Europe* (1973) 85; cf. Martin and Miller, n. 4 above, 323.

[6] E.-J. Thomas, 'Migration in Europe' in A. Dummett, (ed.), *Towards a Just Immigration Policy* (1986) 43, 47.

[7] Cf. E.-J. Thomas, 'Summing-up and Points of Comparison' in E.-J. Thomas, (ed.), *Immigrant Workers in Europe: Their Legal Status, A Comparative Study* (Paris: UNESCO Press, 1982) 211, 232.

[8] R. Stavenhagen, 'New Expressions of Racism in Europe' (1989) 70; International Foundation for Development Alternatives (IFDA) Dossier 47, 50. In a similar context, Thomas has observed that 'immigration has really been the Third World's aid to developed countries': E.-J. Thomas, 'Conclusion' in *Immigrant Workers in Europe: Their Legal Status, A Comparative Study*, *ibid.* 239, 244.

[9] Thomas, 'Summing-up and Points of Comparison', n. 7 above, 232.

[10] S. Castles, 'The Guest-Worker in Western Europe—An Obituary' (1986) 776. Such views are often expressed in concert with the argument that high levels of unemployment in host countries would be reduced significantly if migrant workers were expelled. This argument, of course, contradicts the evidence that nationals are in fact unwilling to take up the low-paid and insecure jobs presently carried out by migrants. See D. Maillat, 'European Receiving Countries' in OECD, *The Future of Migration* (1987) 38, 51.

national working-class. The resulting insecurity experienced by the latter spawns a racism, which, unfortunately, is encouraged by certain political groupings.[11] The worst manifestations of this racism can be seen in the emergence of Neo-Nazi organizations or extreme right-wing parties,[12] and in the proliferation of racially-motivated attacks.[13] The highly-publicized attacks on foreigners in Germany are a pertinent example.[14] Racist attacks have also been reported in the new democracies of central and eastern Europe[15] and in the so-called 'new countries of immigration' in southern Europe. An example is this disturbing excerpt from a newspaper reporting such attacks in Italy in the summer of 1991:

> In June, a gang of youths in wealthy Varese stormed through the city's train station beating up North African immigrants, destroying 14 trailers and injuring two people. Earlier, someone burned down an interracial nursery school in Rome. Immigrant dormitories in Bologna and Florence have been the objects of violent attacks. In late August two Senegalese workers on vacation in Rimini were shot to death in what appears to be a racially motivated incident.[16]

There is undoubtedly a connection between 'systematic institutionalized discrimination' and the prejudicial behaviour towards migrants displayed by the general host population. The root cause of both of these veins of discrimination results from host country treatment of migrants in pure economic terms and a fundamental neglect of their other more human needs:

> The cause [of the discrimination and racism] is not the employment of migrants in itself, but rather, the attempt to treat migrants purely as economic men and women, and to

[11] Castles and Kosack, n. 3 above, 503–4.

[12] In France, Le Pen's Front National obtained 12.5% of the vote in Parliamentary elections in March 1993: L. Doyle, 'Resurgent Right casts Dark Shadow over Europe' *Independent*, 16 Sept. 1993, 10. This success was followed by a 15% share of the total vote in the first round of the Presidential elections in April 1995. See Ch. 6, n. 117 above and accompanying text. In the general election in Austria on 9 Oct. 1994, the far right Freedom Party, led by Jörg Haider, gained 22.6% of the vote. A. Bridge, 'Austria's Chancellor Determined to Hang On' *Independent*, 11 Oct. 1994, 10.

[13] Castles and Kosack, n. 3 above, 503. In 1973, for example, 32 Algerians were murdered in France in a series of racially-motivated attacks. Castles (1986), n. 10 above, 764. See also Commission of the European Communities, *The EC Member States and Immigration in 1993. Closed Borders, Stringent Attitudes* (1993) 78–9, referring to recent attacks in Germany, the Netherlands, and the United Kingdom. Such attacks are frequently unreported and unredressed due to the insecurity of migrant workers in host countries: *Report to the Conference on Migrant Workers from the Mahgreb in the European Community* (1991) 6, para. 1.13.

[14] In a notorious incident on 29 May 1993, five Turkish immigrants were killed after a firebomb attack on a house in the German town of Solingen: D. Gow, 'Turks Ready to Retaliate after Killings/ Solingen' *Guardian*, 31 May 1993, 18; S. Crawshaw, 'Germany's Angry Turks Fight Back—Marchers Clash with Police as Teenager is Arrested over Firebomb Killings' *Independent*, 1 June 1993, 1.

[15] J. Tagliabue, 'Right-Wing Attacks Worry Prague' *New York Times*, 14 Oct. 1991, A3; Topol, n. 1 above, 25; *Rapport de Mission à Prague*, n. 1 above, 3–4; Greenspon, n. 1 above, A12.

[16] A. Stille, 'Bigotry Begins to Fester in Italy' *[Toronto] Globe and Mail*, 11 Nov. 1991, A10. See also *Closed Borders, Stringent Attitudes*, n. 13 above, 79 (n. 203), referring to brutal attacks on Albanians in Greece.

separate between labour power and other human attributes. Because permanent immigration was not expected, and the States concerned refused to take the necessary steps to provide the housing and social amenities needed for orderly settlement, migration has exacerbated some of the underlying problems of Western European societies. It is easier now to blame the victims than to come to grips with the causes.[17]

Racist and discriminatory attitudes towards migrant workers and their families undermine any equal treatment policies in place and hardly serve the task of their integration into the host society.[18] The ILO approach to equal opportunity and treatment, described in Chapter 3, suggests that this integration is more likely to be achieved by the promotion of equality and the elimination of discrimination in practice. Formal prohibition alone is insufficient.[19] Such an approach requires a coherent 'immigrant policy', including special 'integrative' measures directed specifically at the improvement of the condition of migrant workers and their families.[20] These measures, if the particular situation of migrants so demands, may also require the temporary provision of more elaborate rights for migrants than for nationals.[21]

7.2 COE AND EC STANDARDS

It is difficult to speak in terms of true equality between migrants and nationals in European countries of employment when the majority of COE instruments of relevance to migrant workers and their families are unequal from the start, in

[17] Castles (1986), n. 10 above, 776.

[18] ILO, *Some Growing Employment Problems in Europe*, n. 5 above, 88.

[19] In April 1991, the Conference on Migrant Workers from the Mahgreb in the EC, n. 13 above, proposed the following positive action to combat discrimination against migrants: strict enforcement of laws promoting racial harmony, the highest priority to be accorded by the law enforcement authorities to the prevention of acts of racist violence and to combat racist attitudes within their own structure; disciplinary mechanisms and positive awareness campaigns to eliminate such racism; education at school to emphasize that migrants belong fully to society; and anti-racism campaigns to promote religious freedom: *Conclusions of the ICFTU/ETUC/USTMA Conference on Mahgreb Migrant Workers in the European Community*, Tunis, 18–20 April 1991, 6, para. 33.

[20] According to Hammar, these 'integrative' measures form the basis of 'immigrant policy'. Such a policy refers to the conditions provided to resident immigrants that influence their situation, e.g. employment and housing conditions, social benefits and social services, educational opportunities and language instruction, cultural amenities, leisure activities, voluntary associations, and opportunities to participate in trade unions and political affairs. 'Immigrant policy' can be either 'direct' or 'indirect'. The former consists of special measures to improve the situation of immigrants, whereas the latter constitutes general public policy (intended to apply to all without special provision for immigrants) which affects immigrants substantially and which may be 'inequitable' or 'discriminatory' in its application to them. 'Immigrant policy' should be distinguished from 'immigration regulation and aliens control', which is concerned with the technical aspects of an alien's entry into, residence in, and departure from a particular country: T. Hammar, 'Introduction' in T. Hammar, (ed.), *European Immigration Policy: A Comparative Study* (1985) 1, 9.

[21] ILO, *Some Growing Employment Problems in Europe*, n. 5 above, 103. Certain measures, however, particularly in the cultural sphere, should arguably be of a permanent nature in order to remedy a 'permanent' inequality innate in the situation. See R. Cholewinski, *The Positive Cultural and Linguistic Right of Ethnic Minorities* (1988) 160–1.

that they only apply to migrants from other states parties. Moreover, the principle of equality in COE agreements is qualified to a significant degree in areas that are of considerable importance to migrant workers and their families and that serve to facilitate their integration into the host society, such as access to employment, family reunion, political rights, and residence.[22] Free movement of labour within the EC, together with the accompanying rights and benefits, is also confined to nationals of member states.

Combating racism and xenophobia

There are no explicit legally binding provisions in COE Conventions or in EC law requiring states to combat racism and xenophobia directed at foreign migrant workers and their families, although both COE and EC institutions have increasingly referred to this subject at the level of policy.

Within the COE, the heads of state and government of member states, at their summit in Vienna on 9 October 1993, issued a Declaration which included a Plan of Action on combating racism, xenophobia, anti-semitism and intolerance.[23] The plan of action, *inter alia* advocated the launching of a broad European Youth Campaign 'to mobilize the public in favour of a tolerant society based on the equal dignity of all its members' (paragraph 1); invited member states to 'reinforce guarantees against all forms of discrimination, based on race, national or ethnic origin or on religion' (paragraph 2); and established a committee of governmental experts, reporting to the Committee of Ministers, with the mandate to:

— review Member States' legislation, policies and other measures to combat racism, xenophobia, anti-semitism and intolerance, and their effectiveness;
— propose further action at local, national and European level;
— formulate general policy recommendations to Member States; [and]
— study international legal instruments applicable in the matter with a view to their reinforcement where appropriate.[24]

The committee of experts, known as the European Commission against Racism and Intolerance (ECRI), began its work in March 1994.[25] Its working methods

[22] See also cf. A. H. J. Swart, 'The Legal Status of Aliens: Clauses in Council of Europe Instruments Relating to the Rights of Aliens' (1980) Netherlands YBIL 3, 48, 50.

[23] Council of Europe, *Human Rights Information Sheet No. 33 (July–Dec. 1993)* (Strasbourg: Council of Europe, 1994) Doc. H/INF (94) 2, 157–9. See also the earlier Parliamentary Assembly Recommendation 1222 (1993) of 29 Sept. 1993 on the fight against racism, xenophobia, and intolerance.

[24] *Human Rights Information Sheet No. 33, ibid.* 157–8. The European Youth Campaign was launched on 10 Dec. 1994. See Council of Europe, *Human Rights Information Sheet No. 35 (July–Dec. 1994)* (Strasbourg: Council of Europe, 1995) Doc. H/INF (95) 2, 80.

[25] See Council of Europe, *Human Rights Information Sheet No. 34 (Jan.–June 1994)* (Strasbourg: Council of Europe, 1995) Doc. H/INF (95) 1, 105–6. The COE's Directorate of Human Rights produced a document in May 1994 explaining the ECRI's role and relevance in the context of COE activities in the struggle against racism and intolerance: Council of Europe, Directorate of Human Rights, *Activities of the Council of Europe of Relevance to the Work of the European Commission against Racism and Intolerance*, Strasbourg, 5 May 1994, Doc. CRI (94) 4 (hereinafter *Activities of the COE of Relevance to the Work of the ECRI*).

are relatively straightforward. It consists of two working groups, the legal working group and the working group on policies and other measures, which operate in tandem and report back to the plenary sessions of the Commission.[26] One of the first tasks of the ECRI was to commission a report on the legal measures to combat racism and intolerance in COE member states, a preliminary version of which was published in March 1995.[27] Other recent activities include, *inter alia*, the collation of information on 'good practices' in member states and a report on the strengthening of Article 14 of the ECHR (considered below) which has been sent to the Committee of Ministers. In this report, the ECRI proposes a possible additional protocol to the ECHR which would contain a broad protection against racial discrimination.[28] The Parliamentary Assembly has since called for strengthening the mandate of the Commission, 'to include the right to monitor member states' compliance with international legal obligations . . . and to lay down guidelines and common principles for a Europe-wide strategy in this area and increase its resources'.[29]

With regard to EC activity in this area, the Joint Declaration Against Racism and Xenophobia, adopted on 11 June 1986 by the European Parliament, the Commission, the Council of Ministers, and member states, refers explicitly to the positive contribution of migrant workers (including those from third countries) to the development of the member states in which they legally reside, and contains an undertaking to protect the individuality and dignity of every member of society.[30] Since the adoption of this Declaration, the EC has moved steadily in the direction of embracing a uniform policy on racism and xenophobia. At the summit in Maastricht on 9–10 December 1991, the European Council adopted a Declaration on racism and xenophobia requesting Ministers and the Commission 'to increase their efforts to combat discrimination and xenophobia, and to strengthen the legal protection for third-country nationals in the territories of the Member States'.[31] In Edinburgh on 11–12 December 1992, in its Declaration on principles governing external aspects of migration policy, the European Council stressed the need to reinforce the fight against racism and xenophobia.[32] At its meeting in Corfu on 24–5 June 1994, it endorsed a Franco–German initiative on racism and xenophobia, which called for a detailed timetable and work plan with a view to, *inter alia*, the establishment of a Consultative Commission on Racism and Xenophobia with a mandate to issue recommendations on cooperation between governments and the relevant special bodies in favour of encouraging

[26] *Activities of the COE of Relevance to the Work of the ECRI*, *ibid.* 6.

[27] Council of Europe, European Commission against Racism and Intolerance, *Legal Measures to Combat Racism and Intolerance in the Member States of the Council of Europe*, Report prepared by the Swiss Institute of Comparative Law, Strasbourg, 2 March 1995, Doc. CRI (95) 2.

[28] Council of Europe, Directorate of Human Rights, *Human Rights Information Sheet No. 37 (July–Dec. 1995)* (Strasbourg: Council of Europe, 1996) Doc. H/INF (96) 1, 116.

[29] Recommendation 1275 (1995) of 28 June 1995 on the fight against racism, xenophobia, anti-semitism, and intolerance, para. 6(ii).

[30] OJ 1986, C 158/1, recital 3 of Preamble and point 2.

[31] *EC Bulletin*, 12-1991, point I.19. [32] *EC Bulletin*, 12-1992, point I.31.

tolerance and understanding of foreigners and the adoption of a global strategy at the European Union level aimed at combating acts of racist and xenophobic violence.[33] In Cannes on 26–7 June 1995, the European Council welcomed the work carried out by the various EC Council bodies and the Consultative Commission and requested that the latter 'extend its work in order to study, in close cooperation with the Council of Europe, the feasibility of a European Monitoring Centre on Racism and Xenophobia'.[34] The establishment of such a Centre was approved in principle by the European Council at its meeting in Florence on 21–2 June 1996.[35] This activity at the 'high' political level has been supplemented by further recent action to combat racism and xenophobia by the EC Commission and the European Parliament[36] and by the Council of Ministers in the fields of employment and social affairs and education.[37]

On 15 July 1996, the Council also succeeded in reaching a consensus under the Third Pillar of the TEU on a Joint Action concerning action to combat racism and xenophobia. This measure was adopted in accordance with Art. K.1(7) TEU which recognizes judicial cooperation in criminal matters as a matter of common interest. The Joint Action obliges member states to ensure effective judicial cooperation in respect of offences that include behaviour such as, *inter alia*, 'public incitement to discrimination, violence or racial hatred' and 'public dissemination or distribution of . . . material containing expressions of racism or xenophobia'.[38]

[33] Presidency Conclusions, *EU Bulletin*, 6-1994, point I.23. See also D. O'Keeffe, 'The Emergence of a European Immigration Policy' (1995) 20 *EL Rev.* 20, 33 (and n. 46). The EC Council of Ministers presented an interim report on progress made in the fight against racism and xenophobia to the European Council at its meeting in Essen on 9–10 December 1994 and a final report in March 1995. See respectively *EU Bulletin* 12-1994, point 1.33 and *EU Bulletin* 3-1995, point 1.5.9. Parallel reports were also prepared by the Consultative Commission.

[34] Presidency Conclusions, *EU Bulletin*, 6-1995, point I.23. The Consultative Commission submitted an interim report to the European Council meeting in Madrid on 15–16 Dec. 1995 in which it outlined the tasks of such a Monitoring Centre and the arrangements envisaged for its legal basis: *EU Bulletin*, 12-1995, point I.56.

[35] Presidency Conclusions, *EU Bulletin*, 6-1996, point I.5. The European Council, however, requested the Council of Ministers to first examine the legal and budgetary conditions of the future Centre as well as the links between the Centre and the COE and to mandate the Consultative Commission to continue its work until the Monitoring Centre was established.

[36] See respectively Commission of the European Communities, *Communication from the Commission on Racism, Xenophobia and Anti-Semitism and Proposal for a Council Decision designating 1997 as European Year against Racism*, COM (95) 653 final of 13 Dec. 1995, and European Parliament Resolutions of 27 April 1995 and 26 Oct. 1995 on racism, xenophobia, and anti-semitism, OJ 1995, C 126/75 and OJ 1995, C 308/140. On 23 July 1996, the Council of Ministers formally adopted a Resolution declaring 1997 as the European Year against Racism. See Resolution of the Council and of the Representatives of Member States' Governments meeting within the Council concerning the European Year against Racism (1997), OJ 1996, C 237/1.

[37] See the Resolutions of 5 and 23 Oct. 1995 of the Council and of the Representatives of Member States' Governments meeting within the Council on the fight against racism and xenophobia in the fields of employment and social affairs (OJ 1995, C 29/13) and on the response of educational systems to the problems of racism and xenophobia (OJ 1995, C 312/1).

[38] OJ 1996, L 185/5, paras. A(a) and A(e). The Joint Action, in para. B, also calls for judicial cooperation in the investigation of and/or proceedings against offences based on such behaviour. The fulfilment by member states of their obligations under the Joint Action is due to be assessed by the

In addition to these developments, there have also been calls for EC secondary legislation in this area. In 1992, a group of independent experts proposed the adoption of an EC directive against racial discrimination.[39] As demonstrated above, the question of racism and xenophobia has been addressed thus far by way of inter-governmental cooperation under Title VI of the TEU. Although the basis for EC competence in this area presently remains uncertain,[40] the 1996–97 IGC offers an opportunity to argue for the assignment of this area to EC competence.[41] Indeed, most members of the Reflection Group preparing the IGC supported the inclusion in the revised Treaty of a general clause prohibiting discrimination on a number of grounds, including race and religion (thus broadening Article 6 EC which is limited to the prohibition of discrimination on the ground of nationality) as well as an express condemnation of racism, xenophobia, anti-semitism, and intolerance, and a procedure for the enforcement of the clause.[42]

On a final note, it should not be forgotten of course, that in addition to the activity on the European level, individual states have also taken domestic measures to combat racial discrimination.[43]

Equal treatment and non-discrimination

The only COE instrument to apply to all persons residing within the territories of states parties is the ECHR. The ECHR makes no distinction in principle between aliens and nationals, unless this is specifically provided for in the text.[44]

Council by the end of June 1998 (Title II). The adoption of the Joint Action was delayed due to the opposition of the United Kingdom Government to the idea of a 'binding' instrument in an area where it considered domestic law to be adequate. See MNS No. 157/96 (April 1996) 10–11 and MNS No. 153/95 (Dec. 1995) 14.

[39] For an overview of this proposal, see C. Boothman and J. Niessen, 'The European Union and the Starting Line Proposal' in J. Cator and J. Niessen, (eds.), *The Use of International Conventions to Protect the Rights of Migrants and Ethnic Minorities* (1994) 26–30.

[40] O'Keeffe, n. 33 above, 34.

[41] Boothman and Niessen, n. 39 above, 31. For a more detailed overview of the background to developments in this area, including recent activity, see D. Curtin and M. Geurts, 'Race Discrimination and the European Union Anno 1996: From Rhetoric to Legal Remedy?' (1996) 14 NQHR 147. See also the European Parliament Resolutions of 27 April 1995 and 26 Oct. 1995 on racism, xenophobia, and anti-semitism, n. 36 above, recommending that the Commission introduce a proposal for an anti-discrimination directive (points 4 and 6 respectively).

[42] *1996 Intergovernmental Conference, Reflection Group Report* (1996) 22 and 46, para. 39.

[43] See, e.g. the Race Relations Act 1976 (c. 4), which applies to the whole of Great Britain (England, Scotland, and Wales) but not Northern Ireland. For examples of other measures within the EC, see Commission of the European Communities, Directorate General, Employment, Industrial Relations and Social Affairs, *Legal Instruments to Combat Racism and Xenophobia: Comparative Assessment of the Legal Instruments Implemented in the Various Member States to Combat All Forms of Discrimination, Racism and Xenophobia and Incitement to Hatred and Racial Violence* (Luxembourg: OOPEC, 1993). For measures within COE member states, see *Legal Measures to Combat Racism and Intolerance in the Member States of the Council of Europe*, n. 27 above.

[44] For example, see Art. 16 (non-applicability of, *inter alia*, Art. 14 to restrictions imposed on the political activity of aliens) discussed in Ch. 8

However, the non-discrimination provision in the ECHR, Article 14,[45] is limited because it only applies to the rights and freedoms set forth in the Convention:

> The enjoyment of the rights and freedoms set forth in this Convention shall be secured without discrimination on any ground such as sex, race, colour, language, religion, political or other opinion, national or social origin, association with a national minority, property, birth or other status.

Article 14, therefore, has no independent existence and cannot be labelled as a general substantive non-discrimination provision in the same vein as Article 26 of the ICCPR. For Article 14 to apply, however, there does not have to be a violation of another provision in the ECHR. A government measure in conformity with a particular provision of the ECHR may nonetheless be unlawful when considered in the light of Article 14.[46] But not every distinction will amount to a violation. Only discriminatory measures which do not pursue a legitimate or justifiable social aim or which are disproportionate to such an aim are outlawed.[47] These questions are determined by the Strasbourg organs with due regard to a state party's margin of appreciation, which has been interpreted generously.[48] A good illustration of the operation of the non-discrimination clause, which specifically relates to the immigration area, is the European Court's decision in *Abdulaziz, Cabales and Balkandali* v. *United Kingdom*.[49] In this case, the Court concluded that United Kingdom immigration rules, which made it easier for women to join their husbands or fiancés settled in the United Kingdom than for men to reunite with their wives or fiancées, were contrary to Article 14 (discrimination on the ground of sex) taken together with Article 8. The Government argued, *inter alia*, that the reason for these discriminatory immigration rules was to protect the domestic labour market, which would be adversely affected at a time of high unemployment by an influx of immigrant men who were more likely to seek work than female immigrants.[50] Although the Court accepted that

[45] For an overview of recent case law relating to Art. 14, see D. Gomien, D. Harris, and L. Zwaak, *Law and Practice of the European Convention on Human Rights and the European Social Charter* (1996) 345–56.

[46] Application 2299/64, *Grandrath* v. *Federal Republic of Germany* (1965) 8 YBECHR 324 (admissibility decision), (1967) 10 YBECHR 626 (Commission report), 678, para. 38. This position was confirmed by the European Court of Human Rights in the *Case Relating to Certain Aspects of the Laws on the Use of Languages in Education in Belgium (Merits)*, judgment of 23 July 1968, Eur. Ct. H.R., 1968, Ser. A, No. 6, (1979–80) 1 EHRR 241 (hereinafter *Belgian Linguistics Case*) para. 9. See also A. H. Robertson, and J. G. Merrills, *Human Rights in Europe—A Study of the European Convention on Human Rights* (Manchester: Manchester University Press, 1993) 178 and G. S. Goodwin-Gill, *International Law and the Movement of Persons Between States* (1978) 80, 82. In this sense, therefore, Art. 14 can be said to possess autonomous status. A survey of relevant cases, however, reveals that this autonomy is not fully recognized because whenever a violation of a substantive ECHR right or freedom is found, consideration of any additional claim of discrimination under Art. 14 is deemed unnecessary: *Law and Practice of the ECHR and the ESC*, n. 45 above, 349.

[47] *Belgian Linguistics Case*, n. 46 above.

[48] *Law and Practice of the ECHR and the ESC*, n. 45 above, 351.

[49] *Abdulaziz, Cabales and Balkandali* v. *United Kingdom*, judgment of 28 May 1985, Eur. Ct. H.R., 1985, Ser. A, No. 94, (1986) 7 EHRR 471.

[50] *Ibid.* para. 75.

the protection of the domestic labour market constituted a legitimate aim, discrimination between male and female immigrants in furtherance of this aim could not be justified given the importance attached to the advancement of the equality of the sexes in COE member states.[51]

Although Article 14 does not expressly prohibit discrimination on the ground of nationality, it contains illustrative or open-ended language and would, therefore, support a challenge based on other grounds.[52] In a recent case, the Commission of Human Rights adopted a broad approach by asserting that Article 14 'protects individuals placed in similar situations from discrimination in their enjoyment of their rights'.[53] Furthermore, Article 14 does not only impose a purely negative obligation upon states parties, but may also require positive action to be taken so that the enjoyment of the ECHR right or freedom in question can be secured without discrimination.[54]

The principal equality provision in the ESC concerning migrants is Article 19(4), which, unfortunately, has not been accepted by all the states parties to the ESC:[55]

> With a view to ensuring the effective exercise of the right of migrant workers and their families to protection and assistance in the territory of any other Contracting Party, the Contracting Parties undertake:
>
> . . .
>
> 4. to secure for such workers lawfully within their territories, insofar as such matters are regulated by law or regulations or are subject to the control of administrative authorities, treatment not less favourable than that of their own nationals in respect of the following matters:
>   (a) remuneration and other employment and working conditions;
>   (b) membership of trade unions and enjoyment of the benefits of collective bargaining;
>   (c) accommodation.[56]

[51] *Ibid.* para. 78. See also the discussion in Robertson and Merrills, n. 46 above, 180–1.

[52] See also Robertson and Merrills, n. 46 above, 177. Provided of course that the discriminatory measures concerned cannot be justified, either by the proportionality test established under Art. 14, or by reference to Art. 16.

[53] Application 17371/90, *Gaygusuz* v. *Austria* (Commission report, 11 Jan. 1995) para. 48. For a discussion of this opinion and the facts, see the section on social security rights in Ch. 8.

[54] *Belgian Linguistics Case*, n. 46 above, para. 9. The Court, *ibid.*, stated that Art. 14 effectively 'formed an integral part of each of the articles laying down rights and freedoms. No distinctions should be made in this respect according to the nature of these rights and freedoms and of their correlative obligations, and for instance as to whether the respect due to the right concerned implies positive action or mere abstention. This is, moreover, clearly shown by the very general nature of the terms employed in Article 14: "the enjoyment of the rights and freedoms set forth in this Convention shall be secured"'. See also Goodwin-Gill, n. 46 above, 81–2.

[55] In addition to Denmark, Malta, and Iceland, which have not accepted the whole of Art. 19, Austria has not accepted Art. 19(4).

[56] In addition, Art. 19(5) and 19(7) respectively guarantee migrant workers equal treatment with nationals with regard to employment taxes, dues or contributions payable in respect of employed persons, and legal proceedings that relate to matters referred to in Art. 19.

Article 19(4) of the ESC is closely modelled on Article 6(1)(a) of ILO Convention No. 97 of 1949.[57] However, it is considerably narrower in scope than its predecessor because it only applies to migrants originating from countries which have ratified the ESC. It has also inherited similar 'textual weaknesses' to those found in Article 6(1)(a) of ILO Convention No. 97. Fortunately, many of these can be rectified by reading the provision in the context of the ESC as a whole and by its liberal interpretation by the supervisory organs, in particular by the Committee of Independent Experts, which has striven from the very beginning of its work to give Article 19(4) a broad interpretation.

The first textual weakness is that equality in Article 19(4) is limited to matters largely connected with employment. Although accommodation is included, equal treatment in other important areas of concern to migrant workers and their families, such as culture, education, and social security, is not specifically covered by the provision. However, these omissions are to a large extent remedied by the other provisions in the ESC, which also apply to migrant workers from other contracting parties. Secondly, Article 19(4) limits the equality obligation to matters that are 'regulated by law or regulations or are subject to the control of administrative authorities'. Although a strict interpretation of this wording would appear to support the view that private discrimination is not covered *per se*, with the result that, for example, discrimination against migrant workers by landlords in respect of the acquisition of rental accommodation on the private housing market would not be protected by Article 19(4) if such discrimination is not prohibited by national law, one commentator has argued that the Committee of Independent Experts may be moving towards an interpretation of the provision obliging states to counteract this kind of discrimination.[58] Indeed, the Committee of Independent Experts has emphasized that 'it is not enough for a government to prove that no discrimination exists in law alone, but that it is obliged to prove in addition that no discrimination is practised in fact, or to inform the supervisory organ of the practical measures taken to remedy it'.[59] The third apparent weakness, which is clearly related to the second, is that states seem to be under no obligation to take positive action to promote equality. The Committee of Independent Experts, however, observed in its very first Conclusion that Article 19 as a whole should not only ensure equality of treatment between national workers and foreign workers, but also requires the taking of special measures on behalf of the latter group:

[57] See also D. Harris, *The European Social Charter* (1984) 169.

[58] Harris, *ibid.* 169 (n. 908), citing from *Conclusions VII*, 102, with regard to the Swedish report.

[59] *Conclusions III*, 92, cited in Council of Europe, *Case Law on the European Social Charter* (1982) 158. The Governmental Committee, however, has taken a more limited approach to this question, stating that *de jure* equality is sufficient under Art. 19(4): *Report 11(I)* 104 (regarding the Norwegian report), cited in Council of Europe, *Case Law on the European Social Charter—Supplement No. 3* (1993) 143.

[Article 19] goes beyond merely guaranteeing equality of treatment as between foreign and national workers in the sense that, recognizing that migrants are in fact handicapped, it provides for the institution by the Contracting States of measures which are more favourable and more positive to this category of persons than in regard to the States' own nationals . . . Such being the case, *the Contracting Parties should not limit the fulfilment of their obligations under this article to ensuring non-discrimination between their own nationals and foreigners but should pursue a positive and continuous course of action.*[60]

This approach is justified because equality in law between nationals and migrants does not always ensure equality in practice. An example given by the Committee is where a period of residence is necessary for eligibility for government-subsidized housing.[61] Such a requirement, equally applicable in law to both national workers and migrant workers, is likely to have an indirect discriminatory effect on the latter, especially if they have only recently arrived in the country of employment. The interpretation of Article 19(4) as involving a positive duty is also in line with the right of migrant workers and their families, defined in the introductory paragraph of Article 19, as being a right to '*assistance*' as well as to 'protection'.

The objective of the EMW, spelt out in the second recital of the Preamble, is to ensure that migrant workers are '*as far as possible* . . . treated no less favourably than workers who are nationals of the receiving State in all aspects of living and working conditions'.[62] These words appear to concede that full equality is probably unattainable. Moreover, there is no *general* equality or non-discrimination provision in the main text of the EMW as there is in the ESC (though confined to a limited set of matters) and the ECHR.[63]

In EC law, the principle of equal treatment between nationals and migrant workers from other EC member states is enshrined in Articles 6 and 48(2) EC. Whereas the former provision is of broader application and constitutes a general prohibition of 'any discrimination on grounds of nationality',[64] the latter is

[60] *Conclusions I*, 81, cited in *Case Law on the European Social Charter*, n. 59 above, 149 (emphasis added).

[61] *Conclusions V*, 123, cited in *Case Law on the European Social Charter*, n. 59 above, 150. See also the Committee's observations with regard to the Norwegian report: Committee of Independent Experts of the European Social Charter, *Conclusions XI-1* (Council of Europe: Strasbourg, 1989) 159–60.

[62] Emphasis added.

[63] There are, however, *separate* equality provisions in the EMW referring to the following matters: education and vocational training (Art. 14), work conditions (Art. 16), social security (Art. 18), social and medical assistance (Art. 19), occupational safety (Art. 20), inspection of working conditions (Art. 21), taxation on earnings (Art. 23), expiry of contract and discharge (Art. 24), right of access to courts and administrative authorities (Art. 26), use of employment services, (Art. 27), the right to organize (Art. 28), participation in the affairs of the undertaking (Art. 29) and housing (Art. 31).

[64] The present scope of Art. 6 EC is assessed by Peers as follows: 'No right granted by another article of the EC Treaty can be granted independently by Article 6. However, the Article can be used independently to bar Member States from discriminating in fields mentioned by the Treaty, but for which the Treaty does not provide an explicit bar on discrimination': S. Peers, 'Towards Equality: Actual and Potential Rights of Third-Country Nationals in the European Union' (1996) 33 *CML Rev.*

specifically concerned with freedom of movement for workers and provides that such free movement 'shall entail the abolition of any discrimination based on nationality between workers of the Member States as regards employment, remuneration and other conditions of work and employment'.

In contrast with Article 19(4) of the ESC, which, on its face at least, appears not to outlaw discrimination resulting from private action, the Court of Justice has ruled that the prohibition of discrimination in Articles 6 and 48 EC applies not only 'to the action of public authorities, but extends likewise to rules of any other nature aimed at regulating in a collective manner gainful employment . . .'.[65] Equality is also to be ensured in practice and all forms of covert or indirect action, which lead to the same discriminatory result, are prohibited.[66]

The non-discrimination principle, as it applies to free movement of labour, is elaborated in EC secondary legislation, particularly Council Regulation 1612/68/EEC. The Regulation is similar in scope to Article 19(4) of the ESC and prohibits discrimination in respect of employment and work conditions, trade union rights, and housing,[67] as well as vocational training and education.[68] Equal treatment is also extended by EC secondary legislation to social security rights.[69] With regard to economic and social rights therefore, the scope of the equality principle in EC and ESC provisions is comparable. However, EC law also applies equal treatment to other areas such as culture, residence, and political participation. Moreover, because one of the fundamental aims of the EC, as expressed in Article 3(c) EC, is to realize 'an internal market characterized by the abolition, as between Member States of . . . [*inter alia*] obstacles to the free movement of . . . persons . . .', the equality principle is articulated far more forcefully, with the result that EC law contains detailed provisions[70] providing for comprehensive equal treatment between nationals and migrants in those areas that are arguably of great concern to the latter, such as access to employment and residence in the host country.

7, 18. Similar non-discrimination clauses are found in Art. 4 EEA and Art. 9 of the EEC–Turkey Association Agreement. The latter provision prohibits discrimination 'in accordance with the principle laid down in Article 7 of the Treaty establishing the Community [Art. 6 EC]', but it has not yet been invoked before the Court of Justice: Peers, *ibid.*

[65] Case 36/74, *Walrave* v. *Union Cycliste Internationale* [1974] ECR 1405, [1975] 1 CMLR 320, para. 17. The particular rules at issue in this case were the world championship regulations concerned with motor-paced bicycle racing.

[66] See, e.g. Case 152/73, *Sotgiu* v. *Bundespost* [1974] ECR 153, in which the Court of Justice ruled, *inter alia*, that taking into account the fact that workers have their residence in another member state in order to determine the grant of a family separation allowance to such workers may in practice indirectly disadvantage EC migrant workers. See also the fifth recital to Reg. 1612/68/EEC which begins: 'Whereas the right of freedom of movement, in order that it may be exercised, by objective standards, in freedom and dignity, requires that equality of treatment shall be ensured *in fact* and in law' (emphasis added).

[67] Title II, Employment and Equality of Treatment, Arts. 1–6, 7(1), 8 and 9.

[68] Arts. 7(2) and 12. [69] Reg. 1408/71/EEC, as amended.

[70] According to Goodwin-Gill, n. 46 above, 169, provisions concerning themselves with detail are one of the characteristics of an effective freedom of movement regime.

7.3 CONCLUSION

A uniform approach to the principle of equality and non-discrimination in COE instruments is absent. Article 19 of the ESC, which espouses equal treatment between migrants and nationals is, on its face, limited as a substantive equality clause, although it has received a generous interpretation by the Committee of Independent Experts, whereas Article 14 of the ECHR is tied to the rights in that instrument. On the other hand, equal treatment between nationals of EC member states constitutes the keystone to the success of free movement of workers within the EC. This treatment, however, is only applicable to just under one half of the migrant population resident and working in the EC.

8

Economic, Social, Cultural, Political, and Residence Rights

A. ECONOMIC AND SOCIAL RIGHTS

The degree to which the economic and social rights of migrant workers and their families are protected in European states of employment very much depends on whether EC freedom of movement applies. This freedom is accompanied by a series of wide-ranging economic and social entitlements. COE instruments, however, are less effective in safeguarding the economic and social rights of migrants. In particular, rights which affect state sovereign controls regarding the domestic labour market and immigration, such as access to employment and family reunion, and which are commonly subject to significant restrictions by countries of employment, are also the focus of numerous qualifications under COE instruments.

8.1 EMPLOYMENT RIGHTS

Equal work and employment conditions

(a) Background

Immigrant labourers came to Western Europe not only to fill labour shortages, but also to complement the national working class by performing the low-status, manual jobs which the latter had come to spurn.[1] The post-war economic recovery in this region was followed by rapid economic growth, which was sustained by the importation of additional labour.[2] The expanding economy also created employment opportunities further up the occupational ladder which were taken on by better educated national workers, who had previously been in blue-collar positions, leaving incoming migrants to carry out the least desirable, low-paid, and hardest jobs.[3] This phenomenon was succinctly described by an ILO Report in 1973:

[1] R. Stavenhagen, 'New Expressions of Racism in Europe' (1989) 51; S. Castles and G. Kosack, *Immigrant Workers and Class Structure in Western Europe* (1985) 489.

[2] T. Hammar, 'Economy and Ideology' in T. Hammar, (ed.), *European Immigration Policy: A Comparative Study* (1985) 239, 242–3; R. E. Krane, 'Introduction and Overview' in R. E. Krane, (ed.), *International Labor Migration in Europe* (New York: Praeger, 1979) 1, 3.

[3] Hammar, n. 2 above, 244; P. L. Martin and M. J. Miller, 'Guestworkers: Lessons from Western Europe' (1980) 33 *Industr. & Lab. Rel. Rev.* 315, 319.

Rising expectations fuelled by extended education and the mass media as well as a favourable labour market situation have led . . . to the growing aversion of large sections of Western Europe's workers to heavy, dirty, dangerous or unpleasant jobs and latterly also to jobs involving monotonous assembly-type work or inconvenient working hours; these kinds of jobs are classified . . . under the term 'socially undesirable jobs'. Foreign workers have been engaged to fill the vacancies.[4]

As a result, 'immigrant labour quickly became a necessity for the functioning of many of the European economies'.[5] A consideration of the statistical information concerned with the occupational status of migrant workers in some major European immigration countries confirms this analysis. In 1976, most foreign workers were employed in the manufacturing and construction sectors where many manual jobs are found. In western Germany, 73.8 per cent of foreign workers were employed in these occupations, whereas in France and Switzerland the proportion of migrant workers in these sectors amounted to 65.5 and 56.5 per cent respectively.[6] Although the occupational status of migrant workers appears to be improving in some countries,[7] with a trend towards convergence emerging in the sectoral distribution of employment by foreigners and nationals during the 1980s and early 1990s,[8] change is nonetheless gradual. For example, the French National Census of 1982 indicated that the great majority of Mahgreb workers in France were manual workers and that about one half of these were unskilled.[9] In Germany, the number of migrant men in the manufacturing and building occupations remained at the consistently high level of approximately 80 per cent of the total foreign male labour force in both 1972 and 1980.[10] According to figures in 1990, this situation has improved, but the proportion of foreign workers in these sectors remains high: in Germany, the manufacturing and construction sectors continued to employ over 50 per cent of all foreign workers who constituted approximately 10 per cent of the total workforce in these occupations;[11] in Belgium, 63 per cent of non-EC nationals were manual workers compared with 51 per cent of EC nationals and just 29 per cent of Belgian nationals;[12] and

[4] ILO, *Some Growing Employment Problems in Europe: Manpower Aspects of Recent Economic Developments in Europe* (1973) 82.

[5] T. Hammar, 'Introduction' in *European Immigration Policy: A Comparative Study*, n. 2 above, 245.

[6] Martin and Miller, n. 3 above, 323, citing from *SOPEMI 1977*.

[7] E.-J. Thomas, 'Migration in Europe' in A. Dummett, (ed.), *Towards a Just Immigration Policy* (1986) 46; and E.-J. Thomas, 'Summing-up and Points of Comparison' in E.-J. Thomas, (ed.), *Immigrant Workers in Europe: Their Legal Status, A Comparative Study* (1982) 228–9.

[8] *SOPEMI 1994*, 38.

[9] The National Census revealed that 82% of Moroccan workers, 74% of Algerians, and 71% of Tunisians were manual workers: *Report to the Conference on Migrant Workers from the Mahgreb in the European Community* (1991) 4, para. 1.8, citing from ILO, *Jeunes maghrébins: issus de l'émigration*, ILO Working Paper (1986).

[10] Castles & Kosack, n. 1 above, 495–6, citing from Bundesminister für Arbeit und Sozialordnung, (ed.), *Situation der ausländischen Arbeitnehmer und ihrer Familienangehörigen in der Bundesrepublik Deutschland, Repräsentativuntersuchung 1980* (Bonn: Forschunginstitut der Friedrich-Ebert-Stiftung, 1981).

[11] *SOPEMI 1992*, 63 (Table II.11).

[12] *SOPEMI 1990*, 43.

in France, 46 per cent of foreigners were employed in industry and construction and public works (in the construction sector, they constituted almost 17 per cent of the *total* work force).[13] The most recent statistics indicate a significant increase of foreign employment in the service sector,[14] although this does not mean that the proportion of foreign workers is highest in this sector.[15] None of these figures, however, record the occupational status of illegal migrants. It is safe to assume, in the light of the evidence of exploitation faced by this group, that they are likely to be engaged in jobs of the worst kind.

This cursory summary indicates that migrant workers today are still more likely to be found in jobs which traditionally breed the poorest working conditions. With regard to security of employment, recent economic transformations appear not to have resulted in major changes to the foreign labour force, although it would seem that migrant workers are more vulnerable to job cuts as a result of decline, restructuring, and cyclical downturns in the sectors of employment in which they remain concentrated, such as mining, manufacturing, or construction.[16] Furthermore, the rate of unemployment among migrant workers is significantly higher than that of nationals in a number of European countries.[17]

(b) COE and EC standards

Equal treatment between migrant and national workers in respect of work and employment conditions should not be a controversial concept. All migrant workers as 'workers', through the dignity of their labour and as economic participants in society, should be entitled to the same protection as national workers in the workplace and in respect of their conditions of employment.

All the relevant COE instruments, with the exception of the ECHR (which does not deal directly with the matter), and the EC regime, proclaim equality between state party or member state nationals in this regard. Differences, however, exist regarding the extent of protection provided. Unfortunately, the migrant workers who are most likely to suffer from poor work and employment conditions are those who come from countries outside of Europe as well as those in an irregular

[13] *SOPEMI 1994*, 85–6.

[14] *SOPEMI 1993*, 36 (Table I.2); *SOPEMI 1992*, 25–6. In Belgium, Luxembourg, the Netherlands, and the United Kingdom, the service sector employs the most foreign workers: *SOPEMI 1993*, *ibid.* A Dec. 1991 survey conducted in France indicates that most foreign workers in that country are now also employed in the service sector. See Commission of the European Communities, *The EC Member States and Immigration in 1993. Closed Borders, Stringent Attitudes* (1993) 35, citing from the ACEMO (Activity and Conditions of Employment of the Labour Force) survey conducted by the Ministry of Labour.

[15] For example, in Belgium, the hotel and catering industry employs the greatest number of foreign workers, though they still account for less than 10% of the industry's total labour force: *SOPEMI 1992*, 25. In France, 39.5% of foreigners are found in traded services, but they are under-represented in the tertiary sector overall, constituting only 4.6% of the labour force in that sector: *SOPEMI 1994*, 85–6.

[16] *SOPEMI 1994*, 36–7; *SOPEMI 1993*, 41.

[17] *SOPEMI 1994*, 32–3 (Table I.5): Belgium (19.4 to 7.1%), Denmark (28.5 to 10.5%), France (20.7 to 10.8%), Germany (12.7 to 4.9%), the Netherlands (19.7 to 5.8%), Sweden (20.9 to 7.6%), United Kingdom (16.0 to 10.1%).

situation. These groups, with a few exceptions, are unable to benefit from the multilateral and supranational provisions discussed below and must rely on the protection of applicable bilateral agreements or domestic law.

The ECE and EMW both affirm equality with regard to work and employment conditions, but in rather general terms. The ECE refers in Article 17(1) to 'wages and working conditions in general', whereas the EMW merely refers to 'conditions of work' in Article 16(1).[18] Article 24 of the EMW, however, extends the principle of equal treatment between migrant workers and nationals to cases when an employment contract expires, or is due to expire, and to dismissal from employment. The ESC, in Article 19(4)(a), speaks of equality in respect of 'remuneration and other employment and working conditions'. These words have been broadly defined by the Committee of Independent Experts to include promotion, benefits paid to employees for changing jobs or taking up employment for the first time, and access to vocational training.[19] The Committee has also maintained that Article 19(4) provides for equal treatment between nationals and migrants in the event of redundancy or dismissal, which is particularly important in times of recession when governments might be tempted to dispense with foreign workers in order to protect their nationals.[20] Finally, Article 19(5) of the ESC applies the principle of equality between migrants and nationals in employment matters to 'employment taxes, dues or contributions payable in respect of employed persons'.

Article 48(2) EC proclaims that free movement of labour necessitates 'the abolition of any discrimination based on nationality between workers of the Member States as regards employment, remuneration and other conditions of work and employment'. The provision implementing this principle in secondary legislation is Article 7 of Regulation 1612/68/EEC. Article 7(1) guarantees equal treatment between nationals and migrant workers from other EC member states in respect of 'any conditions of employment and work'. Emphasis in this clause is specifically placed on remuneration, dismissal, and reinstatement or re-employment in the event of unemployment. Moreover, the Court of Justice has interpreted the concept of 'conditions of employment and work' to include not only statutory or contractual payments, but also benefits paid voluntarily by employers[21] and general legislative measures applicable to disabled workers with a view to assisting

[18] Under Art. 16(2) of the EMW, the equal treatment principle cannot be derogated from by individual contract.

[19] *Conclusions III*, 92 and 94 and *Conclusions VII*, 103 (regarding access to vocational training), cited in Council of Europe, *Case Law on the European Social Charter* (1982) 159. For a discussion of the separate provisions on vocational training in Arts. 9 and 10 of the ESC, see the section below on the right to education which is also concerned with the right of migrant workers to vocational training and retraining.

[20] During the fourth cycle of supervision, the Committee called upon states parties to 'take specific action to avoid discrimination to the extent that an increase of the level of unemployment is likely to have a particular impact upon migrant workers': *Conclusions IV*, 119, cited by D. Harris, *The European Social Charter* (1984) 171.

[21] Case 152/73, *Sotgiu v. Bundespost* [1974] ECR 153.

them to regain their ability to work.[22] Article 7(2) accords to EC migrant workers the same social and tax advantages as national workers, and is discussed below in the section on social security rights, whereas Article 7(3) guarantees EC migrant workers equal access to vocational training with nationals, a right considered in more detail below in the context of the right to education.

Non-EC nationals whose countries of origin have entered into Association or Cooperation Agreements with the EC can also claim protection under EC law in this area. Decision 1/80 of 19 September 1980 on the development of the Association, adopted by the Association Council under the EC–Turkey Association Agreement, ensures that Turkish workers duly registered as belonging to the labour force of member states are granted treatment 'involving no discrimination on the basis of nationality between them and Community workers', whereas the Cooperation Agreements with the Mahgreb countries guarantee freedom from discrimination based on nationality as regards 'working conditions or remuneration'.[23] The scope of the protection accorded to migrant workers from central and eastern European countries, however, appears to be broader because it extends to 'dismissal'.[24] Given the particular vulnerability of migrant workers to dismissal from employment in difficult economic times, this additional wording is significant. The non-discrimination provision in the Cooperation Agreements with Mahgreb countries, though not tested directly, has been recognized by the Court of Justice as containing a sufficiently clear and precise obligation to confer direct effect in EC countries of employment.[25]

Access to employment

The question of access to employment is of crucial economic and social importance to migrant workers and their families. The connection between restrictions

[22] Case 76/72, *Michel S.* v. *Fonds national de reclassement social des handicapés* [1973] ECR 457.

[23] See respectively Art. 10 of Decision 1/80 and the Cooperation Agreements with Algeria (Art. 38), Morocco (Art. 40), and Tunisia (Art. 39). Decision 1/80 is reproduced in Council of the European Communities, *EEC–Turkey Association Agreement and Protocols and Other Basic Texts* (Brussels/Luxembourg: OOPEC, 1992) 327–46.

[24] Art. 37(1) in both the Europe Agreements with Hungary and Poland, and Art. 38(1) in the Europe Agreements with Bulgaria, the Czech Republic, Romania, and the Slovak Republic. The wording in the draft Euro-Mediterranean Association Agreements with Morocco and Tunisia (Art. 64 in both) and the draft Partnership and Cooperation Agreements with Russia and the former republics of the Soviet Union also refers to 'dismissal'.

[25] Case C-18/90, *Kziber* v. *Office National de L'Emploi* [1991] ECR I-199, para. 22, regarding Arts. 40 and 41 of the Cooperation Agreement with Morocco. In the draft Partnership and Cooperation Agreements, however, only the Russian instrument '*ensures*' this right to non-discrimination (Art. 23(1)), whereas the equivalent clause in the other Partnership and Cooperation Agreements merely '*endeavours*' to ensure it (for example, Agreement with the Ukraine, Art. 19(1)). The latter wording, therefore, is unlikely to confer direct effect. Cf. M. Cremona, 'Citizens of Third Countries: Movement and Employment of Migrant Workers within the European Union' (1995) LIEI No. 2, 187, 112. As discussed in Ch. 6, the conditions of employment of all non-EC nationals legally resident in EC member states, may now be the subject of Directives adopted by the EC Council on a proposal of the Commission under Art. 2(3) of the Agreement on Social Policy. To date, no such Commission proposal has been put forward. See S. Peers, 'Towards Equality: Actual and Potential Rights of Third-Country Nationals in the European Union' (1996) 33 CML Rev. 7, 49.

on access of foreign workers to employment and their continuing low occupational status in society has been identified as one aspect of the 'systematic institutionalized discrimination' ingrained into the temporary migration system. Access to employment is also one area where state sovereignty is prevalent and where countries are least inclined to realize equality between migrant workers and nationals. Chapter 3 described the heated debate surrounding the adoption of Article 14(a) of ILO Convention No. 143 of 1975, which requires all restrictions on access to employment for migrant workers to be lifted after 2 years of employment in the host country or after the completion of the first employment contract (if less than 2 years in duration). Indeed, Article 14(a) is one of the principal reasons why so few countries have ratified this instrument. Restrictions by European countries on the access of foreign workers to the labour market are largely dictated by economic considerations and by the perceived obligation of states to protect their own nationals, and certainly go beyond those permitted by Article 14(a) of the 1975 ILO Convention. Indeed, these restrictions are more consistent with the weaker and more discretionary provisions of the UN Convention concerning this right.

(a) Background

In general, the migrant-receiving countries in Europe give preference to the hiring of their own nationals or nationals of countries that belong to reciprocal free movement of labour regimes, such as the EC, the EEA, or the Nordic Common Labour Market.[26] For example, in Italy, work permits are only issued to foreigners if no Italian or EC nationals possess the occupational qualification in question.[27] Preference may also be given to certain favoured or privileged aliens.[28]

[26] Thomas, 'Summing-up and Points of Comparison', n. 7 above, 218; S. Castles, *Migrant Workers and the Transformation of Western Societies*, Western Societies Program, Occasional Paper No. 22 (New York: Center for International Studies, Cornell University, 1989) 110; Commission of the European Communities, *Member States' National Legislation Applicable to Non-Community Citizens*, Commission Working Paper (1990) 3, 6 and 8 (Denmark, Iceland, and the United Kingdom); R. Kühner 'Participation in Economic Life' in Max Planck Institute of Comparative Law, (ed.), *The Legal Position of Aliens in National and International Law*, vol. 2 (1987) (hereinafter *The Legal Position of Aliens*) 1973, 1975 (*inter alia*, the Netherlands and Switzerland).

[27] Art. 8(3) of Law No. 943 of 30 Dec. 1986 (effective 27 Jan. 1987). See M. Biagi, 'Non-EEC Nationals and the Italian Labour Market: The Institutional Framework' (1992) 8 IJCLLIR, 154, 156 and F. Isgro, 'Italy Enacts Law to Protect Basic Human Rights of Foreign Workers' (1986) 1 *Georgetown Immigr. L.J.* 693, 696. A similar condition exists in Germany regarding the granting of general work permits to foreigners. See M. J. Aukerman, 'Discrimination in Germany: A Call for Minority Rights' (1995) 13 NQHR 237, 243 (n. 34).

[28] See generally Commission Working Paper, n. 26 above, 73 and 74–5, 120–1; and T. Hoogenboom, 'The Position of Those who are not Nationals of a Community Member State' (1991) 367–8. In Greece, for example, preference may be given to ethnic Greeks (*omoyeneis*) and those who have been granted refugee status by the Greek authorities and who are residing legally in the country: Law 1975/1991, Art. 21. See N. Sitaropoulos, 'The New Legal Framework of Alien Immigration in Greece: A Draconian Contribution to Europe's Unification' (1992) 6 INLP 89, 93. In the Netherlands, priority is also given, in addition to Dutch and EC citizens, to workers from those countries with which the Netherlands has entered into bilateral recruitment arrangements: Foreign Employees Act 1978, Art. 8. See L. Betten, 'Immigration Policies and the Labour Market in The Netherlands' (1992) 8 ICJLLIR 140, 144.

As for other foreign workers, the present and expected state of the labour market is normally taken into account first before work permits are issued.[29] Such workers are only engaged in countries of employment if there is a shortage of qualified personnel on the national labour market, necessitating the employment of skilled foreign labour, or if nationals refuse to take up certain manual jobs, in which case less-skilled foreign labour may be called upon.[30] Access to less-skilled positions is now frequently regulated by bilateral agreements, which set fixed quotas and time-limits, or by seasonal contracts.[31]

The employment of migrants in most European countries is regulated by a complex system of work and residence permits, which are usually linked to one another. In some countries, it is the employer who applies for the work permit.[32] In others, the work permit has to be obtained by the migrant worker.[33] There may also be a requirement for the potential migrant worker to apply for the work permit from outside the issuing country,[34] and countries of employment may set a quota for foreign workers.[35]

The scope of the work permit varies. Initially, it tends to be issued for a short period, usually one year, and is often limited to a specific employer, occupation, or geographic region. However, the rights of migrants in respect of occupational mobility normally increase the longer they work and reside in the country concerned.[36] In a number of countries, a minimum period of 5 years of employment

[29] Kühner, n. 26 above, 1975 (Austria, France, and Germany).

[30] Thomas, 'Summing-up and Points of Comparison', n. 7 above, 218.

[31] For an overview of such schemes in Germany, see L. Höfler, 'Migration Programmes of Germany aimed at the Training and Employment of Workers from Developing Countries or Countries of Central and Eastern Europe' (1992) 30 IM (Special Issue: Migration and Development) 335. See also M. Weiss, 'Immigration Policy and the Labour Market in Germany' (1992) 8 IJCLLIR 113, 118–19. In 1993, Germany recruited 180,000 seasonal workers from central and eastern Europe, in particular from Poland (143,000): *SOPEMI 1994*, 89 (Table II.16). The next largest employer of seasonal workers in Europe is Switzerland (72,000), followed by Austria (16,000) and France (11,000): *SOPEMI 1994*, 197 (Table A.6).

[32] See J. Salt, A. Singleton, and J. Hogarth, *Europe's International Migrants* (1994) 39 and 67 (Italy and the United Kingdom). In the Netherlands, both the employer and the migrant must apply for the work permit: *ibid.* 44; Betten (1992), n. 28 above, 143.

[33] Thomas, 'Summing-up and Points of Comparison', n. 7 above, 218–19 (France, Germany, Sweden); *Europe's International Migrants*, n. 32 above, 47 and 58 (Norway and Spain).

[34] See *Europe's International Migrants*, n. 32 above, 22 and 60 (Finland and Sweden).

[35] See *ibid.* 11 and 41 (Austria, where the foreign worker quota for non-EC nationals is 9%, and Italy) and Commission Working Paper, n. 26 above, 37–8 (Greece and Italy). For the position in Austria, see also R. Baubock, 'Austria' in S. Arditti s, (ed.), *The Politics of East–West Migration* (1994) 155, 162 and MNS No. 160/96 (July 1996) 2. In 1993, a quota system, set at 20,600 work permits, was introduced in Spain for foreign workers who are not nationals of an EC member state: *SOPEMI 1994*, 118.

[36] Hoogenboom, n. 28 above, 364, 365; Y. N. Soysal, *Limits of Citizenship. Migrants and Postnational Membership in Europe* (Chicago: Chicago University Press, 1994) 126 (Table 7.5), citing from J. Niessen, 'Migration and (Self-)Employment, Residence, and Work Permit Arrangements in Seventeen European Countries', (Maastricht: European Centre for Work and Labour, 1989) 51. This is not the case in Ireland where migrants are bound to a specific employer throughout their employment: *Europe's International Migrants*, n. 32 above, 37. Restrictions are also in principle maintained in Greece and Portugal on the renewal of the initial work permit: W. R. Böhning and J. Werquin, 'Some Economic, Social and Human Rights Considerations concerning the Future Status of Third-Country Nationals in the Single European Market' (1990) 10 (footnote). In Spain, the duration of

is required before a migrant worker may acquire free choice of occupational activity.[37] In many of these countries, however, the renewal of work permits before unlimited access to employment is realized is subject to the state of the domestic labour market and to the broad discretion of the national authorities.[38] In France and the Netherlands, restrictions on occupational and geographical mobility can be removed after 3 years, and in Italy, after 2 years.[39] A more liberal approach is taken in Sweden. Although entry into the country for the purpose of employment is strictly controlled, some foreigners, mostly highly skilled workers (including employees of multinational companies), are issued work permits which allow for permanent settlement.[40]

The fact that migrant workers are allowed to work in a country does not necessarily mean that members of their families automatically obtain the same permission. Although this is the position in a number of countries,[41] in some, such as Greece and Ireland, the granting of work permits to family members is dependent on the state of the national labour market.[42] In others, such as Germany, a spouse of a migrant worker must reside in the country for 4 years before acquiring a general work permit,[43] and children of migrants, who joined their

the work permit on renewal is dependent on the nationality of the migrant worker. For workers from Spanish-speaking countries permits are valid for 5 years, while other foreigners, such as Moroccans, have to renew their permit every year. See *Closed Borders, Stringent Attitudes*, n. 14 above, 174 (n. 190).

[37] Böhning and Werquin, n. 36 above (Belgium, Denmark (excluding other Nordic nationals to whom free movement of labour applies), Germany, Luxembourg, and Spain). See also 'Comparative Survey of the Hallmarks of Citizenship in Eleven EC Jurisdictions' in J. P. Gardner, (ed.), *Hallmarks of Citizenship* (London: The British Institute of International and Comparative Law, 1995) (hereinafter *Hallmarks of Citizenship Survey*) 71 (Germany) and Bauboek, n. 35 above, 161 (Austria). In Switzerland, restrictions may continue for up to 10 years: Soysal, n. 36 above.

[38] See Thomas, 'Summing-up and Points of Comparison', n. 7 above, 219, 220 (France and Germany). In the United Kingdom, work permits are only granted to individuals to perform work for specific employers: Statement of Changes in Immigration Rules 1994 (1993–1994 HC 395), para. 128. The time-limit on stay, and hence employment, is normally lifted after 4 years' residence on the application of the person concerned (*ibid.* para. 134), and the renewal of work permits before the expiry of this time-period is subject to the discretion of the Department of Employment (*ibid.* para. 132).

[39] Böhning and Werquin, n. 36 above, 10 (footnote); Commission Working Paper, n. 26 above, 54, 56.

[40] This liberal regime must be considered in the light of the fact that since the early 1970s, official immigration of non-Nordic workers into Sweden has virtually ceased. For example, only 200 work permits leading to permanent residence were granted in each of 1992 and 1993: *SOPEMI 1994*, 120. In contrast, between 1982 and 1992, an average of 12,500 temporary work permits were granted every year. These permits, however, are restricted to a specific time period, occupational branch, and employer: *SOPEMI 1994*, *ibid.*

[41] Commission Working Paper, n. 26 above, 77 (France, the Netherlands, Spain, United Kingdom); Thomas, 'Summing-up and Points of Comparison', n. 7 above, 224 (Belgium, the Netherlands, Sweden, the United Kingdom); Bauboek, n. 35 above, 161, 162 (Austria). For the position in the United Kingdom, see Statement of Changes in Immigration Rules 1994, n. 38 above, paras. 195, 198.

[42] Commission Working Paper, n. 26 above, 78.

[43] Act on Employment Promotion of 1969 and the Decree on Work Permits 1980, as amended by the Act on Immigration of 9 July 1990. See Weiss, n. 31 above, 117. The waiting-period in Germany may exceptionally be reduced to 2 years if there is a serious shortage of labour in the economic sector concerned: *ibid.* See also Commission Working Paper, n. 26 above, 79.

parents before the age of 18, are required to reside in Germany for 2 years before they are eligible for a general work permit.[44]

From this fleeting analysis, it is clear that access to employment for migrant workers and their families is strictly controlled and is essentially shaped by economic considerations. Only Sweden appears to make a firm commitment to ensure that some migrant workers and their families enjoy the right to free choice of employment relatively soon after entry into the country, although initial controls on their entry into the Swedish labour market are very rigorous.

(b) COE and EC standards

European standards protecting the right of access to employment for migrant workers and their families vary significantly. Amongst the COE instruments, the ECE and the ESC are the most elaborate on this question, although they also contain numerous qualifications. The ECHR does not deal with the matter, nor in effect does the EMW, largely for historical reasons which are outlined below. Within the EC regime, however, free access to employment in a member state for migrant workers who are nationals of another member state constitutes the *raison d'être* of the free movement of labour principle. It is in this area where differences between the EC regime and COE instruments concerned with the treatment of migrant workers and their families are most striking.

(i) COE standards

The principle of equal treatment between state party nationals under the ECE in respect of access to employment is found in Article 10. Equal treatment, however, may be restricted for cogent economic and social reasons, which, according to Section I(a)(2) of the Protocol to the ECE, are to be judged by 'national criteria'. This 'exceedingly important exception'[45] to the principle of equal treatment in Article 10 arguably undermines the very principle itself, since it effectively provides states parties with considerable discretion to decide who may take up employment in the country. Some of the subsequent provisions in the ECE impose further and more precise restrictions concerning access to employment. Article 13 allows a state party 'to reserve for its own nationals the exercise of public functions or of occupations connected with national security or defence or make the exercise of these occupations by aliens subject to special conditions'. It appears that this provision enables a state party to reserve most civil service and military posts for its own nationals.[46] Article 14 permits restrictions with

[44] Weiss, n. 31 above; Commission Working Paper, n. 26 above. In Italy, both the spouse and unmarried children of the legally resident foreign worker are given authorization to work after one year of residence: Law No. 943 of 30 Dec. 1986, Art. 4(2). See Isgro, n. 27 above, 696. In Denmark and Luxembourg, the waiting-period is 2 and 3 years respectively: Commission Working Paper, *ibid.* 78–9.

[45] A. H. J. Swart, 'The Legal Status of Aliens: Clauses in Council of Europe Instruments Relating to the Rights of Aliens' (1980) *Netherlands YBIL* 3, 23.

[46] Council of Europe, *Commentary on the European Convention on Establishment* (1980) 18, para. 57.

regard to other prescribed occupations,[47] and Article 15 ensures that contracting parties can require nationals from other states parties to possess the same or equivalent occupational qualifications as nationals before being permitted to take up employment.

Despite these restrictions on access to employment, two provisions attempt to make more significant inroads into state sovereignty. Article 11 prevents the imposition of additional restrictions upon migrant workers after they have taken up employment in the host country unless such restrictions are applied to nationals in similar circumstances; and Article 12(1) stipulates that any restrictions on access to employment are to be lifted after 5 years of employment, or after 10 years of residence in that country, or if permanent residence has been acquired.[48] By virtue of Section V(b) of the Protocol to the ECE, the provisions on access to employment are also applicable to the spouse and dependent children of nationals of any state party lawfully residing in the territory of another state party.

In summary, the plethora of restrictions on access to employment that the host country may impose upon nationals from other states parties makes the ECE an ineffective tool for advancing the rights of migrant workers and their families in this important area. According to one commentator, with the advent of the EC regime concerning free movement of workers between member states, Article 12 of the ECE remains the only provision of any practical importance.[49]

The provision dealing with access to employment in the ESC is Article 18, entitled The Right to Engage in a Gainful Occupation in the Territory of Other Contracting Parties:

> With a view to ensuring the effective exercise of the right to engage in a gainful occupation in the territory of any other Contracting Party, Contracting Parties undertake:
> 1) to apply existing regulations in a spirit of liberality;
> 2) to simplify existing formalities and to reduce or abolish chancery dues and other charges payable by foreign workers or their employers;
> 3) to liberalise, individually or collectively, regulations governing the employment of foreign workers; and recognize:

[47] These occupations must be listed at the time of signing the ECE (Art. 14(1)(a)). Otherwise, they may only be introduced later by states parties on account of 'imperative reasons of an economic or social character' (Art. 14(1)(b)).

[48] Art. 12(1) provides a state party with the discretion to opt for one or two of these conditions. Alternatively, by virtue of Art. 12(2), a state party may increase the period of employment in the first condition to 10 years and also declare that it reserves the right to control the change from a wage-earning to an independent occupation. See also *Commentary on the European Convention on Establishment*, n. 46 above, 18, para. 55. Ireland has not accepted the second and third conditions in Art. 12(1) and Sweden has not recognized the first two conditions, while Norway has only accepted the second condition in that provision. On the other hand, Luxembourg has exercised the additional options provided in Art. 12(2). See Council of Europe, Legal Affairs, *Third Periodical Report by the Standing Committee on the European Convention on Establishment (Individuals)* (Strasbourg: Council of Europe, 1977) 110–12 (App. III).

[49] Swart, n. 45 above, 25. As observed in Ch. 5, 11 of the states that have ratified the ECE are also members of the EC.

4) the right of their nationals to leave the country to engage in a gainful occupation in the territories of the other Contracting Parties.

The Committee of Independent Experts has recognized that Article 18 is 'somewhat imprecise'.[50] It is therefore not surprising that this provision has been the subject of much debate during the supervision of state reports, both in the Committee of Independent Experts and the politically-oriented Governmental Committee. Indeed, these bodies have at times taken diametrically opposing views with regard to its interpretation.

The Appendix to the ESC underlines that Article 18 is 'not concerned with the question of entry into the territories of the Contracting parties'.[51] Furthermore, as with the remainder of the ESC, it applies only to migrant workers who are nationals of other states parties. The Committee of Independent Experts has described Article 18 as a 'dynamic' provision, meaning that states are under an obligation to *progressively* improve the situation of migrant workers from other contracting parties with regard to access to employment.[52] Although this interpretation is certainly true of Articles 18(2) and (3), Article 18(1) appears to require the application of 'existing regulations in a spirit of liberality' straight away.[53] Article 18(1) is concerned with administrative practice rather than law and merely requires that discretion is exercised by state authorities in the application of regulations, even if these regulations are restrictive in content.[54] Article 18(2) calls for a procedural relaxation of the formalities governing the employment of foreign workers, such as the fees required for work permits, whereas Article 18(3) is concerned with the relaxation of the substantive rules, such as the grounds upon which work permits are issued, or a change in employment is permitted, and the restrictions imposed in each case.[55] Consequently, Article 18(3) may be considered as being the most important clause to migrant workers from other contracting parties.

The Committee of Independent Experts has asserted that the dynamism inherent in Article 18 requires states parties to show improvements with every report unless the previous situation was already developed to such an extent that no new progress is necessary, but the Committee also recognizes that such improvements may not always be possible in difficult economic times.[56] Nonetheless, a

[50] *Conclusions III*, 83, cited in *Case Law on the European Social Charter*, n. 19 above, 139.

[51] This has also been stressed on a number of occasions by the Committee of Independent Experts and the Governmental Committee: *Conclusions II*, 60, *Conclusions III*, 83 and *Third Report*, 8, cited in *Case Law on the European Social Charter*, n. 19 above, 137, 143, 140 respectively. However, the Committee of Independent Experts has also observed that the aim of Art. 18 would be undermined if the benefits of liberalization in the provision were restricted to those nationals of states parties already in the territory of another state party: *Conclusions XIII-2* (1995) 372.

[52] *Conclusions II*, 59, cited by Harris, n. 20 above, 148.

[53] Harris, *ibid.*

[54] *Conclusions III*, 86, cited by Harris, *ibid.*

[55] Harris, *ibid.* 153.

[56] *Conclusions II*, 60, cited in *Case Law on the European Social Charter*, n. 19 above, 138 and *Conclusions IV*, 108–9, cited by Swart, n. 45 above, 25. See also the position of the Governmental Committee: *Report 10(II)*, 28–9, cited in Council of Europe, *Case Law on the European Social Charter—Supplement No. 3* (1993) 138.

consistent failure to simplify or liberalize measures as well as the tightening of restrictions may lead to the adoption of negative conclusions by the Committee.[57] Although there appears to be no obligation under Article 18 to realize complete equality between nationals and migrant workers with respect to access to employment, the Committee of Independent Experts has noted that the 'letter and spirit of Article 18 mean that the situation of nationals of States bound by the Charter should gradually become *as far as possible* like that of nationals'.[58] The Governmental Committee, however, considers the dynamism in Article 18 to be limited to the extent that the obligations found in this provision occupy the middle ground in a hierarchy of protection, with EC nationals in the most protected position under the EC regime and non-EC nationals as well as those from countries that are not parties to the ESC in the least protected position.[59] In short, therefore, free movement of workers between states parties is not an ultimate objective of the ESC.[60]

[57] During the 13th cycle of supervision, the Committee adopted a negative conclusion in respect of Greece for failing to take steps to simplify procedures under Art. 18(2) for nationals of ESC states parties (who are not EC or EEA nationals) regarding access to the labour market: *Conclusions XIII-2*, n. 51 above, 174–5. This observation led to Recommendation No. R ChS (95) 11, adopted by the Committee of Ministers on 14 Dec. 1995, requesting the Greek Government to take account of the negative conclusion in respect of Art. 18(2). See Council of Europe, *Human Rights Information Sheet No. 37* (1996) 88–9. See also the negative conclusions issued by the Committee of Independent Experts in respect of the Icelandic, United Kingdom, German, Irish, and Danish reports. See respectively: Council of Europe, Committee of Independent Experts of the European Social Charter, *Conclusions XII-1 (1988–89)* (Strasbourg: Council of Europe, 1992) 223–4 (Arts. 18(2) and (3)); Council of Europe, Committee of Independent Experts of the European Social Charter, *Conclusions X-1 (1984–85)* (Strasbourg: Council of Europe, 1987) 142 (Art. 18(3)); *Conclusions XII-2 (1989–90)* (1993) 212 and *Conclusions XIII-2*, n. 51 above, 372 (Art. 18(2)); Council of Europe, Committee of Independent Experts of the European Social Charter, *Conclusions XIII-1* (Strasbourg: Council of Europe Press, 1994) 202 (Art. 18(2)), 203 (Art. 18(3)) and *Conclusions XIII-2*, *ibid.* 180; and *Conclusions XIII-2*, *ibid.* 178–9. Adopting its new role under the Protocol Amending the ESC, the Governmental Committee decided to address a warning to Iceland with a view to making a future recommendation to the Committee of Ministers in respect of that country's failure to comply with Arts. 18(2) and (3): Governmental Committee, *12th Report (I) (1988–89)* (1993) 45, para. 171. This action was not followed up during the 13th cycle of supervision due to assurances by the Icelandic delegate that a law would be introduced to take account of the criticisms made by the Committee of Independent Experts: *13th Report (I)* (1995) 148–9, para. 823 and 151, para. 841. However, the Governmental Committee, *ibid.* 154, para. 863, decided to issue a warning to the United Kingdom for repeated lack of information regarding its compliance with Art. 18(3).

[58] *Conclusions II*, 60, cited in *Case Law on the European Social Charter*, n. 19 above, 138 (emphasis added).

[59] *Fifth Report*, 15, cited in *Case Law on the European Social Charter*, *ibid.* 142; *Eighth Report*, 17, cited in Council of Europe, *Case Law on the European Social Charter: Supplement* (Strasbourg: Council of Europe, 1986) 46 and *Ninth Report (II)*, 25, cited in *Case Law on the European Social Charter—Supplement No. 2* (1987) 28. The Committee of Independent Experts has also partly adopted this view when it emphasized that 'the position of workers nationals of other countries bound by the Charter but not members of the European Communities should be given a more advantageous treatment than nationals of a country not a member of the Communities and not bound by the Charter': *Conclusions VIII*, 198, cited in *Case Law on the European Social Charter: Supplement*, *ibid.*

[60] *Report 11(I)*, 100, cited in *Case Law on the European Social Charter—Supplement No. 3*, n. 56 above, 139.

Article 18 has been interpreted by the Committee of Independent Experts in the light of paragraph 18 of the declaratory Part I of the ESC, which provides that the right of nationals of one state party to engage in any gainful occupation in the territory of another state party on an equal footing with its nationals is subject to 'restrictions based on cogent economic or social reasons'.[61] The Committee recognizes that such restrictions may be particularly appropriate in the event of an economic recession, although special care should also be exercised to protect migrant workers at such a time, because they are affected more than others during a downturn in the economy.[62] Disagreement exists between the Committee of Independent Experts and the Governmental Committee as to who decides when there are 'cogent economic or social reasons' justifying restrictions on the employment of foreign workers. The latter body considers that only the state authorities may determine this matter best,[63] whereas the former has questioned the measures taken by a number of states parties.[64] Harris contends that the correct approach should be to allow for a 'margin of appreciation' to each state party concerning the imposition of restrictions for cogent economic and social reasons, but that the final decision should be taken by the supervisory organs.[65]

The Committee of Independent Experts has ruled that a number of common restrictions imposed by states parties with regard to access to employment are not consistent with the obligation to show improvements when reporting under Article 18(3) of the ESC. Examples of such measures are: the limitation of work permits to certain specified employers, occupations and regions, including restrictions on the freedom of migrant workers to change employers in the first year of employment;[66] the requirement that a work permit is obtained before entering the territory of a state party;[67] and not permitting applications for a vacancy

[61] *Conclusions II*, 60, cited in *Case Law on the European Social Charter*, n. 19 above, 137.

[62] *Conclusions IV*, 107, cited in *Case Law on the European Social Charter*, *ibid.* 139. Furthermore, any restrictions must not be applied in a discriminatory way favouring one state party's nationals or nationals from a non-state party over those from another state party. However, if the country of employment and the country of which the migrant worker is the national are both members of the EC, the migrant worker is entitled to superior treatment by virtue of that regime: *Conclusions III*, 85, 86, and *Conclusions IV*, 109, 111, cited by Harris, n. 20 above, 149.

[63] *Third Report*, 8, cited in *Case Law on the European Social Charter*, n. 19 above, 141.

[64] For example, the Committee of Independent Experts questioned measures taken by Denmark halting the issue of work permits on economic grounds to migrants who were not nationals of EC or Nordic countries. Since these measures, in practice, only adversely affected the nationals of Austria and Cyprus, restrictive provisions applicable to what was effectively a very small group of migrants were hard to justify: *Conclusions VI*, 108, cited in *Case Law on the European Social Charter*, n. 19 above, 145. See also Harris, n. 20 above, 151.

[65] Harris, *ibid.* 151. Consequently, the supervisory organs should only find against a state party if it is *clear* that the restrictions in question cannot be justified on economic and social grounds: *ibid.*

[66] *Conclusions II*, 60, *Conclusions III*, 83 and 84–5, cited in *Case Law on the European Social Charter*, n. 19 above, 137, 139 and 144–5 respectively. The Committee added, however, that economic and social reasons might justify confining migrant workers to specific geographic regions or occupational sectors, but not to a specific employer: *Conclusions II*, *ibid.* This view was restated more recently in *Conclusions XIII-2*, n. 51 above, 368 in consideration of the Belgian report.

[67] *Conclusions III*, 83 and *Conclusions VI*, 114, cited in *Case Law on the European Social Charter*, n. 19 above, 139 and 147 respectively.

from aliens if there is a national applicant.[68] Furthermore, such restrictions should also be relaxed or abolished the longer a migrant worker is resident in a country.[69] The critical approach to these restrictions taken by the Committee of Independent Experts has been diluted somewhat by the Governmental Committee, which views them in a more positive light. It has contended, for example, that the requirement that a work permit is obtained before entry into a country actually provides migrant workers and their families with better social protection by prohibiting employers from hiring those who have entered the country illegally or those who are not in possession of a work permit.[70]

There are no provisions in the EMW affording migrant workers a right of access to employment. Indeed, some clauses in the EMW imply that state sovereignty remains completely intact in this area. A state party is only under a duty in Article 8(1) to issue migrant workers with work permits or to renew them after they have been permitted to enter that country's territory to take up employment there.[71] Article 5 requires migrant workers to possess an employment contract or a definite offer of employment before departure to the receiving country, thus excluding from protection those individuals migrating to seek employment.[72] This provision is buttressed by Article 4(1) which affords migrant workers 'the right to admission to the territory of a Contracting Party in order to take up paid employment', but only after 'being authorised to do so and obtaining the necessary papers'.[73] Finally, by virtue of Articles 25 and 27(2), states parties are required respectively to facilitate the re-employment of migrant workers who lose their jobs for reasons beyond their control, such as redundancy or prolonged illness, and to provide them with the same access as nationals to employment services. These duties, however, include no obligation to guarantee access to

[68] *Conclusions V*, 117 and *Conclusions VI*, 110, cited by Harris, n. 20 above, 154.

[69] *Conclusions II*, 60, cited by Harris, *ibid.*

[70] *Third Report*, 9, cited in *Case Law on the European Social Charter*, n. 19 above, 141. Similarly, measures restricting migrant workers to a particular sector or employer for a certain period of time, according to the Governmental Committee, are primarily designed to protect workers: *ibid.*

[71] See also cf. K. Oellers-Frahm, 'The Contribution of the Council of Europe to the Legal Position of Aliens' (1987) 1749. Some protection is afforded to the migrant worker in Art. 8(2) which stipulates that 'a work permit issued for the first time may not as a rule bind the worker to the same employer or the same locality for a period longer than one year'. As for the obligation to renew a work permit, Art. 9(3) provides that 'this should as a general rule be for a period of at least one year', although with the qualification: 'in so far as the current state and development of the employment situation permits'. Therefore, renewals for a shorter period are not ruled out. This has been justified on the rather tenuous premise that it might not be in the migrant worker's interest 'if the alternative were between renewing [the work permit] for at least one year or not renewing it at all': *Explanatory Report on the EMW* (1978) 15, para. 37.

[72] See also R. Plender, *International Migration Law* (1988) 254.

[73] Moreover, this 'right' to admission 'concerns only the first admission to the territory of the Contracting Parties and hence does not prejudge each Party's right under its own legislation to refuse readmission to a worker who, having left its territory, no longer satisfies the conditions for entitlement to employment and residence': *Explanatory Report on the EMW*, n. 71 above, 12, para. 25. By virtue of Art. 4(2), this right is also 'subject to such limitations as are prescribed by legislation and are necessary for the protection of national security, public order, public health or morals'.

employment for migrant workers on an equal basis with nationals.[74] Clearly, therefore, the EMW stands some way behind the ESC in this respect. Without doubt, the historical context of each instrument constitutes one of the reasons for this striking disparity. The ESC was adopted at a time when the influx of migrant workers into Western Europe was not causing as much concern as at the time of the adoption of the EMW in 1978, only a few years after the energy crisis of 1973–4. The willingness to afford migrants freer access to employment on a par with nationals was greater when their employment was still in demand than when the emphasis was upon controlling labour migration more strictly and upon seeking ways to induce migrant workers to return home.[75]

Despite the contribution of the ESC in Article 18 to loosening the knots of state sovereignty in the sensitive area of access to employment for migrant workers and their families and its superiority to the EMW in this regard, it still lags far behind the EC free movement of persons regime, which cannot be realized fully without *completely* untying these knots. This secondary status of Article 18 is also becoming increasingly marked as more ESC states parties (15 out of 20) join the EC.[76] Article 18, therefore, retains most relevance in relations between EC and non-EC countries. It should be noted, however, that some states parties have not accepted Article 18, either in whole or in part. Cyprus and Norway, which are not EC member states, have rejected Article 18 *in toto*; Malta, another non-EC member, has only accepted Article 18(4); and one EC member state, Austria, has not accepted Article 18(3).

(ii) EC standards

Under Articles 48(2) and 48(3)(a) EC respectively, free movement of workers entails 'the abolition of any discrimination based on nationality between workers of the Member States as regards employment' and the right to 'accept offers of employment actually made'. More detailed provisions concerning access to employment are found in Articles 1 to 6 of Regulation 1612/68/EEC. The clarity of Article 1 stands out in contrast to the provisions and numerous qualifications concerning this subject in the ECE and the rather ambiguous wording of Article 18 of the ESC:

1. Any national of a Member State, shall, irrespective of the place of residence, have the right to take up an activity as an employed person, and to pursue such activity, within the territory of another Member State in accordance with the provisions laid down by law, regulation or administrative action governing the employment of nationals of that State.
2. He shall, in particular, have the right to take up available employment in the territory of another Member State *with the same priority* as nationals of that State.[77]

[74] *Ibid.* 25, para. 90, and 26, para. 95 respectively.

[75] See also Swart, n. 45 above, 28 and Oellers-Frahm, n. 71 above, 1749.

[76] See D. Gomien, D. Harris, and L. Zwaak, *Law and Practice of the European Convention on Human Rights and the European Social Charter* (1996) 404.

[77] Emphasis added.

Furthermore, some of the provisions following Article 1 have as their objective the abolition of many of the measures which states normally make use of to protect their nationals with respect to access to employment, including the imposition of quotas on the employment of foreigners 'in any undertaking, branch of activity or region'.[78] Equal treatment between workers of EC member states in respect of assistance in seeking employment is guaranteed by Article 5 of the Regulation.[79] EC citizens are also permitted to enter another member country to seek employment without the need to apply for a residence permit.[80] The principle of equal access to employment between nationals and migrants from other member states under the EC regime also extends to those EC nationals wishing to establish themselves or to provide services in another member state.[81]

Although the thrust of EC law in this area is to facilitate free movement of workers, restrictions on access to employment for migrant workers from other member states are permissible in certain defined circumstances. The main restrictions concern employment in the public service,[82] those justified on the grounds of public policy, public security or public health[83] and if linguistic knowledge is required 'by reason of the nature of the post to be filled'.[84]

Article 11 of Regulation 1612/68/EEC extends the right of equal access to employment with nationals throughout the territory of the host country to the worker's spouse and children under 21 years of age or to his or her dependent children, regardless of their nationality.[85] Non-EC nationals may also acquire, subject to certain conditions, limited access to employment rights as employees

[78] Arts. 3 and 4(1) respectively.

[79] Moreover, Part II of Reg. 1612/68/EEC, (as amended by Council Reg. 2434/92/EEC of 27 July 1992, OJ 1992, L 245/1), establishes a special mechanism for clearing vacancies and applications for employment.

[80] Case C-292/89, *R v. Immigration Appeal Tribunal, ex parte Antonissen* [1991] ECR I-745, [1991] 2 CMLR 373.

[81] See Arts. 52–8 EC and Arts. 59–66 EC. See respectively Case 2/74, *Reyners v. Belgium* [1974] ECR 631, [1974] 2 CMLR 305 and Case 33/74, *Van Binsbergen v. Bestuur van de Bedrijfsverniging voor de Metaalnijverheid* [1974] ECR 1299, [1975] 1 CMLR 298, holding that the EC Treaty provisions concerned with the right of establishment and the freedom to provide services are directly applicable in national law.

[82] Art. 48(4) EC. See the section below on political rights.

[83] Art. 48(3) EC. See the section below on protection against expulsion.

[84] Reg. 1612/68/EEC, Art. 3(1). The Court of Justice has stated that this exception does not *prima facie* apply if knowledge of the language is not required to perform the work in question: Case C-379/87, *Groener v. Minister for Education* [1989] ECR 3967, [1990] 1 CMLR 401. In *Groener*, however, the Court held that the requirement of knowledge of Irish for the post of commercial art teacher was justified even though English was the normal language of instruction. This was because the requirement was consistent with the legitimate state policy of promoting the Irish language.

[85] Non-EC family members may take up any employment in the member state open to the worker: Case 131/85, *Gül v. Regierungspräsident Düsseldorf* [1986] ECR 1573, [1987] 1 CMLR 501. Furthermore, members of the worker's family may take up employment and reside in a part of the country other than the place of residence of the worker: Case 267/83, *Diatta v. Land Berlin* [1985] ECR 567, [1986] 2 CMLR 164. It is not clear, however, at what point dependent children, who take up their right to work under Art. 11, cease to be dependent on the EC worker. If they become no longer dependent, they would arguably lose their right to work and residence if they are non-EC nationals. See also cf. A. Evans, 'Third Country Nationals and the Treaty on European Union' (1994) 5 EJIL 199, 205 (n. 34).

of EC nationals providing services in another EC member state.[86] They may also obtain independent and fuller access to employment rights as beneficiaries of certain provisions of Cooperation or Association agreements or decisions taken thereunder.

The EC Association Agreement with Turkey and the Additional Protocol contain provisions which aim to progressively realize free movement of labour between Turkey and EC member states.[87] Because of their 'programmatic' character, these provisions have been held not to be directly applicable in national laws.[88] However, the Council of Association set up under the Agreement has issued a number of decisions in this area which the Court of Justice has found to confer direct effect. Article 6(1) of Decision 1/80 of 19 September 1980 on the development of the Association enables Turkish migrant workers lawfully employed in the host country to renew their work permit with the same employer after one year of legal employment if the job is still available. After 3 years of legal employment, such workers may accept work in the same occupation from another employer provided that priority is given to EC workers. Completion of 4 years of legal employment gives rise to the right to take up freely any paid employment in the country concerned. Article 7 of the Decision is concerned with access to employment for the family members authorized to join

[86] Case C-113/89, *Rush Portuguesa Lda* v. *Office National d'Immigration* [1990] ECR I-1417, [1991] 2 CMLR 818; Case C-43/93, *Vander Elst* v. *Office des Migrations Internationales (OMI)* [1994] ECR-I 3803. In *Vander Elst*, a demolition business, operated by a Belgian national and providing services in France, was not required to obtain work permits, and to pay the resulting fee, for Moroccan nationals lawfully in its employment. The Court of Justice stated that the workers must be lawfully employed by the service provider, that their presence in the country where the services are being provided has to be lawful, and that their stay must be temporary to the extent that they do not seek access to the labour market of that country. In *Vander Elst*, the period of employment was for one month only and in *Rush Portuguesa* it was reputedly 6 months, although this is not ascertainable from the text of the judgment. It is not clear when such employment ceases to be temporary. This discussion is partly drawn from a presentation by N. Blake QC on 'European Free Movement Rights and Third Country Nationals: Articles 48, 52 and 59 EC' at a Conference on Practical Problems of UK Implementation of European Union Immigration Law, organized by ILPA, London, 25 Nov. 1994. See also the annotation by S. Peers (1995) 20 *EL Rev*. 303. By analogy with this case law, it might also be argued that the right of EC nationals to freedom of establishment (Arts. 52–8 EC) would be hindered if they were not permitted to transfer third country nationals in their employment to the member state of establishment or to hire non-EC nationals legally resident in another member state. See Peers, n. 25 above, 39, 41–2, who argues that such a right should exist in principle, but if rejected by the Court of Justice, should at least include a right to hire third country nationals in 'managerial or supervisory' posts or those who constitute 'key personnel' in accordance with Art. 54(3)(f) EC.

[87] Art. 12 of the Agreement reads: 'The Contracting Parties agree to be guided by Articles 48, 49 and 50 of the Treaty establishing the Community for the purpose of progressively securing freedom of movement for workers between them'. Art. 36 of the Additional Protocol provides: 'Freedom of movement for workers between Member States of the Community and Turkey shall be secured by progressive stages in accordance with the principles set out in Article 12 of the Agreement of Association between the end of the twelfth and the twenty-second year after the entry into force of that agreement. The Council of Association shall decide on the rules necessary to that end'.

[88] Case 12/86, *Demirel* v. *Stadt Schwäbisch Gmünd* [1987] ECR 3719, [1989] 1 CMLR 421, para. 23.

the Turkish worker in the host member state. Such family members are entitled to respond to any offer of employment after 3 years of legal residence in a member state, subject to the priority to be given to EC workers, and acquire free access to employment after 5 years of legal residence. Article 7 also accords the right of free access to any paid employment to children of Turkish migrant workers who have completed a vocational training course in the country, provided that one parent has been legally employed there for at least 3 years. Article 6(1) and the second part of Article 7 have been successfully invoked before the Court of Justice.[89] The Court has also boldly asserted that the right to the renewal of a work permit necessarily implies a right to a concurrent residence permit if this is required in the country of employment.[90]

The Europe Association Agreements and the Cooperation Agreements are generally silent on the question of access to employment for migrant workers, although it is possible that clauses, discussed in the previous section, guaranteeing 'freedom from any discrimination based on nationality as regards working conditions and remuneration [and dismissal]', might well give rise to a liberal interpretation by the Court in order to ensure that lawfully employed migrants have an automatic right to renew their work and residence permits.[91] As for the

[89] See respectively Case C-237/91, *Kus* v. *Landeshauptstadt Wiesbaden* [1993] 2 CMLR 887 and Case C-355/93, *Eroglu* v. *Land Baden-Württemberg* [1994] ECR I-5113. See also the annotations by N. Burrows (1994) 19 *EL Rev.* 305 and M. Zuleeg (1996) 33 *CML Rev.* 93.

[90] Case C-192/89, *S. Z. Sevince* v. *Staatssecretaris van Justitie* [1990] ECR 3461, [1992] 2 CMLR 57, para. 29; *Kus*, *ibid.* paras. 29–30 and para. 36; *Eroglu*, n. 89 above, paras. 78–9. Johnson and O'Keeffe comment as follows with reference to the *Kus* decision: 'A denial of residence to Turkish nationals meeting the conditions of employment stipulated in Article 6 of the decision would have undermined the *effet utile* of that provision. It is the natural corollary and condition *sine qua non* of the right to work. Even so, the clear ruling of the Court in *Kus* sent shock waves throughout the Community. This was a significant interpretation of the Agreement and of Decisions made under it. Inevitably, it must bring into question the scope of application of the equal treatment principle to Turkish workers living and working in the Community': E. Johnson and D. O'Keeffe, 'From Discrimination to Obstacles to Free Movement: Recent Developments concerning the Free Movement of Workers 1989–1994' (1994) 31 *CML Rev.* 1313, 1342–3. For a negative reaction to this case law, see K. Hailbronner, 'Third Country Nationals and EC Law' (1995) 190 and K. Hailbronner and J. Polakiewicz, 'Non-EC Nationals in the European Community: The Need for a Coordinated Approach' (1992) 3 *Duke J. Int'l & Comp. L.* 49, 56–7, with reference to the *Sevince* judgment.

[91] Indeed, such an approach has been suggested by the Supreme Court of Gibraltar with regard to Moroccan migrant workers in the territory. See *R* v. *Director of Labour and Social Security, ex parte Amini Mohamed* [1992] 3 CMLR 481, para. 21 (per Alcantara J.). This argument has also been forcefully articulated by Guild, writing on the Mahgreb Cooperation Agreements: 'Mahgreb workers, having no free movement rights must have obtained lawful access to the territory and labour market before the protection [under the non-discrimination provision] comes into effect. But once this happens, if they have less security in the labour market than "own nationals" or EC nationals, then discrimination in working conditions must result. For example, uncertainty of residence will be a disincentive to employers considering the promotion of workers. It is also a disincentive for the workers to upgrade their skills and qualifications which may be of use to them only in their country of residence. Discrimination in promotion and training resulting from the uncertain position of the workers in the labour force must inevitably be reflected in their wages. Workers whose position is insecure are likely to remain in the lowest paid and least skilled positions as these are the easiest to fill in the event that the worker is expelled. Similarly, uncertainty in respect of work and residence rights could give rise to discrimination in social security benefits, where the workers may be unable

family members of migrant workers, there is provision under the Europe Association agreements with central and eastern European countries and the Baltic States for the legally resident spouse and children to acquire full access to the labour market in the workers' member state of employment.[92]

Access to employment for non-EC nationals is also governed by the Third Pillar of the TEU, which identifies this area, in Article K.1(3)(b), as an aspect of policy regarding nationals of third countries which member states are to consider as a matter of 'common interest'. As discussed in Chapter 6, the Commission has urged member states to give priority to non-EC nationals who are permanently and lawfully resident in another member state when job vacancies cannot be filled by EC nationals or non-EC nationals lawfully resident in the member state concerned, with a view to progressively realizing full freedom of movement rights for all non-EC nationals lawfully residing in the EC.[93] For the time being, however, this proposal omits those non-EC nationals who are not permanently resident in an EC member state and, by definition, excludes those who wish to be admitted for the purpose of employment. Harsher restrictions are also being imposed on non-EC nationals by way of coordinated action at the EC level in line with some of those applied by individual countries of employment. On 20 June 1994, the Council adopted a Resolution on limitations on admission of third-country nationals to the member states for employment.[94] The Resolution urges member states to implement a number of restrictive measures by 1 January 1996. Its governing principle is that member states are to 'refuse entry to their territories of third-country nationals for the purpose of employment'. Requests

to complete the period of time necessary to accrue the benefit': E. Guild, 'Protecting Migrants' Rights and Community Law: the Cooperation Agreements with Algeria, Morocco and Tunisia' (1993) 7 INLP 15, 16. The argument in favour of an automatic right to renewal of work and residence permits would clearly not succeed if the clause concerning equal work and employment conditions found in the draft Partnership and Cooperation Agreements with Russia and the former Soviet republics were relied upon because of the existence of an explicit provision denying a right of access to the labour market and continued residence in an EC member state (for example, Art. 50 of the Draft Agreement with Russia). Similarly, a joint declaration in the draft revised Euro-Mediterranean Associations Agreements with Morocco and Tunisia asserts that the part of draft Art. 64(1) which relates to redundancy cannot be invoked to obtain renewal of a residence permit and also proclaims, in more general terms, that 'the granting, renewal or refusal of a residence permit shall be governed by the legislation of each Member State and the bilateral agreements and conventions in force between [Morocco and Tunisia] and the Member State'. See also Peers, n. 25 above, 19, 28.

[92] For example, see Art. 37(1), second indent, of the Europe Agreement with Poland and Art. 36(1), second indent, of the draft Europe Agreement with Estonia. Peers, *ibid.* 26, argues that this right, in accordance with the *Kus* (n. 89 above) and *Sevince* (n. 90 above) decisions should give the spouse and children of the migrant worker a right of continued residence for as long as the worker is entitled to reside in the member state concerned.

[93] For example, see *European Social Policy—A Way Forward for the Union: A White Paper* (1994) 29–30, paras. 21–2 and *Immigration and Asylum Policies* (1994) 34, para. 129.

[94] Doc. EN 7760/94. For an outline of this resolution, see *EU Bulletin* 6-1994, point 1.4.5. See also the Resolution relating to the limitations on the admission of third-country nationals to the territory of the member states for the purpose of pursuing activities as self-employed persons (Doc. 11219/94), adopted by the Justice and Home Affairs Council on 30 Nov. 1994. See *EU Bulletin* 11-1994, point 1.4.7.

for admission will only be considered if the positions in question cannot be filled by national or EC workers or by non-EC workers who are lawfully resident on a permanent basis in the member state concerned. Non-EC nationals may also be admitted for the purpose of employment if the work is of a specialist nature and if they hold an offer from the service provider, or if there is a temporary labour shortage which significantly affects the operation of the undertaking. Moreover, non-EC nationals may enter as seasonal workers for a maximum of 6 months in any 12-month period, and as trainees or frontier workers.[95] Authorization for employment must be applied for prior to entry into the country and will normally be restricted, in the first instance, to employment in a specific job with a specified employer.

8.2 TRADE UNION RIGHTS

Background

Trade union rights straddle the divide between economic and social rights and civil rights. A broad definition of trade union rights, as outlined in Chapter 3, encompasses the right to form and join trade unions and works councils, to enjoy the benefits of collective bargaining, and to participate in such organizations by voting in their elections and by being eligible to stand as candidates for office.

The uncontrolled *entry* of foreign workers into the European countries of employment was viewed in a negative light by many national trade unions and their members because the option of cheap migrant labour enabled employers to keep wage increases to a minimum.[96] Nonetheless, from the beginning of post-war guest worker programmes in Western Europe, trade unions insisted, with a view to protecting the wages and working conditions of national workers, that migrant workers be afforded the same work-related rights. It was also in the interest of unions to organize and integrate migrant workers, once they were already employed in the host country, into trade union structures, and to articulate their concerns.[97]

[95] In general, students, trainees, and seasonal workers will not be permitted to extend their period of stay. Other non-EC nationals will be allowed to extend their stay, but, on the first renewal at least, they will have to satisfy the original conditions admitting them to employment. The Resolution also urges member states 'to examine the desirability of issuing a permanent residence permit to third country nationals who have had their restrictions on their employment lifted'. In this regard, see also Council Resolution of 4 March 1996 on the status of third-country nationals residing on a long-term basis in the territory of the member states, OJ 1996, C 80/2, which is discussed below in the section on residence rights.

[96] Vranken also notes that the availability of immigrant workers as cheap labour has frequently been used to weaken the position of trade unions in collective bargaining and industrial conflicts. Moreover, 'migrant workers often lack trade-union experience because they come from countries with a low level of industrialisation and no trade-union tradition': J. Vranken, 'Industrial Rights' in Z. Layton-Henry, (ed.), *The Political Rights of Migrant Workers in Western Europe* (London: SAGE, 1990) 47, 55.

[97] Cf. Vranken, *ibid.* 54, 55; cf. Martin and Miller, n. 3 above, 326; cf. J. Power, *Western Europe's Migrant Workers* (1978) 30.

Trade unions have usually encouraged migrant workers to join, and in some instances have made membership a requirement before employment migration can take place.[98] Most European countries allow migrant workers to establish their own unions,[99] thus recognizing the right to freedom of association which is discussed in the section on political rights below. By and large, however, immigrant workers have joined established unions and have not tried to found their own organizations.[100] Even though migrant workers may join the trade unions of their choice on an equal footing with nationals, union membership among migrants remains proportionately lower, or at best comparable, to that among domestic workers.[101] The reasons for such discrepancies depend to some extent on the industry and enterprise where foreign workers are usually found. Unionization is generally lower in the traditional low-paid industrial sectors, certain service industries, and small and medium-sized undertakings which tend to employ more foreign workers.[102] Migrant workers employed on a short-term basis are also difficult to unionize.[103]

Collective bargaining agreements which focus on issues such as low wages or job classification may have a beneficial impact on the working conditions of migrants, although the inclusion of more specific demands on behalf of migrant workers would be a step forward in realizing some of their employment and related rights.[104]

As noted in Chapter 3, trade unions can exercise considerable influence over the integration of migrant workers and their families into the host society. Examples of specific trade union 'integrative' measures include special welfare sections for migrants, the publication of newspapers in their languages, and various activities advocating improvements in the rights of migrant workers such as language instruction during working hours, longer vacations for those workers

[98] T. Hammar, 'Immigrant Policy' in *European Immigration Policy: A Comparative Study*, n. 2 above, 266. [99] See Kühner, n. 26 above, 1978; Hoogenboom, n. 28 above, 369–74.

[100] Hammar, 'Immigrant Policy', n. 98 above, 266.

[101] Note, 'Migrant Workers and Trade Unions' (Oct. 1982) EIRR 20, citing the report prepared for the Council of Europe by G. Minet in Dec. 1981 on Participation by Migrants in Trade Unions, Trade Union Activities and in the Life of Firms. Figures for 1979 indicated that only 50% of foreign workers were unionized in Belgium in comparison with 80% for all workers. *Ibid.* In France, the unionization rate is much lower generally and only about 15% of foreign workers are unionized in comparison with 20% for nationals. See Vranken, n. 96 above, 62. In Germany and Sweden, however, migrant workers are unionized to approximately the same degree as nationals: T. Hammar and Y. G. Lithman, 'The Integration of Migrants: Experiences, Concepts and Policies' in OECD, *The Future of Migration* (Paris: OECD, 1987) 234, 250.

[102] See respectively Vranken, n. 96 above, 60 and 'Migrant Workers and Trade Unions', n. 101 above, 20. The extent to which the union can influence politics and society and the high regard in which it is held is also important and may well determine the rate of unionization, not just in respect of migrant workers but national workers as well. Cf. Vranken *ibid.* 71.

[103] D. G. Papademetriou, 'International Migration in North America and Western Europe: Trends and Consequences' (1988) 368.

[104] Cf. 'Migrant Workers and Trade Unions', n. 101 above, 21. An example of the latter approach is the position taken by the Dutch CNV (Christian National) union confederation which already bargains on a number of migrant worker-related issues, such as leave for Muslim holidays, adjustment of working hours for Muslim Friday afternoon prayers, and the payment of travel expenses to workers visiting families in the home country: *ibid.*

visiting families in their home country, and strong public stands against discrimination and racism.[105] Indeed, such broad activities undertaken by trade unions on behalf of migrant workers and their families underline their important role in protecting all migrants' rights and not merely those of workers *per se*:

> It is because of [the] identification of 'migrants' with 'migrant workers' that trade unions have been concerned with all migrants and their problems. They were often the first 'welfare agency' for migrants and their first 'political' organisation, defending their basic social and economic rights. Even now that immigration has virtually stopped and the structure of the migrant population is gradually changing, trade unions are still seen by large groups of immigrants as the main defenders of their interests.[106]

COE and EC standards

(a) COE standards

By and large, COE texts protect the right of migrant workers to form and join trade unions and to enjoy the benefits of collective bargaining. Article 11(1) of the ECHR expressly refers to this right within the broader ambit of the right to freedom of peaceful assembly and freedom of association with others, although paragraph 2 of this provision permits restrictions that are prescribed by law and are necessary in a democratic society in the interests of, *inter alia*, national security or public safety and for the prevention of disorder or crime. Article 11 is equally applicable to aliens as well as nationals, but states parties may, by virtue of Article 16 (discussed in the section on political rights below), restrict its operation with respect to aliens if their activities are adjudged to be 'political'.

Article 19(4)(b) of the ESC guarantees equal treatment between nationals and migrant workers from other states parties in respect of, *inter alia*, 'membership of trade unions and enjoyment of the benefits of collective bargaining'. Although there is no explicit reference to a right to 'form' trade unions, such

[105] Power, n. 97 above, 30, referring to some early trade union activities on behalf of migrant workers in France and Germany. For activities in the anti-discrimination field, see *Closed Borders, Stringent Attitudes*, n. 14 above, 81, regarding the work of unions in Denmark and the Netherlands. Other recent specific 'integrative' trade union activities in European countries regarding the promotion of migrant workers' rights include: the publication by the CFDT (Confédération Française Démocratique du Travail) in France of a guide to the rights of foreigners; the establishment by the CISL in Italy of a support centre for migrant workers in Milan, which defends their trade union rights and provides vocational training and language teaching; campaigns by the DGB (Deutsche Gewerkschafts Bund) in Germany disputing the view that compulsory repatriation of foreigners resolves economic problems and unemployment; and calls by the bureau for immigrants of the FNV (the Federation of Dutch Trade Unions) in the Netherlands for positive discrimination in vocational training programmes and public sector employment and minimum employment quotas for migrant workers, in order to eliminate the disadvantages they face in relation to Dutch nationals: *Report to the Conference on Migrant Workers from the Mahgreb in the European Community*, n. 9 above, 5, para. 1.10. The Report also advocates that trade unions establish separate contact units to help migrants in an irregular situation. Furthermore, they should promote progressive policies on migrant workers by, *inter alia*, urging governments to ratify international multilateral agreements concerning the protection of migrants' rights, particularly the ILO Conventions, which few EC countries have ratified, and the recent UN Convention: *ibid.* 21–2, paras. 3.7 and 3.8 respectively.

[106] Vranken, n. 96 above, 47–8.

a right is clearly protected by Article 5 of the ESC which is also applicable, by virtue of paragraph 1 of the Appendix, to nationals of other states parties lawfully resident or working regularly in the State Party concerned. Article 5 guarantees 'the freedom of workers and employers to form local, national or international organizations for the protection of their economic and social interests and to join those organizations'. The EMW is less precise on the question of trade union rights. Article 28 outlines, in general terms, the right of migrant workers 'to organize for the protection of their economic and social interests' on the same conditions as nationals.[107] The implication, however, that this provision encompasses the right to join trade unions and to enjoy the benefits of collective bargaining is confirmed by the Explanatory Report on the EMW, which links Article 28 to the right to organize as defined in Article 5 of the ESC, and to ILO Convention No. 87 of 1948 concerning Freedom of Association and Protection of the Right to Organize.[108]

There is no express provision in COE instruments recognizing the right of migrant workers to participation in trade unions and works councils, which, as discussed in Chapter 3, is still impeded in a number of European countries of employment. The ECE does not refer to trade union rights at all, but there is an obligation upon contracting parties in Article 18 to permit nationals from another contracting party to participate on an equal basis with nationals as electors (or voters) in elections held by economic or professional bodies or organizations. It is not entirely clear, however, whether this provision applies to trade unions.[109] Although a right of migrant workers to participate in trade unions is not expressly mentioned in Article 19(4) of the ESC, nor in Article 5 of the ESC, the Committee of Independent Experts found France in breach of these provisions because of the restrictions imposed on the exercise by migrant workers of certain administrative and managerial functions within French trade unions.[110] As a result of

[107] Indeed, this is one of the few provisions in the EMW which is phrased in terms of 'rights'.

[108] *Explanatory Report on the EMW*, n. 71 above, 27, para. 96. As noted in Ch. 3, ILO Convention No. 87 expressly prohibits discrimination on the grounds of nationality in respect of the formation and membership of trade unions (Art. 2). The Explanatory Report, *ibid.*, also emphasizes that Art. 28 cannot be construed as *requiring* any person to join a trade union.

[109] See also Oellers Frahm, n. 71 above, 1750 and Swart, n. 45 above, 43. In its commentary on the ECE, the Standing Committee fails to clarify this point. It explains, however, that the provision contains 'no corresponding obligation to grant the right to stand for election in the bodies or organizations in question'. Moreover, the Committee concedes that reservations may be justified, in accordance with Art. 26, 'where professional organizations have public law status and are official bodies consulted by the legislature': *Commentary on the European Convention on Establishment*, n. 46 above, 22, paras. 70, 71 respectively. For this reason, a reservation has been made by Luxembourg in respect of elections to trade associations: *Third Periodical Report by the Standing Committee on the European Convention on Establishment*, n. 48 above, 111 (App. III).

[110] *Conclusions VI*, cited by Plender, n. 72 above, 246 and Harris, n. 20 above, 171. During the 13th cycle of supervision, the Committee requested the Belgian Government to provide detailed information on, *inter alia*, the lack of representation of foreign workers on works councils and repeated its question to the German Government on whether the election of foreign nationals as employee representatives in the public sector was subject to restrictions. See *Conclusions XIII-2*, n. 51 above, 379–80.

this negative conclusion, the law in France was amended accordingly.[111] Article 19(4) has also been a catalyst for reform of Spanish law.[112] Finally, the EMW, in Article 29, speaks of equality between nationals and migrant workers in respect of participation 'in the affairs of the undertaking'. States parties, however, are only obliged to 'facilitate' such participation.[113]

(b) EC standards

As with employment rights, EC law relating to trade union rights is remarkably lucid in contrast with some of the ambivalent wording found in COE provisions, especially in so far as the right to participation in trade unions is concerned. Article 8 of Regulation 1612/68/EEC guarantees equal treatment between national workers and those from other member states in respect of 'membership of trade unions and the exercise of rights attaching thereto, including the right to vote and to be eligible for the administration or management posts of a trade union' and 'the right of eligibility for workers' representative bodies in the undertaking' (for example, works councils). The concept of 'trade union' is broadly understood and extends to 'bodies which, while not being in law trade union organisations, perform similar functions as regards defence and representation of workers' interests'.[114] The Court of Justice has also ruled that freedom of movement cannot be restricted under Article 48(3) EC on the ground of public policy because of the worker's involvement in trade union activities.[115]

There is an exception to the right of participation in Article 8 that permits member states to exclude EC migrant workers from taking part in the management of bodies or the holding of an office governed by public law. These functions may be restricted to nationals. This exception is consistent with Article 48(4) EC which excludes certain public service functions from the free movement of labour regime. However, as with Article 48(4) EC, the Court of Justice has adopted a restrictive interpretation, ruling that the consultative function with

[111] Act of 28 Oct. 1982. See also D. Levy-Puech, 'France' in A. Ph. C. M. Jaspers and L. Betten, (eds.), 25 *Years of the European Social Charter* (1988) 145, 148 and Council of Europe, *The European Social Charter, Origin, Operation and Results* (1991) 32.

[112] See Act No. 32 of 2 Aug. 1984, which abolished the reciprocal nationality condition preventing the election of some foreign workers to work committees: Council of Europe, Committee of Independent Experts of the European Social Charter, *Addendum to Conclusions IX-2 relating to the 2nd Report of Spain on the Application of the European Social Charter (1 Jan. 1982–31 Dec. 1984)* (Strasbourg: Council of Europe, 1987) 46. See also *The European Social Charter, Origin, Operation and Results*, n. 111 above, 34.

[113] See also *Explanatory Report on the EMW*, n. 71 above, 27, para. 97, which points out furthermore that the provision is based on the premise that equality in respect of participation in the firm's affairs does not yet exist and that the state duty in Art. 29 merely constitutes an objective to be achieved.

[114] Case C-213/90, *Association de Soutien aux Travailleurs Immigrés (ASTI)* v. *Chambre des Employés Privés* [1993] 3 CMLR 621, para. 16. In this case, an occupational guild was held to perform such tasks: *ibid.* 637, para. 17.

[115] Case 36/75, *Rutili* v. *Minister of the Interior* [1975] ECR 1219, [1976] 1 CMLR 140, para. 31.

respect to certain legislation exercised by an occupational guild was too narrowly drawn to come within the ambit of this exception.[116]

8.3 SOCIAL SECURITY RIGHTS

The right to social security constitutes an important social safety-net for migrant workers and their families. Most European countries of employment have well-developed social security systems. Migrant workers, however, may suffer considerable disadvantages if, for example, they are unable to claim social security benefits in the host country because of strict residence requirements or if the period of employment in that country is not taken into account when they claim benefits in another country or on their return home. The COE and the EC have both developed elaborate standards for protecting the social security rights of member state nationals who work and reside in other member states. While the social security agreements concluded by the COE are largely dependent on further bilateral or multilateral action, EC standards apply directly in member states and the protection of EC law has also been extended to non-EC nationals in certain circumstances. Because of its technical complexity, the following section purports merely to outline the principal features of European social security law.

COE standards

The COE has been concerned with drawing up multilateral instruments in respect of social security from its very outset. In 1953, two European Agreements on Social Security and their Protocols were concluded. The first agreement guaranteed equal treatment for nationals of the states parties with regard to certain social security schemes, whereas the second broadened the ambit of this protection.[117]

The 1953 Agreements were the starting-point for subsequent COE agreements in the field of social security.[118] The next two treaties guaranteeing social security rights are the ESC and the European Code of Social Security, which were both prepared at the same time. As Harris observes, this presented a dilemma for the drafters of the ESC. Because it was not practicable to include a detailed text

[116] *Association de Soutien aux Travailleurs Immigrés*, n. 114 above, paras. 20–1. See also the Opinion in this case of Advocate General Jacobs, *ibid.* 631–2.

[117] European Interim Agreement on Social Security Schemes relating to Old Age, Invalidity and Survivors, and Protocol, 11 Dec. 1953; Council of Europe, ETS No. 12; entry into force 1 July and 1 Oct. 1954 respectively; ratified by 17 States as at 1 July 1996: Belgium, Cyprus, Denmark, France, Germany, Greece, Iceland, Ireland, Italy, Luxembourg, Netherlands, Norway, Portugal, Spain, Sweden, Turkey, United Kingdom. European Interim Agreement on Social Security Schemes other than Schemes for Old Age, Invalidity and Survivors, and Protocol, 11 Dec. 1953, Council of Europe, ETS No. 13; entry into force 1 July and 1 Oct. 1954 respectively; ratified by the same 17 States as at 1 July 1996. In both cases, the Protocols declare the Agreements applicable to refugees within the meaning of the Geneva Convention relating to the Status of Refugees.

[118] Swart, n. 45 above, 34.

outlining social security rights in an instrument concerned broadly with economic and social rights, the drafters decided to insert a provision dealing with social security in more general terms and to leave the specialist instruments to spell out the details.[119] The result was Article 12 of the ESC. The pertinent clause relating to nationals of other member states is Article 12(4) which obliges states parties:

to take steps, by the conclusion of appropriate bilateral and multilateral agreements, or by other means, and subject to the conditions laid down in such agreements in order to ensure
(a) equal treatment with their own nationals or the nationals of other Contracting Parties in respect of social security rights, including the retention of benefits arising out of social security legislation, whatever movements the persons protected may undertake between the territories of the Contracting Parties;
(b) the granting, maintenance and resumption of social security rights by such means as the accumulation of insurance or employment periods completed under the legislation of each of the Contracting Parties.

The Committee of Independent Experts has stated that the first obligation to guarantee equal treatment, when complied with by international action, requires effective and immediate implementation in national law, whereas the second obligation, which may only be effected by international agreements, is merely to *endeavour* to ensure that migrants retain their rights.[120] The weaker standard applied in the case of the second obligation, however, is arguably not justified by the wording, which requires states parties to 'ensure' the standards in *both* paragraphs (a) and (b).[121]

The Committee has taken the view that the words 'by other means' indicate that states parties might be obliged to secure equality of treatment to nationals of other states parties not only by way of bilateral or multilateral agreements, but also by implementing measures unilaterally.[122] This all-encompassing approach has been disputed by the Governmental Committee, which ascribes to the position that states parties might be in conformity with their obligations under Article 12(4) if their arrangements apply only to nationals of *some* of the states parties.[123] Although the Parliamentary Assembly has observed that the wording in Article 12(4) does not support the latter interpretation, it has emphasized that preference regarding the application of the provision is to be given to rules laid down in agreements. According to the Parliamentary Assembly:

[119] Harris, n. 20 above, 110. In this sense, therefore, the role of the ESC is secondary compared with the other more detailed instruments concerned with social security rights: *ibid.* Indeed, the same solution was adopted in respect of the inclusion of social security rights in Art. 9 of the ICESCR (Harris, *ibid.* (n. 588)), Art. 10 of ILO Convention No. 143 of 1975 and Art. 27 of the UN Convention.

[120] *Conclusions III*, 64, cited in *Case Law on the European Social Charter*, n. 19 above, 113. See also Harris, n. 20 above, 119.

[121] Harris, *ibid.*

[122] *Conclusions VI*, 84, cited in *Case Law on the European Social Charter*, n. 19 above, 114.

[123] *Sixth Report*, cited in *Case Law on the European Social Charter*, *ibid.* See also *Report 11(II)*, 38–9, cited in *Case Law on the European Social Charter—Supplement No. 3*, n. 56 above, 119, in connection with the French report.

There is nothing to prevent a state taking unilateral measures of its own accord, but it does not seem realistic to expect every Contracting Party of its own accord to grant equality of treatment to the nationals of other Parties bound by the Charter unless it can ensure that its own nationals enjoy the same rights.[124]

In recent examinations of state reports under this provision, the focus of the Committee of Independent Experts' comments has been on whether the necessary bilateral or multilateral social security agreements have been concluded between COE member states. On occasions, however, the Committee has asked about the possibility of states parties applying unilateral measures to nationals of those parties in respect of whom no social security agreements have been completed. Such measures might well be appropriate in cases where it is not envisaged to complete such agreements in the near future.[125]

The personal scope of Article 12(4) of the ESC is broader than other provisions in the ESC, for it arguably applies to nationals of all states parties, irrespective of whether they are legally resident or working regularly in the host country.[126] In practice, however, it is unlikely that many migrant workers in an irregular situation would come forward to claim social security rights for fear of being detected by the authorities. Moreover, a state party which has accepted Article 12(4) should apply it to the nationals of all the other states parties regardless of whether these countries have themselves accepted the provision.[127]

Although the social security benefits covered in Article 12 are not listed, it may be assumed that Article 12(4) applies to the 9 branches of benefits enumerated in ILO Convention No. 102 of 1952 concerning Minimum Standards of Social Security. This instrument is referred to in Article 12(2) in which states parties are required to maintain a social security system 'at a satisfactory level at least equal to that required for ratification of [the latter Convention]'.[128] ILO

[124] *Report* Doc. 4736, 7–9, cited in *Case Law on the European Social Charter*, n. 19 above, 15.

[125] Indeed, the Committee concluded that France did not comply with Art. 12(4) because it had not extended a number of social security benefits to nationals of those states parties with whom no bilateral or multilateral agreements had been completed. *Conclusions XIII-2*, n. 51 above, 116–19. See also the Committee's request for information in respect of the Icelandic report. *Conclusions XII-1*, n. 57 above, 186.

[126] The application of the ESC to foreigners is expressly limited by the first paragraph of the Appendix to those 'nationals of other Contracting Parties *lawfully resident or working regularly* within the territory of the Contracting Party concerned' (emphasis added). However, this paragraph is to be applied 'without prejudice' to Arts. 12(4) and 13(4). (The latter provision, concerned with equal treatment in respect of social and medical assistance, is considered below.) Unlike Art. 13(4), however, there is no explicit requirement in Art. 12(4) that nationals of other contracting parties be 'lawfully within' the territory concerned. The Committee of Independent Experts has stated that the words 'without prejudice' operate to protect the wider scope of Art. 12(4) in terms of persons protected: *Conclusions VII*, 77–8, cited in *Case Law on the European Social Charter*, n. 19 above, 123. See also Harris, n. 20 above, 118.

[127] Harris *ibid*. Malta, Sweden, and the United Kingdom have not accepted Art. 12(4).

[128] See also Harris, *ibid*. 111. ILO Convention No. 102, discussed in Ch. 3, applies to the following 9 branches of social security: medical care, sickness benefits, unemployment benefits, old-age benefits, employment injury benefits, family benefits, maternity benefits, disability benefits, and survivors' benefits. The revised ESC replaces the ILO Convention in Art. 12(2) with the European

Convention No. 102 applies only to contributory benefits, but the Committee of Independent Experts has confirmed that Article 12(4) of the ESC also covers non-contributory benefits.[129] In this context, it has taken note of the positive developments in social security systems in Europe which 'show a trend towards extending both the categories of persons protected and the range of benefits payable, and in many instances, the abandonment of the traditional connection of social insurance with contribution requirements'.[130] Despite the alignment of its views with such developments, the Committee has endorsed the text of the Appendix to the ESC, which asserts that Article 12(4) permits states parties to impose residence requirements upon nationals from other states parties before granting non-contributory benefits.[131]

The European Code of Social Security and Protocol of 1964 constitute the more detailed texts to which the drafters of the ESC referred.[132] The Preamble to the Code declares, *inter alia*, that one of the objects of the COE's social programme is to encourage member states to 'develop further their systems of social security' and that it is desirable to realize a higher level of protection than that afforded by ILO Convention No. 102 concerning Minimum Standards of Social Security.[133] The Code spells out, in Parts II to X, a comprehensive set of social security standards relating to 9 branches of social security.[134] Article 2(1)(b) of the Code permits states parties to opt out of 4 of these Parts.[135] The personal scope of the Code varies in accordance with the benefit concerned. These provisions were

Code of Social Security which provides for a higher standard of social security. See below for an overview of the European Code of Social Security and the Revised Code.

[129] For example, the Committee ruled that the 'social pension' payable in Italy to persons over 65, who have no other income or whose income does not exceed a certain amount, came within the ambit of social security in Art. 12(4). Consequently, the refusal of Italian authorities to pay 'social pension' to non-Italians was in breach of this provision: *Conclusions III*, 65, cited by Harris, n. 20 above, 111, 120.

[130] *Conclusions VII*, 74, cited in *Case Law on the European Social Charter*, n. 19 above, 114.

[131] *Conclusions VIII*, 158, cited in *Case Law on the European Social Charter: Supplement*, n. 59 above, 40. The Committee has observed, in considering the French Report, that states parties should attempt to set such residence requirements unilaterally in the absence of formal or informal bilateral arrangements to this effect: Council of Europe, Committee of Independent Experts of the European Social Charter, *Conclusions X-2 (1985–86)* (Strasbourg: Council of Europe, 1988) 116.

[132] European Code of Social Security, 16 April 1964; Council of Europe, ETS No. 48; entry into force 17 March 1968; ratified by 17 states as at 1 July 1996: Belgium, Cyprus, Denmark, France, Germany, Greece, Ireland, Italy, Luxembourg, Netherlands, Norway, Portugal, Spain, Sweden, Switzerland, Turkey, United Kingdom. Protocol to the European Code of Social Security, 16 April 1964, Council of Europe, ETS No. 48; entry into force 17 March 1968; ratified by 7 states as at 1 July 1996: Belgium, Germany, Luxembourg, Netherlands, Norway, Portugal, Sweden.

[133] Second and fourth indents. The aim of the Protocol to the Code is to improve on these standards. The first indent of the Preamble to the Protocol reads: 'Being resolved to establish a higher level of social security than that provided for in the provisions of the European Code of Social Security'.

[134] The branches of social security are the same as those listed in ILO Convention No. 102, n. 128 above.

[135] However, Pt II on medical care is to count as two parts and Pt V on old-age benefit as three parts.

strengthened in a revised version of the Code, adopted in 1990 with a view to progressively replacing the original Code and Protocol.[136] The new version has not yet entered into force.[137]

Although the Code is not expressly limited to state party nationals and applies to all employees as well as to all persons who are ordinarily resident in the country concerned, there are no provisions which deal with the special problems faced by migrant workers and their families in the social security field. Indeed, Article 73 of the Code calls for the conclusion of a special social security instrument relating to foreigners and migrants:

> The Contracting Parties shall endeavour to conclude a special instrument governing questions relating to social security for foreigners and migrants, particularly with regard to equality of treatment with their own nationals and to the maintenance of acquired rights and rights in course of acquisition.[138]

In 1972, the COE adopted the European Convention on Social Security and the Supplementary Agreement for its application.[139] The Convention recognizes that 'multilateral co-ordination of social security legislation' constitutes one means of realizing the COE aim of 'greater unity between its Members, in particular for the purpose of facilitating their social progress',[140] and affirms, in the fourth indent of the Preamble, the following two principles:

> [T]he principle of equality of treatment for nationals of the Contracting Parties, refugees and stateless persons, under the social security legislation of each Contracting Party, and the principle that the benefits under social security legislation should be maintained despite any change of residence by the protected persons within the territories of the Contracting Parties.

By virtue of Article 76 of the Convention, the two 1953 social security agreements cease to apply in relations between contracting parties, although ILO instruments and EC provisions concerned with social security are not affected.[141]

[136] See the fifth indent of the Preamble to the revised Code: European Code of Social Security (Revised), 6 Nov. 1990; Council of Europe ETS No. 139; no ratifications as at 1 July 1996 (signed by 14 COE member states).

[137] The revised Code requires two ratifications to come into force (Art. 84(2)).

[138] By virtue of Art. 2(1)(d), the opt-out in Art. 2 cannot be exercised in respect of Pt XIII where Art. 73 is found.

[139] European Convention on Social Security, 14 Dec. 1972; Council of Europe, ETS No. 78; entry into force 1 March 1974; ratified by 8 states as at 1 July 1996. Supplementary Agreement for the Application of the European Convention on Social Security, 14 Dec. 1972; Council of Europe, ETS No. 78; entry into force 1 March 1974; ratified by 8 states as at 1 July 1996. The same states have ratified both instruments: Austria, Belgium, Italy, Luxembourg, Netherlands, Portugal, Spain, Turkey. For an overview of the Convention, see Council of Europe, *Explanatory Reports on the European Convention on Social Security and on the Supplementary Agreement for the Application of the European Convention on Social Security* (Strasbourg: Council of Europe, 1973) 5–12. In addition to this general appraisal, the Explanatory Report contains a detailed article by article commentary on the Convention. See also Plender, n. 72 above, 248–51.

[140] See respectively the second and first indents of the Preamble.

[141] Art. 6(1)–(2).

Indeed, the Convention is based on EC social security provisions,[142] which are examined below. It is a framework and model instrument and only some of its provisions are directly applicable; the implementation of others depends on the negotiation of agreements between the contracting parties.[143] The Supplementary Agreement was adopted at the same time as the Convention. It regulates relations between social security institutions and the procedures to be followed for the application of the provisions of the Convention which are immediately applicable, and it also serves as a guide for the application of those provisions which only become applicable after the conclusion of separate bilateral or multilateral agreements.[144] The Convention and the Supplementary Agreement co-exist; Article 80(3) of the Convention requires states that ratify the former to also ratify the latter.

The principle of equality between nationals of states parties in respect of social security rights is enshrined in Article 8(1) of the Convention.[145] The instrument applies to persons 'who are or have been subject to the legislation of one or more of the Contracting Parties and are nationals of a Contracting Party, or are refugees or stateless persons resident in the territory of a Contracting Party, as well as to the members of their families and their survivors'.[146] By virtue of Article 14 of the Convention, the applicable law in social security matters, as a general rule, is the law of the country of employment, even if the beneficiaries reside in the territory of another state party. The Convention applies to 8 branches of social security[147] and also encompasses contributory and non-contributory benefits,[148] although a state party may impose residence requirements in respect of entitlement to some non-contributory benefits.[149]

By virtue of Article 2(4), however, the Convention expressly excludes social or medical assistance schemes.[150] Such schemes are governed by the COE Convention on Social and Medical Assistance, which is discussed below in the section

[142] *Explanatory Reports on the European Convention on Social Security and on the Supplementary Agreement*, n. 139 above, 6, para. 4. [143] *Ibid.* 6, para. 3.

[144] *Ibid.* 12, para. 22.

[145] Art. 8(1) reads: 'Unless otherwise specified in this Convention, persons who are resident in the territory of a Contracting Party and to whom the Convention is applicable shall have the same rights and obligations under the legislation of every Contracting Party as the nationals of such Party'.

[146] Art. 4(1)(a).

[147] Art. 2(1)(a)–(h). The applicable branches of social security are: sickness and maternity benefits; invalidity benefits; old-age benefits; survivors' benefits; benefits in respect of occupational injuries and diseases; death grants; unemployment benefits; and family benefits.

[148] Art. 2(2). [149] Art. 8(2).

[150] However, under Ch. 1 of Title III of the Convention, which specifically relates to sickness and maternity benefits, Art. 20(1)(a) provides that 'persons who reside in the territory of a Contracting Party other than the competent State and who satisfy the conditions for entitlement prescribed by the legislation of the latter State . . . shall receive in the territory of the Contracting Party in which they are resident: (a) benefits in kind, provided at the expense of the competent institution by the institution of the place of residence in accordance with the provisions of the legislation which the latter institution applies, as if these persons were affiliated to it'. Art. 20, however, is one of those provisions in the Convention the application of which is subject to the conclusion of bilateral or multilateral agreements between the states parties (Art. 26(1)).

on the right to equal access to health care and medical treatment. This instrument also forms the basis of equal treatment between migrants and nationals in these two areas under Article 13(4) of the ESC. The conclusions of the Committee of Independent Experts under this provision have led to the adoption by the Committee of Ministers of two Recommendations to Greece in respect of measures restricting to Greek nationals the payment of a 'pension' to persons over 68 years of age and requiring foreigners to be lawfully resident in the country for at least 6 months in order to qualify for social assistance.[151] Although the latter measure was also applicable to Greek nationals, it constituted indirect discrimination against foreigners who were likely to find it more difficult to meet the residence condition. The condition was incompatible with the ESC because Article 13(4) only requires that the migrant be 'lawfully within' the territory of the state party in order to qualify for social assistance. However, because lawful presence is determined by the host country, this creates obvious difficulties for migrants who have applications for the renewal of their resident permits refused *on the ground that they are in need of social assistance*, with the result that their status in the country is rendered illegal.[152]

The ESC, the Code (and Protocol), and the Convention (and Supplementary Agreement) are the principal COE instruments relevant to the social security rights of migrant workers and their families, although only the latter and Article 12(4) of the ESC are specifically concerned with the unique situation of migrants in this field. Article 18(1) of the EMW also provides for equal treatment between nationals of states parties in respect of social security rights, but the principle of equality is subject to conditions required by national legislation or by international agreements. This very general provision was adopted after the entry into force of most of the other social security instruments. Consequently, the reference to other instruments was considered sufficient.[153] Article 18(2) of the EMW requires states parties to preserve acquired social security rights, but the obligation is only to 'endeavour' to secure such rights to migrant workers and their families and, once again, only through international agreements.

The ESC, Code, and European Convention on Social Security complement and reinforce each other in implementing social security rights in Europe. For example, out of the 20 countries that have ratified the ESC, only Malta, Sweden, and the United Kingdom have not accepted Article 12(4) of the instrument. Both

[151] Recommendation No. R ChS (93) 1 of 7 Sept. 1993 (cited in (1994) 1:1 IHRR 265) and Recommendation No. R ChS (95) 4 of 22 June 1995 (cited in Council of Europe, *Human Rights Information Sheet No. 36* (1995) 68–9). See also *Conclusions XII-1*, n. 57 above, 196 and *Conclusions XIII-2*, n. 51 above, 138–40.

[152] Cf. E-M. Hohnerlein, 'Federal Republic of Germany' in *25 Years of the European Social Charter*, n. 111 above, 105, 126.

[153] *Explanatory Report on the EMW*, n. 71 above, 22, para. 76. Furthermore, in view of this, it was not necessary to make Art. 18 one of those provisions in Art. 36 to which no reservation can be made. *Ibid.* 23, para. 77. The 8 states parties to the EMW are also parties to at least one of the principal COE instruments concerned with social security mentioned above, and 5 (Italy, the Netherlands, Portugal, Spain, and Turkey) have ratified the European Convention on Social Security.

Sweden and the United Kingdom, however, have ratified the European Code of Social Security and the former country has also ratified the 'more progressive' Protocol.[154] Four countries, Belgium, Luxembourg, Netherlands, and Portugal, have accepted all the social security provisions in force in Europe.

Thus far in this section, no mention has been made of the ECHR, which, as discussed in Chapter 5, is of rather minimal relevance to the protection of economic, social, and cultural rights. However, by recently asserting that the right to peaceful enjoyment of possessions in Article 1 of Protocol No. 1 to the ECHR (discussed in the section on the right to housing below) encompasses entitlements to benefits to which contributions have been made, the Court of Human Rights has confirmed the application of the ECHR to the social security field. In *Gaygusuz* v. *Austria*, the Court concluded unanimously that the refusal of the Austrian authorities to grant an advance on a pension by way of an emergency payment to a resident Turkish national who had contributed to the relevant social security fund, on the grounds that he was not an Austrian national, infringed Article 14 of the ECHR taken together with Article 1 of Protocol No. 1.[155]

EC standards[156]

The principle of free movement of labour in the EC would be effectively unworkable if migrant workers and their families from other member states were to be placed at a disadvantage to nationals in the social security field.[157] EC law

[154] Switzerland is one country which has not ratified the ESC, but it has ratified the Code.

[155] *Gaygusuz* v. *Austria*, judgment of 16 Sept. 1996 (not yet reported). See MNS 163/96 (Oct. 1996) 11–12. This decision complements an earlier Court ruling, which established that the duty to pay taxes falls within the application of Art. 1 of Protocol No. 1. See *Darby* v. *Sweden*, judgment of 23 Oct. 1990, Eur. Ct. H.R., Ser. A., No. 187, (1991) 13 EHRR 774, para. 30. In *Darby*, the Court found an infringement of Art. 14 taken together with Art. 1 of Protocol No. 1 in relation to a Finnish national who was obliged to pay the full municipal tax, part of which was a special tax payable to the Church of Sweden with which the applicant had no connection, even though he was deemed not to be a permanent resident. On the other hand, permanent residents had a right to an exemption from this part of the tax.

[156] On EC social security law, see: P. Watson, *Social Security Law of the European Communities* (London: Mansell, 1980); P. Watson, 'Social Security for Migrants' in D. Wyatt and A. Dashwood, *European Community Law* (1993) 311; C. Laske, 'The Impact of the Single European Market on Social Protection for Migrant Workers' (1993) 30 *CML Rev.* 515; Commission of the European Communities, Directorate-General for Employment, Industrial Relations and Social Affairs, *Social Security for Persons Moving Within the Community*, Social Europe 1/92 (Luxembourg: OOPEC, 1993). A compendium of all EC social security cases is provided in Commission of the European Communities, Directorate-General for Employment, Industrial Relations and Social Affairs, *Judgments of the Court of Justice of the European Communities related to Social Security for Migrant Workers. A Systematic Survey* (Luxembourg: OOPEC, 1995). For an overview of recent case law in this area, see E. Eichenhofer, 'Coordination of Social Security and Equal Treatment of Men and Women in Employment: Recent Social Security Judgments of the Court of Justice' (1993) 30 *CML Rev.* 1021.

[157] Stein and Thomsen observe: 'Freedom of movement would be severely compromised if migrant workers within the Community were to lose their entitlement to social security benefits for themselves and for members of their families as a result of their mobility': T. Stein and S. Thomsen, 'The Status of the Member States' Nationals under the Law of the European Communities' (1987) 1821. See also Watson, n. 156 above, 313 and Note (EEC), 'Article 51: Migrant Workers' Social Security Rights' (Sept. 1986) EIRR 17.

is designed to ensure that this does not occur. Article 51 EC obliges the Council, acting on a proposal from the Commission, 'to adopt such measures in the field of social security as are necessary to provide freedom of movement for workers'. The Council is instructed to make arrangements to ensure that EC migrants do not lose their entitlement to benefits by adding all the relevant periods of benefit together (*principle of aggregation*) and to guarantee that benefits are paid in any member state irrespective of whether the migrant is resident or working in that state (*principle of exportability*).[158] However, EC law does not create a uniform supranational social security system by harmonizing national social security arrangements, but only coordinates them in order to ensure that migrant workers moving between member states are afforded adequate social security protection.[159]

The principal piece of EC secondary legislation implementing Article 51 EC is Regulation 1408/71/EEC of 14 June 1971 on the application of social security schemes to employed persons, to self-employed persons, and to members of their families moving within the Community.[160] In order to ensure that EC migrants are not without social security coverage in any member state and also to prevent them receiving simultaneous benefits in two member states or paying double contributions, Article 13 of the Regulation stipulates that the applicable national social security law, as a general rule, is to be that of the country of employment or self-employment.[161] Article 3 enunciates the principle of equal treatment between nationals of member states in respect of social security benefits. In line with the interpretation given to Article 48(2) EC, both direct and indirect discrimination are outlawed under this provision.[162]

By virtue of Article 2(1), Regulation 1408/71/EEC applies to the following persons:

> employed or self-employed persons who are or have been subject to the legislation of one or more Member States and who are nationals of one of the Member States or who are stateless persons or refugees residing within the territory of one of the Member States, as well as to the members of their families and their survivors.

This provision makes a clear distinction between two categories of persons: workers and members of their families and their survivors. Workers can claim

[158] Stein and Thomsen, n. 157 above.

[159] See also *Social Security for Persons Moving Within the Community*, n. 156 above, 13 and Watson, n. 156 above, 314. For a survey of the social security laws of EC member states, see D. Pieters, *Introduction into the Social Security Law of the Member States of the European Community* (Brussels: Bruylant, 1990).

[160] JO Sp. Ed. 1971, 416, JO 1971, L 149/2, as amended and updated. For a consolidated version of the Regulation, see OJ 1992, C 325/1.

[161] See also *Social Security for Persons Moving Within the Community*, n. 156 above, 14 and Eichenhofer, n. 156 above, 1028–9.

[162] See respectively Case 237/78, *Caisse Régional d'Assurance Maladie (CRAM), Lille* v. *Palermo (née Toia)* [1979] ECR 2645, [1980] 2 CMLR 31 and Case 33/80, *Alluè and Coonan* v. *Università degli studi di Venezia* [1989] ECR 1591, [1991] 1 CMLR 283. For a discussion of this case law, see Watson, n. 156 above, 324–5 and Johnson and O'Keeffe, n. 90 above, 1328–9 regarding the latter case.

rights to benefits as rights of their own, whereas members of the worker's family (regardless of their nationality) can only claim derived rights, namely those rights acquired through their status as a member of the worker's family or as his or her survivor.[163] The concept of worker for the purpose of the Regulation is defined broadly by Article 1(a) and effectively applies to all those who are covered by a member state's social security scheme for employed or self-employed persons.[164]

The material scope of the Regulation is governed by Article 4(1), which includes the same 8 branches of social security as those specified in Article 2(1) of the European Convention on Social Security and applies to both contributory and non-contributory benefits.[165] The Court of Justice has asserted that the list of social security benefits is exhaustive.[166] As with the 1972 Convention, social and medical assistance are expressly excluded by virtue of Article 4(4).[167]

Although the list of social security benefits in Regulation 1408/71/EEC is not as comprehensive as the one found in the European Code of Social Security (and the Revised Code), in practice it has been extended by Article 7(2) of Regulation 1612/68/EEC, which espouses equal treatment between EC workers in respect of, *inter alia*, 'social . . . advantages'. The concept of 'social advantage' in this provision has been interpreted broadly by the Court of Justice. It includes all benefits that are generally granted to national workers because of their objective status as workers or by virtue of their residence on national territory, where the extension of such benefits appears suitable to facilitate free movement of labour within the EC.[168] Although 'social assistance' is excluded from the application of Regulation 1408/71/EEC, the concept of 'social advantages' in Article 7(2)

[163] Case 40/76, *Kermaschek* v. *Bundesanstalt für Arbeit* [1976] ECR 1669; Case 157/84, *Frascogna* v. *Caisse des depôts et consignations* [1985] ECR 1739; Case 94/84, *Deak* v. *Office national de l'emploi (ONEM)* [1985] ECR 1873; and Case C-243/91, *Taghavi* v. *Belgian State* [1992] ECR I-4401. See also Watson, n. 156 above, 321. By virtue of Arts. 1(f) and 1(g) of Reg. 1408/71/EEC, the definitions of 'member of the family' and 'survivor' are determined by the applicable national social security law.

[164] *Social Security for Persons Moving Within the Community*, n. 156 above, 24–5. See also Case 75/63, *Hoekstra (née Unger)* [1964] ECR 177, [1964] CMLR 319.

[165] Art. 4(2). The scope of non-contributory benefits covered has been extended by Council Reg. 1247/92/EEC of 30 April 1992, OJ 1992, L 136/1. Under Arts. 67 *et seq.* of Reg. 1408/71/EEC, unemployed EC nationals seeking work in a member state are entitled to receive unemployment benefits for a maximum of 3 months from the member state in which they were formerly employed, provided that they have registered for at least 4 weeks with the employment service of that country. These provisions have been criticized by Eichenhofer, n. 156 above, 1034, as interfering with the freedom of movement principle: 'It might . . . be fair to impose the burden to finance unemployment benefits upon the State where an employed person was last employed, but such a system violates the principle of freedom of movement if the right to unemployment benefits is bound to availability to the employment services of the State of last employment. This restriction is not adequately compensated by the right to look for a job outside the competent Member State for a period of three months, because a fundamental freedom cannot be reduced to a certain period of time'.

[166] Case 249/83, *Hoeckx* v. *Centre Public d'Aide Sociale de Kalmthout* [1985] ECR 973.

[167] Medical treatment, however, is available as a 'benefit in kind' under the head of social security concerned with sickness and maternity benefits. See the section below on the right to health.

[168] Case 207/78, *Ministère Public* v. *Even* [1979] ECR 2019, [1980] 2 CMLR 71; Case 261/83, *Castelli* v. *O.N.P.T.S.* [1984] ECR 3199, [1987] 1 CMLR 465; *Hoeckx*, n. 166 above.

has been interpreted by the Court of Justice to encompass 'social assistance-type benefits' in respect of both EC migrant workers and dependent members of their families.[169]

Regulation 1408/71/EEC has also played an important, albeit indirect, role in securing social security rights for non-EC migrant workers and their families employed in EC member states. The uncertain position of non-EC migrants in the social security field[170] may be alleviated by adopting bilateral treaties or by the insertion of appropriate provisions in Association and Cooperation Agreements concluded between the EC and third countries.[171] Thus far, the two provisions which have been invoked from such agreements have received a generous interpretation from the Court of Justice. The Court has ruled that Article 41(1) of the EC Cooperation Agreement with Morocco and Article 39(1) of the EC Cooperation Agreement with Algeria, which provide for equal treatment between Moroccan and Algerian workers and EC nationals in the field of social security, are directly effective in member states.[172] The Court has also confirmed that these

[169] For example, the concept of 'social advantages' has been found to include: social benefits guaranteeing a minimum means of subsistence, *Hoeckx*, n. 166 above; a non-pension guaranteed income payable to all old persons, *Castelli*, n. 168 above; disability benefits for disabled dependent children, Case 63/76, *Inzirillo* v. *Caisse d'Allocations Familiales* [1976] ECR 2057, [1978] 3 CMLR 596; reductions in rail fares for large families, Case 32/75, *Fiorini (née Cristini)* v. *S.N.C.F.* [1975] ECR 1085, [1976] 1 CMLR 573; and a discretionary interest-free loan for the birth of a child, Case 65/81, *Reina* v. *Landeskreditbank Baden-Württemberg* [1982] ECR 33, [1982] 1 CMLR 744. It is argued that the extension of the definition of non-contributory security benefits by Reg. 1247/92/EEC, n. 165 above, resolves 'to a large extent the problems which have arisen in the past due to the exclusion of social assistance from the scope of . . . [Reg. 1408/71/EEC]'. See Watson, n. 156 above, 323.

[170] The Commission observed in 1974: 'Many categories of social security benefits do not apply to Third Country migrants. Others are subject to long qualifying periods. Family benefits are often confined to children in the host country, and there are severe limitations on the export of other benefits. Periods of employment and insurance are not aggregated for the purpose of determining entitlement to benefit. At the same time Third Country nationals have equal liability for social security charges as compared with nationals': *Action Programme in Favour of Migrant Workers and Their Families* (1974) 6. The Commission, *ibid.* 15, recommended that 'equality of treatment with Community workers *by progressive stages* should be the Community's objective for these migrants whether or not their present situation is governed by association agreements or bilateral agreements' (original emphasis).

[171] In 1985, the Commission reiterated its earlier views, adding that 'from the social standpoint, workers in the same objective situation cannot be treated differently on the sole basis of nationality': *Guidelines for a Community Policy on Migration* (1985) 22, para. 40. The Commission, *ibid.* 23, para. 40, recognized, however, that the direct application of Community provisions 'would not solve the problems of aggregating periods of insurance completed in the Member States and in the country of origin, nor that of transferring the related benefits to the latter. These questions can only be regulated by agreements between Member States and Third Countries founded on the principles established in Community provisions'. Therefore, the Commission, *ibid.*, considered that the conclusion of association and cooperation agreements was vital to the realization of equal treatment in this area.

[172] See respectively *Kziber*, n. 25 above and Case C-103/94, *Krid* v. *Caisse Nationale d'Assurance Vieillesse des Travailleurs Salariés (CNAVTS)* [1995] ECR I-719. The provision concerned with social security in the EC–Turkey Association Agreement is Art. 39 of the 1970 Protocol, which was implemented by Decision 3/80 of the Association Council of 19 Sept. 1980 on the application of the social security schemes of the member states of the European Communities to Turkish workers and members of their families. The decision incorporates the principal provisions of Reg. 1408/71/EEC

provisions apply to members of the worker's family, including his or her survivors, and to persons who are no longer in employment. Moreover, the scope of applicable benefits can be determined by reference to Regulation 1408/71/EEC and the case law thereunder.[173]

8.4 RIGHT TO HEALTH

A comparative survey examining 11 EC jurisdictions indicates that nationality has little relevance in respect of the right to medical treatment. Health care is usually granted to foreigners on the basis of reciprocal medical agreements and is normally dependent on residence in the country.[174] It is arguable, however, that genuine equality between nationals and migrants in respect of health matters can only be effectively realized if adequate account is taken of the special problems migrants face in respect of access to the health care system, medical treatment, and occupational health and safety. The importance of providing such health care for migrant workers and their families was emphasized in Chapter 3. In 1974, the EC Commission identified the particular health problems of migrant workers and their families as follows:

> Medical services, where they are inadequate for the needs of the indigenous population, are even less capable of meeting the particular problems of migrants. Coming from countries of different climate, environment, eating habits and hygiene, the sudden change makes them more vulnerable than the local population to psychological disorders, to certain infectious diseases, parasitical diseases, and industrial accidents.[175]

as it stood in 1980. The Court of Justice has ruled, however, that although some of the provisions in Decision 3/80 are clear and precise, the Decision cannot be applied until further supplementing implementing measures have been adopted by the Council of Ministers: Case C-227/94, *Taflan Met, Altun-Baser, Andal-Bugdayci, Akol* v. *Bestuur van de Nieuwe Algemene Bedrijfsvereniging*, judgment of 10 Sept. 1996 (not yet reported) para. 37. For the text of Decision 3/80, see *EEC–Turkey Association Agreement and Protocols and Other Basic Texts*, n. 23 above, 349–80. The social security provisions in the other Association and Cooperation Agreements are unlikely to confer direct effect. There is no equal treatment clause relating to social security in the Europe Association Agreements. The clause that exists is limited to three specific social security benefits and is subject to implementation by the Association Council (for example, see the Agreement with Poland, Arts. 38 and 39, and the draft Agreement with Estonia, Arts. 37 and 38). The implementation of the equivalent social security clause in the draft Partnership and Cooperation Agreements with Belarus, Moldova, Russia, and the Ukraine is subject to the conclusion of further agreements between the parties following a recommendation from the Cooperation Council (for example, see the Agreement with Russia, Arts. 24–7). For a detailed analysis of these provisions, see Peers, n. 25 above, 34–8. See also Cremona, n. 25 above, 112.

[173] See respectively *Kziber*, n. 25 above, *Krid*, n. 172 above and Case C-58/93, *Yousfi* v. *Belgium* [1994] ECR I-1353. *Krid* concerned the denial of a supplementary allowance to the widow of an Algerian worker, who was resident in France and receiving a survivor's pension there, on the ground that she was of Algerian nationality. *Yousfi* concerned the refusal of a disability allowance to a Moroccan national who, having suffered an occupational injury, was no longer in employment.

[174] See *Hallmarks of Citizenship Survey*, n. 37 above, 97–8 and S. Behzadi, 'Hallmarks of Citizenship' in *Hallmarks of Citizenship*, *ibid.*, 26, 35–6.

[175] *Action Programme in Favour of Migrant Workers and Their Families*, n. 170 above, 19.

Right of equal access to health care and medical treatment

The most influential COE instruments concerned with equal access to health care for migrants are the European Convention on Social and Medical Assistance and Protocol, both adopted in 1953.[176] The Convention 'completes' the social protection accorded to nationals of states parties by the two social security agreements and protocols adopted that same year. Equal treatment between nationals of the host country and nationals of other states parties in respect of social and medical assistance is guaranteed by Article 1 of the Convention, provided that the latter are 'without sufficient resources' and 'lawfully present' in the territory of the state party. Article 6 of the Convention prohibits a state party from repatriating nationals of other state parties who are lawfully resident in its territory on the sole ground that they are in need of social and medical assistance unless certain conditions, enumerated in Article 7(a)(i) to (iii), are satisfied: if the persons concerned have not resided continuously in the territory of the state party for at least 5 years if they entered it before attaining the age of 55 or for at least 10 years if they entered it after that age; if they are in a fit state of health to be transported; and if they have no close ties in the territory in which they are resident. Under Article 8, a state party that repatriates a national of another state party, in accordance with Article 7, must bear the cost of repatriation. Clearly, the 5- and 10-year residency periods are significant limitations on the right of migrants under Article 6 not to be repatriated on the sole ground that they are in need of assistance. Despite the listed exceptions, however, Article 7(b) urges states parties 'not to have recourse to repatriation except in the greatest moderation and then only where there is no objection on humanitarian grounds'. The Protocol extends the protection of the Convention to refugees as defined in the Geneva Convention relating to the Status of Refugees.[177]

The two COE instruments which expressly provide for equality between nationals and migrants in respect of health care both refer to the 1953 Convention. The ESC contains a 'very general'[178] obligation in Article 11 urging states parties to adopt measures concerning the removal of the causes of ill-health, health education, and disease prevention. The more relevant ESC provision, however, is Article 13[179] which requires states parties to ensure that persons without adequate

[176] European Convention on Social and Medical Assistance and Protocol, 11 Dec. 1953; ETS No. 14; entry into force 1 July 1954; ratified by 17 states (the Protocol has only been ratified by 16 states because Malta has only signed and not ratified the Protocol) as at 1 July 1996: Belgium, Denmark, France, Germany, Greece, Iceland, Ireland, Italy, Luxembourg, Malta, Netherlands, Norway, Portugal, Spain, Sweden, Turkey, United Kingdom.

[177] In accordance with Art. 3 of the Protocol, the provisions in the Convention on repatriation are not applicable to refugees in so far as the latter have not ceased to be 'refugees' under the terms of the Geneva Convention. This would appear to be in conformity with Art. 33 of the latter prohibiting *refoulement*.

[178] *Conclusions I*, 59, cited in *Case Law on the European Social Charter*, n. 19 above, 104. See also Harris, n. 20 above, 105.

[179] The revised ESC makes no amendment to this provision.

resources are provided with social and medical assistance and that they do not suffer political and social discrimination because they receive such assistance.[180] Article 13(4) requires states parties to apply these provisions 'on an equal footing with their nationals to nationals of other Contracting parties lawfully within their territories in accordance with their obligations under [the 1953 Convention]'. Compared with the position under the 1953 instrument, however, the Committee of Independent Experts has confirmed that reciprocity is not a feature of the ESC.[181] The Committee has interpreted Article 13(4) as applying to all nationals of states parties *lawfully within* the territory of another state party regardless of whether their country of origin or the country of employment have ratified the 1953 Convention or accepted Article 13(4).[182] Its operation, like that of the Convention, does not depend on the migrant being resident or regularly employed in the state party concerned.[183] The scope of this provision is therefore broader. The 'obligation' in Article 13(4), however, includes the possibility of repatriation and reservations which are permitted by the 1953 Convention.[184] The equivalent provision in the EMW is Article 19, which asserts that states parties are to grant social and medical assistance to migrant workers on the same basis as nationals in accordance with the obligations assumed by virtue of other international instruments and, in particular, by virtue of the 1953 Convention.

There are no explicit provisions in EC law pertaining to equal treatment between EC workers and their families in respect of access to health care.[185] Indeed, Article 4 of Regulation 1408/71/EEC expressly excludes 'medical assistance'

[180] See Arts. 13(1) and (2) respectively.

[181] *Conclusions VII*, 77–8, cited in *Case Law on the European Social Charter*, n. 19 above, 122.

[182] *Ibid.* 123; Council of Europe, Committee of Independent Experts of the European Social Charter, *Conclusions XI-2* (Strasbourg: Council of Europe, 1991) 122–3 and *Conclusions XIII-2*, n. 51 above, 349, with respect to the German reports. See also the Governmental Committee, *Ninth Report*, 24, cited in *Case Law on the European Social Charter: Supplement No. 2*, n. 59 above, 26 and H. Wiebringhaus, 'Introduction' (1988) 15–16. Indeed, the Governmental Committee considered it appropriate to issue a warning to the United Kingdom regarding the position of Cypriot nationals who were not entitled to free medical assistance if they were visiting the country temporarily: *12th Report (I)*, n. 57 above, 43–4, paras. 165–7. See also *Conclusions XII-1*, n. 57 above, 198. During the 13th cycle of supervision, however, both the Committee of Independent Experts and the Governmental Committee noted that this situation had now been remedied in respect of Cypriots as well as Finnish nationals: *Conclusions XIII-2*, n. 51 above, 145 and *13th Report (I)*, n. 57 above, 143, paras. 779–81. Cyprus is the only state party which has not accepted Art. 13. Furthermore, it has not ratified the 1953 Convention.

[183] In accordance with the Appendix to the ESC, (see also Art. 12(4) in respect of social security rights), nationals of states parties need not be *resident* or *working regularly* in the country of employment for Art. 13(4) to apply. This distinction has been confirmed by the Committee of Independent Experts: *Conclusions X-1*, n. 57 above, 119. Illegal migrant workers, however, are clearly excluded by virtue of the wording in Art. 13(4), restricting the rights to those 'lawfully within' the territory.

[184] This interpretation is implicit in the Committee of Independent Experts' request for more information about the conformity of expulsion provisions in Spanish legislation with 'the limitations and conditions concerning repatriation' in the 1953 Convention: *Conclusions XI-2*, n. 182 above, 124. See also Harris, n. 20 above, 128.

[185] It is noteworthy that most EC member states, with the exception of Austria and Finland, are parties to the European Convention on Social and Medical Assistance and to the Protocol.

from the definition of social security. However, health care is implicitly covered in Chapter 1 of Title III of the Regulation which is concerned with sickness and maternity benefits and which entitles EC migrants to 'benefits in kind',[186] including medical treatment.[187] EC Association and Cooperation Agreements with third countries, in the relevant provisions concerned with social security rights, all provide for the principle of aggregation in respect of medical care for migrant workers and their families.[188]

In its 1974 Action Programme in Favour of Migrant Workers and their Families, the Commission observed: 'Insufficient information is at present available on the seriousness and the incidence of illnesses among the migrant population, as well as the factors which make them prone to such illnesses and industrial accidents. This situation is obviously a major obstacle for the development of adequate preventive measures'.[189] Although the right of many migrants to health

[186] Art. 19(1).

[187] The Commission report on *Social Security for Persons Moving Within the Community*, n. 156 above, 33, notes: 'In accordance with the case law of the Court of Justice, one may consider that benefits in kind comprise dental and medical services and the supply of medicines, even if these benefits are granted in the form of a cost refund'. In support, the report cites Case 61/65, *Vaassen (née Göbbels)* [1966] ECR 261, in which the Court of Justice held, *inter alia*, that EC social security legislation (pre-Reg. 1408/71/EEC) also applies to benefits given in the form of reimbursement of expenses for medical treatment, medicines, and nursing.

[188] For example Art. 39(2) of the Cooperation Agreement with Algeria reads: 'All periods of insurance, employment or residence completed by such workers in the various Member States shall be added together for the purpose of pensions and annuities in respect of old age, death and invalidity, and also for that of *medical care* for members of their families resident in the Community' (emphasis added). Near identical provisions are found in most of the other Association and Cooperation Agreements: Morocco (Art. 41(2)); Tunisia (Art. 40(2)); Hungary and Poland (Art. 38(1), first indent); Bulgaria, Czech Republic, Romania, and Slovak Republic (Art. 39(1), first indent); Estonia (Art. 37(1), first indent); Russia (Art. 24(i), first indent). As noted in the section on social security rights, however, the provisions in the agreements with the central and eastern European countries, the Baltic States, and the republics of the former Soviet Union are unlikely to trigger direct effect. The Commission stated that it would present a proposal, in the second half of 1996, to extend to third country nationals 'the provision of immediate medical care and other limited benefits': Commission of the European Communities, *Medium Term Social Action Programme 1995–1997* (1995), 13, para. 3.1.9. Prompted by the European Parliament, the Commission issued a proposal in June 1995 to amend Reg. 1408/71/EEC in order to permit, *inter alia*, non-EC nationals and members of their families, who are insured under the legislation of a member state, to receive urgent medical treatment while staying in the territory of another member state and to obtain authorization to travel to another member state for treatment appropriate to their condition: Commission of the European Communities, *Amended Proposal for a Council Regulation (EC) amending Regulation (EEC) No. 1408/71 on the application of social security schemes to employed persons, to self-employed persons and to members of their families moving within the Community*, COM (95) 284 final of 26 June 1995, 2–3.

[189] See n. 170 above, 20. The Commission recommended measures with a view to 'improving the effectiveness of medical examination on recruitment, preventive medicine, [and of, *inter alia*] socio-medical services': *ibid.* In its 1985 Guidelines, n. 171 above, 21, para. 38, the Commission stated that 'preventive measures, information and, in general, education in health and hygiene are clearly the cornerstone of any policy aimed at meeting the particular needs of the immigrant population'. The Commission declared its intention 'to undertake studies and to develop pilot schemes to examine the possibility of greater cooperation between the institutions and agents involved in the medical welfare of migrants'.

care, with the exception of illegal migrants, may seem to be adequately satisfied in Europe, the observation by the Commission, as regards the *particular* health problems faced by migrant workers and their families, has not been specifically addressed in the provisions examined above.

Occupational health and safety

The right to healthy and safe working conditions is expressly provided for in both the ESC and the EMW. The obligation under Article 3 of the ESC is threefold: to issue safety and health regulations, to enforce these regulations by measures of supervision, and to consult workers' and employers' organizations on measures intended to improve industrial safety and health.[190] The Committee of Independent Experts regards Article 3 as 'establishing a widely recognized principle, stemming directly from the right to personal integrity, one of the fundamental principles of human rights'.[191] By virtue of the Appendix to the ESC, this provision applies to all nationals of states parties lawfully resident or working regularly in the territory of the contracting party concerned.[192] It is rather disturbing, however, that, in view of the importance attached to this right, the provision does not apply to illegal migrant workers who are most likely to find work in dangerous occupations.[193]

Under Article 20(1) of the EMW, migrant workers are guaranteed equal rights and protection with nationals in respect of the prevention of industrial accidents and occupational diseases, and industrial hygiene. The importance of this provision is underlined by the fact that no reservation can be made to it. Furthermore, it does not preclude the taking of special measures in favour of migrant workers.[194] Special measures for migrant workers in this area are vital, since the latter are particularly prone to suffering industrial accidents due to their poor education and linguistic difficulties and, as outlined in the section on equal work and employment conditions, because they continue to occupy the lowest rungs of the occupational ladder where the dirtiest and most dangerous jobs are to be found. In Chapter 3, the observation was also made that additional instruction in occupational health and safety to migrant workers during employment training as well

[190] The revised ESC expands this provision by including two additional obligations: 'to formulate, implement and periodically review a coherent national policy on occupational safety, occupational health and the working environment'; and 'to promote the progressive development of occupational health services for all workers with essentially preventive and advisory functions' (Arts. 3(1) and (4)). Furthermore, *all* the obligations in the revised ESC are to be undertaken 'in consultation with employers' and workers' organizations'.

[191] *Conclusions I*, 22, cited in *Case Law on the European Social Charter*, n. 19 above, 21.

[192] According to the Committee of Independent Experts, self-employed workers are also covered. See *Conclusions II*, 182, cited in *Case Law on the European Social Charter*, *ibid.* 22.

[193] In this regard, it is noteworthy that the Appendix to the revised ESC is also inapplicable to those who are illegally resident in the territory of the state party.

[194] *Explanatory Report on the EMW*, n. 71 above, 23, para. 80.

as the posting of warning signs and symbols in their language might contribute greatly to the prevention of such accidents.[195]

EC secondary legislation on occupational health and safety applies to all workers irrespective of nationality.[196] It is also now well-developed,[197] in line with Article 118a EC which obliges member states 'to pay particular attention to encouraging improvements, especially in the working environment, as regards the health and safety of workers'. Under this provision, the Council is charged with the adoption, by way of directives, of 'minimum requirements' in this field for gradual implementation by member states.[198]

8.5 RIGHT TO HOUSING

Background

During the initial phases of international labour migration in Europe, migrant workers came as single men and women and were usually housed in temporary and provisional accommodation.[199] This housing, generally provided by employers in accordance with bilateral agreements, was far from adequate, although it was nonetheless better than independently secured accommodation, which was frequently excessively expensive and sub-standard.[200] In the late 1960s, the phenomenon of uncontrolled irregular migration, especially to France, coupled with severe housing shortages, led to migrants living in appalling conditions in shanty-towns around large towns and cities.[201] The living conditions in the notorious French 'bidonvilles' are well-documented.[202] Although largely eradicated

[195] The revised ESC adds a new paragraph to Art. 19 obliging states parties 'to promote and facilitate the teaching of the national language of the receiving state, or, if there are several, one of these languages, to migrant workers and members of their families' (Art. 19(11)). The Draft Explanatory Report explains that this provision has been considered important for, *inter alia*, 'the protection of migrant workers' health and safety at work': *Request for an Opinion on the Draft Revised European Social Charter*, n. 128 above, 15 and 46, para. 78 respectively.

[196] See Hailbronner and Polakiewicz, n. 90 above, 65, 71–2.

[197] An important piece of secondary legislation is Council Directive 89/391/EEC of 12 June 1989 on the introduction of measures to encourage the improvements in the safety and health of workers at work, OJ 1989 L 183/1. For an overview of the principal action and legislation in this field, see Commission of the European Communities, Directorate-General for Employment, Industrial Relations and Social Affairs, *Europe for Safety and Health at Work*, Social Europe, Supplement 3/93 (Luxembourg: OOPEC, 1992). For future directions in EC policy, see Commission of the European Communities, *General Framework for Action by the Commission of the European Communities in the Field of Safety, Hygiene and Health Protection at Work [1994–2000]*, COM (93) 560 final of 19 Nov. 1993.

[198] See Arts. 118(a)(1) and (2) respectively. Similar obligations are found under Arts. 2(1) and (2) of the Agreement on Social Policy, annexed to the Protocol on Social Policy of the TEU.

[199] Hammar, 'Immigrant Policy', n. 98 above, 268. This accommodation normally comprised hostels specially aimed at single workers. See Castles and Kosack, n. 1 above, 494.

[200] Papademetriou, n. 103 above, 348.

[201] S. Castles, 'The Guest-Worker in Western Europe—An Obituary' (1986) 20 IMR 761, 764.

[202] See generally S. Castles, 'Bidonville—A French Word for Hell' in *Migrant Workers and the Transformation of Western Societies*, n. 26 above, 5.

in France, 'bidonvilles' can still be found elsewhere in Europe. As this extract from a newspaper report in 1991 indicates, migration to Italy, one of the so-called 'new countries of immigration', has sparked its own problems in this respect:

> [In October 1991], the northern Italian city of Milan dismantled what had come to be called 'the village of shame', a squalid illegal encampment where about 700 North African immigrants were living in trailers without plumbing and electricity . . . The only problem was that the city offered no alternative housing to most of the immigrants. So, within a few days, many of the homeless had taken over an abandoned factory a few blocks from the dismantled camp.[203]

In the more established European labour-receiving countries, the increase in family reunification compelled migrants to seek accommodation on the general housing market. The shift to the regular private and public housing markets did not alleviate the poor conditions experienced by migrants. Immigrant workers and their families tend to face exploitation in the private housing market by unscrupulous and discriminatory landlords and find themselves at the bottom of waiting-lists for accommodation in the public sector.[204] This situation is partly due to the chronic shortage of quality housing in Western European countries of employment. Principally, however, it is the result of the legal, economic, and social status of migrant workers and their families in society. The connection between restrictions on migrants' occupational mobility and their low occupational status was noted in the previous chapter. This low occupational status has also resulted in the geographic concentration of some migrants in certain urban areas and subsequently in the poorest housing in overcrowded inner-city neighbourhoods.[205] The difficult housing situation of migrants is exacerbated by the legal

[203] A. Stille, 'Bigotry Begins to Fester in Italy' (Ch. 7, n. 16) A1. For further examples of the squalor and dilapidated housing conditions, to which immigrants in Italy have been subjected, see *Closed Borders, Stringent Attitudes*, n. 14 above, 85–6 (and n. 216).

[204] Cf. Hammar, 'Immigrant Policy', n. 98 above, 268. For an outline of the difficult and discriminatory housing conditions of foreigners in Germany, see Aukerman, n. 27 above, 244 (footnotes omitted).

[205] Martin and Miller, n. 3 above, 325 (n. 34), observed in 1980 that 50% of the migrant workers in Germany were concentrated in less than 4% of the territory, whereas in France, 34% of the total foreign population lived in the Paris region alone. In Switzerland, the canton of Zurich accounted for one-fifth of the Swiss foreign population. See also Castles and Kosack, n. 1 above, 494. More recent figures for other countries confirm that foreigners are over-represented in urban areas. In Portugal, 71% (mostly non-EC nationals) of the approximately 120,000 legally-resident foreigners have settled in Lisbon and the valley of the Tagus. In Italy, almost 320,000 and 137,000 of the approximately one million foreigners authorized to reside in Italy on 31 Dec. 1992 were living in Rome and Milan respectively. In Belgium, foreign nationals constituted 28% of the population of Brussels (as at 1 Jan. 1993). See *Closed Borders, Stringent Attitudes*, n. 14 above, 17, 18, 121 and 20 respectively. In the Netherlands, a government study revealed that foreigners and ethnic minorities accounted for large proportions of the population of the four largest cities in the Netherlands (Amsterdam, Rotterdam, the Hague, and Utrecht). For example, aliens constituted 15.5% of all the inhabitants of Amsterdam: *SOPEMI 1992*, 71 (Table II.15). More significantly, perhaps, second generation migrants represented over 50% of the total population in the 0–15 age group in these cities: *SOPEMI 1994*, 109. Similarly, 45% of children under the age of 14 in Brussels were second-generation migrants of Turkish or Moroccan origin: *Closed Borders, Stringent Attitudes*, n. 14 above, 20.

restrictions on their political participation in society which preclude them from drawing attention to their plight.[206]

Inadequate accommodation also creates a breeding ground for poor educational performance among the children of migrants: 'the rejection suffered by migrant populations and the very sub-standard conditions of their housing naturally have an adverse effect on the scholastic performance of their offspring'. Moreover, the fact that migrant workers are concentrated in certain regions of the host country in disproportionate numbers to the local population, particularly in the inner cities, leads to a disproportionate enrolment of their children in the local schools. The resulting tensions created in these schools is hardly conducive to a positive educational environment for migrant children.[207] On the other hand, the concentration of migrants in the poorer housing areas of the host country may, paradoxically, have some positive side-effects in terms of cultural, psychological, and physical security. In spite of the difficulties connected with life in these conditions, the formation and existence of migrant communities in such areas assist in the preservation of culture and language.[208] Furthermore, these communities constitute a refuge or haven from the damaging effects of racial discrimination, xenophobia, and isolation experienced by migrants outside.[209]

Special efforts to improve the housing conditions of migrant workers and their families in Europe have been scarce. The 'bidonvilles' in France were vacated and their occupants offered alternative accommodation. In Norway, positive measures have been undertaken to provide housing for migrants.[210] However, it would seem that despite affording general equal treatment to migrants with nationals in respect of the provision of housing, host countries have preferred to treat migrants under the auspices of general housing policy and have been reluctant to recognize their

[206] Castles and Kosack, n. 1 above. See the section on political rights below.

[207] See respectively *Closed Borders, Stringent Attitudes*, n. 14 above, 87 and cf. Hammar, 'Immigrant Policy', n. 98 above, 269. For measures to promote the dispersal of foreign pupils within the school system, see *Closed Borders, Stringent Attitudes, ibid.* 89 (Belgium and Denmark).

[208] Hammar, n. 98 above, writes: 'Immigrants' housing conditions, in particular the concentration of certain nationalities in the same residential area, is of utmost importance for the planning of immigrant policy. It has gradually become obvious that the geographical dispersion of immigrants adversely affects, among other things, the possibilities for communities to arrange language instruction and the education of immigrant children, as well as opportunities to form organizations that can promote these cultural activities'. However, housing policies aimed at the 'dispersal' of migrants have been pursued in a number of countries on the pretext of avoiding tensions in neighbourhoods where there are a large number of foreigners. See *Closed Borders, Stringent Attitudes*, n. 14 above, 86 on policies in Belgium, Denmark, and the Netherlands.

[209] Castles and Kosack, n. 1 above, 494.

[210] Hammar, 'Immigrant Policy', n. 98 above, 269; Report of the ILO Committee of Experts on the Application of Conventions and Recommendations, *General Survey of the Reports relating to Conventions Nos. 97 and 143 and Recommendations Nos. 86 and 151 concerning Migrant Workers* (1980) (hereinafter *ILO General Survey 1980*) 121, para. 429. The Norwegian measures include the provision of grants to local authorities for housing immigrants, and the establishment of a government-financed society to acquire and make such housing available: *ILO General Survey 1980, ibid.*

special difficulties and needs.[211] Express recognition of these difficulties and needs, leading to the improvement in the housing conditions of this disadvantaged group, would undoubtedly serve its integration into the host society.[212]

COE and EC standards

(a) Public and private rental accommodation

Article 19(4)(c) of the ESC articulates the principle of equal treatment between nationals and migrant workers from other states parties in respect of 'accommodation'.[213] The obligation to secure equal treatment in respect of accommodation has been given considerable attention by the Committee of Independent Experts and has been broadly interpreted.[214] Reserving public housing to nationals or EC nationals is contrary to Article 19(4)(c).[215] The allocation of such housing according to quotas is also not permissible.[216] Moreover, Article 19(4)(c) has been interpreted as prohibiting measures dictating where migrants are to live in the country of employment and discrimination with regard to eligibility for government grants for the construction of family housing.[217] Discrimination against migrants in the housing field cannot be justified on the grounds that there is a shortage of housing generally.[218]

[211] See respectively *Hallmarks of Citizenship Survey*, n. 37 above, 81–7 and Hammar, n. 98 above. As discussed below, however, the principle of equal treatment can be undermined significantly by residence conditions for public housing which may result in indirect discrimination against migrants.

[212] *SOPEMI 1990*, 35. The *Report to the Conference on Migrant Workers from the Mahgreb in the European Community*, n. 9 above, 21, para. 3.9, also urges the adoption of 'active' policies on behalf of migrant workers to promote their equal access to housing. The Report proposes issuing housing benefits to migrants to prevent the emergence of ghettos and discusses the urgent need for renovation and 'infrastructural improvement' policies in poor urban areas.

[213] There is no provision concerned with accommodation elsewhere in the ESC. However, the revised ESC introduces a right to housing (Art. 31) which imposes a threefold state obligation: to promote access to housing of an adequate standard; to prevent and reduce homelessness with a view to its gradual elimination; and to make the price of housing accessible to those without adequate resources. The draft Explanatory Report notes that housing of an 'adequate standard' means 'housing which is of an acceptable standard with regard to health requirements': *Request for an Opinion on the Draft Revised European Social Charter*, n. 128 above, 20 and 51, para. 115.

[214] For an overview of the Committee's observations on Art. 19(4)(c), see *Conclusions XIII-2*, n. 51 above, 44–50, paras. 70–83.

[215] *Conclusions XIII-2*, *ibid.* 193, with regard to the legal situation in Italy. The United Kingdom was deemed to be discriminating against migrants from some ESC states parties residing and working in Northern Ireland because access to public housing in the province was restricted to United Kingdom nationals, EC nationals, and those employed in key posts. This restriction was eventually removed: *Conclusions VI*, 122, cited by Plender, n. 72 above, 246 and Harris, n. 20 above, 171–2.

[216] See *Conclusions X-1*, n. 57 above, 148, with reference to a Swedish Supreme Court judgment outlawing refusals to let accommodation to immigrants, in which the Committee of Independent Experts asked whether this judgment had 'put an end to the ethnic quota system practised by some non-profit housing bodies', and *Conclusions XIII-2*, n. 51 above, 379, on the practice adopted by some municipal authorities in Belgium limiting the number of foreigners permitted to reside in their territory.

[217] See respectively *Conclusions VI*, 21, cited by Harris, n. 20 above, 172, with reference to the exclusion of migrant workers from areas of high immigrant population in Germany, and *Conclusions I*, 215, cited in *Case Law on the European Social Charter*, n. 19 above, 160.

[218] *Conclusions IV*, 122 and 123, cited in *Case Law on the European Social Charter*, n. 19 above, 161.

As discussed in the previous chapter, Article 19(4) has been interpreted by the Committee of Independent Experts as requiring states parties to ensure *de facto* equality between migrant workers and nationals. Consequently, measures, such as residence requirements for the allocation of low-cost accommodation which apply to migrants and nationals alike, are prohibited if they constitute discrimination against migrant workers and their families in practice.[219] Article 19(4) also has a positive aspect, which requires states parties to promote housing for migrants. For example, the Committee of Independent Experts has found that a special programme of assistance to encourage the construction of accommodation specifically for the benefit of migrant workers and their families is fully consistent with Article 19(4)(c).[220]

The provision in the EMW concerned with migrant workers' housing is Article 13. Article 13(1) espouses the principal of equality between nationals and migrant workers in respect of access to housing and rents, although, as with Article 19(4) of the ESC, equality only applies to the extent access to housing and rents is covered by 'domestic laws and regulations'. It is clear, from Article 13(3), however, that if these laws and regulations apply to the private rental sector, states parties are under an obligation to protect migrant workers against 'exploitation in respect of rents'. Article 13(4) is an interesting provision obliging contracting parties to ensure 'by the means available to the competent national authorities, that the housing of the migrant worker shall be suitable'. The explanatory document on the EMW maintains that 'suitable' accommodation is to be assessed in accordance with national housing standards. Furthermore, the undertaking in Article 13(4) is general in scope and applies to all types of accommodation, including communal accommodation.[221] It is not clear, however, whether this provision endorses an obligation upon states to take positive action to assist migrant workers and their families to obtain 'suitable' accommodation.[222]

EC law is succinct on the question of the provision of adequate housing for

[219] *Conclusions II*, 68, cited in *Case Law on the European Social Charter*, n. 19 above, 160. The Committee observed in relation to the position in Norway: '[T]he Charter requires that the migrant worker receive treatment "not less favourable" than that of nationals. Where a Norwegian municipality imposes a residence requirement [in respect of low cost housing], it is easier for Norwegians to fulfil that requirement in the town in which they normally live, creating a "de facto" less favourable situation for a foreigner': *Conclusions XI-1* (1989) 159–60. The subsequent Norwegian report claimed that there was no *de facto* discrimination because ordinary labour migration had stopped in 1975. Nonetheless, the Committee insisted that the Norwegian Government provide relevant statistical information to support this assertion: *Conclusions XII-1*, n. 57 above, 234.

[220] *Conclusions II*, 67, cited in *Case Law on the European Social Charter*, n. 19 above. See also the Committee's positive comments in *Conclusions X-2*, n. 131 above, 147, with reference to French efforts to improve migrant workers' housing.

[221] *Explanatory Report on the EMW*, n. 71 above, 21, para. 67.

[222] Swart, n. 45 above, 10, thinks that, in contrast with Art. 19(4)(c) of the ESC, Art. 13(4) of the EMW endorses no such obligation. However, in considering the first Norwegian report under the EMW, the Consultative Committee noted, *inter alia*, that the body specially established to assist migrants to find low-rent housing was a situation in keeping with the EMW: *Fourth Report on the Application of the EMW* (1991) 7, para. 57.

EC migrant workers and their families. Article 9(1) of Regulation 1612/68/EEC maintains that such workers are to 'enjoy all the rights and benefits accorded to national workers in matters of housing', whereas Article 9(2) is specifically concerned with ensuring equality in respect of the allocation of public housing. EC workers have the same right as nationals to place their names on lists for this kind of accommodation. More importantly, the families of migrant workers, if still resident in the country of origin, are deemed to be resident in the region of employment for the purpose of this provision, but only if national workers benefit from a similar presumption. This clause, therefore, appears to deter member states from giving priority to their nationals when allocating public accommodation on the basis that they are in greater need of such accommodation because of the presence of their families.

In its Guidelines for a Community Policy on Migration in 1985, the Commission observed that:

> The conditions in which immigrant workers live are, in general, worse than those enjoyed by nationals with the same income. As a result of discrimination or ignorance of their rights, these workers find it difficult to take advantage of the machinery for obtaining loans and subsidies or to enrol on lists of applicants for priority housing.[223]

The Commission, therefore, urged that information be disseminated to migrants, particularly through the social services, on the possibility of gaining access to financing available for the construction of dwellings or the upgrading of old and unsanitary accommodation.[224] In 1994, the Commission identified adequate housing (together with health) as relevant elements of a successful policy aimed at integrating third country nationals legally resident within member states.[225]

(b) Acquisition of private property

A survey of 11 EC member states indicates that non-EC nationals generally have an unrestricted right to acquire private property and that this right is limited only in a few instances.[226] COE instruments, however, provide for no unrestricted

[223] See n. 171 above, 22, para. 39.

[224] *Ibid.* The Commission, *ibid.*, also proposed to consider the housing of migrant workers in connection with schemes for the renewal of urban neighbourhoods that often contain a large number of migrants.

[225] *Immigration and Asylum Policies*, n. 93 above, 36, para. 135. However, the Commission noted that difficult housing conditions and access to health services were not limited to immigrants and considered these matters as falling within the EC programme against exclusion. See generally Commission of the European Communities, Communication, *Towards a Europe of Solidarity. Intensifying the Fight Against Social Exclusion, Fostering Integration*, COM (92) 542 final of 23 Dec. 1992. See also Commission of the European Communities, Directorate-General for Employment, Industrial Relations and Social Affairs, *Towards a Europe of Solidarity: Combating Social Exclusion*, Social Europe, Supplement 4/93 (Luxembourg: OOPEC, 1994) and Commission of the European Communities, Directorate-General for Employment, Industrial Relations and Social Affairs, *Towards a Europe of Solidarity: Housing*, Social Europe, Supplement 3/92 (Luxembourg: OOPEC, 1992).

[226] *Hallmarks of Citizenship Survey*, n. 37 above, 78–81. Most of the restrictions are limited to non-EC nationals and are found in Denmark (5 years' residence required unless permission granted by the Minister of Justice), Ireland (agricultural land), and Greece, Italy, and Spain (acquisition of property in border regions).

right of aliens to acquire property within COE member states. Indeed, only one instrument deals with this question directly, while two refer to it implicitly.

Article 1 of the first Protocol to the ECHR[227] is concerned with property rights and asserts, in the first paragraph, that 'every natural or legal person is entitled to the peaceful enjoyment of his possessions'. The provision, therefore, does not explicitly protect the *acquisition* of property, although it clearly applies to both nationals and aliens. Nevertheless, the right to enjoy peacefully one's property is subject to restrictions: 'No one shall be deprived of his possessions except in the public interest and subject to the conditions provided for by law and by the general principles of international law'.[228] The Court of Human Rights has confirmed that the phrase 'general principles of international law' refers to the international law standard giving rise to the right of non-nationals to 'prompt, adequate and effective compensation' in the event of expropriation by national authorities.[229] Moreover, specific measures limiting the rights of migrant workers to hold property in the country of employment under Article 1 would also have to satisfy the test under Article 14 of the ECHR, which prohibits discrimination on the ground of, *inter alia*, 'property' in respect of rights and freedoms set forth in the ECHR.[230]

The broad interpretation given to Article 19(4)(c) of the ESC by the Committee of Independent Experts extends the principle of equality between nationals and migrant workers to the acquisition of private property. The Committee has asserted that discrimination between citizens and foreigners in respect of the purchase of real estate is contrary to Article 19(4)(c).[231] However, the acquisition of property by migrant workers for a purpose other than accommodation would not be protected.[232]

The ECE is the only COE instrument which explicitly provides, in Article 4, for equal treatment between host contracting party nationals and those from other states parties in respect of, *inter alia*, 'rights relating to property'. Indeed, it would be unusual for this treaty, the main purpose of which is to facilitate temporary

[227] Protocol to the European Convention on Human Rights, 20 March 1952; Council of Europe ETS No. 9; entry into force 18 May 1954; ratified by 31 states as at 1 July 1996: Austria, Belgium, Bulgaria, Cyprus, Czech Republic, Denmark, Estonia, Finland, France, Germany, Greece, Hungary, Iceland, Ireland, Italy, Liechtenstein, Lithuania, Luxembourg, Malta, Netherlands, Norway, Poland, Portugal, Romania, San Marino, Slovak Republic, Slovenia, Spain, Sweden, Turkey, United Kingdom.

[228] Under the second para. of Art. 1, states parties have further discretion in controlling the use of property in accordance, *inter alia*, with the 'general interest or to secure the payment of taxes or other contributions or penalties'.

[229] *Lithgow and others* v. *United Kingdom*, judgment of 8 July 1986, Eur. Ct. H.R. 1986, Ser. A., No. 102, (1986) 8 EHRR 329, para. 119. The Court recognized in *Lihgow*, *ibid.* para. 116, that this compensation might be more generous for non-nationals than for nationals. See also L. Sermet, *The European Convention on Human Rights and Property Rights*, Human Rights Files No. 11 (Strasbourg: Council of Europe Press, 1992) 43–5; A. H. Robertson and J. G. Merrills, *Human Rights in Europe—A Study of the European Convention on Human Rights* (1993) 215; *Law and Practice of the ECHR and the ESC*, n. 76 above, 318–19; and C. Krause, 'The Right to Property' in *Economic, Social and Cultural Rights: A Textbook* (1995) 143, 152 and n. 35.

[230] Cf. Oellers-Frahm, n. 71 above, 1752; cf. Swart, n. 45 above, 40.

[231] *Conclusions IV*, 121, cited in *Case Law on the European Charter*, n. 19 above, 160–1.

[232] Harris, n. 20 above, 172 (n. 925).

and permanent residence, not to clearly assert this principle. Nevertheless, the effect of Article 4 is reduced by subsequent provisions, which permit the host state to reserve the acquisition of property to nationals or to restrict, *inter alia*, its acquisition by aliens for reasons of national security or defence.[233]

Although COE provisions are generally sympathetic to the right of migrant workers to acquire private property in the country of employment, in contrast with ILO instruments and the UN Convention which are silent on this question, they still lag somewhat behind EC law on this subject. Article 222 EC maintains that the Treaty 'shall in no way prejudice the rules in Member States governing the system of property ownership', but it is clear that the principle of freedom of movement would be fettered considerably if EC nationals were unable to acquire property freely in member states.[234] In *Re Ownership of Landed Property: EC Commission* v. *Greece*, the Court of Justice considered the validity of Greek legislation prohibiting non-Greeks from acquiring or dealing in rights in land in the border regions of the country, which extended to approximately 55% of Greek territory. The Court ruled that access to housing and ownership of property is the corollary of freedom of movement for workers and that the Greek legislation constituted discrimination on the grounds of nationality under Article 48 EC. Furthermore, it also hindered the right of establishment under Article 52 EC. The right to establish oneself and to pursue an occupation in an EC member state necessarily implies the right to acquire, use, or dispose of immovable property in the country.[235] Restrictions, such as the one referred to above, may also infringe Article 9(1) of Regulation 1612/68/EEC, which extends equality between EC workers in respect of matters of accommodation to 'ownership of . . . housing'.

8.6 RIGHT TO FAMILY REUNIFICATION[236]

Family reunion is clearly an important social entitlement. Individuals cannot enjoy their basic rights unless protection is extended to the social context in

[233] Art. 5. The Standing Committee has noted that the reasons for the exceptions in Art. 5 are to be judged according to national criteria: *Commentary on the European Convention on Establishment*, n. 46 above, 15, para. 39. Article 6(1)(a) permits states parties to retain restrictions on, *inter alia*, the acquisition of property already in existence at the time the ECE was concluded for reasons other than those specified in Art. 5. A list of such restrictions is to be transmitted to the COE Secretary General at the time of signature. Further restrictions may only be added 'for imperative reasons of an economic and social character or in order to prevent monopolization of the vital resources of the country' (Art. 6(1)(b)).

[234] See also Stein and Thomsen, n. 157 above, 1819–20.

[235] Case 305/87, *Re Ownership of Landed Property: EC Commission* v. *Greece* [1989] ECR 1461, [1991] 1 CMLR 611. In an earlier case, the Court found Italy in violation of Arts. 52 and 59 EC by allowing only Italian nationals to buy or lease housing, which had been built or renovated with the assistance of public funds, and to obtain mortgage loans at a reduced rate. See Case 63/86, *Re Housing Aid: EC Commission* v. *Italy* [1988] ECR 29, [1989] 2 CMLR 601.

[236] The principal arguments in this section are drawn from R. Cholewinski, 'The Protection of the Right of Economic Migrants to Family Reunion in Europe' (1994) 43 ICLQ 568. The terms 'family reunification' and 'family reunion' are synonymous and are used interchangeably.

which they find themselves. The family, however broadly defined, constitutes the closest attachment human beings possess. Such attachments effectively define who we really are. This truism is in line with modern communitarian thought, which considers an individual, detached from *family*, friends, and community, as 'a person wholly without character, without moral depth'.[237] The right of migrant workers to reunite with their families is essential not only to their own well-being and to the welfare of their families, but also, as argued in Chapter 3, because the realization of this right contributes to social stability in both receiving and sending countries.[238]

Background

As observed in Chapter 6, early European labour migration policy was based on the assumption of temporariness. The objective was to ensure that foreign workers would only stay in the country of employment for a limited period of time. It was to be achieved through the application of the 'rotation principle' which held no place for the 'migrant's role as a family member'.[239] Exclusion of family members from the country of employment served to discourage permanent settlement.

The recession after the oil crisis of 1973–4 threatened to significantly reduce the number of migrant workers in Western Europe. Although some returned to their countries of origin, many of those who had acquired residence rights preferred to stay in the country of employment and to send for their families, rather than risk returning home with the knowledge that this would probably prove to be an irreversible decision. As noted earlier, migrant workers also remained in demand economically because national workers were no longer willing to perform the dirty, manual, and low-status jobs. Moreover, the longer migrant workers stayed in the country of employment, the more likely they would refuse to accept 'the denial of the basic human right of living with their wives, husbands and children'.[240] Such humanitarian grounds, therefore, also denied states the discretion to prevent family members joining those workers who had already established substantial economic and social ties in host communities. This curious combination of economic considerations and rights ensured that the 'rotation principle' was never implemented to the full and that family reunification in

[237] M. Sandel, *Liberalism and the Limits of Justice* (Cambridge: Cambridge University Press, 1982) 179. As an alternative, Sandel offers a constitutive conception of the individual whose bounds are not fixed superficially in advance, but are defined by the individual's affiliations, attachments, and commitments: *ibid.* 63.

[238] It has been asserted that, in addition to being a basic human right, the right to family reunification 'enhances the sense of security of migrant workers and so is a factor for greater stability in society as a whole': *Report to the Conference on Migrant Workers from the Mahgreb in the European Community*, n. 9 above, 23, para. 3.16.

[239] R. Rogers, 'Post-World War II European Labour Migration: An Introduction to the Issues' (1985) 21.

[240] Castles (1986), n. 201 above, 771.

Europe became a reality as well as a major concern. Although the economic downturn caused the relative proportion of foreign workers to decline, especially between 1975 and 1980, the *total foreign population* in Western European countries continues to rise, largely because of the increase in family reunions.[241]

The right to family reunification is legally recognized in all major labour-receiving European countries, although it is by no means applied in a uniform manner and is subject to significant restrictions.[242] Generally-speaking, the definition of 'family' for the purposes of family reunification is confined to the spouse and minor children.[243] In a number of countries, migrant workers are required to work and reside in the country of employment for a certain period of time (usually one year)[244] and possess suitable accommodation before their families are permitted to join them.[245] Further conditions frequently imposed on the entry of families are that migrant workers possess sufficient resources to maintain their families, and that incoming family members are in good health.[246] Restrictions on access to the labour market for dependents, discussed earlier in connection with employment rights can, in practice, be also very influential in determining whether the family members of a migrant worker enter a country.

The conditions imposed on the reunion of migrant workers with their families reflect the broad discretionary control that states exercise in the immigration field, which is also sanctioned by general international law. The extent of these conditions indicates the strictness, or otherwise, of an individual country's policy

[241] This trend continued throughout the 1980s and into the early 1990s, although at a steadier rate: *SOPEMI 1994*, 194 (Table A.1). See also Thomas (1986), n. 7 above, 45.

[242] The right is recognized in different forms in the legislation of all EC member states with the exception of Ireland and Luxembourg, which conform, however, to this principle in administrative practice: *Report to the Conference on Migrant Workers from the Mahgreb in the European Community*, n. 9 above, 23, para. 3.16 and Commission Working Paper, n. 26 above, 7, regarding the position in Luxembourg.

[243] Commission Working Paper, n. 26 above, 19; Rogers, n. 239 above, 17. In some countries, parents may also enter on humanitarian grounds and if they are dependent on their children. See *Closed Borders, Stringent Attitudes*, n. 14 above, 61 (n. 146) (Portugal) and Isgro, n. 27 above, 696, on the position in Italy, where the parents of a foreign worker may enter and reside in the country for family reasons, provided that they do not take up employment: Law No. 943 of 30 Dec. 1986, Art. 4(3). See also Soysal, n. 36 above, 121, 122 (Table 7.2) and S. Thomsen, 'The Legal Position of the Spouse and Family Members' in *The Legal Position of Aliens*, n. 26 above, 1947, 1949.

[244] *ILO General Survey 1980*, n. 210 above, 121, para. 426; Thomsen, *ibid.* 1951. The waiting-period, however, is longer in some countries. For example, in some German *Länder* 3 years are required. See J. A. Frowein, 'Concluding Report to the Heidelberg Colloquium on the Legal Position of Aliens in National and International Law' in *The Legal Position of Aliens*, n. 26 above, 2081, 2084. Moreover, as discussed in n. 298 below, and accompanying text, a longer period of residence is required from second-generation migrants living in Germany. In France, the Act of 24 Aug. 1993 introduced, *inter alia*, a waiting-period of 2 years continuous residence (rather than one year), while in Denmark, non-Nordic nationals can now only be joined by family members after 5 years of residence in the country: *SOPEMI 1994*, 43 and 81 respectively.

[245] Commission Working Paper, n. 26 above, 18; *ILO General Survey 1980*, n. 210 above; Thomsen, n. 243 above; *Closed Borders, Stringent Attitudes*, n. 14 above, 62, 63 (the Netherlands and Spain).

[246] See Commission Working Paper, n. 26 above; *ILO General Survey 1980*, n. 210 above; *Closed Borders, Stringent Attitudes*, n. 14 above (Denmark, the Netherlands, Spain), with regard to the sufficient resources requirement.

towards family reunification.[247] But if both labour-receiving and sending countries are parties to a bilateral labour agreement or belong to a regional arrangement which implements free movement for workers, such as the EC or the EEA, many of these conditions on family reunification are then removed.

Definition of family

European standards concerned with the right of migrant workers to family reunion essentially define 'family' as the spouse and minor dependent children. This basic definition has been expanded, in some cases to a considerably generous extent by the ESC Committee of Independent Experts and the Court of Justice in their respective interpretations of the relevant provisions. In one sense, however, the various definitions of 'family' found in these standards are nothing more than further restrictions on the right to family reunification simply because migrant workers cannot determine for themselves the persons who constitute their 'family'.

The ESC and the EMW each offer different definitions of 'family' in connection with family reunion. The ESC in its Appendix defines the family of a foreign worker for the purpose of the family reunification obligation in Article 19(6) to mean 'at least his wife and dependent children under the age of 21 years'. The words '*at least*' allow for a broader interpretation of the concept of 'family' which, for example, would probably include dependent disabled children over 21 years of age.[248] In examining state practice, the Committee of Independent Experts has found that not all contracting parties conform to the age requirement, particularly if the age of majority in the state party is lower. The most restrictive rules exist in Germany, where young persons over 16 years of age from non-EC countries are excluded from family reunion by the *Länder* on the recommendation of the Federal Government. Children with only one parent resident in Germany cannot enter for the purpose of family reunion either. Moreover, spouses of second-generation migrants are also excluded, unless the latter have already resided in Germany for 8 years, are over 18 years of age and have been married for one year. The Committee maintained that the German provisions are contrary to Article 19(6).[249] The position in the United Kingdom has also given rise

[247] In respect of migrant workers settled in a country of employment, the need for such restrictions for economic reasons is questionable. With reference to third-country nationals residing in EC member states, Böhning and Werquin, n. 36 above, 18–19, para. 43, cite some German studies to argue that the adoption of a more liberal family reunion regime in those countries would only lead to a modest increase in immigration because only a small number of spouses and children remain separated and not all family members eligible to migrate would actually do so.

[248] Harris, n. 20 above, 174 (and n. 938), referring to the drafting process in the Committee of Ministers (Doc. CM (61) 95 rev.3). In this regard, the Committee of Independent Experts has requested information on whether possibilities exist for migrant workers to be reunited with relatives other than the spouse and dependent children under 21 years of age: *Conclusions III*, 95, cited in *Case Law on the European Social Charter*, n. 19 above, 165.

[249] *Conclusions X-2*, n. 131 above, 150–1; *Conclusions XI-2*, n. 182 above, 151. Hohnerlein, n. 152 above, 127, observes that the 16 years age-limit for family reunion has been fixed by all the

to negative conclusions from the Committee. The age limit for the reunion of dependent children with their parents, who are not EC nationals, stands at 18 years of age, although special consideration is given to dependent daughters between 18 and 21 years. An older dependent child may also be admitted if compassionate circumstances exist, for example if he or she is disabled.[250] In some cases, however, the Committee's observations have generated legal reforms. Previously, dependent children aged 20 years would not be admitted into Norway to join their migrant parents unless they had no other family members in the country of origin. The Norwegian Government later provided information to the Committee on its Immigration Act of 1988 and on draft regulations for the Act's implementation which permit entry to, *inter alia*, all unmarried dependent children under *21 years* of age, provided that their maintenance is guaranteed. This law also grants family reunion to co-habitants if they have lived together for 2 years. In the Committee's opinion, these provisions were in conformity with the ESC.[251]

The Governmental Committee recently proposed to the Charte-Rel Committee, charged with revising the substantive content of the ESC, that an amendment should be introduced to take into account legal developments since the ESC's adoption which have resulted in an age of majority of 18 years in all states parties.[252] In the Appendix to the revised ESC, the family of the worker is now redefined to include 'unmarried children, as long as the latter are considered to be minors by the receiving state and are dependent on the migrant worker'.[253] This development has resulted in the Committee of Independent Experts adopting a more relaxed approach towards those states parties with national legislation fixing the family reunion age limit below 21 years. Such states will not be found in violation of Article 19(6) if they are able to demonstrate by providing statistics that no applications have been turned down in practice from children who fall between the national and ESC age thresholds.[254] The amendment in the

Länder with the exception of Bremen and Hessen. Moreover, the Federal Administrative Court has confirmed these restrictions, although none of the decided cases have concerned nationals from the ESC states parties which are not members of the EC.

[250] *Conclusions XII-1*, n. 57 above, 240. The United Kingdom, however, has drawn the Committee's attention to the rarity of such applications from children aged 18 and over from a country bound by the ESC but not a member of the EC, and that such applications are in practice normally accepted: *ibid.*; *Conclusions XIII-2*, n. 51 above, 204. Similar restrictive rules on the admission of young persons over the age of 18 in Austria, Greece, and Italy have also recently drawn negative conclusions from the Committee. See *Conclusions XIII-2*, *ibid.* 200–202.

[251] See respectively Council of Europe, Committee of Independent Experts of the European Social Charter, *Conclusions IX-1* (Strasbourg: Council of Europe, 1985) 109 and *Conclusions XII-1*, n. 57 above, 238–9. The Committee observed, during the consideration of the next Norwegian report, that these immigration regulations had been adopted and had entered into force on 1 Jan. 1991: *Conclusions XIII-1*, n. 57 above, 209–10. The ninth Swedish report also noted that the concept of 'family' covered 'quasi-marital relations'. The Committee responded that the Swedish approach had a positive effect on the family reunification obligation in Art. 19(6): *Conclusions IX-1*, *ibid.*

[252] *12th Report (I)*, n. 57 above, 72, para. 326 and 110–11, para. 95 (App.).

[253] See also *Request for an Opinion on the Draft Revised European Social Charter*, n. 128 above, 31 and 46 (Draft Explanatory Report, para. 76).

[254] *Conclusions XIII-2*, n. 51 above, 53, para. 92.

revised ESC seriously dilutes the protection afforded by the ESC in this area. The position that the age-limit of 21 years for family reunion is antiquated, and should therefore be changed, is questionable given the existence of an even more generous rule in EC secondary legislation, which is discussed below, and in view of the tendency of children to be dependent on their parents for longer periods because of entry into higher education. The new provision in the revised ESC clearly supports more restrictive age-limits on family reunion, such as the 16-year age-limit described above in relation to Germany.[255]

With regard to the requirement for 'dependence' in Article 19(6) in respect of the admission of children, the Governmental Committee has adopted a progressive interpretation which is not confined to economic dependence, but encompasses 'all situations in which there is *de facto* or legal dependence under the relevant laws'.[256]

One unfortunate anomaly of the ESC's definition of 'family' in respect of family reunion is that it does not apply to husbands of female migrant workers, an omission which has been confirmed by the Committee of Independent Experts.[257] The revised version of the ESC makes the necessary amendment by replacing 'wife' with 'spouse'.[258]

[255] The latter argument was advanced by the representative of Portugal in the Governmental Committee in explaining that country's opposition to the proposed change: *12th Report (I)*, n. 57 above, 72, para. 327 and 111, para. 95 (App. VIII). Despite the proposal to amend the ESC in this way, the Committee of Ministers issued Recommendation No. R ChS (94) 3 of 8 April 1994 urging the German Government to take measures to remedy the situation: cited in (1995) 2:1 IHRR. According to representations made in the Governmental Committee, the German Government considers its family reunion criteria to be 'very balanced' given the significant increase in the foreign population. Moreover, the 16-year age-limit is tempered somewhat by admitting the children of non-EC nationals who are aged between 16 and 18 years provided that they can speak German or if their entry is justified on the ground of 'special hardship'. These conditions also apply in cases where children only have one parent resident in Germany: Council of Europe, European Social Charter, Governmental Committee, *12th Report (II) (1989–1990)* (Strasbourg: Council of Europe Press, 1995) 33–4, para. 98. The Governmental Committee, *ibid.* 34–5, para. 100, proposed during the 12th cycle of supervision that the Committee of Ministers issue a recommendation to Germany to amend its legislation allowing all children of migrant workers under 18 years of age and the spouses of second-generation migrant workers to enter Germany for the purposes of family reunion. During the 13th cycle of supervision, the Committee of Independent Experts reiterated its negative conclusion in respect of Germany in spite of new legislation on family reunion, which, however, did not introduce any improvements in the areas of concern: *Conclusions XIII-2*, n. 51 above, 384–5.

[256] *Eighth Report*, 18–19, cited in *Case Law on the European Social Charter: Supplement*, n. 59 above, 51. The Governmental Committee has suggested that this might include psychological and moral dependence. Such an interpretation seems even wider than that proposed by the Committee of Independent Experts which encompasses 'persons who depend, for their existence, on their family, in particular because of economic reasons or, as the case may be, for such reasons as continuation of education without remuneration or for reasons of health': *Conclusions VIII*, 211–12, cited in *Case Law on the European Social Charter: Supplement*, *ibid.* 50.

[257] *Conclusions IV*, 124, cited in *Case Law on the European Social Charter*, n. 19 above, 166. However, the Committee, *ibid.*, has maintained that the notion of 'dependency' includes the children of *women* migrant workers.

[258] See also *Request for an Opinion on the Draft Revised European Social Charter*, n. 128, 31, 46 (Draft Explanatory Report, para. 76).

The overt discrimination on the ground of sex in the ESC is rectified in the EMW which applies to spouses of both sexes. The EMW, however, confines the state obligation regarding family reunification in Article 12(1) to the spouse and unmarried minor dependent children. In contrast with the ESC, therefore, the definition in the EMW expressly requires dependent children to be unmarried. More importantly, this definition only applies to 'minor' children without specifying a minimum age-limit. Consequently, dependent children *below* the age of 21 may lawfully be excluded under the EMW from the state party where the migrant worker is employed if the law of that country stipulates that the age of majority commences earlier.[259]

Article 10(1) of Regulation 1612/68/EEC offers a more detailed and comprehensive definition of family for the purpose of family reunion. Migrant workers from other EC member states may be accompanied to, or joined in, the country of employment by their spouse and children under the age of 21, or by children over 21 if the latter are still dependent on the worker. However, unmarried partners of EC workers who have lived with them in a stable relationship are *not* covered by the word 'spouse', which only applies to marriage partners.[260] The married couple do not actually have to live together. Indeed, they may both pursue occupations in different parts of the same country. Furthermore, they are still regarded as 'spouses' for the purposes of Article 10 even if they are living permanently apart, provided that their marriage has not been formally dissolved.[261] Article 10(1) also applies to dependent relatives in the ascending line of the worker and his or her spouse, namely their parents and grandparents. As far as other relatives are concerned, Article 10(2) obliges member states to facilitate their admission if they are dependent on the worker or living under his or her roof. This does not mean, however, that the members of the worker's family *must* live permanently under the same roof as the worker so long as the accommodation which the worker makes available is considered as 'normal' for the purpose of accommodating family members.[262] In all cases, proof of the relation-

[259] See also Oellers-Frahm, n. 71 above, 1737 and H. Golsong, 'La convention européenne relative au statut juridique du travailleur migrant' (1978) 243. Therefore, the definition of 'family' for the purpose of the family reunion obligation in the revised ESC is in line with the EMW definition. Both the definitions in the ESC and the EMW, however, are narrower in scope than the corresponding definition of 'family' in Art. 13(2) of ILO Convention No. 143 of 1975, which is applicable to *all* dependent children *and parents*. The definition in Art. 44(2) of the UN Convention on Migrant Workers is limited to 'minor dependent unmarried children' but coverage is extended to 'spouses or persons who have with the migrant worker a relationship that, according to applicable law, produces effects equivalent to marriage'.

[260] Case 59/85, *Netherlands* v. *Reed* [1986] ECR 1283, [1987] 2 CMLR 448. Although Art. 10(1) was inapplicable, the co-habitants in this case were permitted to stay together in the Netherlands because 'cohabitation' constituted a 'social advantage' enjoyed by Dutch nationals under Dutch law. As noted above, discrimination between national and EC workers with respect to the enjoyment of 'social and tax advantages' is prohibited by Art. 7(2) of Reg. 1612/68/EEC. In this regard, therefore, Art. 10(1) is narrower in scope than Art. 44(2) of the UN Convention.

[261] *Diatta* v. *Land Berlin*, n. 85 above.

[262] *Ibid.* See also Art. 10(3) of Reg. 1612/68/EEC; See nn. 316–17 below and the accompanying text.

ship or dependency may be required by the authorities of the receiving member country.[263]

The spouse, children, and other relatives, who come to join the migrant worker in the country of employment, need not be nationals themselves of another EC member state. Article 10(1) expressly provides defined family members with the right, '*irrespective of nationality*', to install themselves with a worker who is a national of one of the member states. Moreover, as noted earlier, Article 11 permits incoming family members to take up employment throughout the territory of the state concerned, '*even if they are not nationals of any member State*'.[264]

Potentially at least, the ECHR offers the broadest concept of 'family' for the purpose of protecting the right of migrant workers to family reunion. There is no explicit right to family reunification in the ECHR,[265] but it is clear from the discussion in the next section on jurisprudence under Article 8 regarding 'the right to respect for . . . family life' that the question of family reunion is of concern to the Commission and the Court. 'Family life' has been broadly defined. In addition to the spouse and unmarried dependent children, the Court has maintained that: '"[F]amily life", within the meaning of Article 8, includes at least the ties between near relatives, for instance those between grandparents and grandchildren, since such relatives may play a considerable part in family life'.[266] Family life also encompasses bonds between parents and illegitimate children,[267] and co-habitees in a stable relationship.[268] More distant family relationships, however, such as those between uncle and nephew and aunt and niece, are less likely to qualify under Article 8.[269] Homosexual partners have been expressly excluded from the scope of 'family life' by the Commission, although they are

[263] Art. 4(1) of Council Directive 68/360/EEC of 15 Oct. 1968 on the abolition of restrictions on movement and residence within the Community, OJ Sp. Ed. 1968–69, 485.

[264] Emphasis added. For example, in *Diatta*, n. 85 above, the spouse who came to join the worker, a French citizen employed in Germany, was a Senegalese national.

[265] Similarly, there is no right to family reunification recognized in the ECE. However, Section V(b) of the Protocol to the ECE does contain a definition of the 'family' in respect of access to employment, which encompasses the 'husband or wife and dependent children': see n. 288 below and the accompanying text.

[266] *Marckx* v. *Belgium*, judgment of 13 June 1979, Eur. Court H.R., 1979, Ser. A, No. 31, (1979–80) 2 EHRR 330, para. 45.

[267] See *Marckx*, *ibid.* para. 31, in which the Court observed that the relationship between mother and illegitimate child constitutes 'family', and Applications 7289/75 and 7349/76, *X. and Y.* v. *Switzerland* (1977) 9 D & R 57, in which the Commission stated that the relationship between illegitimate children and their father is included in the concept of family life.

[268] *X. and Y.*, *ibid.*

[269] Application 3110/67, *X.* v. *Federal Republic of Germany* (1968) 11 YBECHR 494 and Application 8353/78, *X.* v. *U.K.* (1979) Eur. Comm. H.R. (unpublished), cited in Council of Europe, *Digest of Strasbourg Case Law relating to the European Convention on Human Rights*, vol. III (Arts. 7–12) (Köln: Heymanns Verlag, 1984) 85–6 and 90–1 respectively. See also A. Drzemczewski, 'The Position of Aliens in Relation to the European Convention on Human Rights: A General Survey' (1985) 369 (n. 84). Relationships between cousins fall into a similar category as well as relationships between engaged couples. See respectively Applications 7768/77 (1977), Eur. Comm. H.R. (unpublished) and 8823/79 (1980), Eur. Comm. H.R. (unpublished), cited in *Digest of Strasbourg Case Law*, *ibid.* 88, 92.

covered by the concept of 'private life' in Article 8.[270] In each case, however, as elaborated below, the degrees of relationship and dependency between family members are the predominant factors in determining whether 'family life' has been established under Article 8. In contrast with the broad definition accorded to the concept of 'dependency' by ESC organs, the Commission views this concept more in financial and material terms. Emotional dependency alone, therefore, would appear to be insufficient to give rise to the protection of Article 8.[271]

The right to family reunification

(a) European Convention on Human Rights

Although there is no explicit clause in the ECHR concerned with the right to family reunion, the understanding is that states parties, by ratifying the ECHR, have implicitly agreed to limit their sovereignty, including their previously unfettered control over the entry and exit of aliens.[272] In the case of family reunification, the guarantee in Article 8(1) of the ECHR that 'everyone has the right to respect for his private and family life, his home and correspondence' has led the Commission of Human Rights to observe that:

> in certain circumstances, refusals to give certain persons access to, or allow them to take up residence in, a particular country, might result in the separation of such persons from the close members of their family which could raise serious problems under Article 8 of the Convention.[273]

A number of stringent requirements have to be satisfied before the refusal of entry to certain family members, or the separation of families as a result of the expulsion of a non-national, are recognized as violating Article 8(1). First, the relationship between the family members concerned needs to be sufficiently close and effective[274] and family life must be actually 'existing'.[275] Secondly, there

[270] Application 9369/81, *X. and Y.* v. *United Kingdom* (1983) 32 D & R 220; Application 12513/86 v. *United Kingdom* (1989) 11 EHRR 49.

[271] Application 10375/83, *S. and S.* v. *United Kingdom* (1985) 40 D & R 196.

[272] In the words of the Commission of Human Rights in Application 434/58, *X.* v. *Sweden* (1958/59) 2 YBECHR 354, 372–3: '[A] State which signs and ratifies the European Convention on Human Rights must be understood as agreeing to restrict the free exercise of its rights under general international law, including the right to control the entry and exit of foreigners to the extent and within the limits of the obligations which it has accepted under that Convention'.

[273] Application 1855/63, *X.* v. *Denmark* (1965) 8 YBECHR 200, 204. This position was confirmed by the Court in *Abdulaziz, Cabales and Balkandali* v. *United Kingdom*, judgment of 28 May 1985, Eur. Ct. H.R., 1985, Ser. A. No. 94, para. 59, (1986) 7 EHRR 471.

[274] For examples of applicable 'close' relationships, see the previous section. As far as 'effective' relationships are concerned, see Application 2992/66, *Singh* v. *U.K.* (1967) 10 YBECHR 478, in which the Commission ruled that because the applicant son had lived apart from his widowed father for a long time, their relationship did not constitute 'effective' family life for the purpose of Art. 8(1).

[275] In Application 7229/75, *X. and Y.* v. *U.K.* (1977) 12 D & R 32, the Commission maintained that Art. 8 guaranteed a right to respect for *existing* family life and that it did not oblige a state party to grant a foreign citizen entry into its territory for the purpose of establishing a *new* family relationship there.

must be a lack of 'respect for family life', and there will be no infringement if it is feasible for family reunion to take place elsewhere.[276] This is a very difficult requirement to satisfy. In *Abdulaziz, Cabales and Balkandali* v. *United Kingdom*, discussed in the previous chapter, the discriminatory immigration rules did *not* violate Article 8 taken alone because the Court concluded that there is no general obligation on states parties 'to respect the choice by married couples of their matrimonial residence and to accept the non-national spouses for settlement in that country'.[277] However, the rules infringed Article 14 taken together with Article 8.[278] In *Gül* v. *Switzerland*, the Court also found that the refusal of Swiss authorities to permit a 12-year-old Turkish boy to join his parents, who were lawfully resident in Switzerland on humanitarian grounds, was not contrary to Article 8 because there were 'no obstacles preventing them from developing family life in Turkey'.[279] Even when a public authority decision or action is found to interfere with the right to respect for family life, it might still comply with Article 8(2), which permits the interference if it is 'in accordance with the law and is necessary in a democratic society in the interests of [*inter alia*] national security, public safety or the economic well-being of the country, for the prevention of disorder or crime [and] for the protection of health'.

All of these stringent requirements have been satisfied in certain claims arising from expulsion.[280] On several occasions, the Court has found an infringement of the right to respect for family life in cases involving second-generation migrants, who had either been expelled, or were under threat of expulsion, because they had been convicted of criminal offences in their country of residence. Although in each case, the expulsions, or threatened expulsions, pursued the legitimate aim under Article 8(2) of preventing disorder or crime, they constituted a disproportionate means of achieving this aim given that the affected individuals had spent most of their lives, together with their immediate families, in the

[276] In Application 7816/77, *X. and Y.* v. *Germany* (1977) 9 D & R 219, the Commission stated that there was no reason why family life could not be established outside of Germany. It made no difference in this case that the wife was a citizen of the country which had ordered the expulsion of her American husband on the ground that he was dealing in heroin.

[277] See n. 273 above, para. 68.

[278] Unfortunately, the government nullified the effect of this decision when it made it equally difficult for women to join their husbands or fiancés who had settled in the United Kingdom. See the commentary by S. H. Bailey, D. J. Harris, and B. L. Jones, *Civil Liberties: Cases and Materials*, 4th edn. (London: Butterworths, 1995) 709–10.

[279] *Gül* v. *Switzerland*, judgment of 19 Feb. 1996, (1996) 22 EHRR 93 para. 42. The Court acknowledged, however, that return to Turkey would not be easy given that the applicant's wife was receiving medical treatment in Switzerland and in view of the length of time which the couple had spent outside their country of origin (over 10 years for the applicant and over 8 years for his wife).

[280] For a recent case concerned with entry, see the Commission report in Application 21702/93, *Ahmut and Ahmut* v. *Netherlands* (17 May 1995), finding that the decision of the Dutch authorities to refuse to grant a residence permit to a 14-year-old boy, so that he could remain with his father in the Netherlands, constituted a violation of Art. 8 and could not be saved by Art. 8(2).

countries concerned and had little or no ties with their country of origin.[281] In cases where the offences committed are particularly serious, however, the Court is less willing to encroach upon the exercise of a state's margin of appreciation under Article 8(2).[282] The development of this case law has resulted in a series of similar applications before the Commission of Human Rights.[283]

The conditions which states usually impose on the right to family reunification, *inter alia* that migrant workers first reside in the country of employment for a

[281] See the judgments of the Court in *Beldjoudi* v. *France*, judgment of 26 March 1992, Eur. Ct. H.R., 1992, Ser. A, No. 234-A, (1992) 14 EHRR 801 and *Moustaquim* v. *Belgium*, judgment of 18 Feb. 1991, Eur. Ct. H.R., 1991, Ser. A, No. 193, (1991) 13 EHRR 802. See also Application 13446/87, *Djeroud* v. *France*, Eur. Ct. H.R., 1991, Ser. A, No. 191-B, (1992) 14 EHRR 68 and Application 16152/90, *Lamguindaz* v. *United Kingdom*, Eur. Ct. H.R. 1993, Ser. A, No. 258-C, which were both settled before the Court in favour of the applicants after the Commission had concluded that there had been an infringement of Art. 8. Recently, these decisions were reinforced by the Court in *Nasri* v. *France*, judgment of 13 July 1995, Eur. Ct. H.R., 1995, Ser. A., No. 324, (1996) 21 EHRR 458, which concerned a deaf and dumb Algerian national facing deportation from France for committing a number of criminal offences, including a conviction for participation in a gang rape. The Court found that the decision to deport the applicant constituted a violation of Art. 8(1) and, moreover, was not justified under Art. 8(2) because it was not proportionate to the otherwise legitimate aims of preventing disorder and crime: 'In view of [the] accumulation of special circumstances, notably his situation as a deaf and dumb person, capable of achieving a minimum psychological and social equilibrium only within his family, the majority of whose members are French nationals with no close ties with Algeria, the decision to deport the applicant, if executed, would not be proportionate to the legitimate aim pursued'. The Court also found a violation of Art. 8 in *Berrehab* v. *Netherlands*, judgment of 21 June 1988, Eur. Ct. H.R., 1988, Ser. A, No. 138, (1989) 11 EHRR 322, which should be distinguished from the cases above on its facts. In *Berrehab*, a father, who was a Moroccan citizen, was separated from his infant daughter after the Dutch authorities refused to renew his residence permit because of divorce from his Dutch wife. The father had lived and worked in the Netherlands for a considerable length of time and had maintained regular contacts with his daughter after the divorce. These considerations could not be outweighed under Art. 8(2) by the Dutch government's legitimate aim of regulating the labour market in the interests of the 'economic well-being of the country'. In contrast with the decisions cited above, the applicant had not lived in the Netherlands for most of his life and had been expelled from that country on grounds unconnected with criminality. For a detailed discussion of this case law, see R. Cholewinski, 'Strasbourg's "Hidden Agenda"?: The Protection of Second-Generation Migrants from Expulsion under Article 8 of the European Convention of Human Rights' (1994) 12 NQHR 287.

[282] In *Boughanemi* v. *France*, judgment of 24 April 1996, (1996) 22 EHRR 228, the Court also found a violation of Art. 8 in respect of a Tunisian national deported from France to Tunisia after he had been convicted of a series of criminal offences. The applicant had lived in France since the age of 8, all his family resided there and he had also been co-habiting with a French national with whom he had had a child. However, the Court, *ibid.* para. 44, concluded that the deportation was nonetheless justified under Art. 8(2) in view of the applicant's continued links with Tunisia and the serious nature of his crimes which had led to a long prison sentence. See also the Commission reports in two similar cases, Application 23078/93, *Bouchelka* v. *France* (6 Sept. 1995) and Application 21794/93, *Chorfi* v. *Belgium* (21 Feb. 1995), in which the seriousness of the crimes convinced the majority of the Commission to conclude that the decision to deport the applicant was in conformity with Art. 8(2). The Commission's conclusion in *Chorfi* was essentially confirmed by the Court in an unanimous ruling delivered on 7 Aug. 1996 (not yet reported). See Council of Europe, European Court of Human Rights, *Press Releases issued by the Registrar of the European Court of Human Rights* (Strasbourg, 10 July–2 Sept. 1996) 5–7.

[283] For recent applications found admissible in connection with this line of case law, see Application 25404/94, *D.B.* v. *France*, Application 25613/94, *A.E.B.* v. *France*, and Application 26102/95, *Dalia* v. *France* (cited in European Commission of Human Rights, *Information Note No. 131* and *Information Note No. 133*, 3 and 2 respectively).

specified period, possess adequate accommodation and sufficient resources, and that incoming family members are in good health, have yet to be directly evaluated by the Court under Article 8 jurisprudence. The Commission has accepted that entry procedures may raise an issue under Article 8(1), but found that a waiting-period of 6 months, which was required of an applicant who wished to join her spouse in the United Kingdom, was not unreasonable given the total number of applicants and the difficulties of verifying their status.[284] Even if the conditions that states impose on family reunion are found to infringe Article 8(1), many of them might no doubt be justified under Article 8(2), provided that the requirement of proportionality is satisfied.

The right to marry and to found a family is protected by Article 12 of the ECHR.[285] Neither the Commission nor the Court, however, have found that this right has been infringed because an applicant has had to leave or has been refused entry into a country. In most cases, the couple are able to marry and live together elsewhere.[286] However, both Articles 8(1) and 12 read together may be interpreted as imposing an obligation to admit a fiancé/e into the country of residence of the partner if marriage and life together outside of that country are deemed impossible.[287]

(b) European Convention on Establishment

There is no right to family reunification in the ECE, which is clearly an anomaly given that one of its aims is to facilitate prolonged or permanent residence in one state party for nationals from other contracting parties. Section V(b) of the Protocol to the ECE provides a definition of the family in respect of access to employment as encompassing the 'husband or wife and dependent children of nationals of any Contracting Party lawfully residing in the territory of another Party *who have been authorized to accompany or rejoin them*'.[288] This wording indicates, in the absence of express provisions to the contrary, that family reunion is at the sole discretion of the receiving country. This discretion, however, is qualified somewhat in the case of expulsion by Section III(c) of the Protocol, which stipulates that family ties are to be taken into account in determining whether to remove a state party national from the territory of another contracting party.

(c) European Social Charter

As noted earlier, the ESC contains an express provision relating to family reunification. Article 19(6) places states parties under an obligation 'to facilitate as far as possible the reunion of the family of a foreign worker permitted to establish

[284] Application 7048/75, *X.* v. *United Kingdom* (1977) 9 D & R 42.

[285] Art. 12 reads: 'Men and women of marriageable age have the right to marry and to found a family, according to the national laws governing the exercise of this right'.

[286] Application 7175/75, *X.* v. *Germany* (1976) 6 D & R 138; Application 9773/82 v. *United Kingdom* (1983) 5 EHRR 296.

[287] Cf. Plender, n. 72 above, 235.

[288] Emphasis added.

himself in the territory'.[289] The duty is only to 'facilitate' and constitutes a watered-down version of a draft text of the ESC which used much stronger language and spoke of family reunification in terms of an express right.[290] Nonetheless, the Committee of Independent Experts has interpreted Article 19(6) broadly, while strictly construing the validity of the restrictions which states often impose on the reunion of migrant workers with their families. The aim of Article 19(6) is to oblige states parties 'to create the conditions which make family reunion possible' and thus 'it should not be interpreted in the sense that it permits the adoption of restrictions likely to deprive the obligation of its content'. The provision is also to be interpreted in the light of Article 16 of the ESC.[291] Article 16 recognizes the obligation of states parties to ensure the 'economic, legal and social protection' of the family, which is regarded as 'a fundamental unit of society', and is a similar provision to those found in universal and other regional human rights instruments (discussed in Chapter 2).

The duty in Article 16 extends, *inter alia*, to the 'provision of family housing'. Most countries of employment require migrant workers to obtain suitable housing before family reunion may take place, and the scarce availability of such accommodation, especially in Western European states, is a considerable obstacle to the realization of this right. In recognition of these difficulties, the Committee of Independent Experts has frequently interpreted the duty to 'facilitate' in Article 19(6) as implying a *positive* obligation to assist migrant workers and their families in finding suitable public or private housing.[292] The Committee has

[289] The Committee of Independent Experts has confirmed that this obligation extends to self-employed workers: *Conclusions IX-2*, 102, cited in *Case Law on the European Social Charter: Supplement No. 2*, n. 59 above, 31.

[290] This version required states to grant migrant workers 'the *right* to be accompanied or joined by their families' and 'to facilitate', without qualification, 'the reunion of their families': Harris, n. 20 above, 174 (emphasis added). The word 'facilitate' is also used in the relevant provisions of the UN Convention and ILO Convention No. 143 on migrant workers. The scope of the duty is also similar. In the former, under Art. 44(2), states parties are to take measures that they '*deem appropriate . . . to facilitate*' family reunion and in the latter, under Art. 13(1), they '*may* take all measures . . . *to facilitate*' family reunion (emphasis added). A similarly diluted obligation concerning family reunion exists in Art. 10(1) of the UN Convention on the Rights of the Child: '[A]pplications by a child or his or her parents to enter or leave a State Party for the purpose of family reunification shall be dealt with by States Parties in a positive, humane and expeditious manner'.

[291] *Conclusions VIII*, 211, 212, cited in *Case Law on the European Social Charter: Supplement*, n. 59 above, 50.

[292] *Conclusions I*, 85, *Conclusions II*, 69, *Conclusions III*, 94, 96, *Conclusions IV*, 124, 126, *Conclusions V*, 136–7 and *Conclusions VII*, 105, cited in *Case Law on the European Social Charter*, n. 19 above, 163–7. In *Conclusions XII-2*, n. 57 above, 225, the Committee asked 'what measures had been taken by the French authorities to help foreign workers find accommodation, particularly in urban areas affected by housing shortages'. See also *Conclusions XIII-2*, n. 51 above, 202 and 383–4, with regard to the Italian and Belgian reports. On examination of the subsequent French report, the Committee took note of a measure (Circular No. 93–10 of 12 March 1993) which enabled those whose applications for family reunion had been rejected on the grounds of sub-standard accommodation to seek assistance: *Conclusions XIII-2*, n. 51 above, 200. Positive state action is not required, however, if housing market conditions are favourable. See *Conclusions III*, 94, *Conclusions V*, 136–7 and *Conclusions VII*, 105, cited in *Case Law on the European Social Charter*, n. 19 above, 164, 167.

keenly observed state practice in this area. For example, it has concluded that stringent residence conditions on the acquisition of public housing are unlikely to be in conformity with the ESC because they do not 'facilitate' family reunion.[293] The call for special housing measures in favour of migrant workers and their families under Article 19(6) is clearly an extension of the principle of equal treatment between migrants and nationals in respect of accommodation under Article 19(4)(c) of the ESC.[294]

The wording of Article 19(6) appears to restrict family reunion to the family of a worker 'permitted to establish himself in the territory' of a state party. This clause should be contrasted with other paragraphs in Article 19 which afford rights to migrant workers 'lawfully within' the territories of states parties,[295] thus excluding undocumented workers from their protection. Although the Committee of Independent Experts has not expressly concluded that Article 19(6) is narrower than the other provisions, the drafting history suggests that it is more limited.[296] The Governmental Committee has also maintained that this wording must exclude certain categories of migrant workers 'recruited for short-term employment, such as seasonal workers and persons on short-term non-renewable contracts'.[297] This restriction on the reunion of such workers with their families finds further support in the acknowledgement by the Committee of Independent Experts that states parties may require migrant workers to reside a certain period of time in their territory before their families are permitted to join them, provided that this period is not too excessive. A 3-year waiting period contravenes Article 19(6) as well as the requirement in Germany that the spouses of second-generation migrants may only enter the country to join them if the latter have resided in Germany for at least 8 years and have been married for at least one year.[298] A blanket refusal of entry to family members of migrant workers who are on renewable fixed-term contracts also violates this provision.[299]

A requirement that migrant workers possess sufficient financial resources to maintain their families is probably another justifiable restriction on family

[293] The Committee was concerned here with the situation in Norway where migrant workers were required to wait 10 years before gaining access to subsidized housing: *Conclusions XI-1*, n. 219 above, 163. See also *Conclusions XIII-2*, n. 51 above, 203.

[294] Harris, n. 20 above, 179.

[295] See also Plender, n. 72 above, 247.

[296] Harris, n. 20 above, 175.

[297] *Eighth Report*, 18–19, cited in *Case Law on the European Social Charter: Supplement*, n. 59 above, 51. On this interpretation, a policy such as the one implemented by Swiss authorities, (Switzerland has signed but not ratified the ESC), which does not permit seasonal workers to bring their families, would not be subject to scrutiny under Art. 19(6). For a description of this policy, see Note (Switzerland), 'New Policy for Foreign Workers' (Sept. 1991) EIRR 14.

[298] See respectively *Conclusions II*, 69, cited in *Case Law on the European Social Charter*, n. 19 above, 163 and *Conclusions XI-2*, n. 182 above, 151. Recommendation No. R ChS (94) 3, issued to Germany by the Committee of Ministers, n. 255 above, urges the German Government to take steps to remedy this situation.

[299] *Conclusions X-2*, n. 131 above, 150–1, concerning the position in Germany. See also *Conclusions XI-2*, n. 182 above.

reunification so long as it is reasonable.[300] The exclusion of family members with a serious disease may also be justified, but only if it poses a threat to 'public health' or, possibly, to 'public interest'.[301] However, a state cannot prohibit on these grounds the entry of sick or disabled children, who require specialized treatment, to join a family of limited means.[302]

(d) The European Convention on the Legal Status of Migrant Workers

The EMW is also specifically concerned with family reunification. Article 12 is entitled 'family reunion', but according to one commentator, its lengthy provisions remain 'in their entirety some way behind' those of the ESC.[303] Although the importance of Article 12 is underlined by the stipulation that no reservations can be made in respect of its provisions,[304] the principle of family reunion is subject to so many 'escape clauses' that the efficacy of Article 12 must be seriously questioned. The families of migrant workers may only enter the country concerned under the same conditions as applied to these workers by the EMW. Before family reunion may occur, Article 12(1) also requires migrant workers to possess family housing 'considered as normal for national workers in the region where the migrant worker is employed'. There is no obligation upon states parties, however, as has been interpreted under Article 19(6) of the ESC by the Committee of Independent Experts, to provide special assistance to migrant workers in obtaining this accommodation.[305] The provision permits the receiving country to impose a discretionary waiting-period of not more than 12 months. In addition, a state party may impose a further condition requiring migrant workers to possess 'steady resources' sufficient to meet the needs of their families. The exercise of state discretion, however, is subject here to a monitoring mechanism by virtue of Article 12(2) which provides that such a condition may only come

[300] In interpreting the words 'as far as possible' in Art. 19(6), the Governmental Committee has stated that the 'obligation is not absolute, in the sense that a member state is not obliged to facilitate the reunion *at all costs* and in all cases' (emphasis added). See *Eighth Report*, 18–19, cited in *Case Law on the European Social Charter: Supplement*, n. 59 above, 50. However, a 'sufficient resources' condition on family reunion that effectively requires migrant workers to attain a higher standard of living than national workers would be unreasonable.

[301] *Conclusions IX-1*, n. 251 above, 108; *Conclusions X-1*, n. 57 above, 150; *Conclusions XII-2*, n. 57 above, 227. See also Plender, n. 72 above, 247. Harris, n. 20 above, 177, observes that the Committee of Independent Experts implicitly justified this restriction on the basis of Art. 31 of the ESC which permits states parties to limit the exercise of ESC rights for the protection of, *inter alia*, 'public health'.

[302] *Conclusions I*, 85, cited in *Case Law on the European Social Charter*, n. 19 above, 163. Unless the sole intention of the migrant worker in seeking employment in the country is to take advantage of the benefits of the health service for this purpose: *Conclusions II*, 69 and *Conclusions III*, 97, cited in *Case Law on the European Social Charter*, n. 19 above, 165.

[303] Oellers-Frahm, n. 71 above, 1737.

[304] Art. 36. See also *Explanatory Report on the EMW*, n. 71 above, 18, para. 53.

[305] See also Oellers-Frahm, n. 71 above, 1737 and Swart, n. 45 above, 10. Norway has reported that, since 1988, it has not subjected migrant workers to a condition that they must possess adequate accommodation before their families can join them: *Fourth Report on the Application of the EMW*, n. 222 above, 4, para. 29.

into operation one month after a declaration to this effect has been addressed to the COE Secretary General. Migrant workers living off unemployment or public assistance benefits are deemed not to possess 'steady resources'.[306]

The most significant 'escape clause' is Article 12(3), which permits Contracting parties to derogate temporarily from the obligation of family reunification for certain parts of their territory. This provision was added to the draft of Article 12 in the final stages of negotiation in order to take account of the special situation of those states parties which are no longer able to cope with the influx of migrant workers' families into certain regions with respect to the provision of housing, education, and health care services.[307] To ensure that this power is not abused, Article 12(3) is subject to a number of inbuilt safeguards, based upon those found in Article 15 of the ECHR which permits derogation from certain rights in time of war and public emergency.[308] The Article 12(3) derogation may only be applied temporarily, although no specific time-limit is expressly provided,[309] and cannot be employed in respect of the whole territory of the country. Moreover, the Secretary General must be informed of the intention to derogate by a declaration stating 'the special reasons justifying the derogation with regard to receiving capacity'.[310] A further safeguard is provided by Article 33(6), by virtue of which any state party may request a meeting of the Consultative Committee whenever Article 12(3) is invoked.[311]

The differences between the ESC and the EMW in respect of acceptable restrictions on the right to family reunification may largely be explained by the time-gap between the two instruments. The EMW was completed after the decline in labour migration to Western Europe in 1973–4. Migrant workers resident in Western European countries during this difficult economic period preferred to bring in their families, rather than risk return to their countries of origin. Fearing, however, that these additional arrivals would eventually lead to an over-concentration of the foreign population in certain regions and thus to problems

[306] *Explanatory Report on the EMW*, n. 71 above, 19, para. 59. This is because Art. 12(1) refers to migrant workers 'lawfully *employed*' in the territory of a state party: *ibid.* (emphasis added). In their replies to a questionnaire prepared by the Consultative Committee, both France and the Netherlands reported that they make family reunion subject to the condition that migrant workers have 'stable and adequate resources' to meet the needs of their families. In each country respectively, the 'guaranteed minimum wage' or 'an income equal to the minimum allowance provided by law' is sufficient to meet this requirement: Council of Europe, *Third Report on the Application of the European Convention on the Legal Status of Migrant Workers* (Reference period: 1 July 1985–31 Dec. 1988) (Strasbourg: Council of Europe, 1990) 7, para. 39.

[307] *Explanatory Report on the EMW*, n. 71 above, 19, paras. 60–1.

[308] *Ibid.* 19, para. 60. [309] Plender, n. 72 above, 255.

[310] Special reasons must be given for derogations from the family reunion obligation for *each* part of the state's territory: *Explanatory Report on the EMW*, n. 71 above, 19, para. 62. The possibility of derogation from *any* obligation in the ESC in the event of war or public emergency threatening the life of the nation is provided to contracting parties by Art. 30.

[311] Golsong, n. 259 above, 244, observes that the availability of such a right of initiative to each state party might lead to genuine multilateral negotiation with respect to the implementation of Art. 12.

of social integration as well as overburdened social, health, and education services, a number of states negotiating the EMW sought to place constraints on the right to family reunion. The result reached was the 'compromise' in Article 12.[312]

(e) EC standards

In contrast with the many qualifications found in applicable COE instruments, the relevant EC provisions on family reunion are far less restrictive. Indeed, the principle of freedom of movement for workers within the EC would become meaningless if migrant workers could not be accompanied by their families or if their families were unable to join them in the country of employment:

> The traditional view of the migrant worker is that of an economic factor of production allowed into the host country, generally for a limited period of time and unaccompanied by his family, to meet particular labour demands. However, the European Community . . . has departed from this pattern. It has set up a common labour market where workers can move freely, taking up employment and residence in any member state on the same conditions as nationals of that state. Far from treating the worker as a temporary immigrant, Community law envisages him as being fully integrated into the social and economic life of the society in which he has chosen to settle . . . One of the most important rights accorded to workers is the right to bring their families to settle in the host member state.[313]

Article 10(1) of Regulation 1612/68/EEC essentially provides that the spouse, children, and the parents of the worker or of his or her spouse have 'the *right* to install themselves with a worker who is a national of one Member State and who is employed in the territory of another Member State'.[314] The obligation in Article 10(2) to 'facilitate' the admission of the worker's other relatives is clearly weaker, since the right in Article 10(1) may be enforced directly in the national courts of each member state, whereas the obligation in Article 10(2) probably does not have this effect.[315]

The only express qualification on family reunion is found in Article 10(3) which provides that the worker must have available housing for the family 'considered as normal for national workers' in the region of employment. This provision 'must not give rise to discrimination between national workers and workers

[312] *Ibid.* 242.

[313] Note (EEC), 'Migrant Workers' Families: Legal Rights' (Dec. 1987) EIRR 18. See also Stein and Thomsen, n. 157 above, 1801.

[314] Emphasis added. For the impact of this right on bypassing more stringent domestic immigration rules in respect of non-EC family members who return with the migrant worker to his or her EC country of origin, see the discussion on 'reverse discrimination' in Ch. 6.

[315] Plender, n. 72 above, 201, argues that the test on the direct effect of EC provisions in national courts, as laid down in Case 41/74, *Van Duyn* v. *Home Office* [1974] ECR 1337, [1975] 1 CMLR 1, might not apply to Art. 10(2). See also P. Oliver, 'Non-Community Nationals and the Treaty of Rome' (1985) 63, citing from T. C. Hartley, *EEC Immigration Law* (Amsterdam: North Holland, 1978) 132.

from the other Member States'.[316] Article 10(3) was the object of an action brought by the Commission against Germany under Article 169 EC. In accordance with Article 10(3), German law allowed EC workers to bring their families if they had appropriate family housing. Residence permits were only granted, however, if the housing remained suitable and these permits could be withdrawn if the level of accommodation fell below the acceptable standards. The Court of Justice ruled that Article 10(3) is only applicable at the time of the arrival of family members and not later when housing conditions may deteriorate below the acceptable standards, for example because more children are born. German law, therefore, discriminated against migrant families from other EC member states in relation to the families of nationals.[317]

Arguably, the need for provisions regulating family reunion is diminishing in the light of moves by EC countries towards greater integration. The EC Treaty now grants a general right of free movement and residence within the territories of member states. This right, however, is 'subject to the limitations and conditions laid down in [the] Treaty and by the measures adopted to give it effect'.[318] Examples of such limitations are the three residence Directives adopted by the Council in 1990, which contain provisions on family reunion that are narrower than those in Article 10 of Regulation 1612/68/EEC.[319] Therefore, Article 10 remains relevant, and particularly in respect of family members from non-EC countries wishing to join EC nationals residing and employed in other member states.[320]

The position of migrant workers from non-EC countries with regard to family reunion is governed by the Third Pillar of the TEU which asserts that policy regarding nationals of third countries is to be a matter of 'common interest'. This policy is to encompass, *inter alia*, 'conditions of residence by nationals of third

[316] In the case of public housing waiting lists, the principle of non-discrimination is satisfied by Art. 9(2) of Reg. 1612/68/EEC, discussed above.

[317] Case 249/86, *Re Housing of Migrant Workers: Commission* v. *Germany* [1989] ECR 1263, [1990] 3 CMLR 540. The German Government's action could not be justified under Art. 48(3) EC on the ground of public policy. The Court, *ibid.* para. 10, also stated that Reg. 1612/68/EEC had to be interpreted in the light of the requirement of respect for family life in Art. 8 of the ECHR, which was one of the fundamental rights recognized by EC law.

[318] Art. 8a(1) EC.

[319] Directive 90/364/EEC of 28 June 1990 on the right of residence, OJ 1990, L 180/26; Directive 90/365/EEC of 28 June 1990 on the right of residence for employees and self-employed persons who have ceased their occupational activity, OJ 1990, L 180/28; and Directive 90/366/EEC of 28 June 1990 on the right of residence for students, OJ 1990, L 180/30, re-issued as Directive 93/96/EC on 29 Oct. 1993, OJ 1993, L 317/59 following the annulment of the original Directive by the Court of Justice in Case C-295/90, *Re Students' Rights: European Parliament* v. *Council* [1992] 3 CMLR 281. The first two Directives preclude the entry of children unless they are dependent, including those children under the age of 21, although dependent relatives in the ascending line of the holder of the right of residence and his or her spouse have a right to be admitted (Art. 1(2) in each Directive). The Directive on the right of residence for students only permits students to bring in spouses and dependent children, but not dependent relatives (Art. 1). See also Peers, n. 25 above, 13 (n. 19).

[320] See also Hartley, who questions whether Art. 8a(1) EC, for the moment at least, 'adds anything to pre-existing immigration rights for Community citizens': T. C. Hartley, 'Constitutional and Institutional Aspects of the Maastricht Agreement' (1993) 42 ICLQ 213, 219.

countries on the territory of Member States, including *family reunion*'.[321] In the communication by the Commission to the Council and the European Parliament on Immigration and Asylum Policies, the Commission proposed the elaboration of a Convention on family reunification:

Family reunification is of considerable importance to third country nationals legally resident in the Community and the success of integration policies can be affected by the policies which apply in this matter. Given the importance of legal certainty in this area for third country nationals legally resident in the Community, a legally binding instrument, such as a Convention, could usefully constitute a firmer basis and could address remaining differences in the practices of Member States in this regard.[322]

Such a Convention would only be acceptable if it serves to increase the rights of non-EC migrant workers to family reunion,[323] and not if it undermines the progress that has been made, for example in the case law of the Committee of Independent Experts under the ESC, by 'harmonizing' the different policies of EC member states into a restrictive approach based on the lowest common denominator. A portent of the restrictive European policy to come is the Resolution on harmonization of national policies on family reunification, adopted on 1 June 1993 by EC Immigration Ministers at a meeting in Copenhagen, which lists a number of so-called harmonization 'principles'.[324] These 'principles' are confined 'to family reunification in respect of persons who are not nationals of a Member State but who are lawfully resident within the territory of a Member State on a basis which affords them an expectation of permanent or long-term residence'.[325] What constitutes such an expectation is to be determined by national

[321] Art. K.1(3)(b) TEU (emphasis added). There are no family reunion provisions in the Association and Cooperation Agreements that the EC and its member states have entered into with third countries. Moreover, the definition of family, for the enjoyment of other rights conferred by these agreements, is to be determined by the host member state concerned. See the joint declarations attached to the Europe Association Agreements with central and eastern European countries, the draft Partnership and Cooperation Agreement with Russia and the draft Euro-Mediterranean agreements with Morocco and Tunisia. With regard to the position of Turkish migrants, Art. 7 of Decision 1/80 (n. 23 above) limits rights of access to employment to those family members who are 'authorized to join' the worker. This wording would seem to indicate that it is for the EC member states to define family members. However, Peers, n. 25 above, 25 argues that 'the most logical approach would be for the [Court of Justice] to find that family members should be understood by the meaning of the identical concept of Article 10 of Regulation 1612/68'. See also Cremona, n. 25 above, 104.

[322] *Immigration and Asylum Policies*, n. 93 above, 21, para. 74.

[323] In 1974, the Commission proposed 'the gradual extension to Third Country migrants of equality of living and working conditions, and particularly the right to be accompanied by their families': *Action Programme in Favour of Migrant Workers and Their Families*, n. 170 above, 27.

[324] Doc. SN 2828/1/93, WGI 1497 REV 1. For a detailed commentary on the Resolution, see P. Boeles and A. Kuijer, 'Harmonization of Family Reunification' in H. Meijers, *et al*, eds., *A New Immigration Law for Europe? The 1992 London and 1993 Copenhagen Rules on Immigration* (1993) 25. These writers, *ibid.* 27–8, criticize the restrictive nature of this resolution and note that it has already resulted in more stringent family reunion policies in some EC member states, such as Luxembourg and the Netherlands. They also point out, *ibid.* 26, that the 'principles' listed fail to refer to such fundamental norms as the right to respect for family life or the right to found a family.

[325] Point 6.

laws and policies, although those non-EC nationals who are present in a member state on a short-term basis, such as students and workers on fixed-term contracts, are not covered.[326] Migrants to whom the resolution applies may be joined in the country of residence by their married partners and by unmarried dependent children below a maximum age, which is to be between 16 and 18 years.[327] This age-limit, therefore, is far more flexible than the definitions of 'family' in connection with family reunion considered above. Consequently, dependent children over 21 years of age will be allowed to join a parent who is an EC national employed in another EC member state, whereas admission might be refused to a dependent child of 17 years wishing to join parents residing in the same country, who are neither EC nationals nor nationals of a COE State that has ratified the ESC or the EMW. Under the Resolution, the spouse and children are required, on admission, to live together with the resident migrant.[328] Article 10(1) of Regulation 1612/68/EEC, however, does not impose such a requirement on the families of EC workers.[329] As for other relatives, member states have reserved to themselves 'the possibility of permitting the entry and stay of [such] family members . . . for compelling reasons which justify the presence of the person concerned'.[330]

The Resolution also permits member states to impose a number of conditions on entry. States may require migrants to be 'lawfully present in their territory for certain periods of time' before family members may join them.[331] The length of this waiting-period is not specified and it seems to be open to each state to determine its own waiting-period. Member states may also require that migrants have available for their families accommodation and sufficient resources, and may also condition entry on the existence of sickness insurance.[332] Consequently, if there are no multilateral or bilateral social security agreements in force involving the receiving or sending countries concerned, family members are likely to be refused entry for the purpose of family reunion on this latter ground. They can also be refused entry and stay on the general grounds of national security, public policy (*ordre public*), and public health.[333]

It is important to emphasize that the principles outlined in this Resolution are *not* legally binding, although member states are urged to ensure that their laws are in conformity with these principles by 1 January 1995.[334] Although the

[326] Principle 1. [327] Principles 2 and 8 respectively. [328] Principle 2.
[329] See *Diatta* v. *Land Berlin*, n. 85 above. [330] Principle 10. [331] Principle 3.
[332] Principle 16.
[333] Principle 17. Furthermore, EC member states may refuse entry to the spouse of a migrant if they determine that the marriage was contracted solely for the purpose of immigration (principle 4). According to Boeles and Kuijer, n. 324 above, 32, this provision effectively introduces the 'primary purpose' rule of United Kingdom immigration law into the laws of other member states. A wife and her children will also be refused entry if the marriage is polygamous and if the husband already has a wife residing with him in the territory of the member state (principle 5).
[334] Point 5. In this regard, Boeles and Kuijer, *ibid.* 28, observe that if 'national parliaments consent expressly or tacitly with the . . . Resolution, it will be difficult if not impossible for them to oppose future legislation based on the Resolution'.

resolution recognizes that family reunion is also governed by international conventions and that the principles do not affect obligations flowing from these Conventions and from basic national laws, these obligations have only been 'taken into account' in the harmonization process and the Resolution fails to specify any of these Conventions by name.[335]

8.7 RIGHT TO EDUCATION

This section discusses the right of migrant workers and their families to education, broadly encompassing both their right to vocational training and retraining, and the right of their children to general education, including higher education and language instruction, in the host country. In previous chapters, these rights were considered separately, in accordance with the separate organization of these standards in the applicable instruments. Although the division is retained in this section for the sake of uniformity, it is somewhat artificial given that the principal European standards do not always attempt to distinguish clearly between these closely related rights.

Vocational training and retraining

The preceding chapters have underlined the importance of equal treatment between migrant workers and national workers in respect of access to vocational training and retraining, including instruction in the language of the host country. Special adult educational and skills training programmes for migrant workers are necessary to end labour force segmentation, particularly in view of the fact that migrant workers often enter the country of employment with linguistic problems and a poor initial education.[336] This right is very important to specific migrant groups. Its effective enjoyment is crucial to second- or third-generation migrants in assisting their integration and economic advancement and in contributing to

[335] Point 3. Moreover, this reference to international obligations flowing from applicable Conventions must be juxtaposed with the following paragraph which recognizes 'a need to control migration flows into the territories of the Member States . . . considered to be one of the factors for the successful integration of immigrants who are lawfully resident within [these territories]'. The EC Commission's observation in its 1994 Communication to the Council and European Parliament on Immigration and Asylum Policies, n. 93 above, 20–1, para. 73, that 'the resolution reflects the principle that family reunification is intrinsically linked to the right of family life as recognized by the European Convention on Human Rights' is a rather questionable statement given the restrictive approach outlined above. Indeed, the European Parliament has stated that the Resolution 'is likely not to respect private life as laid down in the international treaties and to lead to discrimination and uncertainty'. See the Resolution of 15 July 1993 on European immigration policy, OJ 1993, C 255/185, point 1(f). Nonetheless, the Commission communication recognizes somewhat critically that the Resolution leaves certain matters for member states to determine, such as family formation and the criteria for admission of unmarried partners or so-called 'second-degree' relatives: *ibid.* 9–10, para. 35. In this regard, see also Hailbronner, n. 90 above, 202.

[336] *Report to the Conference on Migrant Workers from the Mahgreb in the European Community*, n. 9 above, 20, para. 3.6.

a reduction in their unemployment.[337] A right to language training is also of particular importance to migrant women, especially those who stay at home.[338] Although the right to vocational training and retraining serves to promote the integration of migrants as full economic and social participants in the receiving society, it has its obvious limitations given the restrictions usually imposed upon their access to employment.

(a) COE standards

There is no *express* reference in the text of the ESC to any state obligation to ensure equal treatment between migrant workers and nationals in respect of access to vocational training or retraining. This general principle, however, has been recognized by the Committee of Independent Experts in its interpretation of various ESC provisions. The Committee has interpreted Article 19(4), which guarantees equal treatment between migrant workers and nationals in respect of, *inter alia*, 'employment and working conditions' as applying to vocational training.[339] Moreover, this provision has also been interpreted by the Committee as containing an obligation to provide language training for migrant workers.[340]

By virtue of the Appendix to the ESC, which confirms the ESC's general application to migrant workers who are nationals of contracting parties, the Committee has stated that Article 10 of the ESC, which is concerned with the effective exercise of the right to vocational training, operates to prohibit discrimination against migrant workers.[341] The same principle applies to the right to vocational guidance in Article 9. Under this provision, vocational guidance is to be available

337 Unemployment among young migrants is proportionately greater than among young nationals of working age. P. J. Muus, 'Employment and Vocational Training of Young Immigrants in the Netherlands, Western Germany and Belgium' in OECD, *The Changing Course of International Migration* (1993) 199–200; D. Maillot, 'European Receiving Countries' in *The Future of Migration*, n. 101 above, 51, in relation to the position in Belgium and Germany.

338 *Guidelines for a Community Policy on Migration*, n. 171 above, 18, para. 29.

339 *Conclusions VII*, 103, cited in *Case Law on the European Social Charter*, n. 19 above, 159.

340 *Conclusions IV*, 120, 122, cited by Harris, n. 20 above, 170 and Swart, n. 45 above, 31. The revised ESC adds a new paragraph to Art. 19 which obliges states parties 'to promote and facilitate the teaching of the national language of the receiving State or, if there are several, one of these languages, to migrant workers and members of their families' (Art. 19(11)). The Draft Explanatory report observes that this provision is 'considered important for . . . [*inter alia*] the guarantee of their rights . . . relating to work': *Request for an Opinion on the Draft Revised European Social Charter*, n. 128 above, 15 and 46, para. 78 respectively.

341 *Conclusions VII*, 103, cited in *Case Law on the European Social Charter*, n. 19 above, 159. The Governmental Committee issued a warning to Greece after the Committee of Independent Experts concluded that Greece had failed to comply with this provision because it limited access to certain apprenticeship programmes to nationals and to those foreigners born and living in Greece. See respectively *12th Report (I)*, n. 57 above, 42–3, paras. 161–4 and *Conclusions XI-1*, n. 219 above, 112, 114, 117 and *Conclusions XII-1*, n. 57 above, 162, 167, 171. The Greek delegate later informed the Governmental Committee that amendments to the impugned legislation had been introduced: *12th Report (II)*, n. 255 above, 130, para. 685. The Committee of Independent Experts also adopted a negative conclusion, with reference to Arts. 10(1) and (2), in respect of Malta which reported that its nationals were accorded priority regarding participation in apprenticeship schemes: *Conclusions XIII-2*, n. 51 above, 321 and 323.

free of charge, and the Committee has expressed a particular interest in the application of this right to the children of foreign workers.[342]

Article 10 of the ESC is a comprehensive provision imposing an obligation upon states parties, in paragraphs (1) to (3) respectively, to provide or promote, *inter alia*, the following: 'the technical and vocational training of all persons . . . and to grant facilities for access to higher technical and university education'; 'a system of apprenticeship . . . for training young boys and girls in their various employments'; and training and retraining facilities for adult workers. Article 10(4) obliges states parties 'to encourage the full utilization of the facilities provided by appropriate measures' such as, *inter alia*, 'granting financial assistance in appropriate cases'.[343] The Committee of Independent Experts has observed, with reference to the whole of this provision, that a special effort should be made on behalf of unemployed migrant workers, who are more likely to be seriously affected by economic difficulties, to ensure that they enjoy equal treatment with nationals in respect of vocational training and retraining.[344] The obligation to grant migrant workers the right to vocational training 'cannot be made dependent upon the advantages which may or may not result for the economy of the immigration country'.[345] Moreover, *de jure* or *de facto* restrictions on access to vocational training for migrant workers, such as those preventing foreign workers from applying for financial aid to fund such training or those requiring a prescribed period of employment or residence, are incompatible with Article 10 of the ESC.[346] Indeed, the Committee has emphasized that, irrespective of whether Article 10(4) has been accepted by state parties, the provision of financial assistance is essential for the effective exercise of the right to vocational training in Article 10.[347]

342 *Conclusions IV*, 69, cited in *Case Law on the European Social Charter*, n. 19 above, 94.

343 Art. 10(4)(c). Cyprus and Iceland have not accepted Art. 10 *in toto*, whereas Germany has not accepted Art. 10(4), and Malta has rejected Arts. 10(4)(b) and (c).

344 *Conclusions IV*, xv, cited in *Case Law on the European Social Charter*, n. 19 above, 96.

345 *Conclusions VII*, 60 with respect to Art. 10(1), cited in *Case Law on the European Social Charter*, n. 19 above, 98.

346 For example, the Committee asserted, with regard to Art. 10(3), that measures which only permitted access to financially-assisted vocational training after 6 years of employment potentially discriminated against foreign workers: *Conclusions V*, 84–5, cited in *Case Law on the European Social Charter*, *ibid.* 101. Similarly, a condition that prevented young migrants from the benefit of vocational training before at least one parent had completed 3 years of residence and employment in the host country was incompatible with Art. 10(2): *Conclusions VI*, 71, cited in *Case Law on the European Social Charter*, n. 19 above, 100. See also the Committee's negative conclusions in respect of the position in Austria (with reference to Arts. 10(2) and (3)): *Conclusions XIII-2*, n. 51 above, 220, 221.

347 *Conclusions VII*, 62, cited in *Case Law on the European Social Charter*, n. 19 above, 100 and *Conclusions VIII*, 136, cited in *Case Law on the European Social Charter—Supplement*, n. 59 above, 34 with reference to Art. 10(1): 'The importance of financial assistance in the framework of vocational training is, in fact, so great that the very existence of the right protected by Article 10 of the Charter may depend on it'. See also *Conclusions XIII-2*, n. 51 above, 321. The establishment of a link between Art. 10(1) and (4) has been contested in the Governmental Committee by the German representative: *Report 12 (II)*, n. 255 above, 83, para. 355.

In contrast with the ESC, the ECE and the EMW explicitly recognize the right of migrants to vocational training. Article 20 of the ECE ensures equality of access to institutions for, *inter alia*, 'technical and vocational training', although this access is restricted to 'nationals of school age of any state party lawfully residing in any other state party'. Article 14(1) of the EMW recognizes the principle of equal treatment between migrant workers and their families and nationals in respect of, *inter alia*, vocational training and retraining. The reference to retraining should be read in conjunction with Article 25 of the EMW obliging states parties to promote measures to ensure, as far as possible, the vocational retraining and occupational rehabilitation of those migrant workers who have lost their jobs for reasons beyond their control, such as redundancy or prolonged illness, provided that they plan to continue working in the state concerned afterwards.[348] However, the words 'as far as possible' seem to indicate that Article 25 does not ensure the full equality of nationals and migrant workers in this regard.[349] To promote access to vocational training, Article 14(2) imposes an explicit obligation upon the receiving country to facilitate the teaching of its language or languages to migrant workers and members of their families. Article 14(3) provides that the granting of scholarships for the purpose of, *inter alia*, vocational training, including linguistic instruction, is to be left to the *discretion* of each state party. This clause, therefore, appears to be more restrictive than the interpretation given to Article 10 of the ESC by the Committee of Independent Experts prohibiting discrimination between national and foreign workers in respect of the provision of financial assistance for vocational training.[350] Moreover, the provision of vocational training and retraining for migrants in the EMW is to 'cater as far as possible for the needs of migrant workers with a view to their return to their State of origin'.[351] This clause reflects the difficult economic circumstances at the time of drafting when countries of employment were more concerned to see migrant workers return home rather than take steps to integrate them into the host society.[352]

(b) EC standards

The EC's concern with the education and vocational training of migrants is tied up with the free movement of labour principle, which would be impeded considerably if EC migrant workers residing in member states were unable to enjoy access to educational and vocational training institutions on equal terms with

[348] Cf. *Explanatory Report on the EMW*, n. 71 above, 21, para. 69. However, Art. 25 does *not* apply to the families of migrant workers: *ibid*.

[349] See cf. Swart, n. 45 above, 37.

[350] Art. 20 of the ECE also leaves the grant of scholarships to the discretion of each state party.

[351] Art. 14(5). See also *Explanatory Report on the EMW*, n. 71 above, 21, para. 69.

[352] Indeed, the emphasis in countries of employment today on integration rather than return is reflected in the Norwegian report on this provision: 'No steps have yet been taken to organise training and retraining for immigrant workers with a view to their return to their country of origin, since priority is given to their integration': *Fourth Report on the Application of the EMW*, n. 222 above, 8, para. 62.

nationals.[353] The right of EC migrant workers and their families to equal treatment with nationals in respect of vocational training is guaranteed by a number of provisions in EC secondary legislation. Article 7(3) of Regulation 1612/68/EEC guarantees the right of equal access to 'training in vocational schools and retraining centres' for nationals from EC member states working in other member states,[354] while Article 12 of the Regulation ensures admission for the children of such workers on the same conditions as nationals to, *inter alia*, 'apprenticeship and vocational training courses'. Vocational training has been broadly defined by the Court of Justice to include any form of instruction which prepares for a qualification in a particular profession, trade, or employment or which provides the necessary training and skills, regardless of the age and educational level of the person concerned.[355]

A requirement that migrants from other EC member states, but not nationals, pay tuition fees for vocational training is contrary to Article 6 EC (formerly Article 7 EEC), which prohibits discrimination against EC migrants on grounds of nationality.[356] The Court of Justice has ruled, however, that Article 6 EC, at the present stage of development of EC law, is limited to fees connected with admission to such studies and does not extend to other forms of assistance, such as maintenance grants, which a state may provide to nationals undertaking the training in question.[357] But discriminatory assistance of this kind may be prohibited

[353] Cf. K. Lenaerts, 'Education in European Community Law after "Maastricht"' (1994) 31 *CML Rev.* 7, 12–13.

[354] Lenaerts, *ibid.* 12, notes: 'The purpose of this provision is to secure effective access to the national labour market by allowing migrant workers to obtain locally the vocational training which they need'.

[355] Case 293/83, *Gravier* v. *City of Liege* [1985] ECR 593, [1985] 3 CMLR 1, para. 30; Case 197/86, *Brown* v. *Secretary of State for Scotland* [1988] ECR 3205, [1988] 3 CMLR 403, para. 10. These conditions are fulfilled by university education with the exception of certain special courses, which are intended for persons wishing to improve their general knowledge, rather than to prepare themselves for an occupation. Universities, however, cannot be regarded as 'vocational schools' within the meaning of Art. 7(3) since the latter have a narrower meaning and refer solely to establishments providing instruction in between periods of employment or otherwise closely connected with employment, particularly during apprenticeship. *Brown, ibid.*, para. 12.

[356] Case 152/82, *Forcheri* v. *Belgium* [1983] ECR 2323, [1984] 1 CMLR 334, para. 18. This case concerned the Italian wife of an Italian EC official employed in Brussels, who was required to pay tuition fees for a further education course. Belgian nationals were exempt from paying these fees. See also *Gravier*, n. 355 above, paras. 14–15, and *Brown*, n. 355 above, paras. 17 and 19.

[357] *Brown, ibid.* paras. 18 and 19; Case 39/86, *Lair* v. *Universität Hannover* [1988] ECR 3161, [1989] CMLR 545, para. 15; Case C-357/89, *Raulin* v. *Minister van Onderwijs en Wetenschappen* [1992] ECR 1027, [1994] 1 CMLR 227, para. 25. The Court of Justice views equal treatment under Art. 6 EC in respect of admission by an EC national to vocational training as also implying a right of residence in an EC member state for this purpose. The right of residence is not dependent on the grant of a residence permit, but may be made subject to certain conditions provided that these do not affect the principle of non-discriminatory access to vocational training: *Raulin, ibid.* para. 40. To a certain extent, this decision mirrors Council Directive 93/96/EC on the right of residence for students, n. 319 above. By virtue of this Directive, students, together with their spouses and dependent children, are granted, for the duration of their studies, an independent *right of residence* in EC member states unconnected with the exercise of an economic activity, provided that they have sufficient resources to avoid becoming a burden on the social assistance system of the host state

if it constitutes a 'social advantage' within the meaning of Article 7(2) of Regulation 1612/68/EEC, provided that migrants retain their status as 'workers'. This is satisfied if a link exists between previous employment and the vocational training undertaken,[358] or, in the event of no such link, if the person concerned has become involuntarily unemployed.[359]

Article 127 EC obliges the EC to 'implement a vocational training policy which shall support and supplement the action of the Member States, while fully respecting the responsibility of the Member States for the content and organization of vocational training'.[360] The Council is empowered, acting in accordance with the 'co-operation procedure' under Article 189c EC and after consultation with the Economic and Social Committee, to adopt measures to contribute to the achievement of the objectives referred to in Article 127 EC.[361] In recent years, EC policy, based on the former Article 128 EEC which the above provision partly replaces,[362] has expanded rapidly in this area, with the adoption of vocational training measures aimed at specific groups, such as women and youth, and the implementation of more general schemes with the objective of preparing EC citizens for employment in the single integrated market.[363]

Education of migrant children

(a) Background

The proportion of migrant children enrolled in the education systems of countries of employment is significant and has been rising steadily.[364] Between 1990 and 1994, migrant children represented approximately one tenth of total primary

concerned and are covered by sickness insurance. See also the case annotation by O'Keeffe (1992) 29 *CML Rev.* 1215, 1222 and P. Watson, 'Vocational Training' in Wyatt and Dashwood, n. 156 above, 640, 647.

[358] *Lair*, n. 357 above, paras. 22–4 and para. 39 respectively. Migrants retain their status as workers even if they give up their employment voluntarily in order to pursue full-time education, provided that there is still a relationship between such education and previous work. Case C-3/90, *Bernini* v. *Minister van Onderwijs en Wetenschappen* [1992] ECR 1071, para. 21. Furthermore, the right to such a social advantage cannot be made conditional upon a minimum period of prior employment activity in the host country. *Lair*, *ibid.* para. 42.

[359] *Raulin*, n. 357 above, para. 22.

[360] Art. 127(1) EC.

[361] Art. 127(4) EC.

[362] Art. 128 EEC was replaced by a new Chapter III of Title VIII of the EC Treaty entitled Education, Vocational Training and Youth comprising Article 126 EC (which specifically deals with education and which is discussed below) and Art. 127 EC.

[363] See Watson, 'Vocational Training', n. 357 above, 647–50 for a brief overview of the principal measures. For a more detailed coverage, encompassing the changes introduced by the TEU, see Lenaerts, n. 353 above, 24–40.

[364] Between 1976 and 1985, the number of migrant children in schools rose by 41% and the number of nationals dropped by 13%. The proportion of foreign children enrolled in schools stood at 8.6% in 1985, as against 5.4% in 1976. In real terms, these figures reflect a net increase of 700,000 foreign children and a decrease of almost 4 million nationals. Since 1985, the enrolment of migrant children has continued to increase, but at a much slower rate. See D. Blot, 'Issues Concerning the Education of Immigrants' Children' in OECD, *The Changing Course of International Migration*, n. 337 above, 243, 244.

school enrolment in France (9.3 per cent), Germany (11.3 per cent) and Sweden (11.7 per cent). In Switzerland, the proportion of foreign children enrolled in such schools was higher, standing at 19.4 per cent.[365] Moreover, these figures would probably be even higher if all migrant children of school-age were in education (e.g. the children of illegal migrants, or those who work to supplement the family income).[366]

Although a formal right to education regardless of nationality is recognized in many European host countries, a number of studies reveal that migrant children are disadvantaged educationally in comparison with national children and tend to perform less well than their counterparts.[367] They are over-represented in 'special education' and in short-cycle secondary and vocational education which do not normally lead to prolonged studies and higher education.[368] Many young migrants also leave vocational education without any qualifications.[369] The reasons for these discrepancies have been linked to the educational level of parents, the social origin of parents, and length of stay in the host country, with the latter two variables recognized as predominant.[370] The migration process and the strains of European inner-city life clearly have detrimental consequences for the education of migrant children.[371] Their educational difficulties need to be counteracted by special measures to ensure that they are not disadvantaged with respect to their future training, employment, or entry into higher education. Otherwise, they risk remaining in the same socio-occupational strata as their parents.[372]

365 *SOPEMI 1994*, 48 (Table I.7). The proportionate enrolment of migrant children in secondary education is lower, but this is explained by a lower average age of such children in comparison with that of nationals: Blot, n. 364 above, 244.

366 For instance, in 1970, the German authorities found 97,800 children working illegally in the country in contravention of the compulsory schooling regulations. Power, n. 97 above, 19. It is noteworthy that the laws of all the major European countries embrace the principle of compulsory education, which also encompasses foreign children. See M. Herdegen, 'Political Rights and other Aspects of Resident Status' in *The Legal Position of Aliens*, n. 26 above, 2003, 2013.

367 See respectively *Hallmarks of Citizenship Survey*, n. 37 above, 95–7 and Blot, n. 364 above, who provides an overview of some of these studies.

368 *SOPEMI 1992*, 38; Blot, n. 364 above, 244. The proportion of foreigners to nationals enrolled in 'special education' in countries of employment in 1990–1994 ranged from 9.1% in Sweden, 13.8% in Germany and 16.8% in France, to 42.7% in Switzerland: *SOPEMI 1994*, 48 (Table I.7). A working definition of 'special education' concerns instruction which is 'generally reserved for children with physical, intellectual and sometimes behavioural handicaps'. See Blot, *ibid.* 243 (n. 4).

369 Muus, n. 337 above, 202, 203.

370 Blot, n. 364 above, 245–6.

371 The migration process results in language difficulties, cultural differences, family problems as a result of separation and the new environment, and lack of clear perspectives due to an insecure legal status. The strains of inner-city life include poor housing conditions and a lack of play facilities for children: Castles and Kosack, n. 1 above, 500. See also the section on the right to housing and the implicit connection between inadequate housing and poor educational performance.

372 Castles and Kosack, n. 1 above, 501–2. It has been observed that poor education, together with inadequate social services in run-down areas of towns where migrants tend to live, contribute to a 'vicious circle', whereby children from the area are badly educated and therefore unable to take up better employment than the low-status occupations possessed by their parents: *Report to the Conference on Migrant Workers from the Mahgreb in the European Community*, n. 9 above, 6, para. 1.12, citing from EC Group of Experts, *Politiques d'Immigration et Intégration Sociale des Immigrés dans la Communauté Européenne* (European Commission, 1990) 21–3.

Some of the special measures taken in European countries have included additional language instruction, preparatory and adaptation classes, assistance with homework, and intercultural education.[373] Another special measure involves the teaching to these children of their language and culture of origin. This question is considered separately in the section on cultural rights below.

Castles and Kosack have observed that the special conditions required for ensuring that migrant children enjoy the same educational opportunities as nationals have rarely been available in Europe. One reason for this state of affairs has been the lack of clear and consistent host country policies in the field of education, partly as a consequence of the difficulties many of these countries have encountered in coming to terms with the reality of the permanent settlement within their borders of immigrant worker groups as *de facto* ethnic minorities.[374]

(b) COE standards

Notwithstanding that the ECHR is mainly concerned with civil and political rights, there is a right to education in Article 2 of the first Protocol to the ECHR, which is drawn quite narrowly when compared with other international human rights educational guarantees considered in Chapter 2:

> No person shall be denied the right to education. In the exercise of any functions which it assumes in relation to education and to teaching, the State shall respect the right of parents to ensure such education and teaching in conformity with their own religious and philosophical convictions.

This provision, when read with Article 14, clearly applies on a non-discriminatory basis to both nationals and aliens who are within the territory of a contracting party unless there is an objective and reasonable justification for differential treatment.[375] No children of migrants residing and working in a COE member country which has ratified this Protocol should, therefore, be denied their right to receive an education, even if their parents are in an irregular situation. As discussed above, however, some European countries recognize that the

[373] See Hammar, 'Immigrant Policy', n. 98 above, 270, referring to some of the special measures taken in Switzerland and *ILO General Survey 1980*, n. 210 above, 105, para. 395, referring to the special arrangements in France, Germany, the Netherlands, Sweden, and Switzerland for teaching the language of the host country to children of migrant workers. Language teaching is usually carried out within the framework of general schooling, through intensive courses or special adaptation classes designed to enable the children to participate in the normal school curriculum as soon as possible. See also Note (EEC), 'Focus on Migrant Workers' (April 1984) EIRR 19, 20 concerning the special measures in Germany and the United Kingdom. Other special measures may include supplementing the content of some general courses, such as geography and history, with information more relevant to non-European children in order to encourage their continued interest and also to promote the understanding of European children: *Report to the Conference on Migrant Workers from the Mahgreb in the European Community*, n. 9 above, 21, para. 3.9. For recent developments in this area, see Commission of the European Communities, *Report on the Education of Migrants' Children in the European Union*, COM (94) 80 final of 25 March 1994.

[374] Castles and Kosack, n. 1 above, 500, 501.

[375] Robertson and Merrills, n. 229 above, 223; cf. Swart, n. 45 above, 38.

fundamental right to education must be tailored to the specific needs of migrant children in order to facilitate their integration into society and to ensure that they are not placed at an educational disadvantage to the children of nationals. Formal equality between the children of migrants and those of nationals in respect of access to schooling in the country of employment is therefore insufficient.

There are few COE standards specially designed to protect and promote this kind of education for migrant children. Under Article 10(1) of the ESC, states parties are under a duty to 'grant facilities for access to higher technical and university education, based solely on individual aptitude' in addition to the obligation to 'provide or promote . . . the technical and vocational training of all persons . . .'.[376] As noted above, the obligation in Article 10 also implies equal treatment in respect of the provision of financial assistance. Furthermore, the Committee of Independent Experts has interpreted the state duty in Article 19(2) 'to adopt appropriate measures . . . to facilitate the . . . [*inter alia*] reception of . . . [migrant] workers . . .' as encompassing the need 'to ensure appropriate educational reception' of their children.[377] Arguably, 'educational reception' means the provision of 'special' facilities for these children to ease their adaptation to the educational system of the receiving country. It is clear, however, from the Committee's interpretation of 'reception' that such measures are to be temporary only.[378]

Article 20 of the ECE provides for equal treatment between nationals of school age from any state party legally resident in another party and the nationals of the latter in respect of, *inter alia*, admission to primary and secondary educational institutions where access to education at those establishments is controlled by the state. However, this provision does not apply to higher or university education.[379] Article 14 of the EMW is broader in scope and guarantees, in its first paragraph, equality between migrant workers and nationals in respect of, *inter alia*, general education and 'access to higher education according to the general regulations governing admission to respective institutions in the receiving State'.[380]

[376] During the examination of the first Turkish report, the Committee of Independent Experts noted in respect of Art. 10(1) that although foreign nationals generally had equal access with nationals to all levels of education, there was a quota for foreigners in higher educational establishments admitting foreigners and it seemed that some establishments did not admit foreigners. The Committee observed that this situation 'did not appear to comply with the requirements of [Art. 10(1)] in terms of equality of treatment of foreigners, nationals of Contracting Parties to the Charter', although it decided to defer its conclusion pending receipt of further information: *Conclusions XIII-1*, n. 57 above, 237–8.

[377] *Conclusions IV*, 117, cited in *Case Law on the European Social Charter*, n. 19 above, 155.

[378] The Committee has stated that: '"Reception" must be provided at the time of arrival and the period immediately following, that is to say during the weeks in which immigrant workers and their families find themselves in a particularly difficult position': *Conclusions IV*, 115, cited in *Case Law on the European Social Charter*, n. 19 above, 154.

[379] *Commentary on the European Convention on Establishment*, n. 46 above, 22, para. 73.

[380] The Explanatory Report on the EMW, n. 71 above, 21, para. 68, points out the obvious limitations, applicable to both migrants and nationals, concerning such access: 'Equal entitlement to admission to universities, and higher education establishments in general, does not rule out the possibility of restricting the admission of migrant workers and members of their families, as of nationals, to such establishments on the basis of a *numerus clausus* laid down by a Contracting Party'.

Under both provisions, the granting of scholarships is left to the discretion of each state party, an approach which is in conformity with that taken by other international instruments in this area. Article 14(3) of the EMW, however, attempts to temper the harshness of this rule with respect to the children of foreign workers by specifying that states parties should make 'special efforts' to aim for equal treatment between the children of nationals and migrant workers with regard to the granting of scholarships.[381] In addition to this concession, the EMW also contains a special provision in Article 14(2) requiring the receiving state to *facilitate* the teaching of its language or languages to migrant children in order to promote their access to, *inter alia*, general schools.

(c) EC standards

Article 12 of Regulation 1612/68/EEC guarantees equal treatment between the children of migrant workers from EC member states and the children of nationals in respect of, *inter alia*, 'general educational . . . courses'. Moreover, the provision imposes a positive duty upon member states to 'encourage all efforts to enable such children to attend these courses under the best possible conditions'.[382] The Court of Justice has ruled that equal treatment extends not only to admission to educational courses, but also to the entitlement of all measures which facilitate participation in such courses, such as scholarships and grants.[383] Equal treatment in respect of the provision of financial assistancc for education covers not only the financing of studies, but also ancillary assistance, such as maintenance and other costs.[384] Article 12 also entitles migrant children to continue their

[381] Some state party reports have provided information to the Consultative Committee on the availability of education grants to the children of migrant workers. See respectively *Third Report on the Application of the EMW*, n. 306 above, 9, para. 45 (France) and *Fourth Report on the Application of the EMW*, n. 222 above, 8, para. 61 (Norway).

[382] The Court of Justice has asserted that children benefiting from Art. 12 do not have to fulfil conditions of age and residence or dependency, such as those for family reunion in Art. 10 of Reg. 1612/68/EEC. See Case C-7/94, *Landesamt für Ausbildungsförderung (Nordrhein-Westfalen)* v. *Gaal* [1995] ECR I-1031. With regard to the second half of Art. 12, it would appear that it is not directly effective: '[It] provides merely an admonition to Member States as to the spirit in which they should apply the first paragraph of that Article, and a guide to the courts in its interpretation': D. Wyatt, 'Free Movement of Workers' in Wyatt and Dashwood, n. 156 above, 237, 260.

[383] Case 9/74, *Casagrande* v. *Landeshauptstadt Munich* [1974] ECR 773, [1974] 2 CMLR 423; Case 68/74, *Alaimo* v. *Prefect of the Rhône* [1975] ECR 109, [1975] 1 CMLR 262. In both cases, measures limiting eligibility for educational grants to nationals were held to constitute an infringement of the equality principle in Art. 12. Decision 1/80 on the development of the EC–Turkey Association, n. 23 above, grants the children of Turkish migrant workers, on an equal basis with the children of nationals, admission to 'courses of general education, apprenticeship and vocational training' (Art. 9). This provision, however, does not extend equal treatment to grants and scholarships because member states are given the discretion to decide whether these children can benefit from advantages provided under national legislation. See also Peers, n. 25 above, 27. Protocol 29 (on vocational training) to the EEA Agreement also precludes EEA students from benefiting from equal treatment with nationals in respect of tuition fees (OJ 1994, L1/196). See Peers, *ibid*. 18.

[384] Cases 389–390/87, *Echternach and Moritz* v. *Minister van Onderwijs en Wetenschappen* [1989] ECR 723, [1990] 2 CMLR 305, para. 34.

education in the member state, even if their parents return to the country of origin.[385] It even enables those children, who are resident with an EC worker in a member state, to obtain a grant from that state in order to study in their country of origin, but only if support for study abroad is also available to nationals.[386] Article 12 also covers assistance to those children with special educational needs, such as disabled children.[387]

The need to adopt special educational measures in respect of migrant children is called for in Council Directive 77/486/EEC,[388] which 'clarifies' the legal content of Article 12 of Regulation 1612/68/EEC and which is considered by the Commission to be the 'Community's key instrument on the education of immigrant children'.[389] By virtue of Article 1, the Directive is applicable to all migrant children of compulsory school age who are dependants of an EC migrant worker and who are resident in the member state of employment. The Directive calls for special measures with an emphasis on teaching the language of the host country. Article 2 obliges member states 'in accordance with their national circumstances and legal systems, [to] take appropriate measures to ensure that free tuition to facilitate initial reception is offered in their territory to [these children]'.[390] Measures are to include, in particular, 'the teaching—adapted to the specific needs of such children—of the official language or one of the official languages of the host state'. The rationale for this clause is 'to permit the integration of such children into the educational environment and the school system of the host state'.[391] The Commission has observed that Article 2 has binding force and that 'reception education for pupils with an inadequate or non-existent knowledge of the language in which education is imparted is every child's subjective right'.[392] Although the application of Directive 77/486/EEC is expressly limited to the children of EC nationals, the Council and the member states, in a political declaration attached to the Directive at the time of its adoption, committed themselves to implementing its objectives in respect of children originating from

[385] *Ibid.* para. 23. Particularly if these children, on return to their country of origin, are unable to obtain recognition of diplomas acquired in the host country: *ibid.* para. 21.

[386] Case C-308/89, *Di Leo* v. *Land Berlin* [1990] ECR I-4185, paras. 15 and 17.

[387] *Michel S.*, n. 22 above.

[388] Council Directive 77/486/EEC of 25 July 1977 on the education of the children of migrant workers, OJ 1977, L 199/32. The measures in this Directive were to be applied in full in all member states from 2 Aug. 1981. See Commission of the European Communities, *Report on the Implementation in the Member States of Directive 77/486/EEC on the Education of the Children of Migrant Workers*, COM (88) 707 final of 3 Jan. 1989, 1.

[389] *Report on the Education of Migrants' Children in the European Union*, n. 373 above, 12 and 13 respectively.

[390] The Commission has noted that the purpose of the phrase 'in accordance with their national circumstances and legal systems' is to take account of the position in some member states where the national legislature lacks the power to legislate on the content of the school curriculum: *Report on the Implementation of Directive 77/486/EEC* (1989), n. 388 above, 125.

[391] Preamble, second indent. The second paragraph of Art. 2 also obliges member states to 'take the measures necessary for the training and further training of the teachers who are to provide this tuition'.

[392] *Report on the Implementation of Directive 77/486/EEC* (1989), n. 388 above, 8, para. 3.2.2. and 125 respectively.

third countries.[393] Indeed, in collecting information for its first report on the implementation of the Directive, the Commission asked member states to include information about the existence of measures for the education of these children.[394]

The EC has now been explicitly provided with the competence to encourage cooperation between member states and to support their actions in the sphere of education under Article 126 EC.[395] Before the TEU amendments, educational measures could only be taken within the ambit of vocational training policy under Article 128 EEC. The Council is now empowered, in accordance with the 'co-decision' procedure under Article 189b EC and after consulting the Economic and Social Committee and the Committee of the Regions,[396] to adopt incentive measures for the purpose of contributing to the educational objectives specified in Article 126 EC.[397]

B. CULTURAL, POLITICAL, AND RESIDENCE RIGHTS

In a liberal democratic state, rights to culture, political participation, and residence are at the very root of statehood and are integral to the way the national community defines itself. An inward-looking national community perceives the right of migrants to maintain and develop their cultures and languages as a threat to its cultural homogeneity, and the granting of political and residence rights as undermining its very *raison d'être*.[398] Nonetheless, it is arguable that migrant

[393] *Ibid.* 4, para. 3.1; *Report on the Education of Migrants' Children in the European Union*, n. 373 above, 7. The Directive, however, clearly applies to children who are non-EC nationals, but whose parents possess the nationality of an EC member state. It is noteworthy that the Commission originally proposed that the Directive should apply to non-EC nationals. See Proposal for a Council Directive on the education of the children of migrant workers of 28 July 1975, OJ 1975, C 213/2, Art. 1, para. 2. See also Evans (1994), n. 85 above, 203 (n. 21).

[394] Commission of the European Communities, *Report from the Commission to the Council on the Implementation of Directive 77/486/EEC on the Education of the Children of Migrant Workers*, COM (84) 54 final of 10 Feb. 1984, 4. The European Parliament has called for the extension of the provisions of the Directive, either fully or partially, 'to the children of residents of *all* ethnic minority groups whose language or culture differs from that of the indigenous community amongst whom they reside . . . this should be done irrespective of whether these ethnic minority residents have citizenship of the country in which they are living and even if they are permanently settled': Resolution of 16 April 1985 on the implementation of Directive 77/486/EEC on the education of the children of migrant workers, OJ 1985, C 122/61, para. 6 (emphasis added).

[395] Art. 126(1) EC.

[396] The Committee of the Regions is a body consisting of representatives of regional and local bodies set up under Arts. 198a–c EC to give advisory opinions to the Commission and Council. See also A. Dashwood, 'The Institutions of the Communities and of the Union' in Wyatt and Dashwood, n. 156 above, 19–20.

[397] Art. 126(4) EC. The Council can also adopt recommendations, acting by a qualified majority on a proposal from the Commission.

[398] Indeed, an argument often posited against immigration generally is that the presence of a significant number of new immigrants threatens the cultural and historical make-up of the polity, with the result that a functioning political community may not be possible. For example, Walzer argues that closure in general, including closure at the level of the nation-state, is necessary if the distinctiveness of cultures and groups is to thrive: 'the restraint of entry serves to defend the liberty and welfare, the politics and culture of a group of people committed to one another and to their common life': M. Walzer, *Spheres of Justice: A Defense of Pluralism and Equality* (1983) 39.

workers and their families may lay claim to *all* these rights. They may claim cultural rights on the basis of the communitarian conception of the individual which recognizes the person's close attachment to his or her ethnic or cultural group[399] and they may claim incremental political and residence rights on the basis of their economic and social participation in society. The protection of these rights, however, is limited under COE instruments. On the other hand, the right of residence and the right to remain under EC law are at the core of the free movement rubric which now also embraces political participation at the local and European levels. Some national provisions concerning the protection of rights to culture and political participation are more advanced, however, and these are referred to where appropriate.

8.8 CULTURAL RIGHTS

Background

The *raison d'être* of the maintenance and promotion of the culture and language of migrant workers and their families is to support this vulnerable minority group as a distinct entity in the country of employment and to nurture the identity of individual members. A crucial component of this process is teaching the culture and language of migrants to their children, which also constitutes one of the special measures required to satisfy fully their right to education. Another objective, which is almost of equal importance, is to facilitate the integration of migrants into the host society. Indeed, these objectives are interrelated. It has been shown that mother tongue instruction to migrant children serves to assist their integration into the host country's educational system:

> A growing body of socio-linguistic research shows that mastery of the language spoken at home (mother tongue . . .), contributes positively to the educability of the children, and to their acquisition of the host country's language (second language). Especially for the very young immigrant pupils, the early stages of education are made easier if their first language is recognized and used. This is a sign of recognition of the pupil's identity, and it contributes to the development of a positive self-image. Also, it facilitates the acquisition of the basic conceptual skills which form the basis for all future learning, be they linguistic in nature or not.[400]

A secondary objective of promoting the culture and language of migrants is to assist the reintegration of migrant workers, and particularly of their children,

[399] See the analogous argument with regard to the right of migrant workers to reunion with their families, n. 237 above and accompanying text.

[400] *Report on the Education of Migrants' Children in the European Union*, n. 373 above, App. I, Ia, para. 7.

if they decide to return to their country of origin. Although this objective, if pursued at all, was dominant during the earlier phases of labour migration to Western Europe when it was expected that many migrants would return home, it is no longer prevalent given that most migrant communities have become permanently established in host countries.[401]

Many European countries which have provided for mother tongue instruction to migrant children have usually either placed accent on integration into the host society or repatriation to the country of origin, or have attempted to pursue both policies simultaneously rather than viewing the right of migrant workers and their families to enjoy their culture and language as an end in itself.[402] This should be contrasted with an approach where the mother tongue and culture are taught to children with a view to strengthening their self-esteem and supporting the whole minority group and not solely with the aim of integrating these children into the host society or of preparing their return to the country of origin.[403] Such an approach has been taken in the Netherlands, in Sweden and, to some extent, in France.[404] In Sweden, it is one of the cornerstones of that country's immigration policy, namely freedom of choice, and has received constitutional recognition.[405] Migrants have a genuine choice between retaining and developing their own cultural identity and assuming a Swedish cultural identity.[406] In the sphere of education, this choice is translated into a policy of 'active

[401] *Ibid.* 16, paras. 60–1. The Commission's report, *ibid.*, 7, para. 23, observes, however, that the demand for mother tongue teaching from more skilled migrants is still made in the context of eventual return to countries of origin, or perhaps of continuing migration to another member state.

[402] Castles and Kosack have criticized the 'dual strategy' adopted in Germany of integrating foreign children into German society, while at the same time preparing them for repatriation. In the authors' view, this 'dual strategy' cannot achieve either of its contradictory aims and ends up as 'education for bilingual illiteracy': Castles and Kosack, n. 1 above, 501, citing from U. Akpinar, A. López-Blasco, and J. Vink, *Pädagogische Arbeit mit ausländischen Kindern und Jugendlichen* (Munich: Juventa Verlag, 1977) 45.

[403] Steps in this direction were taken by the Conference of Local and Regional Authorities of Europe in 1982, which stressed the need 'to protect and develop the culture in which the immigrant child is rooted, in particular by providing education in his native tongue (para. 5)' and requested local authorities in COE member states 'to ensure that teaching aids in the mother tongue of migrant children are geared towards the actual situation of migrant families (para. 18)': Conference of Local and Regional Authorities of Europe, 17th Session, 19–21 Oct. 1982, Resolution 129 (1982) on the education of migrant workers' children.

[404] Hammar, 'Immigrant Policy', n. 98 above, 270. A scheme set up in the Netherlands in 1984 enables migrant children, mainly at the primary school level, to receive education in their own language and culture. Over 68,000 children (90% of them Moroccans and Turks) benefited from this scheme in 1991. Less interest, however, was expressed at the secondary level with only 8,000 children taking advantage of the programme: *Closed Borders, Stringent Attitudes*, n. 14 above, 87–8.

[405] T. Hammar, 'The Civil Rights of Aliens' in *The Political Rights of Migrant Workers in Western Europe*, n. 96 above, 74, 83. The Swedish Constitution includes the following policy declaration: 'Opportunities should be promoted for ethnic, linguistic and religious minorities to preserve and develop a cultural and social life of their own' (Ch. 1, Art. 2.4 of the *Regeringsformen* 1974).

[406] Papademetriou, n. 103 above, 358. The policy assumes that a large number of immigrants will probably settle permanently and, therefore, directs initiatives towards assisting such groups to retain their linguistic and cultural identity with public support, if they so desire: *ibid.* 357–8.

bilingualism'.[407] Such an approach to the teaching of the mother tongue and culture to migrant children reflects a commitment to a policy of cultural pluralism and a rejection of assimilation.[408] For immigrant languages to thrive in the second- and third- migrant generations, this approach, however, requires substantial investment.[409]

COE standards

The only COE instrument dealing explicitly with the question of mother tongue or cultural instruction for migrants is the EMW. Article 15, entitled Teaching of the Migrant Worker's Mother Tongue, reads:

> The Contracting Parties concerned shall take action by common accord to arrange, as far as practicable, for the migrant worker's children, special courses for the teaching of the migrant worker's mother tongue, to facilitate, *inter alia*, their return to their State of origin.

Article 15 has been labelled as 'one of the most significant advances contained in the Convention'.[410] It should be viewed in a context where international human rights standards have only rarely been expressly concerned with the cultural rights of minority groups.[411] Nonetheless, Article 15 seems to emulate the same incoherent sense of direction taken by some European countries to this question. This short clause is riddled with qualifications: first, agreement has

[407] Papademetriou, *ibid.* 358; Hammar, 'Immigrant Policy', n. 98 above, 270. Hammar, *ibid.*, observes that this policy has been taken further in Sweden than anywhere else, since immigrant children are not only taught to speak their mother tongue, but it is also used as a language of instruction for other subjects. Nonetheless, instruction in Swedish is predominant. It is essential that immigrants learn the language of the host country, for this is the only way to achieve integration, particularly in the labour market. See T. Hammar, 'Towards Convergence' in *European Immigration Policy: A Comparative Study*, n. 2 above, 292, 301.

[408] In countries of permanent immigration, the original belief was that immigrants would be easily assimilated into the host country culture. See Hammar, 'Towards Convergence', *ibid.* 301.

[409] *Ibid.*

[410] R. B. Lillich, *The Human Rights of Aliens in Contemporary International Law* (1984) 91. But see now Arts. 45(3) and (4) of the UN Convention on migrant workers, discussed in Ch. 4, which are a considerable improvement on Art. 15 of the EMW.

[411] The COE recently adopted a Framework Convention for the Protection of National Minorities, 1 Feb. 1995; ETS No. 157; not in force; ratified by 5 states, Cyprus, Hungary, Romania, Slovakia, and Spain, as at 1 July 1996. This Convention lays down a number of principles which ratifying states agree to implement through legislation or policy. A relevant provision to the discussion is Art. 5(1): 'The Parties undertake to promote the conditions necessary for persons belonging to national minorities to maintain and develop their culture, and to preserve the essential elements of their identity, namely their religion, language, traditions and cultural heritage'. The Convention does not define 'national minority'. According to the Explanatory Report, 'it was decided to adopt a pragmatic approach, based on the recognition that at this stage, it is impossible to arrive at a definition capable of mustering general support of all Council of Europe member States': Doc. H(94) 10 (Strasbourg, Nov. 1994) 13, para. 12. Therefore, whether migrant workers and their families will be afforded protection under this instrument will depend on whether states are prepared to consider this group as a 'national minority'. Countries ratifying the Convention should be urged to adopt the approach taken by the Human Rights Committee in its General Comment on Art. 27 of the ICCPR (as discussed in Ch. 2) and, in principle, apply the Convention to groups of non-nationals, particularly those who have been resident for a considerable time within their territories. The Convention requires ratification by 12 states in order to come into force (Art. 28(1)). As at 1 July 1996, it had

to be reached between sending and receiving countries before any action may be taken in this area and unilateral initiatives are not necessary; secondly, the teaching of other subjects in the language of origin is not required; thirdly, the provision is limited to language instruction and does not contain any specific reference to the teaching of culture; and fourthly, the principal reason for this special education is to facilitate return to the country of origin.[412] Indeed, Article 15 was initially to follow Article 30, which is concerned with return migration, although the drafters eventually decided to place the clause after Article 14, and, in particular, after Article 14(5) which also refers to return migration in the context of ensuring that vocational and retraining schemes cater as far as possible for the needs of migrant workers with a view to their return to their country of origin.[413]

There are no explicit provisions in COE instruments relevant to the protection of migrant workers and their families which are concerned with the promotion of their general cultural activities besides language instruction. Nor are there any measures obliging governments to allocate funds out of grants for the arts, such as theatre and music, in order to reflect the cultures of migrants. Article 10(3) of the EMW, however, contains the state obligation to ensure that migrant workers' freedom of worship is respected and to 'facilitate such worship within the limit of available means'. This implies the provision of positive assistance to migrants, for example, in their quest for appropriate premises in which to worship, although any such assistance can be constrained by financial considerations. In this respect, therefore, the obligation arguably goes further than Article 9 of the ECHR, which guarantees to everyone the 'right to freedom of thought, conscience and religion',[414] but which does not specify the provision of positive assistance to promote or facilitate this right.

been signed by 27 COE member states, but had only received 5 ratifications. The aim of another COE instrument, the European Charter for Regional or Minority Languages, is to protect the historical, regional, or minority languages of Europe (Preamble, second recital). However, Art. 1(a) of the Charter asserts explicitly that the languages of migrants are *not* covered by the term 'regional or minority languages': European Charter for Regional or Minority Languages, 22 June 1992; ETS 148; not in force; ratified by 4 states as at 1 July 1996: Finland, Hungary, Netherlands, Norway (and signed by 11 COE member states).

[412] See Lillich, n. 410 above, 92. Admittedly, the words '*inter alia*' may include other reasons for such education. Nevertheless, the express emphasis here on 'return' is decisive in any interpretation of Article 15. See also R. Cholewinski, 'The Racial Discrimination Convention and the Protection of Cultural and Linguistic Ethnic Minorities' (1991) *Revue de Droit International* 167, 211 (n. 167).

[413] *Explanatory Report on the EMW*, n. 71 above, 21–2, paras. 71–2. The revised ESC inserts the following additional paragraph in Art. 19 which obliges states parties 'to promote and facilitate, as far as practicable, the teaching of the migrant worker's mother tongue to the children of the migrant worker' (Art 19(12)). The draft Explanatory Report, however, persists with the connection between such instruction and return migration: 'The underlying reason for this paragraph is the importance for the children of migrant workers of maintaining their cultural and linguistic heritage, *inter alia* in order to provide them with a possibility of reintegration if and when the migrant returns home': *Request for an Opinion on the Draft Revised European Social Charter*, n. 128 above, 15 and 46, para. 79.

[414] Cf. Golsong, n. 259 above, 237–8.

The scarcity of COE standards regarding the promotion of migrants' cultural rights does not mean that efforts in this regard are not being undertaken at the national level. The case of Sweden is an exemplar of positive initiatives in this area. The Swedish Government, through the National Cultural Council, co-ordinates, promotes, and subsidizes cultural activities among migrants, while promoting cultural cooperation with countries of origin.[415] This role may also be played by the trade unions of the host country in defending migrant workers' interests, particularly when employment matters conflict with their religious obligations.[416]

EC standards

The relevant provision in EC law on the question of mother tongue and cultural instruction to migrant children is Article 3 of Council Directive 77/486/EEC:

> Member States shall, in accordance with their national circumstances and legal systems, and in cooperation with States of origin, take appropriate measures to promote, in coordination with normal education, teaching of the mother tongue and culture of the country of origin for the children referred to in Article 1 [see the section on the right to education above].

In contrast with Article 15 of the EMW, which is limited to language education, this provision extends instruction to the teaching of the 'culture of the country of origin'. But vestiges of Article 15 qualifications remain. Appropriate measures in this field depend on 'cooperation' with the countries of origin. Moreover, the third indent of the Preamble to the Directive reveals the main purpose of Article 3. Measures to promote the teaching of the mother tongue and culture to the children of migrant workers are to take place 'with a view principally to facilitating their possible reintegration into the Member State of origin'. The promotion of this teaching is to be carried out 'in coordination with normal education'. In the Commission's view, this may take the form of 'integrated teaching', where such instruction is coordinated with ordinary teaching and imparted during normal school hours, or 'deferred teaching', where it is coordinated with ordinary teaching but provided immediately before or after normal school hours. 'Private' teaching taking place outside normal school hours without the input of educational authorities does not conform to the Directive's requirements.[417]

[415] Papademetriou, n. 103 above, 358. The Council organizes literary production and allocates funds for the purchase of literature in minority languages for migrants. It also supports the ethnic press and minority theatrical activities and encourages and promotes foreign films, music, and folklore: *ibid.* 358–9. See also Z. Layton-Henry, 'Immigrant Associations' in *The Political Rights of Migrant Workers in Western Europe*, n. 96 above, 94, 106 with reference to Sweden and the Netherlands. In Italy, Law No. 943 of 30 Dec. 1986, guarantees the right of foreign workers to maintain their cultural identity (Art. 1(1)). Art. 9(4) directs regional governments to promote cultural activities for the various national groups of foreign workers, which are to be in the language of the country of origin (Art. 9(5)). See Isgro, n. 27 above, 697.

[416] See n. 104 above regarding the Dutch CNV union confederation's collective bargaining activities on behalf of migrant workers.

[417] *Report on the Implementation of Directive 77/486/EEC* (1989), n. 388 above, 7, para. 3.1.4.

As noted in the section on the right to education, a political commitment was made by the Council and member states at the time of the Directive's adoption to extend its application to the children of non-EC migrants. It is questionable, however, whether this is possible in respect of the teaching of the language and culture of the country of origin, especially as the implementation of Article 3 requires 'cooperation' between member states.[418] Moreover, there seems little scope for the direct application of Article 3 by the Court of Justice. In contrast with Article 2 which was discussed earlier, the Commission has observed that Article 3 has no binding force[419] and that it does not give the children in question 'an individual, subjective right to be taught their mother tongue and culture of their country of origin',[420] although the Commission has indicated that it would be prepared to take infringement proceedings under Article 169 EC against a member state if no efforts had been taken to comply with the provision.[421] By and large, progress in this area depends on the Commission encouraging member states to take positive measures. The Commission's Report on the Directive's implementation, covering the school year 1984–5, found the situation in some member states to be unsatisfactory.[422] This is unfortunate because an increase in language teaching is arguably central to the realization of greater European unity and integration.[423]

418 Oliver, n. 315 above, 73.

419 *Report on the Implementation of Directive 77/486/EEC* (1989), n 388 above, 8, para. 3.2.2: 'Whereas article 2 is so worded as to leave no doubt as to its truly binding force on Member States, this is not the case with article 3. The terms it employs ("*Member States shall . . . take appropriate measures to promote . . .*") are such that the directive merely places an obligation on Member States to deploy efforts along the desired lines' (original emphasis, footnote omitted).

420 *Ibid.* 126.

421 The Commission, *ibid.* 127, has identified three specific cases which might give rise to such an action: 'parents having to bear the cost of the teaching of the language and culture of origin; the host State refusing to cooperate in any way with the State of origin in setting up such teaching; [and] the host State refusing to coordinate the teaching of languages and cultures of origin with normal education'.

422 The Report, *ibid.* 79 and 84 respectively, noted that no measures had been taken to implement the Directive in Greece and Ireland. It also found, *ibid.* 123, that in the United Kingdom 'integrated' or 'deferred' tuition in the language and culture of origin is offered to only 6% of migrant children. Most tuition was 'almost systematically organized outside school (without being linked to ordinary education)'. In Belgium, only 10% of children in primary school education in French-speaking areas and 18% in Dutch-speaking regions received such instruction: *ibid.* 24. In France, this figure stood at 37%: *ibid.* 60. The conclusions of the Commission regarding the position in Denmark and the Netherlands were more positive. In these countries, 55 and 80% of migrant children respectively were taught their own language and culture: *ibid.* 31 and 109. The conclusions on the position in Germany were also positive: *ibid.* 55.

423 Cf. Stein and Thomsen, n. 157 above, 1826. In this regard, see the first indent of Article 126(2) EC, which proposes that EC action in the field of education is to be aimed at 'developing the European dimension in education, particularly through the teaching and dissemination of the languages of the Member States'. See also the Lingua programme established by the EC to improve foreign language skills: Council Decision 89/489/EEC of 28 July 1989 establishing an action programme to promote foreign language competence in the European Community (Lingua), OJ 1989, L 239/24. See now the European Parliament and Council Decision 819/95/EC of 14 March 1995 establishing the Community action programme 'Socrates', OJ 1995, L 87/10, Annex, Chapter III, Action 1 (Promotion of language skills in the Community (Lingua)).

8.9 POLITICAL RIGHTS

Background

Migrant workers and their families enjoy limited participation in the political life of European countries of employment. In general, the right to freedom of expression is constitutionally guaranteed to migrants on the same conditions as nationals in most countries.[424] Rights to freedom of association and assembly, however, are not afforded the same level of official protection[425] and are subject to legal restrictions in some countries or looked upon rather disapprovingly in others, particularly if their exercise involves political activity. In Germany, the right of foreign residents to form political parties is restricted; the political party leaders and the majority of party members must be German citizens.[426] Before 1981, non-nationals wishing to establish associations in France had to obtain prior permission from the Ministry of the Interior, and although the law was changed placing aliens on an equal footing with nationals, the former are still expected to observe a certain moderation in political affairs (*obligation de réservé*).[427] In practice, however, rights to freedom of association and assembly are liberally extended to aliens in most European countries.[428] In Sweden, the right of foreigners to freedom of association is even actively encouraged and foreign organizations have flourished with support from the State.[429]

[424] In Germany, however, *all political activities* of aliens may be limited or prohibited, *inter alia*, in the interests of public security and public order, to prevent damage to the formation of the political will in Germany, or to protect other matters of substantial concern to the country. Moreover, in Portugal, Art. 15 of the Constitution prohibits non-nationals from exercising political activities without express or tacit permission from the government. See E. Lundberg, 'Political Freedoms in the European Union' in A. Rosas and E. Antola, (eds.), *A Citizen's Europe: In Search of a New Order* (1995) 113, 118–19. In Switzerland, aliens must obtain permission from the cantonal government in order to speak on a political issue at an open or private meeting of an association, and are required to exercise political restraint, especially with respect to criticism of domestic institutions and authorities. Hammar, 'The Civil Rights of Aliens', n. 405 above, 74, 85; T. Hammar, 'The Policymaking Process' in *European Immigration Policy: A Comparative Study*, n. 2 above, 288; Herdegen, n. 366 above, 2006.

[425] The Netherlands is one of the few European countries which explicitly extends these rights to non-nationals. Arts. 7 and 9 of the Netherlands' Constitution. However, this right is regulated and limited by law in the interests of public order. See also E. Özsunay, 'Report on the Participation of the Alien in Public Affairs (Political and Associative Life)' in Council of Europe, *Human Rights of Aliens in Europe* (1985) 195, 202; Hammar, 'The Civil Rights of Aliens', n. 405 above, 86; Lundberg, n. 424 above, 119 (n. 26).

[426] Lundberg, n. 424 above, 120. In Portugal, aliens are prohibited from forming or joining political parties: *ibid.*

[427] T. Hammar, *Democracy and the Nation State: Aliens, Denizens and Citizens in a World of International Migration* (Aldershot: Avebury, 1990) 131. See also Lundberg, n. 424 above, 120; Thomas, 'Summing-up and Points of Comparison', n. 7 above, 235; and Herdegen, n. 366 above, 2006.

[428] Özsunay, n. 425 above, 237; Frowein, n. 244 above, 2087; Lundberg, n. 424 above, 119–20; Behzadi, n. 174 above, 31.

[429] Thomas, 'Summing-up and Points of Comparison', n. 7 above, 235–6; Layton-Henry, 'Immigrant Associations', n. 415 above, 105–6. In Sweden, in the early 1980s, there were about one thousand foreigners' associations and 120 nationwide ones. Many of these receive financial support from the state and from individual municipalities without being required to sacrifice their independence: Thomas, n. 7 above.

Sweden is also one of those European countries that has made great strides in granting electoral rights to migrants. Migrants who have legally resided in Sweden for a minimum of 3 years have the right to vote and to run for office in municipal and regional elections. These rights were accorded to migrants for the first time in the municipal elections of September 1976 with considerable success, since 60 per cent of the 220,000 immigrants eligible to vote, exercised their right to do so.[430] This bold step in the direction of electoral emancipation for resident foreigners has been followed by other European countries. In Ireland, resident non-nationals can participate in local elections on the same basis as nationals.[431] Foreigners are also permitted to participate in municipal elections in Denmark and Norway provided they have legally resided in the country for 3 years.[432] Although other Nordic nationals in Finland can vote and stand in local elections after 3 years of residence, all other foreigners have to be resident in the country for 5 years before they can exercise electoral rights.[433] In 1985, the legislature in the Netherlands implemented a constitutional clause which extended to aliens the right to vote in and stand for local elections after 5 years of legal residence.[434] Indeed, this is the first country with a relatively high population of foreigners to have taken this step.[435]

The exercise by non-citizens of electoral rights at the national level is not possible in most European countries, with the exception of Ireland and the United Kingdom, which grant each others' citizens the right to vote in elections to national parliaments.[436]

[430] Thomas, n. 7 above, 235; Hammar, 'The Policymaking Process', n. 424 above, 288; J. Rath, 'Voting Rights' in *The Political Rights of Migrant Workers in Western Europe*, n. 96 above, 127, 134, 143. After these elections, many political parties and trade unions in Sweden advocated the extension of the right to vote for foreigners to the national level. The Swedish Parliament, however, preferred to ease restrictions on the acquisition of citizenship so that migrants could obtain access to political life at the national level by making an outright commitment to Swedish society: Thomas, *ibid.* It is noteworthy, however, that in subsequent local elections the immigrant turn-out has decreased (to 48% in 1985). See Rath, *ibid.* 143.

[431] Rath, *ibid.* 139; *Hallmarks of Citizenship Survey*, n. 37 above, 50, 52.

[432] Frowein, n. 244 above, 2088; Hammar (1990), n. 427 above, 150; Rath, n. 430 above, 136; A. Rosas, 'Union Citizenship and National Elections' in *A Citizen's Europe: In Search of a New Order*, n. 424 above, 135, 144–5; *Hallmarks of Citizenship Survey*, n. 37 above, 49, 52 (Denmark). In Switzerland, foreigners have had the right to vote in the canton of Neuchâtel since 1849 and in the canton of Jura since 1979, although a number of other cantons have expressly rejected the idea of extending political participation to them: Rath, *ibid.* 128.

[433] Rosas, n. 432 above, 146. In Iceland, only Nordic nationals can exercise these rights: *ibid.* 148; Hammar (1990), n. 427 above, 152. In some countries, such as Portugal and Spain, the right to vote and to stand for elections is granted to foreign residents on the basis of reciprocity. Thus far, however, only Brazilian nationals in Portugal have acquired this right. See Commission of the European Communities, *Proposal for a Council Directive laying down detailed arrangements for the exercise of the right to vote and to stand as a candidate in municipal elections by citizens of the Union residing in a member State of which they are not nationals*, COM (94) 38 final of 23 Feb. 1994, 8. See also Özsunay, n. 425 above, 217, 218.

[434] Herdegen, n. 366 above, 2009 and n. 58; Rath, n. 430 above, 138; Hammar (1990), n. 427 above, 150.

[435] Frowein, n. 244 above, 2088.

[436] Hammar (1990), n. 427 above, 151; Herdegen, n. 366 above, 2009; Rosas, n. 432 above, 140. Electoral rights at the national level can also be exercised in the United Kingdom by Commonwealth citizens. Rosas, *ibid.*

In most other European countries, the right to participate in elections is confined in their constitutions to citizens.[437] For example, in Germany, Article 20(2) of the Basic Law (known as 'the popular sovereignty clause') declares: 'All state authority emanates from the people'. In 1989, the *Länder* of Hamburg and Schleswig-Holstein granted certain foreign residents voting rights in municipal elections.[438] However, these reforms were overturned by the Federal Constitutional Court on the ground that foreigners were not considered as falling within the concept of 'people'.[439] The German Constitution has since been amended to bring it into line with developments in EC law,[440] which are discussed below.

With the exception of the provision of limited electoral rights, which are mainly confined to the local level, migrant workers and their families in European countries of employment remain, to a large extent, disenfranchised. As a result, national political parties have generally ignored their interests, apart from perhaps those parties that have traditionally represented the working-class electorate.[441] The assumption has always been that citizenship should be obtained first before electoral rights are granted.[442] In practice, as discussed below, citizenship is difficult to obtain in some countries. Furthermore, many migrants who have the opportunity to acquire the nationality of the host country do not usually apply for it merely to obtain full political rights.[443] It is arguable, however, that once electoral rights have been granted to migrants at the local level, there seems no logical reason why the franchise should not be extended to them at the national level as well.[444]

[437] *Proposal for a Council Directive laying down detailed arrangements for the exercise of the right to vote and to stand as a candidate in municipal elections by citizens of the Union residing in a member State of which they are not nationals*, n. 433 above, 7; *Hallmarks of Citizenship Survey*, n. 37 above, 49–53 (Belgium, France, Germany, Greece, Italy, and Luxembourg). The constitutions of Austria, Cyprus, Liechtenstein, and Turkey also confine electoral rights to citizens. See Özsunay, n. 425 above, 217.

[438] In Schleswig-Holstein, the right to vote was granted, on a reciprocal basis, to nationals of Denmark, Ireland, the Netherlands, Norway, and Switzerland, after 5 years of residence. In Hamburg, all non-nationals were given the right to vote in elections to the borough assemblies within the city after 8 years of residence. See G. L. Neuman, '"We are the People": Alien Suffrage in German and American Perspective' (1992) 13 *Michigan J. Int'l L.* 259, 283.

[439] Neuman, *ibid.* 283–7. See also C. Closa, 'Citizenship of the Union and Nationality of Member States' (1995) 3 *CML Rev.* 487, 501 and Rosas, n. 432 above, 151.

[440] Rosas, n. 432 above; Closa, n. 439 above.

[441] Cf. Hammar, 'The Policymaking Process', n. 424 above, 280.

[442] Hammar, 'Towards Convergence', n. 407 above, 299–300; Herdegen, n. 366 above, 2008. In the American context, the right to vote has been labelled as the 'quintessential right of citizenship' and it has been argued that the possession of full political rights carries 'an important symbolic message about the value and significance of full membership'. See respectively G. M. Rosberg, 'Aliens and Equal Protection: Why not the Right to Vote' (1977) 75 *Mich. L. Rev.* 1092, 1134; and P. H. Schuck and R. M. Smith, *Citizenship Without Consent: Illegal Aliens in the American Polity* (New Haven: Yale University Press, 1985) 6.

[443] Hammar, n. 442 above.

[444] Rosas, n. 432 above, 153, writes: 'From a practical point of view, it can be asked to what extent the distinction between national elections as "political" and local elections as "non-political" holds true. There is a trend in many states to transfer more powers to local and regional government. And, apart from the specific powers of local governments, local elections are perceived as important political signals, for instance, in assessing the political support of the government in power'.

The general political non-participation of migrants and their families in Europe is alarming. Hammar wrote in 1985 that political democracy does not fully function when more than 10 million men and women in Europe are deprived of their voting rights.[445] Some European countries have tried to lessen the negative effect of non-participation by migrants in the political life of their societies with the creation, mainly on the municipal level, of immigrant advisory or consultative councils, composed of migrant representatives who are chosen by their peers.[446] For this reason, such institutions have been set up in Belgium, France, Germany, and Switzerland.[447] The aim of these bodies has been described as twofold: 'to improve the relationships between migrant workers and the native population, and . . . to establish a channel of communication linking foreign migrants to the political system'.[448] With regard to this latter aim, these bodies have not been very successful for a number of reasons. First, migrant councils are usually established on the initiative of the authorities of the host country rather than the initiative of the migrants themselves.[449] Secondly, they have no power to take any decisions and merely exercise an advisory function.[450] Finally, and most importantly, the *raison d'être* of these bodies is to act as a substitute for genuine political participation. As a result, these unique 'representative' structures, created especially to give a 'voice' to migrants in host countries, have been rejected by the migrants themselves, because, in essence, they have served to separate foreign workers and their families from the political reality in these countries:

> It is a mistake to construct programmes for satisfying unimportant needs or creating artificial needs: what is important is to treat people as much as possible like one's own nationals. This alignment of status with that of nationals should, moreover, to be effective, be carried out as a united policy.[451]

[445] Hammar, 'Towards Convergence', n. 407 above, 299.

[446] For a description of these bodies, see: U. Andersen, 'Consultative Institutions for Migrant Workers' in *The Political Rights of Migrant Workers in Western Europe*, n. 96 above, 113; Thomas, 'Summing-up and Points of Comparison', n. 7 above, 236–7; Martin and Miller, n. 3 above, 327; Hammar, 'The Policymaking Process', n. 424 above, 289; Power, n. 97 above, 31.

[447] Andersen, n. 446 above, 125. However, consultative institutions are also to be found in countries which grant voting rights to immigrants: *ibid.* (the Netherlands, Sweden, the United Kingdom).

[448] *Ibid.* 122.

[449] Andersen, n. 446 above, 113, writes: '[B]ecause they are formally organized by local or regional authorities, who lay down the terms of reference and provide the finance and administrative facilities, consultative institutions are not as independent and unconstrained as the associations and organizations established by migrant workers themselves'. See also Thomas, 'Summing-up and Points of Comparison', n. 7 above, 236.

[450] Andersen, n. 446 above; Thomas, n. 7 above, 237; Power, n. 97 above, 31; Martin and Miller, n. 3 above, 327.

[451] Thomas (1986), n. 7 above, 47. See also Thomas, 'Summing-up and Points of Comparison', *ibid.* However, Andersen makes the important observation that consultative bodies can be considered in a positive light as a step to eventual political participation through voting. On another level, the work of such bodies may also be beneficial in those areas where the aspirations of foreign immigrant communities are limited or where the attitude of local politicians is conciliatory: *ibid.* 115, 125.

The access of migrant workers to employment in the public service of European receiving countries is generally restricted on the basis that 'the exercise of certain forms of public authority, typically linked with the status of a civil servant, presupposes a special bond between the office-holder and the authority he or she is supposed to represent'.[452] Although some states only prohibit access to positions which are civil service positions in 'a strict sense',[453] namely those which involve a higher level of policy-making, and exceptions are made for university professors and technical experts,[454] it has nonetheless been observed that a significant number of EC nationals and non-EC nationals are prevented from taking up 'non-sensitive' public sector employment (which constitutes nearly one-fifth of all jobs in the EC labour market) in EC member states.[455]

COE and EC standards

Until recently, the political rights of migrant workers and their families were conspicuous by their absence in COE standards. Indeed, the thrust of relevant COE provisions had been to restrict rather than promote these rights. The position in EC law was similar until recent amendments introduced by the TEU, which grant rights of electoral participation to EC nationals residing in other member states at the local and European levels.

(a) General political activity

As alluded to in Chapters 2 and 5, Article 16 of the ECHR enables states parties to limit the rights to freedom of expression (Article 10), association, assembly (Article 11), and non-discrimination (Article 14) by imposing restrictions on the political activity of aliens. However, this does not mean that states parties can deny fundamental rights to migrants *carte blanche* under this provision. Governments may not, for example, preclude migrant workers from joining trade unions to protect their interests connected with employment or from forming their own

[452] Kühner, n. 26 above, 1979. [453] Kühner, *ibid.* [454] Özsunay, n. 425 above, 240–1.

[455] Böhning and Werquin, n. 36 above, 14, paras. 32, 33. See also cf. Behzadi, n. 174 above, 32. Böhning and Werquin, *ibid.* 14–15, para. 33, observe that this approach is 'like any measure of durable protection, economically unproductive and wasteful'. In Germany, for example, the category of public service employment has been drawn very broadly: Kühner, n. 26 above, 1984. In 1978, the Mikrozensus Survey recorded that there were no foreigners in the public service in Germany: OECD, *Young Foreigners and the World of Work* (Paris: OECD, 1981) 30. See also Castles and Kosack, n. 1 above, 497. This is because of Art. 33(2) of the German Basic Law which proclaims that only German citizens have the right to be equally eligible for public office. EC nationals excepted, German nationality is required in order to obtain the status of civil servant. See *Hallmarks of Citizenship Survey*, n. 37 above, 60. Recent evidence suggests that there have been few changes in practice and that foreigners can only obtain employment in the German public service under exceptional circumstances. See Aukerman, n. 27 above, 243, citing from Institut für Migrations— und Rassismusforschung, *Comparative Assessment of the Legal Instruments in the Various Member States of the European Communities to Combat All Forms of Discrimination, Racism and Xenophobia and Incitement and Hatred and Racial Violence, National Study for the Federal Republic of Germany* (Hamburg, 1992) 37.

associations. Any political implication in these activities, however, may jeopardize the rights and freedoms outlined. The *travaux préparatoires* reveal that the aim of Article 16:

> is to make provision for the fact that, in accordance with a universally admitted practice, the exercise of the fundamental rights by foreigners (non-nationals) may be subject to certain restrictions not applicable to nationals. These restrictions, however, must not violate the general principles of law as recognized by civilized nations.[456]

Although political activity might also be restricted on the basis of the limitations which are built into Articles 10 and 11, Article 16 seems to envisage further restrictions.[457] For example, it has been contended that the prohibition of political demonstrations by migrant workers in the host state against the Government of their country of origin might be justified on the basis of Article 16 'in the interest of good relations with other states'.[458] Moreover, states parties might also have recourse to this provision in order to prevent migrants from criticizing arrangements in the host country.[459] Article 16 was invoked for the first time by France in a recent case decided by the Court of Human Rights, which concerned the decision to expel a German national from the overseas territory of French Polynesia for participating in a peaceful demonstration supporting the independence of the colony and opposing the holding of nuclear tests in the area.[460] The Court, confirming the earlier finding of the Commission, found a violation of the applicant's right to freedom of expression under Article 10(1) and, furthermore, concluded that Article 16 could not be raised against her given that she was a national of an EC member state and a member of the European Parliament in which the people of overseas territories also take part through elections.[461] Although the concept of 'political activity' was not defined by the Court, the Commission seemed to indicate in its opinion that it was unlikely that Article 16 would receive a broad interpretation today. The Commission observed that 'in placing [Article 16] in the Convention those who drafted it were subscribing to a concept that was then prevalent in international law under which a general unlimited restriction of the political activities of aliens was thought legitimate'. The Commission then added, citing earlier Court judgments, that 'the Convention

[456] Drzemczewski, n. 269 above, 355 (n. 25), citing from *Collected Edition of the 'Travaux Préparatoires' of the European Convention on Human Rights*, vol. III (1976) COE Doc. CM/WPI (50) 1, 246, 266.

[457] P. van Dijk and G. J. H. van Hoof, *Theory and Practice of the European Convention on Human Rights*, 2nd edn. (Deventer: Kluwer, 1990) 561; Robertson and Merrills, n. 229 above, 191.

[458] van Dijk and van Hoof, n. 457 above, observe: 'The fact that such activities of aliens often serve to promote and protect the very values on which the Convention is based, unfortunately does not stand in the way of the application of Article 16, since the latter does not contain any reservation in that respect'.

[459] *Ibid.*

[460] *Piermont* v. *France*, judgment of 27 April 1995, Eur. Ct. H.R., 1995, Ser. A., No. 314-A, (1995) 20 EHRR 301. See also Applications 15773/89 and 15574/89, *Piermont* v. *France* (Commission report of 20 Jan. 1994).

[461] *Ibid.* para. 64.

is a living instrument, which must be interpreted in the light of present day conditions and the evolution of modern society'.[462]

The rights of non-nationals to freedom of expression, assembly, and association have received more positive attention in the recently adopted Convention on the Participation of Foreigners in Public Life at the Local Level, which is not yet in force.[463] These rights are guaranteed to lawfully resident foreigners by Article 3 of the Convention and although they are subject to permissible restrictions, which are identical to those found in the equivalent provisions of the ECHR,[464] there is no sweeping limitation clause in the character of Article 16. Moreover, states parties cannot opt out of this clause in the same way as they may opt out of the provisions which afford aliens rights to political participation in their country of residence.[465]

EC standards do not contain any specific right to general political activity for migrant workers from other member states, which is perhaps not surprising given the predominantly economic accent of the EC regime. Nonetheless, the Court of Justice has ruled on a number of occasions that EC law is to be interpreted in accordance with fundamental human rights.[466] These rights find their expression, for the first time, in Article F(2) of the TEU which asserts that: 'The Union shall respect fundamental rights, as guaranteed by the [ECHR] . . . and as they result from the constitutional traditions common to the Member States, as general principles of Community law'. However, this provision is specifically excluded, by Article L TEU, from the jurisdiction of the Court of Justice, and,

[462] Commission Report, n. 460 above, paras. 58 and 59 respectively. See also cf. Lundberg, n. 424 above, 116–17. Given the recent developments in some countries granting aliens the right to vote and electoral participation at the local level and that few European states in practice restrict the other political activities of migrant workers, an argument for removing this 'anachronistic' restriction is a convincing one. See Drzemczewski, n. 269 above, 355, 399; Swart, n. 45 above, 60. Swart, *ibid.*, concludes that Art. 16 'does not befit a Convention on human rights, and hardly does the Council of Europe credit' and observes that there is no comparable provision to Art. 16 in other international human rights instruments, such as the ICCPR. Indeed, Parliamentary Assembly Recommendation 799 (1977) of 25 Jan. 1977 on the political rights and position of aliens effectively recommends its repeal (para. 10(c)).

[463] Convention on the Participation of Foreigners in Public Life at the Local Level, 5 Feb. 1992; ETS No. 144; not in force; ratified by 3 states, Italy, Norway, and Sweden, as at 1 July 1996. The Convention needs to be ratified by 4 states in order to enter into force (Art. 12(1)). It has also been signed by Denmark, the Netherlands, and the United Kingdom.

[464] Arts. 9(2) and (3). Moreover, these permissible restrictions are found in the same provision as the derogation clause (Art. 9(1)), which is similar to Art. 15 of the ECHR, and thus appear to be subject to further safeguards because Art. 9(4) requires that 'any measure taken in accordance with . . . [Art. 9] . . . be notified to the Secretary General of the Council of Europe, who shall inform the other Parties'. For a succinct overview of the principal provisions of this Convention, see H.-J. Bartsch, 'Council of Europe—Legal Co-operation in 1992' (1992) 12 YEL 675, 678–9.

[465] Art. 1(1). See below for a discussion of these provisions.

[466] For example, the Court has held that participation in trade union activity cannot affect adversely freedom of movement within the EC or within individual member states. See *Rutili*, n. 115 above. See also *Re Housing of Migrant Workers: Commission v. Germany*, n. 317 above, para. 10, in which the Court asserted that Art. 8 of the ECHR was also one of the fundamental rights recognized by EC law.

consequently, 'the concrete legal implications of this commitment . . . remain somewhat uncertain'.[467]

(b) Electoral rights

Article 3 of the first Protocol to the ECHR obliges states parties 'to hold free elections at reasonable intervals by secret ballot, under conditions which will ensure the free expression of the opinion of the people in the choice of the legislature'. Both the Commission and the Court of Human Rights have recognized that this provision guarantees the right to vote and the right to stand for election.[468] It is not stated expressly whether this right may be exercised by *everyone* resident in the country. However, because restrictions on the political activity of aliens are permitted by Article 16 in relation to Article 14, it would be open for states parties to discriminate on the basis of nationality by confining the right of electoral participation in Article 3 of the Protocol to citizens.[469]

The Convention on the Participation of Foreigners in Public Life at the Local Level affords non-nationals a number of political rights. In recognizing the reality that 'the residence of foreigners on the national territory is now a permanent feature of European societies', the Convention seeks 'to improve their integration into the local community, especially by enhancing the possibilities for them to participate in local public affairs'.[470] Article 6(1) of the Convention obliges states parties to accord to foreign residents the right to vote and stand as candidates in local elections provided that they have fulfilled the same legal requirements as those applying to nationals and that they have completed 5 years' lawful and habitual residence in the country concerned. Significantly, states parties may opt out of this provision on ratifying the Convention and may also confine its application to the right to vote.[471]

[467] Lundberg, n. 424 above, 122. In a recent opinion, the Court of Justice asserted that the EC has no competence to accede to the ECHR. Accession can only take place by way of an amendment to the EC Treaty. See Opinion 2/94, *Re: The Accession of the Community to the European Convention on Human Rights* [1996] 2 CMLR 265, paras. 35 and 36.

[468] See respectively Application 9267/81, *Moureaux* v. *Belgium* (1983) 32 D & R 97, para. 61 and *Matthieu-Mohin and Clerfayt* v. *Belgium*, judgment of 2 March 1987, Eur. Ct. H.R. 1987, Ser. A, No. 113, (1988) 10 EHRR 1, para. 54. See also *Law and Practice of the ECHR and the ESC*, n. 76 above, 332.

[469] See also van Dijk and van Hoof, n. 457 above, 560. The Commission has confirmed that a state party may restrict voting rights to nationals: Application 7566/76, *X.* v. *U.K.* (1977) 9 D & R 121, 122. See also *Law and Practice of the ECHR and the ESC*, *ibid.*

[470] Preamble, fourth and sixth indents.

[471] Arts. 1(1) and 6(2) respectively. Art. 7 permits states parties to introduce a shorter waiting-period in Art. 6(1). Another relevant provision is Art. 5(1)(a), whereby states parties are obliged to ensure that there are 'no legal or other obstacles to prevent local authorities in whose area there is a significant number of foreign residents from setting up consultative bodies or making other appropriate institutional arrangements designed . . . [*inter alia*] to provide a forum for the discussion and formulation of the opinions, wishes and concerns of foreign residents on matters which particularly affect them in relation to local public life, including the activities and responsibilities of the local authority concerned'. Moreover, under Art. 5(1)(b), states parties undertake 'to *encourage and*

Between 1974 and 1989, the EC Commission and Parliament had advocated, but without any success, that rights to electoral participation at the local level be accorded to EC nationals resident in other member states.[472] This question, however, was taken up by the inter-governmental conference drafting the TEU. With the advent of European citizenship in Part II of the EC Treaty, EC citizens, residing in a member state of which they are not nationals, have obtained the right to vote and to stand as candidates in local and European parliamentary elections in the EC country of residence under the same conditions as nationals of that country. These rights, which are enshrined in Article 8(b) EC, are not directly effective and require the Council, on a proposal from the Commission and after consulting the European Parliament, to adopt detailed arrangements for their implementation. Article 8(b) EC also specifies that 'these arrangements may provide for derogations where warranted by problems specific to a member state'. Arrangements for elections to the European Parliament were adopted at the end of 1993,[473] whereas the arrangements for local elections were adopted at the end of the following year in the form of Directive 94/80/EC.[474] This Directive, contrary to earlier suggestions, provides for no uniform minimum period of

facilitate the establishment of such consultative bodies or the making of other appropriate institutional arrangements' (emphasis added). The representatives of foreign residents participating in these bodies or arrangements are to be elected by the foreign residents in the local authority area or appointed by individual associations of foreign residents (Art. 5(2)). States parties can also opt out of Art. 5 (Art. 1(1)).

[472] For a brief historical background, see *Proposal for a Council Directive laying down detailed arrangements for the exercise of the right to vote and to stand as a candidate in municipal elections by citizens of the Union residing in a member State of which they are not nationals*, n. 433 above, 13. In 1985, the Commission maintained that granting EC nationals resident in other member states the right to vote and to stand for office would constitute 'a decisive element' in the process of 'the social and political integration of migrants': *Guidelines for a Community Policy on Migration*, n. 171 above, 11, para. 19.

[473] Council Directive 93/109/EC of 6 Dec. 1993 laying down detailed arrangements for the exercise of the right to vote and stand as a candidate in elections to the European Parliament for citizens of the Union residing in a member state of which they are not nationals, OJ 1993, L 329/34. The reason for the speedy adoption of this Directive was to ensure that the arrangements were in place for the fourth direct elections to the European Parliament held in June 1994. See Commission of the European Communities, *Report on the Citizenship of the Union*, COM (93) 702 final of 21 Dec. 1993, 6, 7. Between 2 and 24% of non-nationals eligible to vote in their member state of residence participated in these elections and only one non-national candidate was elected in her member state of residence. The novelty of the right to vote for non-nationals, the lack of information on the subject and the propensity to vote for candidates in member states of origin were some of the reasons given for the low turnout by non-national voters in comparison with national voters. See Commission of the European Communities, Report to the Council and the European Parliament, *The Single Market in 1994*, COM (95) 238 final of 15 June 1995, 6–7.

[474] Council Directive 94/80/EC of 19 Dec. 1994 laying down detailed arrangements for the exercise of the right to vote and to stand as candidate in municipal elections by citizens of the Union residing in a member state of which they are not nationals, OJ 1994, L 368/38. This Directive had to be incorporated into the national laws of the member states by 1 Jan. 1996 (Art. 14). As at the end of July 1996, however, only 3 EC member states (Denmark, Finland and Ireland), had informed the Commission that they had adopted measures transposing this Directive into their national legislation. See MNS No. 161/96 (Aug. 1996) 14.

residence.[475] As a general rule, if nationals are required to complete a minimum period of residence in the territory of the member state concerned, this condition is deemed to have been fulfilled by non-national EC citizens if they have resided for an equivalent period in other member states.[476] According to the Directive, the offices of head or members of the executive of the local municipal authority may be restricted to nationals.[477] Moreover, it permits member states, in which the proportion of non-national voters exceeds 20 per cent of the total electorate, to derogate from applying the Directive by imposing, in respect of voting rights, a residence requirement equivalent to one municipal term and, in respect of the right to stand as a candidate for office, a residence requirement equivalent to 2 municipal terms.[478] In practice, the only EC member state that would presently satisfy this threshold is Luxembourg.[479]

475 In a report issued in Oct. 1986, the Commission considered that a waiting-period corresponding to the term of office of a municipal council plus one year was reasonable in the case of the right to vote. This would have resulted in an average minimum period of residence of 5 years in most EC countries. The Commission also proposed that this period be doubled in the case of the right to stand as a candidate in elections. See Commission of the European Communities, Report to the European Parliament transmitted to the Council for information, *Voting Rights in Local Elections for Community Nationals Residing in a Member State Other than their Own*, Doc. COM (86) 487 final of 7 Oct. 1986, 91, 93 respectively. However, in its proposal for Directive 94/80/EC, n. 433 above, 22, the Commission was of the view that a uniform minimum period of residence was inappropriate for the following reasons: 'Politically, it is important to note that any condition as to a minimum period of residence would deprive a considerable number of Union citizens of the right to vote and to stand as candidate in their Member State of residence. Though deprived of these political rights, such citizens would still be subject to the same obligations as everyone else living in their basic local government unit, notably as regards local taxes. Like other residents there, they would be subject also to decisions taken either by the representative council or by the executive in the exercise of local autonomy and affecting their daily lives. Lastly, the smooth integration of non-national citizens requires that they be able to take part not only in the economic and social life of the local government unit in which they live but in its political life as well, and that, in this context, they be allowed to assume joint responsibility for local public affairs'.

476 Art. 4(1). However, under Arts. 4(2) and (3), the rights to vote and stand as a candidate in local elections may be subject to the requirement that non-nationals have their principal residence in the local government unit concerned or that they have spent a minimum period of residence in that unit or in the constituent part of the member state of which that unit forms a part.

477 Art. 5(3). In its proposal for the Directive, n. 433 above, 24, the Commission, justifies these restrictions 'in view of the fact that the local executive also participates in the exercise of official authority and in the safeguarding of the general interest in the territory of the basic local government unit, as defined by the Court of Justice in its judgments on Articles 48(4) and 55 of the [EC] Treaty'. For a discussion of these provisions, see the section below on employment in the public service.

478 Art. 12(1). Art. 12(4) obliges the Commission to submit a report to the European Parliament and to the Council by 31 Dec. 1998, and every 6 years thereafter, for the purpose of reviewing whether any derogations that have been adopted are still justified.

479 See Rosas, n. 432 above, 152 (n. 74). By virtue of Art. 12(2) of the Directive, and in order to take account of the specific linguistic and regional features and balance in that country (Preamble, recital 22), Belgium is permitted to apply the first derogation in Art. 12(1)(a) in respect of voting rights to a limited number of local government units provided that it communicates a list of units to which the derogation is to apply at least one year before elections in those units take place. In a statement attached to the text of the Directive, the Belgian delegation stated that, if it were to make use of the derogation in Art. 12(2), such a derogation would only be exceptionally applied by the Belgian government to some of the local government units in which the number of non-nationals with the right to vote exceeded 20% of the total electorate.

Although granting electoral rights to EC migrants on the European parliamentary and local levels is a significant development, it is arguable that the extension of these rights to the national level would have been more meaningful in the context of the development of Union or European citizenship:

Taking part in the political life in a municipality of a Member State is a far cry from European citizenship: exercise of voting rights for national elections would be a much more relevant aspect of European citizenship, given the involvement of (some) national bodies of representation in the framing and implementation of the European legal and political order.[480]

Because 'citizenship of the Union' is restricted to EC nationals, non-EC nationals are excluded from the exercise of electoral rights granted under Article 8(b) EC, even though some EC member states, as discussed earlier, grant local electoral rights to *all* alien residents regardless of their nationality.[481] The resulting discrimination between EC citizens who are not nationals of the member state in which they reside and other resident aliens in respect of electoral rights might well be a violation of international law.[482] Third country nationals, however, clearly have the right to petition the European Parliament or to make a complaint about EC maladministration to the Ombudsman because these particular rights are not only granted to EC citizens, but also to 'any natural or legal person residing or having his registered office in a Member State'.[483] It is noteworthy, however, that, in so far as petitions to the European Parliament are concerned, only matters falling 'within the Community's fields of activity' can be considered.[484] Given that non-EC nationals are significantly affected by the Third Pillar of the TEU, which is beyond the scope of Community activity, the

[480] H. U. J. d'Oliveira, 'Union Citizenship: Pie in the Sky?' in *A Citizen's Europe: In Search of a New Order*, n. 424 above, 58, 73. See also A. Evans, 'Nationality Law and European Integration' (1991) 16 *EL Rev*. 190, 210: 'From the point of view of the development of Community citizenship, however, participation at the national level might be thought to be more important than participation at the local level, because it is at the former level that decisions of more direct relevance to the work of the Community are taken'.

[481] Art. 1(2) of Directive 94/80/EC asserts explicitly that it does not affect the rights of third country nationals to enjoy such rights where they are granted under domestic law.

[482] D'Oliveira, n. 480 above, 78, writes: 'One may ask whether it is reconcilable with [the] principle of democracy to include nationals of Member States and to exclude all other residents from (local) elections, and thus to distinguish between a group of nationalities and all other nationalities. To create first-class and second-class citizens in this respect will *prima facie* only then not amount to discrimination and lack of democracy, if there are very good reasons for this distinction. I do not think that the social and political ties between Member States amount to such a good reason as to exclude persons who otherwise fulfil the conditions but do not possess the nationality of a Member State'. Indeed, a relevant international law provision here is Art. 1(3) of ICERD, discussed in Ch. 2. See also Evans (1991), n. 480 above, 214 (and n. 16).

[483] Arts. 138d and 138e EC. These rights are granted to EC citizens by Art. 8d EC in accordance with Arts 138d and 138e EC.

[484] Similarly, the Ombudsman can only consider complaints 'concerning instances of maladministration *in the activities of the Community institutions or bodies*, with the exception of the Court of Justice and the Court of First Instance acting in their judicial role': Art. 138e(1). See also d'Oliveira, n. 480 above, 74–5.

wording, if interpreted narrowly, may amount to a considerable restriction on this right.[485]

(c) Employment in the public service

Generally speaking, employment in the public service in European labour-receiving countries is restricted to nationals. Usually, it is the state concerned which decides what constitutes 'public service' for the purpose of such restrictions. Only EC law attempts to place significant external constraints on the normally broad state discretion in this area.

The ECE is the sole COE instrument which expressly deals with this issue.[486] Article 13 of the ECE stipulates:

> Any Contracting Party may reserve for its own nationals the exercise of public functions or of occupations connected with national security or defence, or make the exercise of these occupations by aliens subject to special conditions.

At first glance, this provision appears promising and might be interpreted to mean that only public functions or occupations '*connected with national security or defence*' can be reserved for nationals and that the reserved category of employment is to be defined by an objective reference to the actual function performed, rather than by reference to the legal description given to the position by the state concerned.[487] However, Section I of the Protocol, which specifically refers to Article 13, asserts in paragraph (a)(4) that each state party has the right to judge by 'national criteria', *inter alia*, 'the reasons specified in the Convention for which a Contracting Party may reserve for its own nationals . . . the exercise of certain rights and occupations or may make the exercise thereof by nationals of the other Parties subject to special conditions'. In its Commentary on the ECE, the Standing Committee envisages a wide range of posts that may be reserved for nationals.[488]

[485] However, the amended parliamentary Rules of Procedure (OJ 1995, L 293/1) are broader in scope because they refer to the 'European Union's fields of activity' (Art. 156(1)). See also Marias who expects that the Committee on Petitions will also find those petitions admissible which come within the Union's fields of activity. See E. A. Marias, 'Mechanisms of Protection of Union Citizens' Rights' in *A Citizen's Europe: In Search of a New Order*, n. 424 above, 207, 219. In 1993–94, out of 1,083 petitions submitted to the European Parliament, 21 petitions were submitted by non-EC nationals: *ibid.* 225–6 (Tables 1 and 2).

[486] Art. 18 of the ESC, which grants to nationals of states parties the right to engage in a gainful occupation in the territory of other contracting parties, does not refer to any limitations regarding public service employment. See also Swart, n. 45 above, 43–4. The Committee of Independent Experts appears not to have addressed this question under the provision. It has stated, however, with respect to Art. 19(4), that measures preventing the access of migrant workers to public service employment for security reasons are justifiable under Art. 31 of the ESC: *Conclusions VIII*, 208, cited in *Case Law on the European Social Charter—Supplement*, n. 59 above, 49.

[487] Cf. Plender, n. 72 above, 238.

[488] *Commentary on the European Convention on Establishment*, n. 46 above, 18, para. 57: 'For example, civil service posts and military posts may be reserved for nationals. These are public functions, including judges, notaries, bailiffs and solicitors. Public service posts may be under the authority of the State, municipalities or semi-public institutions'.

The right of free access to employment for EC workers does not, by virtue of Article 48(4) EC, encompass 'employment in the public service'. This permissible derogation from the principle of freedom of movement has been interpreted restrictively by the Court of Justice on the basis that the principle itself must take precedence over the legitimate interest of member states to reserve public service posts for their own nationals.[489] This restrictive interpretation has concerned the notion of 'employment in the public service' which is not defined in the text. From the case law, it is clear that 'public service' is a fixed notion in all member states, defined by reference to the actual activities performed and 'not in terms of the legal status of the holder of the post'.[490] According to the Court of Justice, the public service positions that may be reserved for nationals are those which involve:

> direct or indirect participation in the exercise of powers conferred by public law and duties designed to safeguard the general interests of the State or of other public authorities. Such posts in fact presume on the part of those occupying them the existence of a special relationship of allegiance to the State and reciprocity of rights and duties which form the foundation of the bond of nationality.[491]

What is crucial in this approach to defining 'public service' for the purpose of the derogation in Article 48(4) EC is whether the person in employment possesses the capacity to exercise public law power or the responsibility for safeguarding the general interests of the state.[492] Such power and responsibility is not exercised by railroad workers and nurses employed in public hospitals, nor by trainee teachers, secondary school teachers, and university foreign-language assistants.[493] Moreover, if EC nationals are already employed in the public service of another member state, Article 48(4) EC cannot be used to deny them the protection of EC law regarding, for example, remuneration and other working

[489] Case 149/79, *Commission* v. *Belgium* [1980] ECR 3881, [1981] 2 CMLR 413, para. 19. For commentaries on Art. 48(4) EC, see D. O'Keeffe, 'Judicial Interpretation of the Public Service Exception to the Free Movement of Workers' in D. Curtin and D. O'Keeffe, (eds.), *Constitutional Adjudication in European Community and National Law* (Butterworths (Ireland), 1992) 89; and J. Handoll, 'Article 48(4) EEC and Non-national Access to Public Employment' (1988) 13 *EL Rev.* 223. See also the Commission's strategy for the elimination of restrictions on grounds of nationality in respect of access to posts in the public sector: freedom of movement of workers and access to employment in the public service of the member states—Commission action in respect of the application of Article 48(4) of the EEC Treaty, OJ 1988, C 72/2.

[490] *Sotgiu* v. *Bundespost*, n. 21 above, 172 (Advocate-General Mayras). See also Plender, n. 72 above, 210 and Stein and Thomsen, n. 157 above, 1818.

[491] *Commission* v. *Belgium*, n. 489 above, para. 10.

[492] See also Plender, n. 72 above, 210. Plender, *ibid.* 238, observes that the difficulties with the interpretation of Art. 48(4) EC would be reduced if it were read in its historical context with reference to Art. 13 of the ECE, which links the notion of public service to 'national security or defence'.

[493] See respectively *Commission* v. *Belgium*, n. 489 above; Case 307/84, *Re French Nurses: Commission* v. *France* [1986] ECR 1725, [1987] 3 CMLR 555; Case 66/85, *Lawrie-Blum* v. *Land Baden-Württemberg* [1986] ECR 2121, [1987] 3 CMLR 389; Case C-4/91, *Bleis* v. *Ministère de l'Éducation Nationale* [1991] ECR I-5627; and *Allue and Coonan*, n. 162 above.

conditions,[494] although these workers may still be prevented from aspiring to posts connected with the exercise of public law powers.[495]

The right of establishment is subject to similar restrictions in that, by virtue of the first paragraph of Article 55 EC, it is inapplicable to 'activities . . . connected, even occasionally, with the exercise of official authority'.[496] This provision also lacks a definition in the text and has been interpreted restrictively by the Court of Justice, which ruled in *Reyners* v. *Belgium* that the exemption in Article 55 EC in respect of the right of establishment is limited to activities which in themselves involve a 'direct and specific connection with the exercise of official authority'.[497] Although the Court did not elaborate on this 'connection', it held, on the facts of the case under consideration, that consultation, legal assistance, and representation given by lawyers or *avocats* are not activities linked directly and specifically with the exercise of official authority, even if the performance of these activities is compulsory or is subject to a legal monopoly.[498]

8.10 RESIDENCE RIGHTS AND THE ACQUISITION OF CITIZENSHIP

Background

For those migrants who came to Europe and were accepted as permanent immigrants, particularly those who emigrated from former colonial territories, the assumption was that they would settle indefinitely in the country of employment. However, for those 'temporary' migrants whose residence and employment in a country depends on a residence and work permit system, their legal situation in respect of regular residence, permanent settlement, and naturalization or the acquisition of citizenship is subject to numerous obstacles.

EC migrants and their families have the right to reside in EC member states while employed there. They also possess the right to remain in that state after the completion of their employment.[499] A general right of residence in other EC member states is now recognized for those EC nationals who are not pursuing an economic activity. These rights are analysed in some detail below. In countries

[494] *Sotgiu* v. *Bundespost*, n. 21 above; *Echternach*, n. 384 above; *Allué and Coonan*, n. 162 above.

[495] *Commission* v. *Belgium*, n. 489 above, para. 21.

[496] Art. 55 EC is extended to the freedom to provide services by Art. 66 EC.

[497] *Reyners* v. *Belgium*, n. 81 above, para. 45.

[498] *Ibid.* para. 52. Article 55 EC applies to 'activities' only and not to occupations or professions as a whole. The Court, *ibid.*, para. 47, indicated in *Reyners* that if a profession contained activities that were 'connected, even occasionally, with the exercise of official authority', the right of establishment would still be protected if it were possible to sever these activities from the profession in question. See also D. Wyatt, 'The Right of Establishment and the Freedom to Provide Services' in Wyatt and Dashwood, n. 156 above, 278, 292.

[499] Nationals of Nordic countries have an automatic right to stay in other Nordic countries. See *Europe's International Migrants*, n. 32 above, 20, 59 (Denmark and Sweden).

that do not belong to the EC, or in the case of most non-EC nationals in EC member states, it can take up to 5 years, as outlined earlier in the section on employment rights, before restrictions on migrant workers' free access to employment are lifted. Given that the practice today is to align residence permits with work permits, it may take a similar period of time before restrictions on the duration of residence are removed.[500] The strictest conditions exist in Germany, Switzerland, Greece, and Portugal where a period of 8, 10, 15 and 20 years' residence respectively is normally required before permanent residence status can be obtained.[501]

The removal of restrictions on the duration of a migrant's residence in the country of employment is not the same of course as naturalization and the acquisition of citizenship.[502] In many European countries, at least 5 years' legal residence is required before applications may be lodged by migrant workers of minimum legal age (between 18 and 20 years) for naturalization,[503] and in some countries this qualifying period of residence may be as long as 10 years.[504] However,

[500] Generally speaking, work permits are aligned with residence permits in the following countries: Austria, Finland, France, the Netherlands, Norway, Sweden, and the United Kingdom. See Thomas, 'Summing-up and Points of Comparison', n. 7 above, 221; Baubock, n. 35 above, 167 (Austria); *Europe's International Migrants*, n. 32 above, 22, 47 (Finland and Norway); Plender, n. 72 above, 312 (United Kingdom). In France, migrants are considered as permanent immigrants if they have been issued with residence permits for more than one year, and in Sweden, migrants can obtain permanent residence permits (valid for 3 years and automatically renewable) after one year's residence if they are accepted as immigrants. See *Europe's International Migrants*, n. 32 above, 23 and 59 respectively and Commission Working Paper, n. 26 above, 30 (France). In Belgium and the Netherlands, a permanent residence permit may be issued after 5 years, while in the United Kingdom, indefinite leave to remain may be granted to migrants after a continuous period of 4 years in legal employment (Statement of Changes in Immigration Rules 1994, n. 38 above, para. 134). See Commission Working Paper, n. 26 above, 21 and 30. In Spain, foreigners who have legally resided in the country for 6 years can apply for a permanent residence permit. See MNS No. 156/96 (March 1996) 4.

[501] Thomas, 'Summing-up and Points of Comparison', n. 7 above, 221–2 (Germany and Switzerland); Papademetriou, n. 103 above, 353 (Greece); Commission Working Paper, n. 26 above, 30 (Germany and Portugal). In Germany, residence permits, which constitute pre-conditions for work permits, are regulated by a Decree on Residence which the Federal Minister for Internal Affairs is empowered to issue under s.10(2) of the Act on Immigration of 18 Dec. 1991. The Act affords the Minister very broad discretion in regulating the conditions for the grant of residence permits, (including unlimited residence permits), and in determining their duration. Weiss, n. 31 above, 115–16. In Switzerland, the permit of establishment can be issued after 5 years residence for European migrants, but 10 years residence is still required for non-European migrants. Residence permits in Switzerland are only valid for the canton which issues them: *Europe's International Migrants*, n. 32 above, 62. For the position in Greece, see *SOPEMI 1994*, 92.

[502] For a comprehensive survey of the position in OECD countries, see *SOPEMI 1994*, Pt III, 'Acquisition of Nationality in OECD Countries'.

[503] This is the position in Belgium, Finland, France, the Netherlands, Sweden, and the United Kingdom: *SOPEMI 1994*, 162, 163 (Table III.3); G. de Rham, 'Naturalisation: The Politics of Citizenship Acquisition' in *The Political Rights of Migrant Workers in Western Europe*, n. 96 above, 158, 161, 164–6. In Ireland, the residence requirement is 4 years, and in Denmark and Norway, non-nationals can apply for citizenship after 7 years' residence: *SOPEMI 1994*, *ibid*.

[504] *SOPEMI 1994*, *ibid*. (Austria, Italy (non-EC nationals only), Luxembourg, and Spain). Italian nationality law was tightened up by Law No. 91 of 5 Feb. 1992. Previously, non-EC nationals had to live in Italy for 5 years before they could apply for naturalization. In contrast, the qualifying period of residence for EC nationals is 4 years. See A. Bondi, 'The Reform of Italian Nationality Law' (1995) 9 INLP 89, 90. Similarly, in Portugal, Art. 6 of Statute No. 25/94 (effective 19 Aug. 1994), amending Statute No. 37/81 (effective 3 Oct. 1981), tightens up the naturalization law for

applications by foreign spouses married to nationals are normally subject to a shorter residence qualification.[505] Applicants for naturalization are invariably required to prove good character, which in most cases means the absence of a criminal record, and may also be required to demonstrate sufficient knowledge of the language, and integration into the host society.[506] The rules in Germany and Switzerland are particularly rigorous and worth outlining in greater detail. In Germany, with the exception of so-called 're-migrants' or '*Aussiedler*' who are treated as citizens by right under the German Constitution,[507] at least 10 years of permanent residence are required before migrants can apply for naturalization.[508] The latter must also satisfy a number of further conditions: an ability to

foreigners by increasing the legal residence requirement from 6 to 10 years. However, 6 years lawful residence remains the requirement in the case of citizens of Portuguese-speaking countries. See E. Rule, 'Portuguese Nationality Law in Outline' (1996) 10 INLP 12, 13.

[505] Germany (5 years), Luxembourg (5 years), Switzerland (5 years, if married for 3 years), Denmark (4 years), Finland (3 years, if married for 2 years), Ireland (3 years if Irish spouse is Irish by descent rather than merely 'naturalized'), Norway (2 to 4 years), Sweden (4 years), Netherlands (3 years, including co-habitees in a stable relationship), Spain (one year). See *SOPEMI 1994*, 164 (n. 18); *Europe's International Migrants*, n. 32 above, 22, 38, 40, 48; and de Rham, n. 503 above, 161, 167. In Belgium, Italy, Luxembourg, Portugal, and the United Kingdom, foreign spouses of nationals may apply for naturalization after 3 years of legal residence: *Closed Borders, Stringent Attitudes*, n. 14 above, 92 (Belgium and Italy); Commission Working Paper, n. 26 above, 94 (Luxembourg and the United Kingdom); Rule, n. 504 above, 13 (Portugal). In France, a foreign spouse of a French national may acquire French citizenship from 2 years after the marriage by making a voluntary declaration provided that the French spouse has retained his or her nationality at the time of the declaration and that the couple continue to live together. The qualifying period of 2 years does not apply if a child is born to the couple either before or after the marriage. This residence period was introduced by amendments to the French Nationality Code (Act of 9 Jan. 1973) in 1993 (Act of 22 July 1993). Previously, the waiting-period was only 6 months. See A. Simmons, 'French Nationality Law' (1994) 8 INLP 13, 14–15. In Italy, spouses may obtain Italian nationality if they have lawfully resided in Italy for at least 6 months or if they have been married for 3 years. Bondi, n. 504 above. In Denmark, Finland, Norway, and Sweden, the residence period is reduced to 2 years in respect of applications for naturalization by other Nordic nationals. See *SOPEMI 1994*, *ibid.*

[506] *SOPEMI 1994*, 163 (Table III.3) and 164; de Rham, n. 503 above, 174 (and Table 8.4).

[507] Art. 116. See also Weiss, n. 31 above, 112, 120. In 1992 and 1993, the influx of ethnic Germans into Germany stood at 220,000 and 230,000 respectively: *SOPEMI 1994*, 88. The gulf in treatment between re-migrants and foreigners is criticized by Weiss, n. 31 above, 120: '[E]ven if many . . . [re-migrants] do not speak German and have had no previous ties to Germany, they are treated as Germans in all respects, including the right to vote. If they were also to be treated as foreigners, immigration policy might be treated in a more generous and less discriminatory way. The re-migrants in most cases come to Germany for economic reasons, and for no other reason. If that is considered to be a legitimate justification for them, it is very difficult to justify the different treatment of foreigners who are not covered by Article 116 of the Constitution'.

[508] H. Esser and H. Korte, 'Federal Republic of Germany' in *European Immigration Policy: A Comparative Study*, n. 2 above, 178; Martin and Miller, n. 3 above, 323 (n. 24); Hammar (1990), n. 427 above, 87. The number of long-term foreign residents in Germany is significant: 66% of Turks, 72% of Italians, 76% of persons from the former Yugoslavia and 87% of Spaniards have lived in Germany for 10 years or more, and about 70% of foreign youth were born there. See Aukerman, n. 27 above, 238, citing from Beauftragte der Bundesregierung für die Belange der Ausländer, *Daten und Fakten zur Ausländersituation*, 13. Auflage, 1992, 9 and G. Andres, 'Einwanderungsland Deutschland: Bisherige Ausländer- und Asylpolitik—Lebenssituation der ausländischen Arbeitnehmer und ihrer Familien' in *Einwanderungsland Deutschland: Bisherige Ausländer- und Asylpolitik, Vergleich mit anderen europäischen Ländern*, (Forschungsinstitut der Friedrich Ebert Stiftung, Abt. Arbeits- und Sozialforschung, 1992), 28.

speak and write German; knowledge of the German political system and loyalty to the basic liberal-democratic order; good behaviour, which is not merely defined in terms of the absence of criminal convictions; and a satisfactory means of support, including the possession of personal accommodation and the ability to maintain one's family. The cost of naturalization is also quite high, about 75 per cent of an average monthly salary. Moreover, this process is by no means automatic and the decision whether or not to grant citizenship to the applicant is at the discretion of the German authorities.[509] In Switzerland, the process is even more complex, with the result that citizenship is very difficult to obtain. Foreign nationals have to satisfy the federal, cantonal, and communal authorities before they can obtain Swiss citizenship. Naturalization may be applied for in the commune in which the applicant resides after 12 years of residence. The process lasts 2 years and is completed when the candidate proves, on taking an examination, that he or she is 'sufficiently assimilated' into Swiss society. The award of citizenship is subject to the payment of a high fee, which varies according to income, and to ratification by the legislative assemblies at the cantonal and communal levels.[510]

Given the restrictions on the acquisition of citizenship in European countries, it is hardly surprising that the naturalization rates in many of these countries are particularly low.[511] Moreover, dual nationality is not an option for migrants in a number of countries of employment because acquisition of the new citizenship invariably means renouncing or giving up the citizenship of their country of origin.[512] Without doubt, these difficulties dissuade migrants from applying for citizenship once they are eligible to do so.[513]

In contrast with the principle of birthright citizenship (*jus soli*) applicable in Canada, Ireland, New Zealand, and the USA, citizenship is not obtained at the

[509] de Rham, n. 503 above, 162–3. See also Hammar, n. 508 above and Martin and Miller, n. 3 above.

[510] H.-J. Hoffmann-Nowotny, 'Switzerland' in *European Immigration Policy: A Comparative Study*, n. 2 above, 206, 222; de Rham, n. 503 above, 168–9.

[511] For example, see *SOPEMI 1993*, 50 (Table I.6) regarding the position in Belgium, Switzerland, and Germany, where the naturalization rate in 1991 (compared with the size of the foreign population in 1990) was 0.2, 0.8 and 2.7% respectively. The report notes the steep rise in the number of naturalizations in Germany since 1989, but explains that this increase is due not to any easing or simplification of naturalization procedures but to applications for citizenship from those immigrants from central and eastern Europe who have been able to prove their ethnic German origins: *ibid.* 50.

[512] Generally speaking, dual nationality is not permitted in a number of migrant-receiving countries unless renunciation of the former citizenship is impossible or unreasonable. This is the position in Austria, Denmark, Finland, Germany, Luxembourg, Norway, and Sweden: *SOPEMI 1994*, 163 (Table III.3) and 165. See also de Rham, n. 503 above, 161–9.

[513] In addition to a bar on dual nationality in the country of employment, migrants might also be dissuaded from applying for that country's citizenship if their country of origin does not permit dual nationality. Three further reasons for the reluctance to apply for naturalization may be advanced: migrants truly believe that they will one day return to their home country; they plan to stay permanently but prefer to retain their own national identity, particularly if the acquisition of new nationality means denunciation of the former; and they perceive the host country as a hostile environment. See T. Hammar, 'Immigration Regulation and Aliens Control' in *European Immigration Policy: A Comparative Study*, n. 2 above, 249, 255; Rogers, n. 239 above, 24; and Martin and Miller, n. 3 above, 323.

moment of birth in the territory in many Western European countries of employment. A child's citizenship in these countries depends mainly on the nationality of his or her parents (*jus sanguinis*), although this does not necessarily mean that the nationality acquired at birth is set in stone because, in practice, these states operate a combination of both principles.[514] However, an obvious preference for the *jus sanguinis* principle in some host countries means that many second- and third-generation migrants born there do not automatically become citizens of these countries, but instead retain the citizenship of the country of origin of their parents. Clearly, such an approach is a significant barrier to their successful integration in the host country. It has been argued that any changes introduced to the legal provisions on nationality in host countries 'will be interpreted, depending on whether they are liberal or strict, as a sign of openness and a positive reception, or, on the contrary, as a sign of rejection'.[515]

Children of foreigners who are born in Germany do not become German citizens and have to qualify for this status via stringent naturalization rules.[516] Recent changes to French immigration law have also made it more difficult for French-born children of foreign parents to obtain French citizenship. Previously, these children, save for the special rules applying to those with connections with former French colonies such as Algeria, automatically received French citizenship when they reached the age of 18, provided they had lived in France during the 5 years before their 18th birthday and had not renounced French citizenship in the year immediately preceding that birthday. However, since 1 January 1994, such children who are between the ages of 16 and 21 have had to declare their willingness (*volenté*) to acquire French nationality in addition to satisfying the 5-year residence requirement.[517] In Belgium, the Act of 12 July 1984, which entered into force on 1 January 1985 and which introduced a new Nationality Code, confers the right on second-generation migrants between 18 and 22 years of age to opt for Belgian nationality if they had their principal residence in Belgium for at least one year before the age of 6 with a person to whose authority they were legally subject.[518] These rules were liberalized further by the Act of

[514] Cf. de Rham, n. 503 above, 159–60; cf. *SOPEMI 1994*, 157, 159.

[515] *Closed Borders, Stringent Attitudes*, n. 14 above, 91. The discussion below is largely taken from Cholewinski (1994:2), n. 281 above, 301, 302–3.

[516] Hammar (1990), n. 427 above, 75, 109. The German rules on naturalization were liberalized somewhat by the Act on Immigration of 9 July 1990, which came into force on 1 Jan. 1991. This legislation introduces a simplified naturalization procedure for migrants aged between 16 and 23 who have resided legally in Germany for at least 8 years and have attended school for 6 years, and for adults who have lived in Germany for more than 15 years and could demonstrate that they have a secure income (provided that the application was submitted before 31 Dec. 1995). Anyone wishing, however, to acquire German citizenship must still relinquish his or her former nationality: Aukerman, n. 27 above, 249 (n. 65); *SOPEMI 1992*, 36; Weiss, n. 31 above, 120.

[517] Act of 22 July 1993. See also Simmons, n. 505 above, 14 and (Intégration), 'La manifestation de la volonté de devenir français sera exigée à partir de 1994' *Le Monde*, 27 July 1993, 11.

[518] Art. 13(4) of the Code. Under Art. 12 *bis* of the Code, second-generation migrants born in Belgium can apply for a declaration of Belgian nationality between the ages of 18 and 30 provided that they are able to show they have lived in Belgium for the whole of their lives. I am grateful to Paul Torremans for translating the relevant provisions from the Dutch version of the Code.

13 June 1991 which entered into force on 1 January 1992. Second-generation migrants born in Belgium and under 12 years of age, who have resided in the country since birth, can obtain Belgian nationality at the request of their parents provided that the latter have resided in Belgium for 10 years before the declaration.[519] Children born in the United Kingdom are entitled to citizenship if one of their parents was a United Kingdom citizen or was 'settled' there at the time of birth, or became so before the child reaches the age of 18.[520] Fear of future immigration led to the abolition of citizenship by mere birth in the British Nationality Act 1981,[521] but these rules remain less restrictive than equivalent rules in other Western European countries.

COE and EC standards

In general, both COE and EC standards tie the right of residence to the employment of migrant workers in the host country. Because free access to employment for EC nationals in any member state is a right and an integral aspect of the freedom of movement principle, the right of residence in that country is essentially a formality once employment is found. A right of residence in any EC member state is now also available to EC nationals who are not economically active provided that they have the means to finance their stay in the country concerned. EC standards are also more protective when migrant workers lose their employment.

There are no COE or EC provisions imposing a state duty to facilitate naturalization for migrant workers and their families. This is not surprising given that the COE has adopted a Convention discouraging the acquisition of dual citizenship and that the thrust of EC principles is aimed at reducing the relevance of nationality within a defined geographical region. Rather than promote the acquisition of the citizenship of individual countries, the EC has embraced a concept of 'European citizenship'. However, a right to stay indefinitely in a member state is recognized under the EC regime.

Migrant workers as aliens also remain subject to expulsion or deportation from the country of employment. Although COE standards limit the grounds on which

[519] Art. 11 *bis* of the Belgian Nationality Code. Under Art. 11, *third-generation migrants* born in Belgium automatically acquire Belgian nationality if one of their parents was also born in Belgium and has had his or her main residence there for 5 out of 10 years immediately preceding the birth of the child.

[520] British Nationality Act 1981 (c. 61), ss. 1(1), 1(3). A person is 'settled' for the purposes of the Act if he or she is 'ordinarily resident in the United Kingdom . . . without being subject under the immigration laws to any restriction on the period for which he may remain' (s.50(2)). On the moot question whether an EC national exercising free movement rights and living in the United Kingdom is sufficiently 'settled' in order to confer British nationality on his or her child, see J. McCarthy and S. Hardy, 'Some Implications of European Free Movement Rights on the Acquisition of British Nationality' (1996) 10 INLP 16. Section. 3(1) of the Act confers a discretionary power on the Home Secretary to register any minor as a citizen of the United Kingdom.

[521] I. Macdonald and N. Blake, *Immigration Law and Practice in the United Kingdom*, 4th edn. (London: Butterworths, 1995) 133.

such expulsion may occur and provide procedural protection enabling migrants to challenge unfair expulsion decisions, greater and more substantive safeguards are enjoyed by migrant workers and their families under EC law.

(a) A right of residence

There is no express right of residence under the ECE and the ESC.[522] Article 2 of the ECE imposes a duty upon state parties to facilitate prolonged or permanent residence, although this obligation is subject to the economic and social conditions persisting in the country which are to be judged by national criteria.[523] As discussed earlier, however, both instruments contain provisions on access to employment for migrants, which though limited, necessarily imply a right of residence.

The EMW provides specifically, in Article 9(1), that residence permits are to be aligned with work permits. Residence permits are to be issued for a period equal to the validity of work permits, and if the latter are of indefinite duration, then residence permits are to be issued for at least one year (Article 9(2)). This right of residence, therefore, is inextricably bound up with the right to pursue an occupation, which is in turn wholly subject to the discretion of the country of employment. Neither the ECE nor the ESC contains an express reference to the renewal of residence permits, although a duty to extend residence must be viewed as existing so long as migrant workers retain the right to pursue an occupation in the host country under a valid work permit.[524] This is also evident from the EMW where, as noted above, residence permits are aligned with work permits. Moreover, Article 9(2) of the EMW expressly stipulates that the residence permit is to be *renewed* for the duration of the work permit or for at least one year if such a work permit is valid indefinitely.

The EMW is the only COE instrument which provides a limited right of residence for migrant workers after the termination of their employment. Under Article 9(4), migrant workers have the right to remain in the host country for at least 5 months, but only if they are temporarily unable to work because of illness or accident or are involuntarily unemployed. The 5-month period is to allow workers to recuperate or to find alternative employment in accordance with Article 25 of the EMW, which deals with re-employment.[525] A state party, however, is not obliged to permit migrant workers to remain for a period exceeding

[522] The ECHR and Protocols also contain no right of residence. Nor may such a right be implied from other rights, such as the right to education. Nevertheless, it is arguable that a right of residence would ensue in the rare case when family life is unjustifiably infringed under Art. 8 as a result of measures restricting family reunification. See also cf. Swart, n. 45 above, 11, 16 and the section above on the right to family reunification.

[523] Section I(a)(2) of the Protocol to the ECE. Swart, n. 45 above, 7, maintains that it is difficult to speak of a *right* of residence under such conditions.

[524] See also Oellers-Frahm, n. 71 above, 1738–9.

[525] See respectively Oellers-Frahm, n. 71 above, 1739 and *Explanatory Report on the EMW*, n. 71 above, 16, para. 42.

the period of payment of the unemployment allowance or for more than 5 months if unemployment benefit is payable beyond this period.[526] Article 9(4) has been criticized on a number of grounds: it does not permit migrant workers to stay longer than 5 months even if they continue to receive unemployment benefit; it is inapplicable to workers who have become *permanently* incapacitated; and it does not apply in the event of a refusal to renew a residence permit.[527]

The right of EC workers and their families to stay in a member state for the purpose of employment is recognized in Article 48(3)(c) EC. Although this right flows directly from the EC Treaty,[528] its scope and formal aspects are found in Council Directive 68/360/EEC on the abolition of restrictions on movement and residence within the Community.[529] By virtue of Article 3(1) of the Directive, EC nationals need only produce a valid identity card or passport in order to gain entry into another EC member state. No other checks are permissible.[530] If the Commission's recent proposal for a Council Directive on the elimination of controls on persons crossing internal frontiers comes to fruition, these checks would only apply at the EC's external borders.[531] Article 4(1) of Directive 68/360/EEC obliges member states to grant the right of residence to EC workers and their families and to issue a residence permit on the production of certain documents, which are listed in Article 4(3). In the case of workers, the document with which they entered the territory[532] and a confirmation of engagement from the employer or a certificate of employment are all that is required. Family members have to

[526] See *Explanatory Report on the EMW*, n. 71 above, 16, para. 43, on the latter point. This provision resembles Art. 8(1) of ILO Convention No. 143 of 1975 and paras. 30 to 34 of the accompanying Recommendation (No. 151). See also Arts. 49(2) and 51 of the UN Convention.

[527] Swart, n. 45 above, 15. Despite these criticisms, the practice of states parties to the EMW in this area appears relatively generous. In its third report on the application of the EMW, the Consultative Committee, n. 306 above, 7, para. 36, noted that the legal provisions in the Netherlands, Portugal, Spain, and Sweden were in accordance with Art. 9(4) 'as illness and unemployment do not affect the right of residence'. The Committee, *ibid.*, also observed that in France, 'a migrant worker who is unemployed or incapable of working has the right to remain in the country for a longer period than provided for under the Convention'.

[528] See Case 48/75, *State* v. *Royer* [1976] ECR 497, [1977] 2 CMLR 585.

[529] See n. 263 above. A right of *permanent residence* to self-employed workers who establish themselves within the territory of a host member state is granted by Art. 4(1) of the equivalent Council Directive 73/148/EEC of 21 May 1973 on the abolition of restrictions on movement and residence within the Community for nationals of member states with regard to establishment and services, OJ 1973, L 172/14.

[530] Case C-68/89, *Re Entry into Dutch Territory: Commission* v. *Netherlands*, [1991] ECR I-2637, [1993] 2 CMLR 389. Further enquiries, however, can be made when the EC national applies for a residence permit: *ibid.* See also the discussion below. In Case 321/87, *Re Belgian Passport Controls: Commission* v. *Belgium* [1989] ECR 997, [1990] CMLR 492, the Court of Justice held, *inter alia*, that 'spot checks' at the border, which require EC nationals to produce residence permits in addition to the documentation listed in Art. 3(1), are permissible provided that such checks are not a condition of entry and do not constitute a barrier to freedom of movement by being carried out in a systematic, arbitrary, or unnecessarily restrictive manner.

[531] See Commission of the European Communities, *Proposal for a European Parliament and Council Directive amending Directive 68/360/EEC and Directive 73/148/EEC* (1995)

[532] An identity card is sufficient even if it is only valid within the EC migrant's national territory: Case C-376/89, *Giagounidis* v. *Stadt Reutlingen* [1991] ECR I-1069.

submit the former document and proof of their relationship with the worker, and also, in the case of dependent children over 21 years of age and relatives in the ascending line of the worker or his or her spouse, proof of dependency.[533] No further conditions for granting a residence permit have to be met.[534] The right of residence is also conferred upon non-EC nationals, who are family members of EC workers. Moreover, the Court of Justice has ruled that a right of residence is the logical corollary of any access to employment rights acquired by Turkish workers in an EC member state by virtue of decisions taken by the Council of Association under the EC Association Agreement with Turkey.[535]

Article 6(1) of the Directive stipulates that the permit must be valid throughout the territory of the member state for a period of at least 5 years and be automatically renewable. The permit cannot be withdrawn if a worker has become temporarily incapacitated as a result of illness or accident or involuntarily unemployed, although its duration, on the first renewal, may be shortened to not less than 12 months if the worker has been involuntarily unemployed for more than 12 consecutive months (Article 7). Although renewal is a formality, it would appear that no renewal is possible if the worker voluntarily gives up work or is permanently incapacitated. In the latter case, however, the right to remain may apply (see below).[536]

EC nationals are now entitled to a general right of residence in any other

[533] Although penalties might legitimately be imposed by member states for failure to comply with these formalities, they must not be so disproportionate as to become an obstacle to freedom of movement: Case 8/77, *Republic* v. *Sagulo* [1977] ECR 1495, [1977] 2 CMLR 585; Case 157/79, *R* v. *Pieck* [1979] ECR 2171, [1980] 3 CMLR 220. Consequently, imprisonment or deportation for failure to comply with these formalities is prohibited. *Pieck*, *ibid*. See also *Royer*, n. 528 above. Moreover, penalties which are not comparable to those attaching to minor offences committed by nationals are not permissible. See *Pieck*, *ibid*., appearing to reverse the position of the Court of Justice in *Sagulo*, *ibid*. See also Johnson and O'Keeffe, n. 90 above, 1321 (n. 25). Art. 8(1) of Directive 68/360/EEC stipulates that a residence permit need not be issued to those employed in a member state for less than 3 months and to frontier and seasonal workers, although in each case these workers may be required to report their presence in its territory (Art. 8(2)). Measures requiring EC nationals to register their presence with the police after arrival are allowed, but to require them to register within 3 days of entry and to impose criminal penalties for non-compliance is unreasonable. See Case C-265/88, *Messner* [1989] ECR 4209, [1991] CMLR 545. Furthermore, as noted earlier, EC nationals seeking employment may also reside in a member state for a reasonable period of time. See *Antonissen*, n. 80 above.

[534] In Case C-363/89, *Roux* v. *Belgian State* [1991] ECR I-273, [1993] 1 CMLR 3, the Court of Justice ruled that the refusal to issue a residence permit to a French national employed in Belgium because she failed to register under the national social security scheme was contrary to EC law.

[535] See the cases of *Eroglu* and *Kus*, n. 89 above and *Sevince*, n. 90 above.

[536] See also Stein and Thomsen, n. 157 above, 1797. On the question of voluntary unemployment, Wyatt, 'Free Movement of Workers', n. 382 above, 248, writes: 'It would seem to follow that a worker who is voluntarily unemployed may have his permit withdrawn, i.e. lose his right of residence in the territory. This is certainly in accord with the scheme of Article 48 of the Treaty which guarantees residence for the purpose of seeking or engaging in activities as an employed person. An individual who is voluntarily unemployed can no longer be considered "a worker" within the meaning of Article 48'. He adds, *ibid*. 248 (n. 63), that such an argument follows from the reasoning in Case 53/81, *Levin* v. *Staatssecretaris van Justitie* [1982] ECR 1035, [1982] 2 CMLR 454. See also the discussion on the definition of an EC worker in Ch. 6.

member state regardless of whether they are pursuing an economic activity. The way was paved for such a right by the three residence Directives, adopted by the Council,[537] and the right has been explicitly recognized in Article 8a(1) EC, which was inserted by the TEU: 'Every citizen of the Union shall have the right to move and reside freely within the territory of the Member States, subject to the limitations and conditions laid down in the Treaty and by the measures adopted to give it effect'. The latter phrase indicates, therefore, that the enjoyment of a general right of residence is by no means absolute: for example, the right of residence in the three 1990 Directives is subject to the conditions that migrants are covered by sickness insurance and have sufficient resources to avoid becoming a burden on the social assistance system of the host member state.[538]

(b) Right to remain, naturalization, and acquisition of citizenship

Migrant workers and their families residing in the country of employment have no right under COE instruments to an unlimited period of residence, nor to naturalization and citizenship.[539] The only provision which comes close to providing such a right is the duty imposed upon states parties in Article 2 of the ECE to facilitate prolonged or permanent residence, although as discussed above, this obligation is qualified to such an extent that its usefulness is questionable. Any rights of residence that may be implied from the ESC and the EMW are strictly connected with migrant workers remaining in employment, with the narrow exception provided in Article 9(4) of the EMW. In contrast, the recommendations of COE institutions in this area are far-reaching. For example, Parliamentary Assembly Recommendation 769 of 1975 on the legal status of aliens boldly advocates a basic freedom of choice of COE nationals to reside in any COE member state, including an unrestricted right of residence after a stay of over 3 years in the country.[540] A more recent Recommendation encompasses non-COE nationals and invites member states to 'recognize the right of migrants, *irrespective of their country of origin or nationality*, to reside permanently on their territories when they have resided there for at least five years'.[541] Other Parliamentary Assembly Recommendations propose that member states facilitate the naturalization of migrant workers as well as migrant women and second-generation migrants.[542]

537 Dir. 90/364/EEC, Dir. 90/365/EEC and Dir. 93/96/EC, n. 319 above.

538 Ar'. 1 in all the Directives.

539 S.e also Oellers-Frahm, n. 71 above, 1734. The latter right, of course, would favourably alter the condition of migrant workers and their families in the host country, since so many of the rights that matter to them are tied to nationality. Cf. Swart, n. 45 above, 60.

540 Recommendation 769 of 3 Oct. 1975 on the legal status of aliens, Appendix—Principles on which a uniform aliens law in Council of Europe member states could be based, principle 7.

541 Recommendation 1082 (1988) of 30 June 1988 on the right of permanent residence for migrant workers and members of their families, para. 9(b) (emphasis added).

542 See respectively Recommendation 915 (1981) of 13 Jan. 1981 on the situation of migrant workers in host countries, para. 13(i)(c), and Recommendation 956 (1982) of 9 Nov. 1982 on migrant women, para. 9(iii). See also Committee of Ministers Recommendation (84) 9 of 9 March 1984 on second-generation migrants, in which COE member states are called upon to enable these migrants to acquire the citizenship of the host country or to resume their original nationality (para. III(b)).

The lack of progress by COE member states in facilitating naturalization for resident foreigners is linked, to some extent, to their unwillingness to accept dual nationality. Indeed, in 1963, the COE adopted the Convention on Reduction of Cases of Multiple Nationality and Military Obligations in Cases of Multiple Nationality.[543] The aim of the Convention, as expressed in the second recital of the Preamble, is to discourage dual nationality: '*Considering* that cases of multiple nationality are liable to cause difficulties and that joint action to reduce as far as possible the number of cases of multiple nationality, as between member States, corresponds to the aims of the Council of Europe'. Article 1(1) of the Convention stipulates that contracting party nationals 'who are of full age and who acquire of their own free will, by means of naturalization, option or recovery, the nationality of another Party shall lose their former nationality'.[544] By virtue of Article 1(2), minor children who acquire a new nationality in the same way are also to lose their former nationality.

Thus far, the Convention has only been ratified by 13 COE states and mainly by those countries of employment in which dual citizenship is discouraged. As discussed above, the renunciation of previous citizenship has usually been one of the pre-conditions to a successful application by migrants for naturalization in the country of residence. Often, this rule is applied to all non-nationals within a state in spite of the fact that the Convention only prohibits dual nationality in respect of citizens from other states parties. Indeed, only France appears to apply the Convention in this manner, with the result that citizens from non-states parties find it easier to acquire French citizenship without having to renounce their own nationality.[545] Some of the traditional southern European countries of emigration, such as Portugal and Spain, have either not ratified the Convention or have not accepted Chapter 1 of the instrument, which is concerned with the reduction of cases of multiple nationality, because it has been in the interests of these countries to ensure that their numerous citizens abroad retain their former citizenship even when they become citizens of another country.[546]

[543] Convention on Reduction of Cases of Multiple Nationality and Military Obligations in Cases of Multiple Nationality, 6 May 1963; Council of Europe, ETS No. 43; entry into force 28 March 1968; ratified by 13 states as at 1 July 1996: Austria, Belgium, Denmark, France, Germany, Ireland, Italy, Luxembourg, Netherlands, Norway, Spain, Sweden, United Kingdom. Ireland, Spain, and the United Kingdom have made declarations that they will only apply the Convention's second chapter dealing with military obligations in cases of muliple nationality (Art. 7(1)). See also G. Kojanec, 'The European Convention on Reduction of Cases of Nationality and the Second Amending Protocol' in *The Use of International Conventions to Protect the Rights of Migrants and Ethnic Minorities* (1994) 102 and Hammar (1990), n. 427 above, 112.

[544] de Rham, n. 503 above, 175, notes that the Convention only operates to minimize cases of dual nationality in respect of applications for citizenship by naturalization, registration or recovery and is inapplicable to the acquisition of citizenship by other means.

[545] Hammar (1990), n. 427 above, 113.

[546] Cf. *ibid.* 112. Moreover, in Portugal, there is no obligation on persons seeking Portuguese nationality to renounce their own nationality. Rule, n. 504 above, 12. In Spain, however, foreigners seeking Spanish nationality are required to renounce any other nationality unless they are citizens of countries with which Spain has a 'historic link', such as the Spanish-speaking Latin-American countries: Art. 23 of the Spanish Civil Code 1978 (as amended). See Rule, n. 504 above, 12 (n. 3).

The Convention was adopted in 1963 when international labour migration in Europe was still in its infancy. However, the steep influx of migrant workers into Western European countries of employment until the early 1970s and the subsequent migration of families has resulted in the settlement of large foreign populations.[547] Attitudes towards the concept of dual citizenship are changing, with the result that the principle underlying the Convention 'is increasingly seen as an obstacle to the integration of immigrants into the political and social life of their host countries'.[548] Pressures to revise the 1963 Convention led to the adoption of an Amending Protocol in February 1993.[549] The Explanatory Report to the Amending Protocol recognizes the importance for integration of the acquisition of the host state's nationality by long-term resident immigrants:

> Acquisition of the nationality of the host country is certainly an important, even crucial factor, as far as integration in that country is concerned. Seen from the point of view of states it is not in a country's national interest that a large section of its population should remain from generation to generation without the nationality of the adoptive country. Seen from the viewpoint of immigrants of long standing, who are recognized in the host country in practically all respects, the absence of full participation in its political life can only be regarded as deplorable.[550]

The Amending Protocol relaxes the strict rules of the Convention for 'those groups of immigrants whose integration or need for the new nationality is most urgent', namely second-generation migrants, who were either born in the host country or brought up and educated there, and spouses in mixed marriages and their children.[551] The second recital of the Preamble to the Protocol advocates that second-generation migrants in particular, who have settled permanently in COE member states, should be able to acquire the nationality of their country of residence in order to 'complete their integration'.[552] The Protocol inserts a

Even though Italy has ratified the Convention, Art. 11 of Law No. 91 of 5 Feb. 1992 affirms the dual nationality principle by enabling emigrants to obtain another nationality without losing their Italian citizenship. Bondi, n. 504 above, 90.

[547] See also Bartsch, n. 464 above, 676. Moreover, despite the existence of the Convention, there has also been a considerable increase in the number of dual citizens in Europe. Nonetheless, Hammar, n. 427 above, 107, maintains that the Convention 'has probably partly served its purpose . . . for . . . without [it] . . . the number would probably have been greater'.

[548] Bartsch, n. 464 above, 677.

[549] Second Protocol Amending the Convention on the Reduction of Cases of Multiple Nationality and Military Obligations in Cases of Multiple Nationality, 2 Feb. 1993; Council of Europe ETS No. 149; entry into force 24 March 1995; ratified by 2 states, France and Italy (and signed by the Netherlands) as at 1 July 1996.

[550] Council of Europe, *The Reduction of Cases of Multiple Nationality and Military Obligations in Cases of Multiple Nationality. Explanatory Report: Second Protocol Amending the Convention Opened for Signature on 2 February 1993* (Strasbourg: Council of Europe Press, 1994) 4, para. 6.

[551] *Ibid.* 4, para. 7.

[552] In observing that many members of the younger foreign generation in Western European countries are growing up with dual identities, Hammar (1990), n. 427 above, 108, maintains that, 'from a psychological point of view, dual citizenship could for them be a fair expression of their dual national identity'.

provision into the Convention, which enables second-generation migrants from one state party, on acquiring the nationality of another state party, to retain their nationality of origin at the discretion of the countries concerned.[553] With regard to foreign spouses of mixed marriages and their children, the Explanatory Report to the Amending Protocol asserts that dual nationality would benefit them by assisting their full integration into the country of residence and would also foster family unity.[554] Pursuant to this objective, the Amending Protocol provides that 'in cases of marriage between nationals of different Contracting Parties, each of these Parties may provide that the spouse, who acquires of his or her own free will the nationality of the other spouse, retains the nationality of origin'.[555]

The Amending Protocol may well contribute to easing the difficulties experienced by migrants who have thus far been unable to acquire the nationality of their host country of residence, but it is important to emphasize that the principle in Article 1 of the Convention remains unchanged. States parties are merely given a discretion to depart from the stringent rules concerned with the reduction of multiple nationality; they are under no *obligation* to actually facilitate the acquisition of other nationalities.[556]

EC law does not contain any provisions on facilitating naturalization. The emphasis is on the creation of a distinct kind of 'European citizenship', rather than on the acquisition of the nationality of individual member states.[557] However,

[553] Art. 1(5) of the Convention, inserted by Art. 1 of the Amending Protocol, now reads: '[W]here a national of a Contracting Party acquires the nationality of another Contracting Party on whose territory either he was born and is resident, or has been ordinarily resident for a period of time beginning before the age of 18, each of these parties *may* provide that he retains the nationality of origin' (emphasis added). Although the Explanatory Report, n. 550 above, 6, para. 11, recognizes that 'residence may have begun immediately before the age of 18 . . . the period and legal conditions relating to residence required for naturalization and other forms of acquisition of nationality are determined by the law of the host country'. Therefore, even though the host country may allow for dual nationality in such cases, it may nonetheless impose stringent residence requirements for the acquisition of its nationality by second-generation migrants.

[554] *Explanatory Report to the Amending Protocol*, n. 550 above, 5, para. 9. The third recital of the Preamble also provides that the 'unity of nationality within the same family' is advanced if one spouse is able to acquire the nationality of the other spouse and if children can obtain the nationality of both parents.

[555] Art. 1(6) of the Convention, inserted by Art. 1 of the amending Protocol. The new Art. 1(7) of the Convention affords nationals of contracting parties, who are minors and who acquire the nationality of one of their parents, both of whom are nationals of different contracting parties, the opportunity to retain their nationality of origin.

[556] The Explanatory Report to the Amending Protocol, n. 550 above, 6, para. 10 observes that 'this provision has not been made compulsory, since the aim of the Protocol is to form exceptions to the main principle of Article 1', namely discouraging multiple nationality. However, Kojanec, n. 543 above, 105, observes that some European states (Netherlands and Switzerland) have begun to permit dual citizenship, and expresses the hope that the Amending Protocol might encourage national legislative reform in this area. See also *SOPEMI 1994*, 47, which notes the amendments to Dutch nationality law adopted in 1993, introducing the possibility of dual nationality. The German Bundestag, however, is still opposed to the concept of dual nationality. See *Closed Borders, Stringent Attitudes*, n. 14 above, 93.

[557] Stein and Thomsen, n. 157 above, 1800–1. See also Pt II of the EC Treaty on 'Citizenship of the Union'.

Article 48(3)(d) EC grants EC migrant workers the right 'to remain in the territory of a Member State after being employed in that State', and thus makes it an integral part of the freedom of movement principle.[558] The right to remain is implemented by Commission Regulation 1251/70/EEC, and applies, in Article 1, to 'nationals of a Member State who have worked as employed persons in the territory of another Member State and to members of their families, as defined in Article 10 of [Regulation 1612/68/EEC]'.[559] By virtue of Article 2(1)(a), the right to remain permanently in the territory of an EC member state is accorded to workers who have reached the age of retirement in the country of employment entitling them to an old-age pension, have been employed in that country for at least 12 months, and have resided there continuously for more than 3 years. Workers who have become permanently incapacitated obtain a right to remain after 2 years of continuous residence in the host member state, unless their permanent incapacity is the result of an industrial accident or an occupational disease in which case no residence requirements need to be met for the right to remain to accrue to the worker (Article 2(1)(b)).[560] Article 3(1) extends the right to remain to workers' families if this right has been acquired by the worker.[561] The right, moreover, is not extinguished on the worker's death.[562] Those holding the right to remain under EC law, in the same way as those with a right of residence, are entitled to a 5-year residence permit, which is automatically renewable (Article 6(1)). Article 7 of Regulation 1251/70/EEC underlines that the right to equality of treatment in Regulation 1612/68/EEC also applies to workers with the

558 See also Stein and Thomsen, n. 157 above, 1794.

559 Commission Reg. 1251/70/EEC of 29 June 1970 on the right of workers to remain in the territory of a member state, OJ Sp. Ed. 1970, 402. Identical provisions to those in Reg. 1251/70/EEC are found in Council Directive 75/34/EEC of 17 Dec. 1974 concerning the right of nationals of a member state to remain in the territory of another member state after having pursued therein an activity in a self-employed capacity, OJ 1975, L 14/10. There is no explicit right for family members to remain in a member state after the death of a retired or 'independent' EC migrant to whom the residence Directives apply (n. 319 above), unless the latter has been employed in the member state concerned. As for students, the right of residence is restricted to the duration of the course of studies in question (Art. 2(1) of Dir. 93/96/EC). See also Peers (1996), n. 25 above, 13–14 (n. 20).

560 Under Art. 2(2), the employment and residence requirements for affording retired or incapacitated workers the right to remain are waived if the worker's spouse is 'a national of the member State concerned or has lost the nationality of that State by marriage to that worker'. Workers who have completed 3 years of continuous residence and employment in one member state and then work in another member state as frontier workers, retaining their residence in the first state by returning there each day or at least once a week, may also qualify for the right to remain (Art. 2(1)(c)). All workers eligible for the right to remain are given 2 years to decide whether or not they should exercise it. During this period, they can leave the territory of the member state without forfeiting this right (Art. 5(1)).

561 However, in order for family members who are not EC nationals to benefit from this right under EC law, the worker must have exercised his or her free movement rights. See Joined Cases C-297/88 and C-197/89, *Dzodzi v. Belgian State* [1990] ECR I-3763.

562 If the worker dies before acquiring the right to remain, members of his family may remain regardless, but only if one of the following conditions is satisfied: the worker resided continuously in the member state for at least 2 years before his or her death; the death was caused by an industrial accident or disease; or the surviving spouse is a national of the country of residence or had forfeited that nationality by marriage to the worker (Art. 3(2)).

right to remain. However, migrant workers and their families who have acquired the right to remain permanently in the host member state are still some way from acquiring *de facto* citizenship status. For example, as discussed below, they may still be subject to expulsion from the country of residence on certain specified grounds.

The right to remain is clearly limited to workers who are nationals of EC member states. The Court of Justice has refused to interpret the Association Agreement with Turkey and Council of Association Decision 1/80 as implying such a right for Turkish workers in EC countries of employment.[563] However, the need to integrate long-term resident non-EC nationals by granting them, *inter alia*, firmer residence rights has been recognized by the Justice and Home Affairs Council in its Resolution of 4 March 1996 on the status of third-country nationals residing on a long-term basis in the territory of the member states.[564] Based on the guiding principle that 'the integration of long-term residents contributes to greater security and stability, both in daily life and work, and to social peace in the various Member States (Preamble, third recital)', the Resolution urges member states to grant a 10-year residence permit or an unlimited residence authorization (point III) to those non-EC nationals who can show that they have been residing legally in their territory for at least 10 years (point III, paragraph 1, first indent) and who can demonstrate a stable means of existence, in particular by holding health insurance and the conditions for exercising an occupation (point IV, paragraph 2). The granting of such residence authorizations is subject to public policy or national security reasons (point IV, paragraph 1). The Resolution asserts that long-term residents and members of their families 'should enjoy no less favourable treatment than is enjoyed . . . by nationals of that Member State' in respect of working conditions, membership of trade unions, public policy in the sector of housing, social security, emergency health care, and compulsory schooling (point V, paragraph 2). The Resolution does not refer to political rights and there are no access to employment rights, which clearly is a very negative feature given that the Resolution concerns non-EC nationals who have legally resided in a member state for over 10 years. Point VII merely assets that

[563] Case C-434/93, *Bozkurt* v. *Staatssecretaris van Justitie* [1995] ECR I-1475. See the annotation by S. Peers (1996) 33 *CML Rev.* 103. This decision concerned a Turkish international lorry driver, employed by a Dutch haulage company, who became permanently incapacitated for work as a result of a work accident. The Court ruled that Art. 6(2) of Decision 1/80, n. 23 above, which was concerned with the consequences of certain breaks from employment for the operation of Art. 6(1) relating to access to employment rights, only applied to those still in the labour force or who were temporarily incapacitated for work and could not confer on the applicant a right to remain in the Netherlands.

[564] OJ 1996, C 80/2. The Resolution does not apply to all non-EC nationals. Family members of EC citizens, EEA nationals, non-EC nationals whose status is governed by EC agreements with third countries affording more favourable provisions, and those non-EC nationals admitted to a member state for study or research are not covered (point II, para. 2). Although the Resolution clearly has no binding legal effect at the EC level, member states are expected to make changes to their national laws in the areas covered by the measure and to notify the Council of these changes by 1 Jan. 1997 (point VIII, para. 1).

long-term residents '*should* be able to obtain authorization to engage in gainful activities, *in accordance with the provisions of [the] Member State's legislation*'.[565]

(c) Protection against expulsion

The threat of expulsion seriously impedes any rights of residence which migrants may acquire. However, states that are parties to COE instruments cannot expel aliens and migrant workers at will, but may only do so in accordance with certain criteria. There are two provisions in the Protocols to the ECHR specifically concerned with protecting non-nationals from expulsion. Article 4 of Protocol No. 4 contains a blanket prohibition against the collective expulsion of aliens. In the opinion of the European Commission of Human Rights, aliens cannot be expelled *as a group* without an examination of each individual case on its merits.[566] Article 1(1) of Protocol No. 7 also provides a number of minimum procedural guarantees to lawfully resident aliens who are facing expulsion from the territory of a state party.[567] The lack of substantive guarantees is clearly a weakness of this provision.[568] Moreover, it is only applicable to lawfully resident aliens, and is therefore narrower in scope than Article 4(1) of Protocol No. 4 which clearly applies to *all* aliens, including irregular migrants. The term 'resident' operates to exclude the following categories of aliens from protection: those arriving at the port of entry of a state party who have not yet passed through immigration control; those admitted into the territory of that party for the purpose only of transit or for a limited period for a non-residential purpose;

565 Emphasis added.

566 In *Becker* v. *Denmark*, which was concerned with the refusal of entry and of residence permits to a group of Vietnamese children, the Commission of Human Rights defined 'collective expulsion of aliens' as 'any measure of the competent authority compelling aliens as a group to leave the country, except where such a measure is taken after and on the basis of a reasonable and objective examination of the particular cases of each individual alien of the group': Application 7011/75, *Becker* v. *Denmark* (1975) 4 D & R 215, 235, (1976), 19 YBECHR 416, 454 (admissibility decision). See also van Dijk and van Hoof, n. 457 above, 500 and Robertson and Merrills, n. 229 above, 235. van Dijk and van Hoof, *ibid.*, identify an inconsistency in the Commission's interpretation, and tentatively suggest that the Commission's approach may nonetheless have positive implications for the protection of *all* aliens threatened with expulsion: 'The definition of the Commission, however much it may have to be welcomed *per se*, raises the problem that for the expulsion of an alien who forms part of a particular group certain requirements are made for the examination underlying that expulsion, which were not prescribed for the expulsion of other aliens [for example, see Article 1(1) of Protocol No. 7 to the ECHR, which is discussed below]. Therefore, the issue remains as to when there is a question of a group and why a group deserves more protection than an individual . . . [A] satisfactory solution is reached only if it is assumed that any expulsion of an alien as an alien, without an objective examination having been made of his individual situation and interests, in fact is part of a prohibited collective expulsion, irrespective of whether his expulsion in actual fact is or is not accompanied by the expulsion of other aliens in a comparable situation. It must be admitted, however, that thus the word 'collective' is interpreted in a rather improper sense which seems to be contrary to the genesis of Article 4'.

567 Council of Europe, *Explanatory Report on Protocol No. 7 to the Convention for the Protection of Human Rights and Fundamental Freedoms* (Strasbourg: Council of Europe, 1985) 7, para. 7.

568 Robertson and Merrills, n. 229 above, 239, write: '[A] . . . serious limitation is that Article 1 is wholly concerned with procedure and has nothing at all to say about the grounds on which an alien may be expelled; or, to put the point in a different way, in no sense does this provision confer anything in the way of a right of residence on which an alien can rely'.

and those awaiting a decision on an application for a residence permit. Furthermore, the conditions of 'lawful' residence are determined by domestic law and the term 'expulsion' is broadly drawn, referring to any measure obliging the alien to leave the territory of a state party with the exception of extradition.[569] The procedural safeguards outlined in Article 1(1) of Protocol No. 7 enable aliens to submit reasons against their expulsion, to have their cases reviewed, and to be represented for these purposes before the competent authority.[570] The right to a review, however, does not mean that the case has to be considered by an independent authority. Indeed, a review may be carried out by the same administrative or judicial authority responsible for the original decision. Moreover, a 'review' is not the same as an 'appeal', with the result that in the event of aliens being permitted under domestic law to appeal against the expulsion after the review, there is no requirement under this provision to stay or suspend the expulsion until the appeal is heard.[571] In addition to these provisions in the Protocols, which have *not* been ratified by all the states parties that have accepted the ECHR,[572] a number of other rights' guarantees in the ECHR itself may also be invoked by aliens to challenge a decision of expulsion from the territory of a state party.[573]

[569] *Explanatory Report on Protocol No. 7*, n. 567 above, 7–8. paras. 9–10.

[570] In this respect, therefore, the provision resembles Art. 13 of the ICCPR. The grounds on which these safeguards may be overridden, however, are wider under the Protocol, which allows states parties, in Art. 1(2), to dispense with the safeguards if expulsion is necessary in the 'interests of public order' or for 'reasons of national security'. In contrast, the safeguards may only be overturned under Art. 13 of the ICCPR for 'compelling reasons of national security'. The use of the term 'compelling' clearly means that states parties to the ICCPR would have to show that the measures taken are proportionate to the aim of protecting national security. Although the Explanatory Report on Protocol No. 7, *ibid.* 9, para. 15, indicates that the principle of proportionality, as defined in the case law of the European Court of Human Rights, is relevant in respect of the public order exception, it asserts that expulsion for reasons of national security 'in itself should be accepted as sufficient justification'. See also van Dijk and van Hoof, n. 457 above, 507, who contend, however, that it is unlikely that the Commission and Court of Human Rights would accept the exclusion of their review in this way, although they concede that the provision appears to grant 'a larger discretion on the part of the authorities to expel an alien before he has exercised his rights under [Art. 1(1)]'. This unequivocal deference to a state party's own interpretation of the concept of national security would seem, on one view, 'to be contrary to the spirit of the protocol and to defeat the operation of the supervisory system of the Convention': *Law and Practice of the ECHR and the ESC*, n. 76 above, 366.

[571] *Explanatory Report on Protocol No. 7*, n. 569 above, 8, para. 13.2.

[572] As at 1 July 1996, Protocol No. 4 had been ratified by 24 states and Protocol No. 7 by 19 states.

[573] For example, if the alien threatened with expulsion to another country can show that, if returned there, he or she faces a 'real risk' of torture, or inhuman or degrading treatment or punishment under Art. 3 of the ECHR. This argument was successful in *Soering* v. *United Kingdom*, judgment of 7 July 1989, Eur. Ct. H.R., 1991, Ser. A, No. 161, (1989) 11 EHRR 439, paras. 93–9, in respect of a German national threatened with expulsion to the USA to stand trial for murder. If convicted of the charge, the applicant faced the death penalty and a significant period of time on 'death row'. For a useful overview of the relevant Art. 3 case law, see R. Alleweldt, 'Protection Against Expulsion Under Article 3 of the European Convention on Human Rights' (1993) 4 EJIL 360. Other relevant ECHR guarantees include: the right to a fair hearing in the determination of civil rights and obligations (Art. 6); the right to respect for family life (Art. 8), which has been discussed in some depth above in the section on family reunion; and the right to an effective remedy (Art. 13). See also Swart, n. 45 above, 16–20 and Drzemczewski, n. 269 above, 361–5, for a more extensive discussion of the potential application of these provisions in protecting aliens against expulsion.

In contrast with Article 1 of Protocol No. 7 to the ECHR, the ECE, ESC, and EMW afford more comprehensive safeguards by limiting expulsion to a number of specified substantive grounds, although it must be recalled that these instruments only apply to those aliens and migrants who are also nationals of other states parties. The principal grounds of expulsion common to these agreements are national security, public morality, and various derivatives of public policy.[574] These instruments also provide aliens and migrant workers procedural protection against expulsion, and particularly, in Articles 3(2), 19(8), and 9(5) respectively, a right of appeal to a court, independent authority or person.[575] In the case of the ESC, such a right has been read into Article 19(8) by the Committee of Independent Experts.[576] With the exception of Article 3(2) of the

[574] The grounds of expulsion for each instrument are as follows: national security, public order, or morality (Art. 3(1) ECE); national security, public interest, or morality (Art. 19(8) ESC); and national security, public policy, or morals (Art. 9(5)(a) EMW) and public health (Art. 9(5)(b) EMW). In addition to the three states parties (Denmark, Iceland, and Malta) which have not accepted the whole of Art. 19 of the ESC, Austria and Norway have not accepted Art. 19(8). By virtue of Section I(a)(3) of the Protocol to the ECE, each State party is free to decide by national criteria the scope of these grounds. Under Section III(c) of the Protocol, however, the state's right to expel aliens may only be exercised in individual cases and, in exercising this right, states parties are required to take into account 'the particular relations which exist between the members of the Council of Europe' and, in particular, 'family ties and the period of residence in [the] territory [of States parties] of the person concerned'. See also *Commentary on the European Convention on Establishment*, n. 46 above, 14, paras. 35–6. The grounds of expulsion under the ECE also become more restricted the longer migrants have resided in the state party concerned. For example, under Art. 3(3), nationals of a state party who have been lawfully resident in another state party for more than 10 years can only be expelled 'for reasons of national security or if the other reasons . . . [in Art. 3(1)] . . . are of a particularly serious nature'. Expulsion on grounds of public health under the EMW is only permissible if migrant workers refuse to comply with public health measures specifically issued to them. The EMW also permits expulsion if a condition essential to the validity of the residence permit has not been fulfilled (Art. 9(5)(c)). In connection with the ground of 'public interest' under Art. 19(8) of the ESC, the Committee of Independent Experts has asserted that a state party cannot justify the expulsion of migrant workers for public health reasons unless medical treatment has been unreasonably refused: *Conclusions V*, 138, cited in *Case Law on the European Social Charter*, n. 19 above, 173. The Committee has also emphasized that Art. 19(8) and Art. 13(4) complement each other. (As discussed earlier, the latter provision refers to the European Convention on Social and Medical Assistance, which safeguards foreigners against expulsion on the sole ground that they are in need of social and medical assistance). See *Second Report on Unaccepted Provisions*, 18, cited by *Case Law on the European Social Charter—Supplement No. 3*, n. 56 above, 150. However, the protection under the Convention is not absolute because it allows for repatriation of foreigners on this ground if certain stringent residence conditions are not met. The implication in the Committee's observations, therefore, is that expulsion on health grounds *in conformity with* the Convention on Social and Medical Assistance is permissible.

[575] Under Art. 3(2) of the ECE, procedural protection is only accorded to nationals of a state party who have been lawfully resident in the territory of another state party for more than 2 years. This protection can only be overridden 'where imperative considerations of national security otherwise require'.

[576] The Committee has concluded that 'the right of appeal in the final resort to a court or other independent body must be provided against the possibility of arbitrary decisions in the matter of expulsion of a worker lawfully residing within a Contracting State's territory even in cases where "national security, public interest or morality" are at stake': *Conclusions VII*, 109, cited in *Case Law on the European Social Charter*, n. 19 above, 174. See also *Conclusions IV*, 129, *Conclusions V*, 139, and *Conclusions VI*, 128, cited in *Case Law on the European Social Charter*, n. 19 above, 172–4.

ECE,[577] the ESC and EMW provisions do not make any explicit allowances for the suspension of a migrant worker's expulsion before the outcome of his or her appeal.[578]

On the whole, these provisions are silent on the question of expulsion on economic grounds.[579] As noted earlier, only the EMW expressly obliges states parties

and *Conclusions XII-1*, n. 57 above, 242, in which the Committee added that under the ESC 'all expulsion orders, whatever their nature, must be subject to appeal'. Both Harris, n. 20 above, 185–6 and Swart, n. 45 above, 19, have questioned the Committee's forward interpretation of Art. 19(8). The Committee adopted negative conclusions in respect of the application of Art. 19(8) by Greece, Sweden, and the United Kingdom. In Greece, there is no right to appeal against expulsion orders that are also considered to be 'government acts'. The only 'remedy' is the possibility of subjecting the person issuing the order to disciplinary and penal sanctions if the order is unconstitutional or illegal. In Sweden, expulsion on the ground of national security cannot be challenged before an independent body, whereas the body set up in the United Kingdom to hear representations from aliens issued with deportation orders on political or national security grounds is not, according to the Committee, effective enough because it can only make non-binding recommendations to the Secretary of State. The Committee of Independent Experts also repeated its negative conclusion in respect of the position in Ireland, where there is no right of appeal against a deportation order for persons who are neither EC nationals nor nationals of states parties to the ECE: *Conclusions XIII-1*, n. 57 above, 211. The negative conclusions of the Committee in respect of these countries were reiterated during the 13th cycle of supervision. See *Conclusions XIII-1*, n. 57 above, 211–12 and *Conclusions XIII-2*, n. 51 above, 206–7 and 208–9. These conclusions eventually resulted in the Governmental Committee proposing that the Committee of Ministers address recommendations to the countries concerned, with the exception of the United Kingdom in respect of which information had come to light regarding the practical application of the review procedures. See *13th Report (I)*, n. 57 above, 163–6, paras. 931–51. These recommendations were adopted by the Committee of Ministers on 22 June 1995 (see Recommendations No. R ChS (95) 5 (Greece), 6 (Ireland), and 10 (Sweden), cited in *Human Rights Information Sheet No. 36*, n. 151 above, 69–70, 72–3) and reiterated, in respect of Ireland and Sweden, in Resolution ChS (95) 2 on the implementation of the European Social Charter during the period 1991–92 (13th supervision cycle—part II), adopted by the Committee of Ministers on 14 Dec. 1995 (cited in *Human Rights Information Sheet No. 37*, n. 57 above, 87–8).

577 Under this provision, state party nationals who have been lawfully resident in the territory of another state party for more than 2 years 'shall not be expelled *without first* being allowed . . . [*inter alia*] . . . to appeal to . . . a competent authority or a person or persons specifically designated by the competent authority' (emphasis added). This interpretation is confirmed by the Standing Committee of the ECE, *Commentary on the European Convention on Establishment*, n. 46 above, 14, para. 36.

578 Swart, n. 45 above, also makes this observation in respect of Art. 9(5) of the EMW. With regard to Art. 19(8) of the ESC, however, the Committee of Independent Experts has requested a state party to 'indicate whether expulsion might be delayed to facilitate appeal': *Conclusions V*, 137–8, cited in *Case Law on the European Social Charter*, n. 19 above, 173. Furthermore, during the 12th cycle of supervision, the Committee noted the positive developments in France and Italy in this regard and was able to reiterate its positive conclusions in respect of both countries. In France, the Act of 10 Jan. 1990 had introduced suspensive judicial review of administrative orders to deport foreigners illegally entering or residing in the country. In Italy, by virtue of Art. 5 of Law No. 39/90, appeals by foreigners against a deportation order imposed on them by the Prefect had suspensive effect, (although appeals against such orders issued by the Minister of the Interior were not suspensive for reasons of public order or national security). See *Conclusions XII-2*, n. 57 above, 228 and 229 respectively. However, the Governmental Committee clearly takes the opposite view: '[I]n the case of a threat to national security, the public interest or morality, an expulsion order could be immediately enforceable. It must, however, always be possible for the expelled migrant worker to lodge an appeal from abroad and, if successful, to return to the host country': *Eighth Report*, 19, cited in *Case Law on the European Social Charter—Supplement*, n. 59 above, 52.

579 See also Swart, n. 45 above, 15.

to permit migrant workers to remain in the country in the event of involuntary unemployment, but only for a limited period of time and only if they are still collecting unemployment benefit. The Committee of Independent Experts, however, has interpreted Article 19(8) of the ESC as prohibiting the expulsion of migrant workers solely on the basis that they are of limited means.[580] Another important COE agreement in this area is the European Convention on Social and Medical Assistance, discussed in the sections on social security rights and the right to health, which expressly prohibits the expulsion of lawfully resident aliens on the sole ground that they are in need of assistance. However, this prohibition on expulsion is inapplicable to those aliens who have not been continuously resident in a state party for a considerable period of time (5 years if they entered the state party's territory before the age of 55 and 10 years if they entered it after reaching that age), are in a fit state of health to be transported, and have no close ties in the territory in which they reside.[581]

Under Article 48(3) EC, the right to freedom of movement for workers may be limited on grounds of 'public policy [*ordre public*], public security or public health'. In accordance with the practice of the Court of Justice, this derogation from the freedom of movement principle is to be interpreted strictly.[582] Council Directive 64/221/EEC[583] specifies when these grounds may be invoked by member states and elaborates somewhat on their content. Article 2(1) stipulates that the Directive applies to all measures taken by member states based on these grounds in respect of entry into their territory, issue or renewal of residence permits, or expulsion from their territory.[584] Article 3(1) maintains that 'measures taken on grounds of public policy or of public security shall be based exclusively on the personal conduct of the individual concerned'.[585] Previous criminal

[580] *Conclusions V*, 139, cited in *Case Law on the European Social Charter*, n. 19 above, 173. During the 12th cycle of supervision, in examining the Greek report, the Committee observed that 'in so far as foreign workers are expelled from Greece only for reasons of *ordre public*, this country complies with the Charter. However, it wished to be informed . . . if there were other grounds on which a foreign worker could be expelled, such as lack of financial resources': *Conclusions XII-1*, n. 57 above, 241. This approach should be contrasted with an earlier view of the Committee that Art. 19(8) does not preclude a situation where the loss of employment by migrant workers leads to a loss of residence: *Conclusions II*, 198, cited in *Case Law on the European Social Charter*, n. 19 above, 171 and by Harris, n. 20 above, 186. Such an eventuality is specifically prohibited in ILO Convention No. 143 by Art. 8(1).

[581] See Arts. 6 and 7 respectively.

[582] *Van Duyn*, n. 315 above; Case 67/74, *Bonsignore* v. *Oberstadtdirektor Cologne* [1975] ECR 297, [1975] 1 CMLR 472; *Rutili*, n. 115 above.

[583] Council Directive 64/221/EEC of 15 Feb. 1964 on the co-ordination of special measures concerning the movement and residence of foreign nationals, OJ Sp. Ed. 1963–64, 117. The application of this Directive is extended to those EC nationals and members of their families who exercise the right to remain by Council Directive 72/194/EEC of 18 May 1972, OJ Sp. Ed. 1972, 474 (Art. 1).

[584] 'Measures' include a recommendation for deportation by a court. See Case 30/77, *R* v. *Bouchereau* [1977] ECR 1999, [1977] 2 CMLR 800. The expiry of an identity card or passport used by the EC national to enter the territory of a member state does not justify expulsion from that territory (Art. 3(3)).

[585] 'The concept of "personal conduct" expresses the requirement that a deportation order may only be made for breaches of the peace and public security which might be committed by the individual affected', and cannot be used for reasons of a 'general preventive nature' in order to deter other aliens: *Bonsignore*, n. 582 above, paras. 6–7.

convictions do not in themselves constitute a basis for expulsion on the grounds of public policy or public security.[586] Moreover, restrictions on the basis of public policy may only be imposed if the migrant's conduct constitutes 'a genuine and sufficiently serious threat to the requirements of public policy affecting one of the fundamental interests of society'.[587] Article 4(1) of Directive 64/221/EEC refers to a list of diseases and disabilities in the Annex justifying refusal of entry into a territory or refusal to issue a first residence permit.[588] Expulsion for economic reasons is explicitly prohibited by Article 2(2) which stipulates that the grounds are not to be invoked to 'service economic ends'. As discussed earlier, however, although EC law concerning the issue of residence permits appears to adequately protect migrant workers and their families in the event of unemployment, those EC nationals who have become unemployed and are not entitled to a renewal of the residence permit or the right to remain might be particularly vulnerable to expulsion. Member states are given a margin of appreciation in the application of measures invoking the grounds of public policy, public security, or public health.[589] Although the offensive conduct in question need not be illegal under domestic law,[590] member states cannot make arbitrary distinctions between nationals and EC migrant workers in their assessment of such conduct.[591]

In addition to the substantive protection considered above, extensive procedural protection against the refusal of entry, issue or renewal of a residence permit, and expulsion is afforded EC nationals by Directive 64/221/EEC. Under Article 5(1), member states are required to reach speedy decisions, (within 6 months), whether to grant or to refuse a first residence permit, and to allow workers to remain in the territory until a decision is taken. The procedural protection is in the form of a 'double safeguard'. First, the persons concerned are entitled to be notified of the grounds on which the measures restricting their freedom of movement are based unless interests of state security dictate otherwise (Article 6). These reasons must be precise and comprehensive in order to enable the persons concerned to prepare an effective defence. The second aspect of this safeguard concerns the availability of a right of appeal (Articles 8 and 9).[592] Article 8 grants EC migrants 'the same legal remedies in respect of any decision concerning

[586] Art. 3(2). However, in *R* v. *Bouchereau*, n. 584 above, paras. 28–9, the Court of Justice recognized 'that the existence of a previous criminal conviction can . . . be taken into account in so far as the circumstances which give rise to that conviction are evidence of personal conduct constituting a present threat to the requirements of public policy . . . Although, in general, a finding that such a threat exists implies the existence in the individual concerned of a propensity to act in the same way in the future, it is possible that past conduct alone may constitute such a threat to the requirements of public policy'.

[587] *R* v. *Bouchereau*, n. 584 above, para. 35. See also *Rutili*, n. 115 above, para. 28.

[588] If the prescribed disease or disability, however, is contracted after the issue of the first residence permit, refusal to renew the permit or expulsion from the territory cannot be justified (Art. 4(2)).

[589] For a more detailed discussion of this area, see D. Wyatt, 'Free Movement of Workers', n. 382 above, 271–5.

[590] In *Van Duyn*, n. 315 above, the Court of Justice ruled that a member state may expel an individual for conduct, which though undesirable, need not be tainted with illegality.

[591] Cases 115/81 and 118/81, *Adoui and Cornuaille* [1982] ECR 1665, [1982] 3 CMLR 631.

[592] See *Rutili*, n. 115 above, paras. 37, 39.

entry, or refusing the issue or renewal of a residence permit, or ordering expulsion from the territory, as are available to nationals of the State concerned in respect of acts of administration'. Under this provision, member states are not obliged to postpone expulsion until the end of the appeal process provided that the persons concerned can nonetheless obtain a fair hearing and present their defence in full. If no right of appeal on the merits is available, or where the appeal can have no suspensory effect, Article 9(1) delays the implementation of a decision by the administrative authority to refuse the renewal of a residence permit or to order the expulsion of the permit holder 'until an opinion has been obtained from a competent authority of the host country.' Where Article 9(1) applies, the migrant must be allowed to remain in the country until the relevant competent authority has arrived at its opinion, save in cases of urgency which have to be properly justified by the administrative authority refusing the renewal of the permit or ordering the expulsion under Article 8.[593]

The substantive and procedural safeguards afforded EC migrants, not only from expulsion but also from decisions to refuse entry into the country, or to refuse to issue or renew residence permits, are superior to those available under COE instruments. However, non-EC migrants resident in EC countries of employment have to rely on the latter. Their avenue of complaint will be confined further still, to the ECHR or national law, if they come from outside Europe or if their country of origin, though perhaps a member of the COE, has not ratified any of the relevant instruments, such as the ECE, ESC, and EMW. The lack of applicable safeguards make non-EC nationals vulnerable to expulsion, particularly as the present anti-immigration climate in Western Europe encourages and facilitates the removal of such persons.[594] It is arguable, however, that those non-EC

[593] See Case 98/79, *Pecastaing* v. *Belgian State* [1980] ECR 691, [1980] 3 CMLR 685, paras. 8–20. See also R. C. A. White, 'Procedural Guarantees and Expulsion' (1996) 21 *EL Rev*. 241, with reference to the recent Court of Justice decision in Case C-175/94, *R* v. *Secretary of State for the Home Department, ex parte Gallagher* [1996] 1 CMLR 557, in which the Court confirmed that the administrative authority of a member state cannot, save in urgent cases, take a decision in the circumstances triggered by Art. 9(1) without first receiving the opinion of the competent authority. The Court also ruled that Directive 64/221/EEC does not preclude the competent authority from being appointed by the same administrative authority taking the decision ordering expulsion provided that the former can perform its duties in complete independence and is not subject to any control by the authority empowered to take the measures provided for in the Directive. *Ibid*. paras. 22 and 26 respectively. By virtue of Art. 9(2), a person can refer any decision refusing the issue of a *first* residence permit or ordering his or her expulsion before the issue of that permit to the competent authority under Art. 9(1) for consideration. The individual concerned can submit a defence in person unless this would be contrary to the interests of national security.

[594] For example, see the Recommendation regarding Practices followed by Member States on Expulsion (Doc. SN 4678/92, WGI 1266), adopted by EC Immigration Ministers on 30 Nov. 1992. This Recommendation stipulates that, as a general rule, the following categories of persons, subject to the existence of compelling humanitarian reasons, should be expelled: those who have entered or remained unlawfully in EC member states; those liable to expulsion on grounds of public policy or national security; and those who have failed definitively in an application for asylum and have no other claim to remain. The Recommendation lists a number of safeguards, including: criminal or administrative law should provide for the expulsion; persons should not be expelled without being notified in an appropriate manner of the reasons for the decision, unless national security interests

nationals, whose countries have entered into Association and Cooperation Agreements with the EC, might qualify for additional protection from expulsion which is comparable to that afforded EC nationals.[595]

8.11 CONCLUSION

The protection of the economic and social rights of migrants in respect of their rights to equal work and employment conditions, social security, health care, and housing is given extensive consideration by COE instruments and EC law. COE instruments are clearly weaker, however, in safeguarding trade union rights because they contain no express guarantee concerning the right of migrants to participate in unions. Moreover, in line with general international human rights instruments and with the ILO and UN instruments that are concerned specifically with the protection of the rights of migrant workers and their families, a general right to education is also guaranteed by COE and EC standards, particularly as it pertains to the education of migrant children. In contrast with these other instruments, however, EC provisions extend the right of equal treatment between migrants and nationals in respect of education to the provision of financial assistance, including grants and scholarships.

Arguably, the most important economic and social rights for migrant workers

make such notification undesirable; and they should have a right to be represented and an appropriate means to challenge the expulsion decision. However, it is also proposed that expulsion takes place as soon as possible after the decision to expel has been taken, which leaves little room for suspending the decision until a review is undertaken or an appeal is heard. Moreover, the measure contains positive recommendations to detain persons liable to expulsion, provided that the restriction on liberty is limited to a period necessary to effect the expulsion, and to introduce laws permitting the fingerprinting of those to be expelled in order to assist their identification. Finally, in line with the Resolution on the harmonization of national policies on family reunification, nn. 324–35 above and accompanying text, the Recommendation only 'takes account of' relevant international instruments, although in doing so it does at least specify the ECHR.

[595] In respect of workers under the Mahgreb Cooperation Agreements, Guild, n. 91 above, 17, contends that this protection ought to be equivalent to that afforded EC nationals, or at least comprise a number of uniform grounds for expulsion. There is a stronger argument for EC case law on expulsion to be applicable to Turkish migrants, who have acquired access to employment rights and equivalent rights of residence in an EC member state by virtue of Decision 1/80, n. 23 above. The access to employment provisions in the Decision are subject to 'limitations justified on grounds of public policy, public security or public health' under Art. 14(1). It is argued that EC law should be applied in interpreting this phrase. Such protection would be a logical extension of the approach adopted by the Court of Justice in *Sevince*, n. 90 above and *Kus* and *Eroglu*, n. 89 above, ruling, *inter alia*, that the right of residence is a corollary of a right to remain in employment in the host country concerned. Indeed, a German administrative court has already concluded that a deportation order made under the public policy exception in Art. 14(1) is subject to the rules of EC law. See *Re a Turkish Drugs Pedlar* [1993] 3 CMLR 276 (Administrative Court of Appeal, North-Rhine Westphalia, Case 18 B 4386/92, decision of 29 April 1993). See also Burrows, n. 89 above, 307–8. However, this provision has not yet been considered by the Court of Justice. See Peers, n. 25 above, 46–7 and Cremona, n. 25 above, 103–4. Peers, *ibid.* 47–8, also argues that non-EC nationals in the employment of EC nationals or companies providing services in another member state should also benefit from the more favourable EC law on expulsion because lesser protection might constitute an obstacle to the right of EC nationals to provide services under Arts. 52 *et seq.* EC.

and their families are the right of access to employment and the right to family reunification, which are heavily qualified under COE instruments. The provisions in the ECE regarding access to employment and Article 12 of the EMW on family reunion constitute exemplars of such restrictions. There are encouraging signs, however, that the right to family reunion is being given at least some measure of recognition and respect by certain European human rights enforcement bodies, if not by national governments, in their interpretation of the relevant provisions concerned. The Committee of Independent Experts of the ESC has developed an interesting and detailed jurisprudence in this area despite the limitations of the instrument and the lower esteem in which social rights are held by some states. Similarly, the Commission and Court under the European Convention on Human Rights have succeeded, to a limited extent, in restraining the state's traditional freedom to act with respect to the entry and exit of non-nationals. The discretion granted to states parties generally under COE instruments to impose substantial conditions on the rights to family reunion and access to employment is consistent with their concern to protect national sovereignty, which they perceive as being threatened by the spectre of a mass migration from the developing and underdeveloped parts of the world. In contrast, these rights are considered integral to the successful operation of the EC free movement of workers regime. It is hardly surprising, therefore, that the protection afforded migrants who are nationals of EC member states with respect to these rights is far stronger. They are *rights* in the true sense.

The relatively weak COE standards on rights to culture, political participation, and residence merely reflect the restrictive approaches taken in individual countries of employment, with few exceptions such as the position in Sweden. Cultural rights are very limited as witnessed by Article 15 of the EMW and its numerous qualifications. The right of migrants to vote and stand for office in local elections is only a recent and rather limited COE innovation. Indeed, a number of countries of employment grant foreigners more generous voting rights at the municipal level. There are also no rights in COE instruments to permanent residence or to naturalization. The customary superiority of EC provisions over COE standards is less pronounced in the areas of culture and political participation, and there were fewer significant differences until recently. The right of migrant children to retain and develop the culture and language of the country of origin of their parents is subject to similar conditions to those found in Article 15 of the EMW. With regard to political participation, however, after years of discussion on the policy level, the TEU has recently granted EC nationals, who are not nationals of the member state of residence, the right to vote and to stand for political office in local elections and in elections to the European Parliament. Although EC provisions are silent on the question of naturalization, those EC nationals who reside and work in other member states by and large possess secure rights of residence and may remain there indefinitely after the cessation of economic activity.

Conclusion: Towards Inclusion or Exclusion?

[A]s regards the alien, we must remember that compacts have a particular sanctity; indeed, offences by alien against alien, we may say, compared with sins against fellow-citizens, more directly draw down the vengeance of God. For the alien, being without friends or kinsmen, has the greater claim on pity, human and divine . . . What anxious care, then, should a man of any foresight take to come to the end of life's journey guiltless of offence towards aliens![1]

Chapter 1 concluded with an appraisal of the link between migration for employment and the right to development. A comprehensive agenda aimed at sustainable development in regions of high emigration pressure is recognized as the way forward in reducing labour migration in the long-term. Such an agenda, however, should not be implemented at the expense of the protection of the rights of migrant workers and their families already residing and working in many developed countries of employment. Nor should this protection be merely viewed as a means of serving another end. For example, UN and ILO standards recognize that safeguarding the rights of irregular migrants can serve as a means of deterring clandestine labour. Although this is a valid consideration, it should not inform the overall approach. Migrant workers and their families, simply as human beings and as those who make an economic and social contribution to the society in which they live, are entitled to both national and international protection of their rights in the country of employment independent of any development agenda and the weight to be attached to other policies concerned with migration.

The plethora of international standards concerned with the protection of migrant workers and their families examined in this study may well give the impression that international human rights law has given sufficient attention to the plight of this vulnerable group. On a global scale, general international human rights instruments, such as the International Bill of Rights and the ICERD, and regional treaties in Europe, Africa, and America have generally taken the human being as their starting-point regardless of citizenship status or nationality. Migrant workers and their families have also been the object of specific attention in the ILO since the Organization's inception in 1919. Most ILO standards concerning the protection of people in their working environment are applicable to migrant workers. In addition, specific instruments were adopted for their protection by the International Labour Conference in 1949 and 1975. Since the early 1970s, migrant workers and their families have also been the focus of UN concern which recently generated a lengthy and complex instrument dedicated to their complete protection.

[1] Plato, *The Laws* (London: Dent, 1966) para. 729.

In Europe, additional standards to those found in the European Convention on Human Rights were adopted under the auspices of the Council of Europe (COE) in order to protect migrant workers and their families. In contrast with the universal thrust of the standards mentioned above, these regional norms are characterized by their exclusivity, namely they are not applicable to all migrants residing in a state party which has ratified the instrument in question, but only to those who are nationals of other states parties. Similarly, the European Community (EC) free movement of workers regime is an exclusive 'club' and operates only to protect those member state nationals who work in another member state.[2] The EC system, as examined in the European case study, offers the best arrangement. It is the *crème de la crème* of protection.

The liberal-democratic polity faces a dilemma. In order to preserve itself, it must to some extent exclude newcomers, but the ideals and values on which it is based are universal in application. This dilemma may partly be resolved by according equal treatment with citizen-members to all those who have been invited to participate in the economic, social, and cultural life of society, including perhaps those uninvited guests who have also participated in and contributed to the community for a considerable length of time.

Chapter 2 observed that the bastion of the nation-state order in the world today, the principle of state sovereignty, is being whittled away by the international system for the protection of human rights, which is based on the creed that the dignity of all human beings is the concern of the whole international community and not merely a matter for the sovereign nation-state. Consequently, migrant workers and their families, who find themselves at the mercy of national governments, employers and the general citizenry, are not supposed to be without protection in a country of employment. They have universal and international norms to rely on in times of exploitation and the trampling of their human rights.

The creed of the international system for the protection of human rights is a worthy one, but is it truly viable? Nation-states, no matter how tyrannical or authoritarian, continue to sign international human rights agreements. No country wishes to be perceived as openly acknowledging the oppression of its own members. But can the nation-state order be expected to protect the rights of alien migrant workers and their families? The international system for the protection of human rights maintains that it does, or more accurately, that it should.

Below, the international instruments already examined in the preceding chapters are applied in a general manner, and from a somewhat different perspective, to the hypothetical situation of a particularly vulnerable group of migrant workers and their families residing in one or more of the major European countries of employment. The objective of this examination is to consider how adequately

[2] Although it also provides minimal guarantees in certain limited areas to those migrants who come from countries that have entered into Association and Cooperation Agreements with the EC, such as Turkey and the countries of the Mahgreb and central and eastern Europe.

these instruments interact in protecting this class of migrants, bearing in mind that this group is excluded from most of the regional standards analysed in the European case study.

THE HYPOTHETICAL SITUATION

The migrant group

Consider a group of migrant workers and their families residing in Western Europe and who come from a developing country, such as from one of the countries of the Mahgreb region of North Africa (Algeria, Morocco, and Tunisia), from one of the new democracies in central and eastern Europe (Bulgaria, the Czech Republic, Hungary, Poland, Romania, or Slovakia), or from Turkey and the former Yugoslavia. Leaving aside any possible protection they might be entitled to under the national law of the country of employment and under bilateral agreements signed between sending and receiving states,[3] what further protection might they expect under international human rights law? Consider also the undocumented migrants working and residing in Western Europe. What kind of recourse does this group have to the safeguards afforded by this law?

Universal human rights instruments

As far as universal human rights instruments are concerned, this group of migrants may claim protection under the ICCPR, the ICESCR, and the ICERD, which all the European countries of employment have ratified. As individuals, however, they may not be able to enforce these rights because not all of the countries in question have ratified the Optional Protocol to the ICCPR, nor made a declaration under Article 14 of ICERD accepting the individual right of petition. The only 'countries of employment' with a substantial number of foreigners living within their borders, which have accepted this right under both instruments, are France, Italy, and the Netherlands. In contrast, neither Switzerland nor the United Kingdom has accepted the right of individual petition under the ICCPR and the ICERD.[4]

[3] For example, Ch. 6 noted the adoption of recent bilateral agreements between a number of Western European countries and the newly democratic states of central and eastern Europe, which are particularly concerned with seasonal labour.

[4] As at 1 Jan. 1996, the following European countries had ratified the Optional Protocol to the ICCPR: Armenia, Austria, Belarus, Belgium, Bosnia-Herzegovina, Bulgaria, Croatia, Cyprus, Czech Republic, Denmark, Estonia, Finland, France, Georgia, Germany, Hungary, Iceland, Ireland, Italy, Latvia, Lithuania, Luxembourg, Macedonia, Malta, the Netherlands, Norway, Poland, Portugal, Romania, Russia, San Marino, Slovakia, Slovenia, Spain, Sweden, and Ukraine. The following had made declarations under Art. 14 of the ICERD, allowing for the right of individual petition: Bulgaria, Cyprus, Denmark, Finland, France, Hungary, Iceland, Italy, the Netherlands, Norway, Russia, Sweden, and Ukraine.

Universal human rights instruments specifically relating to migrants

With regard to specific universal standards concerned with the protection of migrant workers and their families, only ILO instruments are relevant for the time being. The UN Convention is not in force and, as has been explained in Chapter 4, it is unlikely that it will come into force in the very near future.[5] The ILO standards are therefore critical. As at 1 January 1996, ILO Convention No. 143 of 1975 had only been ratified by 17 countries, including 9 European countries, namely Bosnia-Herzegovina, Cyprus, Italy, Norway, Portugal, San Marino, Slovenia, Sweden, and Yugoslavia. Italy and Portugal, predominantly countries of emigration in the past, are very relevant to the hypothetical situation discussed. Both have recently experienced an influx of migrants from developing countries that includes a considerable flow of North Africans to Italy. As noted in Chapter 6, many of these immigrant workers are undocumented. Because Part I of this Convention applies to all migrants, including those in an irregular situation, its importance to the migrant group under consideration is apparent. The list of European migrant-receiving countries that have ratified ILO Convention No. 97 of 1949 is lengthier. Belgium, Bosnia-Herzegovina, Cyprus, France, Germany, Italy, the Netherlands, Norway, Portugal, Slovenia, Spain, United Kingdom, and Yugoslavia (Serbia and Montenegro) were all parties to this agreement as at 1 January 1996. Convention No. 97, however, does not apply to illegal migrants.

Regional human rights instruments

With regard to regional human rights instruments in Europe, only the ECHR applies, for the time being, to those migrants who originate from the Mahgreb region, other developing countries, and from the newly democratic states of central and eastern Europe, many of which are also new members of the COE and have also ratified the ECHR. The ECHR has been ratified by 33 COE member states as at 1 July 1996. All the states parties to the ECHR have also made declarations accepting the right of individual petition and the jurisdiction of the European Court of Human Rights. However, COE agreements, such as the ECE, ESC, and the EMW, only protect nationals from other states parties residing and employed in another state party. They are not open, for example, to ratification by countries from the Mahgreb, although they can now be ratified by the new central and eastern European COE member states. As at 1 July 1996, however, none of these countries had ratified the ECE, ESC, or the EMW. Consequently, migrants from the group under consideration are not protected by these instruments except those from Turkey, which has ratified each one. Finally, EC provisions are not applicable to the migrants in question, with the important exception of Association and Cooperation Agreements entered into between their

[5] The UN Convention had not been ratified by a single European state as at 1 November 1996.

countries of origin and the EC. The position taken by the Court of Justice that some of the provisions in these agreements and the decisions taken thereunder can be directly (and successfully) invoked by such migrants before the domestic courts in the country of employment is a significant step forward in advancing the rights of this group in certain important areas, such as employment and social security.

Definition and rights

Given this rubric of international instruments, what kind of rights' safeguards might this particular group of migrant workers and their families expect? Before answering this question, it must be emphasized that even if these migrants are fortunate enough to find themselves in a country which has ratified one or both ILO Conventions concerning migrant workers, the safeguards contained therein might not apply to them if they fall beyond the scope of the definitions of 'migrant worker' in these instruments.[6] For example, if they are self-employed workers, students or trainees engaging in employment, or so-called 'project-tied' workers, (namely workers who have entered a country to work on a specific job and who are required to leave once this job is completed), they cannot claim protection under these Conventions.[7] The definitions in these agreements also exclude illegal migrants, although this group is protected to some extent under Part I of Convention No. 143.

The fundamental rights of migrants from which no derogation is permissible, such as their right to life and their right not to be subjected to torture, are guaranteed by the universal human rights instruments of general application. These rights are also covered by the term 'basic human rights' in Article 1 of ILO Convention No. 143. They are protected in the ECHR and are listed fully in the UN Convention. The international protection of the economic, social, cultural, political, and residence rights (including protection against unfair expulsion) of the group of migrant workers and their families under consideration is less well-defined. The UN Convention is the most comprehensive, but is presently dormant. ILO Conventions, in line with the Organization's mandate, are mainly concerned with the economic and social rights relating to labour and less so with other rights, although references to culture, education, and residence are made in those ILO instruments specifically concerned with the protection of migrants. The ECHR and its Protocols have only limited application; positively, for example by espousing a general right to education and providing procedural safeguards against the arbitrary expulsion of lawfully resident migrants and the collective expulsion of *all* aliens,[8] and negatively, by potentially excluding migrants from political activity in the country of employment.[9]

[6] See Art. 11 in both Conventions No. 97 and 143.

[7] Seasonal migrant workers, however, are not expressly excluded by these definitions.

[8] See respectively Protocol No. 1 to the ECHR, Art. 2; Protocol No. 7, Art. 1; and Protocol No. 4, Art. 4.

[9] ECHR, Art. 16.

In terms of a general right to equal treatment with nationals, laws, regulations, and administrative action which discriminate against migrant workers in respect of employment, social security, accommodation, and membership of trade unions, and the enjoyment of the benefits of collective bargaining are prohibited under ILO Convention No. 97.[10] Consequently, discrimination in the private sector, such as the renting of private accommodation, which is not always regulated by national laws, regulations, or by the action of administrative authorities, is not, strictly speaking, covered, although the Committee of Independent Experts has adopted an expansive conception of equality in its 'case law'. The application of equality under ILO Convention No. 143 is clearly broader, with the result that states parties are under a duty to declare and pursue a national policy which promotes equal treatment between lawfully resident migrant workers and their families and nationals, not only in respect of the aforementioned matters but additional matters as well. Non-discrimination is also a principle found in Article 14 of the ECHR, although this is not a substantive equality clause in the true sense because it only applies to the rights set forth in the ECHR, which are principally civil and political rights.

The right of this particular group of migrants to equal work and employment conditions is guaranteed by the ICESCR,[11] and in more detail by numerous ILO standards, including the instruments specifically concerned with the protection of migrant workers. This right is of particular importance to migrant workers from the Mahgreb and from central and eastern Europe and to those in an irregular situation, because they constitute the lowest tier of labour in Europe and are most likely to be found in the dirtiest and most menial jobs. Association and Cooperation Agreements guarantee equal treatment in this area between nationals and *lawfully* resident migrants, who originate from countries to which these Agreements apply.

The right to form and join trade unions is guaranteed to all workers by the ICESCR, the ICCPR, and the ECHR. ILO standards also safeguard the right of all workers, irrespective of nationality, to establish and to join trade unions.[12] Rights to participate in trade union activities, or to be elected to trade union office, are less pronounced. However, the ILO Committee of Independent Experts on the Application of Conventions and Recommendations has asserted that the term 'trade union rights' in Article 10 of Convention No. 143 encompasses these participatory rights.

In line with Article 9 of the ICESCR, which provides for the right of 'everyone' to social security, both ILO Conventions relating to migrant workers and their families guarantee equal treatment between migrants and nationals in respect of social security rights.[13] Social security is defined in ILO Convention

[10] Arts. 6(1)(a) and (b). [11] Art. 7.

[12] See especially Art. 2 of ILO Convention No. 87 of 1948 concerning Freedom of Association and Protection of the Right to Organize.

[13] Convention No. 97, Art. 6(1)(b) and Convention No. 143, Art. 10.

No. 97. Its contours may also be drawn from more specific ILO standards dealing with this question, such as Convention No. 102 of 1952 concerning Minimum Standards of Social Security. As at 1 January 1996, Convention No. 102 had only been ratified by the following central and eastern European countries: Bosnia-Herzegovina, Croatia, the Czech Republic, Slovakia, Slovenia, and Yugoslavia. Although Turkey had also ratified the Convention, none of the Mahgreb countries had accepted it. This rather poor ratification record is significant given that Convention No. 102, like those social security instruments which follow it, only operates on the basis of reciprocity. Conventions Nos. 97 and 143, however, guarantee social security rights to all migrants lawfully resident in the territory of any state party which has ratified one or both of these instruments. The social security rights of irregular migrants are far less well-defined, although Part I of Convention No. 143 guarantees, on an equal basis with regular migrant workers, their rights arising out of past employment as regards, *inter alia*, social security and other benefits.[14]

Article 12(1) of the ICESCR recognizes the 'right of everyone to the enjoyment of the highest attainable standard of physical and mental health'. Although Convention No. 97 does not refer to medical care, subsequent ILO Conventions on social security have defined 'social security' to include medical care. However, with regard to health and safety at work, ILO standards specifically relating to migrant workers are only found in a Recommendation, which has no legally binding force.[15]

The right of this group of migrants to equality with nationals in respect of accommodation is set out in ILO Convention No. 97.[16] Although Convention No. 143 of 1975 does not specify 'housing' in the equality clause by which states are required to promote equal treatment in practice between migrants and nationals, the accompanying recommendation maintains that migrants should enjoy effective equal opportunity and treatment with nationals in respect of, *inter alia*, 'conditions of life, including housing . . .'. Consequently, a state policy ensuring equal treatment between migrants and nationals in respect of access to accommodation on the private housing market would be in conformity with this provision. The accompanying recommendation also proposes, that states, with a view to facilitating family reunion, should take the needs of migrant workers and their families into account in their housing construction and housing assistance policies.[17]

The right to education, irrespective of nationality and legal status, is guaranteed to 'everyone' in the ICESCR and the ECHR. Strictly speaking, education falls outside of the competence of the ILO, which is primarily concerned with labour-related rights, although as indicated in Chapter 3, the education of migrant children is a question not entirely ignored by ILO standards, especially in

[14] Art. 9(1). [15] Recommendation No. 151 of 1975, paras. 21–2. [16] Art. 6(1)(a)(iii).

[17] See Recommendation No. 151, paras. 2(i) and 16 respectively. See also Recommendation No. 115 of 1961 concerning Workers' Housing, Pt. I, para. 5.

the context of their cultural education and integration into society. If this group of migrants, however, seeks financial assistance or scholarship funding for their children, which is especially relevant to higher education, they are unlikely to have much success, unless national regulations are sympathetic in this area. Among all the standards concerned with education examined in this study, only EC provisions, as interpreted by the Court of Justice, ensure equality between member state nationals in respect of equal access to educational assistance, including access to scholarships and grants, and these provisions would not apply to the group under consideration.

Because of its interrelationship with labour matters, the education of workers is clearly a focus of ILO attention. The right of migrant workers to equal treatment with nationals in respect of access to vocational training, is guaranteed by both Conventions No. 97 and No. 143.[18] In addition, Recommendation No. 151 proposes that migrant workers are also given language instruction within working hours,[19] a crucial component of their integration into the working life of the host country. The Committee of Independent Experts on the Application of Conventions and Recommendations has recognized, however, that the right of equal access to vocational training may be difficult to satisfy in the case of seasonal migrants or migrant workers on short-term contracts.

Rights to free choice of employment, family reunification, culture, political participation, and residence, including the right to stay or remain, naturalization, and safeguards against unfair expulsion, are grouped together below because the protection this group of migrants might expect to receive with respect to these rights is fairly minimal. Indeed, these areas are at the core of the socio-economic, cultural, and political sovereign concerns which states normally have in respect of the presence of migrant workers and their families within their territories.

Article 14(a) of Convention No. 143 is the most enlightened provision in international human rights law regarding the right of migrant workers to free choice of employment. Only the provisions of the EC free movement of workers regime are stronger.[20] Under Article 14(a), migrant workers from central and eastern Europe and the developing world, who are legally resident in countries which have ratified this ILO instrument, such as Italy or Portugal, are entitled to free choice of employment after 2 years of work and residence, or sooner if they have completed their first work contract that is under 2 years in duration. Article 14(a) thus curtails state sovereignty in a significant economic area and is probably the principal reason why so few states have ratified this Convention.

Proclamations that the family is 'the natural and fundamental group unit of society' and hence entitled to the fullest protection by the state abound in international human rights law. However, the reality of ensuring this protection in

[18] Art. 6(1)(a)(i) and Art. 10 respectively. [19] Para. 7(1)(b).

[20] See also Decision 1/80 of the EC–Turkey Association Council, discussed in Ch. 8, which incrementally increases the access to employment rights of Turkish migrant workers after they have worked for a certain specified number of years in an EC country of employment.

respect of migrant families through family reunification is very different as many states view increasing family reunion less from a humanitarian perspective and more from the perspective of a threat to their sovereignty. The right of migrant workers from the group under consideration to reunion with their families is limited. ILO Convention No. 97 only refers to this question from the standpoint of permanent migration, whereas states parties to Convention No. 143 are given the discretion to 'facilitate' the reunion of migrant workers with their spouses, dependent children, and parents.[21] Moreover, the migrant worker should also be in possession of suitable accommodation for his or her family, which meets the standards normally applicable to nationals.[22] Obstructing family reunion, however, may constitute an infringement of the right to 'family life' under Article 8(1) of the ECHR. Recent cases decided by the European Court of Human Rights indicate that a foreigner, who is 'rooted' in a country of employment on account of strong family ties, can only be expelled from that country in the event of a very serious threat to public order or national security.[23] Indeed, migrants from central and eastern Europe and from the developing world are not necessarily in a less protected position with regard to family reunification than other nationals, particularly those whose countries have ratified the ESC and the EMW, since the right to family reunion is qualified considerably under both of these instruments, in particular under the latter.[24] On the other hand, EC law provides for a *right* to family reunification in the strong sense, subject only to the condition that the migrant worker possesses accommodation for his or her family which is considered normal for national workers in the region of employment.[25]

The right of migrants to maintain their culture and language is also limited under the instruments which apply to the group of migrants under consideration. Indeed, only ILO Convention No. 143 refers to this question by obliging states parties to assist and encourage migrant workers and their families to preserve their cultural identity, including the possibility of providing mother-tongue education to migrant children.[26]

Migrant workers and their families possess no express right to political participation in the country of employment in international human rights law. Indeed, any political activity in the host country, if connected with the right to freedom of expression and to freedom of assembly or association, is potentially subject to restrictions under Article 16 of the ECHR, although it is likely that this provision will be interpreted narrowly given the developments in a number of European countries permitting electoral participation to resident foreigners. Electoral

[21] Art. 13. [22] Recommendation No. 151, para. 13(2).

[23] See *Boughanemi* v. *France*, judgment of 24 April 1996, (1996) 22 EHRR 228; *Nasri* v. *France*, judgment of 13 July 1995, Eur. Ct. H.R., 1995, Ser. A., No. 324; *Beldjoudi* v. *France*, judgment of 26 March 1992, Eur. Ct. H.R., 1992, Ser. A, No. 234-A; and *Moustaquim* v. *Belgium*, judgment of 18 Feb. 1991, Eur. Ct. H.R., 1991, Ser. A, No. 193.

[24] ESC, Art. 19(6) and EMW, Art. 12. However, the Committee of Independent Experts of the ESC has adopted a generous interpretation of Art. 19(6).

[25] Regulation 1612/68/EEC, Art. 10. [26] Art. 12(f).

participation is limited to nationals in the ICCPR[27] and in other regional human rights instruments. The instrument which comes closest to referring to such a right for non-nationals is the UN Convention, which obliges states to facilitate the 'consultation or participation of migrant workers and their families in decisions concerning the life and administration of local communities',[28] but without specifically proposing that migrants are to be granted voting rights in local elections. Only EC nationals residing and working in other EC member states have a right under EC law to political participation in local elections in the country of employment. This is also one of the areas where national laws have developed more positively and rapidly than international norms. For example, if migrants from the Mahgreb or eastern Europe have legally resided in certain countries, such as the Netherlands for 5 years, or in Denmark, Norway, or Sweden for 3 years, they acquire the right to vote at the municipal level. Lastly, restrictions on the access of migrant workers to the public service in the country of employment are permissible under all instruments concerned with migrant workers, including ILO Convention No. 143.[29]

In most migrant-receiving countries in Europe, residence permits are aligned with work permits. If migrant workers lose their jobs, their residence status is jeopardized as a result, unless they have acquired more stable status, such as permanent residence. ILO Convention No. 143 stipulates that migrant workers who have been legally employed are not to be considered in an irregular situation on account of loss of employment.[30] Unemployed migrant workers should therefore be permitted to stay in the host country in order to find alternative employment, at least for a period corresponding to that during which they may be entitled to unemployment benefit.[31] There is no right to stay or to acquire naturalization under ILO instruments or under the ECHR. Indeed, no such right exists in international human rights law. However, the recent Second Amending Protocol to the Convention on Multiple Nationality deviates from the guiding principle of the original instrument by encouraging states parties to facilitate naturalization for certain groups, such as second-generation migrants, the foreign spouses of nationals and their children. Only EC provisions allow for a right to remain after the completion of a certain period of employment and residence in the country of employment.[32] As far as protection against unfair or arbitrary expulsion is concerned, migrants from the group under consideration can generally be expelled without too much difficulty provided that the authorities concerned follow the correct legal procedures.[33]

Illegal migrant workers and their families are in the least protected situation. Together with legal migrants, they may lay claim to the protection of their basic

[27] Art. 25. [28] Art. 42(2). [29] Art. 14(c). [30] Art. 8(1).
[31] Recommendation No. 151, para. 31.
[32] Regulation 1251/70/EEC.
[33] ICCPR, Art. 13 and Protocol No. 7 to the ECHR, Art. 1. Under both provisions, the 'correct procedure' includes the right of aliens to have their cases reviewed by the competent authorities.

or fundamental rights under universal and regional human rights instruments. Even these instruments, however, make specific exceptions which limit rights to lawful residence. For example, illegal migrants have no right to freedom of movement within a state,[34] nor any right to procedural protection against expulsion, unless they are expelled collectively as members of a group,[35] and their liberty can be denied under the ECHR with a view to expulsion or deportation.[36] Only the universal instruments specifically relating to migrant workers and their families, namely the UN Convention and ILO Convention No. 143, provide any comprehensive protection to undocumented migrants. The basic thrust of these instruments in this area is to prevent clandestine migration and the abusive conditions which it gives rise to, although both also list some specific rights to which members of this vulnerable group are entitled over and above the basic civil and political guarantees in the universal and regional human rights treaties of general application.

The UN Convention is not yet in force, but it confirms the universality of basic human rights principles in the UDHR, the ICCPR, and the ICESCR, namely that they encompass all human beings regardless of citizenship or legal status. Under Part III of the UN Convention, migrant workers and their families in an irregular situation are guaranteed minimum protection in respect of rights to equal employment and work conditions, membership of trade unions, social security, emergency health care, education and culture. Part I of ILO Convention No. 143 is devoted to the problem of illegal migration. As noted earlier, this instrument is most relevant to the particular group under consideration. Undocumented migrant workers from this group are protected in respect of their rights arising out of past employment. Their employers, therefore, cannot refuse to pay their wages or infringe their rights to social security or other benefits on the ground that their employment is unlawful.[37] Furthermore, as part of its policy to deter and combat clandestine and irregular migration, this instrument obliges states to impose sanctions on employers for hiring illegal migrant labour, but no punishments are to be imposed on undocumented migrants themselves.[38] This approach is reinforced by the stipulation that migrants are not liable for the administrative and judicial costs of their expulsion.[39] Furthermore, Convention No. 143 is supportive of national programmes aimed at the regularization of the situation of migrant workers and their families.[40] It is noteworthy that Italy, which has ratified ILO Convention No. 143, implemented substantial regularization programmes in 1986 and 1990. There are no mechanisms in place, however, which would enable illegal migrants to come forward to claim the rights to which they are entitled without fearing detection by the authorities and, ultimately, expulsion.

[34] ICCPR, Art. 12(1) and Protocol No. 4 to the ECHR, Art. 2(1).

[35] Protocol No. 4 to the ECHR, Art. 4. However, the UN Convention grants illegal migrant workers and members of their families limited procedural protection against expulsion (Art. 22).

[36] Art. 5(1)(f). [37] Art. 9(1). [38] Art. 6(1). [39] Art. 9(3).

[40] Convention No. 143, Art. 9(4) and Recommendation No. 151, para. 8(1).

A HIERARCHY OF PROTECTION

This overview illustrates the rather limited application of existing international human rights instruments to Europe's most vulnerable group of migrants. The UN Convention requires 20 ratifications in order to come into force, unlike most ILO Conventions which only require 2 ratifications. Indeed, if the same rule applied to ILO Convention No. 143, adopted in 1975, it would still not be in force today. For the time being, therefore, this latter instrument is the most relevant to the group of migrants considered above, but it only applies to 4 countries of significance in Europe: Italy and Portugal, for whom the influx of migrant workers is still a relatively new experience; and Norway and Sweden, which, in recent times, have effectively closed their doors to labour immigration. Although the ECHR applies to all migrant workers and their families residing within the jurisdiction of the 33 states which have ratified it and is endowed with superior enforcement machinery, it has, as is evident from this discussion, only a very narrow application to the particular group of migrants under consideration. The ECHR essentially safeguards the fundamental civil and political rights of migrants, although it confers moderate protection in respect of some social rights, such as the right to education and family reunion. It also provides lawfully resident migrants with procedural safeguards against arbitrary expulsion. However, the companion instrument to the ECHR, namely the ESC, which is concerned with the protection of economic and social rights, only applies to nationals of other states parties on the basis of reciprocity.

Indeed, it is disputable whether the protection accorded to nationals of other states parties, including those from Turkey, by the ECE, the ESC, and the EMW is any stronger than that afforded migrants from the Mahgreb or from central and eastern Europe by the human rights treaties of universal application, the ECHR, and the ILO Conventions combined. It should also be emphasized that not all COE member states have ratified these instruments. In theory, therefore, the rights of a large number of migrants depend upon the safeguards conferred by national law or by the provisions of applicable bilateral agreements. The specific COE Conventions elaborate on many of the rights accorded to migrant workers and their families in other international instruments, such as ILO Conventions Nos. 97 and 143, but some of these rights, especially those concerned with areas at the core of the socio-economic concerns of sovereign states, are qualified considerably; for example the right of access to employment in the ECE and the right to family reunion in the EMW. Moreover, the supervision and enforcement machinery in these instruments is very weak compared with the ECHR and the tripartite ILO supervisory procedures. Only the ESC has advanced the rights of migrant workers and their families, and this has largely been through the 'case law' of the Committee of Independent Experts which has given a broad interpretation to the provisions that are concerned with the protection of migrants. Moreover, neither the ESC, the EMW, nor the ECE apply to illegal migrant workers, even if they originate from another COE state which has ratified one of these instruments.

The rather precarious lot of one group of migrant workers and their families in Europe, namely those who originate from regions outside of Europe and from the central and eastern parts of the continent, is in stark contrast with the experiences of 'privileged' migrants who belong to the EC 'club' of states. Fortunately, the position of the former, if they originate from countries which have entered into Association or Cooperation Agreements with the EC, has improved considerably in recent years as a result of a generous interpretation of these agreements by the Court of Justice.

The very *raison d'être* of a system designed by a group of states with the objective of removing obstacles to the realization of, *inter alia*, free movement of labour among its members, demands that many of the rights commonly denied, or significantly restricted in respect of migrant workers and their families, are granted in full. Consequently, the EC regime affords nationals of member states, with few limitations, rights to free choice of employment, social security, family reunification, and a right to remain in the country of employment after having worked and resided there for a defined period of time. With regard to enforcement, EC law is superior to the other instruments described because many of its provisions are *directly* applicable in the national legal systems of member states and can thus be enforced in the domestic courts. In the context of such a system, the principle of state sovereignty loses much of its significance. Even so, some rights considered central to the definition of the national community, such as the right to political participation in the country of employment *at the national level*, for the time being at least remain beyond the reach of EC migrants as well.

FROM NATIONAL EXCLUSION TOWARDS REGIONAL EXCLUSION?

The importance of the EC regime, as an example of the quintessential system of protection of the rights of migrant workers and their families, should not be underestimated. As indicated in the European case study, the EC free movement of labour system operates, for the time being, within the confined context of an integrated group of states with similar economic, social, and political aspirations. Nonetheless, more and more states are clamouring for accession to this unified part of Europe. It is by no means inconceivable that, by the beginning of the 21st century, free movement of labour will be a reality among 20 or more states in Europe and not just among the present fifteen.[41]

The phenomenon of free movement of labour is not confined to Europe. The implementation of trade regionalization in other parts of the world might potentially

[41] Or 17, if Iceland and Norway are included as the EFTA states to which free movement of workers is presently applicable under the EEA.

lead to the development of free movement of labour within these regions. Free trading zones have been set up in central and eastern Europe,[42] North America,[43] South America,[44] and are also under consideration in South-east Asia.[45]

The liberal dilemma, noted earlier, between excluding aliens or non-members from the benefits enjoyed by citizen-members and granting the former rights on the basis of their human dignity and their participation in and contribution to society has been transferred from the domain of the nation-state to the realm of regional economic pacts among countries. Chapter 6 described the dilemma faced by the EC—whether, how, and when to accord protection to non-EC migrant workers and their families on an equal basis with migrants from other EC member states.

As the hypothetical situation described indicates, the gulf between these two groups of migrants is considerable and is a profound aberration in the continent which can *best* provide for the fulfilment of the rights discussed in this study. The powerful unifying forces at play in the European arena that aim to integrate national economic and political systems must not lose sight of the human factor. For it is the people and workers of Europe, regardless of their nationality or social status, who contribute to its development. The contribution of present and future migrant workers to the Europe of tomorrow must not entail the same toil, hardship, and inequality that characterized the contribution of their predecessors. Such an outcome is simply unacceptable on a continent which only so recently celebrated the triumph of human rights over oppression.

[42] Central European Free Trade Agreement (CEFTA), Kraków, 21 Dec. 1992, (1995) 34 ILM 3: Czech Republic, Hungary, Poland, Slovakia, and Slovenia. Indeed, there is already free movement of labour between the Czech Republic and Slovakia as a result of an agreement signed in 1992 before the anticipated dissolution of the former Czech and Slovak Republic. See *SOPEMI 1994*, 141.

[43] North American Free Trade Agreement (NAFTA), Ottawa, Mexico City, Washington, 8–17 Dec. 1992, (1993) 32 ILM 289 and (1993) 32 ILM 605: Canada, Mexico, USA. Presently, NAFTA does not envisage free movement of labour, with the exception of the temporary entry of highly qualified workers. To date, discussions have centred on its potential to reduce illegal Mexican immigration to the USA in the long term by generating economic growth in Mexico. See S. Wientraub, 'North American Free Trade and the European Situation Compared' (1992) 26 IMR 506; and J. C. Vialet, 'The North American Free Trade Agreement and Immigration' (1993) 21 *Migrationworld Magazine* Nos. 2/3, 2. See also *SOPEMI 1994*, 106–7.

[44] At the end of Aug. 1992, four of the five Andean Pact countries, Bolivia, Colombia, Ecuador, and Venezuela, agreed to implement a customs union. See Commission of the Cartagena Agreement Decision 324 of 25 Aug. 1992 on Common External Tariff, Liberation Program and Incentives for Intrasubregional Exports, (1993) 32 ILM 211. By Decision 321 of 25 Aug. 1992, the fifth Andean Pact member state, Peru, suspended its participation in the Andean Group free trade and common external tariff programmes, (1993) 32 ILM 209. See also J. R. Pate, 'Introductory Note' (1993) 32 ILM 143–5. The official codified text of the Cartagena Agreement of 26 May 1969 (as amended) establishing the Andean Pact can be found in (1989) 28 ILM 1165. In the southern cone of the continent, Argentina, Brazil, Paraguay, and Uruguay are also implementing a free trade area: Treaty Establishing a Common Market (MERCOSUR), Asunción, 26 March 1991, (1991) 30 ILM 1041. This common market came into effect on 1 Jan. 1995.

[45] The ASEAN countries, comprising Brunei, Indonesia, Malaysia, the Philippines, Singapore, Thailand, and Vietnam, plan to realize the ASEAN free trade area, or AFTA, by the year 2000. See S. Sucharitkul, 'Introductory Note' (1996) 35 ILM 1063, 1065.

The international human rights instruments examined in this work are attempting to bridge the divide between, on the one hand, a system such as that of the EC which enables those employed in countries other than their own to benefit from protection comparable with that afforded nationals, and, on the other hand, the intransigent and exclusionary walls of state sovereignty. These efforts must continue for the sake of migrant workers and their families who rightly seek national and international recognition as persons with equal moral worth and as fully integrated social beings, and not merely as economic men and women.

The thought of Plato, cited at the beginning of this concluding chapter, should lead us to the conviction that our treatment of the alien or the stranger in our midst, particularly in the form of the immigrant worker and his or her family, is a measure of our humanity. If we succeed in adequately protecting migrant workers and their families, we shall also be advancing and serving the rights and interests of all who live and work within our system of nation-states, including the rights and interests of those we aspire perhaps to protect most, namely citizen-members.

Bibliography

BOOKS

ALSTON, P., (ed.), *The United Nations and Human Rights: A Critical Appraisal* (Oxford: Clarendon Press, 1992).

ANDERSON, B., *Britain's Secret Slaves: An Investigation into the Plight of Overseas Domestic Workers in the United Kingdom* (London: Anti-Slavery International, 1993).

APPLEYARD, R., (ed.), *International Migration Today—Vol. 1: Trends and Prospects* (Paris; Nedlands, Western Australia, The Centre for Migration and Development Studies: UNESCO, 1988).

—— *International Migration: Challenge for the Nineties* (Geneva: International Organization for Migration, 1991).

ARDITTIS, S., (ed.), *The Politics of East–West Migration* (New York: St. Martin's Press, 1994).

BAILEY, S. H., HARRIS, D. J., and JONES, B. L., *Civil Liberties: Cases and Materials*, 4th edn. (London: Butterworths, 1995).

BANTON, M., *International Action Against Racial Discrimination* (Oxford: Clarendon Press, 1996).

BIEBER, R. and MONAR, J., (eds.), *Justice and Home Affairs in the European Union* (Brussels: European Interuniversity Press, 1995).

BÖHNING, W. R., *Studies in International Labour Migration* (London: ILO (published by Macmillan Press), 1984).

—— and SCHLOETER-PAREDES, M., (eds.), *Aid in Place of Migration?: Selected Contributions to an ILO-UNHCR Meeting*, A WEP Study (Geneva: International Labour Office, 1994).

BROWNLIE, I., (ed.), *Basic Documents on Human Rights*, 3rd edn. (Oxford: Clarendon Press, 1992).

CASTLES, S., *Migrant Workers and the Transformation of Western Societies*, Western Societies Program, Occasional Paper No. 22 (New York: Center for International Studies, Cornell University, 1989).

—— and KOSACK, G., *Immigrant Workers and Class Structure in Western Europe*, 2nd edn. (Oxford: Oxford University Press for the Institute of Race Relations, 1985).

—— BOOTH, H. and WALLACE, T., *Here for Good: Western Europe's New Ethnic Minorities* (London: Pluto Press, 1984).

CATOR J., and NIESSEN, J., (eds.), *The Use of International Conventions to Protect the Rights of Migrants and Ethnic Minorities* (1994).

CRAVEN, M. C., *The International Covenant on Economic, Social and Cultural Rights: A Perspective on its Development* (Oxford: Clarendon Press, 1995).

DUMMETT, A., (ed.), *Towards a Just Immigration Policy* (London: Cobden Trust, 1986).

EIDE, A., KRAUSE, C., and ROSAS, A., (eds.), *Economic, Social and Cultural Rights: A Textbook* (Dordrecht: Martinus Nijhoff, 1995).

EIDE, A., *et al.*, (eds.), *The Universal Declaration of Human Rights: A Commentary* (Oslo: Scandinavian University Press, 1992).

FAWCETT, J. E. S., *The Application of the European Convention on Human Rights*, 2nd edn. (Oxford: Clarendon Press, 1987).

GARDNER, J. P., (ed.), *Hallmarks of Citizenship* (London: The British Institute of International and Comparative Law, 1995).

GOODWIN-GILL, G. S., *International Law and the Movement of Persons Between States* (Oxford: Clarendon Press, 1978).

GOMIEN, D., HARRIS, D., and ZWAAK, L., *Law and Practice of the European Convention on Human Rights and the European Social Charter* (Strasbourg: Council of Europe, 1996).

GUILD, E., *The Developing Immigration and Asylum Policies of the European Union. Adopted Conventions, Resolutions, Recommendations, Decisions and Conclusions* (The Hague: Kluwer, 1996).

HAMMAR, T., (ed.), *European Immigration Policy: A Comparative Study* (Cambridge: Cambridge University Press, 1985).

—— *Democracy and the Nation State: Aliens, Denizens and Citizens in a World of International Migration* (Aldershot, England: Avebury, 1990).

HENCKAERTS, J.-M., *Mass Expulsion in Modern International Law and Practice* (The Hague: Martinus Nijhoff, 1995).

HENKIN, L., (ed.), *The International Bill of Rights: The Covenant on Civil and Political Rights* (New York: Columbia University Press, 1981).

HARRIS, D., *The European Social Charter* (Charlottesville, Virginia: University Press of Virginia, 1984).

—— *Cases and Materials on International Law*, 4th edn. (London: Sweet & Maxwell, 1991).

HUJANEN, T., (ed.), *Role of Information in the Realization of the Human Rights of Migrant Workers*, Report of International Conference, Tampere, 19–22 June 1983 (Tampere: University of Tampere, Department of Journalism and Mass Communication, 1984).

JASPERS, A. Ph. C. M. and BETTEN, L., (eds.), *25 Years of the European Social Charter* (Deventer: Kluwer, 1988).

KORELLA, G. D. and TWOMEY, P. M., (eds.), *Towards a European Immigration Policy* (Brussels: European Interuniversity Press, 1995).

KRANE, R. E., (ed.), *International Labor Migration in Europe* (New York: Praeger, 1979).

KRITZ, M. M., LIM, L. L., and ZLOTNIK, H., (eds.), *International Migration Systems: A Global Approach* (Oxford: Clarendon Press, 1992).

LAYTON-HENRY, Z., (ed.), *The Political Rights of Migrant Workers in Western Europe* (London: SAGE, 1990).

LEARY, V. A., *International Labour Conventions and National Law: The Effectiveness of the Automatic Incorporation of Treaties in National Legal Systems* (The Hague: Martinus Nijhoff, 1982).

LILLICH, R. B., *The Human Rights of Aliens in Contemporary International Law* (Manchester: Manchester University Press, 1984).

MACDONALD, I. and BLAKE, N., *Immigration Law and Practice in the United Kingdom*, 4th edn. (London: Butterworths, 1995).

MCKEAN, W., *Equality and Discrimination under International Law* (Oxford: Clarendon Press, 1983).

MAX PLANCK INSTITUTE OF COMPARATIVE LAW, (ed.), *The Legal Position of Aliens in National and International Law*, vol. 2 (Berlin: Springer Verlag, 1987).

MEIJERS, H., *et al.*, (eds.), *Schengen: Internationalisation of Central Chapters of the Law on Aliens, Refugees, Privacy, Security and the Police*, 2nd rev. edn. (Leiden: Stichting NJCM—Boekerij, 1992).

—— *A New Immigration Law for Europe? The 1992 London and 1993 Copenhagen Rules on Immigration* (Utrecht: Dutch Centre for Immigrants, 1993).

MONAR, J. and MORGAN, R., (eds.), *The Third Pillar of the European Union* (Brussels: European Interuniversity Press, 1994).

MURDOCH, J. L., *Article 5 of the European Convention on Human Rights. The Protection of Liberty and Security of Person*, Human Rights Files No. 12 (Strasbourg: Council of Europe Press, 1994).

NOWAK, M., *U.N. Covenant on Civil and Political Rights. CCPR Commentary* (Kehl: Engel, 1993).

PAPADEMETRIOU, D. G. and MARTIN, P. L., (eds.), *The Unsettled Relationship: Labor Migration and Economic Development* (New York: Greenwood Press, 1991).

PIETERS, D., *Introduction to the Social Security Law of the Member States of the European Community* (Brussels: Bruylant, 1990).

PLENDER, R., *International Migration Law*, rev. 2nd edn. (Dordrecht: Martinus Nijhoff, 1988).

—— *Basic Documents on International Migration Law* (Dordrecht: Martinus Nijhoff, 1988).

POWER, J., *Western Europe's Migrant Workers*, Minority Rights Group Report No. 28, rev'd edn. (London: Minority Rights Group, 1978).

RICCA, S., *International Migration in Africa: Legal and Administrative Aspects* (Geneva: International Labour Office, 1989).

ROBERTSON, A. H. and MERRILLS, J. G., *Human Rights in Europe—A Study of the European Convention on Human Rights* (Manchester: Manchester University Press, 1993).

ROGERS, R., (ed.), *Guests Come to Stay: The Effects of European Labour Migration on Sending and Receiving Countries* (Boulder, Colorado: Westview Press, 1985).

ROSAS, A. and ANTOLA, E., (eds.), *A Citizen's Europe: In Search of a New Order* (London: SAGE, 1995).

RUSSELL, S. S. and TEITELBAUM, M. S., *International Migration and International Trade* (World Bank Discussion Papers No. 160) (Washington, D.C.: The International Bank for Reconstruction and Development (World Bank), 1992).

SALT, J., SINGLETON, A., and HOGARTH, J., *Europe's International Migrants* (London: HMSO, 1994).

SANDEL, M., *Liberalism and the Limits of Justice* (Cambridge: Cambridge University Press, 1982).

SEGAL, A., *An Atlas of International Migration* (London: Hans Zell, 1993).

SERMET, L., *The European Convention on Human Rights and Property Rights*, Human Rights Files No. 11 (Strasbourg: Council of Europe Press, 1992).

SCHERMERS, H. G., *et al.*, (eds.), *Free Movement of Persons in Europe: Legal Problems and Experiences* (Dordrecht: Martinus Nijhoff, 1993).

SCHUCK, P. H. and SMITH, R. M., *Citizenship Without Consent: Illegal Aliens in the American Polity* (New Haven: Yale University Press, 1985).

SOYSAL, Y. N., *Limits of Citizenship. Migrants and Postnational Membership in Europe* (Chicago: Chicago University Press, 1994).

STALKER, P., *The Work of Strangers: A Survey of International Labour Migration* (Geneva: International Labour Office, 1994).

THOMAS, E.-J., (ed.), *Immigrant Workers in Europe: Their Legal Status, A Comparative Study* (Paris: UNESCO Press, 1982).

VALTICOS, N., *International Labour Law* (Deventer, The Netherlands: Kluwer, 1979).

VAN DIJK, P. and VAN HOOF, G. J. H., *Theory and Practice of the European Convention on Human Rights*, 2nd edn. (Deventer: Kluwer, 1990).

WALZER, M., *Spheres of Justice: A Defense of Pluralism and Equality* (New York: Basic Books, 1983).

WATSON, P., *Social Security Law of the European Communities* (London: Mansell, 1980).

WRENCH, J. and SOLOMOS, J., (eds.), *Racism and Migration in Western Europe* (Berg: Oxford, 1993).

WYATT, D. and DASHWOOD, A., *European Community Law*, 3rd edn. (London: Sweet & Maxwell, 1993).

ARTICLES

ACHERMANN, A., 'Asylum and Immigration Policies: From Cooperation to Harmonization' in R. Bieber and J. Monar, (eds.), *Justice and Home Affairs in the European Union* (Brussels: European Interuniversity Press, 1995) 127.

ADEPOJU, A., 'Illegals and Expulsion in Africa: The Nigerian Experience' (1984) 18 IMR 426.

ALEXANDER, W., 'Free Movement of Non-EC Nationals. A Review of the Case-Law of the Court of Justice' (1992) 3 EJIL 53.

ALLEWELDT, R., 'Protection Against Expulsion Under Article 3 of the European Convention on Human Rights' (1993) 4 EJIL 360.

ALSTON, P., 'The Committee on Economic, Social and Cultural Rights' in P. Alston, (ed.), *The United Nations and Human Rights: A Critical Appraisal* (Oxford: Clarendon Press, 1992) 473.

ANDERSEN, N. O., 'Free Movement of Labour within the Nordic Countries and within the European Communities' (1988) 57 *Nordic J. of Int'l L.* 384.

ANDERSEN, U., 'Consultative Institutions for Migrant Workers' in Z. Layton-Henry, (ed.), *The Political Rights of Migrant Workers in Western Europe* (London: SAGE, 1990) 113.

ANSAY, T., 'Legal Problems of Migrant Workers' (1977) *Recueil des Cours* (Académie de Droit International, The Hague) 1.

—— 'The New UN Convention in Light of the German and Turkish Experience' (1991) 25 IMR 831.

APPLEYARD, R., 'Migration and Development: Myths and Reality' (1989) 23 IMR 486.

—— 'Migration and Development: A Critical Relationship' (1992) 1 *Asian and Pacific Migration Journal* 1.

—— 'International Migration and Development—An Unresolved Relationship' (1992) 30 IM (Special Issue on Migration and Development) 251.

AUKERMAN, M. J., 'Discrimination in Germany: A Call for Minority Rights' (1995) 13 NQHR 237.

BARSH, R. L., 'The Right to Development as a Human Right: Results of the Global Consultation' (1991) 13 HRQ 322.
BARTSCH, H.-J., 'Council of Europe—Legal Co-operation in 1992' (1992) 12 YEL 675.
BAUBOCK, R., 'Austria' in S. Ardittis, (ed.), *The Politics of East–West Migration* (New York: St. Martin's Press, 1994) 155.
BAYEFSKY, A. F., 'The Principle of Equality or Non-Discrimination in International Law' (1990) 11 HRLJ 1.
BEHZADI, S., 'Hallmarks of Citizenship' in Gardner, J. P., (ed.), *Hallmarks of Citizenship* (London: The British Institute of International and Comparative Law, 1995) 26.
BERCUSSON, B., 'The European Community's Charter of Fundamental Social Rights of Workers' (1990) 53 MLR 624.
BERNHARDT, R., 'Reform of the Control Machinery under the European Convention on Human Rights: Protocol No. 11' (1995) 89 AJIL 145.
BETTEN, L., 'European Social Charter' (1988) 6 NQHR 69.
—— 'The Protocol to the European Social Charter: More Rights; A Better Impact?' (1988) 6 NQHR 9.
—— 'Towards a Community Charter of Fundamental Social Rights' (1989) 7 NQHR 77.
—— 'Immigration Policies and the Labour Market in The Netherlands' (1992) 8 IJCLLIR 140.
—— 'At its 75th Anniversary, the International Labour Organization Prepares Itself for an Active Future' (1994) 12 NQHR 425.
—— 'Committee of Ministers of the Council of Europe—Call for Contracting States to Account for Violations of the European Social Charter' (1994) 10 IJCLLIR 147.
BIAGI, M., 'Non-EEC Nationals and the Italian Labour Market: The Institutional Framework' (1992) 8 IJCLLIR 154.
BLOT, D., 'Issues Concerning the Education of Immigrants' Children' in OECD, *The Changing Course of International Migration* (Paris: OECD, 1993) 243.
BOELES, P., 'Schengen and the Rule of Law' in H. Meijers, *et al.*, (eds.), *Schengen: Internationalisation of Central Chapters of the Law on Aliens, Refugees, Privacy, Security and the Police*, 2nd rev. edn. (Leiden: Stichting NJCM—Boekerij, 1992) 135.
—— and KUIJER, A., 'Harmonization of Family Reunification' in H. Meijers, *et al.*, (eds.), *A New Immigration Law for Europe? The 1992 London and 1993 Copenhagen Rules on Immigration* (Utrecht: Dutch Centre for Immigrants, 1993) 25.
BÖHNING, W. R., 'International Migration in Western Europe: Reflections on the Past Five Years' (1979) 118 ILR 401.
—— *Studies in International Labour Migration* (London: ILO (published by Macmillan Press), 1984) Ch. 1, 'International Migration and the International Economic Order' 3.
—— *Studies in International Labour Migration* (London: ILO (published by Macmillan Press), 1984) Ch. 10, 'International Contract Migration in the Light of ILO Instruments' 233.
—— 'Basic Rights of "Temporary" Migrant Workers: Law vs. Power' in L. F. Tomasi, (ed.), *In Defense of the Alien, Vol. VIII, Immigration Enforcement, Employment Policy, Migrant Rights and Refugee Movements* (Proceedings of the 1985 Annual National Legal Conference on Immigration and Refugee Policy) (New York: Center for Migration Studies, 1986) 99.
—— 'The Protection of Migrant Workers and International Labour Standards' (1988) 26 IMR 133.

—— 'Integration and Immigration Pressures in Western Europe' (1991) 130 ILR 445.
—— 'The ILO and the New UN Convention on Migrant Workers: The Past and Future' (1991) 25 IMR 698.
—— and SCHLOETER-PAREDES, M., 'Introduction' in W. R. Böhning and M. Schloeter-Paredes, (eds.), *Aid in Place of Migration?: Selected Contributions to an ILO-UNHCR Meeting*, A World Employment Programme (WEP) Study (Geneva: International Labour Office, 1994) 1.
—— and WERQUIN, J., 'Some Economic, Social and Human Rights Considerations concerning the Future Status of Third-Country Nationals in the Single European Market', WEP Working Paper (International Labour Office: Geneva, 1990).
BOLTEN, J. J., 'From Schengen to Dublin: The New Frontiers of Refugee Law' in H. Meijers, *et al.*, (eds.), *Schengen: Internationalisation of Central Chapters of the Law on Aliens, Refugees, Privacy, Security and the Police*, 2nd rev. edn. (Leiden: Stichting NJCM—Boekerij, 1992) 8.
BONDI, A., 'The Reform of Italian Nationality Law' (1995) 9 INLP 89.
BOOTHMAN, C. and NIESSEN, J., 'The European Union and the Starting Line Proposal' in J. Cator and J. Niessen, (eds.), *The Use of International Conventions to Protect the Rights of Migrants and Ethnic Minorities* (Strasbourg, 1994).
BORCHARD, E., 'The "Minimum Standard" of the Treatment of Aliens' (1940) 38 *Mich. L. Rev.* 445.
BORGERUD, I., 'Application of the Right of Free Movement for Workers under the European Economic Area Agreement' in J. Kenner, (ed.), *Trends in European Social Policy: Essays in Memory of Malcolm Mead* (Aldershot: Dartmouth, 1995) 189.
BOSNIAK, L. S., 'Exclusion and Membership: The Dual Identity of the Undocumented Worker under United States Law' (1988) *Wisconsin L. Rev.* 955.
—— 'Human Rights, State Sovereignty and the Protection of Undocumented Migrants Under the International Migrant Workers Convention' (1991) 25 IMR 737.
BOUDAHRAIN, A., 'The New International Convention: A Moroccan Perspective' (1991) 25 IMR 866.
BURROWS, N., 'The Rights of Turkish Workers in the Member States' (1994) 19 *EL Rev.* 305.
CAMPANI, G., 'Immigration and Racism in Southern Europe: The Italian Case' (1993) 16 *Ethnic and Racial Studies* 507.
CASTLES, S., 'The Guest-Worker in Western Europe—An Obituary' (1986) 20 IMR 761.
CHESNAIS, J.-C., 'By Way of Introduction' in Council of Europe, *People on the Move. New Migration Flows in Europe* (Strasbourg: Council of Europe, 1992) 13.
CHOLEWINSKI, R., 'The Racial Discrimination Convention and the Protection of Cultural and Linguistic Ethnic Minorities' (1991) *Revue de Droit International* 167.
—— 'The Protection of the Right of Economic Migrants to Family Reunion in Europe' (1994) 43 ICLQ 568.
—— 'Strasbourg's "Hidden Agenda"?: The Protection of Second-Generation Migrants from Expulsion under Article 8 of the European Convention of Human Rights' (1994) 12 NQHR 287.
—— 'The Rights of Non-EC Immigrant Workers and Their Families in European Community Countries of Employment: A Case for Integration' in J. Dine and R. Watt, (eds.), *Discrimination Law: Concepts, Limitations and Justifications* (London: Longman, 1996) 134.
CISSÉ, M., 'The "Right to Live" and the Protection of Migrant Workers at the International

Level' in D. Prémont, (ed.), *Essays on the Concept of A 'Right to Live' in Memory of Yougindra Khushalani* (Bruylant: Brussels, 1988) 133.

CLAPHAM, A., 'The Role of the European Community' (1991) 1 AEHRYB [*Perspectives of an All-European System of Human Rights Protection—The Role of the Council of Europe, the CSCE, and the European Communities—Proceedings of the Poznan Conference* (Engel: Kehl am Rhein, 1991)] 63.

CLAYDON, J., 'International Protection of the Welfare of Migrant Workers' in R. S. J. Macdonald, D. M. Johnston and G. L. Morris, (eds.), *The International Law and Policy of Human Welfare* (Alphen aan den Rijn, The Netherlands: Sijthoff & Noordhoff, 1978) 347.

CLOSA, C., 'Citizenship of the Union and Nationality of Member States' (1995) 32 *CML Rev.* 487.

CREMONA, M., 'Citizens of Third Countries: Movement and Employment of Migrant Workers within the European Union' (1995) LIEI No. 2, 87.

CURTIN, D. and GEURTS, M., 'Race Discrimination and the European Union Anno 1996: From Rhetoric to Legal Remedy?' (1996) 14 NQHR 147.

CURTIN, D. and MEIJERS, H., 'The Principle of Open Government in Schengen and the European Union: Democratic Retrogression?' (1995) 32 *CML Rev.* 391.

DANKWA, E. V. O., 'Working Paper on Article 2(3) of the International Covenant on Economic, Social and Cultural Rights' (1987) 9 HRQ 230.

DASHWOOD, A., 'The Institutions of the Communities and of the Union' in D. Wyatt and A. Dashwood, *European Community Law* (London: Sweet & Maxwell, 1993) 19.

DE JONG, C., 'Towards a European Immigration Policy under the Treaty on European Union' in G. D. Korella and P. M. Twomey, (eds.), *Towards a European Immigration Policy* (Brussels: European Interuniversity Press, 1995) 45.

DE LOBKOWICZ, W., 'Intergovernmental Cooperation in the Field of Migration—From the Single European Act to Maastricht' in J. Monar and R. Morgan, (eds.), *The Third Pillar of the European Union* (Brussels: European Interuniversity Press, 1994) 99.

DE RHAM, G., 'Naturalisation: The Politics of Citizenship Acquisition' in Z. Layton-Henry, (ed.), *The Political Rights of Migrant Workers in Western Europe* (London: SAGE, 1990) 158.

DE VALDERRAMA, C. B. F., (Research Note), 'The New Hosts: The Case of Spain' (1993) 27 IMR 169.

D'OLIVEIRA, H. U. J., 'Expanding External and Shrinking Internal Borders: Europe's Defence Mechanisms in the Areas of Free Movement, Immigration and Asylum' in D. O'Keeffe and P. M. Twomey, (eds.), *Legal Issues of the Maastricht Treaty* (London: Wiley Chancery Law, 1994) 261.

—— 'Union Citizenship: Pie in the Sky?' in A. Rosas and E. Antola, (eds.), *A Citizen's Europe: In Search of a New Order* (London: SAGE, 1995) 58.

DRZEMCZEWSKI, A., 'The Position of Aliens in Relation to the European Convention on Human Rights: A General Survey' in Council of Europe, Directorate of Human Rights, *Human Rights of Aliens in Europe*, Proceedings of the Colloquy on Human Rights of Aliens in Europe, Funchal, Madeira, Portugal, 17–19 Oct. 1983 (Dordrecht: Martinus Nijhoff, 1985) 349.

—— and MEYER-LADEWIG, J., 'Principal Characteristics of the New ECHR Control Mechanism, as Established by Protocol No. 11, signed on 11 May 1994' (1994) 15 HRLJ 81.

EATON, M., 'Foreign Residents and Illegal Immigrants: *os Negros em Portugal*' (1993) 16 *Ethnic and Racial Studies* 536.

EGGERS, A., (Note, Recent Developments in Human Rights), 'The International Convention on the Protection of the Rights of All Migrant Workers and Members of Their Families' (1991) 34 *German YBIL* 429.

EICHENHOFER, E., 'Coordination of Social Security and Equal Treatment of Men and Women in Employment: Recent Social Security Judgments of the Court of Justice' (1993) 30 *CML Rev.* 1021.

EIDE, A., 'Economic, Social and Cultural Rights as Human Rights' in A. Eide, C. Krause, and A. Rosas, (eds.), *Economic, Social and Cultural Rights: A Textbook* (Dordrecht: Martinus Nijhoff, 1995) 21.

ESSER, H. and KORTE, H., 'Federal Republic of Germany' in T. Hammar, (ed.), *European Immigration Policy: A Comparative Study* (Cambridge: Cambridge University Press, 1985) 165.

EVANS, A., 'Nationality Law and European Integration' (1991) 16 *EL Rev.* 190.

—— 'Third Country Nationals and the Treaty on European Union' (1994) 5 EJIL 199.

EVANS, M., 'The European Social Charter' in J. Bridge, D. Lasok, and R. D. Plender, (eds.), *Fundamental Rights: A Volume of Essays to Commemorate the 50th Anniversary of the Founding of the Law School in Exeter, 1923–1973* (London: Sweet & Maxwell, 1973) 278.

FERNHOUT, R., '"The United States of Europe have Commenced", but for whom?' (1993) 11 NQHR 249.

FOX, C., 'European Community Migrant Workers: The Right to Remain and Look for Work' [1992] *J. Social Welfare and Family L.* 85.

FROWEIN, J. A., 'Concluding Report to the Heidelberg Colloquium on the Legal Position of Aliens in National and International Law' in Max Planck Institute of Comparative Law, (ed.), *The Legal Position of Aliens in National and International Law*, vol. 2 (Berlin: Springer Verlag, 1987) 2081.

GEDDES, A., 'Immigrant and Ethnic Minorities and the EU's "Democratic Deficit"' (1995) 33 JCMS 197.

GHOSH, B., 'Trends in World Migration: the European Perspective' (Sept.–Oct. 1991) *The Courier* (African-Caribbean-Pacific (ACP)–European Community) 46.

—— 'The Future of East–West Migration' in S. Ardittis, (ed.), *The Politics of East–West Migration* (New York: St. Martin's Press, 1994) 217.

GINSBURG, G., 'The Case of Vietnamese Gastarbeiters in the Soviet Union' (1989) 35 *Osteuropa Recht* 166.

GOLINI, A., GERANO, G. and HEINS, F., 'South–North Migration with Special Reference to Europe' (1991) 29 IM 253.

GOLSONG, H., 'La convention européenne relative au statut juridique du travailleur migrant' in Société française pour le droit international, (ed.), *Les travailleurs étrangers et le droit international* (Paris: Éditions A. Pedone, 1978) 226.

GOODWIN-GILL, G. S., 'Immigration, Nationality and the Standards of International Law' in A. Dummett, (ed.), *Towards a Just Immigration Policy* (London: Cobden Trust, 1986) 3.

—— 'International Law and Human Rights: Trends Concerning International Migrants and Refugees' (1989) 23 IMR 526.

—— JENNY, R. K. and PERRUCHOUD, R., 'Basic Humanitarian Principles Applicable to Non-Nationals' (1985) 19 IMR 556.

GORDEN, M. E., 'Haitian Forced Labor in the Dominican Republic' (1994) 15 *Comp. Lab. L.J.* 206.

GRECIC, V., 'East–West Migration and its Possible Influence on South–North Migration' (1991) 29 IM 241.

GREENWOOD, C., 'Nationality and the Limits of the Free Movement of Persons in Community Law' (1987) 7 YBEL 185.

GROENENDIJK, C. A., 'The Competence of the EC Court of Justice' in H. Meijers, *et al.*, (eds.), *A New Immigration Law for Europe? The 1992 London and 1993 Copenhagen Rules on Immigration* (Utrecht: Dutch Centre for Immigrants, 1993) 45, 51.

GROENENDIJK, K., 'Migration Policy in Europe and the Role of the CSCE' in A. Bloed and W. de Jonge, (eds.), *Legal Aspects of a New European Infrastructure* (Utrecht: Europa Instituut and the Netherlands Helsinki Committee, 1992) 119.

GUILD, E., 'Protecting Migrants' Rights and Community Law: the Co-operation Agreements with Algeria, Morocco and Tunisia' (1993) 7 INLP 15.

GUNATILLEKE, G., 'Seminar Report: International Response to Trafficking in Migrants and the Safeguarding of Migrant Rights (Eleventh IOM Seminar on Migration, Geneva, 26–28 Oct. 1994)' (1994) 32 IM 593.

GUNDARA, J. S., 'Racism and the National Question in Western Europe' (1988) NQHR (SIM Newsletter Special No. 7—New Expressions of Racism—Growing Areas of Conflict in Europe, Seminar, Amsterdam City Hall, 19–21 Oct. 1987) 30.

HAILBRONNER, K., 'Migration Law and Policy within the Third Pillar of the Union Treaty' in R. Bieber and J. Monar, (eds.), *Justice and Home Affairs in the European Union* (Brussels: European Interuniversity Press, 1995) 95.

—— 'Third Country Nationals and EC Law' in A. Rosas and E. Antola, (eds.), *A Citizen's Europe: In Search of a New Order* (London: SAGE, 1995) 182.

—— and POLAKIEWICZ, J., 'Non-EC Nationals in the European Community: The Need for a Coordinated Approach' (1992) 3 *Duke J. Int'l & Comp. L.* 49.

HAMMAR, T., 'Introduction' in T. Hammar, (ed.), *European Immigration Policy: A Comparative Study* (Cambridge: Cambridge University Press, 1985) 1.

—— 'Economy and Ideology' in T. Hammar, (ed.), *European Immigration Policy: A Comparative Study* (Cambridge: Cambridge University Press, 1985) 239.

—— 'Immigration Regulation and Aliens Control' in T. Hammar, (ed.), *European Immigration Policy: A Comparative Study* (Cambridge: Cambridge University Press, 1985) 249.

—— 'Immigrant Policy' in T. Hammar, (ed.), *European Immigration Policy: A Comparative Study* (Cambridge: Cambridge University Press, 1985) 263.

—— 'The Policymaking Process' in T. Hammar, (ed.), *European Immigration Policy: A Comparative Study* (Cambridge: Cambridge University Press, 1985) 277.

—— 'Towards Convergence' in T. Hammar, (ed.), *European Immigration Policy: A Comparative Study* (Cambridge: Cambridge University Press, 1985) 292.

—— 'The Civil Rights of Aliens' in Z. Layton-Henry, (ed.), *The Political Rights of Migrant Workers in Western Europe* (London: SAGE, 1990) 74.

—— 'Civil Rights and Political Participation of Immigrants' in OECD, *The Changing Course of International Migration* (Paris: OECD, 1993) 251.

—— and LITHMAN, Y. G., 'The Integration of Migrants: Experiences, Concepts and Policies' in OECD, *The Future of Migration* (Paris: OECD, 1987) 234.

HAMMOND, P. R., 'International Agreements—New Convention aimed at improving

Condition of Migrant Workers in Council of Europe Nations' (1977–78) 13 *Texas Int'l L.J.* 353.

HANDOLL, J., 'Article 48(4) EEC and Non-national Access to Public Employment' (1988) 13 *EL Rev.* 223.

HARRIS, D., 'A Fresh Impetus for the European Social Charter' (1992) 41 ICLQ 659.

HARTLEY, T. C., 'Constitutional and Institutional Aspects of the Maastricht Agreement' (1993) 42 ICLQ 213.

HASENAU, M., 'Setting Norms in the United Nations System: The Draft Convention on the Protection of the Rights of All Migrant Workers and their Families in Relation to ILO in Standards on Migrant Workers' (1990) 28 IMR 133.

—— 'ILO Standards on Migrant Workers: The Fundamentals of the UN Convention and Their Genesis' (1991) 25 IMR 687.

HELTON, A. C., 'The New Convention from the Perspective of a Country of Employment: The U.S. Case' (1991) 25 IMR 848.

HERDEGEN, M., 'Political Rights and other Aspects of Resident Status' in Max Planck Institute of Comparative Law, (ed.), *The Legal Position of Aliens in National and International Law*, vol. 2 (Berlin: Springer Verlag, 1987) 2003.

HODGES-AEBERHARD, J., 'The Right to Organise in Article 2 of Convention No. 87—What is Meant by Workers "Without Distinction Whatsoever"?' (1989) 128 ILR 177.

HOFFMANN-NOWOTNY, H.-J., 'Switzerland' in T. Hammar, (ed.), *European Immigration Policy: A Comparative Study* (Cambridge: Cambridge University Press, 1985) 206.

HÖFLER, L., 'Migration Programmes of Germany Aimed at the Training and Employment of Workers from Developing Countries or Countries of Central and Eastern Europe' (1992) 30 IM (Special Issue on Migration and Development) 335.

HOHNERLEIN, E.-M., 'Federal Republic of Germany' in A. Ph. C. M. Jaspers and L. Betten, (eds.), *25 Years of the European Social Charter* (Deventer: Kluwer, 1988) 105.

HONDIUS, F. W., 'Legal Aspects of the Movement of Persons in Greater Europe' (1990) 10 YEL 291.

HOOGENBOOM, T., 'The Position of Those who are not Nationals of a Community Member State' in A. Cassesse, A. Clapham, and J. Weiler, (eds.), *Human Rights and the European Community: Methods of Protection* (Baden-Baden: Verlagsgesellschaft, 1991) 351.

—— 'Free Movement of Non-EC Nationals, Schengen and Beyond' in H. Meijers, *et al.*, (eds.), *Schengen: Internationalisation of Central Chapters of the Law on Aliens, Refugees, Privacy, Security and the Police*, 2nd rev. edn. (Leiden: Stichting NJCM—Boekerij, 1992) 74.

—— 'Integration into Society and Free Movement of Non-EC Nationals' (1992) 3 EJIL 36.

HUJANEN, T., 'The Role of Information in the Realization of the Human Rights of Migrant Workers' (Conference Report of the Final Conference of the Joint Study held at Crêt-Bérard, Lausanne, Switzerland, 23–27 Oct. 1988) (1989) 23 IMR 105.

HUNE, S., 'Drafting an International Convention on the Protection of the Rights of All Migrant Workers and their Families' (1985) 19 IMR 570.

—— 'Drafting an International Convention on the Protection of the Rights of All Migrant Workers and their Families' (1987) 21 IMR 123.

—— 'Migrant Women in the Context of the International Convention on the Protection of the Rights of All Migrant Workers and Members of Their Families' (1991) 25 IMR 800.

—— 'Equality of Treatment and the International Convention on the Protection of the Rights of All Migrant Workers and Members of Their Families' in J. Cator and J. Niessen, (eds.), *The Use of International Conventions to Protect the Rights of Migrants and Ethnic Minorities* (Strasbourg, 1994).

HUNE, S. and NIESSEN, J., 'The First UN Convention on Migrant Workers' (1991) 9 NQHR 131.

—— and —— 'Ratifying the UN Migrant Workers Convention: Current Difficulties and Prospects' (1994) 12 NQHR 393.

'Introduction' in D. G. Papademetriou and P. L. Martin, (eds.), *The Unsettled Relationship: Labor Migration and Economic Development* (New York: Greenwood Press, 1991) ix.

ISGRO, F., 'Italy Enacts Law to Protect Basic Human Rights of Foreign Workers' (1986) 1 *Georgetown Immigr. L.J.* 693.

JAGERSKIOLD, S., 'Freedom of Movement' in L. Henkin, (ed.), *The International Bill of Rights: The Covenant on Civil and Political Rights* (New York: Columbia University Press, 1981) 166.

JENKS, C. W., 'Human Rights, Social Justice and Peace—The Broader Significance of the ILO Experience' in A. Eide and A. Schou, (eds.), *International Protection of Human Rights*, Proceedings of the 7th Nobel Symposium, Oslo, 25–27 Sept. 1967 (Stockholm: Almquist & Wiksell, 1968) 227.

JOHNSON, E. and O'KEEFFE, D., 'From Discrimination to Obstacles to Free Movement: Recent Developments concerning the Free Movement of Workers 1989–1994' (1994) 31 *CML Rev.* 1313.

KAHN-FREUND, O., 'Labour Relations and International Standards—Some Reflections on the European Social Charter' in *Miscellanea W.J. Ganschof van der Meersch*, vol. 1 (Brussels: Emile, 1972) 131.

—— 'The European Social Charter' in F. G. Jacobs, (ed.), *European Law and the Individual* (Amsterdam: North-Holland, 1976) 181.

KAPLANSKY, K., 'The International Labour Organization' in R. Matthews and C. Pratt, (eds.), *Human Rights in Canadian Foreign Policy* (Montréal and Kingston: McGill-Queen's University Press, 1988) 115.

KELLERSON, H., 'International Labour Conventions and Recommendations on Migrant Workers' in A. Dummett, (ed.), *Towards a Just Immigration Policy* (London: Cobden Trust, 1986) 33.

KITAMURA, Y., 'Recent Developments in Japanese Immigration Policy and the United Nations Convention on Migrant Workers' (1993) 27 *UBC L. Rev.* 113.

KLERK, Y., 'Working Paper on Article 2(2) and Article 3 of the International Covenant on Economic, Social and Cultural Rights' (1987) 9 HRQ 250.

KOJANEC, G., 'The UN Convention and the European Instruments for the Protection of Migrants' (1991) 25 IMR 818.

—— 'The European Convention on Reduction of Cases of Nationality and the Second Amending Protocol' in J. Cator and J. Niessen, (eds.), *The Use of International Conventions to Protect the Rights of Migrants and Ethnic Minorities* (Strasbourg, 1994).

KORCELLI, P., 'International Migrations in Europe: Polish Perspectives for the 1990s' (1992) 26 IMR 292.

KRANE, R. E., 'Introduction and Overview' in R. E. Krane, (ed.), *International Labor Migration in Europe* (New York: Praeger, 1979) 1.

KRAUSE, C., 'The Right to Property' in A. Eide, C. Krause, and A. Rosas, (eds.), *Economic, Social and Cultural Rights: A Textbook* (Dordrecht: Martinus Nijhoff, 1995) 143.

KRITZ, M. M. and ZLOTNIK, H., 'Global Interactions: Migration Systems, Processes, and Policies' in M. M. Kritz, L. L. Lim, and H. Zlotnik, (eds.), *International Migration Systems: A Global Approach* (Oxford: Clarendon Press, 1992) 1.

KRUIJTBOSCH, E. D. J., 'Benelux Experiences in the Abolition of Border Controls' in H. G. Schermers, *et al.*, (eds.), *Free Movement of Persons in Europe: Legal Problems and Experiences* (Dordrecht: Martinus Nijhoff, 1993) 31.

KUDAT, A. and SABUNCOUGLU, M., 'The Changing Composition of Europe's Guestworker Population' (1980) 103 *Monthly Labour Review* 10.

KÜHNER, R., 'Participation in Economic Life' in Max Planck Institute of Comparative Law, (ed.), *The Legal Position of Aliens in National and International Law*, vol. 2 (Berlin: Springer Verlag, 1987) 1973.

KURFIS, M., 'The Constitutionality of California's Proposition 187: An Equal Protection Analysis (1995) 32 *California Western L. Rev.* 129.

LASKE, C., 'The Impact of the Single European Market on Social Protection for Migrant Workers' (1993) 30 *CML Rev.* 515.

LAYTON-HENRY, Z., 'Immigrant Associations' in Z. Layton-Henry, (ed.), *The Political Rights of Migrant Workers in Western Europe* (London: SAGE, 1990) 94.

LENAERTS, K., 'Education in European Community Law after "Maastricht"' (1994) 31 *CML Rev.* 7.

LEARY, V. A., 'Migrant Workers and Human Rights' in *Materials for the 18th Study Session of the International Institute of Human Rights*, Strasbourg, France, July 1987 (Strasbourg: International Institute of Human Rights, 1987).

—— 'Lessons from the Experience of the International Labour Organization' in P. Alston, (ed.), *The United Nations and Human Rights: A Critical Appraisal* (Oxford: Clarendon Press, 1992) 580.

LEBLANC, L., 'The Economic, Social and Cultural Rights Protocol to the American Convention and its Background' (1992) 10 NQHR 130.

LEUPRECHT, P., 'Reflections on Human Rights' (Lecture given at the University of Gdansk, Poland on April 25, 1988) (1988) 9 HRLJ 163.

LEVY-PUECH, D., 'France' in A. Ph. C. M. Jaspers and L. Betten, (eds.), *25 Years of the European Social Charter* (Deventer: Kluwer, 1988) 145.

—— 'Espagne' in A. Ph. C. M. Jaspers and L. Betten, (eds.), *25 Years of the European Social Charter* (Deventer: Kluwer, 1988) 171.

LILLICH, R. B., 'The Current Status of the Law of State Responsibility for Injuries to Aliens' in J. F. Murphey, *et al.*, 'State Responsibility, Self Help and International Law' (1979) 73 *Am. Soc. Int'l L. Prcdgs* 242.

LÖNNROTH, J., 'The International Convention on the Rights of All Migrant Workers and Members of their Families in the Context of International Migration Policies: An Analysis of Ten Years of Negotiation' (1991) 25 IMR 710.

LUNDBERG, E., 'Political Freedoms in the European Union' in A. Rosas and E. Antola, (eds.), *A Citizen's Europe: In Search of a New Order* (London: SAGE, 1995) 113.

MCCARTHY, J. and HARDY, S., 'Some Implications of European Free Movement Rights on the Acquisition of British Nationality' (1996) 10 INLP 16.

MCDOUGAL, M. S., LASSWELL, H. D., and CHEN, L., 'Protection of Aliens from Discrimination and World Public Order: Responsibility of States Conjoined with Human Rights' (1976) AJIL 432.

McKean, W., *Equality and Discrimination under International Law* (Oxford: Clarendon Press, 1983) Ch. XI, 'Equality in the Treatment of Aliens' 194.

Mahalic, D. and Mahalic, J. G., 'The Limitation Provisions of the International Convention on the Elimination of All Forms of Racial Discrimination' (1987) 9 HRQ 74.

Mahmood, S., 'The Schengen Information System: An Inequitable Data Protection Regime' (1995) 7 IJRL 179.

Maillat, D., 'European Receiving Countries' in OECD, *The Future of Migration* (Paris: OECD, 1987) 38.

Marias, E. A., 'Mechanisms of Protection of Union Citizens' Rights' in A. Rosas and E. Antola, (eds.), *A Citizen's Europe: In Search of a New Order* (London: SAGE, 1995) 207.

Marie, J.-B., 'International Instruments Relating to Human Rights. Classification and Status of Ratifications as of 1 January 1996' (1996) 17 HRLJ 61.

Martin, P., 'Labor Migration: Theory and Reality' in D. G. Papademetriou and P. L. Martin, (eds.), *The Unsettled Relationship: Labor Migration and Economic Development* (New York: Greenwood Press, 1991) 27.

—— 'Migration and Development: Conference Report' (Tenth IOM Seminar on Migration, Geneva, 15–17 Sept. 1992) (1992) 30 IM 457.

—— 'Epilogue. Reducing Emigration Pressure: What Role can Foreign Aid Play?' in W. R. Böhning and M. Schloeter-Paredes, (eds.), *Aid in Place of Migration?: Selected Contributions to an ILO-UNHCR Meeting*, A WEP Study (Geneva: International Labour Office, 1994) 241.

—— 'Proposition 187 in California' (1995) 29 IMR 255.

Martin, P. L. and Miller, M. J., 'Guestworkers: Lessons from Western Europe' (1980) 33 *Industr. & Lab. Rel. Rev.* 315.

Meijers, H., 'Schengen: Introduction' in H. Meijers, *et al.*, (eds.), *Schengen: Internationalisation of Central Chapters of the Law on Aliens, Refugees, Privacy, Security and the Police*, 2nd rev. edn. (Leiden: Stichting NJCM—Boekerij, 1992) 1.

Miller, M. J., 'Towards Understanding State Capacity to Prevent Unwanted Migration: Employer Sanctions Enforcement in France, 1975–1990' (1994) 17 *West European Politics* (Special Issue on The Politics of Immigration in Western Europe) 140.

Mohr, M., 'The Turin Protocol of 22 October 1991: A Major Contribution to Revitalizing the European Social Charter' (1992) 3 EJIL 362.

Mole, N., 'Freedom of Movement in a Wider Europe: A Comparison of International Instruments' (1991) 1 AEHRYB [*Perspectives of an All-European System of Human Rights Protection—The Role of the Council of Europe, the CSCE, and the European Communities—Proceedings of the Poznan Conference* (Engel: Kehl am Rhein, 1991)] 199.

Monar, J., 'The European Parliament and Immigration Policy: Its Positions and Possibilities of Control' in G. D. Korella and P.M. Twomey, (eds.), *Towards a European Immigration Policy* (Brussels: European Interuniversity Press, 1995) 123.

Müller-Graff, P.-C., 'The Legal Bases of the Third Pillar and its Position in the Framework of the Union Treaty' in J. Monar and R. Morgan, (eds.), *The Third Pillar of the European Union* (Brussels: European Interuniversity Press, 1994) 21.

Muus, P. J., 'Employment and Vocational Taining of Young Immigrants in the Netherlands, Western Germany and Belgium' in OECD, *The Changing Course of International Migration* (Paris: OECD, 1993) 199.

Nafziger, J. A. R. and Bartel, B. C., 'The Migrant Workers Convention: Its Place in Human Rights Law' (1991) 25 IMR 771.

NANDA, V. P., 'The Protection of the Rights of Migrant Workers: Unfinished Business' (1993) 2 *Asian and Pacific Migration Journal* 161.

NANZ, K.-P., 'The Harmonization of Asylum and Immigration Legislation within the Third Pillar of the Union Treaty—A Stocktaking' in J. Monar and R. Morgan, (eds.), *The Third Pillar of the European Union* (Brussels: European Interuniversity Press, 1994) 123.

—— 'The Schengen Agreement: Preparing the Free Movement of Persons in the European Union' in R. Bieber and J. Monar, (eds.), *Justice and Home Affairs in the European Union* (Brussels: European Interuniversity Press, 1995) 29.

NEUMAN, G. L., '"We are the People": Alien Suffrage in German and American Perspective' (1992) 13 *Mich. J. Int'l L.* 259.

NIELSEN, H. K., 'The Concept of Discrimination in ILO Convention No. 111' (1994) 43 ICLQ 827.

NIESSEN, J., 'The Conference on Security and Cooperation in Europe and other European Fora on Migration' (1994) 28 IMR 580.

—— 'Immigrants and Migrant Workers' in A. Eide, C. Krause, and A. Rosas, (eds.), *Economic, Social and Cultural Rights: A Textbook* (Dordrecht: Martinus Nijhoff, 1995) 323.

—— and DE LARY DE LATOUR, H., 'Equality of Treatment: The European Social Charter and the European Convention on the Legal Status of Migrant Workers' in J. Cator and J. Niessen, (eds.), *The Use of International Conventions to Protect the Rights of Migrants and Ethnic Minorities* (1994).

—— and TARAN, P. A., 'Using the New Migrant Workers' Rights Convention' (1991) 25 IMR 859.

NOWAK, M., 'The Right to Education' in A. Eide, C. Krause, and A. Rosas, (eds.), *Economic, Social and Cultural Rights: A Textbook* (Dordrecht: Martinus Nijhoff, 1995) 189.

OELLERS-FRAHM, K., 'The Contribution of the Council of Europe to the Legal Position of Aliens' in Max Planck Institute of Comparative Law, (ed.), *The Legal Position of Aliens in National and International Law*, vol. 2 (Berlin: Springer Verlag, 1987) 1725.

O'KEEFFE, D., 'The Schengen Convention: A Suitable Model for European Integration?' (1991) 11 YBEL 185.

—— 'The Free Movement of Persons and the Single Market' (1992) 17 *EL Rev.* 3.

—— 'Judicial Interpretation of the Public Service Exception to the Free Movement of Workers' in D. Curtin and D. O'Keeffe, (eds.), *Constitutional Adjudication in European Community and National Law* (Butterworths (Ireland), 1992) 89.

—— 'From Mastricht to the 1996 Intergovernmental Conference: The Challenges Facing the Union' (1994) LIEI No. 2, 135.

—— 'The New Draft External Frontiers Convention and the Draft Visa Regulation' in J. Monar and R. Morgan, (eds.), *The Third Pillar of the European Union* (Brussels: European Interuniversity Press, 1994) 135.

—— 'The Emergence of a European Immigration Policy' (1995) 20 *EL Rev.* 20.

—— 'Recasting the Third Pillar' (1995) 32 *CML Rev.* 893.

—— 'Reflections on a European Immigration Policy' in G. D. Korella and P. M. Twomey, (eds.), *Towards a European Immigration Policy* (Brussels: European Interuniversity Press, 1995) 19.

OKOLSKI, M., 'Poland' in S. Ardittis, (ed.), *The Politics of East–West Migration* (New York: St. Martin's Press, 1994) 51.

O'LEARY, S., 'Nationality Law and Community Citizenship: A Tale of Two Uneasy Bedfellows' (1992) 12 YEL 353.
OLIVER, P., 'Non-Community Nationals and the Treaty of Rome' (1985) 5 YBEL 57.
ÖZSUNAY, E., 'Report on the Participation of the Alien in Public Affairs (Political and Associative Life)' in Council of Europe, Directorate of Human Rights, *Human Rights of Aliens in Europe* (Dordrecht: Martinus Nijhoff, 1985) 195.
PAPADEMETRIOU, D. G., 'International Migration in North America and Western Europe: Trends and Consequences' in R. T. Appleyard, (ed.), *International Migration Today—Vol. 1: Trends and Prospects* (Paris; Nedlands, Western Australia, The Centre for Migration and Development Studies: UNESCO, 988) 311.
—— 'Confronting the Challenge of Transnational Migration: Domestic and International Responses' in OECD, *The Changing Course of International Migration* (Paris: OECD, 1993) 207.
—— and MARTIN, P. L., 'Labor Migration and Development: Research and Policy Issues' in D. G. Papademetriou and P. L. Martin, (eds.), *The Unsettled Relationship: Labor Migration and Economic Development* (New York: Greenwood Press, 1991) 3.
PARTSCH, K. J., 'Fundamental Principles of Human Rights: Self-Determination, Equality and Non-Discrimination' in K. Vasak and P. Alston, (eds.), *The International Dimension of Human Rights* (Westport, Connecticut: UNESCO, Greenwood Press, 1982) 61.
PAVLIK, Z. and MARESOVA, J., 'Former Czechoslovakia' in S. Ardittis, (ed.), *The Politics of East–West Migration* (New York: St. Martin's Press, 1994) 111.
PEERS, S., 'Towards Equality: Actual and Potential Rights of Third-Country Nationals in the European Union' (1996) 33 *CML Rev.* 7.
—— 'An Ever Closer Waiting Room?: The Case for Eastern European Accession to the European Economic Area' (1995) 32 *CML Rev.* 187.
—— 'The Queue for Accession Lengthens' (1995) 20 *EL Rev.* 323.
PENNA, L. R., 'Some Salient Human Rights in the UN Convention on Migrant Workers' (1993) 2 *Asian and Pacific Migration Journal* 179.
PENNINX, R., 'International Migration in Western Europe Since 1973: Developments, Mechanisms and Controls' (1986) 20 IMR 951.
PLENDER, R., 'Competence, European Community Law and Nationals of Non-Member States' (1990) 39 ICLQ 599.
RAMCHARAN, B. G., 'Equality and Nondiscrimination' in L. Henkin, (ed.), *The International Bill of Rights: The Covenant on Civil and Political Rights* (New York: Columbia University Press, 1981) 246.
RATH, J., 'Voting Rights' in Z. Layton-Henry, (ed.), *The Political Rights of Migrant Workers in Western Europe* (London: SAGE, 1990) 127.
RICH, R., 'The Right to Development: A Right of Peoples?' in J. Crawford, (ed.), *The Right of Peoples* (Oxford: Clarendon Press, 1988) 39.
ROGERS, R., 'Post-World War II European Labor Migration: An Introduction to the Issues' in R. Rogers, (ed.), *Guests Come to Stay: The Effects of European Labour Migration on Sending and Receiving Countries* (Boulder, Colorado: Westview Press, 1985) 1.
—— 'Western Europe in the 1980s: The End of Immigration?' in R. Rogers, (ed.), *Guests Come to Stay: The Effects of European Labour Migration on Sending and Receiving Countries* (Boulder, Colorado: Westview Press, 1985) 285.
ROSAS, A., 'Article 21' in A. Eide, *et al.*, (eds.), *The Universal Declaration of Human Rights: A Commentary* (Oslo: Scandinavian University Press, 1992) 299.

—— 'Nationality and Citizenship in a Changing European and World Order' in M. Suksi, (ed.), *Law under Exogenous Influences*, Publications of Turku Law School, Vol. 1, No. 1/1994 (Kirjapairo Grafia OY: Turku, 1994) 30.

—— 'Union Citizenship and National Elections' in A. Rosas and E. Antola, (eds.), *A Citizen's Europe: In Search of a New Order* (London: SAGE, 1995) 135.

ROSBERG, G. M., 'Aliens and Equal Protection: Why not the Right to Vote' (1977) 75 *Mich. L. Rev.* 1092.

RULE, E., 'Portuguese Nationality Law in Outline' (1996) 10 INLP 12.

RUSSO, F., 'Migrant Workers: Existing and Proposed International Action on their Rights' (1975) *The Review of the International Commission of Jurists* No. 15, 51.

RUSSELL, S. S., 'Migrant Remittances and Development' (1992) 30 IM (Special Issue on Migration and Development) 26.

SAKSON, A., 'Nowa Fala Migracji w Europie' (1995) *Przegląd Zachodni* (Western Review) No. 1, 75.

SCHERMERS, H., 'The European Court of Human Rights after the Merger' (1993) 18 *EL Rev.* 493.

SCHOKKENBROEK, J. G. C., 'The Results of the Ministerial Conference on the European Social Charter' (1992) 13 HRLJ 177.

SEGAL, A. and MARSTON, L., 'Maps and Keys—World Voluntary Migration 1500–1980' (1989) 27:1 *Migrationworld Magazine* 36.

SIMMONDS, K. R., 'The Concertation of Community Migration Policy' (1988) 25 *CML Rev.* 177.

SIMMONS, A., 'French Nationality Law' (1994) 8 INLP 13.

SIMON, G., 'Migration in Southern Europe: An Overview' in OECD, *The Future of Migration* (Paris: OECD, 1987) 258.

SITAROPOULOS, N., 'The New Legal Framework of Alien Immigration in Greece: A Draconian Contribution to Europe's Unification' (1992) 6 INLP 89.

SKELDON, R., 'International Migration Within and From the East and Southeast Asian Region: A Review Essay' (1992) 1 *Asian and Pacific Migration Journal* 19.

SKOGLY, S., 'Article 2' in A. Eide, *et al.*, (eds.), *The Universal Declaration of Human Rights: A Commentary* (Oslo: Scandinavian University Press, 1992) 57.

STAVENHAGEN, R., 'New Expressions of Racism in Europe' (1989) 70 International Foundation for Development Alternatives (IFDA) Dossier 47.

STEENBERGEN, J. D. M., 'Schengen and the Movement of Persons' in H. Meijers *et al.*, (eds.), *Schengen: Internationalisation of Central Chapters of the Law on Aliens, Refugees, Privacy, Security and the Police*, 2nd rev. edn. (Leiden: Stichting NJCM—Boekerij, 1992) 57.

STEIN T. and THOMSEN, S., 'The Status of the Member States' Nationals under the Law of the European Communities' in Max Planck Institute of Comparative Law, (ed.), *The Legal Position of Aliens in National and International Law*, vol. 2 (Berlin: Springer Verlag, 1987) 1775.

SWART, A. H. J., 'The Legal Status of Aliens: Clauses in Council of Europe Instruments Relating to the Rights of Aliens' (1980) *Netherlands YBIL* 3.

SZOKE, L., 'Hungarian Perspectives on Emigration and Immigration in the New European Architecture' (1992) 26 IMR 305.

TAPINOS, G. P., 'International Migration and Development' (1994) *Population Bulletin of the United Nations* No. 36, 1.

TARDOU, M., 'Migrant Workers' in R. Bernhadt, (ed.), *Encyclopaedia of Public International Law* (Amsterdam: North Holland, 1981) Instalment 8, 372.
THOMAS, E.-J., 'Summing-up and Points of Comparison' in E.-J. Thomas, (ed.), *Immigrant Workers in Europe: Their Legal Status, A Comparative Study* (Paris: UNESCO Press, 1982) 211.
—— 'Conclusion' in E.-J. Thomas, (ed.), *Immigrant Workers in Europe: Their Legal Status, A Comparative Study* (Paris: UNESCO Press, 1982) 239.
—— 'Migration in Europe' in A. Dummett, (ed.), *Towards a Just Immigration Policy* (London: Cobden Trust, 1986) 43.
THOMSEN, S., 'The Legal Position of the Spouse and Family Members' in Max Planck Institute of Comparative Law, (ed.), *The Legal Position of Aliens in National and International Law*, vol. 2 (Berlin: Springer Verlag, 1987) 1947.
TOMUSCHAT, C., 'Protection of Minorities under Article 27 of the International Covenant on Civil and Political Rights' in *Mosler Collection*, Völkerrecht als Rechtsordnung—International Gerichtsbarkeit-Menschenrechte; Festschrift für Hermann Mosler (Berlin: Springer Verlag, 1983) 949.
TOPOL, J., 'Slavery in a Newly Free State' (1990) 3 *Uncaptive Minds* 24.
TREBILCOCK, A., 'Migrant Workers: An Overview of International Labour Standards' in Max Planck Institute for Comparative Public Law and International Law, (ed.), *The Legal Position of Aliens in National and International Law* (Berlin: Springer Verlag, 1987) 1827.
VALTICOS, N., *International Labour Law* (Deventer: Kluwer, 1979) Ch. XIV, 'Foreign and Migrant Workers' 207.
—— 'The Role of the ILO: Present Action and Future Perspectives' in B. G. Ramcharan, (ed.), *Human Rights: Thirty Years after the Universal Declaration*, Commemorative Volume on the Occasion of the Thirtieth Anniversary of the Universal Declaration of Human Rights (The Hague: Martinus Nijhoff, 1979) 211.
—— 'The International Labour Organization' in K. Vasak, (ed.), *The International Dimensions of Human Rights*, vol. 1, revised and edited for the English edition by P. Alston (Westport, Connecticut: Greenwood Press, 1982) 363.
VANDAMME, F., 'The Revision of the European Social Charter' (1994) 133 ILR 635.
VIALET, J. C., 'The North American Free Trade Agreement and Immigration' (1993) 21 *Migrationworld Magazine* Nos. 2/3, 2.
VINCENZI, C., 'European Citizenship and Free Movement Rights in the United Kingdom' (1995) *Public Law* 259.
VRANKEN, J., 'Industrial Rights' in Z. Layton-Henry, (ed.), *The Political Rights of Migrant Workers in Western Europe* (London: SAGE, 1990) 47.
WATSON, P., 'The Community Social Charter' (1991) 28 *CML Rev.* 37.
—— 'Social Security for Migrants' in D. Wyatt and A. Dashwood, *European Community Law* (London: Sweet & Maxwell, 1993) 311.
—— 'Vocational Training' in D. Wyatt and A. Dashwood, *European Community Law* (London: Sweet & Maxwell, 1993) 640.
WEISS, M., 'Immigration Policy and the Labour Market in Germany' (1992) 8 IJCLLIR 113.
WHITAKER, E., 'The Schengen Agreement and its Portent for the Freedom of Personal Movement in Europe' (1992) 6 *Georgetown Immigration L.J.* 191.
WHITE, R. C. A., 'Procedural Guarantees and Expulsion' (1996) 21 *El Rev.* 241.
WIDGREN, J., 'The Position of "Second Generation" Migrants in Western Europe: Policy Failures and Policy Prospects' (1986) 23 *Studi Emigrazione/Etudes Migrations* 7.

WIEBRINGHAUS, H., 'Introduction' in A. Ph. C. M. Jaspers and L. Betten, (eds.), *25 Years of the European Social Charter* (Deventer: Kluwer, 1988) 9.

WIENTRAUB, S., 'North American Free Trade and the European Situation Compared' (1992) 26 IMR 506.

WOLF, F., 'Human Rights and the International Labour Organization' in T. Meron, (ed.), *Human Rights in International Law: Legal and Policy Issues* (Oxford: Clarendon Press, 1984) 273.

WYATT, D., 'Free Movement of Workers' in D. Wyatt and A. Dashwood, *European Community Law* (London: Sweet & Maxwell, 1993) 237.

—— 'The Right of Establishment and the Freedom to Provide Services' in D. Wyatt and A. Dashwood, *European Community Law* (London: Sweet & Maxwell, 1993) 278.

ZEGERS DE BEIJL, R. and BÖHNING, R., 'Combating Discrimination against Migrant Workers: International Labour Standards and Operational Activities' in Commission on Security and Cooperation in Europe, *CSCE Human Dimension Seminar on Migrant Workers: Report, Briefing, Documentation*, Warsaw, Poland, 21–5 March 1994 (Washington, D.C.: Commission on Security and Cooperation in Europe, April 1994) 87.

INTERNATIONAL DOCUMENTS
(in reverse chronological order)

Council of Europe

Council of Europe, *Conventions and Agreements. Chart showing signatures and ratifications of Conventions and Agreements concluded within the Council of Europe*, (Strasbourg: Directorate of Legal Affairs, Treaty Section, 1996).

Council of Europe, Directorate of Human Rights, *Human Rights Information Sheet No. 37 (July–Dec. 1995)* (Strasbourg: Council of Europe, 1996) Doc. H/INF (96) 1.

Council of Europe, European Commission against Racism and Intolerance, *Legal Measures to Combat Racism and Intolerance in the Member States of the Council of Europe*, Report prepared by the Swiss Institute of Comparative Law, Strasbourg, 2 March 1995, Doc. CRI (95) 2.

Council of Europe, Parliamentary Assembly, *Request for an Opinion from the Committee of Ministers to the Assembly on the Draft Revised European Social Charter*, Doc. 7242, 10 Feb. 1995.

Council of Europe, *Human Rights Information Sheet No. 35 (July–Dec. 1994)* (Strasbourg: Council of Europe, 1995) Doc. H/INF (95) 2.

Council of Europe, *Human Rights Information Sheet No. 34 (Jan.–June 1994)* (Strasbourg: Council of Europe, 1995) Doc. H/INF (95) 1.

Council of Europe, Committee of Independent Experts of the European Social Charter, *Conclusions XIII-2* (Strasbourg: Council of Europe Press, 1995).

Council of Europe, European Social Charter, Governmental Committee, *13th Report (I)* (Strasbourg: Council of Europe Press, 1995).

Council of Europe, European Social Charter, Governmental Committee, *12th Report (II) (1989–1990)* (Strasbourg: Council of Europe Press, 1995).

Council of Europe, Directorate of Human Rights, *Activities of the Council of Europe of*

Relevance to the Work of the European Commission against Racism and Intolerance, Strasbourg, 5 May 1994, Doc. CRI (94) 4.
Council of Europe, *The Reduction of Cases of Multiple Nationality and Military Obligations in Cases of Multiple Nationality. Explanatory Report: Second Protocol Amending the Convention Opened for Signature on 2 February 1993* (Strasbourg: Council of Europe Press, 1994).
Council of Europe, Committee of Independent Experts of the European Social Charter, *Conclusions XIII-1* (Strasbourg: Council of Europe Press, 1994).
Council of Europe, *Human Rights Information Sheet No. 33 (July–Dec. 1993)* (Strasbourg: Council of Europe, 1994) Doc. H/INF (94) 2.
Council of Europe, *Case Law on the European Social Charter—Supplement No. 3* (Strasbourg: Council of Europe Press, 1993).
Council of Europe, Committee of Independent Experts of the European Social Charter, *Conclusions XII-2 (1989–90)* (Strasbourg: Council of Europe Press, 1993).
Council of Europe, European Social Charter, Governmental Committee, *12th Report (I) (1988–89)* (Strasbourg: Council of Europe Press, 1993).
Council of Europe, Committee of Independent Experts of the European Social Charter, *Conclusions XII-1* (Strasbourg: Council of Europe, 1992).
Council of Europe, *People on the Move. New Migration Flows in Europe* (Strasbourg: Council of Europe, 1992).
Council of Europe, Committee of Independent Experts of the European Social Charter, *Conclusions XI-2* (Strasbourg: Council of Europe, 1991).
Council of Europe, *Fourth Report on the Application of the European Convention on the Legal Status of Migrant Workers* (Reference period: 1 Jan. 1989–30 June 1990) (Strasbourg: Council of Europe, 1991).
Council of Europe, *The European Social Charter. Origin, Operation and Results* (Strasbourg: Council of Europe Press, 1991).
Council of Europe, *Third Report on the Application of the European Convention on the Legal Status of Migrant Workers* (Reference period: 1 July 1985–31 Dec. 1988) (Strasbourg: Council of Europe, 1990).
Council of Europe, *Collection of Recommendations and Declarations of the Committee of Ministers concerning Human Rights 1949–1987* (Strasbourg: Council of Europe, 1989).
Council of Europe, Committee of Independent Experts of the European Social Charter, *Conclusions XI-1* (Strasbourg: Council of Europe, 1989).
Council of Europe, Committee of Independent Experts of the European Social Charter, *Conclusions X-2 on the Application of the European Social Charter by Austria, Cyprus, the Federal Republic of Germany, France, Ireland, Italy and Spain during the period from 1 January 1985 to 31 December 1986* (Strasbourg: Council of Europe, 1988).
Council of Europe, Committee of Independent Experts of the European Social Charter, *Conclusions X-1 on the Application of the European Social Charter by Denmark, Greece, Iceland, the Netherlands, Norway, Sweden and the United Kingdom during the period from 1 January 1984 to 31 December 1985* (Strasbourg: Council of Europe, 1987).
Council of Europe, Committee of Independent Experts of the European Social Charter, *Addendum to Conclusions IX-2 relating to the 2nd Report of Spain on the application of the European Social Charter (1 January 1982–31 December 1984)* (Strasbourg: Council of Europe, 1987).

Council of Europe, *Case Law on the European Social Charter—Supplement No. 2* (Strasbourg: Council of Europe, 1987).

Council of Europe, Social Affairs, *Case Law on the European Social Charter: Supplement* (Strasbourg: Council of Europe, 1986).

Council of Europe, Committee of Independent Experts of the European Social Charter, *Conclusions IX-1 on the Application of the European Social Charter by Denmark, Iceland, the Netherlands, Norway, Sweden and the United Kingdom during the period from 1 January 1982 to 31 December 1983* (Strasbourg: Council of Europe, 1985).

Council of Europe, *Explanatory Report on Protocol No. 7 to the Convention for the Protection of Human Rights and Fundamental Freedoms* (Strasbourg: Council of Europe, 1985).

Council of Europe, *Digest of Strasbourg Case-Law relating to the European Convention on Human Rights*, vol. III (Arts 7–12) (Köln: Heymanns Verlag, 1984).

Council of Europe, Social Affairs, *Case Law on the European Social Charter* (Strasbourg: Council of Europe, 1982).

Council of Europe, *Commentary on the European Convention on Establishment (adopted by the Standing Committee)* (Strasbourg: Council of Europe, 1980).

Council of Europe, Directorate of Press and Information, *The Council of Europe—Aims, Operations, Activities* (Strasbourg: Council of Europe, 1979).

Council of Europe, *Explanatory Report on the European Convention on the Legal Status of Migrant Workers* (Strasbourg: Council of Europe, 1978).

Council of Europe, Legal Affairs, *Third Periodical Report by the Standing Committee on the European Convention on Establishment (Individuals)* (Strasbourg: Council of Europe, 1977).

Council of Europe, *Explanatory Reports on the European Convention on Social Security and on the Supplementary Agreement for the Application of the European Convention on Social Security* (Strasbourg: Council of Europe, 1973).

European Communities

Commission of the European Communities, *Proposal for a Council and Commission Decision on the conclusion of the Partnership and Cooperation Agreement between the European Communities and their Member States, of the one part, and the Republic of Uzbekistan, of the other part*, COM (96) 254 final of 5 June 1996.

Eurostat, 'Non-nationals make up less than 5% of the Population of the European Union on 1.1.93' (1996) *Statistics in Focus. Population and Social Conditions* No. 2.

Eurostat, *Labour Force Survey Results 1994* (Luxembourg: OOPEC, 1996).

General Secretariat of the Council of the European Union, Information Policy, Transparency and Public Relations, *1996 Intergovernmental Conference (IGC '96): Reflection Group Report and Other References for Documentary Purposes*. Brussels, Dec. 1995 (Luxembourg: OOPEC, 1996).

Commission of the European Communities, *Proposal for a Decision of the Council and the Commission on the conclusion of a Euro-Mediterranean Agreement establishing an association between the European Communities and their Member States, of the one part, and the Kingdom of Morocco, of the other part*, COM (95) 740 final of 20 Dec. 1995.

Commission of the European Communities, *Communication from the Commission on Racism, Xenophobia and Anti-Semitism and Proposal for a Council Decision designating 1997 as European Year against Racism*, COM (95) 653 final of 13 Dec. 1995.

Commission of the European Communities, Communication from the Commission to the European Parliament and the Council, *Possible Application of Article K.9 of the Treaty on European Union*, COM (95) 566 final of 22 Nov. 1995.

Commission of the European Communities, *Proposal for a Council Directive on the Elimination of Controls on Persons Crossing Internal Frontiers*, COM (95) 347 final of 12 July 1995.

Commission of the European Communities, *Proposal for a Council Directive on the Right of Third-country Nationals to Travel in the Community*, COM (95) 346 final of 12 July 1995.

Commission of the European Communities, *Proposal for a European Parliament and Council Directive amending Directive 68/360/EEC on the abolition of restrictions on movement and residence within the Community for workers of Member States and their families and Directive 73/148/EEC on the abolition of restrictions on movement and residence within the Community for nationals of Member States with regard to establishment and the provision of services*, COM (95) 348 final of 12 July 1995.

Commission of the European Communities, *Proposal for a Decision of the Council and the Commission on the conclusion of the Europe Agreement between the European Communities and their Member States, of the one part, and the Republic of Slovenia, of the other part*, COM (95) 341 final of 12 July 1995.

Commission of the European Communities, *Amended Proposal for a Council Regulation (EC) amending Regulation (EEC) No. 1408/71 on the application of social security schemes to employed persons, to self-employed persons and to members of their families moving within the Community*, COM (95) final of 26 June 1995.

Commission of the European Communities, Report to the Council and the European Parliament, *The Single Market in 1994*, COM (95) 238 final of 15 June 1995.

Commission of the European Communities, *Proposal for a Decision of the Council and the Commission on the conclusion of Europe Agreements between the European Communities and their Member States, of the one part, and the Republics of Estonia, Latvia and Lithuania, of the other part*, COM (95) 207 final of 2 June 1995.

Commission of the European Communities, *Proposal for a Decision of the Council and the Commission on the conclusion of a Euro-Mediterranean Agreement establishing an association between the European Communities and their Member States, of the one part, and the Republic of Tunisia, of the other part*, COM (95) 235 final of 31 May 1995.

Commission of the European Communities, Communication to the Council, the European Parliament, the Economic and Social Committee and the Committee of Regions, *Medium Term Social Action Programme 1995–1997*, COM (95) 134 final of 12 April 1995.

Commission of the European Communities, Directorate-General for Employment, Industrial Relations and Social Affairs, *Judgments of the Court of Justice of the European Communities related to Social Security for Migrant Workers. A Systematic Survey* (Luxembourg: OOPEC, 1995).

Commission of the European Communities, Directorate General, Employment, Industrial Relations and Social Affairs, *The EC Member States and Immigration in 1993. Closed Borders, Stringent Attitudes*, Working Document, Synthesis Report of the Information Network on Migration from Third Countries (Rimet) by C.-V. Marie (Luxembourg: OOPEC, 1995).

Commission of the European Communities, *Proposal for a Decision of the Council and the Commission on the conclusion of the Partnership and Cooperation Agreement between the European Communities and their Member States of the one part, and the Republic of Belarus, of the other part*, COM (95) 44 final of 22 Feb. 1995.

Commission of the European Communities, *Proposal for a Decision of the Council and the Commission on the conclusion of the Partnership and Cooperation Agreement between the European Communities and their Member States of the one part, and the Republic of Moldova, of the other part*, COM (94) 477 final of 3 Nov. 1994.

Commission of the European Communities, *Proposal for a Decision of the Council and the Commission on the conclusion of the Partnership and Cooperation Agreement between the European Communities and their Member States of the one part, and the Kyrgyz Republic, of the other part*, COM (94) 412 final of 5 Oct. 1994.

Commission of the European Communities, *Proposal for a Decision of the Council and the Commission on the conclusion of the Partnership and Cooperation Agreement between the European Communities and their Member States of the one part, and the Republic of Kazakhstan, of the other part*, COM (94) 411 final of 5 Oct. 1994.

Eurostat, 'Non-Nationals Form over Four Percent of Total Population in the European Union' (1994) *Rapid Reports. Population and Social Conditions*, No. 7.

Commission of the European Communities, *European Social Policy—A Way Forward for the Union: A White Paper*, COM (94) 333 final of 27 July 1994.

Commission of the European Communities, *Proposal for a Decision of the Council and the Commission on the conclusion of the Agreement on Partnership and Cooperation between the European Communities and their Member States of the one part, and Russia, of the other part*, COM (94) 257 final of 15 June 1994.

Commission of the European Communities, *Proposal for a Decision of the Council and the Commission on the conclusion of the Partnership and Cooperation Agreement between the European Communities and their Member States of the one part, and Ukraine, of the other part*, COM (94) 226 final of 1 June 1994.

Commission of the European Communities, *Report on the Education of Migrants' Children in the European Union*, COM (94) 80 final of 25 March 1994.

Commission of the European Communities, *Proposal for a Council Directive laying down detailed arrangements for the exercise of the right to vote and to stand as a candidate in municipal elections by citizens of the Union residing in a member State of which they are not nationals*, COM (94) 38 final of 23 Feb. 1994.

Commission of the European Communities, Communication from the Commission to the Council and the European Parliament, *Immigration and Asylum Policies*, COM (94) 23 final of 23 Feb. 1994.

Commission of the European Communities, Directorate-General for Employment, Industrial Relations and Social Affairs, 'Towards a Europe of Solidarity: Combating Social Exclusion', *Social Europe*, Supplement 4/93 (Luxembourg: OOPEC, 1994).

Commission of the European Communities, *Report on the Citizenship of the Union*, COM(93) 702 final of 21 Dec. 1993.

Commission of the European Communities, Communication from the Commission to the Council and the European Parliament, *(1) Proposal for a Decision based on Article K3 of the Treaty on European Union establishing the Convention on the Crossing of the External Frontiers of the Member States; (2) Proposal for a Regulation based on Article 100c of the Treaty Establishing the European Community Determining the Third Countries whose Nationals must be in Possession of a Visa when crossing the External Borders of the Member States*, COM (93) 684 final of 10 Dec. 1993.

Commission of the European Communities, Directorate-General for Employment, Industrial Relations and Social Affairs, 'Social Security for Persons Moving Within the Community', *Social Europe* 1/92 (Luxembourg: OOPEC, 1993).

Commission of the European Communities, Directorate General, Employment, Industrial Relations and Social Affairs, *Legal Instruments to Combat Racism and Xenophobia: Comparative Assessment of the Legal Instruments Implemented in the Various Member States to Combat All Forms of Discrimination, Racism and Xenophobia and Incitement to Hatred and Racial Violence* (Luxembourg: OOPEC, 1993).

Commission of the European Communities, *General Framework for Action by the Commission of the European Communities in the Field of Safety, Hygiene and Health Protection at Work [1994–2000]*, COM (93) 560 final of 19 Nov. 1993.

European Union: Selected Instruments Taken from the Treaties, Book I, Vol. I (Luxembourg: OOPEC, 1993).

Council of the European Communities, *EEC–Turkey Association Agreement and Protocols and Other Basic Texts* (Brussels/Luxembourg: OOPEC, 1992).

Commission of the European Communities, Communication from the Commission to the Council and the European Parliament, *Abolition of Border Controls*, SEC (92) 877 final of 8 May 1992.

Commission of the European Communities, Directorate-General for Employment, Industrial Relations and Social Affairs, 'Europe for Safety and Health at Work', *Social Europe*, Supplement 3/93 (Luxembourg: OOPEC, 1992).

Commission of the European Communities, Directorate-General for Employment, Industrial Relations and Social Affairs, 'Towards a Europe of Solidarity: Housing', *Social Europe*, Supplement 3/92 (Luxembourg: OOPEC, 1992).

Commission of the European Communities, Communication, *Towards a Europe of Solidarity. Intensifying the Fight Against Social Exclusion, Fostering Integration*, COM (92) 542 final of 23 Dec. 1992.

Commission of the European Communities, Directorate-General for Employment, Industrial Relations and Social Affairs, 'Immigration of Citizens from Third Countries into the Southern Member States of the European Community: A Comparative Survey of the Situation in Greece, Italy, Spain and Portugal', *Social Europe*, Supplement 1/91 (Luxembourg: OOPEC, 1991).

Commission of the European Communities, *Member States' National Legislation Applicable to Non-Community Citizens (reference date: 31 Dec. 1990)*, Working Paper No. V/1685/90.

Commission of the European Communities, Report to the European Parliament transmitted for information to the Council, *Voting Rights in Local Elections for Community Nationals*, COM (86) 487 final of 7 Oct. 1986.

Commission of the European Communities, Communication to the Council, *Guidelines for a Community Policy on Migration*, COM (85) 48 final of 7 March 1985.

Commission of the European Communities, *Report from the Commission to the Council on the Implementation in the Member States of Directive 77/486/EEC on the Education of the Children of Migrant Workers*, COM (84) 54 final of 10 Feb. 1984.

Commission of the European Communities, *Proposal for a Council Directive concerning the approximation of the legislation of Member States, in order to combat illegal migration and illegal employment*, COM (78) final of 3 April 1978.

Commission of the European Communities, Communication to the Council, *Action*

Programme in Favour of Migrant Workers and their Families, COM 2250 of 18 Dec. 1974.

International Labour Organization

International Labour Conference, 81st Session, 1994, Report III (4A), *Report of the Committee of Experts on the Application of Conventions and Recommendations* (Geneva: International Labour Office, 1994).

International Labour Conference, 81st Session, 1994, *Report of the Director General. Part II: Activities of the ILO, 1992–93* (Geneva: International Labour Office, 1994).

UN, Economic and Social Council, Commission of Human Rights, Sub-Commission on Prevention of Discrimination and Protection of Minorities, 46th Session, *Memorandum Submitted by the International Labour Office*, UN Doc. E/CN.4/Sub.2/1994/5 (17 June 1994).

UN, Economic and Social Council, Commission of Human Rights, Sub-Commission on Prevention of Discrimination and Protection of Minorities, 45th Session, *Memorandum Submitted by the International Labour Office*, UN Doc. E/CN.4/Sub.2/1993/3 (30 July 1993).

International Labour Conference, 80th Session, 1993, Report III (4A), *Report of the Committee of Experts on the Application of Conventions and Recommendations* (Geneva: International Labour Office, 1993).

International Labour Organization, *World Labour Report 1993* (Geneva: International Labour Office, 1993).

International Labour Conference, 79th Session, 1992, Report III (4A), *Report of the Committee of Experts on the Application of Conventions and Recommendations* (Geneva: International Labour Office, 1992).

International Labour Conference, 82nd Session, 1995, Report III (4A), *Report of the Committee of Experts on the Application of Conventions and Recommendations* (Geneva: International Labour Office, 1995).

International Labour Conference, 82nd Session, 1995, Report III (5), *List of Ratifications by Convention and by Country* (as at 31 December 1994) (Geneva: International Labour Office, 1995).

International Labour Organization, *International Labour Conventions and Recommendations, 1919–1991* (Geneva: International Labour Office, 1992).

International Labour Organization, *World Labour Report 1992* (Geneva: International Labour Office, 1992).

International Labour Organization, Governing Body, 249th Session, Geneva, 27 Feb.–2 March 1991, Report of the Director-General (Third Supplementary Report), *Migrant Workers affected by the Gulf Crisis*, ILO Doc. GB.249/15/7.

International Labour Organization, Governing Body, 235th Session Geneva, February–March 1987, *Recent Events in the United Nations System (Draft International Convention on the Protection of the Rights of All Migrant Workers and their Families)* ILO Doc. GB.235/IO/1/3.

International Labour Organization, Governing Body, 229th Session, Geneva, Feb.–March 1985, *International Convention on the Protection of the Rights of All Migrant Workers and Their Families*, ILO Doc. GB.229/IO/1/6.

International Labour Conference, 69th Session, 1983, Report of the Committee of Experts on the Application of Conventions and Recommendations, *General Survey on the Applications of the Conventions on Freedom of Association, the Right to Organize and Collective Bargaining and the Convention and Recommendation concerning Rural Workers' Organizations* (Geneva: International Labour Office, 1983).

International Labour Office, *Report of the Commission of Inquiry appointed under Article 26 of the Constitution of the International Labour Organization to Examine the Observance of certain International Labour Conventions by the Dominican Republic and Haiti with respect to the Employment of Haitian Workers on the Sugar Plantations of the Dominican Republic* (1983) 66 *Official Bulletin*, Series B.

International Labour Conference, 66th Session, 1980, Report of the Committee of Experts on the Application of Conventions and Recommendations, *General Survey of the Reports relating to Conventions Nos. 97 and 143 and Recommendations Nos. 86 and 151 concerning Migrant Workers* (Geneva: International Labour Office, 1980).

International Labour Organization, Governing Body, 212th Session, Geneva, Feb.–March 1980, *Role and Place of the ILO in the Restructured United Nations System*, ILO Doc. GB.212/IO/1/8.

International Labour Conference, 60th Session, 1975, *Record of Proceedings* (Geneva: International Labour Office, 1976).

International Labour Conference, 60th Session, 1975, Report V(2), *Migrant Workers* (Geneva: International Labour Office, 1975).

International Labour Conference, 60th Session, 1975, Report V(1), *Migrant Workers* (Geneva: International Labour Office, 1974).

International Labour Conference, 59th Session, 1974, Report VII(2), *Migrant Workers* (Geneva: International Labour Office, 1974).

International Labour Conference, 59th Session, 1974, Report VII(1), *Migrant Workers* (Geneva: International Labour Office, 1973).

International Labour Organization, Second European Regional Conference, Report II, Geneva, Jan. 1974, *Some Growing Employment Problems in Europe: Manpower Aspects of Recent Economic Developments in Europe* (Geneva: International Labour Office, 1973) Ch. IV, 'Migration of Workers as an Element in Employment Policy' 81.

International Labour Conference, Report of the Director General (Part I), 52nd Session, 1968, *The ILO and Human Rights* (Geneva: International Labour Office, 1968) Ch. IV, 'Equality' 51.

Organization for Economic Cooperation and Development

OECD, *Trends in International Migration—Continuous Reporting System on Migration—SOPEMI 1994* (Paris: OECD, 1995).

OECD, *Trends in International Migration—Continuous Reporting System on Migration—SOPEMI 1993* (Paris: OECD, 1994).

OECD, *The Changing Course of Migration* (Paris: OECD, 1993).

OECD, *Trends in International Migration—Continuous Reporting System on Migration—SOPEMI 1992* (Paris: OECD, 1992).

OECD, *Continuous Reporting System on Migration—SOPEMI 1990* (Paris: OECD, 1991).

OECD, *The Future of Migration* (Paris: OECD, 1987).

OECD, *Young Foreigners and the World of Work* (Paris: OECD, 1981).

United Nations

UN, Centre for Human Rights, *The Rights of Migrant Workers. Fact Sheet No. 24* (Geneva: UN, 1996).

UN, *Report of the Fourth World Conference on Women*, Beijing, 4–15 Sept. 1995, UN Doc. A/CONF.177/20 (17 Oct. 1995).

UN, ECOSOC, Substantive Session of 1995, *International Migration and Development*, Report of the Secretary General, UN Doc. E/1995/69 (14 June 1995).

UN, *Report of the Committee on the Elimination of Racial Discrimination*, 49 UN GAOR Supp. No. 18, UN Doc. A/49/18 (1995).

Report of the International Conference on Population and Development, Cairo, 5–13 Sept. 1994, UN Doc. A/CONF.171/13 (18 Oct. 1994), Ch. X, 'International Migration'.

UN, ECOSOC, Commission of Human Rights, 50th Session, Report of the Secretary-General, *Status of the International Convention on the Protection of the Rights of All Migrant Workers and Members of Their Families*, UN Doc. E/CN.4/1994/62 (10 Jan. 1994).

UN, *Report of the Committee on the Elimination of Racial Discrimination*, 48 UN GAOR Supp. No. 18, UN Doc. A/48/18 (1994).

UN, *Report of the Human Rights Committee*, 47 UN GAOR Supp. No. 40, UN Doc. A/47/40 (1994).

UN Centre for Human Rights, *United Nations Action in the Field of Human Rights* (New York and Geneva: UN, 1994).

UN, ECOSOC, Commission on Human Rights, 49th Session, Report of the Secretary-General, *Status of the International Convention on the Protection of the Rights of All Migrant Workers and Members of Their Families*, UN Doc. E/CN.4/1993/51 (31 Dec. 1992).

UN, General Assembly, 47th Session, Report of the Secretary-General, *Status of the International Convention on the Protection of the Rights of All Migrant Workers and Members of Their Families*, UN Doc. A/47/429 (15 Sept. 1992).

UN, ECOSOC, Commission on Human Rights, 48th Session, Report of the Secretary-General, *Status of the International Convention on the Protection of the Rights of All Migrant Workers and Members of Their Families*, UN Doc. E/CN.4/1992/38 (10 Jan. 1992).

UN, *Report of the Committee on the Elimination of Racial Discrimination*, 46 UN GAOR Supp. No. 18, UN Doc. A/46/18 (1992).

UN, General Assembly, 46th Session, Note by the Secretary-General, *Implementation of the International Convention on the Protection of the Rights of All Migrant Workers and Members of Their Families*, UN Doc. A/46/395 (29 Aug. 1991).

UN, General Assembly, 45th Session, Third Committee, *Report of the Open-ended Working Group on the Drafting of an International Convention on the Protection of the Rights of All Migrant Workers and Their Families*, UN Doc. A/C.3/45/1 (21 June 1990).

UN, Commission on Human Rights, 46th Session, *Report of the International Seminar on Cultural Dialogue Between the Countries of Origin and the Host Countries of Migrant Workers*, Athens, Greece, 18–26 Sept. 1989 (Implementation of the Programme of Action for the Second Decade to Combat Racism and Racial Discrimination), UN Doc. E/CN.4/1990/50 (10 Nov. 1989).

UN, General Assembly, 44th Session, Third Committee, *Report of the Open-ended Working*

Group on the Drafting of an International Convention on the Protection of the Rights of All Migrant Workers and Their Families, UN Doc. A/C.3/44/4 (17 Oct. 1989).

UN, General Assembly, 44th Session, Third Committee, *Report of the Open-ended Working Group on the Drafting of an International Convention on the Protection of the Rights of All Migrant Workers and Their Families*, UN Doc. A/C.3/44/1 (19 June 1989).

UN, *Report of the Committee on the Elimination of Racial Discrimination*, 43 UN GAOR Supp. No. 18, UN Doc. A/43/18 (1989).

UN, Centre for Human Rights, *United Nations Action in the Field of Human Rights* (New York: UN, 1988).

UN, General Assembly, 43rd Session, Third Committee, *Report of the Open-ended Working Group on the Drafting of an International Convention on the Protection of the Rights of All Migrant Workers and Their Families*, UN Doc. A/C.3/43/7 (17 Oct. 1988).

UN, General Assembly, 43rd Session, Third Committee, *Report of the Open-ended Working Group on the Drafting of an International Convention on the Protection of the Rights of All Migrant Workers and Their Families*, UN Doc. A/C.3/43/1 (20 June 1988).

UN, General Assembly, 42nd Session, Third Committee, *Report of the Open-ended Working Group on the Drafting of an International Convention on the Protection of the Rights of All Migrant Workers and Their Families*, UN Doc. A/C.3/42/6 (9 Oct. 1987).

UN, General Assembly, 42nd Session, Third Committee, *Report of the Open-ended Working Group on the Drafting of an International Convention on the Protection of the Rights of All Migrant Workers and Their Families*, UN Doc. A/C.3/42/1 (22 June 1987).

'Limburg Principles on the Implementation of the International Covenant on Economic, Social and Cultural Rights', UN Doc. E/CN.4/1987/17, Annex, reproduced in (1987) HRQ 122.

UN, Commission on Human Rights, Sub-Commission on Prevention of Discrimination and Protection of Minorities, *Exploitation of Labour Through Illicit And Clandestine Trafficking* (Consolidated Report), UN Doc. E/CN.4/Sub.2/1986/6 (1986).

UN, Department of International Economic and Social Affairs, Centre for Social Development and Humanitarian Affairs, *Migrant Workers No. 2. The Social Situation of Migrant Workers and Their Families*, UN Doc. ST/ESA/189 (New York: UN, 1986).

UN, General Assembly, 41st Session, Third Committee, *Report of the Open-ended Working Group on the Drafting of an International Convention on the Protection of the Rights of All Migrant Workers and Their Families*, UN Doc. A/C.3/41/3 (10 Oct. 1986).

UN, General Assembly, 40th Session, Third Committee, *Report of the Open-ended Working Group on the Drafting of an International Convention on the Protection of the Rights of All Migrant Workers and Their Families*, UN Doc. A/C.3/40/6 (15 Oct. 1985).

UN, General Assembly, 40th Session, Third Committee, *Report of the Open-ended Working Group on the Elaboration of an International Convention on the Protection of the Rights of All Migrant Workers and Their Families*, UN Doc. A/C.3/40/1 (20 June 1985).

Deschênes, J. (UN Sub-Commission on Prevention of Discrimination and Protection of Minorities), *Proposal Concerning a Definition of the Term 'Minority'*, UN Doc. E/CN.4/Sub.2/1985/31 (Geneva: UN, 1985).

UN, General Assembly, 39th Session, Third Committee, *Report of the Open-ended Working Group on the Elaboration of an International Convention on the Protection of the Rights of All Migrant Workers and Their Families*, UN Doc. A/C.3/39/4 (11 Oct. 1984).

UN, General Assembly, 39th Session, Third Committee, *Report of the Open-ended Working*

Group on the Elaboration of an International Convention on the Protection of the Rights of All Migrant Workers and Their Families, UN Doc. A/C.3/39/1 (14 June 1984).

UN, General Assembly, 38th Session, Third Committee, *Report of the Open-ended Working Group on the Elaboration of an International Convention on the Protection of the Rights of All Migrant Workers and Their Families*, UN Doc. A/C.3/38/5 (11 Oct. 1983).

UN, General Assembly, 38th Session, Third Committee, *Report of the Open-ended Working Group on the Elaboration of an International Convention on the Protection of the Rights of All Migrant Workers and Their Families*, UN Doc. A/C.3/38/1 (16 June 1983).

UN, Commission for Social Development, 28th Session, 1983, Report of the Secretary-General, *Social Integration. Pertinent Regulations concerning the Welfare of Migrant Workers and their Families*, UN Doc. E/CN.5/1983/10 (1 Dec. 1982).

UN, General Assembly, 37th Session, Third Committee, *Report of the Open-ended Working Group on the Elaboration of an International Convention on the Protection of the Rights of All Migrant Workers and Their Families*, UN Doc. A/C.3/37/7 (19 Nov. 1982).

UN, General Assembly, 37th Session, Third Committee, *Report of the Open-ended Working Group on the Elaboration of an International Convention on the Protection of the Rights of All Migrant Workers and Their Families*, UN Doc. A/C.3/37/1 (11 June 1982).

UN, General Assembly, 36th Session, Third Committee, *Report of the Open-ended Working Group*, UN Doc. A/C.3/36/10 (23 Nov. 1981).

UN, General Assembly, 35th Session, Third Committee, *Report of the Open Working Group*, UN Doc. A/C.3/35/13 (25 Nov. 1980).

UN, Commission on Human Rights, Sub-Commission on Prevention of Discrimination and Protection of Minorities, Study prepared by Baroness Elles, Special Rapporteur, *International Provisions Protecting the Human Rights of Non-Citizens*, UN Doc. E/CN.4/Sub.2/392/Rev.1 (New York: UN, 1980).

CAPOTORTI, F., *Study of the Rights of Persons Belonging to Ethnic, Religious and Linguistic Minorities*, UN Doc. E/CN.4/Sub.2/384/Rev.1 (New York: UN, 1979).

Report of the World Conference to Combat Racism and Racial Discrimination, Geneva, 14–25 Aug. 1978, UN Doc. A/CONF.92/40 (New York: UN, 1979).

UN, Division of Human Rights, *Report of the Seminar on the Human Rights of Migrant Workers*, Tunis, Tunisia, 12–24 Nov. 1975, UN Doc. ST/TAO/HR/50 (1976).

UN, Commission on Human Rights, Sub-Commission on Prevention of Discrimination and Protection of Minorities, 28th Session, *Exploitation of Labour Through Illicit and Clandestine Trafficking: Statement Concerning the Study on Illicit Trafficking in Labour and on the Present Problem of Migrant Workers* (made by Ms Halima E. Warzazi in introducing her final report on the same topic), UN Doc. E/CN.4/Sub.2/L.640 (20 Nov. 1975).

UN, Commission on Human Rights, Sub-Commission on Prevention of Discrimination and Protection of Minorities, 28th Session, *Exploitation of Labour Through Illicit And Clandestine Trafficking* (final report prepared by Mrs Halima E. Warzazi, Special Rapporteur), UN Doc. E/CN.4/Sub.2/L.629 (4 July 1975).

UN, Commission for Social Development, 24th Session, 1975, Note by the Secretary-General, *ILO Action on Behalf of Foreign and Migrant Workers and their Families*, UN Doc. E/CN.5/523 (6 Jan. 1975).

UN, Commission for Social Development, 24th Session, 6–24 Jan. 1975, Report of the Secretary-General, *The Welfare of Migrant Workers and Their Families*, UN Doc. E/CN.5/515 (14 Oct. 1974).

UN, Commission on Human Rights, Sub-Commission on Prevention of Discrimination and Protection of Minorities, 27th Session, *Exploitation of Labour Through Illicit and Clandestine Trafficking: Introductory Statement Concerning the Study on Illicit Trafficking in Labour and on the Present Problem of Migrant Workers* (made by Mrs Halima E. Warzazi in introducing her preliminary report on the same topic), UN Doc. E/CN.4/Sub.2/352 (14 Aug. 1974).

UN, Commission on Human Rights, Sub-Commission on Prevention of Discrimination and Protection of Minorities, 27th Session, *Exploitation of Labour Through Illicit And Clandestine Trafficking* (Preliminary Study prepared by Mrs Halima E. Warzazi, Special Rapporteur), UN Doc. E/CN.4/Sub.2/351 (17 June 1974).

World Bank

World Bank, *World Development Report 1995. Workers in an Integrating World* (New York: Oxford University Press for the World Bank, 1995).

MISCELLANEOUS PUBLICATIONS

BLAUSTEIN, A. and FLANZ, G., (eds.), *Constitutions of the Countries of the World: A survey of updated texts, constitutional chronologies and annotated bibliographies* (Dobbs Ferry, N.Y.: Oceana, 1971–)

Canada, Immigration and Refugee Board Documentation Centre, Question and Answer Series, *The Persian Gulf: The Situation of Foreign Workers* (Ottawa, May 1991).

CATHOLIC INSTITUTE FOR INTERNATIONAL RELATIONS (CIIR), *The Labour Trade* (London: CIIR, 1987).

CHOLEWINSKI, R., 'The Positive Cultural and Linguistic Right of Ethnic Minorities' LL.M. Thesis, University of Saskatchewan, Saskatoon, August 1988 (unpublished).

COMMISSION ON SECURITY AND COOPERATION IN EUROPE, *CSCE Human Dimension Seminar on Migrant Workers: Report, Briefing, Documentation*, Warsaw, Poland, 21–5 March 1994 (Washington, D.C.: Commission on Security and Cooperation in Europe, April 1994).

'Comparative Survey of the Hallmarks of Citizenship in Eleven EC Jurisdictions' in J. P. Gardner, (ed.), *Hallmarks of Citizenship* (London: The British Institute of International and Comparative Law, 1995).

Conclusions of the ICFTU/ETUC/USTMA Conference on Mahgreb Migrant Workers in the European Community (Tunis, 18–20 April 1991).

DATELINE MIGRATION (INTERNATIONAL), 'Repatriation of Vietnamese in Germany' (1995) 23:1 *Migrationworld Magazine* 5.

Documentation and Comment, 'Council of Europe. The Introduction of a System of Collective Complaints' (1995) 3 IJCLLIR 270.

Editorial, 'Legislating Free Movement: An Over-ambitious Commission Package' (1996) 33 *CML Rev.* 1.

EMPLOYMENT AND IMMIGRATION CANADA, *An Approach to International Migration* (Immigration Policy Group, Jan. 1993).

FÉDÉRATION INTERNATIONALE DES DROITS DE L'HOMME, *Rapport de Mission à Prague* (Paris: Fédération Internationale des Droits de L'Homme, 1990).

GIBSON, U. and NIESSEN, J., *The CSCE and the Protection of the Rights of Migrants, Refugees and Minorities in Europe*, CCME Briefing Paper No. 11 (Brussels: Churches Commission for Migrants in Europe, March 1993).

GROUPE D'INFORMATION ET DE SOUTEIN DES TRAVAILLEURS IMMIGRÉS (GISTI) and IMMIGRATION LAW PRACTITIONERS' ASSOCIATION (ILPA), *The Movement of Aliens in the European Area* (GISTI, ILPA, May 1995).

ILPA, *Update: October 1995*.

ILPA, *1996: The Intergovernmental Conference on the Re-Negotiation of the European Union Treaties: The Impact on Asylum and Immigration* (March 1996).

International Confederation of Free Trade Unions (ICFTU), European Trade Union Confederation (ETUC), Union of Arab Mahgreb Workers—Union Syndicale des Travailleurs du Mahgreb Arabe (USTMA), *Report to the Conference on Migrant Workers from the Mahgreb in the European Community* (Tunis, 18–20 April 1991).

International Organization and Integration: Annotated Basic Documents and Descriptive Directory of International Organizations and Arrangements, Vol. I.B, 2nd rev. edn. (The Hague: Martinus Nijhoff, 1982).

Migrants, Refugees and International Cooperation, A joint contribution to the International Conference on Population and Development (Geneva: ILO, IOM, UNHCR, 1994).

NIESSEN, J. and ZEGERS DE BEIJL, R., *International Migration, Economic Development and Human Rights*, CCME Briefing Paper No. 18 (Brussels: Churches Commission for Migrants in Europe, Dec. 1994).

Note, 'The Holy See's Perspective on Migration and Development' (Presented at the Tenth IOM Seminar on Migration, 15–17 Sept. 1992) (1993) 21 2:3 *Migrationworld Magazine* 45.

Note, International, 'Foreign Women in Domestic Service' (1991) ILO SLB 361.

Note, International, 'Increase in Emigration Pressures' (1991) ILO SLB 100.

Note, Switzerland, 'New Policy for Foreign Workers' (Sept. 1991) EIRR 14.

Note, EEC, 'Migrant Workers: A Two-tier Labour Market' (Aug. 1990) EIRR 12.

Note, Egypt, 'Population Growth and Jobs' (1989) ILO SLB 292.

Note, EEC, 'Migrant Workers' Families: Legal Rights' (Dec. 1987) EIRR 18.

Note, EEC, 'Article 51: Migrant Workers' Social Security Rights' (Sept. 1986) EIRR 17.

Note, EEC, 'Focus on Migrant Workers' (April 1984) EIRR 19.

Note, EEC, 'Employing Non-Community Workers' (May 1983) EIRR 24.

Note, 'Migrant Workers and Trade Unions' (Oct. 1982) EIRR 20.

Note, 'The 60th Session of the International Labour Conference, June 1975' (1975) 112 ILR 231.

Note, 'The 59th Session of the International Labour Conference, June 1974' (1974) 110 ILR 277.

The Refugee Council, 'The Asylum and Immigration Act 1996. What it means—Related measures—Timetable' Bulletin (Sept. 1996).

Refugee Policy Group (RPG), The North American-European Dialogue on Politics and Migration, *Changing Migration in and from Eastern Europe and the Soviet Union*, Summary of the Third Meeting in Vienna, 16–17 July 1990 (Washington/Geneva: RPG, 1990). *Refugee Advisers Support Unit*.

United Kingdom, Commission for Racial Equality, *Citizens, Minorities and Foreigners* (London: Commission for Racial Equality, 1994).

U.S. Commission for the Study of International Migration and Cooperative Economic Development, 'Immigration and Economic Development' in D. G. Papademetriou and P. L. Martin, (eds.), *The Unsettled Relationship: Labor Migration and Economic Development* (New York: Greenwood Press, 1991) 221.

Index

Printed in the United Kingdom
by Lightning Source UK Ltd.
106978UKS00001B/13

9 780198 259923